36TH EDITION

STUDENTS WITH DISABILITIES AND SPECIAL EDUCATION LAW

- Autism
- Tuition Disputes
- Gifted Students
- Mainstreaming
- Student Discipline
- Bullying

Center for Education & Employment Law

TABLE OF CONTENTS

CHAPTER SIX
IDEA Procedural Safeguards

CHAPTER SEVEN
Private School Tuition

CHAPTER TEN
Student Civil Rights

CHAPTER ELEVEN
Employment

TABLE OF CONTENTS

CHAPTER TWELVE
School District Operations

REFERENCE SECTION

INTRODUCTION

Federal law requires that school districts provide each child with a disability a free appropriate education. *Students with Disabilities and Special Education Law* has been published in response to the need of school administrators and others involved in providing special education services to have a reference available when confronted with any of the multitude of problems in the special education area. The 34th Edition continues to group cases by subject matter and contains the full text of the Individuals with Disabilities Education Act as amended. The full legal citation is given for each reported case, and all cases have been indexed and placed in a Table of Cases following the Table of Contents.

Although the IDEA has undergone several major amendments – from the EHA to the EAHCA to the HCPA and finally to the IDEA – the book generally uses the abbreviation "IDEA" in place of the others for ease of readability and textual flow.

The intent of this volume is to provide professional educators and lawyers with access to important cases, statutory and regulatory law in the field of special education and disabled students' rights.

Thomas D'Agostino, Esq.
Managing Editor
Center for Education & Employment Law

i

ABOUT THE EDITORS

Carol Warner is the editor of *EducationTechNews.com* and two monthly newsletters: *School Safety & Security Alert* and *Legal Update for Teachers*. She is also a contributing editor for *HigherEdMorning.com* and *Higher Education Legal Alert*. Before joining the Center for Education & Employment Law, she was an editor for two employment law newsletters: *What's Working in Human Resources* and *What's New in Benefits & Compensation*. Ms. Warner is a graduate of The New York Institute of Technology and holds a Bachelor of Arts in English with an emphasis in professional writing.

James A. Roth is the editor of *Legal Notes for Education* and *Special Education Law Update*. He is a co-editor of *Students with Disabilities and Special Education Law* and an adjunct program assistant professor at St. Mary's University in Minnesota. Mr. Roth is a graduate of the University of Minnesota and William Mitchell College of Law. He is admitted to the Minnesota Bar.

Thomas D'Agostino is a managing editor at the Center for Education & Employment Law and is the editor of *Higher Education Legal Alert*. He is a co-author of *Keeping Your School Safe & Secure: A Practical Guide*. He graduated from the Duquesne University School of Law and received his undergraduate degree from Ramapo College of New Jersey. He is a past member of the American Bar Association's Section of Individual Rights and Responsibilities as well as the Pennsylvania Bar Association's Legal Services to Persons with Disabilities Committee. Mr. D'Agostino is admitted to the Pennsylvania bar.

Curt J. Brown is the Editorial Director of the Center for Education & Employment Law. Prior to assuming his present position, he gained extensive experience in business-to-business publishing, including management of well-known publications such as *What's Working in Human Resources, What's New in Benefits & Compensation, Keep Up to Date with Payroll, Supervisors Legal Update,* and *Facility Manager's Alert*. Mr. Brown graduated from Villanova University School of Law and graduated magna cum laude from Bloomsburg University with a B.S. in Business Administration. He is admitted to the Pennsylvania Bar.

HOW TO USE THIS VOLUME

We have designed *Students with Disabilities and Special Education Law* in an accessible format for both attorneys and non-attorneys to use as a research and reference tool toward prevention of legal problems.

Using Your Deskbook to Conduct Research

As a research tool, our deskbook allows you to conduct your research on two different levels – by topics or by cases.

Topic Research

◆ If you have a general interest in a particular **topic** area, our **Table of Contents** provides descriptive section headings with detailed subheadings for each chapter.

✓ For your convenience, we also include an individual chapter table of contents at the beginning of each chapter.

Example:

If you are seeking information on medical services, the Table of Contents indicates that a discussion of that topic takes place in Chapter Eight, under "Transition Services and Related Services," on page 237:

How to Use This Volume

◆ If you have a specific interest in a particular **issue**, our comprehensive **index** collects all of the relevant page references to particular issues.

> **Example:**
> For more information on individualized education programs (IEPs), the index provides references to all cases dealing with IEPs, including those cases dealing with student progress:
>
> Individualized education programs (IEPs), 53-99
>   appropriateness, 71-88
>   maximizing potential, 79-82
>   methodology questions, 71-75
>   particular schools, 85-88
> ➡   student progress, 75-77
>   transfer students, 82-85
>   behavior intervention plans, 95-98
>   functional behavioral assessments, 98-101

Case Research

◆ If you know the **name** of a particular case, our **Table of Cases** will allow you to quickly reference the location of the case.

> **Example:**
> If you wanted to look up the case *T.D. v. Rutherford County Board of Educ.,* you would look in the Table of Cases, which has been arranged alphabetically. The reference to the case is located under section T and directs you to page 245.
>
> **T**
>
> T.B. v. Prince George's County Board of Educ., 23
> ➡ T.D. v. Rutherford County Board of Educ., 245
> T.F. v. Fox Chapel Area School Dist., 17, 276
> T.H. v. Cincinnati Public School Dist. Board of
>   Educ., 111
> T.J. v. Winton Woods City School Dist., 248
> T.K. and S.K. v. New York City Dep't of Educ., 94, 326

✓ Each of the cases summarized in the deskbook also contains the case citation that will allow you to access the full text of the case from a law library. See *How to Read a Case Citation*, p. 521.

How to Use This Volume

◆ If your interest lies in cases from a **particular state**, our **Table of Cases by State** will identify the cases from your state and direct you to the page numbers where they are located.

> **Example:**
> If cases from Arizona are of interest, the Table of Cases by State, arranged alphabetically, lists all of the Arizona case summaries contained in the deskbook.
>
> ## ARIZONA
>
> A.G. v. Paradise Valley Unified School Dist., 15, 15, 338
> Gallagher v. Tucson Unified School Dist., 321
> Hack v. Deer Valley Unified School Dist., 55
> Houston v. Arizona State Board of Educ., 391

✓ Remember, the judicial system has two court systems – state and federal – which generally function independently of each other. See *The Judicial System*, p. 517. We have included the federal court cases in the table of cases by state according to the state in which the court resides. However, federal court decisions often impact other federal courts within that particular circuit. Therefore, it may be helpful to review cases from all of the states contained in a particular circuit.

Reference Tool

As a reference tool, we have highlighted important resources that provide the framework for many legal issues.

◆ If you would like to see specific wording of the **Individuals with Disabilities Education Act Amendments of 1997**, refer to **Appendix A**.

◆ If you would like to review the **Table of Special Education Cases Decided by the U.S. Supreme Court** in a particular subject matter area, our topical list of U.S. Supreme Court case citations located in **Appendix B** will be helpful.

How to Use This Volume

We hope you benefit from the use of *Students with Disabilities and Special Education Law*. If you have any questions about how to use the deskbook, please contact Thomas D'Agostino at tdagostino@pbp.com.

OVERVIEW AND KEY TERMS

The Individuals with Disabilities Education Act (IDEA), 20 U.S.C. §§ 1400 – 1487 is the most important federal law regarding the education of students with disabilities. States also have special education laws that parallel the IDEA. Unlike Section 504 of the Rehabilitation Act and the Americans with Disabilities Act (ADA), the IDEA does not prohibit discrimination on the basis of disability. Instead, it imposes obligations on the states and requires them to comply with IDEA procedures as a condition of receiving federal funds.

Congressional findings in support of the IDEA tell a story about the lack of educational services for students with disabilities both before and after federal involvement began in 1975. Before the Education for All Handicapped Children Act of 1975 (Public Law 94–142) was enacted, the special educational needs of children with disabilities were not being fully met. Congress found that over half the children with disabilities in the U.S. did not receive appropriate educational services that would enable them to have full equality of opportunity.

An estimated one million children with disabilities in the U.S. were excluded entirely from the public school system and did not go through the educational process with their peers. Congress found in 1975 that disability is a natural part of the human experience and in no way diminishes the right of individuals to participate in or contribute to society.

Improving educational results for children with disabilities was declared an essential element of our national policy of ensuring equality of opportunity, full participation, independent living, and economic self-sufficiency for individuals with disabilities. Congress found student disabilities often went undetected. Because of the lack of adequate services within the public school system, families were often forced to find services outside the public school system. The IDEA provides federal funding to local education agencies through grants to the states. To receive IDEA funds, states must demonstrate that they maintain a policy assuring that all children with disabilities have access to a free appropriate public education (FAPE).

Local educational agencies receiving IDEA funds must include satisfactory assurances that they are identifying and providing special education services to all students with disabilities residing within the local jurisdiction.

The IDEA has been reauthorized periodically by Congress, with the most recent reauthorization taking place in 2004 in what was known as the Individuals with Disabilities Education Improvement Act. The 2004 IDEA amendments increased federal funding, adopted terms from the No Child Left Behind Act, and relaxed some student disciplinary provisions.

The IDEA was originally passed as the Education of the Handicapped Act of 1970 (EHA). It was intended to assist the states in providing a FAPE to children with disabilities by establishing minimum requirements with which the states had to comply in order to receive federal financial assistance. Congress amended the EHA in 1975 with the Education for All Handicapped Children Act (EAHCA) (P.L. 94–142), which contains many of the most important legal protections of the legislation now known as the IDEA.

The Handicapped Children's Protection Act of 1986 (HCPA) (P.L. 99–372), further amended the EHA by specifically authorizing awards of attorneys' fees to the families of students with disabilities who prevailed in EHA lawsuits. The HCPA also expressly allowed disabled students to cumulate their available remedies under Section 504 of the Rehabilitation Act of 1973 (29 U.S.C. § 794) and 42 U.S.C. § 1983. The HCPA is found in the present IDEA at 20 U.S.C. § 1415(i)(3) and Section 1415(l).

In 1990, Congress passed the amendment renaming the legislation the Individuals with Disabilities Education Act (IDEA) (P.L. 102–119), and added specific clauses to abrogate sovereign immunity and authorize remedies under both legal and equitable theories (20 U.S.C. § 1403). In 1994, Congress amended the IDEA as part of the Improving America's Schools Act of 1994 (P.L. 103–382). States and LEAs must have in place a number of statutory policies and procedures in order to ensure the receipt of IDEA funds.

School districts must comply with the general requirements of 20 U.S.C. § 1414(a)(1)(A), which requires a full and individual initial evaluation upon a parent request or its own initiative. Districts must comply with IDEA notice and procedural requirements. Parents who have not allowed an evaluation of their children, or who have refused special education, are barred from later asserting IDEA procedural protections in disciplinary cases.

Each IEP includes statements of annual goals, including benchmarks or short-term objectives, related to meeting the student's needs that result from the student's disability, to enable involvement and progress in the general curriculum. IEPs include a statement of the special education and related services to be provided to the student and a statement of the program modifications to be furnished, which will allow the student to advance appropriately toward attaining the annual goals, and be involved and progress in the general curriculum and participate with other students.

Each IEP must explain the extent to which a student will not participate with non-disabled students in regular classes and a statement of any individual modifications that are needed for the student to participate in state or local student achievement assessments. For students age 14 and over, a statement of the student's necessary transition services under the applicable components of an IEP focusing on courses of study must be included.

For those over 16, a statement of necessary transition services must be included which may describe interagency responsibilities. Beginning at least one year before the student reaches the age of majority under state law, the IEP must include a statement that the student has been advised of IDEA rights that will transfer to the student upon the attainment of the age of majority.

The following abbreviations are used in this edition of *Students with Disabilities and Special Education Law*:

ABA – applied behavior analysis

ADA – Americans with Disabilities Act

ADD – attention deficit disorder

ADHD – attention deficit hyperactivity disorder

ALJ – administrative law judge

ARD – admission, review and dismissal

AVT – auditory-verbal therapy

AYP – adequate yearly progress

BIP – behavior intervention plan

CSE – committee on special education

CST – child study team

DTT – discrete trial training

EBD – emotional-behavioral disorder

EEOC – Equal Employment Opportunity Commission

ESY – extended school year

FAPE – free appropriate public education

FERPA – Family Educational Rights and Privacy Act

FIE – full and individual evaluation

FMLA – Family and Medical Leave Act

IDEA – Individuals with Disabilities Education Act

IEE – independent educational evaluation

IEP – individualized education program

IFSP – individual family service plan

IHO – independent hearing officer

IU – intermediate unit

LEA – local educational agency

LRE – least restrictive environment

MDE – multidisciplinary evaluation

MDT – manifestation determination team

NCLB Act – No Child Left Behind Act

OG – Orton-Gillingham

OT – occupational therapy

PPT – planning and placement team

PT – physical therapy

RICO – Racketeer Influenced and Corrupt Organizations Act

TA – teaching assistant

TEACCH – Treatment and Education of Autistic and Related Communication Handicapped Children

TABLE OF CASES

TABLE OF CASES

TABLE OF CASES

TABLE OF CASES

TABLE OF CASES

TABLE OF CASES

TABLE OF CASES

TABLE OF CASES

TABLE OF CASES

TABLE OF CASES

TABLE OF CASES BY STATE

TABLE OF CASES BY STATE

TABLE OF CASES BY STATE

NORTH CAROLINA

RHODE ISLAND

SOUTH CAROLINA

SOUTH DAKOTA

TENNESSEE

TEXAS

CHAPTER ONE

Laws Protecting Students with Disabilities

I. INDIVIDUALS WITH DISABILITIES EDUCATION ACT

A. Background

The Individuals with Disabilities Education Act (IDEA) imposes obligations on the states and requires compliance with IDEA procedures as a condition of receiving federal funds. To receive IDEA funds, states must maintain a policy assuring that all children with disabilities have access to a free appropriate public education (FAPE). "FAPE" refers to appropriate special education and related services provided at public expense that meet state educational agency standards in conformity with an individualized education program (IEP).

B. Minimum IDEA Standards Under *Board of Educ. v. Rowley*

As explained by the Supreme Court in Endrew F. v. Douglas County School Dist. RE-1, *137 S.Ct. 988 (U.S. 2017), the IDEA does not guarantee any particular level of education, nor a particular educational outcome.*

In E.F. v. Newport Mesa Unified School Dist., *726 Fed.Appx. 535 (9th Cir. 2018), the Ninth Circuit court of Appeals explained that the decision in* Endrew F. v. Douglas County School Dist. RE-1 *"did not change, but simply clarified" the FAPE standard set by the Supreme Court in* Board of Educ. of Hendrick Hudson Cent. School Dist., Westchester County v. Rowley, *458 U.S. 176 (1982), (Rowley) in 1982. In* Endrew F., *the Court held the IDEA requires "an educational program reasonably calculated to enable a child to make progress appropriate in light of the child's circumstances." The Court rejected the Tenth Circuit's finding that* Rowley *set a minimal FAPE standard for assessing the progress of students who are not fully integrated into regular classrooms.*

The Endrew F. *case clarified that the Court's ruling in* Rowley *did not endorse a particular standard for determining whether a child is receiving sufficient educational benefits. It stated that **an IEP must be "reasonably calculated to enable a child to make progress appropriate in light of the child's circumstances."***

In I.Z.M. v. Rosemount-Apple Valley-Eagan Public Schools, this chapter, the U.S. Court of Appeals, Eighth Circuit, rejected a student's argument that Minnesota law creates a heightened standard for school districts in the form of an absolute obligation to attain a specific level of instruction.

◆   In *L.H. v. Hamilton County Dep't of Educ.*, 900 F.3d 779 (6th Cir. 2018), the U.S. Court of Appeals, Sixth Circuit, held a student with Down syndrome was improperly segregated from his non-disabled peers. In ruling for the student, the court held children with disabilities may be segregated from their non-disabled peers only when the nature or severity of a disability is such that education in regular classes (with supplementary aids or services) cannot be achieved. The court found a mainstream setting would have provided the student in this case "some" educational benefit. An administrative law judge had improperly held he would have to show "mastery of the regular education grade-level curriculum" in order to be mainstreamed. **In the Sixth Circuit's view, the standard for placing a student with a disability is not mastery of the general-education curriculum. Instead, a student with a disability must progress on his/her IEP goals.** There was evidence that the student's teachers did not properly engage in mainstreaming when he attended general education classes. Staff isolated and removed him from situations that became challenging, and the school provided a curriculum with very low educational expectations, no report cards and no homework. A lower court had incorrectly denied tuition reimbursement to the parents for their private Montessori school costs. Finding the Montessori curriculum "well-suited for children with Down syndrome in many respects," and good for the student in this case, the court returned the case to the lower court for the taking of additional evidence to determine an appropriate amount of tuition reimbursement for the parents.

When the case returned to the lower court, it determined the parents were entitled to reimbursement for the student's educational costs for grades 3-8 at the Montessori school in the sum of $103,274. After the court held the school system had to reimburse the parents for this sum, they sought their attorneys' fees and costs. The court held they were "unquestionably" prevailing parties in their case and awarded them attorneys' fees and court costs of $349,249.50. *L.H. v. Hamilton County Dep't of Educ.*, 356 F.Supp.3d 713 (E.D. Tenn. 2019).

◆   As a Pennsylvania student with learning disabilities prepared to enter high school, his IEP team addressed his lack of focus by specifying that he sit at the front of his classes and receive prompts, clarification and repeated directions. He was allowed additional time for tests and assignments. During his ninth-grade year, he missed over 100 class periods and failed five classes. Even with a 1:1 special education teacher for algebra, the student failed the class. Despite his 0.97 grade average, the IEP team found he was progressing toward his goals. He advanced to grade ten by taking summer classes. During the student's tenth-grade school year, his absences decreased and he did not fail any classes. His grade average rose to 2.04. In grade eleven, the student continued making uneven progress despite increased absences. Significantly, his mother provided the school a note from his doctor describing his anxiety about his English class. The student was provided access to an emotional support classroom. His grade average increased to 2.19. Nonetheless, his mother filed a due process hearing complaint in December of his senior year of high school. She claimed the student's IEPs had been inadequate and denied him a free appropriate public education. A hearing officer denied her request for relief, as did a federal court.

On appeal, the Third Circuit Court of Appeals noted the Supreme Court's decision in *Endrew F. v. Douglas County School Dist.* requires school districts to provide "an educational program reasonably calculated to enable a child to make progress appropriate in light of the child's circumstances." **The court stated that if a school district complies with the *Endrew F*. standard, "it is not liable just because a student does not progress as quickly as his peers."** In this case, the IEPs were appropriate because they addressed the student's behavior and enabled his academic progress. In ruling for the school district, the court found he kept pace with his grade level and went from failing several classes to passing all of them. Not only did the student increase his grade average; he was offered programs addressing his behavior. While he contended his anxiety was evident, the court refused to judge his IEPs in hindsight. Once the district learned of his anxiety, it offered him emotional support. Finding the school district took reasonable steps to assist the student, the court held in its favor. *S.C. v. Oxford Area School Dist.*, 751 Fed.Appx. 220 (3d Cir. 2018).

◆   The Ninth Circuit Court of Appeals held a California school district did not violate federal law by failing to provide a student with autism with the assistive technology (AT) devices his parents wanted. The court held the hearing officer's decision withstood scrutiny under *Endrew F.* **The IEPs were reasonably calculated to enable the student to receive educational benefits and make appropriate progress in light of the circumstances.** The administrative decision recognized the district had failed to assess the student for a high-tech AT device for a one-year period. But the student made progress on his speech and language goals with non-electronic AT devices. There was evidence that children with autistic-like behaviors may begin using electronic AT devices as early as age three. However, the court held for the district on the ADA and Section 504 claims, finding the delay of an electronic AT assessment was not intentional bias. While the district should have assessed the student for a high-tech AT device at an earlier point, the court found its decision not to do so was the result of thorough and good-faith evaluations of the student's skills. The lower court properly held the state-law claims were barred by Eleventh Amendment immunity. Last, the court rejected the parents' arguments for more time to develop the facts. It issued a decision for the school district. *E.F. v. Newport Mesa Unified School Dist.*, 726 Fed.Appx. 535 (9th Cir. 2018).

◆   The U.S. Court of Appeals, Fifth Circuit, upheld the IEPs of a Texas student with multiple disabilities whose parents became disenchanted when school officials reassigned her to a new school. The court held that *Endrew F. v. Douglas County School Dist. RE-1*, 137 S.Ct. 988 (U.S. 2017), did not overrule *Cypress-Fairbanks Independent School Dist. v. Michael F.*, 118 F.3d 245 (5th Cir. 1997), its leading decision for assessing the appropriateness of a student's IEP. The court held the two cases "fit together." Further, a lower court and a magistrate judge had followed *Endrew F.* in upholding the IEPs at issue in this case. The court noted *Endrew F.* rejected the Tenth Circuit Court of Appeals' reliance on a minimal standard for assessing IEPs. *Endrew F.* requires that an IEP be "appropriately ambitious" for each student based upon his or her own individual circumstances. The court found the IEPs offered a free appropriate public education, and rejected the parents' predetermination claim. **Noting "the IEP standard is not perfection," the court found the IEPs were reasonably calculated to allow progress and provided the student a FAPE.** *E.R. v. Spring Branch Independent School Dist.*, 909 F.3d 754 (5th Cir. 2018).

◆ A Minnesota student's grade-nine IEP called for him to use Braille for all his assignments and instruction. His parents claimed he was not consistently provided accessible, accurate and timely Braille instructional materials. They filed a due process complaint against the district, which came before an administrative law judge (ALJ). After the hearing, the ALJ found the "provisions in the IEP were largely, although not perfectly implemented." Evidence indicated the student was progressing in his regular education and honors classes, and "met, and often exceeded, the ability to communicate with the proficiency of his peers." After the ALJ held for the school district, the parents appealed. Later, a federal court upheld the decision for the school district. Appeal then reached the U.S. Court of Appeals, Eighth Circuit.

In reviewing findings that the district may not have perfectly complied with the IEP, the court held "the IDEA does not require perfection." Evidence indicated that the district took steps to timely provide the student with accessible instructional materials. His grades indicated he received educational benefits. According to the student, higher standards imposed by state law may be enforced in an IDEA case. Instead, the court found no heightened standard was placed on the school district so as to create an absolute obligation to guarantee all blind students used Braille instruction to attain a specific level of instruction. Instead, **the IDEA does not guarantee a particular level of education or any particular educational outcome**. This standard was recently discussed in *Endrew F. v. Douglas County School Dist. RE-1*, this chapter. The court found the district complied with an IDEA regulation at 34 C.F.R. Part 300.172 by taking reasonable steps to provide instructional materials in accessible formats. **Prior IDEA cases have found an IEP need not maximize a student's potential or provide the best possible education.** *I.Z.M. v. Rosemount-Apple Valley-Eagan Public Schools*, 863 F.3d 966 (8th Cir. 2017).

◆ A Colorado school district did not adjust the IEP goals and objectives of a student with autism. His parents grew concerned about his lack of progress in a public school, noting his IEP goals and objectives were carried over from year to year. When the school district declined to make the "thorough overhaul" they sought for their son, they placed him in a private school. When the school district offered an IEP that did not meaningfully depart from the prior year's plan, the parents filed a due process request to recover tuition reimbursement.

When the case reached the U.S. Court of Appeals, Tenth Circuit, it held for the school district, noting the student's IEP objectives "were sufficient to show a pattern of, at the least, minimal progress." The parents appealed to the U.S. Supreme Court. In reviewing the case, the Court revisited *Board of*

Educ. of Hendrick Hudson Cent. School Dist., Westchester County v. Rowley, this chapter. *Rowley* rejected a lower court's ruling that a New York student's education "was not 'appropriate' unless it provided her with an opportunity to achieve her full potential commensurate with the opportunity provided to other children." In the Court's view, *Rowley* "carefully charted a middle path between the competing views of the district and the parents." **Under *Rowley*, the Court held no particular level of education is guaranteed, which "reflects the unobjectionable proposition that the IDEA cannot and does not promise any particular outcome."** Reiterating its language from *Rowley*, the Court held an IEP for a fully mainstreamed student with a disability should be "reasonably calculated to enable the child to achieve passing marks and advance from grade to grade." The Court rejected the Tenth Circuit's standard, which would have accepted merely minimal educational progress. Instead, a student's IEP "must be appropriately ambitious in light of his circumstances." Although some students would not make grade-level advancement, the Court held "every child should have the chance to meet challenging objectives." The IEP process ensures parents and educators provide their opinions about the IEP. **The Court held the IDEA "requires an educational program reasonably calculated to make progress appropriate in light of the child's circumstances."** "Appropriate progress" turns on the unique circumstances of each child. The Court returned the case to the Tenth Circuit for further proceedings. *Endrew F. v. Douglas County School Dist. RE-1*, 137 S.Ct. 988, 197 L.Ed.2d 335 (U.S. 2017).

When the case returned to the Tenth Circuit, it noted the Supreme Court had clarified that the standard for IEPs "is markedly more demanding than the 'merely more than *de minimis*' test applied by the Tenth Circuit." In sum, the Tenth Circuit vacated its prior order and returned the case to the trial court for further proceedings consistent with the Supreme Court's decision. *Endrew F. v. Douglas County School Dist. RE-1*, 694 Fed.Appx. 654 (10th Cir. 2017).

After the case returned to the trial court, it reviewed the Supreme Court's FAPE standard, then held the IEPs offered by the school district were insufficient to enable progress in light of the student's unique circumstances. It found the IEPs offered a "continued pattern of unambitious goals and objectives." His progress was found "minimal at best." **Only minor changes were made to the IEPs, and many goals were carried over from year to year or simply abandoned.** In addition, the district did not offer the student support to address his maladaptive behaviors. Further, the parties agreed he was making progress at his private school. As the IEP was not appropriately ambitious in light of the student's circumstances, and his private school was appropriate, the parents were to be reimbursed for their tuition and transportation costs, plus their attorneys' fees and costs. *Endrew F. v. Douglas County School Dist. RE 1*, 290 F.Supp.3d 1185 (D. Colo. 2018; 10th Cir. appeal dismissed 4/5/18).

◆ A New York student attended a private school for children with autism that used the Developmental, Individual Difference, Relationship/Floortime (DIR/Floortime) model. Her parents disagreed with an IEP offer by the New York Department of Education (DOE) and filed a due process complaint. An impartial hearing officer (IHO) held a hearing, then found DOE denied the student a free appropriate public education (FAPE). But a request for private tuition reimbursement was denied. A state review officer found the IEP provided the student a FAPE, and this decision was upheld by a federal district court.

On appeal, the Second Circuit Court of Appeals stated an IEP need not bring a child to grade level, but must aspire to more than minimal progress. In the parents' opinion, the school site selected by the DOE could not have implemented the IEP. They complained that the IEP did not specify DIR/Floortime methodology and had an inadequate student-to-staff ratio. The court found "the IEP implicitly recommended DIR/Floortime methodology and the overall goals set by the private school." It held the review officer reasonably found this methodology was not required. Instead, the IEP goals "reflected commonly used tenets of special education instruction, regardless of methodology employed." The court affirmed the review officer's findings that the IEP did not deny the student a FAPE. Next, the court found the student-to-staff ratio adopted by the IEP was sufficient. Evidence indicated that the DOE selected the student-to-staff ratio in the IEP based on a determination that it would provide a very structured, supported full-time special education setting. The parents relied on impermissible speculation in rejecting the school site selected by the DOE. As they did not show the school site selected for her was incapable of implementing the IEP or reasonably accommodating her allergies and other needs, the court held for the DOE. *N.B. and C.B. v. New York City Dep't of Educ.*, 711 Fed.Appx. 29 (2d Cir. 2017).

◆   Based on dissatisfaction with IEPs offered to their son by the New York City Department of Education (DOE), the parents enrolled him in a private school for students with autism. They requested a due process hearing, seeking tuition reimbursement. After a hearing, an impartial hearing officer (IHO) held the IEPs for two school years were insufficient. In addition to finding the IEP's vocational and transition services deficient, the IHO found the DOE did not give enough notice for one year and provided insufficient goals for both IEPs. Moreover, the IHO found the IEPs were predetermined and called for classroom student-to-educator ratios that would not allow the student to have appropriate social interactions. The IHO also disapproved of the teaching methodology employed in the classrooms and found the recommended school sites ill-equipped to implement the IEPs. A state review officer reversed the decision, finding any DOE procedural violations did not deny the student a FAPE. A federal court also held for the DOE. Appeal then reached the U.S. Court of Appeals, Second Circuit, which declared that the IDEA guarantees "an appropriate education, not one that provides everything that might be thought desirable by loving parents."

Review of an IEP proceeds in two steps. **First, a court examines whether the school has complied with IDEA procedures. Next, it considers whether the IEP is reasonably calculated to enable a child to make progress appropriate in light of the child's circumstances.** Tuition reimbursement based on procedural violations is permitted only when an IEP has (1) impeded a child's right to a FAPE, (2) significantly infringed upon a parent's opportunity to participate in the IEP decision-making process or (3) caused a deprivation of educational benefits. In this case, the parents did not show any procedural violations led to inadequacy of the IEP or affected the decision-making process. There was evidence that the DOE did not conduct an in-person assessment of the student because his parents submitted a private assessment. They declined invitations to bring him to meetings at which postsecondary goals and transition services were discussed because they felt that he could not sit through meetings. Finding the IEPs were reasonably calculated to provide postsecondary goals and transition services required by the IDEA, the court held for the DOE. *R.B. v. New York City Dep't of Educ.*, 689 Fed.Appx. 48 (2d Cir. 2017).

◆ A Texas student with autism and pervasive developmental delays attended special education classrooms with speech and occupational therapy and other services. Dissatisfied with her progress, the parents rejected an IEP proposal and enrolled her in a private school. They filed a due process complaint, seeking reimbursement for their private costs. A hearing officer held for the school district and the parents appealed to a federal court, where they added a disability discrimination claim under Rehabilitation Act Section 504. The court held for the district on both the administrative appeal and the Section 504 claim.

On appeal, the U.S. Court of Appeals, Fifth Circuit, noted the Supreme Court's decision in *Endrew F. v. Douglas County School Dist. RE-1*, this chapter, declared that parents and schools must collaborate to develop an IEP that is "reasonably calculated to enable a child to make progress appropriate in light of the child's circumstances." **An IEP must be reasonably likely to produce progress, not regression, or trivial educational advancement.** While the lower court did not apply the *Endrew F.* test verbatim, the Fifth Circuit found it examined whether the educational benefit to the student had to be more than minimal and likely to produce progress, not regression or trivial educational advancement. As the lower court found, the IEP was appropriately ambitious in view of the student's circumstances. Evidence indicated she was making progress, and that the district adjusted its strategies and altered her school day in response to her parents' concerns. Since the lower court correctly held for the school district, the court affirmed the judgment. *C.G. v. Waller Independent School Dist.*, 697 Fed.Appx. 816 (5th Cir. 2017).

◆ According to the U.S. Supreme Court in the leading case of *Board of Educ. of Hendrick Hudson Cent. School Dist., Westchester County v. Rowley,* the IDEA's precursor – known as the Education for All Handicapped Children Act – was not enacted to maximize the potential of students, but rather to open the door of educational opportunity. Students such as Amy Rowley – an eight-year-old New York student with profound hearing impairments who attended regular classrooms – "would generally require an IEP reasonably calculated to enable the child to achieve passing marks and advance from grade to grade." In view of Amy's excellent progress and array of IEP services, the Court found the school district complied with the free appropriate public education (FAPE) requirement. The Court observed that in passing the IDEA, "Congress sought primarily to make public education available to [children with disabilities]. But in seeking to provide such access to public education, Congress did not impose upon the States any greater substantive educational standard than would be necessary to make such access meaningful." According to the Court, the IDEA imposed no requirement on states to provide equal educational opportunities and Congress recognized that educational opportunity differs among students of varying abilities. Because of the "wide spectrum" of abilities, the Court refused to establish a test to determine the adequacy of educational benefits provided by schools under the IDEA. It held:

> Insofar as a State is required to provide a handicapped child with a "free appropriate public education," we hold that it satisfies this requirement by providing **personalized instruction with sufficient support services to permit the child to benefit educationally from that instruction**. Such instruction and services must be provided at public expense, must meet the State's educational standards, must approximate the grade levels used in the State's regular education, and must comport with the child's IEP. In addition, the IEP, and therefore the personalized instruction, should be formulated in accordance with the requirements of the Act and, if the child is being educated in the regular classrooms of the public education system, should be **reasonably calculated to enable the child to achieve passing marks and advance from grade to grade**.

The Court ruled that the school board was not required to provide the sign-language interpreter. The IDEA required only the development of an IEP that was reasonably calculated to enable the disabled student to derive some educational benefit. **The IDEA created a minimum floor** for the provision of special education services but did not require states to maximize the potential of each disabled child. In this case, the child was advancing through school easily and was not entitled to an interpreter, despite evidence that this would remedy the disparity between her achievement and her potential. *Board of Educ. of Hendrick Hudson Cent. School Dist., Westchester County v. Rowley,* 458 U.S. 176, 102 S.Ct. 3034, 73 L.Ed.2d 690 (1982).

◆   An Alabama student struggled in elementary school and had to repeat a grade. He was placed in special education in middle school. For grade nine, the student passed only two classes. But the IEP team granted his mother's request to place him on a regular diploma track. It also let him "double up" on his grade nine and 10 classes so he could remain with his peers. Asserting that the school board denied her child a free appropriate public education (FAPE), the mother filed a due process hearing request. A hearing officer held the school district provided the student a FAPE. When the case reached the U.S. Court of Appeals, Eleventh Circuit, it found the student's IEP reading goals were not adapted to address his individual needs. His reading skills were assessed at a first-grade level, but the reading goal for the IEP was derived from the state standard for ninth-graders. Moreover, the student's IEP goals remained largely the same from year to year. **The school used "boilerplate IEPs," with goals going far beyond his reading levels that did not provide him educational benefits.** Postsecondary goals and transition services stated in the IEPs did not meet relevant standards. Finding a lack of individualized planning and a program that denied the student a FAPE, the court held for the parent. *Jefferson County Board of Educ. v. Lolita S.,* 581 Fed.Appx. 760 (11th Cir. 2014).

◆ In 2000, the Fifth Circuit Court of Appeals described a test for assessing the appropriateness of an IEP that has been cited in almost 200 cases. The test requires an assessment of: whether (1) the IEP is individualized on the basis of the student's assessment and performance; (2) is administered in the least restrictive environment; (3) services are provided in a coordinated and collaborative manner by the key "stake-holders"; and (4) positive academic and non-academic benefits are demonstrated. *Houston Independent School Dist. v. Bobby R.,* 200 F.3d 341 (5th Cir. 2000).

C. U.S. Supreme Court Cases

◆ Reiterating its language from *Board of Educ. of Hendrick Hudson Cent. School Dist., Westchester County v. Rowley,* 458 U.S. 176 (1982), the Supreme Court clarified in 2017 that *Rowley* did not endorse one standard for determining whether a child was receiving sufficient educational benefits. An IEP "must be appropriately ambitious in light of his circumstances." Although some students would not make grade-level advancement, the Court held "every child should have the chance to meet challenging objectives." The IEP process ensures that parents and educators will provide their opinions on the progress an IEP should pursue. **The Court held the IDEA "requires an educational program reasonably calculated to make progress appropriate in light of the child's circumstances."** It declined to define what "appropriate progress" means, as this turns on each child's unique circumstances. *Endrew F. v. Douglas County School Dist. RE-1,* 137 S.Ct. 988, 197 L.Ed.2d 335 (U.S. 2017).

◆ The Supreme Court granted a Michigan student an opportunity to show she did not have to file an IDEA due process complaint prior to suing a school district because administrators refused to allow her to bring her service dog to school. The IDEA requires exhaustion of its procedures before filing a lawsuit under the ADA, Section 504 or similar laws, when the relief sought is available under the IDEA. If an action seeks a remedy that implicates the provision of a free appropriate education (FAPE), exhaustion is required. **A reviewing court should review the substance of the complaint when determining whether the FAPE obligation is implicated.** A court should examine whether the claim could be brought if the matter took place at a public facility other than a school. If the family could have filed a similar claim against a non-school entity, or a similar action could have been filed by an employee or a visitor, the complaint would be unlikely to involve a FAPE. If a complaint involved a FAPE, a court should also examine the history of the proceedings. If the family has previously invoked IDEA procedures, this suggests the FAPE obligation is implicated. *Fry v. Napoleon Community Schools,* 137 S.Ct. 743, 197 L.Ed.2d 46 (U.S. 2017).

◆ A Maryland student with learning disabilities and a speech impairment attended private schools until the eighth grade, when his parents sought to place him in district schools. The district conducted an evaluation and drafted an IEP that would have placed him in one of two district schools. The parents rejected the offer, seeking a smaller classroom setting with more intensive services. They requested an IDEA due process hearing, where the administrative law judge ruled they had the burden of persuasion and did not meet it. Eventually the case reached the U.S. Supreme Court, which agreed that **parents who challenge IEPs have the burden of proving that the IEPs are not appropriate**. To do otherwise would force courts to assume that every IEP is invalid until the school district demonstrates that it is not. *Schaffer v. Weast*, 546 U.S. 49, 126 S.Ct. 528, 163 L.Ed.2d 387 (2005).

◆ The Supreme Court held that an Iowa school district had to provide a quadriplegic student with a full-time aide to assure his meaningful access to education under the IDEA. **Providing an aide amounted to a necessary related service and not an excluded medical service.** Using a "bright-line" rule, the Court limited medical services to those provided by a physician. *Cedar Rapids Community School Dist. v. Garret F.*, 526 U.S. 66, 119 S.Ct. 992, 143 L.Ed.2d 154 (1999).

◆ The U.S. Supreme Court held that a New York statute that created a special school district for a religious community (which had been incorporated as a village) had to be struck down as violative of the Establishment Clause. **The special school district exceeded the bounds of religious neutrality** required by the Constitution. *Board of Educ. of Kiryas Joel Village School Dist. v. Grumet,* 512 U.S. 687, 114 S.Ct. 2481, 129 L.Ed.2d 546 (1994).

◆ The Court held that the failure of a school district to propose an appropriate IEP and placement for a student with a learning disability justified an award of private school tuition reimbursement by the district, even though the private school was not approved by the state of South Carolina. This was because the private school placement was appropriate and because South Carolina did not publish a list of approved schools. The IDEA requirement to provide a free appropriate public education did not apply to parental placements. **To recover private school tuition costs, parents must show that the placement proposed by the school district violates the IDEA and that the private school placement is appropriate under the act.** Federal courts have broad discretion in granting relief under the IDEA and may reduce tuition reimbursement awards found to be unreasonably expensive. The Court upheld the lower court decisions in favor of the parents. *Florence County School Dist. Four v. Carter*, 510 U.S. 7, 114 S.Ct. 361, 126 L.Ed.2d 284 (1993).

◆ The Establishment Clause of the First Amendment did not bar a public school district from **providing a sign-language interpreter to an Arizona student who attended a parochial school**. The provision of the interpreter was a neutral service that provided only an indirect economic benefit to the parochial school. *Zobrest v. Catalina Foothills School Dist.,* 509 U.S. 1, 113 S.Ct. 2462, 125 L.Ed.2d 1 (1993).

◆ In *Dellmuth v. Muth,* 491 U.S. 223, 109 S.Ct. 2397, 105 L.Ed.2d 181 (1989), the Supreme Court held Congress did not intend that the IDEA permit monetary damages against states in actions brought in federal courts. This permitted Pennsylvania to avoid liability in an IDEA damage suit brought by a student with a learning disability. [In 1990, Congress responded by abrogating sovereign immunity (20 U.S.C. § 1403) in IDEA cases and authorizing both equitable (injunctive and declaratory) and legal remedies for IDEA violations.]

◆   The suspension or expulsion of a special education student constitutes a change of placement under the IDEA, according to the 1988 decision *Honig v. Doe*. School authorities may not unilaterally exclude a child from classes pending administrative proceedings. However, **the IDEA's stay-put provision (20 U.S.C. § 1415(j)) did not prevent school districts from imposing temporary suspensions of 10 school days or less** upon students who present a threat of harm to other persons. *Honig v. Doe*, 484 U.S. 305, 108 S.Ct. 592, 98 L.Ed.2d 686 (1988). The 1997 Amendments address suspensions for disciplinary reasons in 20 U.S.C. Section 1415(k) and allow removal from class for up to 45 days on a case-by-case basis under unique circumstances.

◆   The parents of a Massachusetts student with a learning disability violated the IDEA's stay-put provision by unilaterally enrolling him in a private school. Because the proposed IEP was held appropriate, the parents were not entitled to tuition reimbursement and other costs. The Court noted that in some cases, parents may be reimbursed for unilaterally placing a student in a private school. A court must find the proposed IEP inappropriate to allow this. **Parents who unilaterally change their children's placement do so at their own risk**, because if the proposed IEP is upheld, the parents have to pay for it. *School Committee of the Town of Burlington, Massachusetts v. Dep't of Educ. of Massachusetts,* 471 U.S. 359, 105 S.Ct. 1996, 85 L.Ed.2d 385 (1985).

◆   **A Texas school district had to provide catheterization services for a student with a disability while she attended school because it was a "supportive service" (related service)** under the IDEA, 20 U.S.C. § 1401(26). The Court held that the student's parents were also entitled to receive their attorneys' fees under Section 504 of the Rehabilitation Act. *Irving Independent School Dist. v. Tatro*, 468 U.S. 883, 104 S.Ct. 3371, 82 L.Ed.2d 664 (1984).

◆   A Rhode Island student with cerebral palsy was not entitled to recover attorneys' fees despite prevailing in an IDEA lawsuit against his school district in *Smith v. Robinson*. The Court ruled that there was no evidence that the school district had violated any of the student's procedural safeguards under the IDEA. Congress responded to the *Smith* decision by passing the Handicapped Children's Protection Act of 1986 (P.L. 9-372), which **specifically authorized attorneys' fee awards to students with disabilities who prevailed in IDEA lawsuits**. The same act provided that students may cumulate remedies under Section 504 of the Rehabilitation Act (29 U.S.C. § 794) and 42 U.S.C. § 1983. *Smith v. Robinson*, 468 U.S. 992, 104 S.Ct. 3457, 82 L.Ed.2d 746 (1984).

[In *Fry v. Napoleon Community Schools,* the Supreme Court observed that *Smith v. Robinson* was superseded by law. As the Handicapped Children's Protection Act of 1986 substantially overruled the Court's decision in *Smith*, there is no further summary of the case in this book.]

II. SECTION 504 AND THE ADA

The Americans with Disabilities Act (ADA), 42 U.S.C. Section 12101, et seq., and Section 504 of the Rehabilitation Act, 29 U.S.C. Section 794, prohibit discrimination based on a disability and require reasonable accommodations for qualified individuals with disabilities. Although the ADA requires a person to define disability by reference to an impairment that substantially limits a major life activity, the IDEA instead requires that a student have a qualifying disability that creates a need for special education and related services.

In Ricks v. State of Hawaii Dep't of Educ., *752 Fed.Appx. 518 (9th Cir. 2019), the Ninth Circuit Court of Appeals noted that implementing an IEP is one means of ensuring compliance with Section 504 requirements. It held a lower court properly drew a careful distinction between a claim for denial of a FAPE under the IDEA and a claim for disability discrimination based on denial of meaningful access to education under Section 504.*

The Rehabilitation Act is a federal law intended to promote employment training and habilitation for individuals with disabilities. Its key provision, Section 504 (29 U.S.C. Section 794) prohibits entities that receive federal funds from discriminating against individuals with disabilities in their programs or services. Since school districts, states and educational agencies receive federal funds, Section 504 complaints are commonly filed by students seeking educational benefits, by individuals seeking employment or benefits, and by employees claiming disability discrimination.

Section 504 of the Rehabilitation Act differs from the IDEA in scope, intent and coverage. The congressional objective of Section 504 is the elimination of discrimination against individuals with disabilities.

A. Section 504 Plans

Federal regulations interpreting Section 504 in the educational context specify that disabled students are entitled to a free appropriate public education (FAPE) and reasonable accommodations. Although an IEP is not required for an individual who is a student with a disability under Section 504, the regulations state that providing a student with an IEP is one way to meet Section 504 requirements to provide a FAPE.

In A.G. v. Paradise Valley Unified School Dist., *this chapter, the Ninth Circuit reiterated its opinion that a free appropriate public education (FAPE) is defined differently under Section 504 and the IDEA. The distinction was made in* Mark H. v. Lemahieu, *513 F.3d 922 (9th Cir. 2008). In the court's view, Section 504 regulations gauge the adequacy of services to disabled persons by comparing them to the level of services provided to non-disabled persons. A FAPE as defined by the IDEA instead requires an inquiry into the adequacy of a student's IEP in view of the student's individual needs.*

Beginning with the 2019–2020 school year, Illinois school boards must post notice on their websites and in student handbooks or newsletters that students with disabilities who do not qualify for an IEP under the IDEA may qualify for services under Section 504 of the Rehabilitation Act. Notices must state that qualification under Section 504 requires that a student (i) have a physical or

*mental impairment that substantially limits one or more major life activities, (ii)
have a record of a physical or mental impairment, or (iii) be regarded as having
a physical or mental impairment. One-Hundredth Illinois General Assembly,
P.A. 100-1112. H.B. 5770. Illinois School Code 105 ILCS 5/14–6.01.*

◆   A Georgia student with Attention Deficit Hyperactivity Disorder (ADHD)
performed well in an honors program at a magnet school with accommodations
stated in a Section 504 plan. His parents rejected additional help for fear of
his being stigmatized. He earned high scores on his End of Course Tests and
passed his classes. Two teachers wrote him letters of recommendation for MIT.
Teachers unanimously rejected any suggestion that the student needed special
education prior to his senior year, when his grades plummeted and he amassed
five failing grades. At a meeting to discuss his 504 plan, the student admitted
he had been procrastinating. He completed his senior year coursework, but
was unable to do so in time to graduate with his class. In May of his senior
year, his parents requested a special education evaluation. While the school
went forward with an evaluation, the parents requested a due process hearing.
       An administrative law judge held for the school district and a federal
court affirmed the decision. On appeal, the U.S. Court of Appeals, Eleventh
Circuit, found that for most of his school career, the student met or exceeded
expectations. He demonstrated college readiness, excelled on college entrance
exams and passed honors and AP courses until his senior slump. When the
student failed classes as a high school senior, his school promptly initiated
IDEA evaluation processes. **At meetings to modify his Section 504 plan, he
acknowledged his lack of effort. While ADHD can be an IDEA-qualifying
disability under the other health impairment category, the court found no
evidence that the student's ADHD adversely affected his education prior to
the relevant time.** The court held that special education is generally ill-suited
for students who are making adequate academic progress, but neglect their
work. The court found no violation of the IDEA child-find duty. *Durbrow v.
Cobb County School Dist.*, 887 F.3d 1182 (11th Cir. 2018).

◆   A Pennsylvania student with a complication of Ehlers-Danlos syndrome
called Postural Orthostatic Tachycardia Syndrome (POTS) had symptoms
such as severe dizziness, fainting, headaches, fatigue, difficulty concentrating
and other problems. He fainted twice in a period of less than four years, and
his school district developed a Section 504 plan for him. The plan included
recommendations from his pediatrician, a cardiologist and his parents. Among
other things, the plan stated that if the student felt dizziness or light-headedness,
the school nurse would be called and he would be escorted to the health room
for evaluation. He was to have unlimited access to water and lavatories. After the
student's teacher overheard him say that he felt sick, she sent him to the nurse's
office. Once there, he fainted, fell from a chair and suffered a concussion. The
school later held a meeting to discuss modifications to the Section 504 plan.
       After the meeting, the parents asked to have a medically trained aide
assigned to the student. A pediatrician wrote letters stating his support for the
aide to be immediately available to the student throughout the entire school
day. The district instead developed a medical alert poster to ensure that nurses

and teachers knew of his condition. In addition, the nurse provided training to district staff. The parents filed a due process complaint, seeking an order to require the district to assign a medically trained aide to the student. A hearing officer denied the parents' request, and they appealed to a federal court. **The court found Section 504 of the Rehabilitation Act requires the reasonable accommodation of the needs of a child with a disability to ensure meaningful participation in educational activities and access to educational benefits.** In this case, the parents relied primarily on statements by a pediatrician whom the hearing officer identified as an advocate, rather than an objective expert. By contrast, the school nurse stated that the student did not require an aide. The court rejected claims that the student was twice excluded from activities in a discriminatory manner. As the hearing officer found, the school did not have to provide him a medically trained aide. *Rylan M. v. Dover Area School Dist.*, No. 1:16-CV-1260, 2017 WL 1862337 (M.D. Pa. 5/9/17).

◆   An Arizona seventh-grader attended a program for uniquely gifted students with high IQs and learning or behavioral disabilities. She refused to go to class, destroyed school property, threatened to harm herself, acted aggressively, caused disruption and was noncompliant. After the student did not cooperate with a school resource officer and hit her, the school suspended her and met to amend her IEP. After the IEP meeting, the school district transferred her to a school for students with emotional disturbances. On her second day at the new school, the student resisted entering the building and had to be escorted to an intervention room. She kicked a paraprofessional in the face and a municipal police officer arrested her for aggravated assault and criminal damage. The officer handcuffed the student and detained her until her mother arrived at the school. About six weeks later, a teacher called the same officer to escort the student to the intervention room. The officer tried to handcuff the student, but she said the student resisted and scratched her. As a result, the student was again arrested for aggravated assault. This time, she was placed in juvenile detention.

After pursuing a due process complaint, the parents filed a lawsuit against the district, municipality and the municipal officer who had arrested the student. The parents settled their claims against the officer and municipality. They reached a settlement with the district regarding the IDEA claims. But discrimination claims arising under Section 504 of the Rehabilitation Act and Title II of the Americans with Disabilities Act (ADA) went forward. During pretrial activity, the court held for the school district. The parents appealed to the U.S. Court of Appeals, Ninth Circuit, which explained that there is an implied right of action for monetary damages under Section 504. The court disagreed with the district's argument that the parents had waived their Section 504 and ADA challenge by consenting to placement at the school for emotional disturbances. In the court's view, the lower court had improperly dismissed the Section 504 and ADA claims for denial of meaningful access and reasonable accommodations. It held **the parents presented evidence that placement in the school for students with emotional disturbances denied her meaningful access to educational opportunities, such as art, music and gifted education programming**. In addition, the parents said their child was placed inappropriately in the intervention room. They said the school deprived her of appropriate behavioral supports and offered her deficient IEPs. The lower court would have to reconsider whether certain accommodations would have helped the student remain in her original placement. *A.G. v. Paradise Valley Unified School Dist.*, 815 F.3d 1195 (9th Cir. 2016).

◆   A Pennsylvania high school student attended a rigorous, advanced program for gifted students. In her junior year, she was diagnosed with gastroparesis and was intermittently hospitalized. She received weekly homebound instruction, which her parents supplemented with private tutoring. Although she returned to school for her senior year, she had a relapse and remained at home. The school found the student eligible for a Section 504 service plan allowing her to attend school when her health allowed. Near this time, she was diagnosed with an anxiety disorder. Her parents questioned the effectiveness of homebound instruction, noting a school district instructor was unable to provide substantive guidance in advanced placement courses such as Japanese and Chinese. The student dropped some courses and completed others with tutoring. Although the district sought permission to evaluate the student for eligibility under the IDEA, the parents declined. A Section 504 plan was offered to her with "significantly more permissive accommodations" such as a lack of attendance penalties for medical absences and permission to enter and exit the school as needed. But the student soon fell behind in her classes and began taking refuge in the library.

After finishing the school year at home with the help of private tutoring, the student graduated 21st in her class of 336. But she had to withdraw from college in her second year. Her parents filed a due process complaint against the district. A hearing officer found the district had been careless, but did not act with deliberate indifference to the student's rights. The parents sued the school district in a federal court, claiming it did not properly implement the Section 504 plan. The court held for the district and the parents appealed. The U.S. Court of Appeals, Third Circuit, rejected the argument that state law entitled the student to accommodations that maximized her potential. It found that **virtually every interaction between the parents and school district had led to express action to address the student's concerns**. Homebound services were never intended to be a substitute for in-class learning. On the whole, the district provided the student with a meaningful opportunity to pass advanced courses and allow her to gain admission to a prestigious university. As a result, the court found no discrimination. The parents rejected suggestions to evaluate the child for IDEA eligibility and to coordinate services from the district and her psychologist. **Since there had been no deliberate indifference to the student's rights, the court held for the school district.** *K.K. v. Pittsburgh Public Schools*, 590 Fed.Appx. 148 (3d Cir. 2014).

◆   Due to Klinefelter Syndrome and ADHD, a California student was eligible for Section 504 accommodations. He enrolled in an advanced placement (AP) calculus course, where he struggled and suffered from anxiety and weight loss. His mother asked for permission to drop the class but was told the three-day window for dropping classes had passed. An administrator said no exceptions could be made to the school policy. A hearing officer denied the parent's request for an order requiring the district to pay for a Section 504 evaluation and remove a failing AP calculus grade from the student's records. On appeal, a federal court dismissed the Section 504 claim. It held **the student was prohibited from dropping the AP class under a general rule of the school district, not because of a disability**. But the student had a plausible claim regarding a timeline and procedure to evaluate students who might need Section 504 accommodations. He could refile the claim to allege denial of a service or benefit solely due to a disability. But he could not show any deprivation of a protected interest in not being allowed to drop his AP course. As a due process right is implicated only when exclusion from the entire educational process is at stake, the court dismissed the constitutional claims. *S.M. v. San Jose Unified School Dist.*, No. 14-CV-03613, 2015 WL 1737535 (N.D. Cal. 4/13/15).

◆   Wisconsin parents of a child with Type 1 diabetes worked with their school to develop a Section 504 plan incorporating his doctor's orders to administer insulin doses and snacks at school. The plan required the school to train three employees as "trained diabetes personnel." Although the parents were mostly satisfied during the child's kindergarten year, they maintained only one school nurse had the training to be qualified under the "trained diabetes personnel" designation. Conflict grew when a school nurse supervisor banned the nurse from deviating from insulin dosages recommended by the personal diabetes manager on a "case by case basis." The supervisor believed state law required strict adherence to doctor's orders and did not allow school nurses to follow conflicting parental instructions. After filing an agency complaint, the parents sued the school district in a federal court. The court held for the school district.

On appeal, the Seventh Circuit Court of Appeals held that **for a Section 504 plan violation to be deemed disability discrimination, it must be significant enough to effectively deny a child the benefit of a public education**. As the lower court found, the district trained three people to serve as "trained diabetes personnel" in fulfillment of the 504 plan. Any violation of the plan by the school was minor. The school's refusal to employ the case-by-case approach urged by the parents amounted to a dispute over doctor orders. As the doctor's orders were confusing and the school's refusal to deviate from them was not unreasonable, the court found no discrimination. The court held for the school district. *CTL v. Ashland School Dist.*, 743 F.3d 524 (7th Cir. 2014).

◆   A Pennsylvania student with a severe nut allergy was deemed at risk of life-threatening allergic reactions. Although at least four meetings were held to develop a Section 504 accommodation plan for the student, no agreement could be reached. Believing the district's plan was not sufficiently detailed, the parents gave the school a 19-page proposed plan. The district rejected the plan because some items were already standard district procedures and because the plan was excessively long. Although the district offered new Section 504 plan proposals, the parents rejected them – even one that had been approved by the student's doctor. The parents then filed a complaint against the district with a state agency. A hearing officer found the district did not discriminate against the student or deny him a free appropriate public education.

A federal court held for the school district, and appeal reached the U.S. Court of Appeals, Third Circuit. The court found evidence that a Section 504 plan relating to food allergies had to be accessible and understandable to staff in the event of an emergency. District teachers and staff were trained to identify symptoms of anaphylaxis and to administer epinephrine. **The court held the failure to include each requested accommodation and detail requested by the parents was not a Section 504 violation.** There was evidence that the district worked diligently with the parents to ensure their child participated in school activities and had access to educational benefits. Since the parents did not show their child was denied program benefits or subjected to discrimination, the court held for the district. *T.F. v. Fox Chapel Area School Dist.*, 589 Fed. Appx. 594 (3d Cir. 2014).

B. FAPE Under Section 504

Because Section 504 and the ADA define disability more broadly than the IDEA, some students are covered by Section 504 and the ADA but not the IDEA. A Section 504 regulation, 34 C.F.R. Part 104.33, mandates that schools provide qualified students with disabilities a free appropriate public education (FAPE).

In Mark H. v. Lemahieu, *513 F.3d 922 (9th Cir. 2008), the Ninth Circuit held a Section 504 free appropriate public education (FAPE) is not identical to FAPE under the IDEA. And in* K.M. v. Tustin Unified School Dist., *725 F.3d 1088 (9th Cir. 2013), the court held a valid IEP did not necessarily satisfy ADA Title II communication requirements. The court held that in some cases, the ADA might require schools to provide different services than under the IDEA.*

Revocation of consent to IDEA services does not eliminate the broader protections of Section 504 and the Americans with Disabilities Act. See Kimble v. Douglas County School Dist. RE-1, *925 F.Supp.2d 1176 (D. Colo. 2013), summarized in Chapter Two, Section II.B. of this volume.*

◆ A federal court found New York school officials fully informed a parent at an IEP meeting that her request to place her child in a residential facility was being denied and did not mislead her in any way. According to the parent, the school district's inaction resulted in a "crisis" for her child during the 2011-12 school year. In 2015, she initiated an impartial hearing complaint, asserting claims under the IDEA and Section 504 of the Rehabilitation Act. Because the parent's claims involved a number of school years between 2005-6 through 2011-12, an impartial hearing officer dismissed the IDEA claims as untimely. However, the hearing officer found the district violated Section 504 by failing to provide the student with a residential placement from January to June 2012. A federal court later held for the district, finding the IDEA and Section 504 claims were untimely.

On appeal, the U.S. Court of Appeals, Second Circuit, observed that in cases involving limitation of actions, "the proper focus is on the time of the discriminatory act, not the point at which the consequences of the act become painful." In this case, **the court found the decision to deny a residential placement for the 2011-12 school year was the act underlying the Section 504 claim**. The "crisis" identified by the parent later in the year manifested an act taking place in May 2011. Next, the court rejected the parent's claim that the district made misrepresentations that required extending the time limit on filing her case. There was no merit to her claim that she did not adequately understand her due process rights. Nor was there evidence that the district misrepresented that it resolved the problem forming the basis for her complaint. Finding the action was untimely and that no exception allowed the parent to extend the time for filing suit, the court affirmed the dismissal of the case. *Board of Educ. of North Rockland Cent. School Dist. v. C.M.*, 744 Fed.Appx. 7 (2d Cir. 2018).

◆ A California student had multiple disorders including ADHD, autism, a mood disorder with psychotic features, intermittent explosive disorder and reading and written language disorders. As a kindergartner, she threw a chair, head-butted a teacher and had tantrums. Following two incidents in which she tried to stab others with objects, she was hospitalized as a danger to herself and others. Despite her many behavior problems and outbursts, the student remained in general education classrooms for up to 100% of her school day. While she was in grade two, she was admitted to a psychiatric hospital. For grade three, the student was offered a placement with 95% general education inclusion. Her behavior problems continued, and the school often called her mother to take her home. But by the end of grade three, the student regressed academically and behaviorally. Her parents placed her in a non-public school, where she received counseling and mental health services for grade four. They commenced a due process proceeding against the school district, asserting IDEA violations and retaliation against them when the district revoked funding for an independent educational evaluation of the student's younger brother. A hearing officer held for the parents, ordering the school district to reimburse them for their private school tuition and travel costs. The district appealed to a federal court.

In pretrial activity, the court rejected an argument that the Section 504 claim for denial of a FAPE improperly duplicated the IDEA claim. **As the Ninth Circuit has held, Section 504 and the IDEA have differing FAPE standards.** The IDEA's FAPE provisions permit actions for prospective relief only, while Section 504 broadly prohibits disability-based discrimination. Section 504 may be enforced in a lawsuit seeking prospective relief as well as compensatory damages. In this case, the court found the district did not counter the parents' Section 504 claim. They asserted retaliation in the denial of funding for an IEE for their younger child after the district had approved such funding. Although certain claims against a school employee had to be dismissed, the court otherwise held for the parents. *Bonsall Unified School Dist. v. Richard C.*, No. 17-CV-1386 W (MDD), 2018 WL 638233 (S.D. Cal. 1/31/2018).

◆ A Texas student with cerebral palsy used a wheelchair and needed help with lavatory transfers. Two employees were supposed to accompany disabled children during lavatory breaks under a school policy, but they often made such transfers without help. An aide who was assigned to help the student at school accompanied him alone to the lavatory and sexually molested him there. After the student told his mother of the assault, she reported the aide, who confessed to the misconduct. In a federal court, the mother sued the school district under the ADA, Section 504 of the Rehabilitation Act and Title IX of the 1972 Education Amendments. In pretrial activity, the family settled its claims against the aide. After the court held for the school district on the remaining claims, the family appealed to the U.S. Court of Appeals, Fifth Circuit. Rejecting the ADA claim, the court held the evidence did not support claims by the student that the district denied him an accessible, safe lavatory. It found the lavatory had safety devices for disabled students and that several urinals were accessible. Two employees accompanied the student on the vast majority of his lavatory visits.

Attempts to accommodate a student with a disability, even if imperfect, do not support an intentional discrimination claim. **In order to pursue a Section 504 claim based on failure to provide a free appropriate public education (FAPE), the student had to show some evidence of bad faith or gross mismanagement by the school district.** But the student failed to show a denial of a FAPE. The school district held no less than 28 IEP meetings to formulate his program. Any flaws in his IEPs did not result in the loss of an educational opportunity. Finding insufficient evidence to show the district failed to provide the student with educational opportunities or grossly mismanaged his IEP, the court affirmed the judgment for the district. *Estrada v. San Antonio Independent School Dist.*, 575 Fed.Appx. 541 (5th Cir. 2014).

◆   A Maryland student had ADHD and was eligible for a Section 504 plan. Despite having accommodations, she had difficulty with her classes. By grade six, her parents obtained medical opinions suggesting she needed an IEP instead of a Section 504 plan. But the school system repeatedly declined their requests to consider an IEP. Team members instead discussed removing accommodations that had already been granted. The parents said that as her eighth-grade year went on, teachers did not consistently provide some Section 504 plan accommodations. After removing their child from school, the parents enrolled her in a private school for grade nine and requested a hearing. An ALJ dismissed the complaint. A federal court held **liability under Section 504 in the context of the provision of FAPE requires a showing of bad faith or gross misjudgment by the school system.** While this is a very high standard, the court found the parents set forth facts suggesting the school system denied accommodations it had agreed to provide without explanation. When the student was in eighth grade, the school's diligence in addressing her needs appeared to decline markedly. Teachers insisted that she advocate for her own accommodations even though her language difficulties significantly hindered her ability to do so. Near this time, evaluators were continuing to find the student had additional areas of weakness. Since the facts supported a finding that the district was no longer acting in good faith to fully address the student's needs, the court returned the case to the administrative level for a hearing. *K.D. v. Starr*, 55 F.Supp.3d 782 (D. Md. 2014).

◆   A California student who experienced seizures claimed her school did not allow her reasonable accommodations. When she entered high school, she had a number of seizures in class. She said teachers did not know what to do and often did not follow her seizure plans. By the end of the student's ninth-grade year, her parent said a vice principal told her the seizures "were too much for the school to handle" and that she should be kept at home. Although the school found the student eligible for a Section 504 plan, she was not found IDEA-eligible. After the student had a seizure in jazz choir class, her parent claimed she was required to reaudition. The school district found the student was not

IDEA-eligible. The parent dismissed a due process complaint she had filed, based on the district's finding that the student was not IDEA-eligible. She sued the school district in a federal court for violating Section 504 and the ADA.

Although some of the student's discrimination claims involved denial of a FAPE and failure to accommodate a disability, the court found that there was no IDEA relief available for her. Next, the court held the student qualified for federal disability protection. She said she had been excluded from class, disallowed from making up work or compensating for missed class time and excluded from participating in the jazz choir. Since these actions denied the student the benefits of a full public education, the court held she could pursue her discrimination claims. In addition, **the student asserted intentional discrimination by the district, which was on notice that she needed accommodations to obtain the benefits of a public education**. As the student stated valid Section 504 and ADA claims, she also made out a case under the state civil rights act. The court denied the district's motion for dismissal and to strike parts of the complaint. *S.L. v. Downey Unified School Dist.*, No. CV 13-06050 DDP (PJWx), 2014 WL 934942 (C.D. Cal. 3/10/14).

◆   A Florida school board devised an IEP that placed a child with hearing impairments in a segregated setting for one hour. As his mother felt this was unnecessary and detrimental, she withdrew her consent for the IEP. But at the same time, the mother requested services for her child under Section 504. This included assistive technology for his classes. The board refused to provide the requested services, and the mother sued the school district in a federal court.

In pretrial activity, the court held the parent's withdrawal of IDEA consent was not as extensive as the school board claimed. She had made a request for services, which "can hardly constitute a waiver of those services." **The court found no basis for the district's argument that withdrawal of consent to IDEA services constituted a waiver of services under other laws.** An IDEA regulation (34 C.F.R. Part 300.300) states that if consent is withdrawn by a parent, a school is not to provide special education to a child and it cannot be considered in violation of its duty to provide a FAPE. But the court found the same regulation is limited in that a school district cannot use parental refusal to consent to one service or activity to deny the parent or child any other service, benefit or activity of the school. A student's right to be free from discrimination is independent of eligibility or parental consent for IDEA services. The mother's refusal to provide IDEA consent did not authorize the district to deny her request to provide her child assistive technology. As she stated an adequate Section 504 claim, the court refused to dismiss it. She also stated an adequate claim for retaliation for withdrawing consent to the IEP. *D.F. v. Leon County School Board*, No. 4:13cv3-RH/CAS, 2014 WL 28798 (N.D. Fla. 1/2/14).

I. CHILD FIND DUTY

The IDEA's "child find" duty (found at 20 U.S.C. § 1412(a)(3)(A)) requires states, through their local educational agencies, to "identify, locate, and evaluate all children with disabilities residing within their boundaries." The child find obligation is triggered as an individualized duty to a child when an educational agency "has knowledge" that the child has a disability. When this individualized duty has been triggered, students who have not been identified as eligible for IDEA services may claim IDEA procedural protections when their schools seek to discipline them.

◆ A Texas student convinced the Fifth Circuit Court of Appeals that her school district violated federal law by failing to identify her as a student with a disability. According to the court, **the IDEA child-find duty requires schools to identify, locate and evaluate students with suspected disabilities "within a reasonable time" after receiving notice of facts or behavior likely to indicate a student has a disability**. In finding the school district violated its child-find duty, a lower court had found the student's academic decline, hospitalization and two thefts from her parent were sufficient to cause the district to suspect that her disabilities created a need for special education.

The court found the district's evaluation occurred three months after a request for a due process hearing and some six months after the events which put the district on notice of a need for special education. It held **a six-month delay was unreasonable given the extensive notice to the district and the dire circumstances involved**. Further, the court found the school district did not timely develop an IEP for the student and denied her a free appropriate public education. In rejecting the school district's argument that the hospitalization did not put it on notice of a need for special education, the court found evidence of academic decline by the student at the relevant time. As she was the "prevailing party" in the case, she was entitled to $70,000 in attorneys' fees. *Krawietz v. Galveston Independent School Dist.*, 900 F.3d 673 (5th Cir. 2018).

◆ Despite having Crohn's disease, a Pennsylvania student generally performed well at school through grade six. His behavior and academics worsened significantly when he reached grade seven. In grade ten, the student was disciplined for trying to leave his school during school hours. When he was threatened with expulsion, his parents filed a due process complaint. The school district created a Section 504 plan allowing the student accommodations, including an "any time pass" for access to a lavatory or the nurse's office. Upon a doctor's suggestion, the student was provided with homebound instruction. But when the district tried to provide it, the student was uncooperative. The school board then voted to expel him. At the same time, the district completed an evaluation report of the student. The district found the student had no qualifying disability and was ineligible for special education under the IDEA. The parents then obtained an independent educational evaluation (IEE) suggesting he was eligible for an IEP and offering specific recommendations.

A hearing officer then upheld the school district's finding that the student did not need an IEP. Instead, she found the district appropriately provided him with Section 504 accommodations. The parents sued the school district in a federal court, which held the student was eligible for special education under the IDEA. In ruling for the student, the court held the district violated its IDEA child-find duty and Section 504 by delaying its evaluation. On appeal, the Third Circuit Court of Appeals held the IEE gave a more accurate picture of the student than the district evaluation report. In the court's view, the IEE gave more detail to "the misery" inflicted on the student by Crohn's disease. The court found he needed specially designed instruction and that homebound instruction was insufficient for him. From grade seven on, the student had severe academic and disciplinary issues, and the school should have investigated whether his problems stemmed from his disease. **The court held for the student, finding the district violated its IDEA child-find duty and Section 504.** *Culley v. Cumberland Valley School Dist.*, 758 Fed.Appx. 301 (3d Cir. 2018).

◆ A Maryland student earned good grades in elementary school, but his middle school grades declined steeply. By grade nine, he began to fail classes and his father requested a special education evaluation. An IEP team found the student's lack of progress was not the result of a disability. Teachers noted he failed to follow instructions, did not participate in classes, failed to turn in assignments and had problem behaviors. Because the student failed almost all his classes in grade ten, the school district sought to retain him. His parents requested special education testing and obtained an independent educational evaluation (IEE). The IEE found the student had moderate ADHD, a specific learning disorder in written expression and an unspecified depressive disorder.

After receiving the IEE, the school district transferred him to a different high school for his second year of grade ten. But after only a few days, the student quit attending the school due to panic attacks, asthma and excessive noise. His parents pursued a due process proceeding. While the case went forward, the district evaluated the student and found him eligible for special education with an emotional disability. Although the IEP team recommended a self-contained setting, the student never attended it. Meanwhile, his case came before an administrative law judge (ALJ), who found there was no denial of a free appropriate public education. Instead, the student "simply did not want to go to school." A federal court later held for the school district and the parents appealed. On appeal, the U.S. Court of Appeals, Fourth Circuit, explained that **the IDEA's child-find duty requires the identification of all children suspected of having disabilities who need special education**. In this case, the ALJ found the student's problems were rooted in his refusal to attend school. **Teachers said he could do satisfactory work, but he simply failed to show up for school.** Finding the ALJ relied on "overwhelming evidence" that the student was capable of doing satisfactory work when he wanted and admitted he was not trying, the court held for the school district. *T.B. v. Prince George's County Board of Educ.*, 897 F.3d 566 (4th Cir. 2018; U.S. cert. denied 3/4/19).

◆   A Minnesota student earned As and Bs in a gifted and talented program. She had frequent attendance problems, and by grade eight she quit going to school. A private psychiatric evaluation diagnosed the student with depression and a generalized anxiety disorder. She was admitted to a day treatment program. Although the district referred the student to an intervention team, it decided not to evaluate her for special education based on her excellent grades. Due to her continuing absences, the district dis-enrolled her three times during grades 8-11. The parents later said they were not informed she could take honors courses while enrolled in a special education program. When the student was a high school freshman, she was admitted to an inpatient hospital program. She was diagnosed with ADHD and prescribed Adderall XR. Without evaluating the student, the district created a Section 504 plan for her. She was again placed in the hospital inpatient program and diagnosed with major depressive disorder, ADHD, autism spectrum disorder, generalized panic disorders with obsessive-compulsive disorder features and a borderline personality disorder.

When the student re-enrolled in the district as a high-school junior, her parents were provided notice of their special education rights for the first time. The district conducted an evaluation and found the student ineligible for special education. No functional behavioral assessment (FBA) was completed. The parents hired professionals to conduct an independent educational evaluation (IEE) of their child. After incurring almost $19,000 in IEE costs and obtaining private tutoring for their child, they requested a due process hearing. An administrative law judge conducted a seven-day hearing, resulting in a decision for the parents. A federal court found the district evaluations were deficient. There were no "systematic observations" of the student in her classes, and no FBA was conducted. **It appeared to the court that the student's mental health issues directly impacted her school attendance.** She met state and federal definitions for emotional behavioral disorder and other health impairment and was eligible for special education. Rejecting an argument that the student's excellent grades showed her absenteeism did not adversely affect her educational performance, the court explained that special education is designed to help students progress in the general curriculum. The court found the district's child-find efforts were insufficient, as it knew she was not attending school due to her anxiety. *Independent School Dist. No. 283 v. E.M.D.H.*, 357 F.Supp.3d 876 (D. Minn. 2019; 8th Cir. Appeal filed, 2/20/19).

◆ The Second Circuit Court of Appeals found no improper delays in evaluating a Connecticut student with a high-functioning type of autism who threatened to harm himself and others. It found no violation that denied the student a FAPE or prevented the parents from meaningfully participating in the IEP decision-making process. First, the court found no violation of the IDEA child-find provision, which requires each state to have policies and procedures to ensure the identification and evaluation of each child with a disability.

Federal regulations specify that the child-find obligation extends to all children suspected of having a disability who need special education, "even though they are advancing from grade to grade." Connecticut regulations provided for the implementation of an IEP as soon as possible, and in any event, within 45 school days of a referral or notice, exclusive of time required to obtain parental consent. The court found the district held three PPT meetings after the parents referred him for a special education evaluation. Nothing indicated he was experiencing emotional disturbance over a long time period, and there was evidence that his medication was beginning to help him. The district continued to monitor the student after initially finding him ineligible for special education. During this time, he was hospitalized again, then began homebound tutoring with Section 504 accommodations. **The court found it was reasonable for the PPT to "proceed deliberately when weighing whether a tenth-grader, who has previously done well in school, should be enrolled in special education.** The district's caution was reinforced by the parents' own reluctance to give the district access to their son's psychiatric records. The court declined to find the school board violated the IDEA's child-find duty. *Mr. P and Mrs. P v. West Hartford Board of Educ.*, 885 F.3d 735 (2d Cir. 2018).

◆ A student with learning disabilities began her high school career at a private school in Dallas. She moved to California, where a school district found her eligible for special education. During a summer break, the student had "dramatic symptoms of an emotional breakdown," spent time in a psychiatric hospital and was diagnosed with schizophrenia. Doctors recommended a specialized learning environment for her and deemed her "far too fragile to be placed on a general education campus." The student returned to Dallas, where she was enrolled in a private school for students with learning disabilities. As part of a settlement agreement, the California school district prepared an IEP for her senior year that specified placement in a private school in California.

The parent returned to Dallas and asked the Dallas Independent School District (DISD) for private school tuition reimbursement. The student remained at a private school for her senior year. Her parent and the DISD did not meet to consider an IEP until just before winter break. At the meeting, the DISD rejected the California IEP, indicating it would evaluate the student and develop an IEP. When the district found her ineligible for special education, the parent requested an independent educational evaluation (IEE). After a private psychologist found the DISD's evaluation was defective, the DISD found the student IDEA-eligible. But it did not consider the IEE. The parent requested a due process hearing, seeking private school tuition reimbursement. A hearing officer awarded her over $25,000 in private school tuition costs. A federal court reduced this to $11,942.50, and appeal reached the U.S. Court of Appeals, Fifth Circuit. It held **the IDEA's child-find provision does not require temporary services or "the near-immediate provision of FAPE or comparable services."** The DISD was bound to reimburse the parent for any failure to provide her child a FAPE once it knew she was attending a private school in the district. While the district did not offer a FAPE until just before the school year ended, the parent contributed to the delay. The court held a lower court would have to further consider the parent's reimbursement claim. *Dallas Independent School Dist. v. Woody*, 865 F.3d 303 (5th Cir. 2017).

◆   The District of Columbia Public Schools (DCPS) evaluated a preschool student and found him eligible for services under IDEA Part C. As his third birthday approached, he was evaluated for special education eligibility under IDEA Part B, but he was found ineligible. In the team's opinion, he did not qualify as a child with an autism spectrum disorder, speech or language impairment or developmental delay. The parent disagreed with the DCPS' determination and requested an independent educational evaluation. The DCPS agreed to fund the evaluation. An audiologist found he had an expressive language deficit in verbal language communication. An independent psychologist identified clinical symptoms consistent with global developmental delay, and an occupational therapist found he needed support for fine motor delays.

A DCPS team reconvened and found the student met eligibility criteria for developmental delay and had a qualifying disability under Part B. The parent filed a due process hearing request to review the team's initial finding. A hearing officer held for the DCPS, finding its initial evaluation was comprehensive. On appeal, a federal court found **no federal requirement that an evaluation contain firsthand classroom observations or interviews with parents and teachers**. Federal law and regulations imposed no requirements on the content of a psychological evaluation. The DCPS psychological evaluation was held "technically sound," and was supplemented by evaluation data, parental input and notes from classroom observations. The court found IDEA regulations do not require that a particular professional conduct classroom observations. Nor do they specify when a school district must order updated testing. *Richardson v. District of Columbia*, 273 F.Supp.3d 94 (D.D.C. 2017).

◆   After a Pennsylvania school district identified a student as having a specific learning disability, his parents enrolled him in a private school. He remained there for at least eight years and was twice reevaluated by the district. The first reevaluation found the student had ADHD and an autism spectrum disorder. The second found he was below average in processing information and defining vocabulary, but found him ineligible for special education. The parents obtained two private evaluations which indicated the student had a mixed receptive-expressive language disorder and a reading disorder. The parents filed a due process complaint, seeking compensatory education and other relief. They claimed the district violated the IDEA by denying their child "equitable participation in education" when it failed to timely identify his receptive-expressive language and reading disorders. The hearing officer dismissed the case, finding the parents did not state a claim for relief. On appeal, a federal court found that the IDEA requires the states to identify children with disabilities residing in the state – including those attending private schools – and to conduct a sufficiently comprehensive evaluation to identify all of a child's special education needs. **A school district must assess a student in all areas related to a suspected disability.** The court held the school district should have evaluated and identified the student with a receptive-expressive language disorder and a reading disorder, given his known disabilities and areas of need.

The court found a school district does not fulfill its child-find obligations by identifying "some of a student's disabilities." Since the parents stated a plausible claim that the district failed to identify all of the student's disabilities, the court refused to dismiss their case. *C.F. v. Delaware County Intermediate Unit,* Civ. No. 17-CV-1599, 2017 WL 4467498 (E.D. Pa. 10/6/17).

II. ELIGIBILITY DETERMINATIONS

A. IDEA Eligibility Determinations

The IDEA, at 20 U.S.C. § 1414(a)(1)(A), requires a full and individual evaluation before the initial provision of special education and related services to resident students with disabilities. Evaluations may take place upon a parental request or the school's initiative. Each state must also demonstrate that each resident student with a disability is identified, located and evaluated under 20 U.S.C. § 1412(a)(3), and is provided with an IEP that meets IDEA requirements described at 20 U.S.C. § 1414(d).

In B.G. v. Board of Educ. of City of Chicago, *this chapter, the court rejected an argument that a school board violated an IDEA regulation requiring that assessments and evaluation materials are selected and administered so as not to be discriminatory on a racial or cultural basis. See at 34 C.F.R. Part 300.304(c)(1)(i). Assessments are to be administered in the child's native language or other communication mode, in the form most likely to yield accurate information on his/her knowledge and abilities. The court found the student was no longer considered an English Language Learner.*

On December 20, 2018, the U.S. Department of Education's Office of Special Education Programs (OSEP) issued a guidance letter interpreting IDEA Part C screening requirements for infants and toddlers suspected of being deaf or hard of hearing. The letter explained that newborn hearing screening or screening conducted by an Early Head Start program or health care provider can meet specific Part C evaluation requirements. An IDEA regulation (34 C.F.R. § 303.321(a)(1)) requires states to ensure each child under age three who is referred for evaluation or early intervention services and who is suspected of having a disability must have a timely, comprehensive, multidisciplinary evaluation, unless medical or other records establish eligibility.

◆ The U.S. Court of Appeals, Ninth Circuit, held a California school district violated the IDEA by tying a student's eligibility status to her speech and language disorder, to the exclusion of her hearing impairment. In classifying the student with a speech and language disorder, the school district relied on her "hearing loss which results in a language or speech disorder and significantly affects educational performance." Further, the district found the student did not meet eligibility requirements for hearing impairments because its evaluations did not indicate her hearing loss impaired her ability to process information via her hearing aids. Classification as a child with a hearing impairment required that the student have "an impairment in hearing, whether permanent or fluctuating, that adversely affects a child's educational performance."

In this case, the district evaluations showed the student had a hearing loss that resulted in a language or speech disorder, and which significantly affected her educational performance. In reversing a lower court judgment, the Ninth Circuit found the IEP team had to consider the student's language and communication needs, and her opportunities for direct communications with peers and professionals in her language and communication mode. Further, the court found the IEP team had to consider her academic level and full range of needs. Having improperly determined that she did not have a disability based on hearing impairment, the school district only addressed goals and programs to address her speech and language delay. The court noted the IDEA requires school districts to ensure that students are assessed in all areas of suspected disability. Moreover, the district had an obligation to conduct a full initial evaluation of the student in all areas of suspected disability. **The school district could not circumvent its assessment obligations by conducting "informal observations."** Concluding that the district violated the student's procedural rights under the IDEA and denied her a FAPE, the court reversed the judgment. *S.P. v. East Whittier City School Dist.*, 735 Fed.Appx. 320 (9th Cir. 2018).

◆ A federal court upheld an evaluation by a Maryland school district to assess the eligibility status of a gifted student with attention deficit hyperactivity disorder (ADHD). **The court relied on 20 U.S.C. § 1414(b)(2)(A), an IDEA section stating that in order to conduct an appropriate evaluation, the school district must use a variety of assessment tools and not rely on any single measure or assessment.** After considering the parties' submissions, the court held the evidence supported a conclusion that it appropriately assessed the student's needs. The district's assessments provided sufficient information to the IEP team to make recommendations for the student's IEP in the event he was found eligible for special education. Finding the ALJ based his decision on a thorough, careful and comprehensive review of the evidence by the ALJ, the court held the district conducted comprehensive assessments that complied with the IDEA and relevant state and federal special education regulations.

Appeal reached the U.S. Court of Appeals, Fourth Circuit. In addition to appealing from the ruling that the district evaluations were IDEA-compliant, the parents urged the court to supplement the record with a new independent neuropsychological evaluation of their son. But the court found no error in the lower court's decision for the school district. It rejected the parents' arguments that they should have been allowed to further challenge the evaluation by the district. After reviewing the administrative record and the parents' arguments, the court affirmed the judgment for the school district. *E.P. v. Howard County Public School System*, 727 Fed.Appx. 55 (4th Cir. 2018).

◆ A Pennsylvania high school student earned high grades and scored well on cognitive assessments. But she had a history of family trauma, post-traumatic stress disorder and a major depressive disorder, including a significant sleep disorder that often caused her to fall asleep during classes. When the student's school attendance and grades began to plummet, her school district proposed a psychoeducational evaluation to assess her emotional functioning and attendance. Four of six interviews could not be completed due to her heightened anxiety, fatigue and absences. Based on this review, the district found the student did not require specially designed instruction and was ineligible for special education. Her parent challenged the appropriateness of the evaluation by requesting an independent educational evaluation (IEE). In response, the school district requested a due process hearing to defend its evaluation. A state hearing officer found the district did not evaluate the student in all areas of suspected disability.

On appeal, a federal court found the district did not evaluate the student for an other health impairment (OHI) or an emotional disturbance. Schools must comply with 34 C.F.R. § 300.4 - 300. 11 when determining whether a student has a qualifying disability and a resulting need for special education. A school district must use a variety of assessment tools and cannot rely on any single measure. **While an evaluation does not have to identify and diagnose every possible disability, it must ensure that a student is assessed in all suspected areas of disability.** The court found the evaluation report in this case did not discuss OHI, even though this was an area of suspected disability. In the court's opinion, the district discounted an assessment of the student indicating she had an emotional disturbance. It held a student who is classified as mentally gifted may still meet IDEA eligibility criteria. While the court found the district conducted an adequate assessment for a specific learning disability, it held the district failed to adequately assess the student for an OHI or an emotional disturbance. For this reason, the district had to fund an IEE. *Rose Tree Media School Dist. v. M.J.*, No. 18-cv-1063, 2019 WL 1062487 (E.D. Pa. 3/6/19).

◆ A Texas high school student with dyslexia earned a 3.45 grade average with the help of a Section 504 accommodation plan. Claiming his school district unreasonably denied him a full and individual evaluation during his last semester of high school in violation of its IDEA child-find duty, he filed a due process complaint against the district. Meanwhile, he graduated and received an academic scholarship from a private university. After a two-day hearing, a special education hearing officer held the student did not demonstrate a need for special education. He appealed to a federal court, adding disability discrimination claims against the school district. On appeal, the court rejected the student's argument that the hearing officer could not declare him ineligible for special education. Many decisions indicated Texas special education hearing officers have the authority to find a student eligible or ineligible for services. **The court stated that Fifth Circuit precedents hold that the IDEA does not penalize school districts for failing to timely evaluate students who do**

not need special education. The hearing officer relied on evidence that the student passed his classes, graduated from high school, passed almost all of his state assessments and gained college admission. Although the student claimed the accommodations he received proved his need for special education, the court found these accommodations were typically available to all students in general education programs. Finding he presented no evidence of professional bad faith or gross misjudgment and no need for special education, the court held for the district. *T.W. v. Leander Independent School Dist.*, No. AU-17-00627-SS, 2019 WL 1102380 (W.D. Tex. 3/7/19).

◆ A Washington student's parents rejected an IEP proposal and requested an independent educational evaluation (IEE) at the school district's expense. After the request was denied, both parties requested due process hearings. An administrative law judge (ALJ) held the district's reevaluation was appropriate and denied the parents' request to pay for an IEE. In a separate order, the ALJ held for the district on the remaining claims. A federal court consolidated the cases and held the claims arising from matters taking place over two years prior to the date of filing the action were barred by the IDEA's limitations period.

The court affirmed the ALJ's ruling that the IEP was appropriate. On appeal, the U.S. Court of Appeals, Ninth Circuit, held the lower court improperly found the IDEA's two-year limitations period barred claims relating to the student's preschool and kindergarten years as untimely. This matter was returned to the lower court. In a separate opinion, the Ninth Circuit held the district assessed the student in all areas related to his suspected disability. Although the district did not refer to dyslexia and dysgraphia, the court found it evaluated him for a specific learning disability. In addition, the district reevaluated the student using many of the tests used by the parents' private evaluator. While they claimed the district should have used subtests from the WIAT-II test for dyslexia and dysgraphia, the district used the updated WIAT-III. **Finding the school district assessed the student for reading fluency and fine motor skills in a manner aimed at detecting his writing inefficiencies, the court held it complied with its duty to assess him in all areas of suspected disability.** The case was returned to the lower court, which found the school district adequately assessed the student in all areas related to his suspected disability. Although the district did not refer to dyslexia and dysgraphia, the court found it evaluated him for a "specific learning disability." The Ninth Circuit held the parents did not file their complaint until after the relevant limitations period lapsed. Although the parents raised other arguments in support of their claims, the court found them meritless and held for the school district. *Avila v. Spokane School Dist. 81*, 744 Fed.Appx. 506 (9th Cir. 2018).

◆ Arkansas school officials assumed a gifted student with an autism spectrum disorder and ADHD could not qualify for special education due to his academic success. Because of his trouble with social skills, his parent sought three times to obtain special education services, including speech therapy. But the school district found the students' academic needs were adequately met by his Section 504 plan. In addition to finding him ineligible for special education, the district found his behavior at school was acceptable and did not hinder his learning. The parent filed a due process hearing complaint. A hearing officer held the district denied the student a free appropriate public education by failing to adequately evaluate him for special education. The district was ordered to hire a behavioral analyst, conduct a functional behavioral assessment and evaluate his language and behavior deficits. Further, the district was to hire a health care aide, develop an IEP and allow mental health professionals to observe him if necessary.

On appeal, a federal district court held further evaluation of the student was needed. As the hearing officer found, all prior efforts to evaluate him had been defective. **The court found the school district had taken the erroneous position that a student without academic deficits could not qualify for special education.** Evidence did not clearly indicate whether the district's evaluations complied with IDEA procedures. At the last evaluation conference, a decision was made to simply not test the student. District staff felt a student must have academic deficits in order qualify for special education and an IEP. Since a "twice-exceptional" or "2E" child with average (or above) academic performance may qualify for special education, the court held the hearing officer correctly ordered additional testing of the student. But the court found no intentional discrimination by the district, requiring dismissal of his non-IDEA claims. *Lawrence County School Dist. v. McDaniel*, No. 3:17-CV-00004 BSM, 2018 WL 1569484 (E.D. Ark. 3/30/18).

◆   An 18-year-old New York City student's committee on special education (CSE) relied on reports from a private school he had attended for the past four years to devise his IEP. Although he was due for a triennial reevaluation, the CSE did not conduct one. The parent rejected the CSE's proposal for the student to attend a classroom with a 12:1:1 student-teacher-paraprofessional ratio. After re-enrolling her child in the private school, she requested a due process hearing. The court held for the New York City Department of Education (DOE). On appeal to the U.S. Court of Appeals, Second Circuit, the parent argued the DOE violated the IDEA by failing to state the frequency, location and duration of her child's transition services in his IEP. She said the DOE failed to conduct a required triennial reevaluation, including vocational and transition assessments.

Despite these defects, the court found the DOE did not deny the student's right to a free appropriate public education (FAPE). Procedural violations do not deny a FAPE unless they deprive a student of educational benefits, impede parental participation opportunities, or infringe upon a child's right to a FAPE. **While the IEP did not specify how much time the student would spend receiving academic instruction compared to how much time he would spend in vocational instruction, the court found no FAPE denial.** Next, the court found there was no denial of FAPE caused by the failure to specify whether the student's classroom would be onsite or offsite. The court adopted the review officer's finding that the IEP discussed a vocational program with annual goals and sufficient information to allow the school to provide a FAPE. The court found the parent was involved in important junctures in developing the IEP. The review officer found the CSE considered input from the parent and private school teachers. The court affirmed the decision for the DOE. *M.M. v. New York City Dep't of Educ.*, 655 Fed.Appx. 868 (2d Cir. 2016).

◆ A California student was referred to a child counseling center to address his anger and lack of self-control. Near this time, he was diagnosed with ADHD and began to take Adderall. For most of his third-grade year, he was assigned to a teacher who ultimately proved unable to control his behavior. For grade three, the school developed a behavioral support plan (BSP). But the teacher did not implement it with fidelity, and he had 16 incidents of discipline and 10 days of suspension. Following revisions to the BSP, the student was reassigned to a new teacher who implemented the BSP with fidelity. By year end, the student achieved or neared mastery in most of his academic areas. His behavior improved. A school team found him ineligible for special education, and the parent requested a hearing. When the case reached the Ninth Circuit, the court stated that even if a child has a qualifying disability under the IDEA, he or she does not qualify for special education if support provided through a regular education program is sufficient. While the lower court and ALJ found the student was performing satisfactorily in general education classes, the court found he was receiving many services that were in fact special education.

In the court's opinion, services such as 1:1 assistance from a paraeducator, mental health services and clinical interventions by a school behavior specialist should be considered special education because they met the definition of "specially designed instruction" to meet the unique needs of a child with a disability. **Since the level of services provided to the student had been misstated, the lower court and ALJ incorrectly found he did not require specialized assistance.** The student had threatened and attempted suicide. Yet the lower court found irrelevant his hospitalizations and suicide attempts because they took place outside school. By grade four, the student needed psychotropic medications to attend school. **Since his emotional disturbance adversely affected his attendance and academic performance, the court reversed the decisions finding him ineligible for special education.** Finding the district violated IDEA safeguards and improperly denied the student services, the court returned the case to the lower court. *L.J. v. Pittsburg Unified School Dist.*, 850 F.3d 996 (9th Cir. 2016).

B. Section 504 Eligibility

School districts have child find duties under both the IDEA and Section 504. Where a Section 504 claim is based on the provision of educational services for a disabled child, liability depends upon proof that school officials acted in bad faith or with gross misjudgment. To prove this, a student must show a substantial departure from accepted professional judgment. Section 504 and the ADA do not "create general tort liability for educational malpractice."

◆ A California student was enrolled in the Panama-Buena Vista Union School District (PBVUSD). PBVUSD received a copy of a Section 504 plan and a behavior support plan from Bakersfield City School District (BCSD), where he previously attended school. The student had a behavior incident at a PBVUSD junior high school. PBVUSD asked BCSD for his records, but it did not receive them for over two weeks. The records showed he had a history of discipline at

BCSD schools. BCSD had evaluated him for special education eligibility but determined his attention deficit hyperactivity disorder did not hinder his ability to learn. PBVUSD developed a Section 504 accommodation plan for the student. But he again engaged in misconduct and was disciplined. The district scheduled a manifestation determination meeting. According to PBVUSD, it requested the parent's consent to evaluate the student at least four times. A Spanish-language request for consent was provided, but she did not sign it for nearly four months. A PBVUSD assessment found the student qualified for special education.

The parent then filed a due process hearing request against PBVUSD. A hearing officer found the district did not timely evaluate the student and deprived the parent of participation opportunities by failing to translate certain disciplinary documents into Spanish. A federal court held school districts must identify, locate and evaluate resident children with disabilities up to the age of 21 "within a reasonable time." In this case, the hearing officer incorrectly found PBVUSD's child-find obligation commenced on the student's first day of school. When he entered school, PBVUSD staff had no opportunity to observe his behavior and had not received his records from BCSD. California law prohibits school districts from making special education referrals until a district considers, and where appropriate, utilizes its own general education resources. **Forcing a district to make an immediate decision would require a "rush to judgment."** Although the parent appealed to the Ninth Circuit, she later agreed to voluntarily dismiss the case. *Panama-Buena Vista Union School Dist. v. A.V.*, No. 18-15021, 2018 WL 3398374 (9th Cir. 5/30/18).

◆ A Pennsylvania student with attention deficit hyperactivity disorder was found ineligible for an IEP and offered an accommodation plan under Section 504. Accommodations and strategies were set forth in the 504 plan to increase his attention, focus and organization for the rest of his second-grade year. The parent expressed no further concerns about her son's behaviors until the fall of his fourth-grade school year. At her request, the district again evaluated the student for special education eligibility. This time, it found he needed special education and prepared an IEP for him. During the student's fourth-grade year, his IEP was revised eight times. Later, his parent placed him in a cyber charter school for grade five. She then obtained the result of the IEE, which contained a diagnosis of expressive language disorder. The parent filed a due process complaint against the school district, asserting violation of the IDEA's child find duty and deprivation of a free appropriate public education (FAPE).

A hearing officer found the student was not denied a FAPE. A federal court held additional evidence the parent sought to include did not bear out her theory that the district intentionally misrepresented and withheld information. Even if evidence from the student's second- and third-grade school years had been improperly excluded, the court found no denial of FAPE. His grade-two report showed overall satisfactory performance, work habits and test scores. The court found **the school team considered the student's test scores, assessments and teacher comments when deciding not to evaluate him as a second-grader**. In sum, the court agreed with the hearing officer that the district did not violate its IDEA child find obligation. It was not unreasonable for the district to refrain from rushing to evaluate the student in his early school years, and instead find his needs could be addressed by a Section 504 plan. Although the parent raised other issues, including bias and improper delays by the hearing officer, the court held for the school district. *Price v. Upper Darby School Dist.,* Civil No. 15-131, 2016 WL 6033534 (E.D. Pa. 10/14/16).

◆   Compton Unified School District (CUSD) students filed a federal case asserting they are so traumatized by violence and poverty that they should be deemed to have disabilities. According to the complaint, the neurobiological effects of complex trauma impairs the ability to perform essential activities of education such as learning, thinking, reading and concentrating. The students argued complex trauma amounted to a disability under the Americans with Disabilities Act (ADA), Section 504 of the Rehabilitation Act and Section 504 regulations. The students said CUSD did not properly train its teachers and staff to recognize and address the effects of complex trauma and did not provide staff with evidence-based trauma interventions. The restorative practices sought by the students were said to encourage healthy relationships, address conflicts and violence and permit students to self-regulate in high-stress or anxiety situations. CUSD was accused of subjecting traumatized students to punitive and counterproductive suspensions, expulsions, transfers and referrals to law enforcement that push them out of school and into the criminal justice system.

The court found it unnecessary for impairments to be listed in the Diagnostic and Statistical Manual of Mental Disorders (DSM) in order to state a preliminary case. Trauma was within the DSM definition of "mental disorder." It was claimed that if children repeatedly experience fear, areas of the brain can become over-sensitized, leading to hyperarousal or disassociation triggered by seemingly innocent stimuli. **The students made a valid preliminary claim by asserting they suffered substantial limitations on major life activities such as learning, reading, concentrating, thinking and communicating.** The court found the claims showed the students were denied the benefits of CUSD programs solely by reason of a claimed disability. A group of CUSD teachers could also pursue claims in their own right. *P.P. v. Compton Unified School Dist.,*135 F.Supp.3d 1098 (C.D. Cal. 2015).

◆   A Pennsylvania child with cerebral palsy and ADHD was found ineligible for special education. He earned As and Bs, and his behavior was satisfactory. The parents obtained evaluations diagnosing him with Asperger's syndrome. When the student began grade four, his parents again sought a reevaluation. This yielded a finding that he had a disability in math but still did not need special education. The parents removed him from the district and placed him in a cyber-charter school that found him eligible for special education. They then requested a hearing. A hearing officer upheld the district evaluations. When the case came before a federal court, it held **school districts have a child find obligation under both the IDEA and Section 504**. Once the parents request an evaluation, the school district must evaluate the child in all areas of suspected disability, using a variety of technically sound assessment tools. A school may not rely exclusively on one assessment. The parents complained that the district's use of assessment tools known as DIBELS and GMADE was not sound. But the court found the psychologist used these tools appropriately.

In most areas, the student's achievement not only matched his ability but was in the average range. Observations by a teacher and psychologist provided a sufficient basis to find he did not have an IDEA-qualifying disability. It appeared that the student performed at his best in a regular classroom. The cyber-charter school's later eligibility finding did not undermine the findings of the school district. In the short time between evaluations, the student's situation changed substantially. When he was diagnosed with Asperger's syndrome, the district updated his accommodations. He earned As and Bs, and his behavior was satisfactory. Finding the student meaningfully benefited from his education under a Section 504 plan, the court held for the district. *Timothy F. v. Antietam School Dist.*, No. 12-2719, 2014 WL 1301955 (E.D. Pa. 3/31/14).

◆   Colorado parents agreed to their child's IEPs when she was in elementary school but rejected an IEP proposal as she entered middle school. They revoked their consent to continued provision of special education and related services under the IDEA. A district director of special education notified the parents that the student's "Section 504 plan would be her IEP." But the director also claimed the parental revocation of IDEA services cut off any district obligation to serve the student under the Rehabilitation Act. Later, the parties met and agreed that the child was a qualified individual with a disability under Section 504. But the district offered only to implement the same IEP services that had been rejected months earlier. The parents declined the Section 504 plan and sued the school district. **The court observed that without parental consent, special education cannot be provided.** When the parents revoked consent under the IDEA, the district was required to cease providing special education, with no further obligation to develop an IEP for the student. The court agreed with the parents that their rejection of an IEP devised under the IDEA was not an automatic rejection of a Section 504 plan. **Section 504 regulations suggested that satisfying Section 504 through an IEP offer was only an expediency to avoid a duplicate process and did not establish "a legal equivalency."** Since Section 504 regulations permitted a school district to meet its Section 504 obligations through an IEP, the court held the Section 504 meeting and offer of accommodations was sufficient. *Kimble v. Douglas County School Dist. RE-1*, 925 F.Supp.2d 1176 (D. Colo. 2013).

C. Decertification or Change in Classification

A number of courts have observed that the IDEA is not concerned with "labels," but with whether a student is receiving a free appropriate public education. The IDEA does not provide a specific right for a student to be classified under a particular disability, but requires that the IEP be designed to suit the child's demonstrated needs. See 20 U.S.C. Section 1412(a)(3)(B).

◆   A Washington student qualified for special education with a specific learning disability (SLD) from grades 4-9. Based on a reevaluation, an IEP team found he no longer qualified for special education. A Section 504 plan was created for the student, and he enrolled in general education classes. When his parents asked for reimbursement for certain private services, the district declined. They filed a due process challenge. An administrative law judge (ALJ) held the reevaluation was appropriate and that the decision to exit the student from special education was legally correct. The parents appealed to a federal court, adding disability discrimination and retaliation claims. The court held they did not show the school district's reevaluation failed to assess the student in all areas of suspected disability. **Testimony by school witnesses indicated the IEP team no longer believed the student required special education because his basic writing difficulties were not adversely affecting his academic performance.**

After affirming the ALJ's decision, the court dismissed the discrimination and retaliation claims. On appeal, the U.S. Court of Appeals, Ninth Circuit, found the district's evaluation was appropriate. In the court's opinion, the evaluation report detailed the student's cognitive, attention, social, emotional, medical and physical evaluations. A school psychologist attended his English class for 40 minutes, noted his interactions with peers and saw him working quietly and independently. The court held this satisfied a state regulatory requirement to observe student academic performance. Next, the court found the district provided the parents proper notices, including a description of options considered by the IEP team. It found the district considered all necessary testing in reaching its decision. **The court held that removing the student from special education services did not result in lost educational opportunities.** In sum, the court held the student no longer met the relevant SLD eligibility criteria. *R.Z.C. v. North Shore School Dist.*, 755 Fed.Appx. 658 (9th Cir. 2018).

◆ An Arkansas student's aggressive, inappropriate behaviors increased when he was in fifth grade. A functional behavioral assessment (FBA) was completed, and his primary disabling condition was changed to emotional disturbance. When the student entered junior high school, he was placed in a self-contained classroom. Although he had "notable successes" during grade seven, he began using profanity and threatened teachers and classmates. Shortly after the student's mother warned the school that any violent threat made by her son should be taken seriously, he threatened the school's assistant principal (AP). The AP suspended the student out of school for 10 days. The IEP team did not believe his threats were a manifestation of his disability. But instead of proceeding with a manifestation review, the team reduced the suspension to three days. After the team placed the student on a half-day schedule, the parent rejected the plan and requested a due process hearing.

A hearing officer held the school district violated the IDEA by changing the student's disability category from autism to emotional disturbance. The district appealed to a federal court, which noted the team reviewed recent evaluations, completed a therapy reevaluation, assessed the student's pragmatic skills and completed an FBA before it changed his eligibility category. **The results of the FBA and reevaluations were discussed at an IEP team meeting at which the parent agreed to the change in disability category.** In addition, the court found the change in disability category "did not disregard or override" the student's autism spectrum diagnosis. The reclassification made little substantive change in educational benefits. Next, the court held the school did not violate the IDEA by failing to strictly follow the IEP when the student had behavioral incidents. The IDEA only requires a team to "consider" using positive behavior interventions. The court held the "IDEA does not require that the school strictly adhere to behavior plans when adhering to such a plan would result in a danger to the student or his peers." Finding the student's IEP did not require employees to allow him to leave school grounds, the court found no IDEA violation. *Bentonville School Dist. v. Smith*, No. 5:17-CV-05134, 2019 WL 291641 (W.D. Ark. 1/23/19; 8th Cir. appeal filed 2/26/19).

◆   In a Texas case, a federal court held the IDEA does not require a school district to classify a student into a particular category or assign a particular disability label. **An IDEA section (20 U.S.C. § 1412(a)(3)(B)) states that an eligible student need not be classified by his/her disability so long as the child is regarded as a child with a disability under the act.** Many courts have found a disability diagnosis is often immaterial, since the IEP must be tailored to the student's specific needs. Further, the fact that the parents in this case believed their child was mislabeled did not mean she had been denied a FAPE. They had agreed with the student's IEP goals, accommodations and schedule. Significantly, one of the child's evaluators noted the parents consented to the IEP, but were concerned about their child's diagnostic label. In fact, "their goal was not to obtain any additional services from the school system, but [they] wanted the Autism eligibility added in order to ensure optimal services" from public agencies in the future. As a result, the court held for the school district.

The parents appealed to the U.S. Court of Appeals, Fifth Circuit, which held the child-find and FAPE questions were moot. On the other hand, the attorneys' fees issue was not. While the student prevailed on the issue of misdiagnosis, the court found she had received a FAPE. Significantly, the hearing officer denied all the relief that was specifically requested. The court found no material alteration in the parties' legal relationship. As the family prevailed in only a technical sense, the court found an award of fees would not be consistent with IDEA purposes, and the judgment for the district was affirmed. *Lauren C. v. Lewisville Independent School Dist.*, 904 F.3d 363 (5th Cir. 2018).

◆   A Texas student was found eligible for special education with an emotional disturbance. As a high school freshman, he experienced clinically significant anxiety and depression and talked about suicide. While his grades dropped and he had difficulties with interpersonal relationships, he performed well on state tests and generally earned good grades. Late in the student's sophomore year, the district found him ineligible for special education. The student's father requested an independent evaluation. Without any special education services, the student earned all A grades as a high school junior. He scored in the average range on college entrance exams and was again found ineligible for special education. Although the student maintained his good progress during the first semester of his senior year, his father emailed teachers about his son's home misconduct and asked that the district provide him accommodations.

The father reported that the student felt overwhelmed by his workload and wanted to quit school. Teachers were responsive to his concerns and made accommodations. But the student became truant and eventually left school. The father requested a hearing to challenge the finding that his son was no longer eligible for special education. A hearing officer upheld the district's conclusion, as did a federal court. Appeal reached the U.S. Court of Appeals, Fifth Circuit, which found the school district appropriately considered its own evaluations, an outside evaluation and teacher observations. **The court stated that teacher observations "are especially instructive as they spend more time with students than do outside evaluators." Further, it observed that "there is no presumption in favor of outside evaluators."** The court disagreed with the student's suggestion that the school district had to consider possible future consequences of his disability. **Fear of a student's problems in the future was not a valid basis for IDEA eligibility.** Finding no evidence that his success would be short-lived, the court held for the district. *D.L. v. Clear Creek Independent School Dist.*, 695 Fed.Appx. 733 (5th Cir. 2017).

◆   A Maine student struggled with reading and talking and was found eligible for special education and related services with a specific learning disability (SLD) in grade two. Over time, she improved her reading skills and began to earn good grades. When the student was in grade seven, her IEP team placed her on "consult status" based on her good grades and record of academic achievement. The next year, a school IEP team decided she no longer qualified for special education based on her straight-A grades and average (or above) performance on standardized tests. Moreover, the team found the student achieved adequately in all areas – including reading fluency – without special education. The student's parents obtained private evaluations indicating lower scores on some tests than those identified by the IEP team. After the team again met and found the student ineligible for special education, the parents requested a hearing. A hearing officer affirmed the eligibility decision, finding the student was achieving adequately in all areas and did not require special education.

A federal court held for the school district. When the case reached the First Circuit, it noted the IDEA has two steps for determining eligibility. First, a student must have a qualifying disorder. Second, it must be determined whether the student "needs" special education by reason of the qualifying disorder. In this case, the court found the lower court did not apply the two-part IDEA analysis. **The court found a broader range of assessments, including grades, classroom performance and standardized tests were to be considered in a holistic inquiry.** Federal guidance indicated that students with high cognition, but who struggle with reading and math, may still satisfy the eligibility inquiry. The court returned the case to the lower court for reconsideration of whether the student's academic performance, intelligence, hard work, devoted parents and academic accommodations might have masked an IDEA-qualifying disability. *Mr. and Mrs. Doe v. Cape Elizabeth School Dist.*, 832 F.3d 69 (1st Cir. 2016).

D. Uncooperative Parents

The IDEA requires school districts to reevaluate eligible students with a disability at least every three years. Parents must be informed about and consent to these evaluations, and a district may file a due process request if they do not provide consent. But a school district need not request a due process hearing or obtain an updated evaluation if a parent refuses consent for this.

In V.M. v. North Colonie Cent. School Dist., *954 F.Supp.2d 102 (N.D.N.Y. 2013) a federal court explained that if a parent refuses to consent to special education, or fails to respond to a request to provide consent, a district is not considered in violation of the IDEA's requirement to make a FAPE available.*

◆   New Jersey parents refused to allow their son's school district to reevaluate him. Instead, they obtained a private neuropsychological evaluation and filed a due process petition, seeking to recover $4,400 in IEE costs from the district. An administrative law judge (ALJ) upheld their claim, and they filed a federal court complaint requesting payment of their costs plus attorneys' fees. After a hearing, the court reversed the ALJ's decision. Applying a federal regulation found at 34 C.F.R. Part 300.502, the court found parents may have an IEE at public expense when they disagree with a completed evaluation or reevaluation. As the district argued, the IDEA regulation specified that a parent's right to public reimbursement for an IEE exists when there is a disagreement with an evaluation obtained by a school district and the parents file a due process complaint. New Jersey special education regulations further declared that parents may request an IEE if there is a disagreement with an initial evaluation or reevaluation provided by a school district board of education. The parents tried to justify an additional evaluation based on their child's diagnoses of panic attacks and anxiety. But the district could not go forward with an evaluation, given their decision to revoke their consent for a district reevaluation.

Since the parents did not disagree with an evaluation or reevaluation by the school district, the court held they were not entitled to an IEE at public expense. The district offered to conduct several assessments, and the parents had joined in a reevaluation plan before revoking their consent. In sum, the court held the parents could not seek reimbursement for an IEE after refusing consent to a district reevaluation. The court rejected the parents' additional arguments, including a claim that the school district was required to file a due process complaint in this case. Their withdrawal of consent obviated any such requirement. *S.S. and M.S. v. Hillsborough Township Public School Dist.*, No. 3:18-cv-2325-BRM-DEA, 2019 WL 396956 (D.N.J. 1/31/19).

◆   A California parent and her child's school district haggled over an assessment plan. The parent asked to sit behind a one-sided mirror where she could see and hear the testing. The district allowed her to observe the testing through a window where she could see but not hear the activity. According to school officials, her attendance would alter the testing environment and compromise the accuracy of test results. Although the parties deadlocked over the assessment observation issue, they met twice at IEP meetings and discussed a variety of placement options, including a full inclusion program, a special day class, continuation of homeschooling, and 1:1 instruction. School members of the IEP team proposed placing the student in a nonpublic school that was certified to serve students with autism in a primarily academic setting.

In rejecting a public school inclusion setting, team members noted the student's sensitivity to noise and her three-year absence from a school setting. The parents rejected the IEP and requested a due process hearing. An administrative law judge (ALJ) held for the district, finding they had no legal right to insist on their attendance at the assessments. Nor was the student denied a FAPE. A federal court upheld the ALJ's decision for the school district. On appeal, the U.S. Court of Appeals, Ninth Circuit, held the district did not deny the student a FAPE by excluding the parent from the assessments. **In the court's view, "there is no legal requirement for the District to let R.A.'s mother see and hear R.A. during the behavioral and psychoeducational assessment."** Moreover, the court found no legal obligation for a school district to halt the updating of an IEP pending completion of a due process hearing. The court held the district did not predetermine a placement. At IEP meetings, multiple options were discussed and the parent participated. While the district violated IDEA regulations by not assuring the attendance of a nonpublic school representative at one meeting, the court found no harm was shown. Last, the court held the district's IEP offer did not deny the student a FAPE. As the district placed him in the least restrictive available setting, the court affirmed the judgment. *R.A. v. West Contra Costa Unified School Dist.*, 696 Fed.Appx. 171 (9th Cir. 2017).

◆   A Virginia eligibility determination group found a kindergartner's primary disability was an intellectual disability. On a district form titled "Eligibility Committee Summary," her parent marked a box indicating "I AGREE with the eligibility team's determination." However, she struck out the word "AGREE" and wrote "acknowledge" on the form. The school board interpreted the parent's signature as a consent to eligibility. An official clarified that her signature did not indicate agreement with a placement option. When the IEP team met and presented the parent an IEP, she rejected it and requested a due process hearing. A hearing officer concluded that substituting the word "acknowledge" for the words "agree with" on the summary form did not constitute consent to eligibility. Finding the child ineligible for special education, the hearing officer dismissed the case. A state court affirmed the decision, and the parent appealed.

The Court of Appeals of Virginia explained that state regulations mirrored federal regulations with respect to consent for initial evaluations and the initial provision of services, but added a category not found in federal law. A state regulation required parental consent before "an initial eligibility determination or any change in categorical identification" of a child. **Federal law allows schools to bar the provision of FAPE based on a parent's refusal of consent only if a parent refuses (or withholds) consent for an initial evaluation, or refuses (or withholds) consent for the initial provision of services.** The court found the state agency's interpretation would add a third situation in which a parent's refusal of consent would release a school board from its obligation to provide FAPE. The court held the student was denied a due process hearing by virtue of the board's requirement that her parent mark the "I agree with" box on a form. The parent could pursue her due process complaint. *J.V. v. Stafford County School Board,* 67 Va.App. 21, 792 S.E.2d 286 (Va. Ct. App. 2016).

◆   In 2016, the Ninth Circuit reviewed a dispute between a California school district and a parent who contested each of her child's IEPs until his graduation. She claimed the district failed to assess her child before a 2009 IEP meeting and did not conduct requested independent educational evaluations (IEEs).

But the court held any procedural failure was caused by the parent. In any event, the public school placement specified in the IEP would have provided a FAPE. Although the district did not have updated performance levels at the 2009 IEP meeting, the court found the parent had "thwarted [the district's] great efforts to conduct assessments by being uncooperative." Contrary to the parent's view, the district did not violate the IDEA by failing to conduct the requested IEEs. Six weeks before an IEP meeting, the parent had agreed that only two assessments were required. The court held the parent was not denied participation in IEP discussions. The 2009 IEP did not deny the child a FAPE.

Any procedural violations were excused because they were found to be caused by the parent. As for the 2011-12 IEP, the court rejected the parent's claims that the school district did not assess her child for anxiety and did not determine baselines for his speech and language goals. In fact, the team discussed the student's anxiety but did not propose a goal for it based on evidence that he could manage his anxiety with medication and deep breathing. Next, the court held **"the IDEA does not require a school district to conduct all assessments possible; it requires school districts to decide what data is needed to determine the educational needs of the child, among other things."** As evidence supported finding that the 2011-12 IEP provided the child with a FAPE, the court upheld the decision for the school district. *Baquerizo v. Garden Grove Unified School Dist.*, 826 F.3d 1179 (9th Cir. 2016).

E. Emotional/Behavioral Issues

In Munir v. Pottsville Area School Dist., *723 F.3d 423 (3d Cir. 2013), the parents of a Pennsylvania student who attempted suicide multiple times could not recover the costs of residential placements that were made primarily in response to mental health needs and not for education.*

◆   A federal court held a California school district had sufficient information suggesting a student might have autism spectrum disorder and that a four-month delay before assessing him amounted to a denial of a free appropriate public education (FAPE). The court cited *Timothy O. v. Paso Robles Unified School Dist.*, 822 F.3d 1105 (9th Cir. 2016), in holding that **once a district or the parents suspect a child has a disability, testing must be performed**. The court found the district had sufficient notice that the student might have autism. At an IEP meeting, one of the student's therapists indicated she had found the student had autism and would be providing her report to the parent. The court found the delay was at least in part due to the skepticism of school staff. **The district was obligated to assess the student for autism regardless of the subjective views of staff members.** In the court's opinion, "the onus is on the District, not the parent, to assess children in all areas of a suspected disability." Further, the court found the district made only minimal attempts to obtain the therapist's evaluation report during the relevant four months. Finding the district's four-month delay in assessing the student for autism was unreasonable, the court held FAPE had been denied. *D.O. v. Escondido School Dist.*, No. 3:17-cv-2400-BEN-MDD, 2018 WL 6653271 (S.D. Cal. 12/18/18).

◆   A Montana student was hospitalized for five days after writing to a friend that she wanted to commit suicide. For grade nine, the student attended a public school health and science academy. She was identified as a gifted student, but she struggled with the academy's academic rigors. A school team found the student eligible for a Section 504 plan. When her accommodations did not work out, she was referred for a special education evaluation. After the evaluation, the district found the student was eligible for special education. She was again hospitalized for depression, anxiety and suicidal thoughts, and a psychologist diagnosed her with autism spectrum disorder. After a series of IEP meetings, the IEP team proposed an alternative placement. The parents rejected the offer and declared their intent to place the student in a Utah therapeutic boarding school. After they requested a hearing, the school district evaluated the student and found her eligible for special education.

A hearing officer found the district did not deny the student a FAPE. The parents appealed to a federal court, which affirmed the decision to deny their request for reimbursement. On appeal, the U.S. Court of Appeals, Ninth Circuit, held **the IDEA's child-find duty arises when a disability is "suspected" or when the district has notice of symptoms of a disability**. While the court found the school district arguably knew that the student was hospitalized for suicidal ideation, triggering the child-find obligation, the claim was barred because of the parents' long delay in filing suit. Moreover, the IEP appeared to be reasonably calculated to enable him to progress in a public school. As the school district complied with the IDEA, the court held in its favor. *J.K. and J.C. v. Missoula County Public Schools*, 713 Fed.Appx. 666 (9th Cir. 2018).

◆   A student enrolled in a Pennsylvania school district as a seventh-grader after moving from New York. She had no disability diagnoses at the time. The student was absent frequently. The district filed a criminal truancy complaint against her mother, who requested a special education evaluation. A school psychologist evaluated the student and found she did not have a qualifying disability under the IDEA. The report found her academic problems likely resulted from anxiety related to her relocation. Although the student had a Section 504 plan, she did not regularly use the accommodations it offered. Despite her improved grades and reduced anxiety, her mother filed a due process complaint against the district, claiming it failed to timely and appropriately evaluate her child and to identify her special needs. After a hearing, a special education hearing officer found the district complied with its child-find obligations under the IDEA.

On appeal, a federal court explained that the IDEA creates a continuing obligation to identify and evaluate all students who are reasonably suspected of having a disability. **An evaluation must be held after a school district could have "reasonably suspected" a student has a qualifying disability.** Under Third Circuit case law, a district has "a reasonable amount of time to evaluate that student for an accommodation." Some courts have found that when a student has a diagnosed anxiety disorder, failing grades and chronic absenteeism, a school district has a reasonable basis to believe he/she has a disability. But some federal cases indicated that courts have not construed a student's general anxiety to be a qualifying disability under the IDEA. In this case, the court found the student's undiagnosed, general anxiety did not qualify her for IDEA eligibility. Her absenteeism alone did not give the district a reasonable basis to believe she had a disability. *Karrissa G. v. Pocono Mountain School Dist.*, No. 3:16-CV-01130, 2017 WL 6311851 (M.D. Pa. 12/11/17).

◆   A student with an autism spectrum disorder was evaluated by his school district just prior to his third birthday. Evaluators were unable to engage him in play and could not use standard assessment tools due to his "compliance issues." A school psychologist attended the evaluation for 30 - 40 minutes and observed the student, finding his behavior was not characteristic of an autism spectrum disorder. Relying on this informal observation, the district drafted an IEP identifying the student as having a speech and language impairment. The student had behavior problems in a district school setting, including tantrums, crying and aggressive behavior. Midway through the school year, the parents requested an independent educational evaluation (IEE) at the district's expense.

Although the IEE yielded a diagnosis of autism, the school district did not reassess the student for almost a year. After an administrative law judge and a federal court held for the school district, the parents appealed to the U.S. Court of Appeals, Ninth Circuit. It explained that the IDEA requires that a district with notice that a child has symptoms of a covered disability must assess the child in all areas of that disability. **School districts cannot circumvent their evaluation responsibilities by using informal observations and subjective staff member opinions.** The court found the school district committed IDEA procedural violations that denied the student a free appropriate public education. The "complete failure" to assess the student for autism clearly and substantially violated the IDEA. *Paso Robles Unified School Dist. v. Timothy O.*, 822 F.3d 1105 (9th Cir. 2016). (U.S. cert. denied 4/17/17).

◆   An Arkansas elementary school student missed significant school time due to his behavior. He was suspended once and often sent home for bad behavior or soiling himself. He hit peers, put them in headlocks, chased them and refused to come in from the playground. Despite these behaviors, the principal did not consider referring him for a special education evaluation. Near the middle of his kindergarten year, the parents obtained a physician's diagnosis that found he had an impulsive form of ADHD, functional impairments in social and behavioral domains, a possible sensory processing disorder and hypotonia. After drafting a Section 504 plan, staff documented the student's continuing behavioral problems. His physician contacted the school with recommendations to address his ADHD and curtail paddling and other forms of discipline. Without contacting the parents, the principal referred the student for a special education evaluation. The school held an IEP meeting without the parents and found the student should remain on a Section 504 plan. By then, the parents had withdrawn their consent for testing by the school. They obtained a psychologist's diagnosis indicating their child had autism. The parents filed a due process complaint, charging the district with an IDEA child find violation.

A hearing officer conducted a hearing and held for the parents. On appeal, a federal court rejected the district's arguments that it complied with federal law regarding its efforts to identify all the student's areas of disability. As the hearing officer found, **the district failed to refer the student for a thorough**

evaluation when he had obvious difficulties. The principal admitted "she essentially avoided contact with [the student's] parents out of concern that they were upset with her." **When the Section 504 plan proved unworkable, the district did nothing but document its failures until the end of the school year.** Since the court found the parents were prevailing parties, they were entitled to their reasonable attorneys' fees. *Swearingen v. Ozark Mountain School Dist.*, 225 F.Supp.3d 813 (W.D. Ark. 2016).

◆   A California student's behavior included pulling out her eyelashes, toenails and fingernails and screaming profanities. Due to her maladaptive behaviors, the student was often removed from classes. Her parents felt her program was too difficult and that bad behavior by classmates was harming her. The school district denied their request for a private placement, and they declared their intent to place her in a private school at public expense. The district requested an IEP meeting, but the parents responded that none of the suggested dates were acceptable. Although they expressly stated that they did not consent to an IEP meeting in their absence, the district held a meeting without them.

The parents initiated a due process hearing. An ALJ held for the district. A federal court found no merit to the district's argument that ongoing daily informal observations of the child's support services amounted to an assessment. It held the district's failure to assess the student's behavior and anxiety denied her a FAPE. In addition, the district deprived the parents of their rights by holding an IEP meeting in their absence. Since the district did not try to notify them of the date of the IEP meeting, there was an IDEA violation. The parents were due reimbursement for their private tuition, plus the costs of an independent educational evaluation. The school district appealed to the Ninth Circuit, which found no IDEA violations. According to the court, **the district did not have to reevaluate the student, as less than three years had elapsed since her last evaluation**. As for the ruling on the parents' claim that school district held an IEP meeting in their absence, the court found this issue had never been raised during administrative proceedings and had to be dismissed. Finding no IDEA violations, the court held for the school district. *M.S. v. Lake Elsinore Unified School Dist.*, 678 Fed.Appx. 543 (9th Cir. 2017).

◆   The U.S. Court of Appeals, Sixth Circuit, agreed with Kentucky school officials that an autistic student's home behavior was not relevant to his special education eligibility status. To show a need for special education and related services, the parents had to show their child's autism adversely affected his "educational performance." According to the parents, "educational performance" includes a student's academic, social and psychological needs. They argued their child's problematic behavior at home was relevant to his "educational performance." The court held the term "educational performance" suggested school-based evaluation. Moreover, the court found the parents' argument would require schools to address all behavior flowing from a child's disability, no matter how far removed from the school day. As a result, **the court held the inquiry into the student's educational performance should be confined to classroom and school settings**. The court rejected the parents' attempt to discredit hearing testimony by the board. The student experienced academic success at school. Finding it was not entitled to discount the lower court's view of the evidence, the court held for the board. *Q.W. v. Board of Educ. of Fayette County, Kentucky,* 630 Fed.Appx. 580 (6th Cir. 2015).

◆   A Minnesota child had lymphoma and underwent chemotherapy. She had frequent illnesses, infections and asthma and was diagnosed with generalized anxiety disorder. When the child began kindergarten, she exhibited separation anxiety when being dropped off at school. Although the parents requested a special education evaluation, the school did not comply. After missing about 20% of her school days during kindergarten and first grade, the child missed 39 of the first 102 days of second grade. The parents requested a due process hearing, at which they asserted the school district should have identified their child as eligible for special education with other health disabilities (OHD). An ALJ held the district did not follow its child find procedures and ordered it to verify a medical diagnosis of a chronic or acute health condition and assess the child's eligibility for services. **A federal court held a school district must identify and evaluate all children who are reasonably suspected of having a disability, even if a parent does not request an evaluation.** The court found the district had reason to suspect that a medical evaluation might yield critical information and committed a child find violation. The district had to get a medical assessment and reevaluate the child. *Independent School Dist. No. 413 v. H.M.J.,* 123 F.Supp.3d 1100 (D. Minn. 2015).

F.   Reevaluation

After a student's initial eligibility determination, a school must reevaluate IDEA eligibility every three years, unless the parties agree otherwise. See 34 C.F.R. Part 300.303. In Phyllene W. v. Huntsville City Board of Educ., the Eleventh Circuit Court of Appeals found an Alabama school board had to assess a student's hearing, even though her parent waived her right to a reevaluation based on concerns that the child would test out of IDEA eligibility.

◆   A Pennsylvania student had developmental delays and behavior problems. A comprehensive behavior support plan was implemented, and a behavior specialist began working with him. During the second part of his kindergarten year, the student showed marked improvement and did not have classroom meltdowns. His behavioral and social progress continued into his first-grade year. But his academic and behavioral progress regressed after the winter holiday break, and he experienced increased frustration and extreme crying that disrupted others and impeded his learning. The district did not immediately restore behavioral support, and the student's behavior continued to deteriorate.

The parents asked the district to reevaluate him and filed a due process hearing complaint. By May of the student's first-grade year, the district completed its reevaluation. It identified him with ADHD, anxiety, OCD and speech/language needs. The district revised his IEP, addressing his areas of concerns and resuming weekly sessions with a behavioral specialist. A hearing officer found the district provided the student a free appropriate public education (FAPE) for kindergarten and most of his first-grade year. Although the hearing officer found the district should have known that the student needed to be reevaluated during the second half of his first-grade school year, she found a compensatory education award was unnecessary. The parents appealed. A federal court found that while the failure to timely evaluate a child violates the IDEA, **a school district does not violate its child-find duty by failing to identify a student as disabled "at the earliest possible moment."** Noting that hyperactivity, lack of compliance and tantrums are not atypical during early primary school years, the court found "it would be inappropriate to rush to identify a child that young as disabled." Given the student's age, the lack of indicators of impairments and his unstructured preschool environment, the court held the school district acted reasonably. *D.B. v. Fairview School Dist.*, No. 15-cv-00085, 2017 WL 4923514 (W.D. Pa. 10/31/17).

◆   In 2014, Maryland parents asked their child's school district to pay for an independent educational evaluation (IEE) of their child, noting the district had not formally evaluated him for five years. The district offered to conduct its own evaluation, but the parents declined and filed a due process complaint. An administrative law judge (ALJ) held they were not entitled to an IEE at public expense because they did not disagree with an evaluation obtained by a public agency. On appeal to a federal court, the parents claimed a 2012 reevaluation planning and determination meeting was an "evaluation" with which they disagreed. Like the ALJ, the court found there was no existing school district evaluation with which the parents disagreed. The 2012 meeting was not an "evaluation." An IDEA "evaluation" must comply with federal regulations and be used to determine whether a child has a disability and the nature and extent of special education and related services required by a student.

Evaluators must use a variety of assessment tools and strategies to gather relevant information about a child. They must use technically sound instruments and review existing evaluation data on the child. Since the 2012 meeting only reviewed the 2009 assessment data, report cards and teacher observations, it was not an IDEA evaluation. As a result, the ALJ correctly held there was no existing evaluation in 2014 for the parents to reject. Instead of requesting an IEE, they should have filed a due process request seeking to force the district to evaluate their child. **Had the parents allowed a reevaluation of their child and then disagreed with the results, they could have sought an IEE at public expense.** But as they had refused the offer for a reevaluation, they could not later seek an IEE. The court explained that the parental right to an IEE is not an end in itself. An IEE furnishes parents independent expertise and data to confirm or reject a district evaluation. *F.C. v. Montgomery County Public Schools,* Civ. No. TDC-14-2562, 2016 WL 3570604 (D. Md. 6/27/16).

◆   An Alabama student had seven ear surgeries by age 16 and had significant difficulties in reading, math, organizing her schoolwork and taking standardized tests. Her mother paid for a private tutor for her throughout her K-12 career. Near the end of the student's second-grade school year, she was found to have a specific learning disability that qualified her for special education. At an IEP team meeting during the student's fifth-grade year, the parent notified the

team that her child had tubes implanted in her ears and that her hearing loss
was worsening. But the team did not schedule an evaluation. The next year, a
triennial reevaluation was due, but the team recommended that no evaluation
take place due to fear that she would test out of special education eligibility.

As the student entered grade 10, her reading was assessed at a grade 3.6
level and her math abilities were found to be at a 2.6 grade level. The parent
placed her in a private school and requested a hearing. A private evaluator
found the student qualified for special education with a hearing impairment. A
hearing officer found for the board, as did a federal court. The U.S. Court of
Appeals, Eleventh Circuit, held a proper evaluation would have uncovered the
cause of the student's hearing deficits. **Although the parent agreed to forgo a
reevaluation due to fears that the student would test out of eligibility, the
board was not excused from conducting future reevaluations.** Failure of
a parent to request an evaluation did not absolve the board of its independent
responsibility to evaluate a child suspected of having a disability. *Phyllene W. v.
Huntsville City Board of Educ.*, 630 Fed.Appx. 917 (11th Cir. 2015).

G. Multi-Tiered Systems of Support

*Students needing additional academic and behavioral support in general
education environments may be served with a multi-tiered system of supports
(MTSS) such as response to intervention (RTI) or positive behavioral
intervention. MTSS may also be used to identify children suspected of having a
specific learning disability. Children whose response to intervention is minimal
or who do not respond must be referred for an IDEA eligibility evaluation.*

*Parents may request an initial special education evaluation at any time.
**The use of MTSS, including RTI, cannot be used to delay or deny a full and
individual IDEA evaluation if a child is suspected of having a disability.***

◆ An Alabama board of education placed a fifth-grade general education
student with behavior problems in a pre-referral intervention program where
it implemented positive behavioral interventions. The parents felt the board
knew his asthma medication caused hyperactivity and that he should have been
evaluated for an IEP. Claiming the board violated its IDEA child-find duty,
they filed a due process complaint. After a hearing officer held for the board,
the parents appealed to a federal court. It turned to an Alabama law detailing the
minimum evaluation criteria for students suspected of having an Other Health
Impairment (OHI). The law required evidence that an OHI adversely affected
a student's academic performance. In the court's opinion, interventions and
accommodations were tried in the regular classes but were found unsuccessful.

The Eleventh Circuit Court of Appeals has recently held that the child-
find obligation "does not extend to testing every student who is not successful
when factors other than a disability would also explain the failure to progress."
Further, **the Eleventh Circuit held a school's failure to diagnose a disability
at the earliest possible moment is not a denial of FAPE**. The court held
the board did not overlook clear signs of a disability and was not negligent in
failing to order testing. It found the school justified its decision by showing

that the IEP team used pre-referral interventions for the student, who was still meeting expectations in all academic areas. Since he performed well in classes and did not exhibit bad behavior or other clear signs of disability, the court held the board did not violate its child-find duty. *D.J.D. v. Madison City Board of Educ.*, No. 5:17-cv-00096, 2018 WL 4283058 (N.D. Ala. 9/7/18).

◆   A Tennessee student had developmental delays but was found ineligible for special education in preschool. As the lone four-year-old in her kindergarten class, she fell behind her peers. The school responded with general education interventions including a Response to Intervention (RtI) plan. A General Education Intervention Team (GEIT) monitored the student's progress. Her parents agreed with the school district that she should repeat kindergarten. A Section 504 plan was created, but she continued falling behind. An evaluator found the student's performance was within or above the normal range. Before the evaluation was done, the parents removed her from school and requested a due process hearing. An administrative law judge (ALJ) held for the school system, and a federal court later affirmed this decision. Appeal reached the Sixth Circuit Court of Appeals, which found the IDEA child-find duty requires school districts to take appropriate steps to identify and evaluate all children who are suspected of having a disability and a need for special education, even if they are advancing from grade to grade. To establish a violation of the child-find duty, it must be shown that school officials overlooked clear signs of a disability and negligently failed to order testing, with no rational basis.

In this case, the court found the district evaluated the student during preschool and reevaluated her about 28 months later. It held **the district neither overlooked clear signs of a disability nor lacked a rational justification for not reevaluating her for over two years**. Meanwhile, the district effectively used general education strategies, such as RtI and GEIT, and later implemented a Section 504 plan to help the student. When a school district has conducted a comprehensive evaluation and found a student does not qualify for IDEA services, it must have a reasonable time to monitor his/her progress before exploring whether further evaluation is required. In ruling for the school district, the court relied on *Marshall Joint School Dist. No. 2 v. C.D.*, 616 F.3d 632 (7th Cir. 2010), which held "a physician cannot simply prescribe special education." The court found the district's numerous assessments of the student were a better indicator of her needs than a doctor's prescription. Nothing in the IDEA or its regulations require an IEP team to adopt a doctor's recommendations. *M.G. v. Williamson County Schools*, 720 Fed.Appx. 280 (6th Cir. 2018).

◆   A South Dakota student was involved in a number of behavioral incidents, leading her guardian to ask to have her evaluated for special education. Instead, the school held a teacher assistance team (TAT) meeting and developed a plan to address the student's behavior. Soon, the guardian placed her in a 10-day hospital behavioral health program, followed by a 45-day stay in a residential chemical dependency treatment facility. When she returned to school, her attendance was sporadic and she posted a picture of herself holding a knife on social media. After serving a five-day suspension for assaulting a classmate, the student brought a knife to school and was suspended for the rest of the semester. Her guardian filed a due process complaint based on the school district's failure to conduct a full individual evaluation (FIE). A hearing examiner held the district failed to order an evaluation and violated the IDEA by expelling the student without any procedural protections, despite knowledge of a disability.

While the hearing examiner ordered the district to complete a FIE and implement an IEP if the student qualified for special education, compensatory education was denied. A FIE was completed, and she was found eligible for special education. Later, the guardian sued the school district in a federal court for compensatory education. The court noted she had requested an evaluation soon after the student's problem behaviors intensified. Instead of conducting the FIE, the district initiated the TAT process, which is South Dakota's version of RTI. State rules permit schools to use an RTI process to help with an IDEA evaluation but declare that parents retain a right to step out of the RTI process and obtain a FIE. **Federal guidance of January 21, 2011 clarifies that state and local education agencies must ensure that evaluations of children suspected of having a disability are not delayed or denied because of an RTI strategy.** The court stated that a school district cannot require a student to complete an RTI process before an evaluation, nor can RTI be used to delay an evaluation. A student who has not been declared eligible for special education is still entitled to IDEA procedural protections, if the school has knowledge that the student has a disability. Knowledge is imputed to a school district when a parent requests a FIE. Since the guardian requested the FIE before the suspension, the student was entitled to IDEA procedural protections. The court upheld the administrative decision. Compensatory education was properly denied, as the student had not been found eligible for special education at the relevant time. *Artichoker v. Todd County School Dist.*, 3:15-CV-03021-RAL, 2016 WL 7489033 (D.S.D. 12/29/16).

◆   An Alabama school district did not violate a student's rights, despite delays in providing her parents with assessments and other eligibility data. A federal court explained that the IDEA does not mandate participation in every aspect of the educational process. The parents complained that an observation of their child by a special education teacher was not considered at an eligibility meeting. But the court found no denial of a free appropriate public education.

A "significant fragmentation of information supplied at the eligibility meeting" did not compel the finding that a different conclusion would have resulted had the information been shared with the team. Alabama special education regulations limit the number of observations to be used for determining whether a child has a specific learning disability. **The parents did not show how the failure to include the observation would lead to a different eligibility result.** The court disagreed with their claim that the information at the eligibility meeting was so lacking that the referral team could not have reached an accurate decision. It held a team may determine, on a case-by-case basis, whether supplemental evaluations beyond the minimums specified in state regulations are needed. All the records sought by the parents in this case indicated the student was performing adequately in her curriculum and did not need a different placement. *E.E. v. Tuscaloosa City Board of Educ.*, No. 7:15-cv-01370-LSC, 2016 WL 3618362 (N.D. Ala. 7/6/16).

◆ In 2005, a California school district began to implement a Response to Intervention (RTI) approach to assist struggling learners in general education environments as an intermediate step before special education referrals. Student RTI assessment results were not shared with parents. Via RTI, a kindergartner was found in need of reading intervention and given additional instruction. The next school year, the parents requested an evaluation of their child for learning disabilities. After two student study team (SST) meetings, the school district referred him for a special education evaluation. The student's RTI graphs were not reviewed in the SST meetings and were not shared with the parents. In late April of the student's first-grade year, an IEP team found he had a phonological processing disorder and declared him eligible for special education. But the parties continued to disagree about evaluations, and the parents eventually withdrew the child from his ISP and enrolled him in an intense private reading and comprehension program. They filed a due process complaint with a state agency, asserting 16 claims against the district regarding the child's eligibility.

An administrative law judge (ALJ) held for the district, and the parents filed three federal court cases that were eventually consolidated. When the case reached the U.S. Court of Appeals, Ninth Circuit, it found the school district had incorporated RTI data into the child's initial evaluation and had used a variety of assessment tools (including the RTI data) during the child's initial evaluation. **While the court upheld the evaluation, it held the team violated the IDEA by failing to ensure RTI data was documented and carefully considered by the parents.** The school was required to furnish data to the parents to allow them to give their informed consent for the initial evaluation and the services he was to receive. Even if the district never proposed to use the RTI assessments to determine eligibility, **the IDEA required notice to parents regarding the tests it intended to conduct on a child. The parents had to be informed of those test results.** Without the benefit of the RTI data, the parents were unaware of the discrepancy in reported scores and were unable to meaningfully participate in the IEP process. Finding a denial of FAPE, the court returned the case to the lower court for it to reconsider the parents' claim for reimbursement. *M.M. v. Lafayette School Dist.*, 767 F.3d 842 (9th Cir. 2014).

◆ An Illinois student had behavioral problems in kindergarten that prompted a school counselor to refer him to counseling. The school provided him with academic and behavioral support in the context of response to intervention (RTI). During second grade, the student was admitted to a hospital psychiatric facility and diagnosed with intermittent explosive disorder. His mother requested a due process hearing, asserting the school district violated its IDEA child find duty and failed to respond to her request for a full and individual evaluation (FIE). She also challenged the adequacy of the IEP and related services. A hearing officer found for the school district on the child find and timeliness issues, and a claim for compensatory education was denied. On appeal, a federal court observed that schools are not required to formally evaluate all struggling students. The standard for whether a school failed to identify a student with a disability was whether it overlooked "clear signs of a disability" and was "negligent in failing to order testing," or there was no rational justification for deciding not to evaluate. Under this standard, the court held the hearing officer did not commit an error. **The district could have rationally believed that the interventions provided under RTI might ameliorate the student's behavior up to the time of his hospitalization.** *Demarcus L. v. Board of Educ. of City of Chicago, Dist. 299*, No. 13 C 5331, 2014 WL 948883 (N.D. Ill. 3/11/14).

III. INDEPENDENT EVALUATIONS

In M.Z. v. Bethlehem Area School Dist., 521 Fed.Appx. 74 (3d Cir. 2013), the Third Circuit observed that school districts must reevaluate students with disabilities at least once every three years unless the parents and the district agree otherwise. Parents who disagree with a school district's assessment may request an independent educational evaluation (IEE) at public expense. If such a request is made, a school must either defend its evaluation or pay for the IEE.

◆   A Chicago student with a specific learning disability had behavior and attendance issues. He experienced turmoil while living alternately with his mother and father. After his father died, he was absent for much of a school year and was hospitalized with a variety of health problems. His mother requested a due process hearing, asserting the school district denied him a free appropriate public education. She later requested independent educational evaluations (IEEs) at public expense in seven areas. Instead of funding the IEEs, the board filed a due process complaint. A hearing officer held a hearing at which she found the district's witnesses more credible and persuasive than the mother's experts, who lacked state certification and had never met the student. The board prevailed, and the mother appealed. A federal court held for the board of education, and appeal reached the U.S. Court of Appeals, Seventh Circuit. It stated that a parent who disagrees with a school's evaluation may be entitled to an IEE at public expense.
     If a parent requests an IEE, the district may file a due process request to defend its evaluation. Although the parent challenged the credentials of the district's psychologists, the court found they were sufficiently trained and knowledgeable, and had adequate experience to administer the assessments she disputed. The court also rejected the parent's argument that a test of her son's intellectual ability was not adequately considered. As the hearing officer found, his grief, depression, emotional disability and/or absences caused his emotional issues and a decline in his IQ score. Substantial evidence supported the hearing officer's findings that any errors by the district evaluators were harmless. This included a decision to provide minimal Spanish translation on a particular assessment. Evidence supported a finding that the student was no longer an English Language Learner and that he was instructed in (and spoke) English. Although the parent contested other aspects of the district's evaluations, the court upheld the judgment for the board of education. *B.G. v. Board of Educ. of City of Chicago*, 901 F.3d 903 (7th Cir. 2018).

◆   A Pennsylvania student had anxiety and symptoms of obsessive compulsive disorder. During her first-grade school year, the school district issued her a gifted individualized education plan in reading and math. A Section 504 service agreement was offered for her anxiety issues. Although the student was earning

A and B grades in grade three, her parents claimed she had a specific learning disability in reading and experienced anxiety and difficulties with peers because she had been bullied. The school psychologist who completed the evaluation found the student was not eligible for IDEA services. While this conflicted with the findings of the student's therapist, the parents ultimately consented to revisions of their child's existing Section 504 plan. Soon after the evaluation, the parents placed their daughter in a private day school. They filed a due process complaint against the district, claiming she had been denied a free appropriate public education (FAPE) and seeking reimbursement for private school tuition.

The parents obtained an independent educational evaluation (IEE) and sought reimbursement for it from the school district. Instead, the district filed its own due process hearing request to defend its evaluation. When the parents' due process (FAPE) matter came before a hearing officer, there was no final decision from a hearing officer in the IEE dispute. The hearing officer assigned to the FAPE dispute held for the school district. The parents appealed the FAPE decision to a federal court, which noted that while the hearing officer in the IEE dispute had ordered the district to pay for an IEE, there was still no final decision in that case. As for the FAPE dispute, **the court found ample support for the conclusion that the school district appropriately evaluated the student and found her ineligible for special education and related services**. No evidence supported the claim that the student had a specific learning disability. Instead, the hearing officer found she should remain in a regular education setting with a Section 504 plan. *G.D. v. West Chester Area School Dist.*, No. 17-969, 2017 WL 3582230 (E.D. Pa. 8/18/17).

◆   A Pennsylvania school district was required to pay the parent of a gifted student for the cost of an independent educational evaluation based on a hearing officer's findings that a district evaluation report left the student's special education eligibility in doubt. A federal court found that there was evidence that the student might have a specific learning disability in reading. **The court issued a decision in which it said that the hearing officer who conducted the due process hearing did not err in ordering the district to pay for an IEE.** A hearing officer's factual findings are presumed to be correct and after a thorough review of the evidence, he found the district used flawed methodology. As a result, the judgment requiring the school district to fund an IEE was affirmed. *West Chester Area School Dist. v. G.D.*, No. 16-4471, 2017 WL 379440 (E.D. Pa. 1/25/17).

◆   An Idaho school district reevaluated an eighth-grader and found him ineligible for special education. His parents obtained a private evaluation that diagnosed him with a high-functioning form of autism. They sought a new evaluation, but the district refused. During ninth grade, the student was arrested and placed in a juvenile detention center. The school district in which the detention center was located evaluated him for special education but found no evidence of any adverse effect of disabilities on his educational performance. Noting the other district's evaluation was limited because of his confinement, the parents asked their home district for a reevaluation. But the home district declined to perform its own evaluation. When the student returned home, the parents requested additional assessments and an IEP. The district refused and found him ineligible for special education. His parents requested an IEE, which the home district denied. In a due process proceeding, a hearing officer held the home district failed to conduct an appropriate evaluation. A federal court then issued a preliminary order preventing the district from graduating the student. A district reevaluation then found the student ineligible for special education.

Appeal reached the Ninth Circuit Court of Appeals, which held the parents were entitled to an IEE at public expense. **The conditions for evaluation at a juvenile center were very different from the home setting and evidence indicated the home district relied too heavily on the student's grades in its assessments.** The court found the order to prevent the school district from graduating the student was questionable, since he was not receiving special education. It appeared that since he met graduation criteria, he likely received all the benefits that the district's general education program offered. It had been three years since the preliminary order was issued and it was vacated. *Meridian Joint School Dist. No. 2 v. D.A.*, 792 F.3d 1054 (9th Cir. 2015).

◆   A Georgia school district evaluated a second-grader and found him eligible for special education in its autism and speech impairment programs. Using the same evaluation, a school IEP team met with the parents and prepared an IEP for the next school year. The parents did not object to the eligibility findings or the proposed IEP and also raised no objection to the evaluation or the child's IEP at the next year's IEP meeting. But about two months into the school year, the parents claimed the initial evaluation — now over two years old — was improper. They asked the school district to pay for an IEE. The district denied the request as untimely, relying on a two-year IDEA limitations provision for due process hearing requests. The district then asked the parents for permission to conduct a triennial reevaluation, even though it was not yet due. But the parents declined to consent to a district reevaluation. Both parties then requested due process hearings. An administrative law judge (ALJ) heard the cases and issued separate orders in the district's favor. On appeal, a federal court agreed with the ALJ. The parents appealed to the U.S. Court of Appeals, Eleventh Circuit, which found they did not support their claim for reimbursement or explain how a psychological assessment of the child qualified as an IEE.

There was no evidence that the parents even paid for a psychological assessment. Any claim for an IEE at public expense was limited to two years, and the issue was moot. The initial evaluation was not current because more than three years had passed. Regardless of the merits of the case, the court held any order for an IEE at public expense would be futile. **There was no right to a publicly funded IEE until the parents disagreed with a school reevaluation.** Because a reevaluation was due, the relief sought by the parents would no longer remedy any injury they alleged. Since the case was moot it had to be dismissed. *T.P. v. Bryan County School Dist.*, 792 F.3d 1284 (11th Cir. 2015).

CHAPTER THREE

Individualized Education Programs

I. PROCEDURAL MATTERS

A. Generally

An individualized education program (IEP) is a written statement for each student with a disability that describes the student's present levels of educational performance, progress in the general curriculum, services to be provided, annual goals and many other statutory requirements.

◆ After their son's fourth-grade year, Pennsylvania parents asked that he be retained in his grade. School representatives disagreed, finding he "showed excellent improvement academically and socially." As the disagreement continued, the parents filed a due process complaint. After mediation, they agreed to allow their child to enter grade five. But they rejected a new IEP offer and filed a second due process complaint. A hearing officer held for the parents, finding the IEP was flawed. On appeal, a federal court held for the school district, finding the hearing officer improperly considered the student's post-

53

IEP progress and exaggerated minor IEP shortcomings. The parents appealed to the U.S. Court of Appeals, Third Circuit, which commented that **an IEP is not guaranteed to produce any particular outcome**. It recited its longstanding rule that the adequacy of an IEP is determined as of the time it is offered, not a later date. In this case, the court found the hearing officer improperly relied on the student's post-IEP performance to evaluate the IEP. For this reason, it held the lower court had correctly rejected his decision that the student did not make progress on certain goals. Next, the court rejected the parents' argument that the IEP was flawed because some goals were too subjective or imprecise to be fully measured. Agreeing with the lower court and the school district, the court found any imprecision in the IEP goals did not deny the student a free appropriate public education (FAPE). **As a school witness testified, goals for social skills such as speech are inherently difficult to quantify.**

In the court's view, the district made up for any lack of clarity in the IEP by communicating with the parents. Even if the goals could not be "measured with mathematical precision," the court found "the IDEA does not require perfection." Any procedural flaws were not legally significant, as the parents did not show their son's right to a FAPE was affected. Nor did they show their participation rights were harmed or any deprivation of educational benefits. The court disagreed with the parents' attempt to read a substantive right into an IDEA regulatory requirement that school districts take necessary action to ensure that parents understand the proceedings of the IEP team. Finding the lower court correctly held for the school district, the court affirmed the judgment. *Colonial School Dist. v. G.K.*, 763 Fed.Appx. 192 (3d Cir. 2019).

◆ An Arizona school district advised the parents of a child with a speech language impairment that he was withdrawn from enrollment in the district under state law because he did not attend school for over 10 consecutive days. The parents were notified that they would have to reenroll him if they wanted him to attend preschool for the rest of the current year or kindergarten the next fall. They were advised that they could request an IEP upon reenrollment. The parents filed a due process complaint. An administrative law judge (ALJ) dismissed the case, and they appealed. A federal court reviewed the ALJ's findings that the parents have four sons and that none of them were enrolled in kindergarten until the age of six. It held the district did not improperly withdraw the student and require the parents to reenroll him before holding an IEP meeting. By then, the parents had rejected the IEP and provided the district with a 10-day notice of intent to obtain private services. Nor did the district violate the IDEA by needlessly delaying or placing conditions on a parent-requested IEP meeting. At the relevant time, the student had missed almost two months of preschool services and the court found he would not be immediately affected by a failure to hold an IEP meeting. Only 12 days were left in the school year.

At the start of each school year, a local education agency is required to have an IEP in effect for each child with a disability residing in its jurisdiction. In addition, a school district must make a formal, specific written offer of placement for each such child. **The court held a school violates the IDEA when it withholds an offer of FAPE until parents enroll a child.** Upon request by a parent, a school district must evaluate a child, even if he/she is enrolled in a private school. In this case, the school district knew the student had a qualifying disability. As the district had to create an IEP for the student, the court found an IDEA violation. *Hack v. Deer Valley Unified School Dist.*, No. CV-15-02255-PHX-JJT, 2017 WL 2991970 (D. Ariz. 7/14/17).

◆   A California student's behavior included pulling out her eyelashes, toenails and fingernails and screaming profanities. Due to her maladaptive behaviors, she was often removed from classes. Her parents felt her program was too hard and that bad behavior by classmates was harming her. The school district denied their request for a private placement, and they notified the district that they intended to place her in a private school at public expense. The district requested an IEP meeting, but the parents responded that none of the suggested dates were acceptable. Although they expressly stated that they did not consent to an IEP meeting in their absence, the district held a meeting without them. Later, the meeting was rescheduled without notice. The parents initiated a due process hearing. An ALJ held for the school district, and the parents appealed.

A federal court found no merit to the district's argument that daily informal observations as part of the child's support services amounted to an assessment. No formal tests were administered, and the district did not assess her behavior despite parental requests and ample evidence that she was becoming more aggressive. The court held the failure to assess the student's behavior and anxiety deprived her of educational benefits and denied her a FAPE. The district deprived the parents of their procedural rights by holding an IEP meeting in their absence. **The school district was required to keep records of its calls, correspondence and home visits to document efforts to obtain parental attendance at IEP meetings.** On appeal, the Ninth Circuit found the school district did not have to reevaluate the student, as less than three years had elapsed since her last evaluation. As for the ruling on the parents' claim that school district held an IEP meeting in their absence, the court found this issue was never raised before the ALJ and had to be dismissed. *M.S. v. Lake Elsinore Unified School Dist.*, 678 Fed.Appx. 543 (9th Cir. 2017).

◆   An Oregon student with an autism spectrum disorder and other disabilities began exhibiting signs of psychosis. She was taken to an emergency room and referred to a psychiatric hospital. Her parents obtained a professional opinion that the student had "Psychotic Disorder: Not Otherwise Specified." When the IEP team met, the parents mentioned the psychotic episode. Without more information about it, the IEP team did not adjust the IEP based on her mental health needs. The parties failed to reach an agreement on an IEP and the parents requested a due process hearing. An ALJ held the parents were denied meaningful participation in the student's education. It was found that the district did not provide her appropriate placements for three school years and failed to identify all her areas of suspected disability. The district was ordered to comprehensively evaluate her, hold an IEP meeting to draft a new IEP and provide her compensatory education and counseling. A federal court reversed much of the ALJ's order, and appeal reached the U.S. Court of Appeals, Ninth Circuit. It found **any failure to provide prior written notices, reevaluate the student's mental health, conduct age-appropriate transition assessments**

and provide progress reports did not affect the parents' substantive rights.
The court found no error in determining the student's classroom placement, since the parents actively participated in the IEP process. Nor did the school district deny the student a FAPE. The court found the IEPs contained concrete measurements of the student's progress. Her 2009 and 2010 IEPs appropriately addressed her anxiety. It appeared that the student was making progress and the school district was not required to provide any preferred teaching methodology. *Forest Grove School Dist. v. Student*, 665 Fed.Appx. 612 (9th Cir. 2016).

B. IEP Meeting and Attendance Issues

The makeup of an IEP team is described at 20 U.S.C. § 1414(d)(1)(B). IEP teams include the parents, at least one of the student's regular education teachers, at least one special education teacher of the student, and a local educational agency (LEA) representative qualified to provide (or supervise the provision of) specially designed instruction to meet the student's unique needs and who is knowledgeable about the general curriculum and LEA's resources.

An IDEA regulation (34 C.F.R. Part 300.322) explains the steps necessary to ensure parents are present at an IEP meeting. This section requires ample notice to parents and the scheduling of a mutually agreed-upon time and place to meet. The same regulation (34 C.F.R. Part 300.322) states that if a parent cannot attend an IEP meeting, the school must offer alternatives. A meeting can be held without a parent only if the district cannot convince him/her to attend.

In A.G. v. Placentia-Yorba Linda Unified School Dist., 320 Fed.Appx. 519 (9th Cir. 2009), the Ninth Circuit held the IDEA does not require the child's most current teacher to attend an IEP meeting. It requires a special education teacher or provider who has actually taught the student. The court also held not all of a student's special education teachers need to attend an IEP meeting.

Although it would be preferable to have a staff member with extensive experience in a child's particular disability, a federal court in Kansas held the IDEA does not require this. Huffman v. North Lyon County School Dist., No. 08-2083-KGS, 2009 WL 3185239 (D. Kan. 9/30/09).

◆   A Pennsylvania district did not have IEPs ready for twins with autism as their kindergarten school year approached. The parents wrote to the district, saying that they would enroll the twins in a private school in 10 days and seek tuition reimbursement. Later, they enrolled the twins in an academy they created for students with disabilities. The parents then requested a due process hearing. While continuing to work with the district, the parents pursued reimbursement for the costs of 1:1 assistants plus the costs of speech therapy, occupational therapy and extended school year (ESY) services. A special education hearing officer held the district failed to offer the twins appropriate IEPs before the start of their kindergarten year. She awarded the parents reimbursement for their tuition and transportation costs. The hearing officer denied the parents' request for reimbursement for the cost of 1:1 aides and speech/language and occupational therapy. A federal court affirmed the award of tuition reimbursement but denied the additional costs they sought. In addition, the court held the parents were entitled to tuition reimbursement pursuant to the IDEA stay-put provision pending appeal. As this time period encompassed over two years, the reimbursement totaled almost $228,000. The court also awarded the parents over $185,500 in attorneys' fees and costs.

On appeal, the U.S. Court of Appeals, Third Circuit, held the failure to timely provide IEPs was a procedural violation that significantly impeded parental opportunities to participate in the decision-making process. **Failure to finalize the IEPs by the start of the school year denied the twins a free appropriate public education.** The hearing officer found the parents' conduct in founding an academy and enrolling their children there was "not substantively different from the usual situation of dissatisfied parents exploring potential private placements." They were entitled to the costs of 1:1 aides, speech/language and occupational therapy, as well as ESY services. The court also upheld the award of attorneys' fees and additional stay-put relief. *School Dist. of Philadelphia v. Kirsch*, 722 Fed.Appx. 215 (3d Cir. 2018).

◆ Arizona parents claimed their child's IEPs lacked necessary transition, speech and math services and extended school year (ESY) services. An administrative law judge (ALJ) ordered the school district to provide the student 40 hours of compensatory special education math instruction. But he denied all the other relief sought by the parents. Before a federal court, the parents argued the ALJ disregarded relevant evidence. They claimed the IEP team violated the IDEA by continuing an IEP meeting after they left with their advocate. But the court noted the IEP meeting was scheduled for two hours. When the parents' advocate had to leave, she suggested reconvening the meeting. A team member stated that the IEP had to be finished because the current one was expiring.

Other IEP team members stated that the meeting would reconvene. In fact, two such meetings were held later in the year and the parents attended them. The parents stayed for the full two hours the meeting was intended to run, and left when their advocate left. Upon review by a federal court, it was found that the school district made a reasonable choice of what course of action promoted IDEA purposes and was least likely to result in the denial of a free appropriate public education. **The parents actively participated in most of the meeting and went to two follow-up meetings at which the IEP was amended.** Under the circumstances, the court held the parents were not denied meaningful participation in the IEP process. *Pangerl v. Peoria Unified School Dist.*, No. CV-14-00836-PHX-JJT, 2017 WL 603834 (D. Ariz. 2/15/17).

◆ Hawaii school officials made extensive efforts to arrange for a parent to attend IEP meetings. It went forward with the meeting in his absence, and it later held a meeting while his child was in temporary foster case. The parent lacked parental rights at the time of the second meeting. In his due process case, a hearings officer found that **IDEA regulations permit a school district to hold an IEP meeting without a parent if there are documented efforts by the district to include the parent**. The DOE did not violate the parent's rights by holding an IEP meeting in his absence when his parental rights were taken away. On appeal, a federal court found the administrative decision was supported by the evidence. The hearings officer identified relevant IDEA provisions allowing the IEP meetings to go forward without the parent.

School districts must take steps to ensure that one or both parents are present at each meeting or are afforded an opportunity to participate. If a parent cannot attend, the school must offer other methods of participation such as video or teleconferencing. **An IEP meeting can be held without parents if the school cannot convince them they should attend under an IDEA regulation found at 34 C.F.R. Part 300.322(d).** In such cases, the school must keep a detailed record of its attempts to include the parent in the meeting. Although the parent argued he was entitled to be involved in the development of his child's IEP when the student was removed from his custody, the court found no legal support for this argument. In addition, the court found the school tried to include the parent in the development of the IEP after he regained his child's legal custody. Since the parent failed to respond to the principal's many contact letters and the school made repeated efforts to include the parent in IEP meetings, the court held for the DOE. *P.M. v. Dep't of Educ., State of Hawaii,* No. 15-00437 LEK-RLP, 2016 WL 6434072 (D. Haw. 10/31/16).

◆   **Connecticut parents failed to convince the Second Circuit Court of Appeals that their school board violated the IDEA by holding two IEP meetings while they vacationed abroad.** The court found the board made considerable efforts to include them in the meetings, and they had participated in two PPT meetings before leaving for the summer. The board tried to schedule meetings around their travel plans. In the court's opinion, the board could reject the alternatives suggested by the parents. It found no basis for rejecting a hearing officer's finding that the IEP proposed by the PPT was appropriate. The Second Circuit noted that a parent's right of participation is not a right to veto an IEP. *Dervishi v. Stamford Board of Educ.,* 653 Fed.Appx. 55 (2d Cir. 2016).

◆   The parents of a California student rejected an IEP offered by his school district. After a hearing officer upheld the district's IEP, a federal court upheld the administrative decision. Among the court's findings was that the district satisfied IDEA requirements by ensuring the IEP team included all required members. At issue was the attendance of a particular regular education teacher. In the court's view, this teacher satisfied 34 C.F.R. Part 300.321(a) as a teacher "who is, or may be, responsible for implementing a portion of the IEP." Next, the court upheld four challenged IEP goals regarding the child's need for reciprocal communication. Supportive services were listed in the IEP. Last, the court upheld the student's placement in a general education setting.

On appeal, the Ninth Circuit held **the general education teacher's presence at IEP meetings met an IDEA requirement that "not less than 1 regular education teacher" of the child be in attendance.** Even if there was procedural error, the court found it was harmless. There was no deprivation of educational opportunities or infringement on the parent's participatory rights. The IEP adequately addressed the student's needs and there was no error in placing him in a general education setting. The IEP satisfied the IDEA's preference for placing students with disabilities with their non-disabled peers. Finding no errors by the lower court, the Ninth Circuit held for the district. *Z.R. v. Oak Park Unified School Dist.,* 622 Fed.Appx. 630 (9th Cir. 2015).

C. Parental Participation

In Doe v. East Lyme Board of Educ., *790 F.3d 440 (2d Cir. 2015), the Second Circuit held that parental participation rights do not include a right to be present throughout a school's decision-making process. Relying on a special education regulation at 34 C.F.R. Part 300.501(b)(3), the court found **parental participation does not require parental presence during informal staff conversations**. The court found that if a parent has a meaningful opportunity to offer input, be part of the team and participate in any group decision about the educational placement of the child, IDEA requirements are respected.*

No IDEA provision requires parental consent to amend an IEP at a team meeting. In Hjortness v. Neenah Joint School Dist., *507 F.3d 1060 (7th Cir. 2007), the court held parents do not have a veto power at IEP team meetings.*

◆ A New York parent claimed his child with disabilities was not progressing. He felt the repetition of IEP goals and the child's poor performance showed educational stagnation or regression. Although the parent prevailed in a due process hearing, a state review officer reversed the decision. After a federal court held for the school district, the parent appealed. The Second Circuit noted the district's committee on special education (CSE) met at least eight times during the relevant period. **A review of audio recordings and transcripts of the meetings indicated the parent had ample opportunities to discuss the IEPs.** In addition, the court found that **while the CSE did not agree to each of the parent's requests, he had input into the student's present levels of performance and annual goals, and provided input into each of the IEPs.** Although the hearing officer found the CSE consistently disregarded the parent's valid concerns, the Second Circuit found no procedural violation. **As a federal district court in New York once observed, "professional disagreement is not an IDEA violation."**

Finding no "persistent refusal" by the CSE to discuss the parent's concerns, the court found no denial of FAPE. Next, the court found each of the student's IEPs presented a description of his strengths and challenges. As the review officer found, **the IEPs were modified in response to evaluations of the student or requests by the parent**. The court found no merit to the parent's claim that the repetition of certain IEP goals and poor performance by the student on standardized tests indicated his academic progress was either stagnating or regressing. In the court's opinion, evidence indicated the student was progressing, although not at a pace his parent would have preferred. Last, the court held the IEPs survived scrutiny under *Endrew F. v. Douglas County School Dist. RE-1*, 137 S.Ct. 988 (U.S. 2017). As *Endrew F.* held, an IEP need not specify grade-level advancement, if such progress is not a reasonable prospect for the student. In sum, the court held for the school district. *F.L. v. Board of Educ. of Great Neck Union Free School Dist.*, 735 Fed.Appx. 38 (2d Cir. 2018).

◆ A California school district proposed to change a student's placement from a program operated by a county department of education to a special day class operated by the district. It did so after holding six IEP meetings. The child's parents refused to consent to the new placement, and due process actions were filed. An administrative law judge (ALJ) held the proposed placement would provide the child with a FAPE and held for the school district. The parents sought further review. After a federal district court awarded judgment to the district, they filed an appeal. On appeal, they argued that the district did not adequately involve them in the placement decision. They also said the district did not provide them with a compliant written notice of its placement decision.

The U.S. Court of Appeals, Ninth Circuit, affirmed the ruling for the district. It held the record showed the parents were given "arguably extraordinary" opportunities to participate in the district's placement decision. In fact, the parents visited the site of the proposed placement many times, and at least one of them participated in every single IEP meeting. They also participated in many decisions to change the IEP. Any error regarding the written notice was harmless. **The parents were already on notice of the placement decision at the time the written notice was delivered.** Finding no evidence that the district improperly predetermined the child's placement, the court held for the district. *S.H. v. Tustin Unified School Dist.*, 682 Fed.Appx. 559 (9th Cir. 2017).

◆   Due to an in utero stroke, an Indiana student had hydrocephalus, cerebral palsy, mitochondrial disease and related medical conditions as an infant. He underwent brain surgery to eliminate seizures but lost a substantial part of his vision and developed sensory sensitivities. After allowing their child to attend a public school early childhood services program, the parents began to homeschool him. Some five years later, they discussed returning him to a school. The school system evaluated the student and held a case conference committee meeting. His mother expressed concerns about an IEP proposal, but allowed her child to return to school. Two days into the school year, it became clear that the school could not serve the student. Asserting that the school system did not offer their child an appropriate IEP, the parents enrolled him in a private academy and filed a due process complaint. A hearing officer held the IEP was inappropriate and ordered the school system to prepare an appropriate one. The IEP team was to review data from the private academy and involve academy staff and the parents in facilitating the student's transition. But the parents and the academy failed to provide the school necessary progress reports.

Based on the information before it, the school created a draft IEP placing the student in his local public school. The parents rejected the IEP and requested an independent educational evaluation. When the school declined to pay for one, the parents requested another hearing. A hearing officer held the school system conducted an appropriate evaluation. A new IEP was proposed but the parents rejected it and requested another hearing. This time, the hearing officer upheld the IEP. A federal court held the school system met IDEA requirements. **Though the parents were dissatisfied with the final IEP, the court found they fully participated in the IEP process.** *Ricci v. Beech Grove City Schools,* No. 1:14-cv-00576-TWP-DML, 2016 WL 4088204 (S.D. Ind. 8/1/16).

◆   Following a dispute with their school district about their child's placement, California parents pursued their IDEA remedies. After they placed the child in a private school, the school excluded them from an IEP meeting. The dispute reached a federal court, which held the parents were entitled to their private school tuition costs for a full school year. The school district appealed. In a brief memorandum, the U.S. Court of Appeals, Ninth Circuit, held the lower court had properly found the exclusion of the parents from the IEP meeting was an IDEA procedural violation. **IDEA regulations require that parents participate in meetings concerning the formulation of an IEP and the educational placement of a child.** According to the court, an educational agency can make an educational decision without the parents "only if it is unable to obtain their participation, which was not the case here." Proceeding without the parents could not be justified by the scheduling needs of school employees. The attendance of parents at IEP meetings took priority over the attendance of other members. The school district was not faced with a decision about whether to comply with conflicting procedural requirements. In fact, even if the parents had already decided to enroll their child at a private school, their exclusion from the meeting was impermissible. As a result, the court held the parents were entitled to tuition reimbursement. *D.B. v. Santa Monica-Malibu Unified School Dist.*, 606 Fed.Appx. 359 (9th Cir. 2015).

◆   After a student was diagnosed with an autism spectrum disorder, the New York City Department of Education (DOE) agreed to fund his placement at a private center for students with special needs. He made progress there, but the DOE recommended a public school placement for his fourth-grade school year. No representative of the private center attended his committee on special education (CSE) meeting, but a center report was discussed. CSE members discussed the related services indicated on the prior year IEP and no one objected to continuing them. During the meeting, the parent was consulted on a range of topics. The CSE recommended placing the child in a community school classroom with 12 students, a special education teacher and a paraprofessional.

A final notice of recommendation indicated he would receive occupational therapy, speech and counseling. But it did not detail the frequency, duration or group size for these services. When the parent toured the school where the IEP was to be implemented, she rejected it as too noisy. Noting the IEP did not include specific recommendations for related services, she re-enrolled her child in the center. In a due process proceeding against the DOE, an impartial hearing officer found the DOE excluded related services recommendations from the IEP. The services were offered without consideration for the child's levels of performance and sufficient parental input. A federal court later held that **while the absence of any representative from the private center from the CSE meeting was an IDEA violation, it did not impede the parent's participation**. The center's 20-page progress report was considered at the meeting. The parent attended with her attorney and actively participated in the discussion. **The inadvertent omission of a related services program from the IEP was not as significant as the parent argued.** The court held failure to include the related services in the properly designated space did not render the IEP inadequate, since it was discussed in other areas of the IEP. The parent did not show the DOE's recommended placement was inappropriate. Rejecting all of the parent's arguments, the court held for the DOE. *C.K. v. New York City Dep't of Educ.*, No. 14-cv-836 (RJS), 2015 WL 1808602 (S.D.N.Y. 4/9/15).

◆ A Virginia student attended a public school autism inclusion program with access to the general curriculum. During her transition to middle school, she was assisted by a 1:1 paraprofessional. But the student had many difficulties during middle school and she had a number of outbursts. At an IEP meeting, the parents and IEP team agreed to a more restrictive setting in an autism spectrum program operated by a public school cooperative education program (CEP). Team members and the parents later agreed that the IEP was not working and that the student should remain in a restricted learning lab until her annual IEP review. But the parents once again declined permission for further observations to facilitate a CEP placement. When the school district filed a notice of proposed action placing the student in a more restrictive CEP setting, the parents rejected it. The district then requested a due process hearing. At the hearing, the parents stated the IEP could not be implemented because it did not identify a specific CEP classroom.

A hearing officer upheld the district's IEP. Later, a federal magistrate judge found the IEP would have provided educational benefits to the student. In fact, the parents' refusal to permit a placement observation prevented the identification of a classroom. **While Congress intended parents to be actively involved in placement decisions, the magistrate noted that "this involvement does not rise to the level of a parental veto."** There was "overwhelming and uncontradicted" evidence that the CEP program could meet the student's needs. As the parents were not denied an opportunity to participate in the IEP formulation, and the CEP setting was appropriate, the court adopted the magistrate's recommendation to rule for the school district. *Bobby v. School Board of City of Norfolk,* No. 2:13cv714, 2014 WL 3101927 (E.D. Va. 7/7/14).

◆ A Hawaii student with autism attended a private special education school at the expense of the state education department. After he had been at the school six years, his parent said he was unavailable for an IEP meeting. Another date for a meeting was chosen, but the parent reported he was ill on the day of the meeting. A special education coordinator proposed two other IEP meeting dates. While the parent stated that he might be able to participate, he said he was sick and could not guarantee his attendance. The coordinator said he could participate in an IEP meeting by phone or online, but the parent said he was too sick. As an annual IEP review deadline was nearing, the coordinator decided to proceed with the meeting. Although the parent was absent and no private school representative attended, the IEP team changed the student's placement to a public school program. At a follow-up meeting, the parent rejected the IEP.

A due process hearing officer held for the education department, as did a federal district court. On appeal, the U.S. Court of Appeals, Ninth Circuit, held **the IDEA requires parental participation to assure quality education for disabled students**. Parents represent the best interests of their children and have information that is unavailable from any other source. School districts have to document their attempts to include parents in IEP meetings. **Parents have to be involved in the IEP process unless they affirmatively refuse.** In this case, the parent did not refuse to attend a meeting. While the department was frustrated with his unavailability, the court held this did not excuse its obligation to include him in a meeting when he expressed a willingness to participate. His attendance took priority over that of other team members. There was no merit to the department's claim that it had to cease providing services to a student whose annual IEP review was overdue. A school district faced with conflicting IDEA duties has to decide a reasonable course that promotes IDEA purposes. As a result, the court held for the parent. *Doug C. v. Hawaii Dep't of Educ.*, 720 F.3d 1038 (9th Cir. 2013).

◆   Parents of a Georgia student with Down syndrome agreed with the IEP devised for her for grade one. An IEP meeting was held to discuss concerns by teachers that the student was being disruptive and having trouble keeping up with the first-grade curriculum. The parties were unable to agree on a proposal to change her program and reassign her to a different school. Over the parents' objection, the school district decided to implement changes to the IEP. The parents requested a hearing to challenge the proposal. They claimed they were not provided prior written notice of their IDEA rights. A hearing officer dismissed the case, and a federal court affirmed the decision.

On appeal, the Eleventh Circuit Court of Appeals found that although parental participation is required by the IDEA, **the IDEA does not explain whether IEP teams have to "act by consensus, majority vote, or otherwise."** In this case, any failure by the school district to provide prior written notice before the team meeting was harmless. As the parents participated in two meetings to discuss the IEP proposal and observed the new school proposed for their child, the court held they fully and effectively participated in the IEP process. Agreeing with the school district, **the court held an IEP team can amend the IEP even if the parents do not consent to the proposal**. IDEA provisions addressing IEP amendment procedures allow a school district to amend an IEP at a team meeting without parental consent. *K.A. v. Fulton County School Dist.*, 741 F.3d 1195 (11th Cir. 2013).

D. Specific IEP Elements

In I.Z.M. v. Rosemount-Apple Valley-Eagan Public Schools, 863 F.3d 966 (8th Cir. 2017), the U.S. Court of Appeals, Eighth Circuit, held a Minnesota school district had no duty to perfectly implement the IEP of a student or guarantee a specific level of Braille proficiency. As found by the Supreme Court in Endrew F. v. Douglas County School Dist. RE-1, *137 S.Ct. 988 (U.S. 2017), the IDEA does not guarantee any particular level of education, nor a particular educational outcome.*

In Sytsema v. Academy School Dist. No. 20, 558 F.3d 1306 (10th Cir. 2008), the Tenth Circuit Court of Appeals explained that the failure to provide a student his final IEP did not cause substantive harm. It held procedural violations of the IDEA are not by themselves sufficient to prove an IDEA violation. The violation must also result in some lost educational opportunity.

◆   A District of Columbia student with a learning disability had IEPs calling for 27.5 hours of weekly specialized instruction outside general education. When he entered high school, the district placed him in a school it identified as having the programming to meet his needs. But during his first year and one-half at the school, the district never provided him 27.5 hours of weekly specialized instruction outside of general education as required by his IEPs. The district reduced the student's special education requirement to 20 hours per week, because that was all the school could provide. According to the parent, she was not told about the IEP modification. She filed a due process complaint.

After a hearing, a hearing officer found the school district denied the student a free appropriate public education. But the hearing officer found the time missed by the student was not material. He also found the IEP reducing the student's special education hours was appropriate, and he awarded the student 50 hours of compensatory education. The parent appealed to a federal court, which rejected the hearing officer's finding that the student's lack of academic progress was due to his social maladjustment and not his disability. Evidence indicated that the school never fulfilled the student's IEP requirements. **It appeared that the school could not provide specialized support to students with 20 or more hours of specialized instruction outside general education.** The court held the district denied the student a FAPE during the period up to its reduction in special education hours, as well as the period after the reduction in hours. Unlike the hearing officer, the court found the failure to provide IEP hours was not inconsequential. It also held 50 hours of compensatory education did not make up for the 542 hours of specialized education denied to the student during this time. The court ordered the parties to discuss a remedy. Rejecting the district's argument that the student was to blame for his lack of progress as a result of his poor attendance, the court held the IDEA put the responsibility on the school district to appropriately place him and implement his IEP. *Wade v. District of Columbia*, 322 F.Supp.3d 123 (D.D.C. 2018).

♦ A Pennsylvania student had ADHD, a generalized anxiety disorder, a seizure disorder and learning disabilities. His parents enrolled him in a private K-12 prep school that complied with their evaluator's recommendation for a small, highly structured classroom with a low student-to-teacher ratio. After making the placement, the parents attended an IEP meeting. They rejected the school district's recommendation that he repeat eighth grade in a public middle school. Later in the school year, the parents requested a due process hearing. They rejected the school district's IEP proposal for the next school year, which would have placed their child in a regular classroom in a public high school. The parents filed a new due process complaint against the school district. A hearing officer consolidated the cases and held for the district. A federal court found the district complied with IDEA procedures. But the grade-eight IEP did not say how the district intended to implement the student's program. **The IEP terms were very broad and general as to what classroom accommodations and supports he would have.** Based in part on the lack of detail in the grade-eight IEP, the court reversed the relevant part of the hearing officer's decision.

Next, the court found the grade-nine IEP rephrased its description of instruction and proposed modifications. Finding the grade-nine IEP addressed the student's anxiety and need for a highly structured learning environment with a lower student-to-teacher ratio, the court found the district offered a FAPE. Since the private preparatory school provided the student with a meaningful education in the least restrictive environment, the court approved the parents' request for their tuition and transportation costs for his eighth-grade school year. *Nicholas H. v. Norristown Area School Dist. of Norristown*, No. 16-CV-1154, 2017 WL 569519 (E.D. Pa. 2/13/17, 3d Cir. appeal dismissed, 5/31/17).

◆   A Maryland student had asthma, a swallowing disorder, a seizure disorder and vision problems. His IEP specified that he have a 1:1 aide, instructional, physical and environmental supports, assistive technology, speech-language pathology, physical and occupational therapy and vision services. The IEP called for a marked lunch area where an aide would assist him with his lunch using a feeding protocol. If the student were to choke, his IEP specified an emergency plan to call 911 and have a trained staff member perform the Heimlich maneuver. If he had a respiratory arrest, the plan specified calling 911 and giving CPR. Staff members at the school had CPR and Heimlich maneuver training, and nurses could reach his classroom or the cafeteria in seconds. But the parents became dissatisfied with the IEP because it did not specify that a properly trained staff member stay with their child throughout the school day. They requested a hearing, which resulted in a decision for the school board.

A federal court held the school board had reasonable procedures in place to assure that the student would have help if he needed it. On appeal, the U.S. Court of Appeals, Fourth Circuit, found **there was convincing evidence that the constant support sought by the parents was unnecessary** given the presence of trained personnel in the building who were immediately available in an emergency. After finding the school board was entitled to judgment on the IDEA claim, the court held a lower court would have to address the parents' Section 504 claims. *Se.H. v. Board of Educ. of Anne Arundel County Public Schools*, 647 Fed.Appx. 242 (4th Cir. 2016).

◆   The New York City Department of Education (DOE) had to pay private school tuition for a teenage student with autism and a seizure disorder based on its failure to properly address his medical conditions. **A federal court found the student's IEP was deficient because it did not sufficiently describe the student's medical needs.** The school site selected to implement the IEP lacked air conditioning in the hallways, cafeteria and auditorium. Moreover, the IEP did not instruct staff members to control the student's environment, keep him hydrated and reduce the risks of exposure to strep. Since failure to address the student's medical needs presented a risk that he would regress, the court found there was a denial of a free appropriate public education. Next, the court held the private school selected by the parents would provide him an appropriate education. It also found the equities between the parties favored the parents. It noted they had cooperated with the DOE at all times while the DOE ignored their communications. As a result, the court held the parents were entitled to full tuition reimbursement for their private school costs. *GB v. New York City Dep't of Educ.*, 145 F.Supp.3d 230 (S.D.N.Y. 2015).

◆   An Alabama student struggled in elementary school and had to repeat a grade. He was placed in special education in middle school and passed only two classes in grade nine. But the IEP team agreed to his mother's request to place him on a regular diploma track and let him "double up" on his grade nine and

10 classes so he could remain with his peers. Asserting that the school board denied her child a FAPE, the mother filed a due process hearing request. A hearing officer held the school district provided the student a FAPE. When the case reached the U.S. Court of Appeals, Eleventh Circuit, it found the student's IEP reading goals were not adapted to address his individual needs. His reading skills were assessed at a first-grade level, but the reading goal for the IEP was derived from the state standard for ninth-graders. Moreover, the student's IEP goals remained largely the same from year to year. **The school used "boilerplate IEPs" with goals that did not provide him educational benefits.** The court found another child's name had been printed on a form describing IEP narratives for the student's reading, math and personal management areas. As the lack of individualized planning and IEP denied the student a FAPE, the court held for the parent. *Jefferson County Board of Educ. v. Lolita S.*, 581 Fed. Appx. 760 (11th Cir. 2014).

◆ The parents of a Delaware student with Down syndrome and a severe mental impairment sought compensatory education and private school tuition, asserting that the district did not formulate or implement appropriate IEPs for the student's sixth- and seventh-grade years. An administrative hearing panel agreed that the district denied the student a FAPE, and it awarded compensatory education. The district appealed to a federal court, which reversed. It noted that the **IEP was not defective because of the absence of historical baseline data and stated that there was no strict requirement that an IEP include such data.** The IEP was created with considerable baseline information. *Red Clay Consolidated School Dist. v. T.S.*, 893 F.Supp.2d 643 (D. Del. 2012).

E. Predetermination

The IDEA requires that placement decisions take place at IEP meetings. But an IDEA regulation at 34 C.F.R. Part 300.501(b)(3) contemplates that school staff members will conduct "preparatory activities" to develop IEP proposals for eventual discussion at an IEP meeting with the parents.

In L.A.S. v. Dep't of Educ., State of Hawaii, *this chapter, the Ninth Circuit found that the analysis of a predetermination claim turns on the motivation and intent of an educational agency, not a parent's subjective perception.*

In Nack v. Orange City School Dist., *454 F.3d 604 (6th Cir. 2006), the Sixth Circuit held predetermination is not the same as preparation. IEP team members may prepare reports and come to meetings with pre-formed opinions about the best course of action for a student.*

In H.B. v. Las Virgenes Unified School Dist., *239 Fed.Appx. 342 (9th Cir. 2007), the Ninth Circuit stated that although an educational agency is not required to accede to the parents' desired placement, it must remain open about placement decisions and be willing to consider a parental placement.*

◆ A Texas eighth-grader with autism endured bullying by peers. Although the school offered to investigate, the family did not submit the paperwork required to begin the process. They gave the district a physician's note stating their son had a severe mental illness requiring his hospitalization followed by homebound instruction. After the student missed over two months of school, the parents gave the district another physician's note urging homebound instruction. At an admission, review and dismissal (ARD) meeting, ARD committee members rejected the request, questioning the integrity of the physician and the sincerity of the note. Although he missed almost a full semester of grade eight, the ARD committee approved his promotion to grade nine. An extended school year (ESY) program was recommended, but his parents said he could not participate in it because the summer semester was nearly over when they received formal notice of it. Upon returning to school for grade nine, the student had inconsistent attendance and fought with peers. Despite reports by teachers that he was making "great progress," his parents requested a due process hearing. They sought an IEP that included the use of applied behavioral analysis (ABA).

A hearing officer held the student received a FAPE, finding his parents' refusal to send him to school created his problems. A federal court affirmed the decision, and the parents appealed. **The Fifth Circuit Court of Appeals found no evidence that the district predetermined an IEP that excluded ABA services.** There was evidence that the school district incorporated ABA techniques and other methods. **The parents contributed to the ARD committee discussions, undercutting their predetermination argument.** Next, the court found no merit to a claim that the district failed to provide a prior written notice of the recommendation for the student to attend a summer ESY program before his ninth-grade year. Contrary to the parents' arguments, the district did not fail to timely address bullying. They admitted their son was willing to return to school, and they failed to follow up with requested paperwork for weeks while keeping him at home. Meanwhile, the district made repeated and reasonable accommodation offers. Last, the court disagreed with the parents' claim that the district offered an unrealistic transition plan describing the student's dreams to become a police officer. Evidence indicated the district tried to collaborate with the parents in transition planning. As they failed to show that the school district denied their child a FAPE, the court affirmed the judgment. *Renee J. v. Houston Independent School Dist.*, 913 F.3d 523 (5th Cir. 2019).

◆ A federal court held a gifted Montana student with depression and suicidal ideation was not denied a free appropriate public education (FAPE), despite claims that her school district committed multiple IDEA violations. Although the parents made several arguments in an attempt to prove that a FAPE was denied to their child, the court found they "resisted everything short of a private therapeutic boarding school" placement. As other courts have found, parents are not denied an opportunity to participate in the development of an IEP where they attend IEP meetings and strongly express their disagreement with staff recommendations. In such cases, the school district does not violate the IDEA by failing to adopt the input of parents. The court found no evidence that the district predetermined the student's placement. **The parents participated in the IEP meetings and the district's consideration of the student's needs indicated preparation, not predetermination.**

The court found the adoption and implementation of the IEP did not deny the student a FAPE. The IEP was created by a cooperative effort. The team considered a continuum of placements and complied with the IDEA's least restrictive environment requirement. Finding the district complied with the IDEA, the court held for the school district. On appeal, the U.S. Court of Appeals, Ninth Circuit, held the school district was obligated to identify, locate and evaluate all students with disabilities within its boundaries. The child-find duty arises when a disability is "suspected" or when the district has notice of symptoms of a disability. While the court found the district arguably knew that the student was hospitalized for suicidal ideation, triggering the IDEA child-find obligation, the claim was barred because of the parents' long delay in filing suit. **Evidence indicated the parents participated in the development of the student's IEP. According to the court, the district did not predetermine a placement.** Moreover, the IEP appeared to be reasonably calculated to enable the student to progress in a public school. Concluding that the school district complied with the IDEA, the court upheld the decision in its favor. *J.K. and J.C. v. Missoula County Public Schools*, 713 Fed.Appx. 666 (9th Cir. 2018).

◆   A federal court agreed with the Hawaii Department of Education (DOE) that a parent's interpretation of a letter offering a placement to her child if she responded by a specific date did not mean the DOE had predetermined a public school placement. Despite her suggestion that the DOE letter made a conditional offer, she admitted she did not respond due to family pressures and her busy lifestyle. The parent then appealed to the U.S. Court of Appeals, Ninth Circuit, which found no error in a hearing officer's decision that the DOE did not predetermine a placement. The parent did not show the DOE was unwilling to consider a private school placement. **The court found nothing supported the argument that the predetermination inquiry turned on the parent's interpretation of the DOE letter and not the DOE's intent.** In the court's view, the DOE letter was "troubling." But it found the letter declaring that the child would not be reevalauted if the parent did not contact the public school by a specific date did not indicate a predetermined placement. *L.A.S. v. Dep't of Educ., State of Hawaii*, 692 Fed.Appx. 842 (9th Cir. 2017).

◆   A federal court rejected arguments by Maryland parents of a student who was moved from a diploma track program into a high school certification program. One of the arguments was that the district predetermined the student's placement. **The court found that members of an IEP team may go into an IEP meeting with ideas or opinions.** Although a staff member suggested that the parents come in "ready for a fight," the court found no evidence that the placement decision was made outside the context of the IEP team. *J.R. v. Smith*, No. DKC 16-1633, 2017 WL 3592453 (D. Md. 8/21/17).

◆   A federal court ordered the New York City Department of Education (DOE) to reimburse the parent of a student with autism $97,700 for private school costs. The court found evidence that the DOE refused to consider the restrictive private setting she sought. While mere disagreement with a school's IEP offer does not amount to denial of meaningful participation in the IEP process, the court held **the DOE had to consider whether the student required a more restrictive student-teacher ratio than what was available through the public schools**. Refusal to consider a more restrictive setting than public schools could offer would amount to predetermination of the IEP. Further, the court found that the IDEA does not permit the categorical rejection of placements outside the public school system. Since the DOE was obligated to consider the parent's point of view but failed to do so, the court found a procedural violation of the IDEA. This violation warranted tuition reimbursement because the DOE's course of conduct significantly impeded the parent's opportunity to participate in the IEP process. *J.E. v. New York City Dep't of Educ.*, 229 F.Supp.3d 223 (S.D.N.Y. 2017).

◆ A federal court held a New York school district was liable for tuition reimbursement because it offered a child an inappropriate IEP and predetermined his placement without considering relevant opinions. In addition to global dyspraxia, ADHD and speech language delays, the student suffered from an inability to control his body movements. The court agreed with the parents that the school predetermined a LEAP II placement in advance of a CSE meeting. **Despite the parents' strenuous objection and their presentation of private reports to bolster their concerns, the CSE never altered its IEP proposal for the LEAP II program.** This amounted to a denial of parental participation that violated their IDEA procedural rights. As for the substance of the IEP, the court noted it did not contain a meaningful statement of management needs. This statement was necessary under state regulations to advise teachers of "the nature and degree to which environmental factors and human resources or materials are required to enable the student to benefit from instruction." No strategies or other information were offered to describe how the IEP would meet her needs. Next, the court found the school in which the LEAP II program was offered did not have a classroom with the capacity to implement the IEP goals. One of the student's teachers admitted some of the mastery levels for written goals "could result from pure guessing." As the IEP was not reasonably calculated to produce meaningful progress, the court held the student was denied a FAPE. *P.F. & S.F. v. Board of Educ. of Bedford Cent. School Dist.*, No. 15-cv-507 (KBF), 2016 WL 1181712 (S.D.N.Y. 3/25/16).

◆ A New York child attended a public school integrated co-teaching (ICT) kindergarten class. Her parents felt she struggled in kindergarten, and her report card indicated her reading was below grade-level. She returned to an ICT class for grade one. Due to continuing concerns about the child's development and below-grade-level performance, the parents obtained an evaluation from a private learning center, found a private school, and signed an enrollment contract for the next school year. They requested a CSE meeting to consider a full-time special education placement. Relying on the private reports, the parents urged the CSE to approve the private placement they had already made.

After conducting an updated psychological evaluation of the child, the CSE met three times with the parents to consider an IEP for the next school year. At each meeting, the parents urged the CSE to approve the private placement they selected. Although CSE members attended the meetings with a draft IEP, they agreed to some suggestions of the private reports. But the team rejected a private placement. The team then offered a special education class placement. The parents visited the school where the IEP would be implemented and rejected it.

After a third CSE meeting, the parents rejected the IEP and requested a hearing. An impartial hearing officer awarded them $46,000 in private school tuition. **A federal court found the parents had attended the CSE meetings and had "ample opportunity to participate in the decision-making process." Disagreement with staff IEP recommendations did not amount to denial of meaningful participation in the decision-making process.** In fact, the IEP cited the private report and incorporated aspects of it. The IDEA allows staff members to prepare for a meeting by developing a proposal. While the parents may have wanted a private education for their child, the court held there was no IDEA entitlement to one. *P.G. v. City School Dist. of New York*, No. 14 Civ. 1207 (KPF), 2015 WL 787008 (S.D.N.Y. 2/25/15).

◆   A Hawaii child attended a private school to address his central processing disorder, anxiety, depression and speech/language issues. The state Department of Education (DOE) paid his tuition for some time, but at the start of the 2010-11 school year he remained at the private school without DOE approval. No placement was agreed upon, and the DOE did not propose a specific placement until January 14, 2011. As late as April 20, 2011, the DOE wrote to the parents that the January placement offer was "the final IEP." The parents kept their child in the private school and requested a due process hearing. A hearing officer found the DOE had predetermined its placement offer. In addition to finding the parents were deprived of meaningful participation in the IEP process, the hearing officer found the placement "ill advised, inappropriate, and potentially disastrous to the student." But tuition reimbursement was denied under a state 180-day limitation period. On appeal, a federal court held the hearing officer's decision was an "agreement" between the DOE and the family that rendered the private school placement "bilateral," and not unilateral. It found the decision to re-enroll the student at the private school was the continuation of a bilateral placement. When the case reached the U.S. Court of Appeals, Ninth Circuit, the DOE conceded that it had violated the IDEA by predetermining the placement. **By waiting so far into the school year to propose a placement, the court found the DOE tacitly consented to enrollment of the student at the private school.** The DOE knew he was going to enroll there, and it offered him no other alternative. Had the DOE offered a placement, the court found it might have maintained the position that reimbursement was now time-barred. But the court held the placement was not unilateral, and the 180-day limit did not apply. In addition to affirming the tuition reimbursement award, the court affirmed an award of attorneys' fees to the parents of over $77,000. *Sam K. v. State of Hawaii Dep't of Educ.*, 788 F.3d 1033 (9th Cir. 2015).

◆   A federal court found New Jersey parents who accused their child's IEP team of predetermining his placement did not keep open minds about placing him. An ALJ found the district had predetermined the placement in violation of the IDEA. The school district appealed to a federal court, which found nothing indicated the district had predetermined a placement or denied the parents participation opportunities. It appeared instead that the parents had been inflexible. According to the court, the IEP adequately explained why the student could not be educated in his current setting. Moreover, the IEP team stated that the student needed a placement where a school-wide behavioral plan could be implemented. The court found the IEP detailed the special education services and supplementary aids that the out-of-district placement would provide him.

Moreover, the court found no evidence that the IEP team had impeded the parents' rights or failed to discuss prospective placements for their child. **To the contrary, the evidence showed the school team believed it could not provide a meaningful education for the student and considered several out-of-district alternatives.** But the parents refused to visit any of these programs or discuss an out-of-district setting. The court rejected the parents' remaining arguments and returned the case to the ALJ to reconsider the IEP. *Alloway Township Board of Educ. v. C.Q.*, Civil No. 12-6812 (RMB/AMD), 2014 WL 1050754 (D.N.J. 3/14/14).

II. APPROPRIATENESS OF IEP

A. Methodology Questions

In W.R. and K.R. v. Union Beach Board of Educ., *the Third Circuit Court of Appeals held parents cannot dictate what methodology will be used for their children. Many courts have refused to intervene in questions of educational methodology, finding this area is best left for educators. But in* Deal v. Hamilton County Dep't of Educ., *258 Fed. Appx. 863 (6th Cir. 2008), the Sixth Circuit held the differences between two methodologies may be so great that the provision of a lesser program amounts to a denial of FAPE.*

◆ Colorado parents insisted on an Orton-Gillingham (OG) reading approach for their child, who was a high school sophomore with Tourette Syndrome, dyslexia and ADHD. When the school district evaluated him and found him eligible for special education with a specific learning disability, the parents obtained another evaluation that found he had an intellectual disability. Following the evaluations, the district prepared an IEP for him based on his ability to read at a second-grade level with 80% proficiency. Near the end of the school year, the district prepared an IEP that was substantively identical for the following school year. His parents had him evaluated by a learning specialist at a children's hospital. She recommended reading programs that utilized an OG approach.

During the school year, the parents insisted that the district incorporate the report of the learning specialist by incorporating OG methodology. According to the district's special education coordinator, the district had a Wilson reading program and trainer that incorporated an OG approach. The parents insisted that the student have some alternative reading program, and a school representative stated that the Wilson program would be used. But the student's teacher did not obtain the necessary Wilson training for almost one month and the parents requested a due process hearing. An administrative law judge (ALJ) upheld the IEPs. The parents appealed to a federal court, which noted **the designation of a particular teaching methodology such as the Wilson program is not typically included in an IEP. The IDEA does not require school districts to**

choose specific programs or methodologies. As the ALJ held, the IEPs were reasonably calculated to provide the student educational benefit. Further, the district was not obligated to implement a specific alternative program. The parents improperly argued that the district failed to anticipate the student's reading needs. The district considered their expert's opinion and used an OG approach through the Wilson program. While they advanced other arguments, the court rejected them, holding for the district. *Matthews v. Douglas County School Dist. RE 1*, No. 16-CV-0717-MSK, 2018 WL 4790715 (D. Colo. 10/4/18).

◆ Nevada parents obtained a private evaluation indicating their child needed instruction in the Orton-Gillingham method. The school district agreed to include components of Orton-Gillingham in the student's IEP and to provide a multi-sensory approach. But it declined a request for teachers to have training in Orton-Gillingham methodology. The parents filed a due process hearing complaint, and an impartial hearing officer held the district denied the student a free appropriate public education. In ruling for the parents, the hearing officer found that the school district "predetermined that under no circumstances would [Orton-Gillingham] methodology be put into the IEP." As a result, the parents were entitled to private school tuition and transportation costs. A review officer reversed the hearing officer's decision and the parents appealed.

A federal court held the parents could pursue their federal disability discrimination claims. Independent evaluations showed the student had learning and developmental disorders that substantially limited her academic abilities. A specific methodology was described to overcome these deficits. In the court's view, **the parents plausibly claimed the district violated federal regulations by denying their child the opportunity to participate in educational programs in a manner at least equal to the opportunity afforded to students without disabilities**. Similarly, the parents alleged a violation of ADA regulations by subjecting their child to discrimination and retaliation. Finding they alleged facts showing the district may have been deliberately indifferent to the accommodation they sought, the court denied the district's motion to dismiss their ADA and Section 504 claims. *O.R. v. Clark County School Dist.*, No. 2:17-cv-01541 RFB-NJK, 2018 WL 1568673 (D. Nev. 3/31/18).

◆ Florida parents of triplets who were diagnosed with autism spectrum disorder claimed their school board denied Applied Behavioral Analysis (ABA) therapy in all cases. After they rejected IEPs proposed for the triplets, their school developed "initial, temporary IEPs" with provisions for the triplets to receive Picture Exchange Communication System (PECS) instruction. PECS is considered an ABA-based intervention strategy for teaching communication skills to children with autism spectrum disorders. The parents requested a due process hearing before an administrative law judge (ALJ). After the proceeding, the ALJ denied their request for reimbursement for ABA therapy. The parents appealed to a federal court. While the case was pending, another parent of a student with autism attending school in the district challenged the lack of a specific ABA therapy in her child's IEP and initiated a due process proceeding.

The court consolidated the cases of both families, dismissed certain non-IDEA claims, then held a trial. It held for the parents on a claim related to their exclusion from an initial child study, but otherwise held for the school board. The parents appealed to the Eleventh Circuit, which found ABA is an applied science intended to produce socially significant changes in behavior. ABA is an umbrella for numerous intervention strategies. In fact, the court found the PECS system is one of hundreds of ABA-based methods. Since PECS is an ABA-based therapy and was included in the IEPs, the school board argued the parents had suffered no real injury. The court agreed with the board that the parents could not show they suffered an injury that would confer standing upon them. **All of the IEPs included PECS methodology, which is considered an ABA-based intervention strategy.** As a result, the parents could not show the board had a general policy of refusing to include ABA services in IEPs. *L.M.P. v. School Board of Broward County, Florida*, 879 F.3d 1274 (11th Cir. 2018).

◆ The New York City Department of Education (DOE) placed a student whose IEP had a stair-climbing goal in a one-story building. His parents objected to the site and requested a due process hearing. At the hearing, a DOE witness testified that the school could implement the IEP benchmark by using a model staircase in the classroom and the outside stairs on an adjacent building. An impartial hearing officer held for the DOE, as did a state review officer. A federal court held the DOE did not deny the student a free appropriate public education (FAPE). On appeal, the U.S. Court of Appeals, Second Circuit, held the lower court had correctly deferred to the impartial hearing officer's decision.

In the court's opinion, the impartial hearing officer was entitled to deference because he made credibility determinations about the witnesses and applied his own understanding of educational methodology. A school administrator testified about the IEP and its benchmark goals for using stairs. **The IEP did not prescribe any particular methodology for this goal and did not state that an indoor staircase must be used.** Further, the administrator stated that the IEP goal could be met either by using the model stairs or the outside stairs. Prior Second Circuit cases have held a parent cannot prevail by speculating that a proposed placement with the capacity to implement an IEP will fail because the IEP will not be implemented as written. Testimony that simply explains or justifies services written in the IEP may be received at a hearing, as in this case. *Jusino v. New York City Dep't of Educ.*, 700 Fed.Appx. 25 (2d Cir. 2017).

◆ A federal court upheld the IEPs of a student with dyslexia, rejecting his parents' claim that he was denied a free appropriate public education (FAPE). Among other things, the parents claimed the IEP devised for his fifth-grade school year was not based on peer-reviewed research as required by the IDEA. They claimed the school district did not provide their son Wilson Reading System programming with fidelity and did not provide an acceptable alternative to Wilson programming. But the court found the parents' arguments were not supported by the evidence. It held the record showed the district used a research-based approach to help the student progress in decoding and reading through a balanced literacy program and a writer's workshop. In fact, the school district used the Wilson Reading System as part of its balanced literacy program. The court found "the Wilson program is the brand-name version of the Orton-Gillingham method," which was used at the private school selected by the parents. **While the parents argued the district should have used the Wilson program "with fidelity or exclusively," the court found no requirement that any particular methodology be used, or that it be used exclusively.**

Although the parents made other arguments to support their claim for private tuition reimbursement, the court rejected them. As evidence indicated the student made progress in his areas of academic difficulty, the court held for the school district. *A.G. and J.G. v. Board of Educ. of Arlington Cent. School Dist.*, No. 16 CV 1530 (VB), 2017 WL 1200906 (S.D.N.Y. 3/29/17).

◆   At one of several IEP meetings to consider a Maine student's program, the school proposed a reading program called Specialized Program Individualizing Reading Excellence (SPIRE). The parent responded by requesting a due process hearing. Some days later, she wrote to the district's special education co-directors about errors in a prior written notice (PWN). In her letter, the parent emphatically rejected the SPIRE proposal, stating it is not research-based and thus inappropriate. In response, the school proposed an IEP that did not identify or discuss SPIRE. Despite the parent's criticism of the SPIRE program, she apparently assumed the district would be providing it to her child. But the district abandoned its consideration for SPIRE, based on her emphatic letter.

When the parent realized the district would not provide SPIRE instruction, she enrolled her child in private tutoring sessions using Lindamood Phoneme Sequencing (LiPS). The school declined a request to provide the student LiPS instruction, and the mother requested another due process hearing. A hearing officer held the failure to offer SPIRE instruction did not harm the student. The mother's claim for reimbursement for LiPS tutoring was denied. She appealed to a federal court, which held the school district violated the IDEA and awarded her $4,111.25 for LiPS tutoring. On appeal, the U.S. Court of Appeals, First Circuit, held **the SPIRE system was never a part of the student's IEP**. It held the PWN proposed – but did not promise – a specific educational program. **The IDEA does not require an IEP to include specific instructional methods and does not require additional information in an IEP beyond what is required by 20 U.S.C. § 1414(d)(1)(A)(ii)(I).** In contrast to an IEP, a PWN is meant to present "a clear record of what placements and educational services were offered" to a student. A PWN is meant to spell out more specific, but not binding proposals to implement that framework. Finding the IEP did not specify that the student was to receive SPIRE instruction, the court reversed the judgment. *Ms. M. v. Falmouth School Dep't*, 847 F.3d 19 (1st Cir. 2017).

◆   A six-year-old New York student with autism attended a private special education school in a classroom with a 1:1 student-teacher ratio (six teachers and six students). He received 1:1 applied behavioral analysis (ABA) therapy. At a committee on special education meeting, the student's private educators urged that he continue receiving ABA therapy. But the CSE instead proposed placing the student in a public school with a 6:1:1 ratio (six students, one teacher and one paraprofessional aide). The parents objected to the IEP and filed a due process hearing complaint against the New York City Department of Education (DOE). An impartial hearing officer agreed with them that the DOE committed a number of IDEA procedural violations. But the IHO found the parents did not show that any of the IDEA procedural violations, either individually or in the aggregate, caused a denial of a free appropriate public education (FAPE). Appeal reached the U.S. Court of Appeals, Second Circuit, which found the procedural violations did not amount to a denial of a FAPE.

The court found overwhelming evidence that the student needed ABA and significant amounts of 1:1 instruction in order to make progress toward his IEP goals. It appeared to the court that the 6:1:1 placement offer was inadequately designed to address the student's educational needs. The court found the consensus of evaluative materials and all witnesses familiar with the student stated he needed ABA support in a 1:1 setting. As a result, it held the IEP was not reasonably calculated to enable the student to receive educational benefits. *A.M. v. New York City Dep't of Educ.*, 845 F. 3d 523 (2d Cir. 2017).

B. Student Progress

There is no requirement that special education guarantee a particular outcome. Under Board of Educ. v. Rowley, *458 U.S. 176 (1982), an IEP need not assure academic success, but must be reasonably calculated to lead to a meaningful educational benefit. Courts and hearing officers are to evaluate IEPs as of the time they are developed and not judge them based on later events.*

In E.G. v. Great Valley School Dist., *this chapter, the court relied on* Endrew F. v. Douglas County School Dist. RE-1, *137 S.Ct. 988 (2017). It held an IEP must be calculated to enable progress in view of the student's specific disabilities. The Supreme Court also found that if grade-level progress is not achievable, an IEP need not aim for grade-level advancement.*

◆ A Pennsylvania student underwent testing prior to her first-grade year, revealing she had a low-average IQ of 87 and ADHD. For grade one, the student divided her time between a regular education and a special education teacher. The IEP called for supplemental learning support and extended year services. For grade two, the student's IEP increased her baselines for certain areas, but some of her goals were not changed. The parents became dissatisfied with her summer programing and asked for dyslexia and dysgraphia testing and a Wilson reading program. During her second-grade school year, the district began offering Wilson reading and it updated the student's IEP. For the student's third-grade year, the IEP team offered an IEP with modified goals, more instructional time and new reading programs. But the parents rejected it, withdrew her from school and placed her privately. In their due process complaint, the parents charged the school district with violating the IDEA. A hearing officer upheld the IEPs and a federal court affirmed the decision.

The parents appealed to the Third Circuit, which rejected their theory that *Endrew F. v. Douglas County School Dist. RE–1*, 137 S.Ct. 988 (2017) implicitly overruled its previous FAPE standard. In the Third Circuit's view, *Endrew F.* language "mirrors our longstanding formulation: the educational program must be reasonably calculated to enable the child to receive meaningful educational benefits in light of the child's intellectual potential and individual abilities." **Third Circuit case law declared that an IEP must be "likely to produce**

progress, not regression or trivial educational advancement." In this case, the court found the district offered the student IEPs that were reasonably calculated to enable her to make appropriate progress, in light of her circumstances. The court held that, given the student's impairments, her "fragmented progress could reasonably be expected." Further, the court held her slow progress did not prove her IEPs were deficient. **An IEP must aim for student progress and courts cannot rely on hindsight to second-guess an IEP that was reasonable at the time.** *K.D. v. Downingtown Area School Dist.*, 904 F.3d 248 (3d Cir. 2018).

♦   As a Pennsylvania student with learning disabilities prepared to enter high school, his IEP team addressed his lack of focus by specifying that he sit at the front of his classes and receive prompts, clarification and repeated directions. He was allowed additional time for tests and assignments. During his ninth-grade year, he missed over 100 class periods and failed five classes. Even with a 1:1 special education teacher for algebra, the student failed the class. Despite his 0.97 grade average, the IEP team found he was progressing toward his goals. He advanced to grade 10 by taking summer classes. During the student's tenth-grade school year, his absences decreased and he did not fail any classes. His grade average rose to 2.04. In grade 11, the student continued making uneven progress, despite increased absences. Significantly, his mother provided the school a note from his doctor describing his anxiety about his English class. The student was provided access to an emotional support classroom. His grade average increased to 2.19. Nonetheless, his mother filed a due process hearing complaint in December of his senior year of high school. She claimed the student's IEPs had been inadequate and denied him a free appropriate public education. A hearing officer denied her request for relief, as did a federal court.

On appeal, the Third Circuit Court of Appeals noted the Supreme Court's decision in *Endrew F. v. Douglas County School Dist.* requires school districts to provide "an educational program reasonably calculated to enable a child to make progress appropriate in light of the child's circumstances." **The court stated that if a school district complies with the *Endrew F.* standard, "it is not liable just because a student does not progress as quickly as his peers."** In this case, the IEPs were appropriate because they addressed the student's behavior and enabled his academic progress. In ruling for the school district, the court found he kept pace with his grade level and went from failing several classes to passing all of them. Not only did the student increase his grade average, he was offered programs addressing his behavior. While he contended his anxiety was evident, the court refused to judge his IEPs in hindsight. Once the district learned of his anxiety, it offered him emotional support. Finding the school district took reasonable steps to assist the student, the court held in its favor. *S.C. v. Oxford Area School Dist.*, 751 Fed.Appx. 220 (3d Cir. 2018).

♦   In *L.H. v. Hamilton County Dep't of Educ.*, 900 F.3d 779 (6th Cir. 2018), the U.S. Court of Appeals, Sixth Circuit, held a student with Down syndrome was improperly segregated from non-disabled peers. In ruling for the student, the court held children with disabilities may only be segregated from their non-disabled peers when the nature or severity of a disability is such that education in regular classes (with supplementary aids or services) cannot be achieved. The court found a mainstream setting would have provided the student in this case "some" educational benefit. An administrative law judge had improperly held he would have to show "mastery of the regular education grade-level curriculum" in order to be mainstreamed. **In the Sixth Circuit's view, the standard for placing a student with a disability is not mastery of the general-education curriculum. Instead, a student with a disability must progress on his/her IEP goals.** There was evidence that the student's teachers did not properly engage in mainstreaming when he attended general education classes. Staff isolated and removed him from situations that became challenging, and the school provided a curriculum with very low educational expectations, no report cards and no homework. A lower court had incorrectly denied tuition reimbursement to the parents for their private Montessori school costs. Finding the Montessori curriculum "well-suited for children with Down syndrome in many respects," and good for the student in this case, the court returned the case to the lower court for the taking of additional evidence to determine an appropriate amount of tuition reimbursement for the parents.

When the case returned to the lower court, it determined the parents were entitled to reimbursement for the student's educational costs for grades 3-8 at the Montessori school in the sum of $103,274. After the court held the school system had to reimburse the parents for this sum, they sought their attorneys' fees and costs. The court held they were "unquestionably" prevailing parties in their case and awarded them attorneys' fees and court costs of $349,249.50. *L.H. v. Hamilton County Dep't of Educ.*, 356 F.Supp.3d 713 (E.D. Tenn. 2019).

◆   Pennsylvania parents requested tutoring for their son in a particular reading program. The school district offered a new IEP that included the reading program. Near the start of the student's fifth-grade school year, the district complied with his parents' request for a reevaluation. But after discussions broke down, the parents rejected an IEP offer and enrolled him in private academy summer program. The parents kept their son at the private academy for grade six and filed a due process complaint. They claimed their son was denied FAPE from his second-grade year through the date of their hearing request. In addition to seeking tuition reimbursement, the parents sought compensatory education. A hearing officer barred relief for any matter prior to two years before the filing of the case. Next, the hearing officer held the school district did not deny the student a FAPE for the two most recent school years. As a result, the claim for tuition reimbursement was denied. The parents appealed to a federal court, which found the school district presented cogent explanations for how the student's IEP would ensure his progress. While the parents suggested the district did not provide Wilson Reading System tutoring with fidelity, an evaluation showed he was mastering his current Wilson level and was making progress in most academic areas. **Evidence indicated the student made "meaningful real-world progress relative to the severity of [his] disability."**

Significantly, the hearing officer found he generalized Wilson skills across settings. Finding the student's severe reading disability made grade-level achievement an unreasonable prospect, the court held the district provided him a FAPE. Next, the court reversed the decision to bar all claims arising two years before the filing date. Utilizing a "discovery rule," the court held it was necessary to determine the date the parents knew or should have known of an IDEA violation. This issue was returned to the hearing officer. If he found for the parents, the hearing officer would have to consider their claim for compensatory education. *E.G. v. Great Valley School Dist.*, No. 16-5456, 2017 WL 2260707 (E.D. Pa. 5/23/17).

◆   A parent asked her child's IEP team to refer him to the California School for the Deaf in Riverside (CSDR). Because no meeting attendee knew about available resources for the child's needs, a CSDR placement was not discussed. Two "addendum meetings" were held. Although the mother sought more intensive services for her child, the school district offered only to maintain the current placement for grade seven. A school psychologist assessed the child's articulation skills in the 4- to 7-year-old range. The mother filed a due process action, seeking an order for a CSDR referral. At a meeting to discuss the student's grade-eight IEP, the parent again asked about a CSDR referral. But the team refused to discuss placement because of the pending due process proceeding. An ALJ issued a decision for the school district, and the mother appealed. A federal court found that the student could not read many first-grade words and had progressed less than a year in reading in the past three years.

The absence of key school personnel from IEP meetings was a significant IDEA violation, hampering discussion of a CSDR placement. The court held it was a violation of the mother's rights to tell her that a CSDR placement would be discussed at a later date. **Failure to properly staff IEP meetings violated the IDEA, as did the team's refusal to discuss placement because of a due process request.** The IDEA stay-put provision does not excuse a district from the duty to have a valid IEP in place at the start of each school year. Finding the proposed IEP did not meet the student's needs, the court held the district denied him a free appropriate public education. The district was ordered to refer him to the CSDR. Any placement decision had to be made by a full IEP team. *J.G. v. Baldwin Park Unified School Dist.*, 78 F.Supp.3d 1268 (C.D. Cal. 2015).

◆   A Pennsylvania student with a specific learning disability was at a 3.5 grade level in reading in grade five. An assessment noted his anxiety and depression, and at school he sometimes seemed lonely and sad. When the student was in grade eight, he was involved in a series of incidents at school and on his school bus. His mother said he endured constant bullying and was threatened on the bus. Although school staff did not observe any bullying or difficult peer interactions, the mother removed him from school for homebound instruction.

Soon, the parents notified the district that they were seeking a private placement at district expense. They requested a due process hearing. Prior to the start of the next school year, the district issued a reevaluation report identifying the student as having general anxiety and a disability in mathematics. An IEP team drafted a behavioral intervention plan and an IEP addressing his social-emotional needs. A hearing officer denied any relief to the parents. On appeal, a federal magistrate judge found the student was making progress in reading and receiving a meaningful educational benefit. His teachers had credibly testified about his progress in reading, and changes to his IEP reading goals from year to year bore this out. Although his writing progress was mixed, the magistrate judge found **"mixed results do not equate to a lack of progress."** The parents did not show the student's emotional needs or social issues were not being served. Finding he received a FAPE, the magistrate recommended judgment for the district. A federal court later adopted the recommendation. *N.M. v. Cent. Bucks School Dist.*, 992 F.Supp.2d 452 (E.D. Pa. 2014).

◆ A New York preschool child with autism had delays in social attention, speech and language, motor skills, chewing and eating. An IEP was drafted that placed him in a children's readiness center operated by a board of cooperative education services (BOCES). As the school year progressed, the mother grew concerned about the student's feeding program and began coming to school early to remove him from the school for feeding. The parents eventually advised the BOCES of their intent to place the child in a private school and to seek tuition reimbursement. At the student's annual IEP review, **the team reported that he had progressed on many of his goals, including following his class routines and increasing his time on task**. The BOCES found the student was independently putting a spoon in his mouth 88% of the time and was no longer crying during feedings. After rejecting placement offers by the district, the parents placed their child in a private school and sought reimbursement.

Appeal reached a federal court, which found the child was putting food in his mouth 88% of the time, swallowing his food and staying in his seat 100% of the time at lunch. A home food therapist found he was making progress in using proper bite and chew patterns, and he appeared to be gaining weight. The court held for the BOCES, finding it had offered the child a FAPE. *L.M. v. East Meadow School Dist.*, 11 F.Supp.3d 306 (E.D.N.Y. 2014).

C. Maximizing Potential

Courts have long held the IDEA does not require schools to maximize student potential or offer the best education available. As the Supreme Court held in Endrew F. v. Douglas County School Dist. RE-1, *137 S.Ct. 988 (U.S. 2017), the IDEA does not guarantee any particular level of education, nor a particular educational outcome. The Court held IEPs "must be appropriately ambitious in light of [the] circumstances, just as advancement from grade to grade is appropriately ambitious for most children in the regular classroom."*

◆ Due to attention difficulties, speech and language impairments, dysgraphia and learning disabilities, a Pennsylvania high school student had special needs in reading, math, written expression, speech and language and other areas. Over a four-year period, he made progress on his IEP goals, with a few exceptions. For example, in the first year, he fell 5% short of a goal to achieve 80% correct on inferential reasoning in social scenarios. He met all his other IEP goals during that school year. The following year, the student made progress in all goals except written expression conventions. He mastered his speech and language goal, indicating he no longer required special services in that area. The parents informed the school district of their intention to enroll their son in a private school and seek reimbursement for their costs. They later changed their minds and met with the IEP team to revise his IEP. But before the school could implement the IEP, the parents again notified the district of their intent to place him privately and seek tuition reimbursement. In a due process complaint, they challenged the IEPs and related services provided to their son for four school years.

In addition to private school tuition and tutoring costs, the parents sought compensatory education. A hearing officer found that with isolated exceptions, the student made meaningful progress. The parents appealed to a federal court, which found the adequacy of an IEP turns on the unique circumstances of the child. **A school district is not required to provide the best possible education or maximize the potential for each child.** The court found no error in the hearing officer's findings. He considered whether the IEPs were reasonably calculated to yield meaningful educational benefit and afforded the student the opportunity for significant learning in light of his individual circumstances. As the hearing officer found, any failure to make progress was isolated and the IEPs enabled the student to make significant and meaningful progress. *J.G. v. New Hope-Solebury School Dist.*, 323 F.Supp.3d 716 (E.D. Pa. 2018).

◆ A Maryland child with Down syndrome had a low full-scale IQ. His parents asked their school IEP team to place him at a private school with an Orthodox Jewish curriculum. Instead, the team proposed a public school placement. In response, the parents requested a due process hearing, seeking a placement at their school of choice plus tuition costs. They argued their child could not generalize between his home and school environments. The parents sought an IEP including Hebrew literacy, identification of Kosher symbols and other bicultural and bilingual measures. When the case came before a federal court, it rejected their claim that the school had denied the child an appropriate IEP by not allowing the student to access the curriculum while remaining a part of his religious community. On appeal, the U.S. Court of Appeals, Fourth Circuit, explained that in *Endrew F. v. Douglas County School Dist. RE-1*, 137 S.Ct. 988 (2017), the Supreme Court disapproved of the "merely more than *de minimis*" FAPE standard formerly relied upon by the Tenth and Fourth Circuit Courts of Appeals. But it found the FAPE duty does not implicate equal educational opportunities for students with disabilities in comparison to non-disabled peers. **The court held the IDEA does not guarantee any particular level of education or require the maximization of a student's potential.**

Moreover, the evidence in this case indicated the school district would make reasonable accommodations for the family's religious preferences. The court found the parents' interpretation of the IDEA would impose requirements that are not present in the act. Federal regulations supported the finding that IDEA funds are not to be used to provide religious and cultural instruction. In sum, the lower court correctly held religious and cultural instruction is not within the FAPE duty. The district stated it would make reasonable accommodations for the student's religious needs. *M.L. v. Smith*, 867 F.3d 487 (4th Cir. 2017).

◆ A Rhode Island parent removed her child from public school and placed him in a private school. She filed a due process complaint against the school district, seeking tuition reimbursement. An administrative hearing officer found the school district provided the student an appropriate IEP during the two school years at issue. On appeal to a federal court, the parent argued her son's most recent IEP misclassified him as eligible for special education based on anxiety, rather than autism. But the court noted that no qualified expert or educator testified regarding the eligibility determination performed by the school district. Next, the parent objected to the IEP, asserting it called for a program that was not an immersion model geared toward addressing her son's executive functions and reading deficiencies. The court found she did not show how the IEP proposal was not reasonably calculated to provide the student with educational benefits. It held the public school placement suggested by the school district was appropriate. In ruling for the district, **the court commented that the IDEA does not require school districts to provide the best education available, or one that maximizes a student's abilities**. As for the parent's argument that the district did not comprehensively evaluate her son, the court found she did not show what impact this had on his educational benefits. Since the school district provided him with a FAPE, the court held the parent was properly denied tuition reimbursement. *Joanna S. v. South Kingstown Public School Dist.*, No. 15-267 S, 2017 WL 1034528 (D.R.I. 3/17/17).

◆   Pennsylvania parents frequently expressed concern about their son's IEPs, which were updated many times. They claimed their son struggled in school and needed more support. Dissatisfied with his progress, the parents obtained two independent educational evaluations (IEEs). In preparation for the student's fifth-grade school year, the IEP team met with the professional who conducted the second IEE. Her recommendations were considered, but the team did not implement direct instruction in executive functioning. Although the student made progress in speech and earned satisfactory grades during grade five, his parents felt his IEP was not fully addressing his needs. They requested a due process hearing. A hearing officer denied relief to the parents, who appealed to a federal court. In the court's opinion, **a school district need not maximize the potential of each student with a disability, "but it must provide an education that confers a 'meaningful benefit.'"** The court held the school district provided the student with a FAPE. The district did not have to provide the program or methodology requested by the parents.

While the parents argued his test scores were in decline, the court found this may have reflected the higher demands as he progressed through school, not regression. The student's IEPs were updated to add goals regarding executive functioning. Like the hearing officer, the court disagreed with the parents that the student's grades were inflated. District progress reports, evaluations and teacher testimony indicated he was making meaningful academic progress. Since there was no IDEA violation, the court found the family's disability discrimination claims necessarily failed. *Parker C. v. West Chester Area School Dist.*, No. 16-4836, 2017 WL 2888573 (E.D. Pa. 7/6/17).

◆   The parents of a Texas student with autism requested a due process hearing because they felt he was falling behind peers. A hearing officer held the school provided the student with a FAPE and denied the parents' request for relief. A federal court explained that Fifth Circuit precedent declares that **the progress of a student with a disability is measured individually and not in relation**

to peers. The evidence did not indicate that the IEP was inappropriate. As the Fifth Circuit has held, an IEP need not provide the best possible education or maximize a student's potential. Instead, the IDEA requires that an IEP provide an education and related services designed to permit a student to benefit from instruction. The court found evidence that the school district had considered the student's needs in formulating his IEP and complied with the IDEA by setting measurable goals for him. His program was administered in the least restrictive environment, in a coordinated manner and in collaboration with key stakeholders. In fact, the record did not show the parents made any request that was not addressed in the ARD meetings. There was evidence that positive academic and nonacademic benefits were provided to the student, who earned all As and Bs and made social and behavioral progress. As a result, the court held for the school district. *Shafi v. Lewisville Independent School Dist.*, No. 4:15-CV-599, 2016 WL 7242768 (E.D. Tex. 12/15/16).

D. Transfer Students

In Termine ex rel. Termine v. William S. Hart Union High School Dist., *90 Fed.Appx. 200 (9th Cir. 2004), the Ninth Circuit Court of Appeals recognized that school districts need not replicate a program created by a previous district for a transfer student.*

◆ A Texas student with ADHD, a speech impairment, impaired concentration and a history of life-threatening seizures attended a life-skills program at an elementary school that was not her home school. After the district opened a life-skills program at her home school, it transferred her there. To address the parents' concerns about the transfer, the district transferred an aide who was familiar with the student. Her teacher took steps to ensure open communication with the parents, including giving them her cell phone number and sending them frequent texts. Several weeks into the school year, the teacher received an unfavorable medical diagnosis and resigned from the district. The parents withdrew the child from the district and placed her in a private school. In a due process complaint against the school district, they requested private school tuition reimbursement. They rejected an IEP offer and re-enrolled their child in the private school. A hearing officer upheld two IEPs and denied the parents' request for tuition reimbursement. They appealed to a federal court, which accepted a federal magistrate judge's recommendation to hold in the school district's favor.

On appeal, the Fifth Circuit explained that *Cypress-Fairbanks Independent School Dist. v. Michael F.*, 118 F.3d 245 (5th Cir. 1997), was its leading decision for assessing IEPs. It held *Michael F.* "fit together" with *Endrew F. v. Douglas County School Dist. RE-1*, 137 S.Ct. 988 (U.S. 2017). Further, the lower court and magistrate judge followed *Endrew F.* in upholding the IEPs. *Endrew F.* requires that an IEP be "appropriately ambitious" for each student based upon individual circumstances. The court found the IEPs offered the student a free appropriate public education (FAPE). The parents' complaints about her present levels of academic achievement and functional performance surfaced only after the district sought to transfer her. They signed the relevant

IEP, undercutting their current objections. The court found no evidence that the district limited the student's IEPs to "critical needs" and did not adequately inform the parents about her IEPs. **It was unnecessary for the school district to hold an ARD meeting to announce the transfer of the student to another school. Prior cases have held parents do not have to be involved in site selection.** Noting "the IEP standard is not perfection," the court found the IEPs were reasonably calculated to allow progress and provided FAPE. Although the parents raised other arguments, the court held for the school district. *E.R. v. Spring Branch Independent School Dist.*, 909 F.3d 754 (5th Cir. 2018).

◆ As a California student neared the end of his ninth-grade year in the Acalanes Union High School District, his parent disagreed with his IEP proposal and filed a due process complaint. Acalanes settled the case by agreeing to pay for an independent educational evaluation (IEE). The parent enrolled her son in a private academy for the next school year. She moved into the Mt. Diablo Unified School District (MDUSD) during the summer. Although the parent provided MDUSD a copy of Acalanes' last IEP, she did not mention she had never consented to it. MDUSD officials then held an "interim IEP meeting." MDUSD offered the student the services and placement described in the final Acalanes IEP offer, with some modifications. The mother rejected the MDUSD IEP offer, then filed a new due process complaint. A state administrative hearing officer found MDUSD failed to make a formal, specific written offer of a free appropriate public education. MDUSD failed to assure all the required IEP team members attended the meeting. After denying tuition reimbursement, the hearing officer awarded the student 20 weeks of speech/language services.

A federal court found MDUSD improperly excused a general education teacher from the IEP meeting because the student "had no definite class schedule." Nothing in the IDEA allows excusing a team member from a meeting for reasons other than those specified by law. MDUSD was not excused from the IEP meeting staffing requirement based on the theory that the parent had no intention of placing her child in a district school. The court held MDUSD improperly relied on an IDEA provision for an interim IEP when a student transfers midyear from one district into another with an IEP in effect. This was not a midyear transfer case. **The court held it is a school district's responsibility to obtain a student's IEP and records from a prior school district.** Despite finding the MDUSD violated the IDEA, the court upheld the decision to deny private school tuition reimbursement. As the hearing officer found, the student was inappropriately retained in grade nine at the private academy and was repeating classes there for which he had already received high school credit. But the court upheld the award of compensatory education, amounting to 20 weeks of group speech/language services. *S.H. v. Mt. Diablo Unified School Dist.*, 263 F.Supp.3d 746 (N.D. Cal. 2017).

◆ A student with disabilities moved with his family from California to Pennsylvania. His parents asked the Pennsylvania school district to continue services under the California IEP, which specified a residential placement. A district director responded that an evaluation would have to be conducted. The parents registered the student in the school district and provided a copy of the

California IEP. At an IEP meeting, the district instead recommended an autistic support program, pending the evaluation results. The parents rejected the IEP and filed a due process complaint. They referenced the district's reliance on the IDEA's interstate student transfer provision, found at 20 U.S.C. § 1414(d)(2)(C) (i)(II). A hearing officer found the school district had denied the student a free appropriate public education (FAPE). He applied the IDEA's stay-put provision, rather than the interstate transfer provision. On appeal, a federal court held the district correctly argued for application of the interstate transfer provision. **The court held the IDEA's interstate transfer provision applies to students who transfer within a school year to a new school with an IEP in effect in another state.** The interstate transfer provision requires a receiving school district to provide a FAPE to a student, "including services comparable to those described in the previously held IEP, in consultation with the parents until such time as the local educational agency conducts an evaluation" and develops a new IEP.

As the student transferred from California during the same school year, the Pennsylvania district was required to provide him with a FAPE by offering "services comparable to those described in the previously held IEP" until a new IEP could be developed that complied with state and federal law. As the student had no "then-current educational placement" in Pennsylvania, the court found the stay-put provision offered no relief. For this reason, the court held for the school district and returned the case to the hearing officer. *Braden O. v. West Chester Area School Dist.*, No. 16-0071, 2017 WL2869397 (E.D. Pa. 7/5/17).

◆   While enrolled in Torrance (California) Unified School District, a student with autism had an IEP specifying 1,950 minutes with a 1:1 aide per week and 720 minutes of monthly supervision from a Board Certified Behavior Analyst (BCBA). After the death of the student's mother, his father made plans to move to Delano, California, where he could obtain childcare from relatives. A Delano Union School District IEP team proposed a 30-day interim IEP that would eliminate support to the student from a 1:1 aide and greatly reduce his BCBA supervision. The parent rejected the interim IEP proposal and began splitting his child's time between Torrance and Delano. The child attended school in Torrance four days each week and lived with his grandmother in Delano during the rest of the week. Delano never provided the student with services because he remained enrolled in Torrance schools. After filing a due process petition against Delano, the parent sought an order under the IDEA stay-put provision.

An administrative law judge denied the request, and the parent sought a federal court order to compel Delano to replicate the Torrance IEP. But the court held the family did not qualify for a temporary restraining order (TRO). It found the parent's actions had helped to defeat his attempt to show irreparable harm, which is required for a TRO. **While the student spent part of the week with his grandmother and uncle in Delano, the court found this did not establish his residency there.** Under California law, a child can have only one residence. The parent's return to Torrance made it impossible to order the relief he sought. Delano had no responsibility to provide the student a free appropriate public education, since he did not reside there. *R.F. v. Delano Union School Dist.*, No. 1:16-cv-01796-LJO-JLT, 2017 WL 633919 (E.D. Cal. 2/15/17).

◆   A Maryland child with autism was placed in a multiple intensive needs classroom. An IEP team proposed another school believed to be similar to his present setting. But the transfer school did not have a 12-month session, and the parents objected to it. A school district autism specialist said the transfer school could provide a "bridging" period of five weeks for the summer. The parents filed a due process hearing request. After a hearing, an administrative law judge (ALJ) held for the school district. The parents then appealed to a federal court, which noted the transfer school had an 11-month program with five weeks of summer services. Moreover, the district's autism specialist had said that all the IEP components were in place at the transfer school, including staff training in autism methodology. One of the parents' witnesses had only observed the child for an hour and could not testify about the ability of the school to implement his IEP. Another had been found to lack necessary experience and firsthand knowledge of the child's unique circumstances. By contrast, school witnesses had worked with the child and were able to testify about the school's ability to implement his IEP. Moreover, **the ALJ found the transfer school could equal the program at the student's current school through "bridging services."**

In the court's opinion, the ALJ had carefully weighed the credibility and persuasiveness of all the witnesses. She had found them more credible because of their testimony and not "simply because of who they were." Although the parents complained that the ALJ had improperly relied on retrospective testimony about the IEP, the court held the testimony was relevant regarding whether the district could sufficiently implement the IEP. This was not improper "retrospective testimony." Rejecting the parents' other arguments, the court affirmed the judgment for the school district. On appeal, the U.S. Court of Appeals, Fourth Circuit, affirmed the judgment. *S.T. v. Howard County Public School System,* 627 Fed.Appx. 255 (4th Cir. 2016).

E. Particular Schools

In Oliver v. State of Hawaii Dep't of Educ., *the U.S. Court of Appeals, Ninth Circuit, held that a change in location alone is not a "change in placement" under the IDEA's stay-put provision. As a result, it held Hawaii parents were not entitled to preserve their child's placement when they moved to a different school district.*

In Luo v. Baldwin Union Free School Dist., *677 Fed.Appx. 719 (2d Cir. 2017), the U.S. Court of Appeals, Second Circuit, noted that parents have input into the IEP process, but not veto power over the particular school site where an IEP will be implemented. Citing its own decision in* T.Y. v. N.Y.C. Dep't of Educ., *584 F.3d 412 (2d Cir. 2009), the court explained that "educational placement" refers generally to the type of educational program a child will receive and not the "bricks and mortar" of the specific school site.*

◆   Due to Trisomy 21 and other medical issues that required use of a tracheostomy and a pacemaker, a Hawaii student received special education and related services under the other health disability category. While he was in preschool, his parents moved from Honolulu to a district located across the island. The transfer district determined the student's IEP could be implemented in one of its elementary schools. But the parents objected and requested a due process hearing, seeking to preserve his placement in Honolulu. A state hearings officer denied the parents' petition for a stay-put order and held the placement proposed by the transfer district was appropriate. A federal court affirmed the decision and the parents appealed to the U.S. Court of Appeals, Ninth Circuit.

Prior Ninth Circuit decisions have held that a change in location alone does not qualify as a change in a student's educational placement. Instead, the decisions indicted "a change in placement occurs when there is a significant change in the student's program." The court found the evidence confirmed the hearings officer's conclusion. It found the transfer district could successfully implement the student's IEP and that the school selected by the transfer district did not constitute a "change in educational placement." As there was no error by the lower court or the hearings officer in finding the school could accommodate the student's IEP, the court affirmed the judgment. *Oliver v. State of Hawaii Dep't of Educ.*, 762 Fed.Appx. 413 (9th Cir. 2019).

◆   A Hawaii student with Down syndrome attended a private school. Under a settlement agreement from a prior year, her tuition was paid by the Hawaii Department of Education (DOE). At an IEP meeting, the DOE offered to implement her IEP "on a public school campus." At the time of the meeting, the parties understood the "public school campus" meant Kalani High School. A few months later, the family moved about 20-30 miles away. Although the parents insisted upon another private placement at public expense, the DOE declined. The DOE advised the parents that enrollment in a private school would be considered a unilateral placement at their expense. Although the DOE sought their new address, they did not provide it. The parents filed a hearing request.

A hearings officer held for the DOE, as did a federal court. On appeal, the U.S. Court of Appeals, Ninth Circuit, reviewed 20 U.S.C. § 1414(d)(1) (A)(i)(VII). This IDEA section requires a statement of the projected date for the beginning of services and modifications, plus "the anticipated frequency, location, and duration of those services and modifications." While the parent claimed the term "location" in the section refers to the specific school where an IEP will be implemented, the court disagreed. Neither the IDEA nor its regulations define the term "location." **The U.S. Department of Education has interpreted "location" to mean a child's general setting or classroom environment – such as a regular classroom or a resource room.** In this case, the court found the parents avoided registering their child in a new school. Characterizing their unilateral placement as a "gambit" to obtain private school tuition reimbursement, the court held for the DOE. *Rachel H. v. Dep't of Educ., State of Hawaii*, 868 F.3d 1085 (9th Cir. 2017).

◆   A New York student attended a private school in a classroom with eight students, one teacher and three paraprofessionals (known as an 8:1:3 setting). At an IEP meeting, the child's committee on special education proposed a 6:1:1 setting made up of six students, one teacher and a paraprofessional. The parents objected, noting this would reduce the overall student-to-adult ratio. In response, the IEP was amended to provide a full-time paraprofessional to help the student's transition to a public school. This maintained the 2:1 student-to-adult ratio sought by the parents. They filed a due process challenge against the New York City Department of Education (DOE). After appearing before two levels of administrative review and a trial court, the case reached the U.S. Court of Appeals, Second Circuit. According to the parents, school officials denied them meaningful participation in selecting the site where the IEP would be implemented. And they said the IEP lacked provisions for parent counseling.

The court recited federal court authority declaring that schools need only provide a basic floor of opportunity for each child with a disability. Any flaws in the IEP process did not impede the child's right to a free appropriate public education or deprive him of educational benefits. Nor was there a significant infringement upon the parents' participation. **The court held parents were not assured a role in selecting the "bricks and mortar of the specific school."** While the IEP did not specify parent counseling and training, the court held they were assured of receiving it by virtue of a state regulation. In addition, the DOE offered to maintain the 2:1 student-to-adult classroom ratio the parents sought. **The court held it was only speculation that the school to which the child was assigned could not have implemented the IEP.** Since speculation was not an appropriate basis for a parental challenge, the court held for the DOE. *R.B. v. New York City Dep't of Educ.*, 603 Fed.Appx. 36 (2d Cir. 2015).

◆ New York parents challenged the school selected for their child by the New York City Department of Education (DOE). Without designating a school site, the DOE proposed a 12-month program for the child in a 6:1:1 classroom (six students, a teacher and a paraprofessional). Later, the DOE identified a public school assignment for the student. After visiting the school proposed by the DOE, the parents decided it would not meet their son's needs. They advised the DOE that their child would attend a private school, then requested a hearing.

After the conclusion of impartial hearing proceedings, a federal court upheld a review officer's decision. Although the parents said no IEP was provided to them until two weeks before the school year, the court held they timely received a copy of the IEP. **State and federal regulations only required that "an IEP must be in effect for the student at the beginning of the school year."** The court found the parents attended the relevant CSE meeting. It appeared to the court that any procedural violation did not harm the child. Finally, **the court held the IHO and review officer had appropriately declined to consider the challenge to the DOE's selection of a school site.** *B.P. v. New York City Dep't of Educ.*, No. 14 Civ. 1822 (LGS), 2014 WL 6808130 (S.D.N.Y. 12/3/14).

◆ A New York student with autism attended public school special education programs from kindergarten through junior high school. His parent enrolled him in a private school, which the city school department funded for two school years. A committee on special education (CSE) proposed a public school IEP for the student but did not identify the school he would attend. A final notice of recommendation (FNR) from the CSE called for a 12-month program in a specialized school with counseling and weekly therapy sessions. The IEP called for placing the student in a 12:1:1 classroom (a setting with a ratio of 12 students to one teacher and a paraprofessional). By the time a FNR was sent to the parent, she had already signed an enrollment contract with a private school.

On the parent's third visit to the school, the assistant principal said the student would attend a 6:1:1 classroom. As no 12:1:1 placement was available at the school, the parent sought a hearing. An impartial hearing officer agreed with the parent that the DOE had denied the student a FAPE. A state review officer reversed the decision, and the parent appealed. A federal court held the CSE had based the IEP on sufficient evaluative data. But the court held the DOE's failure to offer a 12:1:1 classroom and the school's inability to provide adequate speech instruction services violated the IDEA. The DOE repeatedly failed to respond to the parent's concerns, and the court held the student was entitled to tuition reimbursement. **As the parent was never shown a 12:1:1 classroom, the court held the DOE did not show it could implement the IEP.** *Scott v. New York City Dep't of Educ.*, 6 F.Supp.3d 424 (S.D.N.Y. 2014).

III. IMPLEMENTATION OF IEPs

A. Generally

In I.Z.M. v. Rosemount-Apple Valley-Eagan Public Schools, 863 F.3d 966 (8th Cir. 2017), the court held "the IDEA does not require perfection." Prior IDEA cases have found an IEP need not maximize a student's potential or provide the best possible education.

In D.D. v. New York City Board of Educ., 465 F.3d 503 (2d Cir. 2006), the Second Circuit Court of Appeals held IEPs must be implemented as soon as possible after being developed. The IDEA does not require immediate implementation. But IDEA regulations specify that there can be no undue delay.

◆ A Maryland student had complex, challenging and disruptive behaviors, such as hyperactivity and aggression. An IEP team met to address her behavior and create an IEP for grade one. Her parents objected to the IEP and requested a private school placement at the district's expense. In response, the district held a second IEP meeting where team members decided to place her in an intensive communication support classroom (ICSC). The district did not perfectly implement the student's behavior intervention plan. Her teacher did not keep her behavior and performance data after compiling it into monthly progress reports. About three weeks into the student's first-grade year, the teacher noticed her struggles with transitions and her difficulty in general education settings. He gradually began keeping her in the ICSC for longer periods than specified in her IEP in response to her daily needs. The team met in December of her first-grade year to reduce her time in general education classes. Under the December IEP, the student's time outside general education was increased to 29 hours per week. Although the parents opposed any general education placement, they objected to the school district's approach and sought a private placement. When the team disagreed, they filed a due process complaint. After a hearing, an administrative law judge found the teacher violated some IDEA procedural protections, but held no substantive harm resulted from his actions. As a result, the school district did not deny the student a free appropriate public education (FAPE).

A federal court affirmed the decision and the parents appealed to the Fourth Circuit. While they argued the ICSC was overly segregated for their child, the court disagreed. It also rejected their claim that the teacher denied their child a FAPE by increasing her hours in the ICSC beyond the time specified in her IEP. A school must provide prior written notice to parents before changing a student's placement. But in this case, **the court found the teacher's decision to provide more instruction in the ICSC than her IEP specified was "reasonably calculated to enable her to make progress appropriate in light of her circumstances."** The district held another IEP meeting to incorporate the changes into the IEP. The parents attended this meeting and fully participated in it. The court found no merit to the parents' claim that the school denied their child a FAPE or violated their participation rights. Although the parents claimed the IEP was inadequate, the court upheld it under the Supreme Court's FAPE analysis from *Endrew F. v. Douglas County School Dist. RE-1*. *R.F. v. Cecil County Public Schools*, 919 F.3d 237 (4th Cir. 2019).

◆   A Michigan school district did not comply with the IEP of a student with autism who was expected to graduate from high school. Although his IEP called for evenly splitting his time between special education and general education classes, the district instead placed him in a community-based inclusion setting for two periods of his school day. After his parent objected, the school district provided him instruction in the principal's office, where he was segregated from peers. The parent filed a due process complaint, asserting the district denied her son a free appropriate public education (FAPE). She withdrew him from the district and placed him privately. An administrative law judge (ALJ) held the district denied the student a FAPE. On appeal, a federal court affirmed the ALJ's findings of multiple FAPE deficiencies. But unlike the ALJ, the court held the student was entitled to an award of compensatory education.

After additional proceedings, including an appeal to the Sixth Circuit, the court held the school district should pay the student for 1,200 hours of tutoring. A special master appointed to oversee the compensatory award ordered the district to pay the family over $210,000 in attorneys' fees and litigation costs. The case eventually returned to the Sixth Circuit, which held the case was not moot, even though the student had turned 24 and was no longer attending district schools. It held the lower court did not abuse its discretion by awarding compensatory education. **As the district admitted, it denied the student a FAPE by assigning him to a program that was contrary to his IEP.** But the court rejected the parent's argument that the 1,200-hour compensatory education award and year of transition planning was not enough to remedy her son's loss of benefits. As a result, the compensatory education award was affirmed. *Somberg v. Utica Community Schools*, 908 F.3d 162 (6th Cir. 2018).

◆   The parent of a California student with blindness and developmental delays did not believe his IEP would provide him a free appropriate public education (FAPE). She filed a due process hearing complaint. During the due process case, the school district admitted the IEP incorrectly offered the student 240 minutes of monthly TVI (teacher of the visually impaired) services. According to the district, it unilaterally amended the IEP a month after the IEP meeting to change the offer of TVI services to 240 minutes per week. But it did not inform the mother about this. At the hearing, school witnesses testified that the student was offered 300 minutes of weekly TVI services. An administrative law judge (ALJ) found no IDEA violation based on the unilateral amendment of the IEP.

A federal court affirmed the decision for the school district. On appeal, the U.S. Court of Appeals, Ninth Circuit, held the district interfered with the parent's participation in the IEP process. **The court found an IEP is a contract that embodies a binding commitment.** The school district is obligated to notify the parent and seek her consent for an IEP amendment. Without consent from the parent, the school district was bound by the IEP as written, unless it sought to reopen the IEP process and propose a new one. Because the district failed to do so, the IEP in force at the time of the hearing was the one signed by the parties. Since the unilateral amendment to the TVI minutes and failure to identify the assistive technology to be provided infringed upon the parent's participation opportunities, the court held in her favor. The lower court would have to consider whether the district had offered an appropriate IEP. *M.C. v. Antelope Valley Union High School Dist.*, 852 F.3d 840 (9th Cir. 2017).

◆ The parents of a New York City student with autism did not convince a federal court that the City Department of Education (DOE) provided him an inappropriate IEP or could not implement the IEP. After a state due process proceeding, they argued the IEP was drafted before a CSE meeting and was improper because the DOE repeated its recommendation for a 6:1:1 setting for three or four years in a row. While the IEP was drafted before the meeting, the court noted the final placement recommendation showed the committee considered alternative placements, defeating the parents' claim that the IEP had been improperly predetermined. Significantly, the final IEP reflected comments and concerns expressed by the parents at the meeting. While parents are entitled to provide input into the IEP process, the court stated that "they do not have the right to veto decisions with which they disagree." Moreover, **the court held the parents did not show the school site selected by the DOE could not implement the IEP.** In fact, the school used the Applied Behavior Analysis method they sought. Although the parents disputed other IEP matters, the court found their arguments did not warrant a new hearing. As a result, the administrative judgment for the DOE was affirmed. *J.S. and R.S. v. New York City Dep't of Educ.*, No. 15cv355 (DLC), 2017 WL 744590 (S.D.N.Y. 2/24/17).

◆ A federal court held the parents of a student with mobility issues did not show the New York City Department of Education (DOE) had to consider a private placement once it determined it could serve the student in its own schools. Nor did the DOE have to prove in advance that it could properly implement her placement. Due to cerebral palsy, the student has physical and cognitive challenges and uses a walker or wheelchair. During grade two, she attended an integrated co-teaching (ICT) classroom attended by students both with and without disabilities. A committee on special education (CSE) recommended continued placement in an ICT classroom for the next school year, with a full-time 1:1 paraprofessional, physical and speech therapy sessions and counseling. But the parents asked the CSE to consider another placement. In response, the CSE conducted an evaluation of the student and later reconvened to consider the results. It then modified its recommendation for an IEP to specify a classroom placement made up of 12 students, a teacher and one paraprofessional. Expressing concern about her mobility needs, the parents requested consideration of a placement in a "full time special education school." They then requested an impartial due process hearing.

After a hearing, an impartial hearing officer found the DOE denied the student a free appropriate public education (FAPE) by carrying over IEP goals from the previous year. A state review officer held the DOE offered the student a FAPE, and the parents appealed. A federal court held the CSE considered relevant evaluations, including one conducted at the parents' expense. The court rejected a claim that IEP goals were improperly recycled. It found the goals were adequate, finding only one goal that had been repeated from a prior IEP. **The parents could not simply speculate that the DOE would not properly implement the IEP.** In the court's view, they did not show the placement school could not implement the IEP. Nor did the DOE have to prove in advance that it would properly implement the IEP. Last, the court found the CSE did not have to consider a special school placement once it found a public school placement was appropriate. As the DOE's proposal provided the student a FAPE, the court held in its favor. *M.B. v. New York City Dep't of Educ.,* No. 14 CV 3455-LTS, 2017 WL 384352 (S.D.N.Y. 1/25/17).

◆ A New York student with an intellectual disability attended public schools through grade eight. Her parent placed her in a private school for students with disabilities for grade nine. Near the end of the student's ninth-grade school year, a committee on special education met and recommended a public school placement. When the parent visited the school site identified in the final notice of recommendation, she felt it was too restrictive and would not provide appropriate support for her child. She returned her child to the private school and filed a due process complaint against the New York City Department of Education (DOE). An impartial hearing officer (IHO) found the IEP offered the student a free appropriate public education. Appeal reached the U.S. Court of Appeals, Second Circuit. It held the parent relied on speculation that the school identified by the DOE could not provide the services required by her child's IEP. With respect to related services, the parent identified a report stating that the school had not always delivered the required services to all of its students.

But the court found this was not the kind of non-speculative evidence that could lead to a conclusion that the school proposed by the DOE could not implement the student's IEP. It would be "entirely speculative" to conclude that the school could not assist the student in achieving her math goals. Next, the court found the parent's arguments and evidence contradicted her claims. She complained that the school site did not use small group instruction, but her due process complaint admitted the school used such instruction. As a result, **the court found the IHO and state review officer properly found an absence of non-speculative evidence regarding the school's ability to implement the IEP.** Rejecting all the parent's arguments, the court held for the DOE. *Y.F. v. New York City Dep't of Educ.,* 659 Fed.Appx. 3 (2d Cir. 2016).

◆ A Washington student with severe health needs suffered a wheelchair accident and four accidents involving her G-Tube at school. The final accident caused a serious injury. The parties participated in mediation to work on a new IEP for the next school year. As a result of mediation, an IEP was drafted that would require the provision of a 1:1 nurse for the student instead of a 1:1 paraeducator. But when the district issued a prior written notice proposing to amend the IEP, it stated if a nurse was not available on a given day, the parents would be notified and have the option of attending school with their child. The parents filed a due process hearing complaint, asserting the district denied their child a free appropriate public education by not providing a 1:1 nurse when her regular nurse was absent, among other things. An administrative law judge (ALJ) held the mediated IEP denied the student a FAPE. She ordered the district to provide the student with two days of compensatory education for the days on which the nurse was absent, and to provide a substitute nurse or two substitute paraeducators if her regular 1:1 nurse was absent. On appeal, a federal court agreed with the school district that the ALJ applied an incorrect analysis and should have considered the issue of substitute coverage under the IEP implementation standard. Citing recent case law precedent from the Ninth Circuit, the court declared that **"when a school district does not perform exactly as called for by the IEP, the district does not violate the IDEA unless it is shown to have materially failed to implement the child's IEP."**

When the administrative hearing was held in this case, the nurse had only been absent from school twice during the current school year. The court found there was no evidence that these absences impeded the student's educational progress. For this reason, there had been no material failure by the school district to implement the IEP and thus no IDEA violation. As a result, the court reversed the ALJ's decision that the IEP was substantively inappropriate and denied the child a FAPE. *Kent School Dist. v. N.H. and D.M.*, No. C16-0492RSM, 2016 WL 6525814 (W.D. Wash. 11/3/16).

◆ Through his sophomore year in high school, an Illinois student earned As and Bs in honors classes with accommodations. He said some teachers stopped giving him study guides and extra time, claiming it was wrong to provide such assistance in advanced classes. Teachers also said extra time hurt him, and they pressured him to drop advanced placement and honors classes, claiming they would be too difficult for him. The student said that without accommodations, he started to fail advanced placement and honors classes. He refused to drop them and said teachers did not record his good grades, lowered some scores and ignored his questions about assignments. During the student's junior year, his parents withheld their consent for a mandatory triennial evaluation. The school district filed a due process complaint to overrule the need for parental consent.

Later, the student responded with a complaint alleging denial of educational services, discrimination and retaliation. By the time a hearing officer dismissed the complaint, the student was 19 years old and in college. A federal court held the parents lacked standing to file suit. After the lower court closed the case, the U.S. Court of Appeals, Seventh Circuit, found enough detail in the complaint to put the district on notice of a claim based on denial of a free appropriate public education. The student asserted his high school had denied him study guides and extra time to complete tests and homework as required in his IEP. The court reversed the dismissal of the claims. **The student said teachers tried to push him out of classes, refused to comply with his IEP and required him to work on group projects despite a disability that prevented him from working with peers.** While he did not allege a valid claim for retaliation, the court found the parents could proceed with theirs. Since the IDEA guarantees certain rights to parents that were implicated here, the court held they could proceed with claims under the IDEA, ADA and Section 504. The case was returned to the lower court for further activity. *Stanek v. St. Charles Community Unit School Dist. #303,* 783 F.3d 634 (7th Cir. 2015).

B. Bullying and FAPE

School district are obligated to address student-on-student bullying and respond to reasonable requests by parents about student special education programs. An October 21, 2014 "Letter to Colleague" from the U.S. Department of Education's Office for Civil Rights (OCR) declares that bullying of students with disabilities may result in a finding of disability-based harassment or a denial of a free appropriate public education under Section 504. See http:// www2.ed.gov/about/offices/list/ocr/letters/colleague-bullying-201410.pdf.

◆   A Hawaii parent removed her son from his public school and placed him in a private autism center due to peer bullying. In a due process proceeding filed to challenge the student's IEP, a hearings officer found he was the victim of bullying at school. His learning opportunities were limited and the private placement was held appropriate. The school department responded by offering the student an IEP that provided counseling and a behavior support plan with peer mediated instruction and intervention. The IEP provided for transition of the student back to his home school and included a crisis plan specifying close adult supervision at all times. The parent declined the IEP offer and kept her son at the private school. The department notified her that it would only fund the placement up to the date of a prior written notice confirming a placement at the student's home school. The parent filed another administrative complaint against the department. A hearings officer found the IEP proposal was tailored to the student's individual needs and provided him with educational benefits. The IEP provided 1:1 support at all times to prevent bullying. As the IEP was appropriate, the parent could not be reimbursed for private school tuition.

A federal court affirmed the judgment, and the parent appealed to the Ninth Circuit Court of Appeals. In the court's view, the revised IEP was expressly designed to overcome deficiencies from the prior IEP. Included was a full-time aide, a crisis plan and a protocol for stopping further bullying. Under the revised IEP, the student's interactions with peers would be monitored by an adult. The IEP had many of the suggestions for combating the bullying of students with disabilities from an October 21, 2014 "Dear Colleague" letter issued by the U.S. government. The court declined the parent's argument that the federal guidance on bullying should have the force of law. **While she urged the court to adopt a minimum standard for IEPs based on the 2014 letter, the court found such**

guidance letters are not legally binding. Finding the lower court correctly held the parent did not show her son would be unable to make appropriate progress in light of his circumstances under the revised IEP, the court affirmed the judgment. *J.M. v. Matayoshi*, 729 Fed.Appx. (9th Cir. 2018).

◆ New York parents said their third-grade daughter was subjected to bullying almost every day and that staff members did not confront bullies. Classmates pushed and tripped her, laughed at her and called her "ugly," "stupid" and "fat." When the parents sought to raise the issue of bullying with the IEP team (called a committee on special education or CSE in New York), they said the principal "flatly refused to discuss the issue with them." The parents said team members told them bullying was "an inappropriate topic to consider" during an IEP meeting. They located a private school for students with learning disabilities and placed her there. The parents then filed a due process action against the department to obtain private school tuition reimbursement.

An impartial hearing officer (IHO) held for the department and a review officer affirmed the decision. A federal court held for the parents, finding that significant, unremedied bullying may deny a free appropriate public education (FAPE). After further administrative and court activity, the case reached the Second Circuit. On appeal, the court found the DOE denied the student a FAPE by refusing to discuss bullying with her parents, despite their reasonable concerns. Three staff members confirmed that the student was constantly teased, excluded from groups and subjected to a hostile environment. **Since the DOE's persistent refusal to discuss bullying at important times in the IEP process significantly impeded the parents' participation rights, the court found a procedural denial of FAPE.** Finding the balance of equities favored the parents, the court upheld the award of private school tuition reimbursement. *T.K. and S.K. v. New York City Dep't of Educ.*, 810 F.3d 869 (2d Cir. 2016).

◆ A Hawaii student received special education as a child with an other health disability. He had stomach issues, allergies, asthma, febrile seizures, arthritis and behavior problems. Until the student reached grade four, he was homeschooled. During that school year, the parents briefly placed him in a charter school. After the student attended a public elementary school for grade five, the parents placed him in a new charter school that was in the process of "getting organized." Significantly, the school did not obtain a copy of the student's IEP until a week or two into the school year. Near this time, the parents became convinced that the charter school could not serve their child. They briefly enrolled him in a private school before returning him to a homeschool program. When the Hawaii Department of Education (DOE) denied the parents' request for private school tuition reimbursement, they filed an IDEA proceeding. A hearing officer held the DOE did not fail to implement the IEP and did not deny the child a free appropriate public education (FAPE).

Before a federal court, the parents argued the DOE should have classified their child as having autism. But the court noted the DOE was unaware of any autism diagnosis when the IEP team met. In any event, there was no evidence that a difference in category would have yielded different programs or services in the IEP. **Ninth Circuit cases held any claim based on failure to implement**

an IEP must show a "material failure to implement an IEP" to prove an IDEA violation. In this case, the court held any failure to implement the IEP was not "material" and therefore did not implicate a possible denial of FAPE. Although the parents made much of the failure of the charter school to have an IEP by their child's first day of school, the court found this fact alone did not prove a denial of FAPE. Evidence showed the school promptly responded to the mother's bullying concerns. Rejecting the remaining arguments of the parents, the court affirmed the decision for the DOE. *Tyler J. v. Dep't of Educ., State of Hawaii*, Civ. No. 14-00121 DKW-KSC, 2015 WL 793013 (D. Haw. 2/24/15).

IV. BEHAVIOR INTERVENTION

A. Behavior Intervention Plans

Schools must consider positive behavioral interventions and supports, and other strategies when behavior impedes a child's learning. In D.W. v. Milwaukee Public Schools, *526 Fed.Appx. 672 (7th Cir. 2013), the Seventh Circuit found the IDEA has no substantive requirements for behavior intervention plans (BIPs).*

In 2017, Oregon and Minnesota legislators amended their laws concerning the use of behavior intervention plans and positive behavioral interventions and supports (PBIS). The Minnesota amendments define PBIS as an evidence-based framework for preventing problem behavior, providing instruction and support for positive and prosocial behaviors, and supporting social, emotional and behavioral needs for all students. Character education curriculum and programs may be used to support the implementation of key components of PBIS.

PBIS is the use of a continuum of evidence-based interventions that is integrated and aligned to support academic and behavioral success for all students. *PBIS uses a team-based approach to support effective implementation, monitoring of progress and evaluation. Ninetieth Minnesota Legislature, 2017 First Special Session, Ch. 5. H.F. No. 2. Minn. Statutes § 122A.627.*

◆   A Missouri student's IEP had a behavior plan (BIP) addressing her hallucinations and difficulty distinguishing fantasy from reality. At the beginning of her eighth-grade school year, she was diagnosed with schizophrenia. Her IEP for grade eight reduced her time in general classrooms from 80% of the day to 40%. Although the student was scheduled to be in regular education settings less than 40% of the time when she entered high school, this was not immediately implemented. During her first semester of high school, her psychotic symptoms increased and she became aggressive and suicidal at times. At an IEO meeting, the parent agreed to an evaluation of the student. During later examinations, the student had a hallucination and exhibited other symptoms of schizophrenia. Her reading level had declined from a third-grade level to a first-grade level.

A new BIP was devised to address the student's schizoaffective disorder with therapeutic counseling. But the parent filed a due process complaint, asserting the district improperly placed her child in classes with large groups of non-disabled peers. She asserted the district did not modify the IEP to adopt and implement goals, objectives, a BIP and a safety plan to address her child's schizophrenia. A due process hearing was delayed when the parent provided the district with nearly 800 pages of medical records. A new IEP was drafted changing the student's placement to a private separate day facility. A hearing officer denied the parent's due process complaint. On appeal, a federal court found the IEP in place at the time the parent filed the case called for the student to attend general education classrooms 40% of the time. As her psychological problems progressed, the school increased her special education time. **The court found the school district's actions were in line with the IDEA's least restrictive environment requirement.** Evidence indicated the student was doing well in regular classes and that school officials used their best professional judgment. Moreover, the district communicated with the student's medical professionals and completed a full reevaluation. The court held for the school district. *Johnson v. St. Louis Public School Dist.*, No. 4:17 CV 2204 SNLJ, 2018 WL 4383277 (E.D. Mo. 9/14/18; 8th Cir. appeal filed 12/4/18).

◆ At the age of 10, a California student qualified for special education under the emotional disturbance and other health impairment categories. Since kindergarten, he had attended an intensive behavior intervention program in a district elementary school. After two behavior incidents during which the student was placed in prone restraints, an IEP meeting was held. At the meeting, a therapist relayed her conclusion that he had autism spectrum disorder. Team members agreed to conduct a functional behavioral assessment of the student. But the team found no need for an interim behavior plan at the time. Instead, it found there were numerous interventions in place and there was a need to collect additional data. When the therapist produced a report suggesting the student might have autism, the parent did not share it with the school district.

Some three months later (and about seven months after the IEP meeting), the report was supplied to the school district. The district sought to review the therapist's report before making its own assessments, as some test results could be invalidated by more testing. The parent filed a due process complaint against the district, alleging various procedural violations denied her child a FAPE. An administrative law judge held for the district, and the parent appealed to a federal court. According to the court, **the district's failure to document the reasons it failed to develop an interim behavior intervention plan following the prone restraint incidents did not deny the student a FAPE**. While California law required schools to provide such documentation, the court found no evidence that this failure harmed the student or violated his parent's participation rights. Evidence indicated the IEP team discussed what could be done to amend the IEP. The court found it unnecessary for the team to document why it did not create an interim behavior plan. But as the district's four-month delay in assessing the student for autism was unreasonable, the court held there was a denial of FAPE during that time. *D.O. v. Escondido School Dist.*, No. 3:17-cv-2400-BEN-MDD, 2018 WL 6653271 (S.D. Cal. 12/18/18).

◆ Based on dissatisfaction with the IEPs created for their child for two school years, New York parents enrolled him in a private school. They then requested an impartial hearing under the IDEA, seeking reimbursement for their private school costs. A hearing officer rejected the parents' arguments and held for the school district. After a state review officer affirmed the decision, the case reached a federal court. Although the parents sought pretrial dismissal of the case, the court denied their motion. It issued a decision finding the IEPs were procedurally and substantively adequate and deeming appropriate the services offered by the district. The parents appealed to the U.S. Court of Appeals, Second Circuit, which rejected a claim that the hearing officer was biased against them because he had previously served as a school superintendent.

According to the parents, the student's behavior intervention plan (BIP) could not have been implemented or updated on a timely basis. They based this claim on their past experiences with the district. The court found the parents' objection to the BIP was speculative and based on a "pattern and practice" of failing to develop and implement BIPs and functional behavioral assessments in a timely fashion. In this case, the BIP was developed in time to be included in the relevant IEP. **There was no support for the claim that the school district would not be able to implement and update the BIP.** Last, the court rejected the parents' claim that the BIP was not created by an adequate process. Finding none of their arguments had merit, the court held for the school district. *C.E. v. Chappaqua Cent. School Dist.*, 695 Fed.Appx. 621 (2d Cir. 2017).

◆ Illinois parents disagreed with the placement of their son in a segregated program for grade one. His school wanted to place him in a social-emotional learning foundations (SELF) program with a behavior intervention plan (BIP). Because the parents rejected the SELF program, the student continued school in his general education setting, where he struggled with the new BIP. At an end-of-school-year IEP meeting, district members of the IEP team again recommended the SELF program and placed him there for grade one, over the parents' objections. The SELF program was housed in a different school located in another school district. Arguing the SELF program was overly restrictive for their child, the parents obtained a stay-put order to preserve his current placement, pending resolution of the case. As a result of the stay-put order, the student was never moved to the SELF program.

Later, a hearing officer upheld the district's proposed IEP. A federal court affirmed the hearing officer's decision. The parents appealed to the Seventh Circuit Court of Appeals, which noted that the parties agreed to a new IEP for the student for grade three that did not involve the SELF program. As a result, the dispute over his grade one IEP was now moot. **The court held the parents could not pursue the present case to insulate themselves from a future proposal for a SELF placement.** Since they relied on speculation regarding a new SELF placement at some time in the future, the court found the case to be moot. *Ostby v. Manhattan School Dist. No. 114*, 851 F.3d 677 (7th Cir. 2017).

◆ A California student attended special education resource room classes for 115 minutes per day with the rest of his day spent in a general education classroom. His IEP was designed to address his aggression, but he exhibited behaviors such as screaming, crying, throwing objects, hitting and kicking. The student's parent participated in the making of a functional analysis assessment report that formed the basis for a behavior intervention plan (BIP). The BIP called for consequences if the student engaged in "extreme maladaptive behaviors." But the parent later objected to any consequences, and the school stopped implementing that part of the BIP. The student's behavior became markedly worse. At an IEP meeting, the team agreed to transfer him to a special day class to focus on his behavior. On his second day in the new class, the student refused to do an assignment, then tried to run from staff. He charged employees and had to be restrained and taken to a safe room. Once in the safe room, the student began banging his head against the wall. A sheriff's deputy who happened to be in the building handcuffed the student. Later, the IEP team discussed a modified BIP with new consequences. The team agreed to home instruction with counseling, but the parent requested a due process hearing. The district held an IEP meeting in her absence and devised a new IEP. Instead, the parent placed her son in a Catholic school. Before an administrative law judge (ALJ), the parent argued the school did not properly implement the IEP. "

The ALJ found no material failure to implement the IEP. On appeal, a federal court upheld the ALJ's findings and conclusions. **Expert testimony showed the BIP was developed with the use of a functional analysis assessment. In addition, the parent agreed to the BIP.** Persuasive testimony indicated the staff worked with the student to implement his BIP with fidelity. Moreover, the parent presented no expert testimony to counter that of the school team members. In sum, the court found no material failure to implement the IEP, and upheld the IEP proposal offered to the student after the handcuffing. When the case came before the U.S. Court of Appeals, Ninth Circuit, it adopted the lower court's decision in a brief memorandum order, finding the school district had properly implemented the student's IEP. *C.L. v. Lucia Mar Unified School Dist.*, 646 Fed.Appx. 524 (9th Cir. 2016).

B. Functional Behavioral Assessments

While failure to conduct an FBA is a "serious procedural violation," it will not deny a free and appropriate public education "if the IEP adequately identifies problem behavior and prescribes ways to manage it." See R.E. v. New York City Dep't of Educ., *694 F.3d 167 (2d Cir. 2012), and* A.C. and M.C. v. Board of Educ. of Chappaqua Cent. School Dist., *553 F.3d 165 (2d Cir. 2009).*

The IDEA does not specify the substantive requirements for behavior intervention plans. In P.S. v. New York City Dep't of Educ., *No. 13 Civ. 04772 (LGS), 2014 WL 3673603 (S.D.N.Y. 7/24/14), the court held the absence of a functional behavioral assessment did not violate the IDEA, so long as the IEP adequately identified a student's behavioral impediments and implemented strategies to address that behavior.* **The IDEA only requires a school district to consider the use of positive behavior interventions and supports and other strategies when a child's behavior impedes learning.**

◆   An Arkansas student threw things, climbed on equipment, screamed and banged her head on a table while at school. Her parent said the school did not use data from daily observation notes to measure her child's progress toward behavior goals. Claiming the school district did not appropriately address her child's maladaptive behaviors, she filed a due process complaint. A hearing officer held for the district, and the parent appealed to a federal court. It held the district did not have to conduct a new functional behavioral assessment (FBA) or include a new behavior intervention plan (BIP) in the child's IEPs under 34 C.F.R. § 300.530. It noted the student was never removed from her current educational placement for over 10 school days for conduct that was a manifestation of her disability. Further, the student was never placed in an alternative educational placement for behavior involving weapons, drugs or the infliction of serious bodily injury. While the parent argued the district should have provided a new FBA and a new BIP, the court held the IEP team was only required to consider the use of positive behavioral interventions and supports, and other strategies to address her classroom behaviors.

The court found the parent incorrectly claimed the failure to conduct a new FBA and include a new BIP in her child's IEP violated the IDEA. The student's IEPs indicated her behavior was not impeding her learning. Although the parent offered additional arguments to bolster her procedural violations claim, the court rejected all of them. Eventually, the district conducted an evaluation of the student over the parent's wishes, without filing a due process complaint. In the court's opinion, this was a "procedural shortcoming" that made "no substantive difference in the end." In holding for the school district, the court found evidence of the student's progress could be seen in areas such as reading, math, grammar, syntax, play and leisure, social interaction, group instruction and classroom routines. *Albright v. Mountain Home School Dist.*, No. 3:17-CV-3075, 2018 WL 5794164 (W.D. Ark. 11/5/18).

◆ Due to autism, obsessive compulsive disorder, mental retardation, mood disorder, asthma and pica, a New York student attended a special classroom in a public school. Among his behaviors were punching, and scratching himself and eating staples. After he turned 14, his committee on special education (CSE) proposed an IEP describing his sudden personality changes and verbal and physical aggression. Although the IEP called for a behavior intervention plan, no attempt was made to identify the root causes of the student's behavior problems and no functional behavioral assessment (FBA) was done. Over the next two school years, the CSE did not make substantial changes to the student's IEPs. At 17, he began refusing to attend school. His parents filed an impartial hearing complaint. They said the DOE did not use any evaluations or assessments when creating his IEPs. An impartial hearing officer denied the parents any relief, as did a state review officer. A federal court found the IEPs were consistent with evaluative materials available to the CSE at the relevant time.

On appeal, the U.S. Court of Appeals, Second Circuit, found the CSE's neglect of evaluation materials in creating the three challenged IEPs was a significant procedural error that denied the student a FAPE. Had the CSE conducted an FBA, the student's problem behaviors might have been better addressed. None of the BIPs attempted to identify the root causes of his behavior problems. **The court held the failure to conduct an adequate FBA was a serious IDEA procedural violation that prevented the CSE from obtaining necessary information about the student and precluded effective court review.** In addition, the court found failure to provide the student with necessary speech and language instruction was a serious IDEA violation. Critically, the CSE never developed FBAs or attempted to address the causes of the student's interfering behaviors. In sum, the court found a pattern of indifference to IDEA requirements and carelessness in formulating IEPs. *L.O. v. New York City Dep't of Educ.*, 822 F.3d 95 (2d Cir. 2016).

♦   The parents of a child with autism filed a challenge to IEPs proposed for the child by the New York City Department of Education (DOE). When the case reached the U.S. Court of Appeals, Second Circuit, it found the IEP proposed a full-time behavior management program with a paraprofessional assigned to the child. **In its previous cases, the court held that a failure to conduct a functional behavioral assessment is a serious IDEA procedural violation. But it is not legally actionable if the IEP adequately identified the problem behavior, addressed it and prescribed ways to manage it.** In this case, the court found the DOE gave extensive consideration to behavioral concerns at a meeting attended by the parents. At the meeting, committee members were guided by recommendations of staff at the child's school. With this input, the committee developed a behavioral intervention plan that the court found was reasonably calculated to address his behaviors. The committee's failure to conduct its own functional behavioral analysis did not deny the student a FAPE. *F.L. v. New York City Dep't of Educ.*, 553 Fed.Appx. 2 (2d Cir. 2014).

♦   A New York child with autism and other disabilities had behavioral and social-emotional problems which led him to under-perform academically. Early in his elementary school career, his parents rejected an IEP offer and placed him in a private school where he continued to have behavioral issues. Prior to the next school year, the New York City school department recommended placing the child in a general education room with integrated co-teaching services.

As the child's behavior seriously interfered with his instruction, the IEP included a behavioral intervention plan (BIP). But the BIP was not based on a functional behavioral assessment (FBA). The parents rejected the IEP and again placed their child in a private school. Seeking reimbursement for their private school tuition, they filed a due process hearing request. When the case reached the U.S. Court of Appeals, Second Circuit, it found the lack of an FBA did not make the IEP inadequate. State regulations did not deem an IEP without an FBA improper. **The IDEA required consideration for positive behavioral interventions and supports, and other strategies, when behavior impeded learning.** The court held the lack of an FBA did not render an IEP inadequate, if the IEP identified a student's behavioral impediments and implemented strategies to address them. In this case, the court held the BIP described the student's behavior problems and provided a broad, collaborative approach to implement specific strategies to modify his behavior. *M.W. v. New York City Dep't of Educ.*, 725 F.3d 131 (2d Cir. 2013).

♦   A Nebraska child with autism experienced behavior problems. By second grade, he became aggressive, and the school had to use calming strategies. When the student reached grade-three, he began to harm school staff members. Before the end of his third-grade year, his parents took him to a rehabilitation facility for a functional behavioral assessment. A behavior analyst found the calming room increased his aggressive behavior. A three-level behavior plan was devised to eliminate use of a calming room. The first level of intervention was a 30-second baskethold. When the parents presented these findings to the school district, a behavior specialist found it conflicted with her understanding of appropriate responses to aggressive behavior by autistic children. The district devised a behavior intervention plan that replicated parts of the rehabilitation facility plan, but it continued to rely on the calming room.

The parents objected, placed their child in a private setting and requested a hearing. When the case reached the U.S. Court of Appeals, Eighth Circuit, it found the student was progressing and the school district was addressing his behavior. A detailed behavior intervention plan was attached to the IEP with the approach devised by the rehabilitation facility. The court found it "largely irrelevant if the school district could have employed more positive behavior interventions as long as it made a good-faith effort to help the student achieve the educational goals outlined in his IEP." **An IEP team does not have to adopt all the parents' recommendations, and does not have to change methodologies based on parental preferences.** Since there was evidence supporting continued use of a calming room, the court held for the district. *M.M. v. Dist. 0001 Lancaster County School*, 702 F.3d 479 (8th Cir. 2012).

C. Restraint and Seclusion

In Miller v. Monroe School Dist.*, this chapter a federal court addressed a Washington parent's concern for restraint and isolation of her child at school by noting any future use of restraint or isolation would be limited by a state law cited as RCW 28A.600.485(3)(b). Under this provision, "restraint or isolation of any student is permitted only when reasonably necessary to control spontaneous behavior that poses an imminent likelihood of serious harm."*

◆   A Hawaii parent said her son's preschool teacher occasionally seated him in a Rifton chair, even though this was not stated in his IEP or behavior plan. She further asserted this conduct violated a Section 504 regulation found at 34 C.F.R. Part 104.33(b)(1)(i) that requires educational aids and services to be designed to meet a child's individual educational needs. A federal court held a jury trial and found no violation of Section 504 of the Rehabilitation Act. On appeal, the Ninth Circuit Court of Appeals noted that implementing an IEP is one means of ensuring compliance with Section 504 requirements. The court held the parent incorrectly argued that use of a Rifton chair – when not specified in an IEP – necessarily violated Section 504 regulations requiring the provision of a free appropriate public education (FAPE). Further, the court found disputed facts regarding the chair that made a trial appropriate on the Section 504 issues.

Next, the court held the lower court properly dismissed the state-law claims of assault and battery and infliction of emotional distress. It found **state officials who act in the performance of their duties enjoy a qualified or conditional privilege against liability for tortious acts unless it is proven by clear and convincing evidence that they were motivated by malice**. The court held the evidence was insufficient to show any employee demonstrated the level of malice required to overcome the qualified privilege defense. Last, the court held the lower court did not commit error in formulating jury instructions. The lower court properly drew a careful distinction between a claim for denial of a FAPE under the IDEA and a claim for disability discrimination based on denial of meaningful access to education under Section 504. *Ricks v. State of Hawaii Dep't of Educ.*, 752 Fed.Appx. 518 (9th Cir. 2019).

◆   A Pennsylvania fourth-grader had a history of behaving aggressively. He had a difficult transition to a new school, where he bit, kicked and scratched teachers and peers. A teacher responded to his misbehavior with force. She pushed, choked, dragged, slapped and improperly restrained him. After the teacher was charged with abusing the student, the district transferred him to another school. Because the parents feared that any restraint of their son could trigger traumatic memories, they urged the district to create an IEP minimizing physical contact with staff. Over the next six months, the parents and district staff met and refined the IEP numerous times. **The amended IEPs included de-escalation procedures and allowed restraint of the student only as a last resort.** Despite the revisions, staff continued to restrain him. After the parents removed their son from school, the district filed an administrative complaint with a state agency.

A hearing officer upheld the IEP and the parents appealed to a federal court. In addition to appealing the administrative decision, they asserted state law, Fourteenth Amendment and Rehabilitation Act claims arising from the abusive teacher's misconduct. According to the court, the non-IDEA claims were not exhausted, requiring dismissal of the entire case. On appeal, the Third Circuit held the parents' IEP challenge had been properly exhausted in the state administrative proceeding. It did not matter that the school district had filed the case. In fact, the district admitted the teacher's abusive conduct was unrelated to the IEP dispute. Once the hearing officer issued a decision, the parents had no further administrative recourse and could only appeal to a court under 20 U.S.C. § 1415(i)(2)(A). The hearing officer held an extensive hearing, finding the district provided the student a free and appropriate public education. **Finding the parents properly submitted their IEP challenge to a hearing officer, the court returned the case to the lower court for consideration of the IEP.** *E.R. v. Stroudsburg Area School Dist.*, 755 Fed. Appx. 166 (3d Cir. 2018).

◆   Kentucky parents did not convince the Sixth Circuit Court of Appeals that school officials knew a special education teacher assigned to their non-verbal child with disabilities may have mistreated the child. The court found no liability based on deliberate indifference by the board. In fact, the board had no notice of the alleged misconduct until the parents reported it to the sheriff's department. **In sum, the board could not be held liable for deliberate indifference to the student's rights when it did not know of the incidents.** Next, the court held the parents could not rely on an argument that the board failed to adequately train classroom aides regarding their duty to report abuse in the classroom. It found this claim largely repeated a meritless vicarious liability theory it had already rejected. There was no authority supporting the parent's claim that a lack of training could support a legal finding of deliberate indifference where the school district had no knowledge of the relevant facts supporting the claim.

Last, the court declined to accept the parents' claim that shoddy interviews by the board and poor communications amounted to deliberate indifference to the rights of their son. Ruling that the lower court correctly held for the board of education, the court affirmed the judgment. *K.C. v. Marshall County Board of Educ.*, 762 Fed.Appx. 226 (6th Cir. 2019).

◆ A federal court held a Minnesota school district did not deny a fourth-grade student with Down syndrome a free appropriate public education, despite claims that she was restrained by improperly trained staff and placed in an overly segregated setting. After an administrative law judge held for the school district, the case reached a federal court. It held that **although the restraints were improper, the district acted appropriately by holding an IEP team meeting, amending the IEP and conducting an FBA**. The parent did not show the revised IEPs were not reasonably calculated to enable her child to make progress. *Denny v. Bertha-Hewitt Public Schools, ISD No. 786*, No. 16-1954 (DWF/LIB), 2017 WL 4355968 (D. Minn. 9/29/17).

◆ New York parents found the school site proposed for their child inappropriate because the child would have difficulty remaining regulated in a large school attended by children with behavior issues. In particular, the parents expressed concern over the presence of security guards at the school and the need for their child to pass through metal detectors. They said she would associate the guards with dangerous situations, which could heighten her anxiety. After rejecting the placement and notifying the DOE of their intent to seek private tuition reimbursement, the parents requested a hearing. After administrative decisions for the DOE, the dispute came before a federal court. It found the parents had contributed meaningfully to the IEP discussion. The court found no suggestion that the parents were excluded from the IEP process.

There was no evidence that they voiced any disagreement with the IEP at the meeting. Despite the lack of a functional behavioral analysis, **the CSE appropriately addressed the student's interfering behaviors and devised a BIP based on a significant discussion**. The court upheld administrative findings that the IEP's 16 annual goals and 42 short-term objectives were sufficiently measurable to meet the student's identified areas of need. There was no evidence that the DOE would not have properly implemented the IEP at the designated school site. Concerns about the size of the school, its security procedures and student population were impermissible attacks on the proposed school site. As these concerns were found irrelevant to the school's ability to implement the IEP, the court held for the DOE. *M.T and T.W.-S. v. New York City Dep't of Educ.*, No. 1:14-cv-10124, 2016 WL 1267794 (S.D.N.Y. 3/29/16).

◆ A 13-year-old New Mexico student with Down syndrome became involved in an altercation with school employees. According to the school district, its employees "physically managed" him under a district policy statement and a best practices manual. The student's parent claimed the district applied a discriminatory restraint policy only to students with disabilities. In her lawsuit against the school district, a federal court found a district "Staff Conduct with Students" policy allowed physical management of students to quell a threat to serious, imminent bodily harm. A provision of the Staff Conduct with Students policy applied to use of restraints on students who received special education. It stated that any use of restraints beyond the policy had to be identified in a student's IEP as part of his or her behavior plan. A second district policy called "Best Practices for Use of Physical Management for Students with Disabilities" supplemented the general policy by stating that physical management is always a last resort after less restrictive interventions have been exhausted or ruled out.

The court found the district required the provision of additional procedures and documentation whenever a disabled student was restrained. In the court's view, the Best Practices memo only amounted to guidelines. It found the parameters for physical intervention were drawn from the "Staff Conduct with Students" policy, which applied to all students. **The policy did not rely on stereotypes about disabled persons, as the parent argued. In any event, the court held the school was justified in its conduct.** *Hernandez v. Board of Educ. of Albuquerque Public Schools*, 124 F.Supp.3d 1181 (D. N.M. 2015).

◆ A Washington parent said her child's school committed multiple IEP violations and did not tell her when he was being isolated. She requested a due process hearing. The school district asked for many continuances and an ALJ did not issue a decision for 217 days after the parent's request. She petitioned a federal court for an order requiring the district to pay for a private placement. The court held the child had been denied a free appropriate public education during the 142-day period between the date a due process decision was due and the date it was issued. Although the parent claimed the district did not use the isolation safeguards in her child's IEP, the court found staff members were in the quiet room with the student. Since he was not alone at these times, the court held they could not be considered "isolation" and there was no IDEA violation.

Next, the court held the parent did not show the district failed to document or inform her about restraints. The draft IEP included an amended aversive intervention plan and a behavior intervention plan permitting isolation when needed. The district let the parent review its draft IEP before the meeting, and she had ample time to present her concerns at the meeting. In the court's view, **the district was justified in preserving some ability to restrain the child, given his physical reactions and prior record of harming educators**. The parent was granted partial reimbursement for her costs arising from the 142-day period during which a hearing was delayed, but she was otherwise denied relief. *Miller v. Monroe School Dist.*, 131 F.Supp.3d 1107 (W.D. Wash. 2015).

CHAPTER FOUR

Placement

I. PLACEMENT IN SPECIAL EDUCATION PROGRAMS

A. Educational Benefit Generally

In R.E. v. New York City Dep't of Educ., *694 F.3d 167 (2d Cir. 2012), the U.S. Court of Appeals, Second Circuit, explained that "educational placement" of a child with a disability "refers only to the general type of educational program in which the child is placed." Placement "does not refer to a specific location or program." For this reason, a school district did not have to specify the school or classroom where a disabled student's IEP would be implemented.*

◆ In *C.D. v. Natick Public School Dist.*, the U.S. Court of Appeals, First Circuit, held its precedents regarding the free appropriate public education (FAPE) standard were consistent with *Endrew F. v. Douglas County School Dist. RE-1*, 137 S.Ct. 988 (2017). The court rejected arguments by Massachusetts parents who said *Endrew F.* requires courts to "ask not only whether an IEP offers meaningful educational progress, but also, separately, whether the IEP's objectives are ambitious and challenging." Instead, the court held "*Endrew F.* used terms like 'demanding,' 'challenging,' and 'ambitious' to define 'progress appropriate in light of the child's circumstances,' not to announce a separate dimension of the FAPE requirement." **Under *Endrew F.* and prior First Circuit cases, courts evaluating whether an IEP offers a FAPE must determine whether the IEP is reasonably calculated to confer a meaningful educational benefit in light of the child's circumstances.** Depending on the context, determining whether an IEP was reasonably calculated to offer meaningful progress to a student "may or may not require a sub-inquiry into how challenging the plan is." The lower court correctly followed *Endrew F.* and *Johnson v. Boston Public Schools*, 906 F.3d 182 (1st Cir. 2018). Given the student's intellectual disability and serious language deficits, the court held she could make meaningful progress. The court made additional rulings that are summarized in Section II.A of this chapter. *C.D. v. Natick Public School Dist.*, 924 F.3d 621 (1st Cir. 2019).

◆ When a Pennsylvania student with learning disabilities reached high school age, his IEP team addressed his lack of focus by specifying that he sit at the front of his classes and receive prompts, clarification and repeated directions. He was allowed additional time for tests and assignments. During his ninth-grade year, he missed over 100 class periods and failed five classes. Even with a 1:1 special education teacher for algebra, the student failed the class. Despite his 0.97 grade average, the IEP team found he was progressing toward his goals. He advanced to grade ten by taking summer classes. During the student's tenth-grade school year, his absences decreased and he did not fail any classes. His grade average rose to 2.04. In grade eleven, the student made uneven progress, despite increased absences. His mother provided the school a note from his doctor describing his anxiety about his English class. The student was provided access to an emotional support classroom. His grade average increased to 2.19. But his mother filed a due process complaint, claiming the student's IEPs were inadequate and denied him a free appropriate public education. A hearing officer denied her request for relief, as did a federal court.

On appeal, the Third Circuit Court of Appeals noted the Supreme Court's decision in *Endrew F. v. Douglas County School Dist. RE-1* requires school districts to provide "an educational program reasonably calculated to enable a child to make progress appropriate in light of the child's circumstances." **The court stated that if a school district complies with the *Endrew F.* standard, "it is not liable just because a student does not progress as quickly as his peers."** In this case, the IEPs were appropriate because they addressed the student's behavior and enabled his academic progress. He kept pace with his grade level and went from failing some of his classes to passing all of them. The student was offered programs addressing his behavior. While he contended his anxiety was evident, the court refused to judge his IEPs in hindsight. Once the school district learned of his anxiety, it offered him emotional support. Finding the district took reasonable steps to assist the student, the court held in its favor. *S.C. v. Oxford Area School Dist.*, 751 Fed.Appx. 220 (3d Cir. 2018).

◆ The Los Angeles Unified School District (LAUSD) delayed requesting a due process hearing when the parent of a child with autistic-like behaviors refused to consent to a placement. When the case reached the U.S. Court of Appeals, Ninth Circuit, it rejected a lower court's finding that the IDEA foreclosed LAUSD from initiating a due process hearing as required by state law. In ruling for LAUSD, the lower court relied on 20 U.S.C. § 1414(a)(1)(D) (ii)(II), which states that a school district must obtain parental consent before providing special education. A federal regulation forecloses a district's ability to file a due process complaint if the parent fails to respond to a request for (or refuses to consent to) the initial provision of special education. As the parent had consented to the provision of special education, the lower court committed an error in finding LAUSD was not free to initiate a due process hearing. State law required the district to request a due process hearing in this case.

The court held the district could not continue to hold more IEP meetings in lieu of a hearing. While a district was entitled to some flexibility in deciding when to request a hearing, the court held **LAUSD did not act reasonably in keeping the child in a general education placement for almost two years when it had decided he should be in special education classes**. A delay of over a year in requesting a due process hearing was held unreasonable. Finding LAUSD had concluded that the child was not receiving a FAPE in her current placement, **the court found the child lost educational opportunities and was deprived of educational benefits**. *I.R. v. Los Angeles Unified School Dist.*, 805 F.3d 1164 (9th Cir. 2015).

B. Neighborhood Schools

In J.T. v. Dumont Public Schools, 533 Fed.Appx. 44 (3d Cir. 2013), the Third Circuit explained that while a district must take into account the proximity of a placement to a student's home, it is not obligated to place students in their neighborhood schools. Since the IDEA's key requirement is providing a free appropriate public education, the court found students are to be educated in the schools they would attend if not for a disability, unless their IEPs require placement elsewhere. According to the court, no federal appeals court has recognized a right to attend a neighborhood school under the IDEA.

◆   A California student could pursue a discrimination case against his school district based on the theory that he was removed from his neighborhood school because he has the genetic marker for cystic fibrosis. According to the parents, their child was removed from his neighborhood school because district staff believed he had cystic fibrosis. The parents said their child does not actually have the disease, but instead only has the genetic marker for it. Further, they said because the staff believed the child had cystic fibrosis, he posed a threat to other students attending his school who actually have cystic fibrosis. The parents said the school informed other parents of students who had cystic fibrosis about their child, then removed him from his neighborhood school.

In a federal court, the parents sued the district under the Americans with Disabilities Act (ADA) and Section 504 of the Rehabilitation Act. They added a claim under the First Amendment and a state law negligence claim. After the court dismissed the case, the case reached the U.S. Court of Appeals, Ninth Circuit. It held the complaint was adequate to pursue the ADA and Section 504 claims based on the perception that the student had a disability. **Moreover, the court found the lower court would have to further consider whether the student had a right to attend his neighborhood school.** In proceedings before the lower court, it was found that the student presented a "direct threat" to the safe operation of the neighborhood school. But the parents asserted the school district did not make an individualized assessment of whether he presented a direct threat to the health or safety of others. Next, the court held the lower court committed error by finding the district did not intend to violate the ADA or Section 504. It held the standard under these laws does not require a showing of bad motive, ill will, animosity or intent to cause injury. Although the parents could pursue the discrimination claims on behalf of their child, the court held the First Amendment and negligence claims were properly dismissed. *Chadam v. Palo Alto Unified School Dist.,* 666 Fed.Appx. 615 (9th Cir. 2016).

◆ Students attending the Springfield (Massachusetts) Public Day School (SPDS) claimed SPDS was segregated and provided inferior services to those offered at neighborhood schools. According to the students, they could not access extracurricular activities and were subjected to dangerously punitive discipline. They claimed the segregated SPDS denied their access to educational services that were equal to those enjoyed by nondisabled students, in violation of the Americans with Disabilities Act. **A key assertion by the students was that the school district did not offer school-based behavior services (SBBS) in neighborhood schools.** In order to remedy this, the students sought an order compelling the district to provide them with SBBS in their neighborhood schools. After denying a motion by the school district to dismiss the case, a federal court considered a motion to certify the case as a class action. Although the students and their expert described SBBS as a single program that had been subjected to peer-reviewed research, they admitted the term "SBBS" was created for this litigation. The court noted factual differences in their cases, yet only one of the proposed class members requested a hearing.

The students did not claim an exception to the IDEA exhaustion rule, instead relying on their claim to class status. Even if the administrative exhaustion rule did not apply, the court found the requirements for class certification were not met. Since individual determinations would have to be made for each student, the court found there was no available class-wide remedy. **As the students did not exhaust their administrative remedies and class certification was inappropriate, the court denied their motion.** *S.S. v. City of Springfield, Massachusetts,* 146 F.3d 414 (D. Mass. 2016).

◆ Kentucky parents insisted that their diabetic child attend his neighborhood school. But their school district refused because no school nurse worked at the site. Although full-time nurses worked at two other district schools, the parents rejected both sites. School nurses believed he needed assistance from a nurse and that his insulin injections were a nursing function. The district again denied enrollment at the neighborhood school, and the child began attending a district school that was staffed by a nurse. His parents sued the school board in a federal court for violations of the Americans with Disabilities Act (ADA), Section 504 and the Kentucky Civil Rights Act. In ruling for the board and superintendent, **the court found the student had no right under Section 504 to attend a neighborhood school**. In 2012, the U.S. Court of Appeals, Sixth Circuit, returned the case to the trial court for further proceedings. The court again held for the board of education, and the case returned to the Sixth Circuit.

According to the court, a recent change to Kentucky law barred a school from excluding students on the sole basis that it does not have a full-time nurse. Since state law forbade the actions which the student sought to enjoin, the court found his request was now moot. Next, the court considered the student's claims for damages under the ADA, Section 504 and state law. It found no evidence that the board of education knew it would likely violate the student's rights by assigning him to a school with a full-time nurse. As a result, the federal claims failed. Kentucky Civil Right Act claims are treated like federal claims, so the state law claim also failed. *R.K. v. Board of Educ. of Scott County, Kentucky*, 637 Fed.Appx. 922 (6th Cir. 2016).

◆   A New Jersey student with autism attended an inclusion preschool class in his neighborhood school for half days. For kindergarten, the school district proposed an inclusion class that was not in his neighborhood school. His parent objected and filed a federal class action suit against the school district for systemic IDEA violations and discrimination. The court dismissed the case for failure to exhaust administrative remedies. Since the federal court had declined to consider the state law claims, the parent filed a new state court case against the district for discrimination under the state Law Against Discrimination (LAD). She sought an order requiring neighborhood school placements whenever possible. The court found the child thrived in his kindergarten class.

Since nobody in the proposed class was harmed by not attending a neighborhood school or by being bused, the case was dismissed. On appeal, a state appellate court found the federal claims had already been resolved against the student by the Third Circuit. The state court rejected the parent's claim that attending a neighborhood school was a benefit protected by the LAD. It rejected an argument that disabled children were stigmatized by having to take smaller school buses. **Federal courts have held that if a disabled child is not entitled to a neighborhood placement under the IDEA, there is no entitlement under Section 504 of the Rehabilitation Act.** There was no evidence that the student or any class member had been denied a free appropriate public education. Since there is no entitlement to a neighborhood school placement, the court dismissed the case. *J.T. v. Dumont Public Schools*, 438 N.J.Super. 241, 103 A.3d 269 (N.J. Super. Ct. 2014).

◆   Parents of a Massachusetts student with pervasive developmental disorder obtained a private psychologist's recommendation that their child attend school in an enclosed classroom. Since all first-grade classrooms at his neighborhood school were open, the parents sought to place him in a school with enclosed rooms. They signed an intra-district request form in which they agreed to provide transportation for their child. Later, the parents filed an IDEA due process request, asserting procedural violations by the IEP team and stating the team coerced them into signing the transportation form in order to secure their preferred placement. A hearing officer held for the school committee, but a federal court returned the case to the hearing officer for additional proceedings.

Before the hearing, the parents declined an offer by the school committee to reimburse them for their transportation costs. A hearing officer then found no coercion in their signing of an intra-district placement form and no procedural violations of legal significance. When the case returned to the court, it held the parents were not deprived of participation opportunities. A FAPE had not been denied, nor had there been a deprivation of educational benefits. The student remained at the school chosen by his parents, and there was insufficient evidence that he would not have received a FAPE at the school recommended for him. **The fact that the parents had chosen to voluntarily incur transportation costs did not deny their son a FAPE.** As there had been no coercion, the school committee prevailed. *Doe v. Attleboro Public Schools*, 960 F.Supp.2d 286 (D. Mass. 2013).

C. Extended School Year Services

Extended school year (ESY) services must be provided where necessary to provide students with a free appropriate public education. ESY services are typically required if a student with disabilities would otherwise experience significant regression because of an interruption in the instructional program.

◆ After determining a middle school student with dyslexia and dyscalculia required extended school year (ESY) services, the Hawaii Department of Education (DOE) determined she should have four hours of summer daily special education services. When the parents told their child about the summer placement, she refused to attend. But the parents did not advise the DOE about this. Just before the summer semester, they wrote to the DOE that they intended to make a private placement for their child and would seek public reimbursement for it. They then requested a due process hearing. A hearings officer held equitable considerations did not warrant tuition reimbursement or compensatory education. In response, the parents sued the DOE in a federal court. They argued the hearings officer improperly relied on *T.M. v. Cornwall Cent. School Dist.*, 752 F.3d 145 (2d Cir. 2014), a non-binding Second Circuit decision.

The court held that in order to support a private tuition reimbursement award, the school district must have denied the student a FAPE. Second, the private placement selected by parents must be found appropriate by a hearing officer or court. A court may reduce the amount of reimbursement if the parents do not timely inform the IEP team that they are rejecting an IEP and enrolling their child in a private school. Courts have established that to qualify for an award of tuition reimbursement at public expense, the equities must favor it. In this case, the court held the parents did not timely notify the DOE that they were rejecting the ESY proposal for their child. **As the parents did not provide the student a private school placement during the summer, reimbursement was not warranted.** Even if the student had been denied an appropriate placement for the next school year, the court found the equities did not support full tuition reimbursement. Finding it reasonable for the hearings officer to rely on the *T.M.* case, the court held for the DOE. *W.U. and L.U. v. State of Hawaii, Dep't of Educ.*, No. 18-000197 JAO-RT, 2019 WL 1128754 (D. Haw. 3/12/19).

◆ A New York student with autism attended private preschools, and his district provided special education through private providers. When he turned five, the district's committee on special education (CSE) decided he needed a 12-month educational program to prevent substantial regression. The parties reached an agreement for the student to attend a regular classroom with special education services from the same providers that he had worked with previously. Although the CSE offered to place the child in one of two summer programs, the parents rejected them as overly restrictive. The school district did not offer any summer program for general education students, and it did not offer to place the student in any public or private general education program for the summer months. The parents filed a due process complaint and invoked their rights under the IDEA's stay-put provision. After the case went through the administrative process, it reached the U.S. Court of Appeals, Second Circuit. The court held the district's offer to place the student in special education classrooms for the summer violated the IDEA's least restrictive environment (LRE) requirement.

The court held that if a child needed extended school year services to prevent substantial regression, they had to be an integral part of the child's 12-month program. Here, the district failed to offer the student a FAPE in the LRE for the summer months. As a result, the court returned the case to the lower court for it to consider whether tuition reimbursement was required. But the school district correctly argued that it had been improperly ordered to continue reimbursing the parents for pendency services they were obtaining from private providers. It was up to the district to decide how to offer such services. *T.M. v. Cornwall Cent. School Dist.,* 752 F.3d 145 (2d Cir. 2014).

◆   A 10-year-old Ohio student was nonverbal due to autism, Down syndrome, speech apraxia, sensory integration and cognitive impairments. For two years, the district provided him ESY services including therapy and 1:1 services from a paraprofessional. According to the student's mother, the student could not participate in many of the ESY activities. At an IEP meeting, team members presented the parents with two options. After rejecting both proposals, they expressed interest in ESY programs at an autism center. At a subsequent IEP meeting, the team found the student was eligible for ESY services in reading, math and communication. The offer for a classroom or recreation center ESY program was renewed. The parents continued to press their claims for an autism program setting. Just before school ended, the parents sought federal court relief.

The court held that **to support a claim for ESY services, parents must show, in a manner specific to a child, that "an ESY [program] is necessary to avoid something more than adequately recoupable regression."** In this case, the parents did not show the student would suffer irreparable harm without court intervention. The parents did not present any expert testimony supporting the claim for an ESY autism center program. There was no evidence indicating irremediable regression. The parents had demanded a private autism program and did not truly engage in a constructive dialogue with the school district. As a result, the court dismissed the case. *T.H. v. Cincinnati Public School Dist. Board of Educ.,* No. 1:14-cv-516, 2014 WL 2931426 (S.D. Ohio 6/27/14).

◆   The parents of a California student with autism placed the child in a private preschool setting. At some point in time, the student's Part C eligibility expired. After the student's Part C eligibility expired, the school district proceeded to take steps to hold an IEP meeting. Though it held the meeting, it did a poor job of communicating with the student's parents. In addition, the school district declined to offer a special education placement for the student. The parents proceeded to file a due process request. A hearing officer made a determination that procedural violations had occurred. As a result, the hearing officer ordered the school district to pay for the private program until the school district could offer the student a free appropriate public education. The hearing officer also ordered the provision of ESY services and a transition plan to a district program. As part of the school district's offer, the student would stay in his ESY program and would then transition to public school in the fall. However, the parents disliked the IEP and sought tuition reimbursement for the private school, asserting that it was the student's stay-put placement. A federal court disagreed with the parents. **The ESY services could not support a request for a stay-put order at the private school.** *Huerta v. San Francisco Unified School Dist.*, No. C 11–04817 CRB, 2011 WL 5521742 (N.D. Cal. 11/14/11).

II. LEAST RESTRICTIVE ENVIRONMENT

The IDEA, at 20 U.S.C. § 1412(a)(5)(A), requires that schools provide a free appropriate public education in a disabled student's "least restrictive environment" or LRE. A student's LRE is the one that, to the greatest extent possible, satisfactorily educates the student together with non-disabled peers. Ideally, this would be in the same school the disabled student would attend if he or she were not disabled, but courts have held such placements are only appropriate to the extent that the student with a disability is properly served.

A. Appropriateness

In Beth B. v. Van Clay, *282 F.3d 493 (7th Cir. 2002), the Seventh Circuit Court of Appeals held the IDEA's preference for placing students in their least restrictive environment does not suggest making regular classroom placements that would provide them with an unsatisfactory education.*

Courts continue to rely on a test from Sacramento City Unified School Dist. v. Rachel H., *14 F.3d 1398 (9th Cir. 1994), to evaluate the restrictiveness of placements. In* Rachel H., *the court recited four factors to assess whether a placement was in the least restrictive environment: 1) the educational benefits of placement of the student in full-time regular classes; 2) the non-academic benefits of such a placement; 3) the effect the disabled student has on the teacher and other children in a regular class; and 4) costs of mainstreaming.*

◆ Massachusetts parents filed a due process request to seek reimbursement for a private school placement of their child, who had learning disabilities. Among other things, they claimed she was not placed in her least restrictive appropriate environment and that her IEPs did not provide her a free appropriate public education (FAPE). A hearing officer held the IEPs were appropriate, and a federal court then denied the parents' request for pretrial judgment. It returned the case to the hearing officer to determine whether the IEPs were reasonably calculated to provide the student a FAPE in the least restrictive environment (LRE) possible. Later, the hearing officer held the IEPs complied with the LRE requirement. When the parents appealed to the court again, it held **the benefits of mainstreaming must be weighed against the education available in a more**

restrictive setting. When a child's unique needs cannot be met in a general education classroom, the presumption in favor of mainstreaming is overcome, and the student does not have to be placed in a general education classroom.

In ruling for the district, the court noted the IEP team appropriately considered a range of settings for the student. When the case reached the U.S. Court of Appeals, First Circuit, it held the lower court properly applied its precedents. First Circuit cases issued prior to *Endrew F. v. Douglas County School Dist. RE-1*, 137 S.Ct. 988 (2017), were consistent with *Endrew F.* The court upheld the lower court's findings that the IEPs did not violate the IDEA's LRE requirement. Contrary to the parents' arguments, **the lower court appropriately weighed the LRE and FAPE requirements in affirming the IEPs**. It considered the nature and severity of the student's disability and the impact of supplementary aids and services on any potential placement. Last, the court rejected the parents' claim that the lower court ignored IDEA transition requirements. As none of their arguments had merit, the court held for the school district. *C.D. v. Natick Public School Dist.*, 924 F.3d 621 (1st Cir. 2019).

◆ In *L.H. v. Hamilton County Dep't of Educ.*, 900 F.3d 779 (6th Cir. 2018), the U.S. Court of Appeals, Sixth Circuit, held a student with Down syndrome was improperly segregated from non-disabled peers. In ruling for the student, the court held children with disabilities may only be segregated from their non-disabled peers when the nature or severity of a disability is such that education in regular classes (with supplementary aids or services) cannot be achieved. The court found a mainstream setting would have provided the student in this case "some" educational benefit. An administrative law judge had improperly held he would have to show "mastery of the regular education grade-level curriculum" in order to be mainstreamed. **In the Sixth Circuit's view, the standard for placing a student with a disability is not mastery of the general-education curriculum. Instead, a student with a disability must progress on his/her IEP goals.** There was evidence that the student's teachers did not properly engage in mainstreaming when he attended general education classes. Staff isolated and removed him from situations that became challenging, and the school provided a curriculum with very low educational expectations, no report cards and no homework. As a lower court had incorrectly denied tuition reimbursement to the parents for their private Montessori school costs, the court returned the case to the lower court for the taking of additional evidence to determine an appropriate amount of tuition reimbursement for the parents.

When the case returned to the lower court, it determined the parents were entitled to reimbursement for the student's educational costs for grades 3-8 at the Montessori school in the sum of $103,274. They were prevailing parties in their case and were awarded attorneys' fees and court costs of $349,249.50. *L.H. v. Hamilton County Dep't of Educ.*, 356 F.Supp.3d 713 (E.D. Tenn. 2019).

◆ A California student with Down syndrome attended a general education program with resource specialist support and a 1:1 instructional aide. Noting that she met only 40% of her IEP goals for grade seven, her IEP team sought to place her in special education academic classes for grade eight. Teachers noted that the student was not making progress in a general education setting and was beginning to show signs of frustration and withdrawal. Based on the student's lack of progress and evidence of regression, school members of the team proposed an IEP in which she spent 42% of her time in a special day class with the balance in regular classrooms for extracurricular and non-academic activities. The parents declined the IEP, and after another meeting at which no agreement was reached, the district filed a due process complaint to determine whether its IEP offer provided a free appropriate public education. Following a three-day hearing, an administrative law judge (ALJ) held for the school district.

The parents appealed to a federal court, which affirmed the ALJ's decision. On appeal, the U.S. Court of Appeals, Ninth Circuit, found the ALJ was in the best position to determine the credibility of the witnesses. It rejected the parents' argument that the ALJ improperly found their expert unpersuasive. Further, the lower court correctly analyzed the placement issue under *Sacramento City Union School Dist. v. Rachel H.*, 14 F.3d 1398 (9th Cir. 1994). There was evidence that the student was not benefiting from a general education curriculum. Teachers testified that she did not understand material or participate in classes and often put her head on her desk in frustration. **Because the student functioned at a level of six to seven years behind her peers, she could not make progress even with a heavily modified curriculum and a 1:1 aide.** Moreover, evidence indicated she was regressing and beginning to withdraw. In the court's view, the *Rachel H.* factors indicated a special education day class offered the least restrictive environment for the student. Finding the ALJ and lower court made permissible findings under *Rachel H.*, the court held for the school district. *Solorio v. Clovis Unified School Dist.*, 748 Fed.Appx. 146 (9th Cir. 2019).

◆   A Hawaii parent objected to the segregation of his first-grade son in special education settings for language arts and math. After an IEP meeting, the parent accused the school department of not discussing alternative placements. He began home-schooling his child and later advised the department that he would place him in a private school. The parent filed a due process complaint, which went before an administrative hearing officer. After the hearing officer held for the department, a federal court considered the parent's least restrictive environment argument. According to the parent, his son was not far behind his peers, had no behavior problems and felt isolated in special education classes. But the court rejected his argument that the special education language arts and math placements were overly restrictive. There was evidence that the student had struggled in math and language arts in general education settings, despite the provision of many accommodations. It appeared to the court that the parent was relying on his own opinion that his son was not that far behind his peers.

The court denied the parent's request for private tuition reimbursement and held for the department of education. He appealed to the U.S. Court of Appeals, Ninth Circuit, which considered the inclusion analysis from its decision in *Sacramento City Unified School Dist. v. Rachel H.*, 14 F.3d 1398 (9th Cir. 1994). **To determine if a placement is overly restrictive, the Ninth Circuit balances the educational and non-academic benefits of placement full-time in regular classes, the effect the student has on the teacher and classmates in regular classes, and the costs of mainstreaming.** Applying this analysis, the court held the IEP did not deny the student a free appropriate education. Evidence showed he was far behind his peers in reading and math, and had already received accommodations that did not help in general education settings. The parent did not present any reasons why his son could not obtain non-academic benefits while remaining in general education classes for the better part of the school day. Moreover, the student's general education teacher testified about the difficulty of teaching multiple grade levels in her classroom. The court rejected other arguments by the parent and held for the department. *B.E.L. v. Hawaii Dep't of Educ.*, 711 Fed.Appx. 426 (9th Cir. 2018).

◆   A New Jersey student had a traumatic brain injury during his infancy. He began a preschool program, and a team found him eligible for special education. After he spent a few days in a district preschool program, his parents moved him to a private setting. They later returned him to a public school and worked with the school district to draft his IEPs. Although the IEP team revised and amended the student's IEP several times, the parents objected to a proposal for his second-grade year. The parents rejected the IEP and placed their child in a private prep school. Following unsuccessful mediation efforts, the parents filed a due process complaint, seeking reimbursement for their private tuition costs.

An administrative law judge (ALJ) conducted a hearing. Finding the school board did not deny the student a free appropriate public education (FAPE), the ALJ denied the complaint. The parents appealed to a federal court, adding a Section 504 discrimination claim. **On appeal, the court noted the general rule that the IDEA has a preference for placing students with disabilities in the least restrictive environment that will provide "a meaningful educational benefit."** The ALJ found the IEP offered by the district was appropriate and in the least restrictive environment. The parents did not offer sufficient evidence to overturn the ALJ's findings. In the court's view, the IEP proposing a self-contained setting of no more than 12 students for academics, with integrated individual/group physical therapy and a social skills group, was appropriate. Many recommendations suggested by the parents' neuropsychiatrist were included in the IEP. While finding the IEP proposal "may not have been perfect," the ALJ found it would have provided meaningful benefit to the student. As the court found no support for the IDEA and Section 504 claims, it held for the school board. *C.S. and S.S. v. Montclair Board of Educ.*, No. 16-3294 (JLL), 2017 WL 4122433 (D.N.J. 9/18/17).

B. Behavior Issues

In Nathan M. v. Harrison School Dist. No. 2, *the court rejected a claim to continue a preschool student's attendance at an autism center where he made little academic progress and had no opportunity to be with non-disabled peers.*

◆   A Colorado preschool student attended an autism center that emphasized behavior intervention for two years at his school district's expense. An IEP team proposed transitioning him into a public school setting. In response, the student's parent filed a complaint with the state education department. Near this time, the school district proposed placing three other students who had been attending the autism center into public schools. Their families joined the proceeding. A state complaint officer found the district predetermined public school placements for the students. As a result, they remained at the autism center. Two years later, the district again sought to place the student in a public school. It reevaluated him and held a series of IEP meetings. The parent attended the meetings, but rejected an IEP that would have placed her son in a public school autism program with access to a communications and social development program. The IEP would allow him to attend school with non-disabled peers and receive instruction at a higher level. The school was also closer to the family's home. But the parent filed a due process complaint.

A state complaint officer found the school district violated IDEA procedural requirements and ordered it to fund a private placement. In addition, the district was to provide an independent educational evaluation and hold another IEP meeting. The school district filed a due process complaint and, after a hearing, an administrative law judge held for the school district. A federal court then considered the case. It found evidence that the center emphasized behavioral intervention but had no certified teachers. Significantly, the student made little academic progress and had no opportunity to interact with non-disabled peers there. **At the public school site offered by the district, the student would have opportunities to participate with non-disabled peers at lunch, music, art, extracurriculars, science and social studies.** The court noted the district planned an incremental transition to a public school. Last, the court rejected the parent's claim that the IEP was predetermined. She participated meaningfully in the IEP process and staff members listened to her and responded to her input. *Nathan M. v. Harrison School Dist. No. 2*, No. 18-cv-00085-RPM, 2018 WL 6528127 (D. Colo. 12/12/18; 10th Cir. appeal filed 1/9/19).

◆ A Missouri student's IEP had a behavior plan (BIP) addressing her hallucinations and difficulty distinguishing fantasy from reality. At the beginning of her eighth-grade school year, she was diagnosed with schizophrenia. Her IEP for grade eight reduced her time in general classrooms from 80% of the day to 40%. Although the student was scheduled to be in regular education settings less than 40% of the time when she entered high school, this was not immediately implemented. During her first semester of high school, her psychotic symptoms increased and she became aggressive and suicidal at times. At an IEP meeting, the parent agreed to an evaluation of the student. During later examinations, the student had a hallucination and exhibited other symptoms of schizophrenia. Her reading level had declined from a third-grade level to a first-grade level.

Although a new BIP was devised to provide therapeutic counseling, the parent filed a due process complaint, asserting the district did not modify the IEP to adopt and implement goals, objectives, a BIP and a safety plan to address her child's schizophrenia. A due process hearing was delayed when the parent provided the district with nearly 800 pages of medical records. A new IEP was drafted changing the student's placement to a private separate day facility. A hearing officer denied the parent's due process complaint. On appeal, a federal court found that as the student's psychological problems progressed, the school increased her special education time. **The court found the school district's actions were in line with the IDEA's least restrictive environment**

requirement. Evidence indicated the student was doing well in regular classes and that school officials used their best professional judgment. Moreover, the district communicated with the student's medical professionals and completed a full reevaluation. *Johnson v. St. Louis Public School Dist.*, No. 4:17 CV 2204 SNLJ, 2018 WL 4383277 (E.D. Mo. 9/14/18; 8th Cir. appeal filed 12/4/18).

◆ A Texas student with autism, behavior problems and a speech impairment was placed in a classroom that was divided into "zones" by partitions in response to her serious behavioral issues. A school district autism consultant implemented the zoning structure, which separated the student from non-disabled peers except during lunch, recess and special events. But the parents objected that the classroom structure was implemented without their knowledge and expressed concern about their child's transitions from home to school.

The parents asked the ARD committee that school staff have training in ABA methodology. The ARD committee felt the student was already in the least restrictive environment. A school district psychologist conducted an FBA and issued a report. Both reports made recommendations to enhance the student's communication skills. At an ARD committee meeting, the district proposed an IEP that would have placed the student in a self-contained special education classroom. The parents responded to the proposal by placing their child in a private education program. After the parents requested a due process hearing, a special education hearing officer found the school district complied with the IDEA when proposing its IEP. The parents appealed to a federal court, which found no error in the hearing officer's decision for the school district. Evidence indicated the IEP was appropriately individualized on the basis of the student's assessments, including the private assessment. **The court found the parents relied on speculation in arguing that the school violated the LRE requirement.** Next, the court rejected a claim by the parents that ABA teaching strategies were needed. A school district did not have to maximize a student's potential and the court found the IEPs in this case were appropriately individualized. The court held the school district appropriately placed the student in her least restrictive environment. *C.G. v. Waller Independent School Dist.*, No. 4:15-CV-00123, 2016 WL 3144161 (S.D. Tex. 6/6/16).

C. Homebound Instruction

In R.L. v. Miami-Dade County School Board, 757 F.3d 1173 (11th Cir. 2014), the U.S. Court of Appeals, Eleventh Circuit, rejected a Florida school board's argument that no IDEA provision authorizes reimbursement for 1:1 home programs selected by parents. Instead, the court held the IDEA definition of "special education" includes home instruction.

In School Dist. of Wisconsin Dells v. Z.S., 295 F.3d 671 (7th Cir. 2002), the court upheld the assignment of a student with autism to a temporary homebound placement. He had a "disastrous history" in regular placements and failed to function well in any setting except a residential facility.

A California law states that a pupil with a temporary disability making regular or alternative class attendance impossible or inadvisable must receive individual instruction at home, in a hospital or a residential health facility other than a state hospital. Under the amended law, home instruction is to be provided by the district in which the pupil resides, while hospital or residential facility instruction is to be provided by the district in which the facility is located. California 2017-18 Legislative Session, Ch. 167. A.B. 2109. California Educ. Code §§ 48206.3, 48207, 48207.3, 48207.5, 48208, 4824, 51225.5.

◆ Due to the severity and complexity of a Colorado student's disabilities, his IEP team determined that his least restrictive environment for education was at home. The parents claimed the district denied their son instruction in language arts, math, science, history, civics and government, geography, economics, art, foreign language, social sciences, technology, library, visual arts, theater, music and physical education. They further asserted he received no gifted/talented instruction. The parents filed a due process action, challenging failure by the school district to address many academic areas in their son's IEPs. The district later changed his placement to a residential facility, over their objection. After a due process hearing, an administrative law judge (ALJ) held the school district violated the IDEA by failing to offer the student a free appropriate public education (FAPE). But the ALJ held the residential placement was reasonably calculated to provide him with a FAPE. In a federal court, the parents challenged the adverse ruling on the residential placement.

The student's parents claimed the district treated their son and other students in homebound placements differently from similarly situated students who were educated in school settings. In making this claim, the parents sought to compare their son with other students with disabilities in the district. The court found the issue was whether students with disabilities who are educated in classrooms are similarly situated to those who are educated at home. At this early stage of the case, the court refused to dismiss an equal protection claim. **The complaint sufficiently described educational services the student was entitled to receive, but did not.** *C.W. v. Denver County School Dist. No. 1*, No 17-CV-2462-MSK-MEH, 2018 WL 3861157 (D. Colo. 8/14/18).

◆ A New Mexico student with autism and significant delays in cognitive abilities, sensory processing, communication and daily living skills was non-verbal and not toilet-trained. During his sixth-grade school year, he was placed in a "hybrid" program calling for two hours per day in the emerging autism classroom and the rest of the school day in an intensive support program. After the student spent two days in the hybrid program, the parents removed him from school and filed a due process complaint. A hearing officer held the school district denied the student a free appropriate public education and that he could only progress through 1:1 applied behavioral analysis (ABA) therapy. She found the lack of a functional behavioral assessment and a behavior intervention plan interfered with the student's access to services. The school district appealed to federal court, which rejected the hearing officer's findings.

Evidence indicated the IEP team considered the student's autism-related needs and appropriate strategies, then implemented appropriate classroom ABA techniques. The court found the hearing officer ignored evidence of the student's global learning deficits. As many courts have held, educational methodology is for school districts to determine. And the IDEA does not promise any particular educational outcome. The court reversed findings that the student needed an exclusive ABA program. **Evidence indicated ABA therapy is not an appropriate exclusive classroom methodology, even if it might be in home settings.** The hearing record did not support a finding that the district failed to document autism-based strategies. Although the parents claimed the district was required to implement research-based teaching methods, the IDEA only requires this "to the extent practicable." The court found the IEP incorporated numerous teaching techniques, including ABA, which satisfied IDEA requirements. Since the student was making meaningful progress in view of his multiple disabilities, the court held for the school district. *Board of Educ. of Albuquerque Public Schools v. Maez,* No. 16-cv-1082 WJ/WPL, 2017 WL 3278945 (D.N.M. 8/1/17).

◆ A Minnesota student's family relocated to a new school district. At an IEP meeting, the school offered to continue providing him with the 1:1 instruction he had been receiving at his old school for the first six weeks of the school year. After six weeks, the new school intended to reevaluate the placement. The parent rejected a number of IEP proposals that did not ensure at-home instruction. She felt anything but home instruction would interfere with her son's high school football participation. The parent requested a hearing. Prior to a hearing, the parties reached an agreement and the parent signed a prior written notice (PWN) that modified the IEP. Instead of providing 1:1 instruction, the modified IEP called for a shortened in-school schedule. Later in the school year, the parent requested another hearing. School officials proposed a new IEP that would call for the student to receive all his instruction at school on a full-day schedule. After hearing testimony from both parties, the ALJ denied the parent's request for an at-home placement for her son plus compensatory education. In addition, the ALJ granted the district's motion to approve its IEP.

The parent appealed to the state court of appeals, which explained that the student's IEP called for five hours of weekly 1:1 services, but did not specify the location or time for the services. The court held the new district provided the parent with notice of an IEP meeting to either adopt the student's old IEP or draft a new one. The parent signed a PWN calling for a shortened school day with no at-home instruction. At the time of the hearing, the student's IEP consisted of the new district's IEP as modified by the PWN and a later PWN. None of these documents specified at-home instruction. **The court held substantial evidence supported the ALJ's finding that the parent agreed to the IEP as modified by the PWNs.** The new district followed proper procedures in adopting the IEP. It was not error for the ALJ to approve the proposed IEP for a full-day in-school placement. *In the Matter of J.J.E. v. Independent School Dist. 279 (Osseo Area Public Schools)*, No. A16-0828, 2017 WL 164432 (Minn. Ct. App. 1/17/17).

◆ A Pennsylvania high school student attended a rigorous, advanced program for gifted students. In her junior year, she was diagnosed with gastroparesis and was intermittently hospitalized. She received weekly homebound instruction, which her parents supplemented with private tutoring. Although she returned to school for her senior year, she had a relapse and remained at home. The school found the student eligible for a Section 504 service plan allowing her to attend school when her health allowed. Near this time, she was diagnosed with an anxiety disorder. Her parents questioned the effectiveness of homebound instruction, noting a school district instructor was unable to provide substantive guidance in advanced placement courses such as Japanese and Chinese. The student dropped some courses and completed others with tutoring. Although the district sought permission to evaluate the student for eligibility under the IDEA, the parents declined. A Section 504 plan was offered to her with "significantly more permissive accommodations" such as a lack of attendance penalties for medical absences and permission to enter and exit the school as needed. But the student soon fell behind in her classes and began taking refuge in the library.

After finishing the school year at home with the help of private tutoring, the student graduated 21st in her class of 336. But she had to withdraw from college in her second year. Her parents sued the school district, claiming it did not properly implement the Section 504 plan. A federal court held for the district, and the parents appealed. The U.S. Court of Appeals, Third Circuit, rejected the argument that state law entitled the student to accommodations that maximized her potential. **Homebound services were never intended to be a substitute for in-class learning.** As a result, the court found no discrimination. *K.K. v. Pittsburgh Public Schools*, 590 Fed.Appx. 148 (3d Cir. 2014).

◆   A Georgia student with disabilities was placed on a strict diet and began taking nutritional supplements every 45 minutes. Based on the need to follow her regimen in a low-stress setting, her parents requested home-based services for the last three months of the school year. After first offering to provide the student her diet in school, the district agreed to provide in-home services until the end of the school year. It also suggested in-home extended school year services and a return to school in a classroom for students with severe autism.

The parents rejected the placement and filed a due process complaint, urging in-home services to maintain their child's diet. An administrative law judge dismissed the case, and a federal court upheld the decision. On appeal, the U.S. Court of Appeals, Eleventh Circuit, held the parents' demand for an in-home placement conflicted with the IDEA's preference for educating students with disabilities with their non-disabled peers. **Separate education or other removal of a child from regular educational settings was to take place only when the nature or severity of the disability prevented education with non-disabled peers.** In the court's view, the evidence did not justify in-home education. The student did not have a life-threatening condition, and her strict diet was not prescribed by a doctor. Evidence indicated she would best be served by reintegrating into school. The court affirmed the judgment. *A.K. v. Gwinnett County School Dist.*, 556 Fed.Appx. 790 (11th Cir. 2014).

◆   An Idaho student with autism and anxiety disorder had significant cognitive and developmental deficits and had behavior problems such as hitting, kicking and exposing himself. Prior to his entry into junior high school, his school prepared a functional behavioral assessment (FBA) and behavioral intervention plan. After his teacher reported he had stabbed her in the arm with a pencil and hit her in the face, the parents began keeping him at home. They refused to attend an IEP meeting but asked the school to conduct a new FBA and to update his IEP. The parents later rejected proposals for a new IEP. The district claimed the student could return to school any time and did not formally assess a homebound placement. Near the end of the school year, the district agreed to his gradual return to school. A federal court found there was no disciplinary exclusion. Although the district did not deny the student a free appropriate public education before his prolonged absence, it did not adequately evaluate his need for homebound services. **The court held it was improper to reject a request for homebound services without evaluating the student's need for an alternative placement and reintegration plan.** The court held the district had a continuing duty to provide him a FAPE during the protracted dispute and found a denial of FAPE. *Rodriguez v. Independent School Dist. of Boise City No. 1*, No. 1:12-cv-00390-CWD, 2014 WL 1317697 (D. Idaho 3/28/14).

III. PRIVATE SCHOOL PLACEMENT

An IDEA provision allows school districts to place children with disabilities in private schools and facilities in accordance with their IEPs as one means of carrying out their duty to provide special education and related services. See Woods v. Northport Public School, *487 Fed.Appx. 968 (6th Cir. 2012).*

In Blount County Board of Educ. v. Bowens, *the Eleventh Circuit held a board's failure to offer an adequate program to a preschool child with autism resulted in consent to a private placement made by the parents. For more cases involving private school tuition payment disputes, see Chapter Seven.*

◆   A Massachusetts student with a language-based learning disability attended a private, out-of-district special education school under IEPs developed by her school district for grades 3-8. Her grandparents (who served as her guardians) urged placement in a certain college prep school for grade nine where other family members had attended. IEP team members expressed concern that the school did not offer the type of special education curriculum offered at the student's current school. Later, the district offered to place the student in a public high school. The grandmother wrote a letter to state officials to complain about the district's decision. Because of the IEP dispute, the student's current school became her stay-put placement. But the school announced it could not meet her needs for grade nine. By this time, the grandparents had hired an attorney, who wrote to the district to request the college prep school as the stay-put placement. The district proposed a placement in a state-approved, private special education school. The grandparents accepted this, and the school became the student's new stay-put placement. Within a short time, she became unhappy with the school's lack of rigor and her long commute. IEP team members drafted a new IEP that would maintain her stay-put placement while offering a transition plan with goals of completing high school and advancing to a four-year college. Although the grandmother accepted the IEP, she rejected its implementation at the school designated as the stay-put placement. She notified the district of her intent to place the student at the college prep school and sought reimbursement for her tuition costs. Meanwhile, the district offered the student a new IEP that would place her in a partial inclusion program at a public high school. After rejecting the IEP, the family initiated a due process proceeding.

A hearing officer denied the grandparents' request for tuition reimbursement for the college prep school. Further, the hearing officer found the district's failure to offer a transition plan for the student during grade nine was cured by later IEPs. Later, a federal court held that while the district did not provide sufficient transition planning, the student was not denied access to a FAPE. Because of the family's placement decision, she never received the related services specified in the challenged IEPs. The court held the IEPs were reasonably calculated to provide a FAPE. **Evidence suggested that the IEP challenge was based on a specific desire to place the student at the college prep school.** As substantial evidence supported the hearing officer's decision to deny private school tuition reimbursement, the court held for the school district. *Doe v. Belchertown Public Schools*, 347 F.Supp.3d 90 (D. Mass. 2018).

◆ A Minnesota student attended a Catholic school from kindergarten until grade five. She struggled in her classes, and her parents obtained an evaluation from the Minneapolis Public Schools (MPS) which found she needed special education and related services. MPS then began busing the student from her private school to a public school for special education services. The parents grew dissatisfied with MPS and filed a complaint requesting an impartial due process hearing. An administrative law judge found the MPS had denied the student a free appropriate public education (FAPE). The MPS appealed to a federal court, which rejected the argument that private school students in the state do not have individual rights to a FAPE or a due process hearing.

On appeal, the Eighth Circuit Court of Appeals found the 1997 IDEA amendments substantially limited the rights of students whose parents enroll them in private schools. Minnesota followed suit in 1998 by limiting services offered to students with disabilities "to the extent required in federal law," but later deleted this language to restore the law to its prior form. State law prohibited the denial of special instruction and services to a student "on a shared time basis because of attendance at a nonpublic school." While federal law assures private school students a "proportionate share of funds only, without any individual entitlement to the provision of special education services," Minnesota law does not discuss proportionality. For this reason, **the court held private school students in the state have a state-law right to a FAPE on a shared-time basis.** The court rejected the MPS' remaining arguments, finding Minnesota's shared-time statute does not require public schools to constantly monitor private schools. Instead, a school district must provide appropriate services for the part of the regular school day when the student is in attendance. Finding Minnesota law grants students in nonpublic schools rights to a FAPE and due process hearings, the court held for the parents. *Special School Dist. No. 1, Minneapolis Public Schools v. R.M.M.*, 861 F.3d 769 (8th Cir. 2017).

◆ A student with attention deficit hyperactivity disorder had a Section 504 accommodation plan for grade two. The District of Columbia Public Schools (DCPS) found her eligible for special education as a child with an other health impairment/attention deficit disorder the next year. Without rejecting the IEP, the parents investigated private schools for their child and ultimately found a private day school. After notifying the DCPS of their intent to make a private placement and seek funding for it, the parents enrolled their child in the private school. There, she received 35 hours of weekly specialized instruction and related services in a self-contained, intensive, individualized, remedial special education program. While the student attended the private school, the DCPS arranged for evaluations and a functional behavior assessment. After an IEP team created an IEP that would have placed the student in a public school, the parents filed a due process hearing complaint. A hearing officer held they did not prove the DCPS denied their child a free appropriate public education.

The parents appealed to a federal court, which found **the opinions of IEP team members at the time of the creation of the IEP were more relevant than the student's private school progress**. It held the parents did not show the IEP was not reasonably calculated to enable their child to receive educational benefits. At the time the IEP was offered, her parents requested a private placement. But they did not present persuasive evidence that keeping her in DCPS was not viable. **Strong policy considerations counseled against unilateral parental placements before a public school could implement or adjust an IEP.** Since the parents did not show the IEP was inadequate and would have denied their child a FAPE, the court denied private school tuition reimbursement. *Z.B. v. Dist. of Columbia*, 202 F.Supp.3d 64 (D.D.C. 2016).

◆   A federal court ordered a Pennsylvania school district to reimburse parents for privately placing their autistic child after they rejected an IEP calling for online academy services before transitioning to a high school. In the court's view, the student needed small group instruction and/or tutoring, structure and consistency. A hearing officer had found it questionable whether a virtual environment could provide such structure. Nor could the online academy's drop-in center adequately address concerns about the student's need to learn social skills and experience successful peer interactions. The student had significant psychological and behavioral problems, leading the court to find the hearing officer did not commit error in finding the district denied her a free appropriate public education. **The court held the hearing officer considered the student's PTSD diagnosis and evidence that her symptoms** might be triggered by seeing an African-American student she had fought with and students who were present at the time of the incident. The hearing officer had found serious problems with the IEP. As the evidence indicated the IEP was inadequate, the court held for the student. Last, the court rejected the school district's argument that the parents acted unreasonably and should be denied reimbursement. It found they kept open minds and affirmed the award of tuition reimbursement and transportation costs. *School Dist. of Pittsburgh v. C.M.C.*, No. 16-cv-92, 2016 WL 4273175 (W.D. Pa. 8/12/16).

◆   New York parents found a private school for their child and signed an enrollment contract for the next school year. Relying on private reports, the parents urged the committee on special education (CSE) to approve the private placement they had already made for the child. Team members met three times with the parents to consider an IEP for the next school year. Although CSE members attended the meetings with a draft IEP, they agreed to some of the suggestions from the private reports. But the team rejected the parents' request for a private school placement. At one meeting, the team offered a special education class placement in a room with 12 students, a special education teacher and paraprofessional. Despite a suggestion by a team member that a smaller class would be too restrictive, the parents rejected the IEP and requested a hearing.

An impartial hearing officer (IHO) awarded them the $46,000 they had paid for tuition. Later, a state review officer reversed the IHO's decision. On appeal, a federal court found the parents had "ample opportunity to participate in the decision-making process." Changes had been made to the IEPs in response to their concerns. **Disagreement with staff IEP recommendations was not a denial of meaningful participation in the decision-making process.** In fact, the IEP cited the private report and incorporated aspects of it. The IDEA allows staff members to prepare for a meeting by developing a proposal. The court held the IEP was reasonably calculated to confer educational benefits on the child and provide her with a free appropriate public education. While her parents may have wanted a private education for her, the court held there was no IDEA entitlement to one. *P.G. v. City School Dist. of New York*, No. 14 Civ. 1207 (KPF), 2015 WL 787008 (S.D.N.Y. 2/25/15).

◆ A federal court held **New York City's Department of Education could not be ordered to place a child in a school that was not approved by the state**. Case law authorizing parents to place children in non-approved facilities did not apply to a public agency's placement. *Florence County School Dist. Four v. Carter*, 510 U.S. 7 (1993), distinguished parental placements from district placements. *Z.H. v. New York City Dep't of Educ.*, 107 F.Supp.3d 369 (S.D.N.Y. 2015).

◆ The parents of an Alabama preschool child with autism attended IEP team meetings where a speech and language pathologist represented the board of education. Although the speech and language pathologist offered three placement options for the child, none of them met the child's needs. The parents felt a private school for children with autism could best serve their child. At one of the meetings, the speech and language pathologist agreed with them that the private school was "an excellent placement option." But the meeting closed with no offer of placement. As a new school year approached, the parents asked for private school tuition reimbursement. The board offered another program, which they declined. At a due process hearing, the parents said the speech and language pathologist seemed to be unaware of relevant services in the county.

A hearing officer held for the parents, finding the board did not offer any appropriate services or facilities. Moreover, as the board's representative, the speech and language pathologist had acquiesced to the parental placement. A federal court affirmed the decision, and the board appealed. The U.S. Court of Appeals, Eleventh Circuit, held the parental action was not unilateral. **The speech and language pathologist (and by extension, the board) had agreed to the school located by the parents.** Since the board had agreed to the private placement, the court held the parents had no duty to notify the board they were seeking reimbursement. The board had a duty to offer the child an appropriate education and could not wait and see if they would seek reimbursement. The court held for the parents, finding the board had presented them with inadequate placement options and now sought to wash its hands of its IDEA obligations. *Blount County Board of Educ. v. Bowens*, 762 F.3 1242 (11th Cir. 2014).

IV. RESIDENTIAL SCHOOL PLACEMENT

A. Appropriateness

In Richardson Independent School Dist. v. Michael Z., *580 F.3d 286 (5th Cir. 2009), the Fifth Circuit denied a request for a residential placement. It held the parents did not show the placement was necessary for educational (rather than medical or behavioral) reasons. A parental placement must be made for educational reasons to qualify for reimbursement by a school district.*

◆   A New York parent sought a residential placement for her child during a committee on special education (CSE) meeting held near the end of the 2011 school year. The CSE denied the request and confirmed the decision by mailing her a copy of the 2011-12 IEP. According to the parent, the school district's inaction result in a "crisis" for her child during the 2011-12 school year. In 2015, she filed a due process complaint. While the IDEA claims were dismissed as untimely, **the hearing officer found the district violated Section 504 of the Rehabilitation Act by failing to provide the student with a residential placement from January to June 2012**. After a state review officer affirmed the decision on the IDEA claim, the parent appealed. A federal court held for the school district, finding the IDEA and Section 504 claims were untimely.

On appeal, the U.S. Court of Appeals, Second Circuit, found the "crisis" identified by the parent was a manifestation of the consequences of actions taken at an IEP meeting in May 2011. As a result, the claims under the IDEA and Section 504 accrued by May or June 2011. It rejected the parent's claim that the district made misrepresentations that required extending the limitation on filing her case. There was no merit to her claim that she did not adequately understand her due process rights. An advocate attended the May 2011 CSE meeting to help argue for a residential placement. The parent acknowledged she received notice of her procedural safeguards. Finding the action was untimely and she was not entitled to any exception allowing her to extend the timeline for filing, the court held the case was properly dismissed. *Board of Educ. of North Rockland Cent. School Dist. v. C.M.*, 744 Fed.Appx. 7 (2d Cir. 2018).

◆   A New York parent said a school district committee on special education (CSE) did not address her child's nonverbal learning disability "whatsoever" and that committee members "reflected general ignorance of this disability" in the IEP process. Further, the parent asserted the school district denied the student a FAPE because the CSE did not conduct testing that would have helped create an appropriate IEP. She noted the lack of an assessment for assistive technology. Relying on evaluations and a report from the parent's consultant, the CSE found the student should attend her home school and not a residential school. When the case reached a federal court, it found the IEP was reasonably calculated to enable the student to receive educational benefits. On appeal, the U.S. Court of Appeals, Second Circuit, noted the CSE considered a private report submitted by the parent. In addition, the court found the CSE considered the same information and similar techniques as the private consultant recommended.

Further, the recommended techniques were included in the IEP. While the parent made much of the district's failure to identify her child's nonverbal learning disability, the court found this was of little significance. It found the student's needs were appropriately addressed in the IEP. The court found "nonverbal learning disability" is not a recognized diagnosis. As the IEP would have provided the student with a FAPE at a district school, the court found it was not necessary to consider the appropriateness of the private residential placement preferred by the parent. In finding the IEP adequate for the student, the court rejected a claim by the parent that school district staff lacked training and experience in handling students with nonverbal learning disabilities. It found **the IDEA requires personalized instruction with sufficient support services to allow a child to benefit from instruction. Schools must offer IEPs that are reasonably calculated to enable a child with a disability to make progress appropriate in light of the child's disability.** Since the IEP was specifically designed to address the student's nonverbal deficits, the court upheld it. *D.B. v. Ithaca City School Dist.*, 690 Fed.Appx. 778 (2d Cir. 2017).

◆   A Washington student had a history of truancy, juvenile detention and behavior issues. He used illegal drugs, ran away from home and was placed in a psychiatric hospital. After a 28-day elopement, the student was readmitted to a hospital. The parents notified the district of their intention to place him in a residential facility and to seek reimbursement. They enrolled the student in a Utah residential facility with a locked campus and structured environment and requested a due process hearing. An administrative law judge held for the parents, and the district appealed to a federal court. The court found the dispute centered on whether the residential placement was a service related to the student's education or an excluded "medical service."

After examining IDEA definitions of "special education" and "related services," the court found the residential school provided "related services" and/ or the type of services that would be offered in a school nurse's office. These included psychological services, therapeutic recreation, social work services, medication management and counseling. **Further, the court found evidence that the student had to receive the services in a structured residential setting. This was due to his tendency to elope and his truancy resulting from the "perfect storm of his disabilities."** In the court's view, the IEP offered by the district was not reasonably calculated to enable the student to progress. His impulsiveness, hallucinations and cognitive disorganization made it highly unlikely that he would attend school in the absence of constant monitoring. Finding the parents established violations of the IDEA that warranted tuition reimbursement, the court held in their favor. *Edmonds School Dist. v. A.T.*, No. C16-1500RSL, 2017 WL 5157941 (W.D. Wash. 11/7/17).

◆   After a New York school committee on special education (CSE) identified a student as having autism and found him eligible for special education, the CSE and his parent began having disputes about his IEPs. Eventually, the parties entered into a resolution agreement covering three school years. Under the agreement, the district agreed to pay up to $36,562.50 toward tuition at a particular private school. Alternatively, the district agreed to pay the tuition at another New York private school of the parent's choosing upon receipt of proof of enrollment. At the end of a school year, the dean of students at the private school told the parent that the student needed a therapeutic environment and should not remain at the school. According to the parent, she contacted a therapeutic residential school and was told that the district needed to provide a referral for her son before she could begin the application process. According to the parent, the school district failed to provide a referral when she sought one.

Asserting breach of the resolution agreement, the parent sued the school district in the state court system. The court held for the school district and the parent appealed to the New York Supreme Court, Appellate Division. On appeal, the parent argued the district breached an implied covenant of good faith and fair dealing under the agreement by failing to provide the referral her son needed to begin the process of enrolling in the therapeutic residential school as she sought. The court found New York case law holds that every contract contains an implied covenant of good faith and fair dealing. A breach occurs when a party acts in a manner that would deprive the other party of rights to benefits under the resolution agreement. **The court found the agreement did not require the school district to provide a referral for the student to enroll in a residential therapeutic school.** It refused to impose a term upon the parties that was not included in their agreement and held for the school district. *Guzman v. North Syracuse Cent. School Dist.*, 158 A.D.3d 1287, 71 N.Y.S.3d 279 (N.Y. App. Div. Ct. 2018; motion for reargument or leave to appeal to the New York Court of Appeals denied 4/30/18).

◆   A Texas student had a drug habit and attempted suicide. He had attention deficit hyperactivity disorder, emotional deficits, anxiety and depression. But the student's academic achievement was found average or above in every tested area. An admission, review and dismissal (ARD) committee met and offered him an IEP with in-class support and meetings with a school psychologist. After entering high school, the student refused to do his schoolwork and told teachers he intended to sell marijuana. Although the ARD committee met to discuss his progress, his IEP remained unchanged. Early in the student's ninth-grade year, his parents placed him in a Utah wilderness camp. The school district declined their request for reimbursement for the camp, and they placed him in a Missouri mental health facility where he was diagnosed with reactive attachment disorder (RAD). The parents sought tuition reimbursement for both placements.

A hearing officer found the district denied the student a free appropriate public education and ordered reimbursement for the Missouri placement. The Utah facility was ineligible for IDEA reimbursement. A federal court agreed with the parents and ordered the district to reimburse them for the Missouri placement. On appeal, the U.S. Court of Appeals, Fifth Circuit, held the parents did not show the Missouri placement was appropriate. The student's progress at the facility was to be primarily judged by educational achievement. By relying on evidence that the Missouri school would focus on the root cause of his RAD, the lower court committed an error. The court held the benefits to the child were irrelevant if they were only incidental to the parents' reasons for making the placement. **The court found the parents made the Missouri placement over concerns that their son would again attempt suicide and because of his continuing drug problem.** As no educational reason was given for the placement, the court held for the school district. *Fort Bend Independent School Dist. v. Douglas A.*, 601 Fed.Appx. 250 (5th Cir. 2015).

◆ A New York student with a learning disability was placed in a residential facility for more than four years under an agreement between her parents and her school district. She earned mostly As and Bs but had oppositional behavior, poor social skills, verbal aggression, tantrums and social problems. In her last year at the facility, the student earned some Cs and Ds but made academic and behavioral progress. Her mother had concerns about the school's administration of asthma medication and the program's restrictiveness. She obtained a private evaluation of the child, removed her from the facility and sought home tutoring.

A school committee on special education (CSE) recommended a state-approved residential placement. The parent enrolled the student in a private academy and filed an impartial hearing request. An impartial hearing officer found the school district did not offer the student a FAPE for part of the school year. A state review officer found no denial of FAPE during the year of the unilateral private placement. It was also found that the private academy was not an appropriate placement, so reimbursement was denied. On appeal, a federal court affirmed the review officer's decision, and the parent appealed to the U.S. Court of Appeals, Second Circuit. It found **the facility had a specialized curriculum that enabled the student to achieve academic success and improve her behavior**. As the review officer had conducted a thorough review of the record, the court upheld the decision. And since the lower court had correctly found the private academy inappropriate, the court held for the school district. *Ward v. Board of Educ. of Enlarged City School Dist. of Middletown, New York*, 568 Fed.Appx. 18 (2d Cir. 2014).

◆ After a Pennsylvania student made multiple suicide attempts, his parents placed him in a New Hampshire therapeutic residential center. Upon review of an analysis by the center, the student's school district accepted a diagnosis of emotional disturbance and offered him an IEP. Although the IEP incorporated most of the center's recommendations, the parents rejected it because it did not offer the student small classes or the kind of counseling he had been receiving at the center. For the next school year, the parents located a private residential school in Pennsylvania that offered small classes and a supportive environment.

When the dispute reached the Third Circuit, it held **a school district was only liable for a residential placement that was "necessary" to provide a student with special education and related services**. No reimbursement was required if a parental placement was a response to medical, social or emotional problems that were segregable from the learning process. Further, there had to be some "link" between the private services and the child's educational needs.

The court held the student was placed in the New Hampshire facility to address his mental health. Any educational benefit he received there was incidental. As the school district's IEP offer had complied with the IDEA, the court held for the district. *Munir v. Pottsville Area School Dist.*, 723 F.3d 423 (3d Cir. 2013).

◆   Since birth, a Rhode Island student struggled with attentional, emotional and behavioral disabilities. His parents became upset that his sixth-grade IEP did not include goals or objectives relating to his social, emotional or behavioral functioning. They placed him in a residential school and sought to keep him there. A hearing officer agreed that a residential placement was necessary, and a federal court upheld that determination. The court noted that **a residential placement is necessary when consistent instructional and therapeutic interventions are needed throughout the day for the student to make meaningful educational progress**. The district's IEP denied the student a FAPE by failing to address his behavior. *Coventry Public Schools v. Rachel J.*, 893 F.Supp.2d 322 (D.R.I. 2012).

B. Behavioral/Emotional Problems

In assessing claims for residential placements based on behavioral or emotional problems, courts focus on whether the student's behavior problems may be separated from the learning process. In Independent School Dist. No. 284 v. A.C., *258 F.3d 769 (8th Cir. 2001), the Eighth Circuit upheld a residential placement, finding a student would not receive educational benefit until her behavior was addressed in a residential setting. It held that if she could not reasonably be expected to benefit from instruction in a less restrictive setting, residential placement would be found educationally necessary.*

By contrast, in State of Wisconsin v. Randall H., *257 Wis.2d 57, 653 N.W.2d 503 (Wis. 2002), the Wisconsin Supreme Court held that a child was placed in a residential facility under a child-protection order for reasons separate from his educational needs. An IEP prepared after his residential placement did not demonstrate that the placement was necessary to meet his educational needs.*

◆   After being adopted by a New York couple as an infant, a Russian-born child was diagnosed with an autism spectrum disorder. A private psychiatrist who worked with her described her as "the most unique patient she had come across in her years of practice." The student had hallucinations and saw spirits that she believed were real and physically present with her. As she advanced to high school, her hallucinations began to increase significantly, and she had difficulty separating fantasy from reality. She expressed the desire to "kill her spirit self." The student's parents were unable to agree with school officials on an appropriate placement after the student had a psychotic episode and was hospitalized. The parents rejected a day school identified by the district and enrolled their child in a residential school. According to the parents, the district denied the student a free appropriate public education (FAPE) by declining to approve the school they selected. An impartial hearing officer agreed with the parents, but a state review officer reversed the decision and held for the school district.

A federal court then affirmed the review officer's decision, and the parents appealed. When the case reached the Second Circuit Court of Appeals, it found the review officer's decision was entitled to deference. It found the parents' claim for tuition reimbursement depended on the school district's ability to show the IEP provided the student a FAPE. The court held the review officer correctly relied on testimony from the student's private psychiatrist and other witnesses. In addition, the court noted that the review officer considered the student's IEP and a private diagnostic report supplied by the parents. In the review officer's opinion, **the day school identified by the district struck an appropriate balance between the student's therapeutic needs and the need to place her in the least restrictive environment**. Concluding that the review officer's decision was thorough and well-reasoned, the court deferred to it and affirmed the judgment for the school district. *R.C. and D.C. v. Board of Educ. of Wappingers Cent. School Dist.*, 705 Fed.Appx. 29 (2d Cir. 2017).

◆ Due to a genetic disorder known as Prader-Willi Syndrome (PWS), a Colorado student developed hyperphagia – persistent extreme hunger and an inability to feel satisfied. He had a constant feeling of hunger and obsession with food to the point that he could not focus on anything else. Because even seeing or smelling food could cause extreme anxiety and could cause overeating to the point of injury and even death, the school district and parents included food security measures in his IEPs. The student was hospitalized several times for severe anxiety, aggression, obsessive-compulsive behavior and other symptoms. After being hospitalized, he remained out of school for the first half of what would have been his ninth-grade year. The parents rejected a public school IEP and filed a due process hearing request. They sought to hold the district responsible for their private school costs. After an administrative law judge held for the school district, the parents appealed to a federal court.

According to the parents, residential placement at a PWS-specific facility was necessary to provide adequate food security. They insisted upon "total food security" as suggested by one of their experts. But the IEP specified that the student have no unsupervised access to food, a planned and predictable menu, and no unnecessary food exposure. This was in line with the recommendations of professionals who worked with him during his last hospitalization. The court held the district showed awareness for food security and provided for it in the past. **District staff took actions to accommodate the student's needs.** During the IEP process, the parents made clear they would seek a hearing if their child was denied a residential placement. Finding no history of food security issues that prevented him from accessing his education prior to his hospitalization, the court held for the district. *Zachary G. v. School Dist. No. 1*, Civ. No. 15-cv-02399-RPM, 2016 WL 5815283 (D. Colo. 10/5/16).

◆ An Iowa student with Asperger's syndrome and obsessive-compulsive, mood and adjustment disorders was gifted academically. She ranked high in her class and participated in show choir, a school musical and volleyball. Her IEP specified a program for high-functioning students with autism spectrum disorder. During a family vacation, the student was raped by two men. Mental health providers recommended she return to a routine as quickly as possible.

An interim IEP was offered to maintain her IEP and ease her transition back to school. Due to the circumstances, both parents waived any objection to an IEP meeting in their absence. Finding it would be best to delay a comprehensive IEP review until fall, the rest of the team decided to retain the current IEP. When she returned to school, the student began to have social problems with peers. She falsely accused a male show choir member of holding a knife to her throat, slapped another member of the school musical and used foul language. After an audition near the end of the school year, the student was not selected for show choir. Her parent filed a civil rights action in a federal court, seeking an order to require the school district to place her child in the upper-tier show choir. A judge denied the request for relief. No evidence showed the show choir selection process had anything to do with a disability. At an IEP meeting held just before the onset of a new school year, the parent pushed for placing her child in the upper-tier choir. Staff meeting notes indicated she repeatedly conditioned her child's return to school on upper-tier choir participation. In her action, the parent sought tuition reimbursement for placing her child at a special school in Connecticut. An administrative law judge (ALJ) held for the district, as did a federal court. On appeal, the U.S. Court of Appeals, Eighth Circuit, found the parent had consented to an IEP meeting in her absence. It found the school district responded to the student's changed circumstances. While she suffered setbacks due to the rape, she made significant progress at school until being excluded from the show choir. Her progress continued at summer volleyball workouts, where she was getting along with her peers. **Although the parent claimed the student's emotional changes after the rape required more than minor changes to the IEP, the school did not find her behaviors were new.** In sum, the court held the district provided the student appropriate educational opportunities and did not deny her a free appropriate public education. *Sneitzer v. Iowa Dep't of Educ.*, 796 F.3d 942 (8th Cir. 2015).

◆ A New York child with an emotional disturbance had some oppositional issues but made progress in regular education classes. During her ninth-grade year, her academic performance began to decline, and her behavior became more problematic. After she was diagnosed with bipolar disorder and put on medication, she was arrested for shoplifting and placed in a diversion program that required her to receive mental health counseling. By the end of the student's ninth-grade year, she was failing most of her classes and had been disciplined 25 times. The student had to repeat grade nine and was ordered by a family court to undergo a 30-day psychiatric evaluation and a 10-day hospitalization. Soon after returning to her high school, the student tried to commit suicide. This led to another hospitalization and diagnosis of an unspecified mood disorder.

The district and parents then agreed to place the student in a program in which she received daily tutoring. A school psychologist evaluated her and found that "outside mental health factors appeared to be causing significant disruption" in her life. The school district held a CSE meeting but did not create an IEP. The parents said the student then collapsed into depression. They placed her in a therapeutic boarding school that used a 12-step program. While at the boarding school, the student met with a counselor and her grades improved. The parents kept her there for another year before seeking tuition assistance. The district denied their request, and the parents asked for a hearing. The IHO found the district had denied the student a free appropriate public education for two school years. But a review officer found little objective evidence to support this. When the case reached the U.S. Court of Appeals, Second Circuit, **it found the review officer had reasonably found there was insufficient evidence about the boarding school's instruction to support the parents' claim for tuition reimbursement**. As a result, the court held for the school district. *Hardison v. Board of Educ. of Oneonta City School Dist.*, 773 F.3d 372 (2d Cir. 2014).

◆ A Pennsylvania student functioned well academically but had many home behavior problems. She attended religious schools before making an apparent suicide attempt. After the student was hospitalized, her mother put her in a public school homebound program. A school psychologist evaluated her and found her eligible for special education with an "other health impairment." After another suicide attempt, the student was placed in an inpatient substance abuse rehabilitation center. Although the district offered to place her in a public school with full-time emotional support, the parent rejected the offer. She filed a due process complaint, placed her child in a residential 12-step treatment facility and sought tuition reimbursement. A hearing officer held for the school district, and the case reached a federal court. It noted the hearing officer had found the case "was really about the Parent's desire for a residential setting to address [the student's] drug addiction and out-of-control home behaviors." As the IEP called for specially designed instruction and services through a positive behavior support plan, full-time emotional support, counseling and social skills instruction, the court found it appropriate. **The parent's choice was a rational response to her child's drug addiction, but the court held it did not address her disability.** As the district was not responsible for treating drug addiction, family problems and delinquency, the court held for the district. *EK v. Warwick School Dist.*, Civil No. 09-4205, 2014 WL 737328 (E.D. Pa. 2/26/14).

CHAPTER FIVE

Changes in Placement and Student Discipline

I. CHANGES IN PLACEMENT

A. Generally

The IDEA requires a school district to provide parents prior written notice whenever it "(A) proposes to initiate or change; or (B) refuses to initiate or change, the identification, evaluation, or educational placement of the child, or the provision of a free appropriate public education to the child." See 20 U.S.C. § 1415(b)(3). This notice requirement also applies when a school district proposes graduating a student with a disability and awarding the student a regular education diploma. See 34 C.F.R. Part 300.122(a)(3)(iii). A hearing must be granted to parents wishing to contest a change in placement.

Many courts have held a change in schools is not a change in placement of a student with a disability. But in Melodee H. v. Dep't of Educ., State of Hawaii, *No. 07-000256 HG-LEK, 2008 WL 2051757 (D. Haw. 5/13/08), the court found the placement of a student in a large school where he felt unsafe could be emotionally, educationally and psychologically detrimental to him. Under the circumstances, the new school amounted to a change in his placement.*

◆   An eight-year-old Tennessee student with autism had aggressive behaviors that caused injuries to himself, classmates and teachers. A case management team found he should attend a therapeutic behavioral comprehensive development classroom (TBCDC). According to his parents, their child should remain in his placement with his current behavior intervention plan. They filed a due process complaint, challenging the district's proposal to move their son into a TBCDC. As a result of the filing, the school board was required by the IDEA stay-put provision to maintain his current placement pending the case outcome. After a hearing, but before an administrative law judge (ALJ) issued a final order, the parents withdrew the student from school and placed him privately. They asked the ALJ to dismiss their complaint. Instead, the ALJ relieved the board of maintaining the stay-put placement and permitted a 45-day TBCDC placement After a hearing on the remaining issues, the ALJ issued a final order for the board, finding the TBCDC was appropriate.

The parents appealed to a federal court, which explained that the IDEA stay-put provision mandates that a child must remain in his/her "then current educational placement pending the completion of an IDEA proceeding, absent an agreement by the parties. In the court's view, the stay-put rule protects students against unwanted classroom removals by schools, but "does not protect against consequences of improvident unilateral removal by their parents." According to the parents, their withdrawal of the student from the school system made the temporary placement decision moot. On the other hand, they argued their federal court complaint was not moot, as they wished to challenge the ALJ's decision that the board could temporarily avoid the stay-put requirement. The court found **the parents sought to circumvent IDEA procedural requirements by withdrawing the student from the school district**. By asking the ALJ not to enter a decision, they abandoned their complaint and made their claims moot. Rejecting the parents' arguments, the court held for the board. *L.D. v. Sumner County Schools*, 299 F.Supp.3d 901 (M.D. Tenn. 2018).

◆   A student who attended a New York City public high school for gifted and talented students had medical conditions including mononucleosis, Crohn's Disease, irritable bowel syndrome, convergence insufficiency, pediatric sleep apnea and chronic fatigue syndrome. Because of his frequent absences, he had many incomplete grades. The student's IEP specified five hours of weekly direct Special Education Teacher Support Services (SETSS) and 10 hours of indirect SETSS. After he filed a due process complaint, a hearing officer determined she would not consider his claims under Section 504 and the Americans with Disabilities Act. Later, the hearing officer issued an interim order confirming that the student's pendency placement would be the one described in his current IEP. The student then requested a preliminary order from a federal court.

Among other things, the student sought implementation of the pendency order, five hours of weekly 1:1 teacher services at a rate of at least $150 per hour and at-home private tutoring. The student sought the adjustment of grades, the removal of failing grades from his transcript and permission to make up certain assignments and exams. He sought guidance for his college applications, and a cover letter to colleges explaining the school's grading policy and certain grades on his transcript. The student sought a flexible school day for all classes and partial-day, home-based instruction when he was not well enough for school. He sought relief from an IEP provision requiring a parent or chaperone to be present for him to receive home instruction. **Agreeing with the school department, the court held the student failed to show his IEP was not being implemented.** The IEP did not specify that SETSS must be provided at his home. Some claims went beyond the student's current IEP. Others addressed the provision of a free appropriate public education and were within the hearing officer's authority. As the student's requests had to be addressed by the hearing officer, the court denied his request for a preliminary order. He would be allowed to renew his request if he showed an unjustifiable delay. *J.Z. v. New York City Dep't of Educ.*, 281 F.Supp.3d 352 (S.D.N.Y. 2017).

◆   A Kentucky child had autism and apraxia. A school admissions and release committee (ARC) placed him in a private school for one year. But the parents grew unhappy with the program and placed him at another private school. When the ARC reconvened, the parties could not agree on a placement. After going through mediation, the school district agreed to pay part of the parents' tuition and transportation costs. They agreed to discuss a transition plan for the child to return to a district school for the next year but then requested a due process hearing. In challenging the district's IEP proposal, the parents asked the hearing officer to deem the private school they had selected as their child's stay-put placement pending the outcome of the case. A hearing officer held the IEP would have denied the child a FAPE and the school selected by the parents would be the child's stay-put placement throughout the proceeding. As a result, the district was ordered to reimburse the parents for their private school costs.

A federal court held the child's operative placement was the parentally selected private school, and it ordered the district to reimburse the parents for it. On appeal, the U.S. Court of Appeals, Sixth Circuit, held **a school district is not required to pay for private education costs unless a court or hearing officer finds that a FAPE was denied**. An IDEA regulation at 34 C.F.R. Part 300.116 indicates that **a school district must approve of a placement decision in some manner to be subject to reimbursement**. Parents could not unilaterally decide which school was the child's stay-put placement. In this case, the last "agreed-upon" placement was the school from which the parents had removed the child before the mediated settlement. Since none of the parents' stay-put arguments had merit, the court denied reimbursement. *N.W. v. Boone County Board of Educ.*, 763 F.3d 611 (6th Cir. 2014).

B. Notice and Hearing

A Maryland school district did not violate the rights of a student with disabilities by increasing her time in special education without prior notice, according to the Fourth Circuit Court of Appeals. While the parents argued the change resulted in an overly segregated placement for their child, the court disagreed. It held the student's teacher did not improperly increase her hours in the segregated setting beyond the time specified in her IEP. While the court found this was an IDEA procedural violation, it found no resulting denial of FAPE. **A school must provide prior written notice to parents before changing**

a student's placement. But in this case, the court found the teacher's decision to provide more instruction in the segregated setting than her IEP specified was "reasonably calculated to enable her to make progress appropriate in light of her circumstances." The district held another IEP meeting to incorporate the changes in hours into the IEP. The parents attended this meeting and fully participated in it. The court found no merit to the parents' claim that the school denied their child a FAPE or violated their participation rights. In fact, their complaint said she was spending too much time in general education settings. The court found no significant infringement of the parents' rights in this case. Although they claimed the IEP was inadequate, the court upheld it under the analysis from *Endrew F. v. Douglas County School Dist. RE-1*, 137 S.Ct. 988 (U.S. 2017). *R.F. v. Cecil County Public Schools*, 919 F.3d 237 (4th Cir. 2019).

◆   A New Jersey school district placed a child with autism in a private school offering an intensive program of ABA therapy. After three years, the district sought to move him to a public school. The private school's director said the child was progressing, no longer needed intensive private school services and would benefit from a less restrictive setting. Based on the director's comments, the district recommended an in-district, special class for students with autism. This recommendation was incorporated into the IEP, but no school site was indicated. The parents filed a due process petition. After the parents visited their child's school assignment, they sought a stay-put order to preserve his private placement. An ALJ credited the private school director's testimony and held the IEP proposal would not deny the child a free appropriate public education (FAPE). In a federal district court action, the parents said the private school retaliated against them because they had invoked their stay-put rights to preserve his current placement. But the court held for the district. On appeal, the U.S. Court of Appeals, Third Circuit, held the school district provided the parents adequate written notice of the proposal to change the IEP.

Although the classroom was not identified in the district's notice, the IDEA only required a description of the general type of educational program, such as the type of classes, individualized attention and services to be provided. The court held the notice did not have to describe the "bricks and mortar" of a school. Next, the court held the IEP proposal offered the child a FAPE. A school district does not have to incorporate every program requested by the parents and does not have to describe the particular methodology in the IEP. As the IEP was reasonably calculated to provide the child with educational benefits, the court held for the school board. *M.A. v. Jersey City Board of Educ.*, 592 Fed. Appx. 124 (3d Cir. 2014).

◆   An Arkansas student with severe autism had low verbal and cognitive skills and great difficulty with personal interactions. He was often violent at school, and his IEPs called for self-contained special education classes with constant monitoring by staff. When he was 11, he punched a paraprofessional aide, causing her to lose consciousness and go to the hospital. After suspending the student for four days, the school moved up a scheduled IEP meeting five days. At the meeting, team members urged the parents to accept a homebound setting for the child. Instead, they withdrew him from school, requested a due process hearing and sought reimbursement for a private placement. A hearing officer found the school district provided inadequate notice of a change in placement, but denied reimbursement. A federal court held the change in agenda converted the meeting into a manifestation determination review without adequate and proper notice. But the parents had sufficient information to actively participate.

As the student was progressing, the court held the parents were not entitled to private school tuition reimbursement. On appeal, the U.S. Court of Appeals, Eighth Circuit, found the failure to provide proper notice of the meeting was a procedural error. But it found the error was mitigated, because the parents knew before the meeting that their child's behavior and the safety of staff would be discussed. The team did not make a placement decision before the meeting. And the parents had many chances to meet with staff to agree on a placement. Eighth Circuit cases held **neither the IDEA nor its regulations prohibit schools from coming to IEP meetings with tentative recommendations prepared in a parent's absence**. The court denied the parents' request for reimbursement. *W.K. v. Harrison School Dist.*, 509 Fed.Appx. 565 (8th Cir. 2013).

II. STAY-PUT PROVISION

A. Generally

The IDEA's stay-put provision, found at 20 U.S.C. Section 1415(j), was included in the IDEA to protect eligible children and their parents during due process proceedings. The stay-put provision states in relevant part: "during the pendency of any proceedings conducted pursuant to this section, unless the State or local educational agency and the parents otherwise agree, the child shall remain in the then-current educational placement of the child." A state hearing officer's decision is considered an "agreement" that binds the parties.

A child's "then-current educational placement" is "the operative placement actually functioning at the time the dispute first arises." If an IEP has been implemented, the placement specified in the IEP will be the one subject to the stay-put provision. But where the dispute arises before any IEP has been implemented, the "current educational placement" will be the operative placement under which the child is actually receiving instruction at the time the dispute arises. In A.D. v. State of Hawaii Dep't of Educ., 727 F.3d 911 (9th Cir. 2013), the Ninth Circuit held students have "an automatic right" to stay put. A stay-put placement remains the student's current educational placement from the time a due process complaint is filed until the case is resolved.

◆   A Connecticut child attended a private school at his school district's expense. His parent later grew dissatisfied with his progress and placed him in a private religious school outside the district that provided no special education. The parent paid the school's tuition while the district paid for related services. School officials discontinued the agreement at the end of the year and suggested placement in a public school in the district. But the parent rejected this and filed a due process complaint. A hearing officer held for the school board, finding the IEP offered a free appropriate public education (FAPE). The private school was found an inappropriate setting as it provided the child no special education.

The parent appealed to a federal court, which held the IEP offered the child a FAPE. But the court held the board violated the stay-put provision by refusing to fund the related services described in the IEP. Appeal reached the U.S. Court of Appeals, Second Circuit. Throughout the dispute, the student was a resident of the district and the board violated the IDEA by not offering him an IEP. **There was no merit to the board's argument that once a child was enrolled at a school outside the district, any IDEA obligations were terminated.** But the court refused to reverse the findings that the private religious school was an inappropriate placement. It offered no special education and did not modify its curriculum to accommodate the student. In the court's opinion, **the board violated the stay-put provision by discontinuing the provision of related services at the private school**. It held the stay-put provision applies to related services. As the parent argued, she was entitled to the full value of services which the board was required to fund from the time of the due process request until the end of the proceeding. *Doe v. East Lyme Board of Educ.*, 790 F.3d 440 (2d Cir. 2015).

After the case returned to the lower court, it held a trial, then ordered the board to reimburse the parent for $127,302.90 in expenses plus interest. The board had already paid her $97,445. A transportation reimbursement amount was also due the parent, making her total award $36,556, plus interest to be determined by the court. Next, the board was ordered to place $203,478 into an escrow account for the student as a compensatory education award equivalent to the value of related services that were never provided. The parent appealed to the Second Circuit, which found the lower court had yet to complete its calculation of damages. As there was no final judgment, the appeal was dismissed. *Doe v. East Lyme Board of Educ.*, 747 Fed.Appx. 30 (2d Cir. 2019).

◆   Illinois parents disagreed with the placement of their son in a segregated program for grade one. His school wanted to place him in a social-emotional learning foundations (SELF) program with a behavioral intervention plan (BIP). Because the parents rejected the SELF program, the student continued school in his general education setting, where he struggled with the new BIP.

At an end-of-school-year IEP meeting, district members of the IEP team again recommended the SELF program and placed him there for grade one, over the parents' objections. The SELF program was housed in a different school located in another school district. Arguing the SELF program was overly restrictive for their child, the parents obtained a stay-put order to preserve his current placement, pending resolution of the case. As a result of the stay-put order, the student was never moved to the SELF program. Later, a hearing officer upheld the district's proposed IEP. A federal court then affirmed the hearing officer's decision. The parents appealed to the Seventh Circuit Court of Appeals, which noted that the parties agreed to a new IEP for the student for grade three that did not involve the SELF program. As a result, the dispute over his grade-one IEP became moot. The court held the parents could not pursue the present case to insulate themselves from a future proposal for a SELF placement. **Nor could they claim their qualification for stay-put relief amounted to an enforceable judgment or settlement in their favor.** According to the court, the chance that the district would revive its proposal for a SELF program placement was not enough to allow this case to proceed. Nor could the case proceed to simply advise the parties which side was correct about an outdated IEP. Since they relied on speculation regarding a new SELF placement at some time in the future, the court found the case to be moot. *Ostby v. Manhattan School Dist. No. 114*, 851 F.3d 677 (7th Cir. 2017).

◆   Colorado parents used the state's school choice law to enroll their child in a charter school. But staff members determined that the IEP devised by the school district (of which the charter school was a part) was inadequate for him. Although the student's IEP listed the charter school as his school of attendance, staff advised the parents that he would not be readmitted the next school year because the school could not implement his IEP. The parents filed a due process complaint against the school district, charging it with IDEA violations. An ALJ denied their request to enroll the child at the charter school, since they did not show the district could not implement the IEP. In a federal court, the child's mother sought an order under the IDEA stay-put provision that would require the school district to fund a private placement pending the outcome of the proceeding.

The court granted an order requiring the charter school to enroll the child and keep him there throughout any appeal, limited to 90 days. But the court denied the mother's request for public funding of a private placement under the stay-put provision. When the case came before the Tenth Circuit, it observed that while the student was not attending the charter school at the time of the hearing, the school was listed in his current IEP as his school of attendance. Although the mother argued her child would be properly placed at a private school, the court held this would not comply with the stay-put provision. **Since the lower court correctly identified the charter school as the student's stay-put placement, the court held the school district was not required to fund a private placement.** *Smith v. Cheyenne Mountain School Dist. 12*, 652 Fed. Appx. 697 (10th Cir. 2016).

◆   A Maryland student with Down syndrome completed eighth grade at a charter school. Her IEP team prepared a plan for her entry into high school. Although school district officials were invited into the IEP process, no representative from the district attended. As a result, the IEP was crafted by charter school staff members and the parents. Later, the school district rejected a private placement recommended by the team. The parents disagreed with the district's proposal and placed their child in a private school. After mediation, the parties agreed that the child would attend the private school for the rest of the year at the district's expense. Near the end of the school year, the school district determined the child should be removed from the diploma track and placed in a certificate program. The parents requested a due process hearing. An ALJ found the child was entitled to remain at the private school pending resolution of the case. But the district refused to pay her tuition. In response, the parents filed a federal case. The court granted their request for a preliminary order.

While an appeal to the Fourth Circuit was pending, the ALJ held the parents did not prove the IEP was inadequate. A school district official wrote to the parents that the child would be reassigned. Days later, a bus was sent to take the child to a district school. According to the parents, the district approved an IEP on the same day. They asked the court for an order to maintain the private placement. In addition to asserting IDEA violations, they included Rehabilitation Act and Americans with Disabilities Act (ADA) claims. The court held the parents could pursue their discrimination claims against the district based on "blatant disregard" of the stay-put order. **Since the ALJ found the private school was the child's stay-put placement, the school district had to fund the placement for the duration of the case.** There is no personal liability under Section 504 or the ADA, so claims against the staff members were dismissed. *A.B. v. Baltimore City Board of School Commissioners*, Civ. No. WMN-14-3851, 2015 WL 4875998 (D. Md. 8/13/15).

◆ Pennsylvania parents withdrew their child from her public school and placed her in a private setting. A hearing officer held the school district denied the child a FAPE. Compensatory education was awarded to the parents for part of their child's first-grade year and all of grade two. The district was ordered to reimburse some of their tuition and transportation costs. A federal court reversed the hearing officer's decision. It held the district's IEP proposal would have offered a FAPE. Later, the U.S. Court of Appeals, Third Circuit, affirmed the judgment in *Ridley School Dist. v. M.R.*, 680 F.3d 260 (3d Cir. 2012).

The parents sought reimbursement for their costs under the stay-put provision. After the school district denied the request, they filed a new federal case, claiming funding of the private placement until the conclusion of the prior lawsuit. The court agreed and awarded them $57,658. On appeal, the Third Circuit explained that **the stay-put provision acts as an automatic preliminary injunction, fixing a child's "then-current educational placement" as the status quo for the duration of an IDEA proceeding**. When a hearing officer holds for parents, a school district has to fund the private stay-put placement. Despite the district's success on appeal, the private school remained the child's stay-put placement. *M.R. v. Ridley School Dist.*, 744 F.3d 112 (3d Cir. 2014).

B. Settlements and Administrative Cases

IDEA stay-put language at 20 U.S.C. Section 1415(j) declares that a child is to remain in the "then-current educational placement" during the pendency of any IDEA proceeding, unless the parents and educational agency otherwise agree. A state hearing officer's decision changing a placement is deemed an "agreement" of the parties under the stay-put provision. When a hearing officer holds for the parents, a school district must fund the private stay-put placement. As the Supreme Court has held, the stay-put provision reflects a Congressional policy choice that all students with disabilities are to remain in their placements during IDEA disputes, regardless of the merits of their cases.

◆ A Rhode Island parent requested a due process hearing in an effort to obtain a private school placement for her disabled son. She also sought eight new evaluations of him. In return for dismissal of the action, the school committee agreed to pay for private school tuition and to perform four evaluations. The settlement recited that the parent relinquished any right to the other evaluations.

After the parties reached the agreement, the school committee conducted the required evaluations. But a month after the student enrolled at the private school, the parent requested 10 more evaluations. The school committee filed a new request for a hearing. A hearing officer found some of the evaluations done by the school committee were inappropriate. The school committee was ordered to pay for an occupational therapy evaluation and a psychoeducational evaluation. In response, the committee filed a federal court action.

The court held the settlement agreement released the committee from the claim to a new psychoeducational evaluation. On appeal, the U.S. Court of Appeals, First Circuit, found evidence that some of the assessments were adequate. The school committee did not agree to a psychoeducational evaluation. Moreover, **the parent had given up her right to seek evaluations beyond the four specified in the agreement**. Although a change in circumstances would have allowed her to obtain a new evaluation, she did not argue there had been any changed conditions. But the school committee did not challenge a finding by the hearing officer that the educational evaluation had been inappropriate. *South Kingstown School Committee v. Joanna S.*, 773 F.3d 344 (1st Cir. 2014).

◆   A Colorado student with learning disabilities, anxiety and attention deficit hyperactivity disorder had trouble with class sizes and the pace of instruction as she transitioned to middle school. In grade seven, she failed her classes and was bullied and teased by classmates. Her parents placed her in a private academy for students with learning difficulties. They reached a settlement agreement with the school district by assuming "full responsibility for her education." In return, the district paid the parents $16,681 and required them to notify the district whether or not they intended to return their child to a public school for the 2012-13 school year. If they did so, the parties agreed to develop an IEP.

The parents further agreed that the private school would not be deemed the student's stay-put placement in the event of an IEP dispute. Near the end of the school year, the parents asked to renew the settlement for the 2012-13 school year. The district refused and proposed an IEP for a public high school. After rejecting the IEP, the parents returned the child to the private academy. An ALJ held for the parents, finding the district did not assess the student in all areas of suspected disability and denied her a free appropriate public education. They then asked a federal court to order the district to pay their private placement costs from the date of the ALJ's decision. The court held the ALJ's decision shifted the stay-put placement to the private academy. Under 34 C.F.R. Part 300.518(d), **an administrative decision is an "agreement" between the parties to change a student's placement**. The court rejected a claim that the agreement governed a stay-put placement even after the ALJ's decision. *Taylor F. v. Arapahoe County School Dist. 5*, 954 F.Supp.2d 1197 (D. Colo. 2013).

◆   The mother of a Hawaii student with autism placed him in a private school for one year under a settlement agreement with the department of education, agreeing to allow the department to observe him at the private school and to transition him to public school the following year, "if appropriate." She placed limitations on observation and did not attend an IEP meeting, so the department finalized an IEP without her that placed the student in a public school. She kept her son in the private school for several years and then sued for tuition reimbursement, claiming that it was the stay-put placement under the IDEA. A federal district court and later, the Ninth Circuit disagreed. **The court held the settlement agreement was only for the one school year, and the IEPs offered by the department were valid.** *K.D. v. Dep't of Educ., State of Hawaii*, 665 F.3d 1110 (9th Cir. 2011).

C. Transfers and Grade Transitions

An IDEA provision at 20 U.S.C. § 1414(d)(2)(C)(i)(l) governs cases where a child with a disability transfers between school districts during the same school year. If a child transfers into a new school district with an IEP from another school district, the receiving district is required to provide the child a free appropriate public education. This includes "services comparable to those described in the previously held IEP, in consultation with the parents until such time as the [district] adopts the previously held IEP or develops, adopts and implements a new IEP that is consistent with Federal and State Law."

In Johnson v. Special Educ. Hearing Office, *287 F.3d 1176 (9th Cir. 2002), the Ninth Circuit stated the change in responsibility for an autistic student's education from an individualized family service plan (IFSP) to an IEP necessarily changed the status quo of a student placement.* **When a student transfers from one public agency to another, the receiving agency is required only to provide a program that conforms to the last agreed-upon placement.**

The term "then-current educational placement" is undefined in the law, but the Ninth Circuit has held the term refers to the setting in which a student is enrolled at the time the parents request a due process hearing. This is the placement set forth in the student's last implemented IEP. **During a summer break, it is artificial to refer to any "then-current placement," since "literally, there is none."** *N.E. v. Seattle School Dist., 842 F.3d 1093 (9th Cir. 2016).*

◆   Hawaii parents of a child with Trisomy 21 and other medical issues sought to preserve his placement when they moved to a different school district. After a hearing officer and a federal court held the IEP could be implemented by the new school district, the U.S. Court of Appeals, Ninth Circuit, affirmed the decision. It held that **a change in location alone is not a "change in placement" under the IDEA's stay-put provision.** The IDEA's stay-put rule requires that a student remain in the "then-current educational placement" while an IDEA proceeding is pending. **Courts have interpreted the term "then-current educational placement" to mean the one described in the student's last implemented IEP.** While the parents argued the transfer district failed to provide an appropriate prior written notice of the placement, the court instead found the district provided prior written notice. They were also notified of the changes by phone and in a meeting.

Last, the court found no evidence that the parents were denied meaningful participation in IEP meetings or that their son's placement had been predetermined. It appeared that the decision to move the student to a school in the transfer district was based on several factors, including the need to decrease extended transportation time and the possibility of a medical emergency during a long bus ride. As there was no error by the lower court in finding the school could accommodate the student's IEP, the court affirmed the judgment. *Oliver v. State of Hawaii Dep't of Educ.*, 762 Fed.Appx. 413 (9th Cir. 2019).

◆   A Washington student spent most of his instructional time in general education settings until he began to have serious behavioral problems in grade three. Bellevue School District (BSD) proposed a two-stage IEP for him. Stage one specified that the student finish the 2014-15 school year in an "individual class" in which he was the only student with his teacher and a paraeducator. Stage two would begin on the first day of the 2015-16 school year in a self-contained BSD classroom. After the end of the 2014-15 school year, the family moved to Seattle, where the parents enrolled their child in the Seattle School District (SSD). They requested a placement for him in an individual classroom like the one provided by BSD in stage one of his 2014-15 IEP. SSD officials instead proposed a self-contained classroom for the student resembling stage two of his 2014-15 BSD IEP. The parents filed a due process complaint, seeking stay-put relief. An administrative law judge (ALJ) held the self-contained classroom specified in stage two of the IEP would be the student's stay-put placement pending the outcome of the case. The parents asked a federal court for a temporary restraining order to prohibit SSD from placing their son in a self-contained classroom under the stay-put order. The court denied the parents' request and they appealed to the U.S. Court of Appeals, Ninth Circuit.

The court held that **during the pendency of any IDEA proceeding, a child is to remain in the "then-current educational placement" unless the parents and state or local educational agency otherwise agree**. It held the IEP drafted by BSD described the student's then-current placement. As a result, the court held for SSD. *N.E. v. Seattle School Dist.*, 842 F.3d 1093 (9th Cir. 2016).

The case returned to the trial court, which noted the relevant school year was over. The parents argued that an actual controversy still existed. They also appealed the Ninth Circuit's decision to the Supreme Court. In order to bring their appeal, the parents had stipulated to the dismissal of their due process complaint before the ALJ. Noting that the underlying due process complaint had been dismissed, the trial court found the case was moot, notwithstanding claims for tuition reimbursement and the pending Supreme Court appeal. As the parents no longer had a live claim, the court held the case was moot and it denied their request for reconsideration. *N.E. v. Seattle School Dist.*, No. C15-1659JLR, 2017 WL 2806801 (W.D. Wash. 6/29/17, 9th Cir. appeal filed, 7/28/17).

Later, the Supreme Court refused to review the Ninth Circuit's decision that a transfer student cannot use the stay-put rule to preserve a placement from an IEP drafted by another school district pertaining to a prior school year. The appeal to the Ninth Circuit was then voluntarily dismissed. *N.E. v. Seattle School Dist.*, No. 16-1285, 138 S.Ct. 69 (U.S. cert. denied 10/2/17).

◆   The parents of a New Jersey student with learning disabilities agreed with Westwood Regional School District on an IEP placing him in a private school. But before the school year, the parents moved into the Byram School District. Byram officials reviewed the IEP and decided the student's program could be implemented within the district. After mediation failed, the parents initiated an

IDEA due process proceeding. An administrative law judge (ALJ) denied their request to approve the private placement under the IDEA stay-put provision.

A federal court agreed with the ALJ. On appeal, the U.S. Court of Appeals, Third Circuit, found **the stay-put provision preserves the educational status quo during the pendency of an IDEA proceeding**. Unless agreed otherwise, a child must remain in his "then-current educational placement" for the duration of a due process proceeding. In the court's view, the case did not implicate the stay-put provision, because the parents had acted unilaterally. If a child transfers to a new school district with an IEP from a different school district, the receiving district is required to provide the child a free appropriate public education. In *Michael C. v. Radnor Township School Dist.*, 202 F.3d 642 (3d Cir. 2002), the court held that in the context of interstate transfers, unilateral family relocations can override the stay-put provision. Stay-put protections are "inoperative" until a new placement is agreed upon. In this case, the court held the parent's choice to move to Byram made the stay-put provision inoperative. Byram could meet its IDEA obligations by complying with 20 U.S.C. § 1414(d) (2)(C)(i)(l), which governs cases where a child transfers during a school year. Byram offered services comparable to those stated in the Westwood IEP, complying with the IDEA. Both the ALJ and the lower court noted the parents' refusal to cooperate with Byram over any placement beside the private school described in the Westwood IEP. As a result, the court held for Byram. *J.F. v. Byram Township Board of Educ.*, 629 Fed.Appx. 235 (3d Cir. 2015).

◆   Hawaii education department officials proposed moving a student with autism to a public school after he had attended a private school for 10 years with state funding. It was recommended that he prepare for post-high school goals and obtain a diploma. The parents disagreed with the IEP and refused to participate in transfer meetings to discuss a move to a public school setting. The dispute came before a hearings officer who found the IEP did not deny the student an appropriate education as it had accurate goals, objectives and baseline data. The parents appealed to a federal court, which held they did not show the IEP lacked baseline information or had goals that were insufficient.

The hearings officer had correctly found the IEP goals and objectives were measurable. **While placements must be in the least restrictive setting, this must also "be the least restrictive environment which also meets the child's IEP goals."** The court found no evidence of predetermination. It instead found the department had investigated and addressed the concerns of the parents. It was appropriate to await the development of a transition plan until after the IEP meeting took place and the IEP was completed. As a result, the court held for the department of education. *Anthony C. v. Dep't of Educ., State of Hawaii*, No. 12-00698 DKW-BMK, 2014 WL 587848 (D. Haw. 2/14/14).

◆   A Wisconsin ninth-grader attended a multi-categorical classroom in which she studied a core academic curriculum with modifications. Late in the school year, the district determined it could not meet her special education needs in a multi-categorical setting. It proposed a self-contained classroom aligned to extended grade-band standards at a different school. Because of the functional and non-grade-level standards associated with the self-contained classroom, most of the classes in the setting were ineligible for credit toward graduation.

The parents requested a due process hearing and obtained a stay-put order pending review. An administrative law judge (ALJ) held for the school district, and the student remained in her school pending appeal to a federal court. Over a year later, the court upheld the decision to place the student in self-contained classes at the transfer high school. A federal court lifted the stay-put order and the U.S. Court of Appeals, Seventh Circuit, affirmed the decision. But on the first day of the next school year, the parents returned their child to the school at which she attended multi-categorical classes. After a few weeks, she began to attend the transfer high school. Her parents sought a new order, arguing they were not informed about the transfer to the new school. The ALJ held they had been informed of the transfer, and the case returned to federal court. This time, the parents argued their child was placed in an unsafe classroom made up of boys with behavioral disabilities. **The court upheld the ALJ's decision for the school district, finding a placement with students who had minor behavioral problems could still be found adequate.** *Williams v. Milwaukee Public Schools*, No. 13-C-207, 2014 WL 7156830 (E.D. Wis. 12/12/14).

D. Other Stay-Put Issues

When a hearing officer issues a decision approving of a private parental placement, the private school becomes the "stay-put" placement by an "agreement" of the parties. In such cases, the school district is required to fund the private stay-put placement through the duration of the proceeding. The stay-put provision intends to ensure educational stability until a placement dispute is resolved, regardless of the merits of a claim.

A Michigan court held the filing of a juvenile petition was not a change in placement under the IDEA. Since the student was never suspended for more than 10 days, he was not entitled to a manifestation determination hearing. In re Nicholas Papadelis, *No. 291536, 2010 WL 3447892 (Mich. Ct. App. 9/2/10).*

◆   A federal court held an Alaska student will remain in a residential placement at his school district's expense despite the passing of the final date for the placement set in a hearing officer's stay-put order. When the specified date passed, the district refused to continue funding the placement. The court explained that the stay-put provision requires that a student remain in the "current educational placement" pending the result of an IDEA proceeding. The student would stay at the residential school as the case continued, notwithstanding the passing of the final date. While the hearing officer clearly contemplated a transition of the student back to his school district of residence, the court found no decision to create a multi-stage IEP ending on a specific date.

The school district appealed to the Ninth Circuit, which found no error in the lower court's decision to maintain the stay-put placement beyond the deadline set by the hearing officer. Under the IDEA's stay-put rule, the student was entitled to remain in his then-current educational placement until the resolution of his IDEA claim. **Because the hearing officer confirmed that the residential placement was appropriate, the school was the student's**

current educational placement for stay-put purposes. The court affirmed the judgment requiring the district to maintain the placement pending further proceedings, even though the funding timeline set by the hearing officer had expired. *Anchorage School Dist. v. M.G.*, 738 Fed.Appx. 441 (9th Cir. 2018).

◆   The parent of a District of Columbia student who had never attended public schools and had no IEP filed a due process case against the District of Columbia Public Schools (DCPS). After a hearing, a hearing officer found the DCPS had denied the student a free appropriate public education by refusing to provide an IEP despite finding her eligible for special education. The hearing officer also found the private school placement made by the parent was proper. As a result, the DCPS was ordered to "place and fund the Student" at the private school for the rest of the 2012-13 school year. Although the DCPS funded the placement for the rest of the 2012-13 school year, it refused to develop an IEP.

The parent asked a federal court for a preliminary order to retroactively fund the private placement until the completion of the proceeding. As the student showed an IDEA proceeding was pending, the court held the stay-put rule applied. Next, the court rejected the DCPS's assertion that in the absence of an IEP, the student had "no educational placement to be maintained." **Nothing in the IDEA indicates an "educational placement" is limited to the placement identified in an IEP.** Instead, the court held the provision expressed the intent to preserve the status quo at the time a dispute first arises. Where no IEP had been prepared or implemented, the court found a child's current placement was the place where the child was actually receiving instruction when the dispute arose. Failure by the DCPS to maintain the placement ordered by the hearing officer (by denying funds) was grounds for stay-put relief. *District of Columbia v. Oliver*, 991 F.Supp.2d 209 (D.D.C. 2013).

◆   In *A.D. v. State of Hawaii Dep't of Educ.*, 727 F.3d 911 (9th Cir. 2013), the U.S. Court of Appeals, Ninth Circuit, explained that **the stay-put provision functions as an automatic preliminary order by prohibiting changes to a child's educational placement pending resolution of a case.**

III. STUDENT DISCIPLINE

A. Generally

If a school seeks a change in placement that would exceed 10 school days and the behavior that gave rise to the violation is determined not to be a manifestation of the child's disability, the disciplinary procedures applicable to children without disabilities may be applied to the child in the same manner and for the same duration in which the procedures would be applied to children without disabilities, so long as this does not deny the student a free appropriate public education. Children with disabilities who are removed from their placements for disciplinary reasons must continue to receive educational services to enable their participation in the general education curriculum, although in another setting, and to progress toward meeting their IEP goals.

Such students must receive appropriate functional behavioral assessments, behavioral intervention services and modifications to address the violation.

An IDEA provision found at 20 U.S.C. Section 1415(k) allows schools to consider any unique circumstances on a case-by-case basis when determining whether to change the placement of a child with a disability who violates a code of student conduct. Schools may place a child with a disability who violates a code of student conduct in an appropriate interim alternative educational setting, another setting, or suspension, for not more than 10 school days, if such alternatives apply to children without disabilities. Schools may remove a student to an interim educational setting for up to 45 days if a child carries or possesses a weapon at school, knowingly possesses or uses illegal drugs (or sells or solicits the sale of a controlled substance) at school, or inflicts serious bodily injury upon another person while at school.

A recent amendment to Virginia law states that except as provided otherwise, no student in preschool through grade three shall be suspended for more than three school days or expelled from attendance at school, unless (i) the offense involves physical harm or a credible threat of physical harm to others; or (ii) the local school board or the division superintendent or his/her designee finds that aggravating circumstances exist. Virginia Regular Session, Ch. 585, S.B. 170. Code of Virginia, § § 22.1–277.

In Olu-Cole v. E.L. Haynes Public Charter SC, this chapter, a federal court explained that under 34 C.F.R. Part 300.530(g), special circumstances allow the removal of a student to an interim alternative educational setting for not more than 45 days. According to the court, **a hearing officer may order a change of placement for a 45-day period, which may be renewed.** *Olu-Cole v. E.L. Haynes Public Charter SC, 292 F.Supp.3d 413 (D.D.C. 2018).*

◆ A Missouri high school student with autism spectrum disorder, Tourette syndrome, emotional disturbance, major depression, obsessive-compulsive disorder and ADHD had an IEP addressing his medical and educational needs. After an unspecified incident, he was suspended for 10 days. IEP team members held a manifestation determination hearing. According to the team, the student's conduct manifested his disability. **Under the IDEA, the team's conclusion indicated that the student should be readmitted to school or have modifications to his behavior plan.** But the local school superintendent instead notified him by letter that he was being suspended for 180 days.

The parent filed a due process challenge to the imposition of this exclusion. Later, the parties reached a private agreement, and the case was dismissed. But the parent filed suit against the county and local school district and the superintendent. She included claims under the IDEA and Constitution, and added discrimination claims under the Americans with Disabilities Act (ADA) and Section 504 of the Rehabilitation Act. Finding the parent failed to exhaust her administrative remedies as required by the IDEA, the court dismissed the case. Appeal reached the U.S. Court of Appeals, Eighth Circuit, which found the complaint implicated the denial of a free appropriate public education (FAPE). As the Supreme Court held in *Fry v. Napoleon Community Schools*, 137 S.Ct. 743 (2017), **the prior pursuit of IDEA remedies may provide strong evidence that a claim implicates the denial of a FAPE.** In this case, the parent acknowledged that her due process complaint concerned the denial of a FAPE for her son. She had resolved the case with both school districts prior to filing suit. Rejecting the parent's additional arguments for not applying the exhaustion rule, the court affirmed the judgment for the districts and superintendent. *Smith v. Rockwood R-VI School Dist.*, 895 F.3d 566 (8th Cir. 2018).

◆ *Honig v. Doe* is a U.S. Supreme Court case interpreting IDEA disciplinary procedures. The case involved two emotionally disturbed children in California who were given five-day suspensions from school for misbehavior that included destroying school property and assaulting other students. Pursuant to state law, the suspensions were continued indefinitely during expulsion proceedings. The students argued that the suspensions violated the stay-put provision, which provides that students must be kept in the "then current" educational placement during proceedings to change placement. The case reached the U.S. Supreme Court, which declared that the purpose of the stay-put provision is to prevent schools from changing a child's educational placement over a parent's objection until all review proceedings are complete. While the IDEA provided for interim placements where parents and school officials were able to agree on one, no emergency exception existed for dangerous students.

However, **where a disabled student poses an immediate threat to the safety of others, school officials may temporarily suspend him or her for up to 10 school days**. This ensures that school officials can protect others by removing dangerous students, seek a review of the student's placement and try to persuade the student's parents to agree to an interim placement, and seek court rulings to exclude students whose parents adamantly refuse to permit any change in placement. Schools may seek a court order without exhausting IDEA administrative remedies "only by showing that maintaining the child in his or her current placement is substantially likely to result in injury either to himself or herself, or to others." Indefinite suspensions violated the stay-put provision. Suspensions up to 10 days do not constitute a change in placement. In addition, **a school may use "its normal procedures for dealing with children who are endangering themselves or others," such as "timeouts, detention, the restriction of privileges," or suspension**. And states could be required to provide services directly to disabled students where a school district failed to do so. *Honig v. Doe*, 484 U.S. 305, 108 S.Ct. 592, 98 L.Ed.2d 686 (1988).

◆ A Janesville (Wisconsin) student was expelled after a hearing. His mother unsuccessfully tried to enroll him in the Oregon School District. Oregon relied on a state law permitting a school district to deny enrollment to a student who is subject to expulsion by another district. Later, the student's mother sued the Oregon School District, asserting the violation of her son's state constitutional right to public education. She also claimed Oregon violated his right to due process by failing to offer notice or a hearing prior to the decision denying his enrollment application. Oregon began providing the student special education services. The court then held for the district, and the parent appealed to the state court of appeals. While the parent argued the student was entitled to a hearing before being denied enrollment, the court noted she was not challenging the expulsion by Janesville. For this reason, any claim to a hearing was forfeited. The student had received notification of his possible expulsion and a hearing by Janesville. At the time he sought enrollment in Oregon, he was subject to a pending expulsion order by Janesville.

A district could undisputedly expel a student for violating rules. The parent claimed "expulsion" meant the "exclusion of a student from a physical school while still being required to provide alternative educational services." But the court found the state department of public instruction has long held **a school district has no responsibility for providing an education to an expelled student**. There was no state law responsibility to provide services in expulsion cases, and no requirement for a separate notice and hearing. As state law did not require a district to enroll an expelled student while an order of expulsion was in effect in another district, the court held for the Oregon school district. *Patricia L. v. Oregon School Dist.*, 354 Wis.2d 323 (Table) (Wis. Ct. App. 2014).

B. Manifestation Determinations

The IDEA manifestation determination requirement, found at 20 U.S.C. Section 1415(k)(E), states that within 10 school days of any decision to change an eligible student's placement based on discipline, the educational agency, parent and relevant members of the IEP team (as determined by the parent and educational agency) must review all relevant information in the student's file, including the IEP, teacher observations, and any relevant information provided by the parents, to determine if the conduct in question was caused by or had a direct, substantial relationship to the child's disability or was the direct result of the agency's failure to implement the IEP. If the local educational agency, the parent, and relevant members of the IEP team determine that either the conduct in question was caused by or had a direct, substantial relationship to the child's disability, or was the direct result of the agency's failure to implement the IEP, the conduct will be determined to be a manifestation of the child's disability. If a child's conduct was a manifestation of a disability, the IEP team must conduct a functional behavioral assessment and implement a behavioral intervention plan. If the child already had a behavioral intervention plan, the team is to review and modify it, as necessary, to address the behavior. In the absence of special circumstances, the student must then return to the placement from which he or she was removed, unless the parent and the local educational agency agree as part of the modification of the behavioral intervention plan.

◆   A Colorado student with ADHD and an impulse control disorder was taken off an IEP in middle school. He said peers bullied him but nothing was done to stop it. When the student threatened to "shoot up the school," the school held an expulsion hearing. He claimed there was no manifestation determination as required by federal regulations. Although the school later held a manifestation hearing, the student claimed the school district held an expulsion hearing (without providing proper notice) and expelled him. His parents filed a complaint that led to an investigation and a voluntary resolution agreement. The district agreed to monitoring and an investigation by a federal agency. As part of the settlement, the district agreed to hold another expulsion hearing. But after a hearing, it again decided to expel the student. His parents sued the district in a federal court for violating the IDEA, Rehabilitation Act Section 504 and the ADA.

The student claimed the district failed to protect him from disability-based bullying and wrongfully expelled him based on his disabilities. The court dismissed the case, finding the family failed to first file a due process hearing request. On appeal, the Tenth Circuit Court of Appeals held that if a party seeks relief under the ADA, Section 504 or other federal laws that is available under the IDEA, he or she must first exhaust IDEA administrative remedies. **While the parents claimed the agency complaint and voluntary resolution agreement satisfied the exhaustion requirement, the court found these actions did not meet IDEA requirements.** *A.P., IV v. Lewis Palmer School Dist. No. 38*, 728 Fed.Appx. 835 (10th Cir. 2018).

◆   A District of Columbia student went before the disciplinary committee of his charter school for a marijuana offense. After a hearing, the committee expelled him. A manifestation determination review was then held at which the entire team – including his mother – agreed that his behavior was not a manifestation of a disability. As required by law, the student was placed in an interim alternative education setting for the rest of the school year. Although the school board granted another appeal, it affirmed the expulsion decision. The mother then filed a due process complaint to challenge the interim placement. A hearing officer agreed with her arguments and ordered a new placement for the student in a private special education day school. As a new school year approached, the mother sought to re-enroll the student in the charter school. When she was turned down, she filed another due process complaint. This time, a hearing officer held the charter school was not prohibited from barring the student based on his expulsion the prior year. The student appealed to a federal court, which held the charter school did not violate the IDEA by disallowing his re-enrollment. **Because the student's behavior was not a manifestation of a disability, the school could discipline him in the same way as any other student.**

The court rejected the student's argument that the school had an obligation to re-enroll or place him during the school year after his expulsion. Because he had learning and emotional disabilities, the school had to provide an interim alternative placement for the rest of the school year in which he was expelled. But the school complied with this requirement and it was not obligated to assist in his current placement efforts. Federal regulations at 34 C.F.R. Part 300.530(b) and (d)(4) refer to a school's duty to provide access to education during the same school year in which the discipline occurs, not in a later school year. There was no Section 504 violation, as the student was unable to show bad faith or gross misjudgment by the school officials. The court rejected his constitutional claims, finding he had no constitutional right to multiple hearings and no right to the preservation of the evidence that he had possessed marijuana. As a result, the court dismissed the case. *D.P. v. Washington Leadership Academy Public Charter School*, No. CV 18-2868, 2019 WL 1317235 (D.D.C. 3/22/19).

◆   A Minnesota student had diagnoses indicating attention deficit hyperactivity disorder, a major depressive disorder and post-traumatic stress disorder. His Section 504 plan addressed his lack of confidence in academics and struggles with self-advocacy and organization. Another student at his school discovered racist graffiti written in whiteout in a school lavatory stall. Students publicized this through social media, "causing significant tension." School staff members reported being "fully occupied responding to distraught and concerned students." They described receiving "an avalanche of calls" about the graffiti, including at least 20 media inquiries. After an investigation identified the student as the suspected graffiti writer, the school held a manifestation determination. Following its review, a school team determined his behavior was not a manifestation of his disabilities. Although options to avoid expulsion were discussed, the parents rejected them and challenged the finding of misconduct.

After an expulsion hearing, a hearing officer recommended expelling the student for 12 months. The school board upheld the recommendation, and the parents sued the school district in a federal court. In rejecting their arguments, **the court explained that federal regulations permit a manifestation determination hearing as one way to provide a Section 504 hearing**. Further, the court rejected an argument by the parents that the district had to reevaluate their child prior to initiating discipline. They claimed Section 504 requires a reevaluation for any "significant change in placement." **The court held that IDEA procedures allow schools to discipline students with disabilities in the same manner as non-disabled students, if the behavior at issue is not a manifestation of a disability.** Ruling that the district properly found the student's misconduct was unrelated to his learning disability, the court held there was no need to fully reevaluate him under Section 504. *Doe v. Osseo Area School Dist., ISD No. 279*, 296 F.Supp.3d 1090 (D. Minn. 2017).

◆ An Ohio student did not have to await a result in a due process challenge to his school's denial of a manifestation determination before pursuing a separate challenge to the decision to expel him from his high school. After a disciplinary incident, the school expelled the student without holding a manifestation determination. His parents filed a due process hearing complaint, while separately appealing the expulsion to the state board of education. While the due process complaint was pending, the board affirmed the expulsion. In response, the parents appealed to an Ohio county court. After the expulsion case was dismissed, appeal reached the Court of Appeals of Ohio. It held **the parents did not have to wait until the due process matter concluded before appealing the expulsion decision**. *P.D. v. Copley-Fairlawn City School Dist.*, No. 28436, 2017 -Ohio- 9132 (Ohio Ct. App. 12/20/17).

◆ A California high school student with ADHD had a verbal confrontation with a classmate. His school suspended him and moved for expulsion. An assessment was completed to consider whether his conduct was caused by or had a direct and substantial relationship to his ADHD. Finding no such relationship, the assessor found the conduct was not a manifestation of the student's disability. The parents requested a Section 504 hearing under the school district's policies and procedures. A hearing officer upheld the district's manifestation determination, finding the conduct was neither caused by nor had a direct and substantial relationship to the student's disability. He appealed to a federal court, adding Section 504 claims for discrimination and retaliation, and charging the district with applying an incorrect legal standard to evaluate his ADHD and not providing a proper review process. In his challenge, the student argued the district improperly used the IDEA's manifestation review standard, instead of the standard described in a Section 504 regulation at 34 C.F.R. Part 104.36. The court found the district's Section 504 notice of rights and procedural safeguards incorporated procedures from IDEA manifestation determinations. It rejected the student's claim that the Section 504 regulation required more specific findings than those required by the IDEA and the district's policy. Further, the court found 34 C.F.R. Part 104.36 states that **compliance with IDEA procedural safeguards is one means of satisfying Section 504 requirements**.

Under Section 504 regulations, the court found "IDEA compliance is sufficient, but not necessary." Finding the student did not show the district used an incorrect standard or lacked clear and understandable procedures, the court dismissed the discrimination claim. Next, the court considered a retaliation claim based on the student's assertion that the district refused to turn over his records to his new school despite many requests. While he asserted the district acted due to advocacy by his parents, he did not identify any protected activity. Despite ruling for the district, the court allowed the student an opportunity to amend and refile a complaint. *J.M. v. Liberty Union High School Dist.*, No. 16-cv-05225, 2017 WL 2118344 (N.D. Cal. 5/16/17).

◆ A 15-year-old Ohio student with attention deficit hyperactivity disorder, oppositional defiant disorder, anxiety and learning disabilities was accused of telling his school principal that he was "going to terrorize the school." He was suspended for 10 days after a manifestation determination found his behavior was unrelated to his disabilities. A similar incident took place some two weeks later. This time, the student was expelled without a meeting to determine the services he needed while out of school. The parents filed a complaint with the Ohio Department of Education (ODE). The ODE found the school district violated the IDEA by excluding the student from school without services. The ODE ordered the district to hold a manifestation determination, develop a new IEP and provide the student compensatory education. But the district did not comply with a deadline assigned by the ODE for compliance and the parents filed a due process complaint. They then sued the ODE and the school district, seeking a temporary restraining order to obtain services for their child.

According to the parents, the ODE knew the district was not providing services well before they began filing enforcement actions. They claimed the ODE should have stepped in to provide direct services. The court found that while the IDEA allows states to hold school districts financially responsible for failing to provide FAPE, **the IDEA does not provide for "immediate relief," as the parents sought**. Although the ODE had ordered the district to take corrective action, it never found the district could not provide the student a FAPE. While the district's breach of duty violated the IDEA, the court held the state should have a reasonable opportunity to compel local compliance. Since the parents did not show the ODE acted with bad faith or gross misjudgment, their Rehabilitation Act claim failed. *Johnston v. New Miami Local School Dist. Board of Educ.*, No. 1:14cv973, 2016 WL 5122536 (S.D. Ohio 9/21/16).

◆ A New Jersey student was sent home early for inappropriately touching a teacher during horseplay. He was suspended for 10 school days. In a state court, he sued the school board for violating state and federal anti-discrimination laws and his state constitutional right to free, appropriate public education. He sought monetary damages, maintaining he had been denied a manifestation determination hearing to review whether his misconduct related to a disability.

The court dismissed the claims as capable of being redressed by the IDEA. It found no merit to the claim for a manifestation hearing, since the student was not suspended for over 10 days. On appeal, a New Jersey Appellate Division Court explained that before the filing of a civil action seeking relief that is available under the IDEA, there must be an exhaustion of IDEA administrative remedies. The student's claims could be addressed in an IDEA proceeding, since they all sought services and identification of his needs. The case should have been dismissed on the ground that the student waited two years to file it. **The court held the manifestation hearing requirement was not triggered, since the student was not suspended for over 10 days. Sending him home early on the day of the incident was not "an additional day in which he was removed" from his educational placement.** *L.W. v. Egg Harbor Township Board of Educ.*, 2015 WL 1013164 (N.J. Super. Ct. App. Div. 3/10/15).

◆ A day after a note was found stating a bomb would go off at an Illinois high school, police took custody of a student and interviewed him for four hours. Despite the extensive questioning, the police did not call the student's parents. He was arrested on suspicion of making the bomb threat. The school then held an IDEA manifestation determination hearing, at which it was determined that his actions were a manifestation of his autism and/or other impairments.

A disorderly conduct charge was filed against the student in juvenile court. His parents sued school officials in a federal court, charging them with violating the IDEA, the U.S. Constitution and the Illinois school code. They asserted false imprisonment, slander, assault, battery and infliction of emotional distress. In pretrial activity, the court explained that administrative exhaustion applies not only to IDEA claims but to any claim seeking relief that is also available under the IDEA. The relevant question was not the form of relief preferred by the parent, but whether the claimed injuries "could be redressed to some degree by the IDEA's administrative procedures." In this case, the actions were said to have deprived the student of access to an education under the IDEA. Since this is what the IDEA administrative process is designed to redress, the court held the exhaustion rule was not excused. **After holding the federal claims had to be dismissed for failure to exhaust administrative remedies, the court held the state claims could be refiled in the state court system.** *Watson v. St. Rich Cent. High School, Board of Educ., Rich Township High School Dist. 227*, No. 14 C 7530, 2015 WL 1137658 (N.D. Ill. 3/10/15).

◆ A Tennessee student was disciplined 55 times from kindergarten through grade three. Early in his third-grade school year, he was found eligible for special education based on ADHD and an adjustment disorder. In his third-grade school year, the student hit four first-graders on their heads while passing them in the hallway. As a result, the school suspended the student and notified his mother of its intent to expel him for a calendar year for "willful/persistent violation of school rules," "other conduct prejudicial to good order," and bullying. At a manifestation determination meeting, the parent agreed to sign a form reciting that her son's ADHD diagnosis did not "cause a substantial impact on his consistent willful disobedience with all adults making requests." While she agreed with the manifestation determination, she appealed further. The parent rejected an offer to place her son in an alternative learning center, and he finished his third-grade year in homebound education. When the dispute reached a Tennessee chancery court, it found the evidence supported discipline.

On appeal, the Court of Appeals of Tennessee held substantial evidence supported the discipline. There was evidence that the student was disciplined 55 times during his elementary school career. According to the parent, her child's behavior issues were linked to his disability. But the court held **the IDEA did not eliminate a school's ability to discipline a disabled student for misbehavior**. A manifestation review is required to determine whether the conduct was caused by (or had a direct and substantial relationship to) a disability. It must also be determined if the conduct in question was the direct result of a school's failure to implement the IEP. In this case, the parent had agreed that neither her son's diagnosis nor any failure to implement his IEP were direct causes of his misbehavior. She also refused an alternative placement for him. As the evidence supported the disciplinary decision, the court held for the board. *Link v. Metropolitan Nashville Board of Public Educ.*, No. M2013-00422-COA-R3-CV, 2013 WL 6762393 (Tenn. Ct. App. 12/19/13).

C. Interim Placements

"Special circumstances" permit school personnel to remove a student to an interim alternative educational setting for not more than 45 school days without regard to whether the behavior is determined to be a manifestation of the child's disability. This authority exists only if the child: (1) carries a weapon or possesses a weapon at school, on school premises or school functions; (2) knowingly possesses or uses illegal drugs, or sells or solicits the sale of a controlled substance, while at school, on school premises, or at a school function; or (3) has inflicted serious bodily injury upon another person while at school, on school premises, or at a school function. In those cases, the child remains in the interim alternative educational setting. See IDEA regulations published at 34 C.F.R. Parts 300.530 and 300.533.

A parent who disagrees with a placement decision or a manifestation determination may request a hearing. Likewise, if a local educational agency believes that maintaining the current placement of the child is substantially likely to result in injury to the child or to others, it may request a hearing.

◆   A 17-year-old District of Columbia student had an emotional disturbance and a history of violent incidents at school. He received weekly counseling and spent 98% of his instructional time in general education settings. The student repeatedly punched a classmate in the head, causing a concussion and other serious injuries. A school manifestation determination review panel determined the student's behavior was a manifestation of his disability. Despite this finding, the school went forward with a 45-day, out-of-school removal, during which it provided him with homebound tutors. As the end of the 45-day removal period drew near, the school sought approval to transfer the student to a different school. This request was denied by the Office of the State Superintendent for Education (OSSE), and he tried to return to school. After refusing to admit the student, the school filed a due process complaint with the OSSE Office of Dispute Resolution. As the case remained pending, the 45-day removal period elapsed, and the student remained at home. His mother asked a federal court for a temporary restraining order (TRO) and a preliminary injunction requiring the school to accept him back pending the outcome of the due process hearing.

The court denied the request for a TRO and then considered the request for a preliminary injunction. It stated that the IDEA and its regulations allowed the school to place the student in an interim alternative educational setting for up to 45 days due to his violent behavior. Because the 45-day period had expired, the school could not unilaterally exclude him. **The court held the process of requesting a hearing about the appropriateness of an interim alternative educational setting "may be repeated in continued 45-day increments."** At the end of a 45-day removal, the stay-put provision governs any placement until a due process hearing officer issues a decision. In the court's view, the parent did not show the student would suffer irreparable harm if the preliminary order was not granted. It appeared to the court that the school had made a good-faith effort to address her concerns to enable her son to meet his IEP goals. Next, the court found a preliminary order for the student would present a risk of safety to himself and others. As the school argued, this was not his first violent act, and returning him to the school would create an unacceptable risk of injury. Last, the court found the public interest strongly favored the school based on the significant interest in school safety. *Olu-Cole v. E.L. Haynes Public Charter SC*, 292 F.Supp.3d 413 (D.D.C. 2018, D.C. Cir. appeal filed 2/27/18).

◆ A Minnesota student was suspended from school for 10 days for possessing and brandishing a BB gun on school grounds. While suspended, he had access to his school work and many of his teachers met with him to discuss his academic work. The school district assigned an intervention specialist to help the student with his academics and to help him make better choices. A few days after suspending the student, the district sent him notice that he would be suspended for five more days pending an expulsion. He was sent a notice of proposed expulsion under the Minnesota Pupil Fair Dismissal Act and advised of a hearing. After the hearing officer recommended expulsion, the school board voted to adopt the recommendation. The student sued the school district in a federal court, seeking to halt the expulsion proceeding. He argued the district failed to provide him with proper alternative education services prior to initiating the expulsion, in violation of his due process property rights.

The court agreed with the school district that it should abstain from hearing the case, since the student had a state administrative forum to appeal his case and could seek judicial review in the state court system. In addition, the court held the student could not satisfy the requirements for injunctive relief. In fact, the student and his mother admitted the school continued to provide him access to his school work and teachers during the expulsion proceeding. He was also assigned an intervention specialist to help him with academics and coach him regarding his choices. **Both the student and his mother said that they were satisfied with the educational services provided by the district.** The school district offered to allow the student to withdraw, promising to help him enroll in another district. He admitted possessing a BB gun that resembled a handgun, presenting strong evidence of an immediate and substantial danger to himself and others. *B.L. v. Mahtomedi School Dist., ISD No. 832*, No. 17-1193, 2017 WL 1497855 (D. Minn. 4/26/17). A year after denying the student' motion for temporary relief, the court dismissed his case. *B.L. v. Mahtomedi School Dist., ISD No. 832*, No. 17-1193 ADM/SER, 2018 WL 1972474 (D. Minn. 4/26/18).

◆   A Texas student with severe ADHD photographed another student while he was using a toilet. A school administrator found this justified a suspension. The student's parents claimed the administrator then encouraged the parent of the student who was photographed to file a criminal charge. A manifestation determination review (MDR) committee found the incident did not result from the student's ADHD, and he was placed in a disciplinary alternative educational placement (DAEP) setting for 60 days. After the criminal charges were dismissed, the MDR did not revoke the DAEP. After a hearing officer upheld the discipline, the parents appealed to a federal court, where they added claims under Section 504 of the Rehabilitation Act and constitutional theories.

Appeal reached the U.S. Court of Appeals, Fifth Circuit, which found **the complaint was conclusory and did not show discrimination under federal law**. Instead, the parents charged school officials with a conspiracy based on their child's disability. The parents did not attribute any misconduct to the school district that was based on the student's disability. In fact, the student was not placed in a DAEP until after the MDR determination found his behavior was not the result of a disability. Since the parents did not sufficiently plead that any of the school's actions were taken on the basis of a disability, the Section 504 claim was properly dismissed. *C.C. v. Hurst-Euless-Bedford Independent School Dist.*, No. 15-10098, 2016 WL 909418 (5th Cir. 3/9/16). In late 2016, the U.S. Supreme Court declined to hear the case without issuing an opinion.

◆   During a Michigan student's sixth-grade school year, seven IEP meetings and 12 behavior planning sessions were held to address his disruptive and dangerous behavior. The school evacuated classrooms eight times in response to incidents, and emergency responders were called five times before his parents agreed to a home program. An IEP was finalized for the student's transition to middle school proposing to divide his school days between general education classes and a classroom for students with autism spectrum disorder (ASD). The student's grade seven IEP discontinued reliance on a 1:1 aide, which was felt to trigger his aggressive behavior. On the fourth day of seventh grade, he cursed and threatened others, threw chairs, bit a support staff member (drawing blood) and ran away. The school sought to impose long-term discipline and held a meeting to determine whether his conduct was a manifestation of a disability.

The district urged a 45-day interim alternative setting for the student, but the parents did not agree to the center-based program selected by the IEP team. They resumed a home program for him and requested a due process hearing.

An administrative law judge (ALJ) held the district did not properly implement the student's seventh grade IEP. It was found that staff lacked proper training and the IEP was inappropriate. As a result, the ALJ ordered a placement with a 1:1 ASD trained psychologist. The school district appealed to a federal court, which found significant changes were made to the student's placement without a meeting or changes to the IEP. No formal notice was sent to the parents, and his status was unclear to them for several weeks. Supports were not in place for the student at the time of a significant behavior episode. The parents felt the alternative placement was predetermined and that their child was regressing. Based on the district's procedural errors, the court found IDEA violations. Last, the court denied the district's request for an order excluding the student from school. **Evidence indicated he could be educated in general education classes with the right support and an appropriate IEP.** *Troy School Dist. v. K.M.*, No. 12-CV-15413, 2015 WL 1495334 (E.D. Mich. 3/31/15).

D. Regular Education Students

Section 1415(k)(5)(B) of the IDEA addresses the issue of regular education students seeking IDEA protections in disciplinary cases. A student who has not been found eligible under the IDEA may assert the act's procedural protections if the school has knowledge that the student was a child with a disability prior to the misconduct giving rise to discipline. A school may be deemed to have knowledge that a child has a disability if (i) before the behavior leading to discipline, the child's parent "has expressed concern in writing" to a teacher or to supervisory or administrative personnel that the child is in need of special education or related services; (ii) the child's parent has requested an individual initial evaluation to determine if the child has a disability; or (iii) the child's teacher, or other school personnel, "has expressed specific concerns about a pattern of behavior demonstrated by the child, directly to the director of special education of such agency or to other supervisory personnel of the agency."

◆   A New York honor student with no history of discipline earned a lead role in the school play. He had depression and anxiety, severe allergies and other medical conditions, but he did not have an IEP or a Section 504 plan. During the student's senior year, he submitted an essay for a writing course which triggered his teacher's belief that he committed plagiarism. The student claimed to be experiencing a great deal of school-related stress, exacerbated by his health issues and lead role in the play. He claimed he was falsely charged with plagiarism and had no intent to claim outside material as his own work. As punishment, the school assigned the student an F and imposed a two-day, after-school detention. He was also barred from participating in the school play. The student claimed the discipline became known in the community and damaged his reputation.

After graduating, the student sued the school district in a federal court for due process violations. The court held a due process claimant must demonstrate a protected liberty or property interest exists and has been deprived without due process of law. **A two-day detention did not violate a protected property right.** In any event, the student served no detention, since the principal revoked it. Nor did his exclusion from the school play amount to an event or activity of constitutional importance. The court held the student failed to show a constitutional deprivation without due process. Next, the court rejected the student's disability-related claims. It found no violation of equal protection based on a disability. Although the student claimed he should have been identified as having a disability and received IDEA protections, the court found he did not first file a due process complaint and pursue a hearing under the IDEA. Since the student did not exhaust his IDEA remedies, he could not pursue a Section 504 claim, and the court dismissed the case. *Harrington v. Jamesville Dewitt Cent. School Dist.*, No. 5:17-CV-53 (TJM/DEP), 2017 WL 1327719 (N.D.N.Y. 4/11/17, 2d Cir. appeal filed 5/11/17).

◆   An Oregon student was charged with bullying two disabled students as they left school. After investigating, administrators found the student engaged the disabled students in a conversation about sexual topics. In his federal court case, the student advanced claims based on free speech. But the court held schools may suspend students in response to an identifiable threat of school violence, even if it occurs off campus. Schools need not wait until an actual disruption occurs and may rely on a reasonable forecast of disruption. A due process claim also failed, despite his argument that he was not notified of the sexual harassment charge. On appeal, the U.S. Court of Appeals, Ninth Circuit, found the district reasonably deemed the conduct to be sexual harassment. The conduct included verbal conduct of a sexual nature, including sexually oriented kidding, teasing or jokes. Prior Ninth Circuit cases held schools may regulate off-campus speech. **Other federal appeals courts have held off-campus speech may be regulated where there is a connection to the school or if it is reasonably foreseeable that disruptive speech would reach the school.**

Schools may restrict speech that might reasonably lead school authorities to forecast substantial disruption of or material interference with school activities. Speech may also be regulated if it collides with the rights of other students to be secure and let alone. In this case, the court found the offensive comments were made just as school was letting out, a few hundred feet from school property. It was reasonable for the school to be concerned with the well-being of its students. Had administrators not intervened, the younger students would have been deprived of their right to be secure at school. In the court's view, schools must have authority to discipline students for engaging in harassing speech. Next, the court found that since the harassment took place so close to the school, administrators could have reasonably expected its effect to spill over into the school environment. Administrators could not disregard the possibility that the older students would continue to harass the younger students on school grounds. Finding the school's actions were reasonable, the court upheld the discipline. *C.R. v. Eugene School Dist. 4J*, 835 F.3d 1142 (9th Cir. 2016).

◆   A Texas student wrote a "shooting list" in his English journal, identifying classmates he wanted to harm. The principal found the list violated the student conduct code and assigned the student to a disciplinary alternative placement for 35 days. Within days, a team met for a manifestation determination review (MDR). At the meeting, the parents presented a report diagnosing their son with an autism spectrum disorder. Although the ARD committee offered to evaluate the student for autism, the parents withdrew from the MDR proceedings. After a second MDR meeting, the team found the shooting list incident was not a manifestation of an other health impairment or an emotional disturbance.

Instead of reporting to the disciplinary alternative school, the student stayed at home for the last three weeks of the school year. His parents filed a due process request. A hearing officer found the school district failed to diagnose him with autism two years prior to the shooting list incident. A federal court held the parents could not now challenge an evaluation that took place over two years prior to the lawsuit. In any event, the court found it irrelevant that the student was later diagnosed with autism. For most of two years before the shooting list incident, he made academic and non-academic progress. **As the hearing officer applied an incorrect standard in reversing the manifestation findings**, the court held for the school district. *Z.H. v. Lewisville Independent School Dist.*, No. 4:12cv775, 2015 WL 1384442 (E.D. Tex. 3/24/15).

IV. GRADUATION

Graduation with a regular diploma constitutes a change in placement, requiring written prior notice to the parents and a student who has reached age 18. An IDEA regulation (34 C.F.R. Part 300.122) declares that the obligation to make a free appropriate public education (FAPE) available to all children with disabilities does not apply to those who have graduated from high school with a regular high school diploma. This exception does not apply to students who have graduated but have not been awarded a regular high school diploma.

An existing provision of California law permitting foreign exchange students to receive honorary high school diplomas upon returning to their home countries was amended in 2018 to allow the award of an honorary high school diploma to a pupil who is terminally ill. California 2018 portion of 2017-18 Legislative Session, Ch. 167. A.B. 2109. California Educ. Code §§ 48206.3, 48207, 48207.3, 48207.5, 48208, 4824, 51225.5.

A. FAPE Issues

◆ The parents of an 18-year-old Virginia student with Down syndrome claimed his school tried to prevent him from graduating with a regular high school diploma. They said his IEPs had included rigorous goals since he was in grade two and the ultimate goal for him was to graduate with a standard diploma. But the parents claimed that shortly after their son entered high school, he was denied services specified in his IEP. They accused certain teachers and specialists of choosing not to work with him on some IEP goals. According to the parents, their child was allowed to avoid academic participation and watched videos on YouTube instead. Next, they claimed special educators at the school began suggesting new IEPs that did not contain the rigor shown in prior IEPs. They refused to consent to the IEPs and filed a due process complaint.

A hearing officer held the school district provided the child a FAPE. Later, the parents challenged the decision in federal court. They added claims against the district for disability discrimination and retaliation against them in violation of Section 504 of the Rehabilitation Act and the Americans with Disabilities Act (ADA). **The court held that students with disabilities must show either bad faith or gross misjudgment by school officials to prevail on an ADA or Section 504 claim.** In this case, the court found the parents made a sufficient showing of bad faith or gross misjudgment by the district to proceed with their discrimination and retaliation claims. Finding they would be granted relief on their discrimination and retaliation claims if their assertions were proven true, the court denied the school district's dismissal motion. *B.D. v. Fairfax County School Board*, No. 1:18-cv-1425, 2019 WL 692804 (E.D. Va. 2/19/19).

◆   A Tennessee student had ADHD, autism and asthma but was ineligible for special education. He and his mother stayed at a domestic violence shelter, and relocated seven times during a school year. The student's parent said the district refused to enroll her son for the next school year, and she filed a federal action asserting violations of the McKinney-Vento Homeless Assistance Act. The parties settled the case with a stipulation of dismissal, and the student returned to his school. A psychologist conducted an independent evaluation and found the student "may be eligible for special services," as he met the criteria for autism spectrum disorder. Meanwhile, the student turned 18. When he met with school staff members to consider the evaluator's report, he said he did not need special education. The mother disagreed, but he remained in the general education curriculum and earned high grades in advanced placement classes. At the end of the school year, the student graduated with a regular diploma. In a federal court, the mother sued the school board for discrimination and violations of the IDEA, the Fourteenth Amendment and the McKinney-Vento Act. As she is not an attorney, and Tennessee law emancipates people at age 18, the court held she could not pursue these claims.

Next, the court dismissed the disability discrimination claims, as the mother did not identify her son's disability or show he was excluded from a district program, denied any benefits or subjected to discrimination. Before graduating, he participated in the general education curriculum with his peers. Since the mother did not request a due process hearing, the court held she could not pursue the IDEA claims. **Moreover, the IDEA states that when a child turns 18, all rights of the parent transfer to the child.** Since the student was 18 when he declined special education, his position was controlling over his mother's preference. He earned high grades in his general education classes and met Tennessee graduation requirements. Prior to filing this case, the parent had sued the board for violating the McKinney-Vento Act. That case was dismissed, barring litigation between these parties on the claim. Although she sought to advance new legal theories, the court did not allow them and it dismissed the case. *Harris v. Cleveland City Board of Educ.*, No. 1:17-cv-00121 REEVES/ LEE, 2018 WL 1124961 (E.D. Tenn. 3/1/18).

◆   An Ohio student who was diagnosed with depression was on track for graduation. She did not have an IEP or a Section 504 plan. After earning "decent" grades, the student's academic performance began to decline. Her mother believed this was due to her depressive disorder. In December of the student's senior year, her mother emailed teachers about the student's academic performance and emotional well-being. Before the student graduated, the family filed a due process complaint against the school district, asserting denial of a free appropriate public education (FAPE), violation of the IDEA's child-find duty and failure to provide appropriate accommodations and services. As the student had earned enough credits to graduate, the district graduated her and moved to dismiss the due process complaint as moot. An independent hearing officer (IHO) then held a hearing. The IHO found the family did not show the district committed retaliation. It was found that the student had earned the necessary credits to graduate. Next, the IHO found the district did not provide timely notice of its refusal to evaluate the student. But this failure resulted in no harm. Although the IHO found the district's failure to identify a disability violated its child-find duty and denied the student a FAPE, the IHO found she did not show she needed special education and related services. A state review officer affirmed the IHO's decision and the family appealed to a federal court.

The court stated that in the context of education, there must be a showing of bad faith or gross misjudgment before a Section 504 violation may be shown. In this case, the court held the student met this standard by asserting more than a failure to be evaluated. She said the district deliberately ignored information regarding her depression and refused requests to evaluate her based on a predetermined decision that she had no disability. **While the district was on notice of concerns about the student's emotional well-being in December of her senior year, no meeting was held for two months.** Since the student asserted enough facts to allow an inference of bad faith or gross misjudgment by the school district, she could pursue some of her Section 504 claims. *Burton v. Cleveland Heights-University Heights City School Dist. Board of Educ.*, No 1:17 CV 134, 2017 WL 4348915 (N.D. Ohio 9/29/17).

◆ An Idaho school district reevaluated an eighth-grader and found him ineligible for special education. His parents obtained a private evaluation that diagnosed him with a high-functioning form of autism. They sought a new evaluation, but the district refused. During ninth grade, the student was arrested and placed in a juvenile detention center. The school district in which the detention center was located evaluated him for special education but found no evidence of any adverse effect of disabilities on his educational performance. Since the other district's evaluation was limited because of his confinement, the parents asked their home district for a reevaluation. But the home district declined to perform its own evaluation. When the student returned home, the parents requested additional assessments and an IEP. The district refused and found him ineligible for special education. By this time, the student was in grade 11. His parents requested an IEE, which the home district denied. In a due process proceeding, a hearing officer held the home district failed to conduct an appropriate evaluation. A federal court issued a preliminary order preventing the district from graduating the student. It held the parents were entitled to an IEE at the district's expense, plus attorneys' fees. After a second round of hearings, a finding of ineligibility was confirmed. The parents appealed to a federal court, which held the student was not IDEA-eligible.

On appeal, the U.S. Court of Appeals, Ninth Circuit, held the parents were entitled to an IEE at public expense. Since the student was ineligible for IDEA services, the parents did not meet the IDEA definition of "parent of a child with a disability" and were ineligible for IDEA attorneys' fees. **The court found the order to prevent the school district from graduating the student was questionable, since he was not receiving special education.** It appeared that since he met graduation criteria, he likely received all the benefits that the district's general education program offered. It had been three years since the preliminary order was issued. As any benefit from the order was now exhausted, the court vacated it. *Meridian Joint School Dist. No. 2 v. D.A.,* 792 F.3d 1054 (9th Cir. 2015).

◆   Georgia parents wanted their son to graduate with a college preparatory diploma despite his apraxia, language impairments, and reading and executive functioning deficits. Just before his fourth year of high school, school members of his IEP team sought to change his diploma track because they felt he would not be able to pass the state-required high school exit examination. The student had failed a practice test and was currently failing U.S. history a second time. To graduate with an employment-preparatory diploma, he would not have to pass U.S. history and only had to master related IEP goals and objectives. He needed only four courses, including U.S. history, to obtain a college preparatory diploma. The student's mother refused to participate in a second IEP meeting, as she had already rejected the IEP. She notified the district that she would make a private placement and would seek reimbursement for it. An ALJ held he could have been educated in regular classes with supplemental aids and services. But she held he would not receive FAPE in the self-contained classes stated in the IEP. Although the ALJ found the private school selected by the parents was appropriate, she awarded them only half the tuition because they had refused to attend the second IEP meeting. When the case reached a federal court, it held the student could have remained in the regular classes he had attended before the change proposed by the IEP team. He was passing his classes with appropriate aids and services, and **it appeared that "the IEP team just wanted A.V. to graduate in the next year, and the fastest way to do this was to place him in access classes for his core classes."**

As the ALJ's decision was supported by evidence, the court held the district denied the student a FAPE by changing his classes and diploma track. In addition, the court found the private school selected by the parent was appropriate. As the ALJ had found, there was fault on both sides of the dispute. A 50% reduction in reimbursement was held appropriate. *Cobb County School Dist. v. A.V.,* 961 F.Supp.2d 1252 (N.D. Ga. 2013).

◆   A Rhode Island student with Asperger's syndrome, ADHD and severe social anxiety was working toward a high school diploma. She received notice that her right to a FAPE would terminate upon her 21st birthday. Based on this notice, the parent brought an action on her behalf in federal court against the state department of elementary and secondary education. In reviewing the IDEA, the court noted the act requires states to make a FAPE available to resident students with disabilities between the ages of 3 and 21, inclusive. But another section of the act makes the obligation to offer a FAPE inapplicable to those aged 18-21 – if this would not be consistent with the state's law or practice regarding the provision of public education to general education students in the same age range. A Rhode Island special education regulation provides that FAPE must be available to eligible children between the ages of 3-21, inclusive, but only until the child's 21st birthday or the receipt of a regular high school diploma. According to the court, the state regulation would terminate the eligibility to receive a FAPE on a student's 21st birthday.

While the department said the mother lacked standing to pursue the case, the court found this could be easily cured. It allowed the student 30 days to file an amended complaint in her own right. **As she had stated a desire to add a person to represent a class of students in her age range she could also add a class representative.** Since the case involved only legal questions, the court excused the student from exhausting her administrative remedies. It denied the department's dismissal motion. *K.S. v. Rhode Island Board of Educ.*, 44 F.Supp.3d 193 (D.R.I. 2014).

B. Academic Requirements

Delaware legislators amended a law governing state high school diploma requirements by eliminating the certificate of performance. Under the amended law, students who have met the requirements of their IEPs but will not complete high school graduation course credit requirements will receive a diploma of alternate achievement standards. One-Hundred Forty-Ninth Delaware General Assembly, Second Regular Session, 2018 Delaware Laws, Ch. 229, H.B. 287. Delaware Code, Title 14, § 152.

A Mississippi state law amendment makes the state occupational diploma for students with disabilities unavailable to any student entering grade nine beginning in the 2017-2018 school year, pending state board of education approval of new graduation options. The amended law states that career track programs for students not pursuing a baccalaureate degree will not be available to students entering grade nine, beginning in the 2017-2018 school year. Mississippi 2017 Session Laws, S.B. No. 2432, Mississippi Code Sections 37-16-11, 37-16-17, 37-23-147.

Louisiana law allows persons who are no longer enrolled in public schools to petition their former school systems to determine their eligibility to receive a high school diploma. Petitions may be filed by students who were identified as exceptional students and failed to receive a diploma (or were denied graduation) solely for failing to meet relevant exit exam requirements. The provision does not apply to gifted and talented students. Requests for a diploma will not change graduation rate calculations for any school or school district. Louisiana Revised Stat, §§ 17:24.4, 154.2 17:3991.

◆ A federal court held a Texas student with dyslexia who earned a 3.45 grade average and graduated from high school could not show his school district improperly failed to find him eligible for special education and related services. **Decisions by the Fifth Circuit Court of Appeals have held the IDEA does not penalize school districts for failing to timely evaluate a student who does not need special education.** The court found the hearing officer adequately considered other matters raised by the student. The hearing officer relied on evidence that he passed all his classes, graduated from high school, passed almost all of his state assessments and gained college admission. Although the student claimed the many accommodations he received while in high school proved his need for special education, the court found these same accommodations were typically available to all students in general education programs. School liability under Section 504 and ADA requires proof of intentional discrimination based on a disability. In the Fifth Circuit, this is shown by facts creating an inference of professional bad faith or gross misjudgment. Finding the student presented no evidence of professional bad faith or gross misjudgment and no need for special education, the court held for the school district. *T.W. v. Leander Independent School Dist.*, No. AU-17-00627-SS, 2019 WL 1102380 (W.D. Tex. 3/7/19).

◆   A Pennsylvania charter school student had attention deficit/hyperactivity disorder. His parents requested teaching and testing accommodations for him while he attended the school. According to the parents, the school agreed to make accommodations when it admitted the student for grade nine. But they later said the school either could not or would not provide the accommodations. Charging the school with failing to reasonably accommodate his disability in violation of the Americans with Disabilities Act (ADA), the parents filed a lawsuit seeking injunctive relief on behalf of the student and all similarly situated charter school students and applicants. In addition to the ADA claim, the family asserted state-law claims against the school including breach of contract and infliction of emotional distress. During pretrial activity, the student graduated from high school and enrolled in a university. Noting the student's graduation, the court dismissed the case for lack of standing and mootness. It declined to hear the state-law claims, which went to a state court. On appeal, the U.S. Court of Appeals, Third Circuit, explained that the U.S. Constitution allows federal courts to consider "actual cases and controversies only, not moot ones."
A case is moot if the party filing suit no longer has a personal stake in the outcome of the case or the court can no longer grant the requested relief. **Graduation may eliminate a personal stake in the outcome of a case, and it typically moots a claim for an injunction or a declaration.** In this case, the student's graduation meant he would never again be subjected to the charter school's teaching methods. As the case was mooted by the student's graduation, the court held he could not "rescue" the ADA claim via an existing exception to the mootness doctrine. Next, the court rejected an invitation to recognize a new exception to mootness based on the student's "constructive expulsion" from the charter school. The student could not obtain relief for any "residual reputational or psychological trauma" under the ADA, but could continue seeking damages in a state court. As the lower court had correctly found the case moot, the court held for the charter school. *Mirabella v. William Penn Charter School*, 752 Fed. Appx. 131 (3d Cir. 2018).

◆   The parents of a New York special education student placed him in a private school, and their district paid part of the cost. They later notified the district that they intended to place him in a Connecticut residential school. The district sought his transcripts to determine how close he was to graduation, but the parents refused to cooperate. When they sought tuition reimbursement, a federal court ruled that **they were not entitled to it because the student had earned enough credits at the private school to earn a Regents diploma**. His graduation made him ineligible for further tuition reimbursement; also, the parents' actions weighed against any tuition award. *T.M. v. Kingston City School Dist.*, 891 F.Supp.2d 289 (N.D.N.Y. 2012).

◆ The mother of a California student with autism learned in May of her son's senior year that district staff did not intend to award him a diploma. She pulled him from school, after which the district offered an IEP that would return him to school the next year or have him attend a transition program. She challenged the education he'd been given, and an administrative law judge found in her favor on three of the 15 claims she raised. A federal court then held **the district had been properly ordered to devise a placement that would allow the student to work toward a diploma**. The mother was also a prevailing party because she received significant relief that materially altered the relationship of the parties. However, she was not entitled to reimbursement for the private school where she placed her son. *Struble v. Fallbrook Union High School Dist.*, No. 07CV2328-LAB (CAB), 2011 WL 291217 (S.D. Cal. 1/27/11).

◆ An Indiana school district offered special education to a learning disabled student until his parents decided to homeschool him. Later, they sought to reintegrate him into public schools and obtained private evaluations showing he had autism. The district did not identify an autism spectrum disorder until he was 17. When he was 19, the district awarded him a diploma. His parents challenged the graduation, asserting that the student should continue to receive special education. Using the stay-put provisions of the IDEA, federal court ordered the district to continue educating the student in a college preparatory program. **The parents' challenge to the validity and good faith of the decision to graduate their son warranted a stay-put placement.** *Tindell v. Evansville-Vanderburgh School Corp.*, No. 309-CV-00159-SEB-WGH, 2010 WL 557058 (S.D. Ind. 2/10/10).

C. Graduation Ceremonies

New York Education Law requires each school district's board to establish a policy and adopt procedures to allow students to participate in the graduation ceremony of their high school graduating classes and all related activities, under specified circumstances. Students may participate in graduation ceremonies, if they have been awarded skills and achievement commencement credentials or career development and occupational studies commencement credentials, but do not otherwise qualify for regents or local diplomas. Boards are to provide annual written notice to all students and their parents or guardians about the school district's policy and procedures. Nothing requires a student to participate in high school graduation ceremonies and activities. Two-Hundred Forty-First New York Legislature, Ch. 32; S. 7311. New York Education Law §§ 3204, 4402.

Delaware legislators amended a law governing state high school diploma requirements by eliminating the certificate of performance. Students who have met the requirements of their IEPs but will not complete high school credit requirements will receive a diploma of alternate achievement standards. One-Hundred Forty-Ninth Delaware General Assembly, Second Regular Session, 2018 Delaware Laws, Ch. 229, H.B. 287. Delaware Code, Title 14, § 152.

◆   An African-American student was disciplined for misconduct by an Illinois private school near the end of his senior year. He said that other students were suspended for three days for similar conduct but that he alone had to finish the semester at home. The student claimed he was not allowed to attend his graduation ceremony and the school prom. He said the school denied his request for a meeting to review the discipline. The student's family asked a federal court for an order requiring the school to allow his attendance at the graduation ceremony. The court denied the request. Later, the court found the student made only vague and conclusory allegations of discrimination. It held he did not provide necessary facts to draw a causal inference between the school's action and any discrimination. His statement "that non-black students received substantially better treatment" was insufficient to continue this claim.

The court found the student's Section 504 disability discrimination claim provided little detail to support an inference of intentional discrimination. It was not alleged that the student's accommodation plan was disregarded or that the coaches retaliated against him for seeking accommodations. **Numerous courts have held Section 504 regulations do not create a private cause of action to enforce any due process rights.** This defeated the student's claim based on refusing to hold a Section 504 hearing regarding discipline. After dismissing the federal claims, the court held he could refile his state claims in a state court. *Thurmon v. Mount Carmel High School*, 191 F.Supp.3d 894 (N.D. Ill. 2016).

◆   An Alabama student with a specific learning disability under the IDEA was removed from school after he was found with a handgun that had the serial number filed off. After a manifestation determination hearing, he was expelled for one year. He received education services at a private school for a year and a half. His mother sought to have him graduate with his former classmates at the public school, but the district denied the request. When a lawsuit resulted, a federal court held that **the student did not have the right to walk with his former classmates at the graduation ceremony**. The court found nothing to indicate that a graduation ceremony was part of the IDEA's FAPE guarantee. *Jefferson County Board of Educ. v. S.B.*, 788 F.Supp.2d 1347 (N.D. Ala. 2011).

CHAPTER SIX

IDEA Procedural Safeguards

I. DUE PROCESS HEARINGS

IDEA safeguards include an "impartial due process hearing" under 20 U.S.C. § 1415(f) when parents or guardians are dissatisfied with any matter relating to the identification, evaluation, or educational placement of the child, or the provision of a free appropriate public education to the child.

Many states provide for a single due process hearing opportunity, but New York and North Carolina retain two-tier systems. In E.L. v. Chapel Hill-Carrboro Board of Educ., 773 F.3d 509 (4th Cir. 2014), the Fourth Circuit upheld a challenge to North Carolina's two-tier administrative review scheme.

◆ A Delaware court held the expulsion of a student with disabilities for fighting a classmate violated his due process rights in several respects, notably the school board's failure to present witnesses for cross-examination at his expulsion hearing. **The court explained that school board decisions will be upheld unless they are contrary to law, not supported by substantial evidence or are arbitrary or capricious.** Moreover, a board's disciplinary decision will be upheld unless the punishment was so disproportionate to the offense as to be shocking to one's sense of fairness. **Due process requires that students have certain procedural safeguards at hearings, including the right to cross-examine witnesses.** Although the expulsion report included statements from the principal and two witnesses, these persons did not testify at the hearing and were not made available for cross-examination. The court held this was "fundamentally unfair and a violation of due process."

Finding the state board correctly held that cross-examination was necessary to assure minimal due process in an expulsion hearing, the court refused to set aside the decision. Next, the court held the decision to expel the student was arbitrary and capricious, since the school board relied on a code provision that applied only to out-of-school criminal conduct. As the incident took place in school, the court held the expulsion was not supported by the evidence. *Board of Educ. of Smyrna School Dist. v. E.D.*, No. N18A-03-001 ALR, 2018 WL 6566754 (Del. Super. Ct. 12/11/18).

A. Generally

◆   The parents of a New York City student with autism challenged the IEP proposed for their child. Prior to a school year, they enrolled him in a private school and notified the New York City Department of Education (DOE) of their decision to reject the IEP and seek reimbursement for their tuition costs. They requested an impartial hearing. During prehearing activity, the parents' counsel requested adjournment of the hearing and the recusal (disqualification) of the impartial hearing officer (IHO). After the request was renewed, the IHO again denied it. Another attorney from the counsel's law firm attended the hearing with the parents. When he tried to record the hearing (which was already being recorded) the IHO directed him to turn off his device. But the attorney refused to do so and the IHO ended the hearing. The IHO terminated the proceeding, but reinstituted it a few days later and scheduled a new hearing.

The parents requested permission to present evidence through live testimony. They again sought to adjourn the case and unseat the IHO. Although the IHO denied the parents' requests, she allowed the hearing to begin earlier in the day and let one parent testify. She later issued a decision for the DOE. A state review officer affirmed the decision, and the parents appealed to a federal court. There, they argued the IEP was drafted before the meeting and was improper because the DOE repeated its recommendations for three or four years in a row. But the court found the committee considered alternative placements, defeating the parents' claim that the IEP had been predetermined. Further, they did not show the school selected by the DOE could not implement the IEP. **Last, the court agreed with the DOE that the conduct and impartiality of the IHO were not at issue.** As the IHO's actions were within her discretion, the judgment for the DOE was affirmed. *J.S. and R.S. v. New York City Dep't of Educ.*, No. 15cv355 (DLC), 2017 WL 744590 (S.D.N.Y. 2/24/17).

◆   Claiming their child's school district denied him a free appropriate public education, New York parents enrolled him privately and requested a hearing. An impartial hearing officer (IHO) delayed issuing a decision for months after its due date. Despite prompting by the New York State Education Department

(NYSED), the IHO did not comply with notices to issue a decision, including a warning that her certification would be suspended or revoked if she did not do so. Eventually, the NYSED revoked her IHO certification. But two replacement IHOs recused themselves from the case for unspecified reasons. Both the parents and the school district initially agreed to extend a new IHO's deadline to allow her to review the record. But days later, the parents filed a lawsuit against the school district and NYSED in a federal court, asserting the delay in a decision deprived them of their rights to due process. Among other things, the parents sought an order preventing all IHOs who did not have a license from practicing law. Meanwhile, the new IHO issued a decision granting the parents' request for reimbursement of their tutoring costs for a school year. But the IHO denied their request for tuition reimbursement for two subsequent school years.

A state review officer affirmed the IHO's decision, and the school district and NYSED obtained dismissal of the federal court action. Appeal reached the U.S. Court of Appeals, Second Circuit. Although the parents claimed it would have been futile to fully pursue their administrative remedies, **the court noted they had agreed to extend the deadline for an IHO decision only days before filing their lawsuit**. The court found their filing set in motion a possible resolution. Since it appeared a resolution was imminent, the court found it was not futile for the parents to await the outcome of their impartial hearing. *H.B. v. Byram Hills Cent. School Dist.*, 648 Fed.Appx. 122 (2d Cir. 2016).

◆ In separate cases, parents filed complaint resolution proceedings with the California Department of Education (CDE). They charged their school districts with failing to provide disabled children with appropriate educational services. After both parents prevailed in their state complaint resolution proceedings, the districts sued the state in a federal court, asserting the CDE routinely violated IDEA procedures in special education disputes. The districts sought a court order declaring certain CDE practices unlawful. They objected to the CDE's frequent reconsideration of its "final" decisions. In one case, the CDE first held for the parents and then held for the school district. Upon reconsideration, the CDE reversed itself and held for the parents. According to the school districts, the CDE considered conduct outside a relevant one-year statute of limitations from a federal regulation published under the IDEA (at 34 CFR Part 300.153(c)). And the districts claimed the CDE improperly imposed the burden of proof on the districts when it should have instead burdened the parents. After the cases were dismissed, the districts appealed to the U.S. Court of Appeals, Ninth Circuit. In the court's view, the only IDEA provision that could conceivably allow the districts to sue the CDE was 20 U.S.C. § 1415(i)(2)(A).

This IDEA provision describes the appeal process from a due process hearing. In advancing their argument, the districts acknowledged the lack of language allowing them to sue the state. But they argued Section 1415 gave them an implied right to sue. The court noted prior cases rejecting an implied right in cases where the underlying dispute involved a due process proceeding. In *Lake Washington School Dist. No. 414 v. Office of Superintendent of Public Instruction*, 634 F.3d 1065 (9th Cir. 2011), the Ninth Circuit found school districts may only litigate IDEA issues raised by parents in a due process complaint. The court explained that **IDEA procedures are "intended to**

safeguard the rights of disabled children and their parents," not the rights of school districts. Since the lower court had correctly dismissed the cases, the court held for the CDE. *Fairfield-Suisun Unified School Dist. v. California Dep't of Educ.*, 780 F.3d 968 (9th Cir. 2015).

◆ The guardian of a Missouri student with disabilities was denied further review of a decision by the state court of appeals, which held she could not pursue a due process complaint against the student's former school district. The court held any claims based on denial of a free appropriate public education (FAPE) were barred because of the student's withdrawal from the district. Applying federal Eighth Circuit precedent, **the court held the failure to file a due process complaint before the child left district schools barred any claim based on the provision of a FAPE.** *A.H. v. Independence School Dist.*, 466 S.W.3d 17 (Mo. Ct. App. 2015). (Rehearing and/or transfer denied, 6/2/15).

B. Evidence

In B.S. v. Anoka Hennepin Public Schools ISD No. 11, this chapter, Minnesota parents did not convince the Eighth Circuit Court of Appeals that a prehearing agreement limiting the time for the parties to present their cases to an administrative law judge violated their child's due process rights.

◆ Maryland parents were denied permission to present a report by an evaluator who conducted an independent educational evaluation (IEE) of their child, then made a "tactical decision" to delay the completion of the IEE until after their due process hearing. In opposing the parents' motion to allow the evaluator's report, the district said they delayed requesting the IEE as a strategic maneuver. The court explained that when parents request an IEE at public expense, a school district must either file a due process hearing complaint or pay for the IEE. If a due process decision advances to a court, the parties may ask the court to consider additional evidence beyond the administrative record. Typical reasons for supplementing the record include gaps in a transcript, consideration of testimony that was previously unavailable, improper exclusion of evidence by a hearing officer, or relevant events taking place after a hearing.
    The court held additional evidence to supplement an administrative record must be limited to protect the role of the due process hearing as the primary forum for resolving IEP disputes. It held courts must not convert judicial review into a chance for a new trial. In the court's view, the timing of the report showed it was clearly commissioned for the purposes of this litigation. It appeared to the court that the parents made a "tactical decision to reserve the expense – and the impact" of the evaluator's report instead of providing it to the ALJ. As a result, they could not now submit the IEE report to support their claims. Appeal reached the U.S. Court of Appeals, Fourth Circuit. In addition to appealing from the ruling that the district evaluations were IDEA-compliant, the parents urged the court to supplement the record with a new independent neuropsychological evaluation of their son. But the court found no error in the lower court's decision for the school district. It rejected the parents' arguments

that they should have been allowed to further challenge the evaluation by the district. After reviewing the administrative record and the parents' arguments, the court affirmed the judgment for the school district. *E.P. v. Howard County Public School System*, 727 Fed.Appx. 55 (4th Cir. 2018).

◆   A Pennsylvania school district was required to pay the parent of a gifted student for the cost of an independent educational evaluation (IEE) based on a hearing officer's finding that a district evaluation report left the student's special education eligibility in doubt. A federal court found evidence that the student might have a specific learning disability in reading, and it held the hearing officer who conducted the due process hearing did not err in ordering the district to pay for an IEE. After reviewing the evaluation report and considering testimony from the parent, school officials and teachers, the hearing officer found the student had a pattern of strong comprehension with works of narrative, but markedly less comprehension in works of exposition. It was unclear to the hearing officer where the student's fluctuating reading level actually stood. **A hearing officer's factual findings are presumed to be correct and after a thorough review of the evidence, he found the district used flawed methodology.** As a result, the judgment requiring the district to fund an IEE was affirmed. *West Chester Area School Dist. v. G.D.*, No. 16-4471, 2017 WL 379440 (E.D. Pa. 1/25/17).

◆   A New York student had Tourette's syndrome and a generalized anxiety disorder. A committee on special education (CSE) recommended placing him in an integrated co-teaching (ICT) class. The parents objected, saying the ICT class would have been "a disaster" for the student and that he needed a smaller group setting. They advised the school department of their intent to enroll the child in a private school and seek reimbursement. After classes started, the parents visited the school recommended by the department and rejected it for several reasons. They believed the recommended school served predominantly non-native English speakers and was a "dumping ground for special ed students." The parents requested a hearing to seek tuition reimbursement.

An impartial hearing officer disagreed with their claim that the IEP was inappropriate. A state review officer also held for the school department, and a federal court affirmed the judgment. On appeal to the U.S. Court of Appeals, Second Circuit, the parents claimed the hearing officers and the lower court did not analyze all the evidence. They said each tribunal failed to consider testimony by experts who had not attended the relevant CSE meeting and that the testimony of one their child's private school teachers was disregarded. **The court disagreed with the parents, finding the review officer explicitly considered the private school teacher's testimony and the independent evaluation.** It appeared to the court that the review officer exercised appropriate discretion in determining how much weight to put on the teacher's testimony. The court found the question of whether the student had made enough progress to join an ICT classroom was the type of educational policy question on which courts generally defer, as it relies on specialized knowledge. *J.S., L.S. on behalf of D.S. v. New York City Dep't of Educ.*, 648 Fed.Appx. 96 (2d Cir. 2016).

◆   A Massachusetts student was involved in several behavioral incidents and his parents grew concerned about bullying. Near the end of the school year, the student was hospitalized for 10 days in a pediatric psychiatric unit due to increased anxiety and symptoms of OCD. After the student spent the summer in a wilderness residential therapeutic program, the parents had him evaluated.

Near this time, the parents notified the school district that they were placing their child in a residential school. But the student left the school before the school year ended and the school district resumed tutoring services. The parents requested a hearing, seeking retroactive reimbursement for their placement. At an IEP meeting, the team considered the recommendations of a transition counselor hired by the parents. But this report was not provided to the IEP team until five days before the hearing. Over the district's objection, the hearing officer went forward with the hearing. But due to the lateness of the report, she did not consider it when deciding whether the IEP was appropriate. After the hearing officer upheld the IEP, the parents appealed to a federal court. It found the IDEA did not require the parents to provide copies of an independent report or evaluation to the school district. They complied with an IDEA requirement to share an evaluation with the other party within five business days of receiving the report. But the court held compliance with this requirement did not assure the hearing officer would review the report. **The decision by the parents to "wait until the eve of the hearing to provide the expert report to the school district did not merely inconvenience the School District, but circumvented the collaborative TEAM process established under the IDEA."** In sum, the court found the hearing officer had reason to discount the parents' evidence, and it held for the school district. *Doe v. Richmond Consolidated School Dist.*, No. 15-30027-MGM, 2016 WL 3064056 (D. Mass. 6/20/16).

◆   Unable to reach an agreement with their child's school district over his program, Minnesota parents requested a due process hearing. During a pretrial conference, an administrative law judge (ALJ) asked counsel how long they needed to present their cases. The parents' counsel said one and a half days. The school district's attorney asked for one day. On the first day of the hearing, the parents' attorney questioned a special education administrator for five hours.

When the parents' time expired the next day, the ALJ offered to let their attorney introduce evidence through additional witnesses. She instead chose to make an informal offer of proof of additional evidence she had hoped to present. Later, the ALJ held for the school district. After a federal court held for the district, the U.S. Court of Appeals, Eighth Circuit, found **the IDEA requires open hearings, the creation of a hearing record, the right to be advised by counsel, the right to present evidence and confront witnesses, and rights to access hearing transcripts, findings of fact and decisions**. Beyond these minimums, states may devise their own procedures. At the time of the hearing, Minnesota law required ALJs to set hearing times. State regulations added that the amount of time each party had to present its case was determined by balancing the due process rights of the parties with the need for administrative efficiency. In the court's view, there was no due process violation. *B.S. v. Anoka Hennepin Public Schools ISD No. 11*, 799 F.3d 1217 (8th Cir. 2015).

◆ A federal court in New York explained that the U.S. Court of Appeals, Second Circuit, has held **school officials may not present evidence that they would have provided any services not specified in an IEP in seeking to justify an IEP proposal. This is called "retrospective testimony."** Instead, the Second Circuit has held an IEP must be evaluated "prospectively as of the time of its drafting." *M.T. v. New York City Dep't of Educ.*, 47 F.Supp.3d 197 (S.D.N.Y. 2014).

◆ When a Maryland private school student with learning, language and other health impairments did not succeed despite the school's small size, significant accommodations and his receipt of additional services, his parents contacted a school district and sought special education. The district found the student eligible and proposed a draft IEP calling for the student's placement in a public middle school. The parents requested a due process hearing and enrolled the student in a different private school. The administrative law judge (ALJ) assigned the burden of proof to the parents. Since they could not meet this burden, the district prevailed. On appeal, a federal court held that the hearing officer had erroneously allocated the burden of proof to the parents. The Fourth Circuit vacated and remanded the case, and the ALJ held for the parents, finding that the IEP offered by the district was inadequate. A federal court agreed with the ALJ that the district did not provide the student with a FAPE during the year it first proposed an IEP. It awarded the parents full reimbursement for the costs of private school during the first year. Because the parents did not exhaust their administrative remedies concerning the two subsequent years of private school tuition, the court denied those claims. The Fourth Circuit reversed the district court, and the case reached the U.S. Supreme Court, which agreed with the court of appeals that **parents who challenge IEPs have the burden of proving that the IEPs are not appropriate**. To do otherwise would force courts to assume that every IEP is invalid until the school district demonstrates that it is not. *Schaffer v. Weast*, 546 U.S. 49, 126 S.Ct. 528, 163 L.Ed.2d 387 (2005).

On remand, the parents challenged the student's eighth-grade IEP by presenting evidence of the changes made to his tenth-grade IEP. A Maryland federal court ruled for the district, and the Fourth Circuit affirmed. *Schaffer v. Weast*, 554 F.3d 470 (4th Cir. 2009).

C. Hearing Officer Bias and Authority

In M.S. v. Utah Schools for the Deaf and Blind, *822 F.3d 1128 (10th Cir. 2016), the U.S. Court of Appeals, Tenth Circuit, held hearing officers in IDEA due process cases must resolve concrete issues in dispute. They may only delegate ministerial decisions that support their orders. The court relied on a California federal court decision holding that* **hearing officers cannot give IEP teams authority to change or reduce a remedy in any way**.

◆ A federal court rejected arguments by Washington parents that an administrative law judge (ALJ) had been biased against them. **It found no evidence that the ALJ acted questionably or that the extensive hearings had been unfair in any way.** In ruling for the school district, the court restated the longstanding rule that the IDEA does not require a district to maximize its effort and resources on any single student. Instead, schools are only required to provide students with a basic floor of opportunity. After the lower court held for the school district, the parents appealed to the Ninth Circuit, which again held for the district. In view of the evidence, the court held the parents failed to file their complaint until after the limitations period lapsed. Moreover, the parents did not show any exception to the statute of limitations applied. Although they raised other arguments, the court found them meritless and held for the school district. *Avila v. Spokane School Dist. 81*, 744 Fed.Appx. 506 (9th Cir. 2018).

◆   Based on dissatisfaction with the IEPs created for their child for two school years, New York parents enrolled him in a private school. They then requested an impartial hearing under the IDEA, seeking reimbursement for their private school costs. A hearing officer held for the school district. After a state review officer affirmed the decision, the case reached a federal court. According to the parents, the hearing officer was biased against them because he had previously served as a school superintendent. They claimed that as a non-attorney he was incompetent to serve as a hearing officer and that he fell asleep during the hearing. The court rejected the attack on the hearing officer's competence and found no bias that would exclude him from the case. Although the parents sought pretrial dismissal of the case, the court denied their motion.

The parents appealed to the U.S. Court of Appeals, Second Circuit, which rejected a claim that the hearing officer was biased against them because he had previously served as a school superintendent. According to the parents, the student's behavior intervention plan (BIP) could not have been implemented or updated on a timely basis. The court found the parents' objection to the BIP was speculative and based on a "pattern and practice" of failing to develop and implement BIPs and functional behavioral assessments in a timely fashion. In this case, the BIP was developed in time to be included in the relevant IEP. There was no support for the claim that the school district would not be able to implement and update the BIP. **While the parents claimed the hearing officer slept through parts of the hearing, a review of the record confirmed that he was awake and attentive.** There was evidence that the hearing officer spoke frequently, often directly questioning witness, and making rulings on the evidence and objections by counsel. Finding none of the parents' arguments had merit, the court held for the school district. *C.E. v. Chappaqua Cent. School Dist.*, 695 Fed.Appx. 621 (2d Cir. 2017).

◆   During the 2010-11 school year, a Connecticut parent claimed her child's school board violated IDEA procedures by holding two IEP meetings while the family was out of the country. In a due process proceeding, a hearing officer found the board offered the student an appropriate IEP and denied the parent's request for reimbursement for a home program. On appeal, a federal court rejected a claim that the board violated the IDEA by holding IEP meetings while the parents were abroad. In addition to finding the 2010-11 IEP appropriate, the court denied the parents' request to be reimbursed for the home program they provided him under the stay-put provision. On appeal, the Second Circuit found the parents participated in IEP meetings and the board repeatedly tried to schedule a meeting around their summer plans. It held the board was entitled to reject alternative placement options suggested by the parents. In a separate lawsuit, the parent challenged IEPs for her child for the 2011-12, 2012-13, 2013-14 and 2014-2015 school years. Unlike the previous case, she did not file a due process hearing request before filing suit. She added claims under the Americans with Disabilities Act and Section 504 of the Rehabilitation Act.

The court dismissed the case, and the parent appealed to the Second Circuit. It noted the lower court found the board of education provided appropriate notices. **No evidence supported a claim that an impartial hearing officer would be biased against the family.** Last, the court rejected a claim that exhaustion was excused because the family sought an award of money damages. Although the parent advanced other arguments in support of her case, including failure to notify her of her procedural rights under the IDEA, the court rejected each of them and held for the board. *Dervishi, on behalf of T.D. v. Stamford Board of Educ.*, 691 Fed.Appx. 651 (2d Cir. 2016).

◆ A North Carolina parent filed two federal court complaints regarding his son's education without hiring an attorney. After complaining to the state board of education, he agreed to participate in a facilitated IEP meeting in lieu of pursuing a complaint. But the parent claimed an official assigned to resolve the dispute delayed taking action on his complaint. He stated that the official then abandoned resolution efforts when he learned that the parent had filed two complaints against the school district. In response to the official's abandonment of his complaint, the parent filed a federal court action against education officials. In addition to alleging conspiracy and violations of the IDEA, the parent asserted constitutional violations. He requested a court order requiring the officials to provide adequate services to his son and assistance in forming adequate IEPs and behavior plans, as well as a declaration that they violated his constitutional rights. First, the court dismissed the IDEA claims, finding the parent's filing of a complaint seeking dispute resolution was not a petition for a due process hearing. Since the parent did not file a due process complaint, the court dismissed his IDEA claims, including those asserting retaliation for exercising his IDEA rights. In addition, the court dismissed all constitutional claims relating to his son's IEP and behavior intervention plan.

As for the parent's equal protection claim, the court found he did not claim that he was treated any differently than any similarly situated individual or that such treatment arose from intentional discrimination. There was no due process violation based on the parent's claim that the state official failed to move ahead with a facilitated IEP meeting. It was not shown that the procedures employed by the state were inadequate. Last, the court rejected the parent's claims based on civil conspiracy by the officials. **He identified no improper motive by the officials. Nor did he assert any concrete facts showing an agreement to deprive him of his constitutional rights.** The court dismissed the parent's remaining claims, including his request for appointment of counsel to represent him. When the case reached the U.S. Court of Appeals, Fourth Circuit, it found no error by the lower court and affirmed the judgment for the reasons stated by the lower court. *Justice v. Hussey*, 670 Fed.Appx. 785 (4th Cir. 2016).

II. NOTICE

To discourage unilateral action, the IDEA mandates notice to parents when a school seeks to initiate or change the identification, evaluation, placement or provision of a free appropriate public education to a child with disabilities, or refuses to initiate or change a child's identification, evaluation, or placement.

A. Generally

◆ A federal appeals court held an IDEA regulation assuring meaningful parental participation is only a procedural safeguard and does not create a substantive right that allows parents to dictate the outcome of an IEP by claiming they do not understand a child's IEP goals. The court disagreed with an attempt by Pennsylvania parents to read a substantive right into an IDEA regulatory requirement that school districts take necessary action to ensure that parents understand the proceedings of the IEP team. The court held an IDEA regulation found at 34 C.F.R. Part 300.322(e) does not create a substantive right, as the parents argued. Instead, it is a procedural safeguard requiring districts to take necessary action to assure understanding by parents who needed interpreters. **The court rejected the parents' interpretation of "meaningful participation" as perfect comprehension of all aspects of an IEP.** It found the regulation does not give parents a right to dictate outcomes by claiming to misunderstand IEP goals that were reasonably clear. In this case, the district facilitated the parents' participation throughout the IEP process. Finding a lower court correctly held for the school district, the court affirmed the judgment. *Colonial School Dist. v. G.K.*, 763 Fed.Appx. 192 (3d Cir. 2019).

◆ In an important case interpreting free appropriate education (FAPE) issues, the Fifth Circuit Court of Appeals upheld the IEPs of a Texas student with global delays and multiple disabilities whose parents became disenchanted when she was transferred to a new school. After the school district prevailed before a hearing officer and a lower court, the parents appealed to the Fifth Circuit. The court held *Endrew F. v. Douglas County School Dist. RE-1*, 137 S.Ct. 988 (2017), was not in conflict with *Cypress-Fairbanks Independent School Dist. v. Michael F.*, 118 F.3d 245 (5th Cir. 1997), a longstanding precedent setting forth relevant factors for assessing IEPs. After finding the IEPs offered the student a FAPE, the court rejected the parents' claim that the first IEP had been predetermined. They were active participants in the IEP development process and their complaints about the child's present level of academic achievement and functional performance surfaced only after the district sought to transfer her. They signed the relevant IEP, undercutting their current objections. The court found no evidence that the school district limited the student's IEP to "critical needs" and did not adequately inform the parents regarding her IEPs.

As the lower court found, the student was making progress at her home school. Noting "the IEP standard is not perfection," the court found the IEPs were reasonably calculated to allow her to make progress and provided her a FAPE. **In the court's opinion, it was unnecessary for the school district to hold an ARD meeting to announce the transfer of the student to another**

school. Prior federal cases have held that parents do not have to be involved in site selection. Although the parents raised additional arguments, the court rejected them and affirmed the judgment for the school district. *E.R. v. Spring Branch Independent School Dist.*, 909 F.3d 754 (5th Cir. 2018).

B. Prior Written Notice

Prior written notices (PWNs) – also known as notices of recommended educational placement (NOREPs) – have been described as the form completed at the end of the IEP development process that must be provided whenever a school district proposes to change the placement of a student with a disability. See 34 CFR §300.503, for the relevant IDEA regulation. See also https://sites. ed.gov/idea/files/modelform_Procedural_Safeguards_June_2009.pdf.

◆ A Pennsylvania parent claimed his child's school used notices of recommended educational placement (NOREPs) coercively to force him to accept an IEP including parent training. He filed a due process complaint against the district. After a hearing officer ordered an independent educational evaluation (IEE) of the student, the parent sued the school district in a federal court. Over the next months, he filed additional complaints against the district that were consolidated before a hearing officer. The school district initiated its own lawsuit against the parent, and he answered with counterclaims against the district. Among other things, the parent challenged the need for the IEE and claimed the district used NOREPs in an abusive way calculated to force him to accept parent training. He filed still another lawsuit, asserting NOREPs were used maliciously. Later, the court consolidated the cases and directed the parent to file an amended complaint. Instead of complying with the order and despite warnings that noncompliance would result in dismissal, he sought reconsideration of the prior rulings. The court denied reconsideration and again directed the parent to file an amended complaint. But he did not comply and the court dismissed the cases.

The parent appealed to the U.S. Court of Appeals, Third Circuit, which held that in general, a party has no right to maintain two separate actions involving the same subject matter, at the same time, in the same court and against the same party. Finding the action to consolidate the cases was for administrative efficiency, the court upheld the dismissal of the consolidated cases. Next, the court rejected the parent's claim that use of the NOREPs to force him into parent training amounted to a malicious abuse of process. **The court described a NOREP as a form completed at the end of the IEP development process that must be provided whenever a school district proposes to change the placement of a student with a disability.** Although the parent submitted other arguments, the court held for the school district. *Luo v. Owen J. Roberts School Dist.*, 737 Fed.Appx. 111 (3d Cir. 2018; U.S. cert. denied 1/7/19).

◆ A Maryland student with autism had neuromuscular deficits, was non-verbal and needed adult assistance at all times. She had "complex, challenging, disruptive behaviors such as hyperactivity and aggression." Her first-grade

IEP placed her in an intensive communication support classroom (ICSC). The district did not perfectly implement the student's behavior intervention plan. Her teacher did not keep her behavior and performance data, and he gradually began keeping her in the ICSC for longer periods than specified in her IEP. He did not tell the parents of this. According to the teacher, he reduced the student's time in general education settings in response to her daily needs. Midway through her first-grade year, an IEP team met to reduce her time in general education classes. Although the parents opposed any general education placement, they objected to the school district's approach and sought a private placement in a school for children with autism. When the team disagreed, they filed a due process complaint against the district. An administrative law judge found the teacher violated a number of IDEA procedural protections, but held the district did not deny the student a free appropriate public education (FAPE).

A federal court affirmed the decision, and the parents appealed to the Fourth Circuit Court of Appeals. It rejected the parents' argument that the ICSC was overly segregated for their child. Next, the court declined to hold that the teacher denied her a FAPE by increasing her hours in the ICSC beyond the time stated in her IEP. **A school must provide prior written notice to parents before changing a student's placement. But in this case, the court found the teacher's decision to provide more instruction in the ICSC than her IEP specified was "reasonably calculated to enable her to make progress appropriate in light of her circumstances."** The district noted an IEP meeting was held to incorporate the changes in hours into the IEP. The court found no significant infringement of the parents' rights in this case. *R.F. v. Cecil County Public Schools*, 910 F.3d 237 (4th Cir. 2019).

III. EXHAUSTION OF ADMINISTRATIVE REMEDIES

Before a party may file a lawsuit under the IDEA (or seek relief which may be available under the IDEA), the party must exhaust IDEA administrative remedies by going through IDEA due process procedures. The exhaustion of remedies doctrine provides that "no one is entitled to judicial relief for a supposed or threatened injury until the prescribed administrative remedy has been exhausted." Myers v. Bethlehem Shipbuilding Corp., 303 U.S. 41 (1938).

The U.S. Supreme Court, in McKart v. U.S., 395 U.S. 185 (1968), explained that the exhaustion doctrine allows for the development of an accurate factual record, thereby allowing more informed judicial review, encouraging "expeditious decision making," and taking advantage of agency expertise.

A. Operation of the Exhaustion Doctrine

◆ A Michigan parent claimed her child's school district denied him a free appropriate public education (FAPE) by classifying him as a student with a mild cognitive impairment, rather than autism. Although the case was dismissed due to her failure to exhaust IDEA administrative remedies, the court allowed her to refile the action after she filed a due process complaint and exhausted it. An administrative law judge (ALJ) held the student was denied a FAPE and imposed several corrective actions against the district. Eight months after the Michigan Department of Education (MDE) found the district was in compliance with the administrative order, the parent sought to reopen her federal court complaint. She claimed the district did not comply with the ALJ's order. The court referred the case to a federal magistrate judge, who found her remedy was to participate in a state complaint resolution procedure.

Instead of complying with the magistrate judge's instructions, the parent filed a second federal lawsuit, naming the MDE and her son's school district as parties. The court directed the parties to participate in facilitated meetings, and they reached an agreement for the student's current school year. But the parent refused to dismiss the second action, arguing the district should be ordered to pay for a private placement. The court dismissed the MDE from the case, then dismissed the claims against the school district based on the parent's failure to exhaust her administrative remedies. In 2018, the parent filed a third lawsuit against the school district, without appealing from the ALJ's decision. She admitted all her complaints stemmed from her belief that the district failed to timely evaluate her son in preschool some 13 years earlier. **Finding the parent filed a federal action concerning the provision of a FAPE without exhausting her administrative remedies, the court dismissed the case.** A few weeks after the court issued its order, the parent filed a motion for reconsideration. The court found she was trying "to refashion and re-argue her case by reiterating her feelings about how the educational system has disappointed her and presenting a generalized grievance regarding ... the existing special education system." Finding the parent's motion for reconsideration failed to identify any palpable defect in its prior decision, the court denied it. *Sharbowski v. Utica Community Schools*, No. 18-cv-10869, 2019 WL 1471483 (E.D. Mich. 4/3/19).

◆   A Pennsylvania fourth-grader had a history of behaving aggressively. He had a difficult transition to a new school, where he bit, kicked and scratched teachers and peers. A teacher responded to his misbehavior with force. She pushed, choked, dragged, slapped and improperly restrained him. After the teacher was charged with abusing the student, the district transferred him to another school. Because the parents feared that any restraint of their son could trigger traumatic memories, they urged the district to create an IEP minimizing physical contact with staff. Over the next six months, the parents and district staff met and refined the IEP numerous times. **The amended IEPs included de-escalation procedures and allowed restraint of the student only as a last resort.** Despite the revisions, staff continued to restrain him. After the parents removed their son from school, the district filed an administrative complaint with a state agency.

A hearing officer upheld the IEP and the parents appealed to a federal court. In addition to appealing the administrative decision, they asserted state law, Fourteenth Amendment and Rehabilitation Act claims arising from the abusive teacher's misconduct. According to the court, the non-IDEA claims were not exhausted, requiring dismissal of the entire case. On appeal, the Third Circuit held the parents' IEP challenge had been properly exhausted in the state administrative proceeding. It did not matter that the school district had filed the case. In fact, the district admitted the teacher's abusive conduct was unrelated to the IEP dispute. Once the hearing officer issued a decision, the parents had no further administrative recourse and could only appeal to a court under 20 U.S.C. § 1415(i)(2)(A). The hearing officer held an extensive hearing, finding the district provided the student a free and appropriate public education. **Finding the parents properly submitted their IEP challenge to a hearing officer, the court returned the case to the lower court for consideration of the IEP.** *E.R. v. Stroudsburg Area School Dist.*, 755 Fed. Appx. 166 (3d Cir. 2018).

◆   A Maine student with autism, cognitive impairments and Landau-Kleffner Syndrome could not speak. After school officials disallowed his parents' request to allow him to wear a recording device at school, they filed a due process complaint for denial of a reasonable accommodation. A hearing officer held for the school district. When the parents appealed to a federal court, they added disability discrimination and speech rights claims. But the court held they did not exhaust the IDEA administrative process. Following their appeal to the First Circuit, the parents filed a second due process complaint, arguing the district's refusal to allow a recording device deprived their child of a free appropriate public education. A hearing officer dismissed the second due process case. On appeal, the U.S. Court of Appeals, First Circuit, found the parents filed the second action to comply with the lower court's order. Finding the parents had exhausted all the process required by the IDEA, the court returned the case to the trial court, where they would have an opportunity to present their case. *Pollack v. Regional School Unit 75*, 660 Fed.Appx. 1 (1st Cir. 2016).

When the case returned to the trial court, it held the administrative findings precluded the parents from establishing that a recording device was a reasonable accommodation. After a trial, the court held for the school unit. On appeal, the First Circuit held the administrative findings had the same preclusive effect as a state court judgment. It held the parents could not mount an ADA challenge based on an argument that a device for their son to record his school day would be effective in providing him meaningful access to school benefits. According to the parents, the school unit's special education director agreed to allow them to view recordings of their child's speech-language therapy sessions, but only if they promised not to use the recordings as a basis for a complaint. **Finding the parents could not show a recording device would benefit their child, the court held for the school unit.** *Pollack v. Regional School Unit 75*, 886 F.3d 75 (1st Cir. 2018).

◆   A California student attended a school district's functional life skills special day class, spending 85% of her school day in segregated settings. According to her parent, her home behavior began to change due to inappropriate and "stressful disciplinary tactics" by school staff. She claimed the school district did not allow her child to go on a school trip, eat in the cafeteria or attend the general education classes that were supposed to make up 15% of her school day. Based on her claim that a staff member shoved her child into a desk, the parent filed complaints with the school district and the U.S. Department of Education's Office for Civil Rights. The staff member was placed on administrative leave and police investigated. After an incident in which the parent claimed her child was injured when leaving a school lavatory, the parent sued the district and two staff members in a federal court. She included claims under the Americans with

Disabilities Act, the Rehabilitation Act, the state Unruh Civil Rights Act and negligence theories. In pretrial activity, the district sought dismissal, arguing the parent had to file a due process complaint before proceeding to a court. Meanwhile, the parent filed a due process complaint with a state agency.

The court explained that **a due process action must precede any case involving federal laws protecting the rights of children with disabilities, when the relief sought is available under the IDEA**. In this case, the parent stated she was seeking to have her child's "education plan adjusted." She further claimed the district failed to accommodate her child's disability by providing the aids and supports she required. Finding the parent was contesting the adequacy of her child's IEP, the court held she had to exhaust her claims in an IDEA due process proceeding before filing a lawsuit. But the court granted her given permission to amend her complaint to establish other viable federal causes of action. *A.L. v. Clovis Unified School Dist.*, No. 1:17-CV-0358 AWI MJS, 2018 WL 1567835 (E.D. Cal. 3/30/18; 9th Cir. appeal filed 9/5/18).

◆   Due to chronic sinusitis, allergic rhinitis and intermittent asthma, a New Jersey student had a Section 504 plan for grade nine. According to his parents, the plan required him to "teach himself the curriculum and try to identify and understand assignments that had been explained when he was absent." They said he continued to fall behind his peers and accumulated absences. Despite his many absences, the student passed his classes and was promoted to grade 10. During his tenth-grade year, the school board enacted a new attendance policy requiring the retention of students with over 33 absences in a school year. This policy applied regardless of whether absences were excused, approved or unexcused.

During grade 10, the student had 37 medically excused absences, which would trigger grade retention under the new policy. Asserting the policy targeted their son and was discriminatory, the parents sued the board in a federal court for violating the Rehabilitation Act and the Americans with Disabilities Act. The parties reached a settlement by which the student was allowed to advance to grade eleven. But the parents decided to pursue their federal case, adding claims for compensatory education, compensatory damages and punitive damages. The court dismissed the case based on their failure to exhaust IDEA administrative remedies. On appeal, the U.S. Court of Appeals, Third Circuit, affirmed the judgment, finding the claims were educational in nature and related to the provision of a free appropriate public education. Months later, the Supreme Court granted the student's petition for review. It vacated the judgment and returned the case to the Third Circuit for further consideration in light of its recent decision in *Fry v. Napoleon Community Schools*, this chapter. When the case returned to the Third Circuit, it found the discrimination claims raised questions about whether the student's Section 504 plan addressed his needs. While the complaint asserted violations of Section 504 and other federal laws, it also implicated rights under the IDEA. **As the complaint emphasized charges that the board failed to provide for the student's educational needs arising from his disability, the court held the parents had to exhaust their claims through the IDEA administrative process before filing a lawsuit.** *S.D. v. Haddon Heights Board of Educ.*, 722 Fed.Appx. 119 (3d Cir. 2018).

◆   A Maryland student with attention deficit hyperactivity disorder and oppositional defiant disorder attended a summer program at a public school. He said another student dragged him into a school lavatory, and that a group of students taunted, antagonized, threatened, harassed and ultimately assaulted him. In addition, the student claimed one of the students recorded the assault incident, then posted a recording of it on social media. He claimed the principal called him into the office several days later and showed him the recording. Although the student told the principal he did nothing wrong, he was expelled from the summer program. His mother claimed she did not receive notice of the expulsion or any information about her options. The student was deemed eligible for grade eight the next fall, but he refused to reenroll and was subsequently committed to a behavioral health institution. He was diagnosed with post-traumatic stress disorder and manic depressive disorder with suicidal ideation.

The student sued the school district for negligence, violations of the IDEA, violation of Section 504 of the Rehabilitation Act and educational malpractice. A federal court held each of the claims charged the district - either directly or indirectly - with depriving the student of a free appropriate public education (FAPE). The court noted the absence of any due process proceeding. **Since state law and the IDEA both required the family to exhaust available administrative remedies before filing a lawsuit, the federal claims had to be dismissed.** Applying *Fry v. Napoleon Community Schools*, this chapter, the court found the gravamen of the federal claims asserted that the student had been denied a FAPE. As a result, the court held the IDEA exhaustion rule applied, requiring dismissal of his federal law claims. The state law claims could return to the state court. *Tawes v. Board of Educ. of Somerset County*, No. RDB-17-2375, 2017 WL 6313945 (D. Md. 12/11/17).

◆   The parents of an Ohio student with autism reached an agreement with their school district to place him in a specialized school in Pennsylvania. A year later, the parents moved to Nicaragua "to pursue a lifelong humanitarian calling." They had a grandparent execute a power of attorney document to assume responsibility for his care. Although the parents believed the power of attorney would entitle the student to continuing education at the Pennsylvania school, the Ohio district disagreed. Taking the position that the student was no longer a district resident, the board filed an action in an Ohio juvenile court to invalidate the power of attorney. In response, the parents requested a temporary restraining order from a federal court that would require the district to pay the Pennsylvania school for the student's placement. The court agreed with the board that the parents did not meet the requirements for injunctive relief. Their arguments hinged on the determination of issues currently before a juvenile court.

Moreover, the court observed that a party seeking relief that involves the provision of a FAPE must exhaust available administrative remedies under the IDEA prior to filing a lawsuit. The Supreme Court clarified the exhaustion rule in *Fry v. Napoleon Community Schools*, this chapter. As the Supreme Court held, the IDEA exhaustion rule hinges on whether a lawsuit seeks relief for the denial of a free appropriate public education (FAPE). If an action charges a school with such a denial, the parents cannot escape the exhaustion requirement by asserting non-IDEA claims. **The court held the claims in**

this case involved the provision of a FAPE and fell squarely within the exhaustion rule as articulated in *Fry.* This was true even though the parents added disability discrimination claims against the district. In denying relief to the parents, the court noted they had filed a due process request. As the decision was due within a specific time-frame, the court found no reason to excuse the parents from the exhaustion rule. *J.D. v. Graham Local School Dist. Board of Educ.,* No. 3:17-cv-143, 2017 WL 1807626 (S.D. Ohio 5/5/17).

◆ A Michigan student with severe cerebral palsy had a service dog trained to help her with mobility and activities such as opening doors, turning on and off lights and transferring on and off a toilet. Her parents asked school officials to allow the dog to accompany their child to school. After a brief trial period, the dog was not allowed at school. In response, the parents removed their child from school and began homeschooling her. They filed a federal agency complaint, charging the school district with violating the ADA and Section 504 of the Rehabilitation Act. The agency held the district did not comply with the ADA and Section 504, even if a 1:1 aide provided the student a FAPE. School officials allowed the dog to accompany the student to school. But the parents felt the administration would resist their child's return to school, so they placed her in another district, where the dog and student were welcomed. The parents sued the school district and a regional school district in a federal court for failing to reasonably accommodate their child under Section 504 and the ADA.

The court dismissed the case because the parents did not first file an IDEA due process complaint. On appeal, the Sixth Circuit Court of Appeals affirmed the judgment and appeal reached the U.S. Supreme Court. It found that a party cannot escape the exhaustion requirement by simply filing an action under a law other than the IDEA. If the action seeks a remedy that implicates a FAPE, exhaustion is required. This is because the only relief an IDEA hearing officer can order is relief from the denial of a FAPE. **Courts should review the substance of a complaint when determining whether the FAPE obligation is implicated.** To illustrate its decision, the Court offered two considerations. A court should examine whether the same claim could be brought if the alleged conduct took place at a public facility other than a school. Next, a reviewing court should examine whether an employee or visitor to a school could have brought the same kind of grievance. If the family could have filed a similar claim against a non-school entity, or a similar action could have been filed by an employee or a school visitor, the complaint would be unlikely to involve a FAPE. If a complaint appeared to involve the FAPE duty, a court should still examine the history of the proceedings to determine whether the family has previously invoked IDEA procedures. *Fry v. Napoleon Community Schools,* 137 S.Ct. 743, 197 L.Ed.2d 46 (U.S. 2017).

◆ New York parents said their children's school district used their children's chronic fatigue syndrome diagnoses as an excuse to deny them appropriate educational opportunities. They said both children were not allowed to pursue homeschool programs for two years. Before removing their children from school, the school district reported the parents to child protection authorities. They claimed the school district prevented both children from graduating from high school before reaching the age of 21, and they sued the district and officials for violating Section 504, the Americans with Disabilities Act (ADA) and the Equal Protection Clause, among other things. The court held for the school district and officials. On appeal, the U.S. Court of Appeals, Second Circuit, held the parents should have first filed a due process complaint.

Although the parents argued they should not have had to exhaust IDEA remedies, **the court found the theory behind their complaint was that the children's diagnoses were used as an excuse to deny them appropriate educational opportunities**. It held the IDEA would provide relief for their grievances. IDEA coverage extends broadly to children requiring home instruction. The court found that if the "theory" behind a claim relates to the education of a disabled child, IDEA procedures apply. Since a due process hearing would have helped to resolve the homebound instruction dispute, the court held the ADA, Section 504 and equal protection claims were properly dismissed on exhaustion grounds. Next, the court held the parents could not pursue a conspiracy claim against the school district employees. Case law established that it is legally impossible for members of the same entity to engage in a conspiracy. Last, the court held the parents' retaliation claim based on a report to child protective services had been properly dismissed as untimely. *L.K. v. Sewanhaka Cent. High School Dist.*, 641 Fed.Appx. 56 (2d Cir. 2016).

B. Exceptions to the Exhaustion Doctrine

The administrative exhaustion doctrine does not apply when it would be futile to file a due process case. Delay by an agency in making a decision, or the fact that the agency may not be empowered to grant relief, may excuse the exhaustion requirement. The unavailability of a state or local remedy or a predetermined result by an agency may also excuse the requirement.

◆   Missouri parents sought specific accommodations for their son's intellectual disabilities from Down syndrome before he began kindergarten, including use of an iPad to compensate for his speech and fine motor delays. They sought to have his teachers integrate the iPad into their lessons. Negotiations between the parents and school officials lasted for about a year. The district offered IEPs that would have required special education classes, while the parents sought Section 504 accommodations that would allow their son to remain in regular education classes. After rejecting the IEP offers, the parents pulled him out of school and sued the school district in a federal court for disability discrimination.

Finding the parents' complaint asked for relief that would be available in an IDEA due process proceeding, the court held for the district. On appeal, the U.S. Court of Appeals, Eighth Circuit, noted the parents' argument that their decision to opt out of any special education for their son under the IDEA excused their failure to exhaust IDEA administrative remedies prior to filing suit. **The court held there is no exception to IDEA administrative exhaustion based on the opt out of special education and related services.** In *Fry v. Napoleon Community Schools*, 137 S.Ct. 743 (U.S. 2017), the Court held parents must exhaust IDEA administrative remedies whenever a free appropriate public education is at issue. While the claims in this case asserted disability discrimination under Section 504 and the Americans with Disabilities Act, the court noted that conduct violating these statutes may also implicate the IDEA. **Parents who seek relief under multiple statutes must still exhaust their administrative remedies prior to filing a lawsuit.** There was no categorical exception to the exhaustion requirement for parents who refused all IDEA services on behalf of their children. Concluding that "opting out of IDEA services does not unlock a pathway around exhaustion," the court held for the school district. *E.D. v. Palmyra R-I School Dist.*, 911 F.3d 938 (8th Cir. 2018).

◆   Tennessee parents asserted their child's school district and the Tennessee Department of Education (TDOE) were complicit in violating IDEA procedures to the extent of causing systemic violations. They said emails from the TDOE to district officials showed clear bias by the TDOE to decide special education complaints in favor of school districts. Convinced that their son would not receive an appropriate IEP, the parents enrolled him in another school system. Instead of requesting a due process hearing, they sued the district in a federal court, asserting IDEA, Rehabilitation Act and Americans with Disabilities Act claims. They said the TDOE did not investigate their charge and relied solely on the district's account. The school district and the TDOE sought dismissal.

After explaining the IDEA's administrative exhaustion requirement, the court held that an exception applies when relief is sought on the basis of "systemic IDEA violations." While the parents argued there was a systemic problem with the state complaint resolution process, the court found the case challenged one district, with a "secondary nominal challenge" to state processes. The systemic violations exception did not apply where a complaint focused on the particularized concerns of one family. The parents only argued the TDOE and the district had a "chummy relationship" that allowed the TDOE to easily explain inconsistencies. **While the parents wanted a more thorough investigation, their claim against the TDOE did not implicate the systemic violations exception to IDEA exhaustion.** Further, the IDEA contemplates that IEP disagreements such as this one be directed into a due process hearing. As a result, the court dismissed the case. *C.P. v. Tennessee Dep't of Educ.*, No. 3:16-cv-02938, 2018 WL 1566819 (M.D. Tenn. 3/30/18).

◆   A federal court held a case asserting the improper restraint of a 10-year-old student with disabilities on his school bus was properly dismissed. Although the student's parents argued exhaustion did not apply to physical damages, the court held this was incorrect. It discussed the Supreme Court's decision in *Fry v. Napoleon Community Schools*, this chapter. In *Fry*, the Court held a student seeking relief available under the IDEA must exhaust the law's administrative procedures before filing a lawsuit. **Exhaustion of remedies is required whenever a lawsuit implicates the denial of a free appropriate public education (FAPE).** Courts must examine the substance of the complaint to see if FAPE is implicated. A court should first consider whether the same claim could have been brought against an entity other than a school. Second, a court should ask whether an adult could have brought essentially the same claim. According to the Supreme Court, if the answer to both questions is no, the complaint likely involves the denial of FAPE. The family's complaint and each of the claims sought relief for the deprivation of a FAPE. Numerous factual allegations referred to the student's entitlement to special education and transportation. The complaint cited the IEP process, the relationship between the student's IEP and the claims, his educational programs and services, the educational setting, his special education needs and a FAPE. Even the student's negligence claim referred to his IEP, asserting the transportation company failed to comply with it. As the student sought relief available under the IDEA, he had to exhaust his administrative remedies before filing suit. *J.L. v. Wyoming Valley West School Dist.*, 722 Fed.Appx. 190 (3d Cir. 2018).

♦ A Colorado student claimed he had depression and post-traumatic stress disorder due to years of bullying by peers at his school. He had behavioral outbursts in response to peer misconduct and was placed on behavior contracts, which were characterized as unsuccessful. Eventually, his misconduct escalated into threats, including a threat to "shoot up the school." Based on the student's misconduct, the school held an expulsion hearing. But he claimed it did not first determine whether his conduct was a manifestation of his disabilities, as required by regulations implementing Section 504 of the Rehabilitation Act. Although the school later held a manifestation hearing, the student claimed it was still defective. He stated that the district held an expulsion hearing without providing proper notice, then expelled him. The student's parents filed a federal complaint that led to an investigation by the Department of Justice's Office for Civil Rights (OCR). This led to a voluntary resolution agreement specifying OCR monitoring and an investigation. As part of the agreement, the district agreed to hold another hearing. But after the hearing, it again decided to expel the student. His parents sued the district in a federal court for violations of the IDEA, Section 504 and the Americans with Disabilities Act. In sum, the student claimed the expulsion was wrongful because it was based on his disabilities. He further claimed the district violated federal laws. The court dismissed the case, finding the family failed to exhaust its IDEA administrative remedies.

On appeal, the Tenth Circuit Court of Appeals noted **a party seeking relief under federal laws such as the ADA and Section 504 must exhaust IDEA administrative remedies before filing suit, if the relief sought is available under the IDEA.** According to the family, administrative exhaustion was not required for at least three reasons. These included futility, failure by the district to provide appropriate notice of available remedies, and systemic violations by the district. The court found the parents never raised these arguments before the lower court. For this reason, they could not raise them at this stage of the case. The judgment for the school district was affirmed. *A.P., IV v. Lewis Palmer School Dist. No. 38*, 728 Fed.Appx. 835 (10th Cir. 2018).

♦ The parent of a student with schizencephaly (a congenital brain malformation) disputed conduct by three Missouri school districts, challenging them on matters including residency, requests to evaluate her child and denial of special education services. She sued the Special School District of St. Louis County (SSD), Hazelwood School District and Riverview Gardens School Districts and a state agency in a federal court. The parent said the state agency colluded with SSD "to give Hazelwood and SSD time to cover up their improper denial of [her] requests for an IEP and 504 evaluations for R.M." She accused agency staff of altering the transcript of a prehearing conference call to make it appear she had agreed to certain actions. Critically, the parent did not appeal from the dismissal of a due process complaint she filed previously. Among other things, she sought an order requiring SSD and Hazelwood to evaluate her child and immediately implement an IEP. She sought reimbursement of her expenses from all three school districts, as well as compensatory and punitive damages.

The court noted the Supreme Court recently clarified (in *Fry v. Napoleon Community Schools*, this chapter) that the IDEA administrative exhaustion rule hinges on whether a lawsuit seeks relief for the denial of a FAPE. If such a denial is alleged, **a party cannot escape administrative exhaustion simply by filing suit based on a law other than the IDEA**. The parent claimed it would have been futile to pursue administrative remedies. But the court found the child's eligibility for an IEP was the "central dispute" of the litigation. As compensatory education is "relief available" in an IDEA due process proceeding, the court found the parent could not show it would have been futile to request a due process hearing prior to filing suit. Further, the court found the Section 504 claims asserted the denial of a FAPE. In any event, the parent did not show the school districts intentionally failed to provide her child a FAPE in bad faith. Finding the claims involved the denial of a FAPE, the court held they were barred by the exhaustion rule. *Swift v. SSD of St. Louis County*, No. 4:16CV00314 AGF, 2017 WL 4237010 (E.D. Mo. 9/25/17).

On appeal, the Eighth Circuit Court of Appeals affirmed the judgment, modifying it so the parents could not further amend their complaint. *Swift v. SSD of St. Louis County*, No. 17–3223, 2017 WL 8810737 (8th Cir. 11/7/17).

◆   A Tennessee student who took medication for ADHD was recommended for a second year of kindergarten. The parent filed four administrative complaints against the school district and a complaint with the state education department that led to an investigation. The department found two procedural violations by the district and ordered it to take corrective action. The parent filed a due process complaint against the school district that was settled prior to a hearing. She then filed two more complaints against the district with the education department, which found no IDEA violations. The parent filed yet another due process complaint against the district, asserting it breached their settlement agreement by moving her child from a Tier III to a Tier II setting.

An administrative law judge (ALJ) dismissed the parent's most recent due process complaint. After she was given an opportunity to amend her complaint, the ALJ found she raised some claims that might have merit. The parent then voluntarily dismissed her complaint and sued the school district and the state education department in a federal court for violations of the IDEA, Section 504 of the Rehabilitation Act and the ADA. In addition, the parent claimed the district breached the settlement agreement by not properly implementing her child's IEP. The court held the parent's most recent complaint did not meet minimal requirements. She voluntarily withdrew her remaining claims, even though the ALJ deemed them viable. The court held the proper procedure for review of the department's findings was an impartial due process hearing.

The Section 504 and ADA claims failed because the parent did not request a hearing. But she could pursue her breach of settlement claim. And **the parent could pursue a claim asserting systemic practices of failing to prepare and implement IEPs on a wide scale.** As she did not have to exhaust administrative remedies regarding potential systemic IDEA violations and breach of the agreement, the court refused to dismiss those claims. *A.G. and C.F. v. Tennessee Dep't of Educ.*, No. 1:16-cv-00027, 2017 WL 112526 (M.D. Tenn. 1/11/17).

◆   An Indiana parent claimed administrators ignored her requests to evaluate her son's special education needs and her request for a due process hearing. She asked the principal of her son's school to test him because of his many impairments but said he never followed through. When the principal was replaced, the parent said the successor principal ignored the same request. In a federal court complaint, the parent said her son was placed with a teacher who wrongfully and excessively disciplined him. She said the principal did not take the school's bullying policy seriously. Asserting she had no other choice, the parent pulled her child from the school and tried online education before suing the board in federal court. The court noted that the parent had filed her action without the assistance of an attorney. In her supplement to the complaint, the parent asserted violations of the IDEA and the No Child Left Behind Act.

The court held there is no private right of action to enforce the No Child Left Behind Act. **Since the IDEA does not provide for individual liability, the court dismissed the IDEA claims against two school administrators.** But the court rejected the school board's argument that the IDEA claims had no validity under any view of the facts. Since the parent was not represented by counsel, the court held her complaint had to be construed liberally. It held she might be able to show she had exhausted available remedies. While the board was entitled to judgment on the pleadings, the parent was allowed 30 days to file an amended complaint to either pursue her IDEA administrative remedies or explain how such efforts were futile. *Hudson-Harris v. Board of School Commissioners of City of Indianapolis*, No. 1:16-cv-00245-TWP-DML, 2017 WL 605177 (S.D. Ind. 2/15/17).

◆   West Virginia parents brought a due process complaint against their child's board of education. A hearing officer ordered the board to contract with an educational service provider within five days and to train the child, his parents and school staff to use his speech-generating device. The board also had to develop and implement an applied behavior analysis program. Over a month later, the parents informed the board it was violating the order by failing to contract with the provider. They advised the board they would transport their child to receive the services ordered by the hearing officer, even though the board had not contracted with the provider. The board filed an action to appeal the hearing officer's decision. The parents responded and added counterclaims under the Rehabilitation Act, the Americans with Disabilities Act and the IDEA. A federal court denied the board's request to stay (temporarily block) implementation of the administrative order. It held the IDEA's stay-put provision has been interpreted as making a school system financially responsible for the cost of a placement during the pendency of an IDEA dispute.

Since the board's request to stay the administrative order ran afoul of the stay-put provision, the court held for the parents. It rejected a claim that the parents failed to exhaust their administrative remedies. It appeared that the parties had fully run the IDEA administrative process. A second round of administrative proceedings did not have to be brought before the parents could raise counterclaims for money damages. **The court held the case should not be dismissed as it was an original civil action, not an IDEA appeal.** *Board of Educ. of County of Boone, West Virginia v. K.M.*, Civ. No. 2:14-cv-10563, 2015 WL 1481775 (S.D. W.Va. 3/31/15).

C. Claims for Money Damages

In J.B. v. Avilla R-XIII School Dist., *721 F.3d 588 (8th Cir. 2013), this chapter, the Eighth Circuit dismissed a case in which Missouri parents were seeking to recover their educational costs without first requesting a hearing. The court found they were asking for relief that was available under the IDEA.*

◆ The parents of an Iowa teenager with polycystic ovarian syndrome and depression did not convince the Eighth Circuit Court of Appeals that it should hear their discrimination claims against a school district that denied her open enrollment application. According to the court, they should have first exhausted their administrative remedies. It noted that exhaustion is not limited to IDEA claims. Instead, the exhaustion rule applies when a party files an action under federal laws protecting children with disabilities, if the claims seek relief that is also available under the IDEA. In *Fry v. Napoleon Community School Dist.*, 137 S.Ct. 743 (U.S. 2017), the U.S. Supreme Court clarified that **IDEA exhaustion applies if "the substance or gravamen" of the complaint is the denial of a free appropriate public education (FAPE).** In this case, the court found the claim that the district of residence had mishandled the open enrollment application essentially stated that FAPE had been denied. It was claimed that the district of residence was unable to meet the student's educational needs and failed to make reasonable accommodations to enable her to receive a FAPE.

The court rejected the parents' claim that any exception to the administrative exhaustion rule applied. Moreover, it found their complaint to the state board was separate and distinct from the claims they now asserted. **The court found the fact that the parents sought monetary damages in the present action did not preclude them from filing a due process complaint.** They could have filed a due process challenge against the district for failing to identify their child and to provide her with a FAPE. In sum, the court dismissed the case due to failure by the parents to exhaust available IDEA administrative remedies. *Nelson v. Charles City Community School Dist.*, 900 F.3d 587 (8th Cir. 2018).

◆ A federal appeals court held the restraint and isolation of a Missouri student with autism and other disorders involved the implementation of his IEP and thus required his parent to pursue a due process proceeding before suing their school district. The court held the student's IEP was the central dispute at issue. The complaint challenged the repeated use of isolation and restraint that was "not permitted within his IEPs." **Although the parent claimed she sought monetary relief that is unavailable under the IDEA, the court held the administrative exhaustion requirement still applied.** Finding the case involved the failure to implement the student's IEP regarding discipline and thus implicated the FAPE obligation, the court held for the school district. *J.M. v. Francis Howell School Dist.*, 850 F.3d 944 (8th Cir. 2017).

◆   After being diagnosed with Torticollis, an Ohio child was referred to an IDEA Part C provider for therapy. Later, the child was diagnosed with autism. Although the autism assessment recommended 25-40 hours of weekly applied behavior analysis (ABA) therapy, the local Part C provider did not provide it. The child's parents began providing ABA therapy at their own expense and then sued the Ohio Health Department and its IDEA Part C coordinator in a federal court, asserting a systematic and predetermined deprivation of early intervention services. They included claims under the IDEA, the ADA, Rehabilitation Act Section 504 and the Equal Protection Clause. The parents sought declaratory relief and monetary damages to help their child achieve the development level they felt he would have received had necessary services been provided earlier. Finding the parents had simply recast IDEA claims under other federal laws, the court dismissed the case for failure to exhaust IDEA remedies.

On appeal, the U.S. Court of Appeals, Sixth Circuit, found that IDEA Part C has an exhaustion provision that operates the same as the one in IDEA Part B. **The court found the parents could have obtained relief in an administrative hearing, including reimbursement for services.** Since the relief was available under the IDEA, administrative exhaustion was not excused. Next, the parents claimed exhaustion was futile because they asserted systemic violations of law by the state that a hearing officer lacked the power to address. The court found this theory failed because the only systemic relief sought by the parents was a declaration that the state violated the rights of infants and toddlers with disabilities. The court dismissed the equal protection claim and other claims. *W.R. v. State of Ohio, Health Dep't*, 651 Fed.Appx. 514 (6th Cir. 2016).

◆   An Alabama grandparent who failed to mention a Section 504 claim in an IDEA appeal notice regarding her grandchild could not pursue any Section 504 claim at the hearing. When the case reached the Eleventh Circuit Court of Appeals, it noted the grandparent's notice did not mention Section 504 other than to say that the child had once been found eligible for Section 504 services. **For any claim seeking relief available under the IDEA, the act's due process procedures must be used.** The rule applies to Section 504, Americans with Disabilities Act and constitutional claims. Since the grandparent did not seek a due process hearing for her Section 504 claims, she could not now pursue them. Because she did not exhaust her administrative remedies and did not show it would have been futile to do so, the case was properly dismissed. *Laura A. v. Limestone County Board of Educ.*, 610 Fed.Appx. 836 (11th Cir. 2015).

◆   During a home economics class, a Michigan student stopped working on a project. He said this caused his teacher to become enraged and yell "why don't you just go kill yourself" to the class. According to the student, the teacher then ripped his project from his hands and threatened to lock him in a room. In a state court, the student sued the teacher and school district for intentional infliction of emotional distress. Finding reasonable minds could differ regarding whether the teacher's conduct was "extreme and outrageous," the court held it had been error for the trial court to dismiss the case. As an alternative argument, the teacher said that the case could not go forward due to the family's failure to first exhaust available IDEA administrative remedies. Other courts had applied the exhaustion doctrine to actions filed under federal laws seeking relief that was available under the IDEA. **But the court found no authority declaring that the IDEA administrative requirement applied to a tort case.** *Melson v. Botas*, No. 315014, 2014 WL 2867197 (Mich. Ct. App. 6/19/14).

IV. LIMITATION OF ACTIONS

An IDEA provision states that a parent or educational agency must request an impartial due process hearing within two years of the date the parent or agency knew (or should have known) about the facts forming the basis of the complaint. But if the state has an explicit time limitation for requesting such a hearing, the state time period applies. The IDEA's two-year limitation period does not apply if the parent was prevented from requesting a hearing because the local educational agency made specific misrepresentations, or if the local educational agency has withheld information from the parent.

◆   A New York parent sought a residential placement for her child during a committee on special education (CSE) meeting held near the end of the 2011 school year. The CSE denied the request and confirmed the decision by mailing her a copy of the 2011-12 IEP. According to the parent, the school district's inaction result in a "crisis" for her child during the 2011-12 school year. In 2015, she filed a due process complaint. While the IDEA claims were dismissed as untimely, **the hearing officer found the district violated Section 504 of the Rehabilitation Act by failing to provide the student with a residential placement from January to June 2012**. After a state review officer affirmed the decision on the IDEA claim, the parent appealed. A federal court held for the school district, finding the IDEA and Section 504 claims were untimely.

On appeal, the U.S. Court of Appeals, Second Circuit, found the "crisis" identified by the parent was a manifestation of the consequences of actions at an IEP meeting in May 2011. As a result, the claims under the IDEA and Section 504 accrued by May or June 2011. It rejected the parent's claim that the district made misrepresentations that required extending the limitation on filing her case. There was no merit to her claim that she did not adequately understand her due process rights. An advocate attended the May 2011 CSE meeting to help argue for a residential placement. Further, the parent acknowledged she had received notice of her procedural safeguards. Finding the action was untimely and she was not entitled to any exception allowing her to extend the timeline for filing, the court held the case was properly dismissed. *Board of Educ. of North Rockland Cent. School Dist. v. C.M.*, 744 Fed.Appx. 7 (2d Cir. 2018).

◆   A Maine tenth-grader earned four Fs and a D- and was identified as a student with a disability. He engaged in inappropriate internet use and said he was cyberbullied. During the student's eleventh-grade school year, he often missed classes and his parent sometimes kept him home to avoid bullying. Based on a report that the student stole shoes while at school, the school board voted to expel him. He was offered interim tutorial services and attended a partial-day program at an integrated alternative school. Although the student thrived in the placement, his parent objected to the school's shortened school day and her lengthy commute. She placed him in a Massachusetts residential school and filed a due process complaint, seeking reimbursement for over $115,000 in private school tuition costs. A hearing officer dismissed claims that arose during the student's ninth- and tenth-grade years as time-barred. Although the claims relating to his eleventh- and twelfth-grade years were found timely, the hearing officer held his IEPs for those years were reasonably calculated to provide a free appropriate public education (FAPE). A federal court found the time limitation was valid and held the student received a FAPE in grades eleven and twelve. When appeal reached the First Circuit Court of Appeals, it returned the case to the lower court for more consideration of the limitations question. But the court held the student received a FAPE in grades eleven and twelve.

When the case returned to the lower court, it allowed the state education department to intervene regarding the validity of its regulations. In 2019, the case returned to the First Circuit, which found **the IDEA's two-year limitation period requires a parent or school district to file an action within two years of the date the facts forming the basis of the complaint were known (or should have been known).** The court explained that an exception to this timeline applies where a parent was prevented from requesting a hearing due to specific misrepresentations by the school district. Maine enacted a time limitation in 2007 that tracked IDEA language. According to the parent, the state rule was invalid because the department failed to follow necessary rulemaking procedures. The court found that even if the rule was improperly made, the two-year IDEA limitation period barred claims arising from the student's ninth- and tenth-grade years. *Ms. S. v. Regional School Unit 72*, 916 F.3d 41 (1st Cir. 2019).

◆   A federal court held the parent of two Washington students with learning disabilities could not pursue time-barred claims for private school tuition from a school district. The court found evidence that the parent knew (or should have known) well before she filed her complaint of the underlying facts supporting her claim that the school district failed to provide a FAPE to her children. Lack of progress by a student is not itself sufficient to trigger the knowledge requirement. Instead, a parent's "knew or should have known" date is triggered when there is a lack of progress attributed to the school district.

Under Washington law, an action must be filed within two years after a party knows or should have known about the action forming the basis of the complaint. Over three years before she filed her due process complaint, the parent stated that she believed the district was "out of compliance." She said the district acknowledged it had a "limited curriculum" and did not recognize dyslexia as a learning disability over two years before she filed the due process complaint. For this reason, the court held the hearing officer had correctly refused to consider the IEPs from school years prior to her placement of the children in a private school. But the court held the complaint was unclear about whether the parent was challenging an IEP for a third school year after she had made the private placement. It returned the case to the hearing officer for further consideration. *Vandell v. Lake Washington School Dist.*, No. C18-0785-JCC, 2019 WL 1123566 (W.D. Wash. 3/12/19).

◆   In a Montana student's case, the U.S. Court of Appeals, Ninth Circuit, held **an IDEA provision bars claims filed more than two years after parents "knew or should have known about the actions forming the basis of the complaint."** In the court's opinion, the parents knew or should have known of the basis for a complaint as of the time they enrolled their daughter in middle school. As they waited more than five years from that time to file an action, many of their older claims were barred. Next, the court found the school district was obligated to identify, locate and evaluate all students with disabilities within its boundaries. The IDEA child-find duty arises when a disability is "suspected" or when the district has notice of symptoms of a disability.

While the court found the school district arguably knew that the student was hospitalized for suicidal ideation, triggering the child-find obligation, the claim was still barred because of the parents' long delay in filing suit. Evidence indicated they participated in the development of the student's IEP. According to the court, the district did not predetermine a placement. Moreover, the IEP appeared to be reasonably calculated to enable the student to progress in a public school. Concluding that the school district complied with the IDEA, the court upheld the decision in its favor. *J.K. and J.C. v. Missoula County Public Schools*, 713 Fed.Appx. 666 (9th Cir. 2018).

◆   Connecticut parents claimed their child's school district did not appropriately "label" him, leading to the failure to provide him with a FAPE during his K-8 school years. They placed him in a private school and filed a due process hearing in which they sought reimbursement for their private school tuition, medical expenses and transportation costs. An impartial hearing officer held they were not entitled to these costs. On appeal, a federal court declined the school board's invitation to dismiss certain claims as arising outside the two-year limitations period established by the IDEA. In doing so, it noted **the IDEA's limitation period requires parents to file a complaint no more than two years after they "knew or should have known about" a violation**. Since the relevant limitation period is two years from the date the parents reasonably should have known of an IDEA violation, further fact-finding was necessary. The two-year limit did not apply if the parents were prevented from requesting a hearing or if the board withheld information from them. *Wong v. State Dep't of Educ.*, No. 3:16-cv-1873 (VAB), 2018 WL 500642 (D. Conn. 1/22/18).

◆   In 2006, Washington parents asked their school to evaluate their five-year-old child due to his behavior. A school psychologist evaluated him and found his behavior was not severe enough to make him IDEA-eligible. A year later, the parents enrolled their child in kindergarten. A private third-party physician diagnosed him with Asperger's Disorder, and they requested a reevaluation. This time, a school psychologist found the student eligible for special education as a student with autism. After multiple IEP meetings during 2008-2009, the parties signed an IEP in 2009 and the student began attending a district program for students with autism. In 2010, after another reevaluation, the parents rejected a district IEP proposal. The district declined to pay for an independent educational evaluation (IEE). After the parents requested a due process hearing to contest the IEP, the school district requested a hearing to defend its evaluation. An administrative law judge (ALJ) found the school district's reevaluation appropriate and denied the parents' request to fund an IEE. The ALJ held for the district on the remaining claims, finding any claims based on matters taking place more than two years prior to the filing date were time-barred. Included was a claim that the district denied the student a free appropriate public education (FAPE) by failing to identify him as a student with autism in 2006, then failed to evaluate him in all areas of suspected disability in 2006-07. A federal court agreed with the ALJ that the claims arising from matters taking place over two years prior to the date of filing the action were barred by the IDEA's limitation period. In addition, the court affirmed the ALJ's ruling that the 2010 IEP was appropriate and that it provided the student a FAPE. On appeal, **the U.S. Court of Appeals, Ninth Circuit, held the "discovery rule" governs the IDEA's filing period at 20 U.S.C. § 1415(f)(3)(C).** Under the rule, the limitations period begins to run when a party discovers (or could have discovered) the existence of a claim. Section 1415(f)(3)(C) pertains to the timeline for requesting a hearing. **Public policy reasons and legislative history supported use of the discovery rule.** Since the lower court's decision to bar the claims was based on when the objectionable conduct occurred, rather than use of the discovery rule, the case had to be reconsidered. Awareness of the 2006-07 evaluations did not trigger the parents' knowledge or reason to know of a claim. *Avila v. Spokane School Dist. 81*, 852 F.3d 936 (9th Cir. 2017).

After the lower court held for the school district, the parents brought a new appeal to the Ninth Circuit, which again held for the district. In view of the evidence, the court held the parents failed to file their complaint until after the limitations period lapsed. Moreover, the parents did not show any exception to the statute of limitations applied. Although they raised other arguments, the court found them meritless and held for the school district. *Avila v. Spokane School Dist. 81*, 744 Fed.Appx. 506 (9th Cir. 2018).

♦   An 18-year-old Texas student with autism and severe intellectual disabilities had a developmental age of about three. He was aggressive toward school staff. After many meetings with school representatives, his parents stated they would transfer their son to a specialized school. They requested a due process hearing, asserting physical abuse by staff and failure to provide him appropriate services. Before the hearing officer, the school district challenged the mother's authority to file a due process case on behalf of her son, who was no longer a minor. Within weeks, the parents obtained a state court order declaring the student incompetent and appointing them to serve as his guardians. The due process complaint included claims under the IDEA and Rehabilitation Act Section 504, but the parents did not mention Section 504 during the proceeding.

In her decision, the hearing officer did not discuss the Section 504 claims and held most of the IDEA claims were barred by a one-year state limitations period. As for the remaining three-month period at issue, she found no IDEA violations. A federal court held for the school district, and appeal reached the U.S. Court of Appeals, Fifth Circuit. It noted the IDEA, at 20 U.S.C. § 1415(m) (2), applies to children who have reached the age of majority and who have not been determined to be incompetent, yet do not have the ability to provide informed consent. At the relevant time, the state of Texas had not complied with the provision. But the court found the state's inaction did not prevent the parent from obtaining a determination of incompetency from a state court at an earlier time. In addition, the hearing officer had excused the parent's lack of capacity to request a due process hearing. Next, **the court held the state's one-year limit on appeals was appropriately applied in this case.** Since most of the conduct at issue took place over a year prior to the filing, the limitations period barred much of the case. And because all of the claims directly related to the student's education, the IDEA's administrative exhaustion rule applied. *Reyes v. Manor Independent School Dist.*, 850 F.3d 251 (5th Cir. 2017).

V.   OTHER IDEA PROCEEDINGS

A. Class Actions

◆   In 2005, the parents of students with disabilities ages three to five sued the District of Columbia for violating the IDEA child-find duty. They charged the district with failing to provide special education to their children, as well as hundreds of other preschool students. After a federal court certified the suit as a class action and entered a comprehensive order designed to bring the District into compliance with the IDEA, the case reached the U.S. Court of Appeals, District of Columbia Circuit. In 2013, the appeals court held the requirements for class certification were not satisfied. In returning the case to the lower court, the appeals court held the case involved different policies and practices of the district. Moreover, the students who sought to represent the class were at differing stages of the district's child find process, making them unsuitable representatives of the proposed class. The case returned to the lower court, which considered arguments by the parents that their children's cases could be considered in four subgroups. At the time, the students were 10-15 years of age and no longer subject to IDEA child find processes. Agreeing with the parents, the court denied the district's motion to decertify the class and granted re-certification of the claims for reimbursement and compensatory education.

In 2017, the case returned to the District of Columbia Court of Appeals. It found that at the relevant time, the district was failing to identify 98-515 students per month as having disabilities. The district acknowledged that in 2007, it had the nation's lowest special education enrollment. **As the lower court found, the district had yet to attain a period of sustained IDEA compliance. The parents obtained proper class certification before their claims became moot.** Significantly, the court upheld an order requiring the district to ensure that preschool students with disabilities received eligibility determinations within 120 days of being referred. Next, the court approved of subgroups of students and their parents as found by the lower court. Although the district advanced other arguments, the court found no error in the lower court's judgment. *DL v. Dist. of Columbia*, 860 F.3d 713 (D.C. Cir. 2017).

◆   Springfield Public Schools (SPS) operated the Springfield Public Day School (SPDS). A group of students claimed the segregated SPDS denied their access to educational services that were equal to those enjoyed by nondisabled SPS students, in violation of the Americans with Disabilities Act (ADA). A key assertion by the students was that the SPS did not offer school-based behavior services (SBBS) in neighborhood schools. In order to remedy this, the students sought an order compelling SPS to provide them with SBBS in their neighborhood schools. After denying a motion by SPS to dismiss the case, a federal court considered a motion to certify the case as a class action. Although the students and their expert described SBBS as a single program that had been studied and subjected to peer-reviewed research, they admitted the term "SBBS" was created for this litigation. In addition, the court noted factual differences in their cases and found only one of the proposed class members filed a due process hearing request to challenge his placement.

This challenge was unsuccessful, and his parents did not appeal. A party seeking relief that may be available in an IDEA case must exhaust administrative remedies by first filing a due process complaint. The rule requires exhaustion of any claims relating to the identification, evaluation or educational placement of a child, or the provision of a free, appropriate public education. The students did not claim an exception to the IDEA exhaustion rule, instead relying on their claim to class status. **Even if the IDEA administrative exhaustion rule did not apply, the court held the requirements for class certification were not met.** Since individual determinations would have to be made for each student, the court found there was no available class-wide remedy. As the students did not exhaust their administrative remedies and class certification was inappropriate in this case, the court denied their motion. *S.S. v. City of Springfield, Massachusetts,* 146 F.3d 414 (D. Mass. 2016).

◆   A group of Compton Unified School District (CUSD) students convinced a federal court that their claims to disability law protection based on their traumatic circumstances have merit. (A summary of the case appears in Chapter Two, Section II.B. of this volume.) However, the court issued separate orders denying the students' requests for preliminary relief and certification of the case as a class action. The court found the disability issues were novel, and the evidence supporting the claim of trauma-induced disability was too unclear to justify preliminary relief. In a separate order, the court denied the student's request to certify a class action. It found **the students could not currently estimate the size of a proposed class of present and future CUSD students with trauma-induced disabilities**. The students' estimate of the proposed class required more than a good-faith guess. Even if the court accepted the student's methodology and found their expert testimony persuasive, it found questions remained that prevented class certification at this time. But the court left open the possibility that the requirements for class certification could be met based on a fuller record. *P.P. v. Compton Unified School Dist.*, No. CV 15-3726-MWF (PLAx), 2015 WL 5752770 (C.D. Cal. 9/29/15).

◆   In 1992, a group representing disabled students in Chicago Public Schools (CPS) filed a class action against the Illinois State Board of Education (ISBE) and CPS to challenge the placement of students by disability category alone. Of over 500,000 students enrolled in CPS schools, at least 10% were classified as disabled. A federal court certified a class representing certain disabled students in CPS schools. In 1998, the CPS agreed to a consent decree, which committed it to a series of reforms to bring the system into compliance with the IDEA. The ISBE went to trial, which resulted in a finding that it had violated the IDEA.

The ISBE was ordered to submit to a compliance plan, then entered into a consent decree with the students outlining its duties. In 2005, a court-appointed monitor set a formula for a district-wide maximum by which the percentage of students with disabilities in any CPS school could not exceed 20% of the school's total student population. Although CPS could seek waivers from the 20% cap, it failed to do so until the consent decree expired in 2006. CPS then sought waivers for 96 schools. The court complied with the monitor's request to extend the term of the decree for four years and to keep a 20% ceiling. When appeal of the enrollment cap issue reached the U.S. Court of Appeals, Seventh Circuit, it found the challenge premature. The case returned to the district court, which set dates for termination of the consent decrees. While the CPS consent decree had terminated in 2012, CPS moved to decertify the class and vacate the original 1998 consent decree. The court denied the motion, and CPS appealed to the Seventh Circuit. It found the only remaining aspect of the case was the filing of a report by the monitor. Since there was no longer a consent decree, **the court found no live controversy remaining between the parties and it held the case was moot**. Although the CPS suggested that information from the monitor's pending report might provide the grounds for future lawsuits, the court found this did not create a live controversy. It dismissed the CPS motion. *Corey H. v. Chicago Board of Educ.*, 528 Fed.Appx. 666 (7th Cir. 2013).

B. Parent Actions and Representation

A general rule is that non-attorneys cannot represent the legal rights of others. For this reason, non-attorney parents may not advance claims on behalf of their children. In Winkelman v. Parma City School Dist., *550 U.S. 516, 127 S.Ct. 1994, 167 L.Ed.2d 904 (2007), the Supreme Court held parents have enforceable IDEA rights that are independent of their children's rights. As a result, the Court held Ohio parents could pursue an IDEA claim on their own behalf against a school district.*

◆   In 2014, a Florida parent sued educators and corporate and government entities for gross negligence and violating the Florida Deceptive and Unfair Trade Practices Act, the Thirteenth Amendment and Title VI of the Civil Rights Act of 1964. According to the parent, his children were denied adequate IEPs based on their race. He said they were harmed by the prescription drugs Abilify and Risperdal. **A federal magistrate judge advised the parent that a non-lawyer cannot represent his/her children.** Because he asserted claims on only his children's behalf, the case would be dismissed unless he obtained counsel. Instead, the parent filed a new complaint asserting claims on his own behalf and that of his spouse. After the magistrate judge recommended dismissing the case, the court held his IDEA claims were not exhausted administratively and were dismissed. The parent filed a new action against the Florida Agency for Health Care Administration (AHCA) and the Desoto County School Board for civil rights and constitutional violations. This time, he said the AHCA permitted the board to produce IEPs that incorrectly classified some of his non-verbal children as English proficient. Despite the court's warning in the 2014 proceeding, the parent failed to exhaust his IDEA administrative remedies. The case was dismissed with a warning that any future filing would be subject to summary dismissal unless he exhausted his IDEA remedies. In 2016, still unrepresented by counsel, the parent filed a third federal court complaint against state and federal entities and officials, including the Desoto County School Board.

The court noted the parent's history of litigation and its previous warning that any cases he filed in connection with his children's IEPs would be dismissed unless he exhausted his IDEA administrative remedies. As he did not file a due process complaint and was not excused from exhausting IDEA processes, the court dismissed the case. On appeal, the Eleventh Circuit Court of Appeals affirmed, rejecting the parent's argument that inclusion of non-IDEA claims relieved him of the exhaustion requirement. Later, the U.S. Supreme Court declined to hear his appeal. *Prunty v. Desoto County School Board*, No. 18-6522, 139 WL 821 (U.S. cert. denied 1/7/19).

◆   A federal court approved the report and recommendation of a magistrate judge who found a Montana school district did not violate the rights of a parent with a disability by limiting his access to the school attended by his disabled child based on his disruptive conduct. He engaged in a pattern of conduct that eventually led the school principal to restrict his access to the school. Problems arose when he contacted staff members to discuss his son's conduct or progress. In the parent's federal disability discrimination lawsuit, the magistrate judge found **the principal responded to the history of misconduct by the parent and his interactions with staff members, and did not discriminate against him**. *Lagervall v. Missoula County Public Schools*, No. CV 16-57-M-DLC-JCL, 2017 WL 4896103 (D. Mont. 10/30/17).

◆   A Chicago parent sought to have her child's open-enrollment charter school perform an evaluation to assess her for special education eligibility. According to the parent, the child began receiving services under Section 504 of the Rehabilitation Act but an IEP meeting and case study were delayed. When an IEP meeting was finally held, the parent declared it a sham and filed an IDEA due process hearing request. The hearing officer found the school had ample evidence that the child needed special education and ordered the school to pay for 25 sessions with a pathologist, plus an award of compensatory education. The parent appealed the hearing officer's decision to a federal court.

The court held the parent could not represent her child since she was not a lawyer. While she had enforceable IDEA rights of her own, it held she was not "aggrieved" by the hearing officer's decision. Claims for reimbursement for the cost of her child's sessions with a speech and language pathologist were not before the hearing officer, and since the parent was not awarded any other relief, she had no valid IDEA claim. On appeal, the U.S. Court of Appeals, Seventh Circuit, clarified that parents of a child with a disability have their own enforceable rights under the IDEA. But the court rejected the parent's argument that she could represent her child in an IDEA action without a lawyer. **Seventh Circuit authority prohibits nonlawyers from representing others in court.** But the court held the parent's own claims should not have been dismissed. It held she stated sufficient facts that her parental rights were violated under the IDEA. These claims deserved further consideration by the lower court. *Foster v. Board of Educ. of City of Chicago*, 611 Fed.Appx. 874 (7th Cir. 2015).

◆   A Vermont grandparent said a teacher assaulted her learning disabled grandson. When she learned the teacher had also been involved in an argument with a parent, she claimed the teacher received lighter punishment by the school for his misconduct based on the grandchild's African-American race. After police involvement regarding the student's home placement, the grandparent claimed police and child protection authorities did not handle his case properly. She said he had emotional detachment disorder, oppositional defiant order and attention deficit hyperactivity disorder. In a federal court, the grandparent sued state, local and school authorities. She claimed some of the student's conduct was not his fault but was attributable to his disabilities. She sought damages because she claimed he had been a discrimination victim and had been suicidal.
     The court explained that a non-lawyer may not represent another person or entity in a federal court. Despite the grandparent's claim to have been given a power of attorney for his affairs, the court held she could not provide him with representation. The court held it could not rule on the case unless the student himself appeared on his own behalf or through counsel. He was given 30 days to appear on his own behalf (or with counsel), or to amend his complaint. Some of the claims would still be dismissed as untimely or barred by a $10,000 settlement agreement signed by the grandparent in return for the release of her claims against the district. *Miller v. Town of Morrisville*, No. 2:14-cv-5, 2015 WL 1648996 (D. Vt. 4/14/15).

C. Settlement

In Smith v. Rockwood R-VI School Dist., *this chapter, a federal court held a voluntary dismissal or settlement agreement does not satisfy the IDEA administrative exhaustion requirement.*

◆   A Missouri high school student with autism spectrum disorder, Tourette syndrome, emotional disturbance, major depression, obsessive-compulsive disorder and ADHD had an IEP addressing his medical and education needs. After an unspecified incident, he was suspended for 10 days. IEP team members held a manifestation determination hearing. According to the team, the student's conduct manifested his disability. **Under the IDEA, the team's conclusion indicated that the student should be readmitted to school or have modifications to his behavior plan.** But the local school superintendent instead notified him by letter that he was being suspended for 180 days. The parent filed a due process challenge to the imposition of this exclusion. Later, the parties reached a private agreement, and the case was dismissed. But the parent filed a federal case against the county and local school district and the superintendent. She included claims for violations of the IDEA and U.S. Constitution, and added discrimination claims under the Americans with Disabilities Act and Section 504 of the Rehabilitation Act.

Finding the parent failed to exhaust her available administrative remedies as required by the IDEA, the court dismissed the case. Appeal reached the U.S. Court of Appeals, Eighth Circuit, which found the gravamen of the complaint was the denial of a free appropriate public education (FAPE). As the Supreme Court held in *Fry v. Napoleon Community Schools*, 137 S.Ct. 743 (2017), **the prior pursuit of IDEA remedies may provide strong evidence that a claim implicates the denial of a FAPE**. In this case, the parent acknowledged that her due process complaint concerned the denial of a FAPE for her son. She had resolved the case with both school districts prior to filing suit. Rejecting the parent's additional arguments for not applying the exhaustion rule, the court affirmed the judgment for the districts and superintendent. *Smith v. Rockwood R-VI School Dist.*, 895 F.3d 566 (8th Cir. 2018).

◆   A Pennsylvania student suffered a head injury while playing flag football in a P.E. class. A few weeks later, he suffered another head injury while holding a sideline marker at a school football game. A player ran into the student and knocked him over, causing the second injury. A CT scan indicated he had a post-concussive syndrome. Eventually, the student's mother removed him from school. She asked the school district to evaluate the student for special education eligibility, but the school found him ineligible. It offered him a Section 504 plan, but she claimed the school resisted offering him accommodations. The student later graduated from a private school, and his parents filed a due process complaint. A settlement agreement was reached, by which the family released the school district and its employees from liability. Despite the agreement, the student sued the school district and a high school principal in a federal court for violating Section 504 of the Rehabilitation Act and the Americans with Disabilities Act. The court dismissed the case, and the student appealed.

On appeal, the Third Circuit Court of Appeals found the claims principally related to the student's education. Citing the U.S. Supreme Court's recent decision in *Fry v. Napoleon Community Schools*, this chapter, the court found **administrative exhaustion is required for non-IDEA claims, if a party seeks relief that is also available under the IDEA**. As the school district argued, the claims sought relief that could be remedied under the IDEA. Applying the approach used by the Court in *Fry*, the court considered the "gravamen" or crux of the student's complaint. In the court's view, the student's claims all involved the provision of a free appropriate public education, and were subject to exhaustion. It found each of the claims stemmed from an alleged failure to accommodate his condition and fulfill his educational needs. As the student essentially claimed that he was denied accommodations and had released all claims related to the denial of a free. appropriate public education, the court found the case had to be dismissed. *Wellman v. Butler Area School Dist.*, 877 F.3d 125 (3d Cir. 2017).

◆   A California school district settled a due process matter in 2003 concerning a child with autism. A term of the agreement required the parents to indemnify the school district from claims arising from a breach in performance under the agreement, plus attorneys' fees and costs. After the school district began implementing the settlement, the parents grew dissatisfied with providers used for the student's behavior services, occupational therapy and speech-language services. They hired an attorney, prompting the district to use its own lawyers. This resulted in a cost of $39,526 in attorneys' fees for the district. In 2005, the parents filed a due process action against the district, asserting violations of the IDEA and breach of the 2003 settlement agreement. In 2007, they filed two complaints regarding services provided to their child from 2004 through 2007.

After the cases were consolidated, a federal court held in the district's favor. The parents filed a new federal court complaint against the district, again alleging breach of the settlement agreement. The court found the parent simply re-argued issues that had already been decided. Although the court denied the district's claim for $39,526 in fees related to implementing the settlement agreement, it approved of $83,129 in attorneys' fees under the indemnity provision of the settlement. It held the fees claimed by the school district were reasonable. In 2017, the parents appealed to the U.S. Court of Appeals, Ninth Circuit. First, the court found no error in the dismissal of a 42 U.S.C. § 1983 claim. Prior Ninth Circuit decisions have held a Section 1983 claim cannot be based on an IDEA or Rehabilitation Act Section 504 violation. **The court found the record did not support the parents' claim that the school district breached the settlement agreement.** It held any lack of performance by the district was a result of their lack of cooperation with the district. *Pedraza v. Alameda Unified School Dist.*, 676 Fed.Appx. 704 (9th Cir. 2017).

◆   A Missouri student with a Cochlear implant experienced electric shocks due to magnetic fields inside school buildings. One shock required hospitalization. After a school electrician was unable to eliminate the electrical fields from the school building, the student stayed out of school. It was later found that the school district had no building that was safe for the student. But it refused to pay for her to attend school in another district and created a home education program for her eighth-grade year. After the student skipped to grade nine, her parents said the district refused to provide Communication Access Real-time Transcription (CART) services. When the district later offered CART services, the parents said one teacher refused to use it and another did not know how.

After the parents filed a due process complaint against the school district, they agreed to a mediated settlement of their IDEA claims. Under the agreement, the district agreed to provide the student with compensatory educational services. In a separate case, the parents pursued a Missouri Human Rights Act (MHRA) claim. They later sued the district in a federal court. In addition to asserting claims under the U.S. Constitution, ADA and MHRA, the parents included personal injury claims. **The court disagreed with the district's argument that the mediated settlement blocked the action.** Although the settlement called for the parents to dismiss their due process complaint, it did not address compensatory damages or the release of any claims. Further, the court held the parents exhausted their administrative remedies with regard to their claims for compensatory education. **Mediation is included as one of the IDEA administrative procedures that must be exhausted prior to filing suit.** The court found no requirement that a parent be aggrieved by a due process hearing in order to file suit. Since the parents obtained all the relief the IDEA could provide via mediation, they were not required to pursue further IDEA remedies prior to filing an action for compensatory damages. While the MHRA claim was untimely under a state 90-day limitations period, the court held the parents could pursue damage claims for personal injuries and constitutional violations. *R.M. v. City of St. Charles Public School Dist., R.-VI*, No. 4:15-CV-706 CAS, 2016 WL 2910265 (E.D. Mo. 5/19/16).

◆   **The parent of a Pennsylvania student with disabilities was denied enforcement of a settlement agreement with a charter school because it was made outside the due process context.** The court agreed with the school that because the agreement was not finalized until six weeks after an IDEA resolution meeting, it was not "reached at" the meeting. It declined to expand upon IDEA language and other cases as urged by the parent and found the settlement agreement was a "private" agreement. *T.L. v. Pennsylvania Leadership Charter School*, No. 16-1230, 2016 WL 7188226 (E.D. Pa. 12/12/16).

◆   A New Mexico parent charged her dyslexic child's school district with failing to address her needs and requested a hearing. Before the hearing, she sought mediation. After the mediation, the parties reached a settlement and the parent asked the state administrative agency to dismiss her IDEA claims. She then sued the district in a federal court for discrimination under Section 504 of the Rehabilitation Act. Finding the parent did not exhaust her administrative remedies, the court dismissed the case. On appeal, the U.S. Court of Appeals, Tenth Circuit, found the parent's complaint from the administrative action and her current federal complaint were nearly identical in scope. In order to bring a lawsuit under any federal law that seeks relief that is also available under the IDEA, the procedures of the IDEA found at 20 U.S.C. § 1415 subsections (f) and (g) must first be exhausted. In prior decisions, the Tenth Circuit has held a party must file an IDEA administrative complaint if the party has alleged injuries that could be redressed to any degree by the IDEA's administrative procedures and remedies. Moreover, the party must be "aggrieved" by a decision in the administrative proceeding. In this case, the parent admitted she was seeking relief that was available under the IDEA. And the court held she was not "aggrieved" by any IDEA proceeding. According to the parent, her pursuit of mediation satisfied the requirement of administrative exhaustion.

But the court disagreed, ruling that by choosing to settle her IDEA claims and dismiss the administrative complaint, the parent had barred the present case. In affirming the judgment for the school district, the court pointed out that the parent was not aggrieved by the findings and decision of a hearing officer.

Since mediation did not count as exhaustion, the court held for the school district. *A.F. v. Espanola Public Schools*, 801 F.3d 1245 (10th Cir. 2015).

◆   The mother of a 20-year-old former student with cerebral palsy and other disabilities claimed staff members of a Tennessee school district often left him unattended in school lavatories. She said her son had a seizure in one case and was returned to class with bloody underwear in another. In addition to stating that aides regularly failed to help her son clean himself, the parent said an aide sexually abused him. After the parties attended a resolution session under the IDEA, they agreed to a settlement by which the parent dropped her IDEA and state law claims. It was recited in the agreement that the settlement did not cover any claims arising after the date of the agreement and that the agreement was made in a resolution session and could be enforced in a state or federal court. The parent then sued the school district in a federal court for breach of the settlement agreement and violations of the U.S. Constitution, Rehabilitation Act Section 504 and the Americans with Disabilities Act. The court held for the school district, finding the claims were subject to administrative exhaustion.

On appeal, the U.S. Court of Appeals, Sixth Circuit, held the student alleged non-educational injuries that had no IDEA remedy. **Since the constitutional claims did not "arise under the IDEA," the court held they were not released by the settlement agreement.** Moreover, the settlement was reached at an IDEA resolution session and was, by its terms, enforceable in a court. As a result, the court held the breach of contract claim was not subject to the IDEA exhaustion rule. *F.H. v. Memphis City Schools*, 764 F.3d 638 (6th Cir. 2014).

D. Other Proceedings

◆   A Michigan school district sued the Michigan Department of Education (MDE) and its special education director in a federal court, claiming the state conspired with the parents of a child with Down syndrome and speech apraxia to prevent the use of a trial placement agreement to resolve a special education dispute. The district claimed the MDE and its director violated constitutional provisions, the IDEA and other laws by limiting its use of trial placement agreements to resolve special education disputes. In asserting the claims against the MDE and the director, the district argued that the parents were not acting in the best interests of their child. It said "the Parents really do not care about their son getting a FAPE at all, they just want him schooled where it is most convenient for them, and that is why they are pursuing this appeal."

Arguing that it needed to be the student's "voice" in pursuing a FAPE, the school district asked that he be realigned with the district as a party. Under the school district's proposed scenario, the student and the school district would be adverse parties to the parents, the MDE and the director. The court rejected the school district's argument, agreeing with the parents' claim to their fundamental right to advocate for their child and make decisions regarding his care, custody and control. **As the parents argued, they had no place in any dispute between the school district and the MDE concerning the use of trial placement agreements to resolve special education disputes.** In fact, a separate case had been filed to consider that matter. The court found the school district's request to realign the parties was misplaced and without legal merit. *A.A. v. Walled Lake Consolidated Schools*, No. 16-14214, 2017 WL 4913920 (E.D. Mich. 10/31/17).

◆   A federal appeals court reversed a lower court judgment that would have required the family of a disabled student to pay sanctions for filing frivolous cases during a protracted IDEA dispute with a Florida school district. During the course of his K-12 career, his family filed at least three due process requests against the district. In ordering sanctions, the lower court relied on a case involving the merits of an IDEA claim. When the case reached the Eleventh Circuit, it held the present dispute concerned the student's entitlement to injunctive relief, not the merits of an IDEA claim. **Since the parent's request for an injunction was not frivolous, the appeals court held she should not have been sanctioned.** *A.L., P.L.B. v. Jackson County School Board*, 652 Fed. Appx. 795 (11th Cir. 2016).

◆   After the parents of a special education student obtained reimbursement for tuition at a private school, they sought reimbursement for the cost of an educational consultant they used during the course of litigation. A New York federal court awarded them $8,650 of the $29,350 in fees they claimed, reducing the award because the consultant did not keep contemporaneous time records. The Second Circuit upheld the award, noting that the IDEA permits the recovery of fees and costs for individuals with "special knowledge." On further appeal, the U.S. Supreme Court held **the IDEA does not authorize prevailing parents to recover expert fees**. The Court noted that the IDEA was enacted under the Spending Clause, and that it does not even hint that the acceptance of IDEA funds makes a state responsible for reimbursing prevailing parents for the services of experts. The statute simply adds reasonable attorneys' fees to the list of recoverable costs. Further, the expert witness fees could not be deemed costs so as to be reimbursable. *Arlington Cent. School Dist. Board of Educ. v. Murphy*, 548 U.S. 291, 126 S.Ct. 2455, 165 L.Ed.2d 526 (2006).

CHAPTER SEVEN

Private School Tuition

I. TUITION REIMBURSEMENT

A. Unilateral Placement by Parents

1. Generally

An IDEA section – 20 U.S.C. § 1415(i)(2)(C) – authorizes a court to "grant such relief as [it] determines is appropriate" when reviewing a due process challenge to the provision of a free appropriate public education (FAPE). Many courts have held this authorizes private school tuition reimbursement where a school district fails to offer an IEP that would provide a FAPE.

The Supreme Court's standard for evaluating claims for reimbursement of private school tuition costs is derived from School Committee of the Town of Burlington, Massachusetts v. Dep't of Educ. of Massachusetts, *471 U.S. 359 (1985) and* Florence County School Dist. Four v. Carter, *510 U.S. 7 (1993). First, the child must be denied a free appropriate public education. Next, the private placement selected by parents must be held appropriate. Third, the equities must favor an award of tuition reimbursement.*

In L.H. v. Hamilton County Dep't of Educ., *900 F.3d 779 (6th Cir. 2018), the Sixth Circuit Court of Appeals explained that a unilateral private placement does not satisfy the requirements of the IDEA unless it, "at a minimum, provide[s] some element of special education services in which the public school placement was deficient." According to the court, "parents are not entitled to reimbursement for private school just because the private placement is less restrictive than the public school placement."*

◆ According to the parents of a New York City student with speech and language impairments and delays in all areas of intellectual functioning, the New York City Department of Education (DOE) failed to provide him a free appropriate public education. They rejected his IEP, which called for a "12:1+1" classroom made up of no more than 12 students, a teacher and a paraprofessional aide. In a due process complaint, the parents sought tuition reimbursement from the DOE, seeking payment for a private placement they had made. After a due process hearing, an impartial hearing officer held for the parents. A state review officer reversed the decision, and the parents appealed.

A federal court held the review officer's decision was fully supported. Evidence indicated the DOE's committee on special education (CSE) considered a range of placements for the student. Additionally, a 12:1+1 classroom would have provided support from a paraprofessional to access classroom lessons and activities and address his management needs. He would have had supervised and coached "semi-structured social situations" for social growth. Evidence indicated smaller classrooms would not be appropriate for the student and that the DOE wanted to offer him a "balanced program" with opportunities for group academics and group socializing. Appeal reached the U.S. Court of Appeals, Second Circuit, which found the review officer's decision was well supported. A review of federal court decisions, including *Endrew F. v. Douglas County School Dist. RE–1*, 137 S.Ct. 988 (2017), indicated that "the question for a court is whether the IEP is reasonable, not whether the court regards it as ideal." **Further, the IDEA requires an appropriate education, not one that provides "everything that might be thought desirable by loving parents."** In this case, the record showed the review officer considered all the evidence and found the IEP provided sufficient individualized support to enable the student to make meaningful and appropriate educational progress. Second Circuit authority held that the adequacy of 1:1 support from non–teachers was "precisely the kind of educational policy judgment to which we owe the state deference if it is supported by sufficient evidence." Although the parents made further arguments in seeking tuition reimbursement, the court held for the DOE. *J.R. v. New York City Dep't of Educ.*, 742 Fed.Appx. 382 (2d Cir. 2018).

◆ The Second Circuit Court of Appeals held a New York student with disabilities was making educational progress, despite claims by his parent that the repetition of IEP goals and poor performance indicated stagnation or regression. Although an impartial hearing officer held for the parent after a due process hearing, a state review officer reversed the decision. A federal court held for the school district, and the parent appealed to the Second Circuit. In approaching the case, the court employed the longstanding analysis applied by the courts in IDEA reimbursement claims. This required a determination of whether the IEP proposal violated the IDEA. Only if the school district denied a student a FAPE would a court consider whether a parental placement was appropriate for the student. Even if a parental placement is found appropriate, equitable considerations must favor reimbursement of the placement costs. Although the parent claimed the school district committed IDEA procedural violations that denied a FAPE to his son, the court found none. It noted the district's committee on special education (CSE) met at least eight times during the relevant three-year period. Evidence indicated the CSE meetings were attended by no fewer than 10 persons. A review of audio recordings and transcripts of the meetings indicated the parent had ample opportunities to discuss the IEP. In addition, the court found that while the CSE did not agree to each of the parent's requests, he had input into the student's present levels of performance and annual goals, and provided input into each of the IEPs. Although the hearing officer found the CSE had consistently disregarded the parent's valid concerns, the Second Circuit found no procedural violation. **As a federal district court in New York once observed, "professional disagreement is not an IDEA violation."**

Finding no "persistent refusal" by the CSE to discuss the parent's concerns, the court found no IDEA procedural violation amounting to a denial of FAPE. Next, the court found each of the IEPs presented a description of the student's strengths and challenges. It found the IEP goals were consistent with the information before the CSE at each of its meetings. As the review officer found, **the IEPs were modified in response to evaluations of the student or requests by the parent**. The court found the IEPs were reasonably calculated to provide the student meaningful benefit. It also found no merit to the parent's claim that the repetition of certain IEP goals and poor performance by the student on standardized tests indicated his academic progress was either stagnating or regressing. In the court's opinion, evidence indicated the student was progressing, although not at a pace his parent would have preferred. Last, the court scrutinized the IEP in view of *Endrew F. v. Douglas County School Dist.*, 137 S.Ct. 988 (U.S. 2017). As *Endrew F.* found, an IEP need not specify grade-level advancement, if such progress is not a reasonable prospect for the student. Instead, a student's IEP must be "appropriately ambitious in light of his circumstances." Finding the IEPs in this case satisfied the *Endrew F.* standard, the court held for the school district. *F.L. v. Board of Educ. of Great Neck Union Free School Dist.*, 735 Fed.Appx. 38 (2d Cir. 2018).

◆   A New York student with disabilities attended public schools for his K-3 school years and transferred to a private school for grades 4-6. Proposed IEPs for his fifth- and sixth-grade school years called for classroom settings of 12 students, one teacher and two teaching aides or assistants (a 12:1:2 classroom). The student's parents hired two neuropsychologists who recommended placing him in a classroom of eight students, one teacher and one teaching aide (an 8:1:1 classroom). Seeking reimbursement for their private placement, the parents initiated a due process proceeding. An impartial hearing officer (IHO) held they were entitled to reimbursement for the child's fifth- and sixth-grade school years. A state review officer reversed the IHO's decision. He found the ratio of adults to students in a 12:1:2 class is the same as in an 8:1:1 class.

On appeal, a federal court held for the parents. When the case reached the Second Circuit Court of Appeals, it held that if a child with a disability is denied a free appropriate public education (FAPE), the parents may make a private placement and seek tuition reimbursement. **To prevail, the parents had to show that the school district failed to provide their child a FAPE, the private placement was appropriate, and the equities favored their request for tuition reimbursement.** In the court's view, the review officer's reasons for dismissing the 8:1:1 class proposal did not take certain evidence into account.

It found the total number of students in the classroom counted, not just the student-adult ratio. Next, the court found none of the evidence relied upon by the review officer suggested the student's problems with distractions could be resolved without an 8:1:1 classroom setting. A 12:1:2 classroom would not have provided the student a FAPE. The court upheld the IHO's findings that the private school was appropriate. Further, the equities favored the parents, who cooperated with the district. *J.C. v. Katonah-Lewisboro School Dist.*, 690 Fed. Appx. 53 (2d Cir. 2017).

◆   The Ninth Circuit Court of Appeals held a lower court would have to reconsider a claim for private school tuition reimbursement by the parents of a Hawaii student with sensory and developmental disabilities. According to the Ninth Circuit, the lower court improperly denied reimbursement without considering all the relevant elements. **After parents establish that a school district has denied their child a free appropriate public education and show the private placement is appropriate, a court "then must exercise its 'broad discretion' and weigh 'equitable considerations' to determine whether and how much, reimbursement is appropriate."** Under prior cases, a placement is proper if it is specially designed to meet the unique needs of a child, supported by such services as are necessary to permit the child to benefit from the instruction. In this case, the lower court found the student did not progress at a private school. In fact, he regressed there. While the lack of progress is an equitable consideration for a district court to weigh, the Ninth Circuit held it is an unsuitable basis for determining whether a placement was proper. As the lower court did not evaluate the "equitable considerations" that might support the claim for reimbursement, the Ninth Circuit returned the case to the lower court to evaluate the equitable considerations. *J.T. v. Dep't of Educ., State of Hawaii*, 695 Fed.Appx. 227 (9th Cir. 2017).

◆   A New York school's committee on special education (CSE) recommended placing a student with autism in a classroom made up of 12 students, a teacher and one paraprofessional (a 12:1:1 setting) for his kindergarten year. The CSE also proposed weekly sessions of occupational therapy (OT), physical therapy (PT) and speech-language therapy (SLT). Before the school year, the student attended a preschool where he received 20 hours of weekly applied behavioral analysis (ABA) therapy. A committee on preschool special education (CPSE) developed an IEP for the summer that specified a 1:1 setting in a classroom of six students and six staff members, with OT, PT and SLT. Noting the sharp contrast between the CSE's 12:1:1 proposal and the CPSE's 1:1 proposal, the parents placed the student in a private center. There, he received instruction in a 1:1 setting with ABA instruction. Outside school, he received weekly home and community-based SLT, OT and PT services. In a due process case, the parents asked for reimbursement for the private placement and the cost of home and community-based services. An impartial hearing officer (IHO) issued an order preserving the 1:1 services from the CPSE's summer IEP. So the department had to fund these services during the pendency of the dispute. Another IHO then held a hearing on the merits of the complaint, at which the department conceded it did not provide the student a FAPE for his kindergarten school year.

The IHO held the parents did not show the combination of private school with home and community-based services was an appropriate placement. A state review officer found reimbursement for the private school was appropriate, but held equitable considerations did not justify fully reimbursing the parents. A federal court upheld the review officer's decision. On appeal, the U.S. Court of Appeals, Second Circuit, held **courts are to consider all the relevant factors in IDEA tuition reimbursement cases, including the appropriate and reasonable levels of reimbursement**. Courts do not interpret the IDEA as requiring the optimal program. As the review officer found, some of the services provided by the parents were not necessary for the student to progress. **The lower court correctly held the parents were not entitled to reimbursement for services provided in excess of a FAPE.** The lower court was directed to further consider several remaining issues, such as whether the department's reimbursement rate for services was set too low. *L.K. v. New York City Dep't of Educ.*, 674 Fed.Appx. 1oo (2d Cir. 2017).

◆ In *School Committee of the Town of Burlington, Massachusetts v. Dep't of Educ. of Massachusetts,* the U.S. Supreme Court held that parents who unilaterally place children in private schools may nevertheless receive tuition reimbursement from the school district if the IEP proposed by the school is later found to be inappropriate. Parents who place a disabled child in a private educational facility are entitled to reimbursement for the child's tuition and living expenses if a court later determines that the school district proposed an inappropriate IEP. Conversely, reimbursement could not be ordered if the school district's proposed IEP was appropriate. The Court observed that to bar reimbursement claims under all circumstances would violate the IDEA, which requires appropriate interim placement for children with disabilities. **Parents who unilaterally change the placement of a child during the pendency of IDEA proceedings do so at their own financial risk.** If the courts ultimately determine that a proposed IEP is appropriate, the parents are barred from obtaining reimbursement for an unauthorized private school placement. *School Committee of the Town of Burlington, Massachusetts v. Dep't of Educ. of Massachusetts,* 471 U.S. 359, 105 S.Ct. 1996, 85 L.Ed.2d 385 (1985).

2. Behavioral Challenges

In Jenna R.P. v. City of Chicago School Dist. No. 229, *2013 IL App (1st) 112247, 3 N.E.3d 927 (Ill. Ct. App. 2013) the Illinois Appellate Court explained that for parents to qualify for tuition reimbursement for a unilateral private placement, the school they select must be consistent with IDEA purposes. A private placement must offer the student at least some element of special education services in which the public school placement was deficient.*

◆ A Rhode Island student missed 154 school days during a school year and failed her classes. Prior to the next school year, she was again hospitalized for self-cutting and her mother placed her in a residential treatment center. At an IEP meeting, the mother and her attorney urged the district to offer the student a residential placement. When the IEP team declined, they abruptly left. The mother later requested a due process hearing. At a prehearing conference, the mother specified that she sought to place her child at a certain private school. In response, the school district offered an alternative education plan. The hearing went forward and after the proceeding, a hearing officer found the school district did not offer a free appropriate public education (FAPE) to the student. But the hearing officer found the private school sought by the student's mother was inappropriate, and he declined to award any compensatory relief.

A federal court held the private school was not an appropriate placement for the student. According to the court, **a private placement must offer the student at least some element of special services in which the public-school placement was deficient. There was evidence that the school did not provide necessary dialectical behavioral therapy and failed to offer a medically necessary level of family and community involvement.** Next, the court found the student was entitled to an award of compensatory education. The IEP team had set unrealistic expectations for attending school and repeated programming that had previously been unsuccessful for her. As the hearing officer found, the mother's conduct in walking out of an IEP meeting with her attorney hindered the collaborative process. The court found her conduct had been unreasonable. While the court found the mother proved her child had been denied a FAPE, the case was returned to the hearing officer for a determination of the amount of compensatory education due, taking into account the behavior of the parties. The court further instructed the hearing officer to consider an appropriate compensatory award for a five-month time period during which the student's initial IEP lacked any goals and other minimum IDEA requirements. *S.C. v. Chariho Regional School Dist.*, 298 F.Supp.3d 370 (D.R.I. 2018).

◆   New York parents placed their child privately and requested an impartial hearing to claim private tuition reimbursement. An impartial hearing officer (IHO) held for the school system, as did a state review officer and a federal court. **On appeal, the Second Circuit Court of Appeals found the relevant question when assessing an IEP is whether the program is reasonable, not whether a court regards it as ideal.** In this case, the court found the IEP proposal was reasonably calculated to enable the child to make progress appropriate in light of his circumstances. The court rejected the parents' argument that the review officer did not consider the record as a whole. Contrary to their argument, the IHO considered the disparity between the student's preschool IEP and the one at issue in this dispute.

The court also found the lower court did not have to consider IEPs prepared for future school years as evidence that the IEP was not substantively adequate. Finding the administrative decisions well-reasoned and supported by the record, the court refused to overturn them on substantive grounds. Next, the court found the school system complied with the IDEA by conducting an adequate functional behavioral assessment (FBA) and a behavioral intervention plan (BIP). In reaching this conclusion, the court rejected the parents' claim that the school system violated state regulations concerning FBAs and BIPs. While the school system did not comply in all respects with the regulations, the court found no procedural violation that rose to the level of a denial of a free appropriate public education. Rejecting the parents' other arguments, the court affirmed the decision denying reimbursement. *J.P. v. City of New York Dep't of Educ.*, 717 Fed.Appx. 30 (2d Cir. 2017).

◆   A Washington student had a history of truancy, juvenile detention and behavior issues. He was expelled from his school, used illegal drugs, ran away from home and placed in a psychiatric hospital. After a 28-day elopement, the student was readmitted to a hospital. The parents notified the district of their intention to place him in a residential facility and to seek reimbursement. They enrolled the student in a Utah residential facility with a locked campus and structured environment and requested a due process hearing. An administrative law judge (ALJ) held for the parents, and the district appealed to a federal court.

The court found the dispute centered on whether the residential placement was a service related to the student's education, or an excluded "medical service." After examining IDEA definitions of "special education" and "related services," the court found the placement in this case was not an excluded "medical service." It rejected the district's theory that any support the student received there was aimed at medical issues. The court found the residential school provided "related services" and/or the type of services that would be offered in a school nurse's office. These included psychological services, therapeutic recreation, social work services, medication management and counseling. **Further, the court found evidence that the student had to receive the services in a structured residential setting.** This was due to his tendency to elope and his truancy resulting from the "perfect storm of his disabilities." In the court's view, the IEP offered by the district was not reasonably calculated to enable the student to progress. His impulsiveness, hallucinations and cognitive disorganization made it unlikely that he would attend school in the absence of constant monitoring. Finding the parents established violations of the IDEA that warranted tuition reimbursement, the court held in their favor. *Edmonds School Dist. v. A.T.*, 299 F.Supp.3d 1135 (W.D. Wash. 2017).

◆   New York parents obtained private educational evaluations of their child with autism, which recommended 1:1 Applied Behavioral Analysis (ABA) instruction. Seeking the services recommended for their child, they enrolled him in a private center that offered a 1:1 ABA teaching program. There, he had 33.5 hours of weekly ABA instruction with daily individual speech/language and occupational therapy sessions. A committee on special education (CSE) met and proposed a special class in a New York City Department of Education (DOE) school with a student-teacher-paraprofessional composition of 6:1:1.

The parents rejected the IEP offer and filed a due process complaint against the DOE. An impartial hearing officer (IHO) found the DOE's offer denied the child a free appropriate public education (FAPE), but a state review officer substantially reversed the decision. On appeal, a federal court noted evidence that the CSE did not consider a 1:1 setting, but only a spectrum of placements in a 6:1:1 setting. Testimony by educators and therapists who worked with the child indicated a 6:1:1 placement would be inappropriate for him. One professional said his autism was so severe he could only sit still for 2-3 minutes at a time. The court found a key DOE witness gave contradictory testimony and did not address the testimony of the parents' experts. He did not explain how a 6:1:1 program could provide the child with individualized support. **Since the evidence supported the IHO's findings, the court upheld the claim for 1:1 instruction.** Evidence indicated the private school could provide the student an appropriate program and the relevant factors supported an award of tuition. *S.B. v. New York City Dep't of Educ.*, 174 F.Supp.3d 798 (S.D.N.Y. 2016).

◆   A New York student struggled to complete his school work and acted out in classes. Private testing yielded a diagnosis of dyslexia, but a committee on special education found him ineligible for special education. He was offered a Section 504 accommodation plan that provided him reading and writing lab classes. The parents instead placed their son at a private residential school for students with dyslexia. Later in the school year, the district found the student eligible for special education with an other health impairment based on his ADHD. It offered to place him in an integrated, co-taught program at a public high school. The parents rejected the placement, returned him to the residential school and requested a hearing. An impartial hearing officer (IHO) held for the parents and ordered tuition reimbursement for three school years. A state review officer found the student's behavior remained an issue at the private school and held reimbursement was due for only one of his three years there.

On appeal, a federal court held the school district did not offer persuasive reasons for reversing the IHO's findings that tuition reimbursement should be made for all three of the school years at issue. The district found the student ineligible for special education, despite his history of behavioral difficulties and academic struggles. Moreover, the district knew of the student's dyslexia and ADHD, yet failed to consider what effect they might have on his academic difficulties and disruptiveness. Each of the IEPs failed to provide the student a free appropriate public education. **In finding the IEPs insufficient, the court found a school district must consider whether a student's behavior impedes his learning or that of others. Where behavior impedes learning, the district may consider a functional behavior assessment and a behavior intervention plan.** As the school district knew of significant interfering and work-avoidance behaviors that affected the student's classroom ability, the court reinstated the decision awarding the parents $187,000 for three years of tuition. *A.W. & N.W. v. Board of Educ. of Wallkill Cent. School Dist.*, No. 1:14-CV-01583 (DNH/DJS), 2016 WL 4742297 (N.D.N.Y. 9/12/16).

◆   The U.S. Court of Appeals, Fifth Circuit, reversed a lower court decision awarding Texas parents tuition reimbursement for a Missouri residential school placement. The court held the placement was made over concerns that the student would attempt suicide and because of his continuing drug problem. **The parents made the placement for noneducational reasons, and no educational reason was given for it.** Evidence did not show the student's progress at the facility was judged primarily by educational achievement. Instead, the goal had been to treat his reactive attachment disorder. Since the lower court committed error, the court held for the school district. *Fort Bend Independent School Dist. v. Douglas A.*, 601 Fed.Appx. 250 (5th Cir. 2015).

◆   The parents of a child with autism asked the New York City Department of Education (DOE) to continue a program of ABA he had received at a private school. They said he needed a 1:1 setting to address his behavior problems. But a CSE proposed a class with a 6:1:1 student-teacher-paraprofessional ratio. The IEP did not have a functional behavioral assessment (FBA), but it included a behavior intervention plan (BIP). The parents rejected the IEP and returned their child to the private school. An impartial hearing officer held reimbursement was proper, finding the DOE failed to create an individualized program and FBA, and did not offer parent training or counseling.

On appeal, the U.S. Court of Appeals, Second Circuit, explained that schools must conduct an FBA where necessary to identify student behaviors and how they related to the environment. **If a student's behaviors impeded learning despite consistent interventions, a school was required to consider a BIP based on the FBA.** The court found the DOE did not develop an FBA or an adequate BIP for the student. Nor did the DOE provide for parent counseling and training as required by state regulations. As the parents argued, the DOE ignored the recommendations for a 1:1 placement. While the lack of an FBA was not an automatic IDEA violation, the DOE did not create and implement behavioral strategies in the BIP. It did not match strategies to specific behaviors, instead simply listing behaviors and strategies. In addition, the IEP was deficient and denied the student a FAPE. In sum, the court found the private placement was appropriate and the equities favored the parents. *C.F. v. New York City Dep't of Educ.*, 746 F.3d 68 (2d Cir. 2014).

3. Preferred Placement or Methodology

In W.D. v. Watchung Hills Regional High School Board of Educ., *this chapter, a federal appeals court found the IDEA does not require an IEP to describe instructional methodologies. In fact, the U.S. Department of Education has a longstanding position that the instructional methodologies in an IEP are left up to the IEP team. Nothing in the IDEA requires a school to provide parents information about the qualifications of teachers or service providers.*

The Ninth Circuit held in B.D. v. Puyallup School Dist., *456 Fed.Appx. 644 (9th Cir. 2011), that school officials may select the method for implementing an IEP. But in* Deal v. Hamilton County Dep't of Educ., *258 Fed. Appx. 863 (6th Cir. 2008), the Sixth Circuit held the differences between methodologies may be so great that providing a lesser program may amount to a denial of FAPE.*

◆   A Massachusetts student with a language-based learning disability attended a private, out-of-district special education school under IEPs developed by her school district for grades 3-8. Her grandparents (who served as her guardians) urged placement in a certain college prep school for grade nine where other family members had attended. IEP team members expressed concern that the school did not offer the type of special education curriculum offered at the student's current school. Later, the district offered to place the student in a public high school. The grandmother wrote a letter to state officials to complain about the district's decision. Because of the IEP dispute, the student's current school became her stay-put placement. But the school announced it could not meet her needs for grade nine. By this time, the grandparents had hired an attorney, who wrote to the district to request the college prep school as the stay-put placement. The district proposed a placement in a state-approved, private special education school. The grandparents accepted this, and the school became the student's new stay-put placement. Within a short time, she became unhappy with the school's lack of rigor and her long commute. IEP team members drafted a new IEP that would maintain her stay-put placement while offering a transition plan with the goals of completing high school and advancing to a four-year college. Although the grandmother accepted the IEP, she rejected its implementation at the school designated as the stay-put placement. She notified the district of her intent to place the student at the college prep school and sought reimbursement for her tuition costs. Meanwhile, the district offered the student a new IEP that would place her in a partial inclusion program at a public high school. After rejecting the IEP, the family initiated a due process proceeding. A hearing officer denied the grandparents' request for tuition reimbursement for the college prep school. Further, the hearing officer found the district's failure to offer a transition plan for the student during grade nine was cured by later IEPs.

Later, a federal court held that while the district did not provide sufficient transition planning, the student was not denied access to a FAPE. Because of the family's placement decision, she never received the related services specified in the challenged IEPs. The court held the IEPs were reasonably calculated to provide a FAPE. **Evidence suggested that the IEP challenge was based on a specific desire to place the student at the college prep school.** As substantial evidence supported the hearing officer's decision to deny private school tuition reimbursement, the court held for the school district. *Doe v. Belchertown Public Schools*, 347 F.Supp.3d 90 (D. Mass. 2018).

◆   Hawaii parents withdrew their son from a public school for homeschooling and 1:1 services through an autism center. They objected to an IEP proposal on multiple grounds and requested an impartial hearing. At the conclusion of the proceeding, a hearing officer held the IEP denied the student a free appropriate public education. The hearing officer's order further stated that the IEP was developed without the parents' participation. A revised IEP was then issued, followed by a prior written notice indicating that the student would attend his neighborhood school. Dissatisfied with the IEP, the parents filed another due process complaint. A hearing officer recommended dismissal of the complaint because they did not show the revised IEP was inappropriate.

The parents appealed to a federal court, which held the hearing officer failed to determine whether the evidence indicated a need for 1:1 instruction. After the case returned to the hearing officer, he found the student required 1:1 services and that the parents were entitled to reimbursement for the student's private services for a period of one year. A federal court reversed the hearing officer's decision, finding the evidence did not indicate the student needed 1:1 services. When the case reached the U.S. Court of Appeals, Ninth Circuit, the court upheld the hearing officer's conclusion that the student required 1:1 instruction. The case was returned to the lower court, which accepted administrative findings that the student needed 1:1 instruction. **In ruling for the parents, the court held the revised IEP denied the student a FAPE.** They were entitled to be reimbursed for one year of 1:1 autism services. *Howard G. v. State of Hawaii, Dep't of Educ.*, Nos. 11-00523 DKW KSD, 13-00029 DKW KSC, 2018 WL 605897 (D. Haw. 1/29/18).

◆   Dissatisfied with IEPs offered to their son in two consecutive school years, New York parents enrolled him in a private school for students with autism. They requested an impartial hearing to seek tuition reimbursement from the New York City Department of Education (DOE). An impartial hearing officer (IHO) found the IEPs for both school years were insufficient. In addition to finding the recommended vocational and transition services deficient, the IHO found the IEPs were predetermined and called for classroom student-to-educator ratios that would not allow the student to have appropriate social interactions. Further, the IHO disapproved of the teaching methodology employed in the classrooms and found the recommended school sites ill-equipped to implement the IEPs. A state review officer later reversed the IHO's decision, as did a federal court.

   On appeal, the U.S. Court of Appeals, Second Circuit, noted that in *Endrew F. v. Douglas County School Dist. RE-1,* 137 S.Ct. 988 (2017), the Supreme Court held **an IEP need not bring a student to grade-level achievement, but it must aspire to provide more than minimal educational progress**. Review of an IEP proceeds in two steps. First, a court examines whether the school has complied with IDEA procedures. Next, it considers whether the IEP is reasonably calculated to enable a child to make progress appropriate in light of the child's circumstances. In this case, the court rejected the parents' claim that the failure to assess the student in person undermined the development of his IEPs. They did not show the IEP was inadequate. Even assuming there was an IDEA procedural violation, the court found the parents did not show it impeded the student's right to a FAPE, deprived him of educational benefits or significantly impeded their participation opportunities. Finding the IEPs were reasonably calculated to provide the student postsecondary goals and transition services required by the IDEA, the court held for the DOE. *R.B. v. New York City Dep't of Educ.,* 689 Fed.Appx. 48 (2d Cir. 2017).

◆   A student with attention deficit hyperactivity disorder had a Section 504 accommodation plan for grade two. The District of Columbia Public Schools (DCPS) found her eligible for special education as a child with an other health impairment/attention deficit disorder the next year. Without rejecting the IEP, the parents investigated private schools for their child and ultimately found a private day school. After notifying the DCPS of their intent to make a private placement and seek funding for it, the parents enrolled their child in the private school. There, she received 35 hours of weekly specialized instruction and related services in a self-contained, intensive, individualized, remedial special education program. While the student attended the private school, the DCPS arranged for evaluations and a functional behavior assessment. After an IEP team created an IEP that would have placed the student in a public school, the parents filed a due process hearing complaint. A hearing officer held they did not prove the DCPS denied their child a free appropriate public education.

   The parents appealed to a federal court, which found **the opinions of IEP team members at the time of the creation of the IEP were more relevant**

than the student's private school progress. It held the parents did not show the IEP was not reasonably calculated to enable their child to receive educational benefits. At the time the IEP was offered, her parents requested a private placement. But they did not present persuasive evidence that keeping her in DCPS was not viable. **Strong policy considerations counseled against unilateral parental placements before a public school could implement or adjust an IEP.** Since the parents did not show the IEP was inadequate and would have denied their child a FAPE, the court denied private school tuition reimbursement. *Z.B. v. District of Columbia*, 202 F.Supp.3d 64 (D.D.C. 2016).

4. Failure to Cooperate

In Rohn v. Palm Beach County School Board, No. 11-81408-CIV, 2013 WL 6479294 (S.D. Fla. 12/10/13), *a federal court held the parents of Florida twins were not entitled to private school tuition reimbursement after they removed the children from school based on their lack of trust of school officials.*

◆ A North Carolina parent disputed the placement of her child in an elementary classroom made up of non-verbal students with maladaptive behaviors. She believed school officials did not consider his evaluation data and did not explore any potential alternative programs. Moreover, the parent claimed the school board did not develop a behavior intervention plan for the child and did not notify her that he was engaging in self-harming behaviors. After requesting a due process hearing, the parent dropped the case. A year later, she refiled the complaint, seeking compensatory damages, reimbursement of private school tuition, travel expenses, and other relief. For months, the parties engaged in contentious pretrial activity, during which the case was reassigned to another administrative law judge (ALJ). The board sought to dismiss the case based on the parent's refusal to participate in the fact-finding activity known as "discovery." When the parent did not disclose information by a required deadline, the ALJ dismissed the case. A state review officer affirmed the decision, as did a federal district court. Since non-attorney parents cannot litigate the claims of their minor children, the court dismissed the claims she advanced on behalf of her son.

To the extent that the parent advanced IDEA claims in her own right, the court found she did not exhaust her administrative remedies. Next, **the court found the ALJ acted correctly in barring the parent's evidence after the deadline and dismissing the case.** The parent appealed to the U.S Court of Appeals, Fourth Circuit, which affirmed the judgment for the board of education. As the lower court held, her failure to cooperate with orders to disclose information warranted case dismissal. Although the parent appealed to the U.S. Supreme Court, it declined her petition. *Hayes v. Cumberland County Board of Educ.*, No. 17-7777, 138 S.Ct. 1334 (U.S. cert. denied 3/26/18).

◆ Massachusetts parents sought reimbursement after privately placing their child with autism. A federal court agreed with a hearing officer's decision not to rely on an evaluation report they supplied five days before a hearing to consider his IEP. In the court's view, the decision by the parents to "wait until the eve of the hearing to provide the expert report to the school district did not merely inconvenience the School District, but circumvented the collaborative TEAM process established under the IDEA." **Parents who unilaterally place their children in a private school face a heavy burden when seeking tuition reimbursement.** This burden is increased for parents who prematurely abandon the IDEA's collaborative process. Parents who obstruct or interrupt the IEP process should not be allowed to benefit from their refusal to fully cooperate with a school district. Reports and test scores showed the student was progressing in a public school. Since the IDEA does not assure that a student who is being provided an adequate IEP has the right to a different placement, the court held for the school district. *Doe v. Richmond Consolidated School Dist.*, No. 15-30027-MGM, 2016 WL 3064056 (D. Mass. 6/20/16).

◆   After a school IEP team offered to place a disabled preschool child in a two-day per week placement with same-age peers in a typical setting, the parents believed she was being dismissed from her school. They removed the child and her twin sister from the school system, enrolled them in a private pre-kindergarten and requested a due process hearing. After the hearing officer held for the school district, the dispute came before a federal court. It found the district had timely evaluated the twins. **The district's decisions to reduce services resulted from a reasonable evaluation of their current performance.** Nothing indicated that a change in placement was incorrect. Changing the classification of one twin from the "developmental delay" category to "other health impaired" was not improper. Finally, the removal of the students from their public school program after only two days based on lack of trust did not support reimbursement for private school tuition. Since the hearing officer did not commit error by ruling for the school board, the decision was affirmed. *Rohn v. Palm Beach County School Board*, No. 11-81408-CIV, 2013 WL 6479294 (S.D. Fla. 12/10/13).

◆   An 18-year-old Hawaii private school student read at a grade 3-6 level. But his parent said he could do high school level math and had taken a pre-algebra class at a community college. An IEP proposed for the student stated that he would not participate with non-disabled peers but would attend a workplace readiness program in a self-contained classroom for students on track for a certificate of completion. He was to "participate with non-disabled peers in activities of his own choosing." At IEP meetings, the parent told other team members that he wanted his child to remain at the private school. But he did not voice any specific concerns about the IEP and did not seek a general education setting. Two months later, the parent filed a due process hearing request. An impartial hearing officer found the IEP team did not consider general education classes and did not consider whether the student's goals and objectives could be implemented in general education classes. In addition, the hearing officer found the IEP was not properly individualized in that it allowed the student to select his own participation opportunities with non-disabled peers. Since the private school was found appropriate for the student, the hearing officer awarded the parent the cost of tuition and related services there for a full year. A federal court then considered the department's claim that the IEP was appropriate.

According to the department, the parent had withheld his complaints about the IEP offer until the hearing. Although previous IEPs had contained similar provisions, the court found student needs changed from year to year. It held the department had failed to even consider placing the student in general education classes for math. Since the school district failed to place the student in the least restrictive environment, the court affirmed that aspect of the decision. Like the hearing officer, the court found the IEP provision allowing the student to select his own nonacademic peer participation opportunities was not specific enough to address his socialization needs. **In the court's opinion, the "parent's conduct was unreasonable and tainted what should be a collaborative IEP process."** He failed to express relevant concerns and withheld opinions until the time of the administrative hearing, and the court found his sole concern was to obtain the private school placement. It appeared to the court that the department had made a good-faith effort to provide an IEP. As a result, the court reduced the tuition reimbursement by half, based on the parent's unreasonable conduct. *Dep't of Educ., State of Hawaii v. S.C.*, 938 F.Supp.2d 1023 (D. Haw. 2013).

5.   Least Restrictive Environment

In C.L. v. Scarsdale Union Free School Dist., 744 F.3d 826 (2d Cir. 2014), the court held New York parents should not be denied tuition reimbursement on the sole ground that the private school they selected for their child was not his least restrictive environment (LRE). Parents are not held to the same standard as school districts when making private placements.

◆   The U.S. Court of Appeals, Sixth Circuit, held a student with Down syndrome was improperly segregated from non-disabled peers. In ruling for the student, the court noted a strong preference in federal law for mainstreaming students with disabilities. Children with disabilities may only be segregated from non-disabled peers when the nature or severity of a disability is such that education in regular classes (with supplementary aids or services) cannot be achieved. The court found a mainstream setting would have provided the student in this case "some" educational benefit. **In the Sixth Circuit's view, the standard for placing a student with a disability is not mastery of the general-education curriculum. Instead, a student with a disability must progress on his/her IEP goals.** There was evidence that the student's teachers did not properly engage him in mainstreaming when he attended general education classes. It appeared to the court that staff isolated and removed him from situations that became challenging. As the parents argued, the school provided a curriculum with very low educational expectations, and no report cards or homework. The court held students with disabilities may be educated separately only when (1) they would not benefit from regular education, (2) such benefits would be far outweighed by the benefits of special education, or (3) a student would disrupt regular classes. It held the lower court had incorrectly denied an award of tuition reimbursement for their private school costs. It found clear evidence that a Montessori school selected by the parents provided the student a personalized curriculum, "an involved, qualified teacher and an individual aide." Finding the Montessori curriculum "well-suited for children with Down syndrome in many respects," and good for the student in this case, the court returned the case to the lower court for the taking of additional evidence to determine an appropriate amount of tuition reimbursement for the parents. *L.H. v. Hamilton County Dep't of Educ.*, 900 F.3d 779 (6th Cir. 2018).

When the case returned to the lower court, it determined the parents were entitled to reimbursement for the student's educational costs for grades 3-8 at the Montessori school in the sum of $103,274. After the court held the school system had to reimburse the parents, they sought their attorneys' fees and costs. The court held they were "unquestionably the prevailing party in their IDEA case," and approved an award of attorneys' fees and court costs of $349,249.50. *L.H. v. Hamilton County Dep't of Educ.*, 356 F.Supp.3d 713 (E.D. Tenn. 2019).

◆   The New York City Department of Education (DOE) paid the tuition of a student with special needs for several years. After his third year at a private school, he was enrolled in a Skills and Knowledge for Independent Living and Learning program designed for students ages 18-21 with cognitive and developmental delays or severe language-based disabilities. The DOE then sought to place the student at a public school with a 15:1 student-teacher ratio. According to the student's father, the school was an inappropriate placement. He reenrolled the student at the private school, then filed an impartial hearing request, seeking tuition reimbursement. An impartial hearing officer (IHO) granted the relief he requested, but a state review officer reversed the decision.

Appeal went before a federal court. In finding a 15:1 placement would be appropriate for the student, the review officer had relied solely on a teacher's testimony that the placement would be the least restrictive environment and would allow for opportunities to interact with typically developing peers. Significantly, the teacher's description of the class did not specifically refer to the student's circumstances. Next, the review officer did not consider testimony by a private school teacher who had worked with the student for the past two school years. The teacher explained that a 15:1 classroom was too large for him. **The court found no discussion by the CSE indicating the student was ready to learn in a larger classroom.** The equities favored the parent's claim for reimbursement. The court deferred to the IHO's decision that a 15:1 classroom placement denied the child a free appropriate education. *L.R. v. New York City Dep't of Educ.*, 193 F.Supp.3d 209 (E.D.N.Y. 2016).

◆   A Pennsylvania student had specific learning disabilities in reading and written language. Her parents rejected her IEP and placed her in a private school with a curriculum based on creative thinking and "strong experiences that stir the emotions." The parties reached a settlement under which the school district paid the student's tuition at the private school for a school year. But prior to the next school year, the parents rejected an IEP that would have placed their child in a public school.

A hearing officer agreed with the parents that the school district did not seriously consider supplementary aids and services that might have kept her in regular classes. The district did not place her in the least restrictive setting.

The case reached the U.S. Court of Appeals, Third Circuit. On appeal, the court held the district did not counter evidence that it did not adequately consider greater opportunities for inclusion. A school district must comply with the least restrictive environment requirement by considering whether education can take place in regular classes, with supplementary aids and services. Schools must offer a continuum of placements to meet the needs of a disabled child. They must seriously consider including a child in a regular classroom with supplementary aids and services and to modify the regular curriculum. The district did not show what steps it took toward full inclusion, and the court upheld findings that the district did not show it considered the whole range or continuum of possible placements as required by the IDEA. **But because the parents did not show the private school they selected for their child was appropriate, their request for tuition reimbursement was denied.** *H.L. v. Downingtown Area School Dist.*, 624 Fed.Appx. 64 (3d Cir. 2015).

◆   A New York student had a Section 504 plan to assist him with problems arising from ADHD, anxiety, stuttering, motor development and coordination. As he prepared for grade four, his parents asked the school district to determine if he was entitled to an IEP. But the district found him ineligible for special education. Instead of accepting another Section 504 plan, the parents enrolled the student in a private Connecticut special education school. They then filed a due process hearing request, seeking reimbursement for their private school tuition costs. An impartial hearing officer (IHO) agreed with the parents that the district had denied their child a free appropriate public education (FAPE). As the IHO found the private school was appropriate, the district had to reimburse the parents for their tuition costs. A state review officer found that the private school selected by the parents was not the student's least restrictive environment under the IDEA. For this reason, reimbursement was denied.

A federal court affirmed the review officer's decision and the parents appealed to the U.S. Court of Appeals, Second Circuit. It held **parents are not barred from obtaining private school tuition reimbursement when the school selected does not meet the IDEA definition of a FAPE.** Parents whose children are denied a FAPE by their school districts are often forced to turn to private placements that are "necessarily restrictive." As a result, the court found that when a public school system denies a child FAPE, the restrictiveness of a private placement cannot be measured against that of a public school option. In this case, the review officer should not have solely relied on the restrictiveness of the private school placement. It appeared to the court that the parents cooperated with the school district in its efforts to meet its duties under the IDEA. Agreeing with the IHO's decision, the court held reimbursement for the private placement was proper. *C.L. v. Scarsdale Union Free School Dist.*, 744 F.3d 826 (2d Cir. 2014).

◆   The mother of a Hawaii student with autism placed him in a private school that used verbal behavior science and applied behavioral analysis methods. She then sought tuition reimbursement. A hearing officer noted the state's failure to address the student's transition needs but also noted the student's lack of progress in many areas and the mother's failure to cooperate with the department of education. A federal court agreed with the hearing officer that the mother was not entitled to tuition reimbursement. It held the private school was inappropriate for the student, not only because of his lack of progress there, but also because it was found to be an overly restrictive setting. On appeal, the U.S. Court of Appeals, Ninth Circuit, affirmed the judgment denying reimbursement for the cost of the private school. School officials acknowledged that the IEP proposal for a public school violated the IDEA, but **the Ninth Circuit found the private school offered only "meager" educational benefits**. In support of these findings, the court found the student made no progress at all in a "host of essential areas" despite spending more than a year in a private setting. In addition, the court found both the private school and the parents hindered the development of the child's IEP through their uncooperativeness. As a result, the court held for the public school officials. *M.N. v. State of Hawaii, Dep't of Educ.*, 509 Fed.Appx. 640 (9th Cir. 2013).

6. Other Issues

In authorizing reimbursement for 1:1 home programs for a Florida student, the Eleventh Circuit held the IDEA definition of "special education" includes home instruction. See R.L. v. Miami-Dade County School Board, *757 F.3d 1173 (11th Cir. 2014). In* A.C. v. Maple Heights City School Dist. Board of Educ., *No. 1:13CV2710, 2014 WL 953387 (N.D. Ohio 3/11/14), a federal court held Ohio law precluded a claim by parents that their child's IEP did not do enough to address her attendance issues. The court found no support for their argument that schools, not parents, are responsible for getting children to class on time.*

◆ A Washington administrative law judge issued an order against the parents of a student with a disability in a due process proceeding. When they appealed to a federal court, they sought to hold the district's superintendent and its executive director of special services liable for certain educational expenses, private school tuition, tutoring, transportation costs, legal fees and related costs. When the administrators sought to be dismissed from the case, the court refused to do so. It found no case law authority holding that they could not be sued in their individual capacities under the IDEA. Four months later, the parents asked the court to add a school principal, director of special education and a school psychologist as parties. They sought to hold them individually liable for their child's educational expenses, private placement and other costs. The court noted IDEA language about due process appeals refers to parents and local educational agencies, but is silent regarding employees and school officials.

In the court's view, the applicable IDEA provisions reference the ability of a court to award attorneys' fees to "a prevailing party who is either the parent, a state educational agency, or a local educational agency." The IDEA does not list an individual party as a possible prevailing party or a party against whom the award can be made. **The court found the right to reimbursement originates from a school district's failure to provide appropriate education, not the actions of district employees.** Given the language and intent of the IDEA, and the lack of available remedies against individual school district employees or officials, the court found **the appropriate redress for IDEA violations is against school districts, not individual employees**. As a result, the court denied the parents' motion to draw the principal, director of special education and school psychologist into the action. It also dismissed the district superintendent and the executive director from the case. *Crofts v. Issaquah School Dist.*, No. C17-1365RAJ, 2018 WL 1517671 (W.D. Wash. 3/28/18).

◆ A gifted Maryland student struggled with learning disabilities, dyslexia, a central auditory processing disorder and attention deficit hyperactivity disorder. After his third-grade school year, his parents enrolled him in a private school. They said he thrived there but quickly became depressed upon returning to his public school for grade four. In response to the parents' concerns, the county school system agreed to conduct further testing of the student. After the testing, the system accepted him into its talented and gifted program, effective the next school year. In this setting, the student would continue receiving his IEP accommodations and have an instructional assistant. Instead of returning their son to the public school system, the parents enrolled him in the private school he had attended the previous summer. They requested a due process hearing, claiming he was denied a free appropriate public education. After a hearing, an administrative law judge (ALJ) held for the school system.

Appeal reached the U.S. Court of Appeals, Fourth Circuit, which found the ALJ used appropriate fact-finding procedures and thoughtful determinations about the credibility of the witnesses. She found the school experts credible, and their conclusions were corroborated by the student's teachers. By contrast, the ALJ found the parents' experts gave opinions that were almost entirely based on generalized knowledge or information provided by the parents. **She noted they had already decided to enroll their child in a private school months before the school system completed revisions to his IEP.** In the Fourth Circuit's view, the lower court consistently rejected the ALJ's credibility determinations without providing a rationale. Prior Fourth Circuit case law admonished district courts against substituting their own credibility assessments for those of an ALJ without explanation. The court of appeals returned the case to the lower court for further proceedings. *N.P. v. Maxwell*, 711 Fed.Appx. 713 (4th Cir. 2017).

◆ A Florida student had autism and other conditions that caused anxiety, obsessive-compulsive behavior and sensory processing problems. By grade seven, his parents removed him from school because he was becoming violent. While the student was out of school, the school district provided him 1:1 home instruction, which the parents supplemented at their own expense. A private treatment team found the student was regressing from the sensory overload of a large school environment. At a pair of IEP meetings, the parents urged a high school placement in a small magnet school. Over their objection, the IEP team placed the student in a large high school. His symptoms worsened, and his home behavior became almost uncontrollable. The parents withdrew their child from school and designed a home 1:1 program for speech and occupational therapy. The board then requested a due process hearing. When the case reached the U.S. Court of Appeals, Eleventh Circuit, it stated that if parents reject an IEP and make an alternative placement, they may claim reimbursement only if the IEP did not provide a FAPE. A court must also find the parents' alternative was appropriate. Like the ALJ, the court found the school's IEP offer was so deficient that it would not matter where it was implemented. So the parents were entitled to reject the IEP and seek reimbursement. Since the 1:1 program created by the parents was reasonably calculated to confer some educational benefit upon the student, the court held they were entitled to reimbursement.

Rejecting the board's argument that no IDEA provision authorized reimbursement for 1:1 home programs, the court found the IDEA definition of "special education" included home instruction. *R.L. v. Miami-Dade County School Board*, 757 F.3d 1173 (11th Cir. 2014).

B. Placement in Unapproved Schools

In Florence County School Dist. Four v. Carter, *the Supreme Court held parents who placed their children in unapproved private schools could claim tuition reimbursement despite the lack of state approval. The Court focused on the appropriateness of the placement selected by the parents and the inability of a local school district to provide an appropriate alternative.*

◆ A New Jersey student with autism, ADHD, epilepsy and hearing impairments was found ineligible for special education after his first year in a public school. His parents placed him in a private school and filed a due process hearing petition. An administrative law judge (ALJ) found the student was denied a FAPE for two school years and awarded him compensatory education. But the parents argued he should have received a larger award, and they appealed to a federal court. The parties reached an agreement on a placement for a subsequent school year. But the school they selected could not implement the IEP and the student missed 12 days of school. During this time, the parents provided home instruction. They rejected a placement offer by the school district and unilaterally placed their child in a private, unaccredited school that agreed to modify its kindergarten program to provide first grade instruction. When the case came before the court, it upheld the finding that the student was ineligible for special education after his first year of preschool. It further held there should be no compensatory education for his second preschool year. But the court held the student should have six hours of compensatory instruction for each of the 12 days of school he missed, not the 10 hours per week as allowed by the ALJ.

Unlike the ALJ, the court held the parents were entitled to be reimbursed for more than just the cost of gas for their transportation to and from the private school. The award was increased by over $1,000 to reflect the standard IRS rate for business travel. But the court disallowed the parents' claim to reimbursement for their travel time to and from the private school at a minimum wage rate. Last, the court held they should be reimbursed for the seven-week period when their child attended a private school, awaiting a public school placement. **Although the school was unaccredited, the court found it had modified its program by creating a first-grade inclusion class, providing the student with a meaningful educational opportunity.** *A.S. v. Harrison Township Board of Educ.*, No. 14-147, 2016 WL 1717578 (D.N.J. 4/29/16).

◆ A New York child with autism had many behavior problems, including severe tantrums. She once jumped from a first-floor window and later jumped from a school bus. After the child attended a public school from grades three through six, her parent concluded her behavior was not improving and that she was not being challenged academically. She was withdrawn from school in favor of home instruction. But the child's negative behaviors continued, and her home instructor struggled with them. Soon after the child returned to a public school, she had a bus altercation that led to her handcuffing. Her parent rejected a private school placement located by the school staff. She then filed a due process hearing request. Following a hearing, an impartial hearing officer (IHO) held the child should be referred to the Central Based Support Team for consideration of all placement options. The IHO agreed with the parent that any school search should include private schools that were not approved by the state of New York. The New York City Department of Education (DOE) appealed to a state review officer, who held the DOE could only contract with approved schools.

Appeal reached a federal court, where the parent cited a line of federal court authority governing reimbursement to parents who unilaterally place children in an unapproved school. This included the U.S. Supreme Court's leading precedent concerning private school tuition reimbursement, *Florence County School Dist. Four v. Carter*, 510 U.S. 7 (1993). But the court found *Carter* involved a parent's right to independently place a child in a private school over a district's objection. Moreover, **school districts must satisfy state approval requirements when placing a child with a disability in a private school**. Since *Carter* did not rule that a school district could be ordered to place a child in an unapproved private school, the court found the review officer had correctly rejected the parent's arguments and held in favor of the DOE. *Z.H. v. New York City Dep't of Educ.*, 107 F.Supp.3d 1369 (S.D.N.Y. 2015).

◆ The parents of a South Carolina ninth-grader with a learning disability disagreed with the IEP proposed by their school district. The IEP called for mainstreaming in most subjects, with individual instruction three periods a week, and specific goals of increasing the student's reading and mathematics levels by four months for the entire school year. The parents requested due process and unilaterally placed their daughter in a private school that specialized in teaching students with disabilities. A hearing officer held that the IEP was adequate. After the student raised her reading comprehension three full grades in one year at the private school, the parents sued the school district for tuition reimbursement. A federal court found that the educational program and achievement goals of the proposed IEP were "wholly inadequate" under the IDEA. Even though the private school did not comply with all IDEA procedures – by employing noncertified staff members, for example – it provided the student with an excellent education that complied with IDEA substantive requirements. The court awarded tuition reimbursement, a result upheld by the Fourth Circuit. The district appealed to the U.S. Supreme Court.

The Court expanded upon its decision in *School Committee of the Town of Burlington, Massachusetts v. Dep't of Educ. of Massachusetts,* where it held that parents had the right to unilaterally change their children's placement at their own financial risk. To recover private school tuition costs, parents must show that the placement proposed by the school district violates the IDEA and that the private school placement is appropriate under the act. Here, **the failure by the school district to provide an appropriate placement entitled the parents to an award of tuition reimbursement, even though the private school was not approved by the state**, because the education provided at the private school had been determined by the district court to be appropriate. The decisions in favor of the parents were upheld. *Florence County School Dist. Four v. Carter*, 510 U.S. 7, 114 S.Ct. 361, 126 L.Ed.2d 284 (1993).

C. Notice

IDEA provisions require notice by parents who decide to unilaterally enroll their children in a private school. These provisions are listed at 20 U.S.C. § 1412(a)(10)(C)(iii). Before reimbursement can be limited under this section, the school district must have previously provided the parents with all applicable IDEA notices. Parents seeking private school tuition are required to notify the district, in writing, of their objections to the district's program and their intent to enroll their children in private programs before actually doing so. Failure to do so may result in denial or reduction of a reimbursement claim.

◆ A New York student had Tourette syndrome, ADHD, a developmental coordination disorder, a central processing disorder, dyscalculia and dyslexia. A school committee determined he should be placed in a classroom made up of 15 students, a special education teacher and a teaching assistant for grade seven (a "15:1+1 classroom). His parents visited the school site. Teachers there reiterated that the student would attend a 15:1+1 classroom. In a letter to the district's director of pupil personnel services, the parents indicated their intent to make a private placement. They said they did not receive a copy of the IEP and could not review it. The school district responded by sending the parents a copy of the IEP. However, the district notice indicated a 12:1+1 classroom placement for English, math, social studies and science. The district later admitted the reference to a 12:1+1 classroom was a clerical error. The student began the school year at a private school, and the parents filed a due process complaint. After a resolution meeting, the school district developed a second IEP that changed the class size to 15:1+1. An impartial hearing officer held the student received a free appropriate public education. A review officer reversed the decision, finding the district was precluded from relying on the second IEP by *R.E. v. New York City Dep't of Educ.*, 694 F.3d 167 (2d Cir. 2012). On appeal, a federal court agreed with the review officer that the initial IEP was the operative document. As the school district admitted, it was unable to offer the student a 12:1+1 classroom at the beginning of his seventh-grade school year.

The court rejected the school district's argument that it corrected a good-faith IEP error and properly amended it while verbally informing the parents of its intent. In *R.E. v. New York City Dep't of Educ.*, the Second Circuit Court of Appeals barred a school district from rehabilitating or amending an IEP after-the-fact through testimony about services not specified in an IEP. Moreover, the court found the school district failed to send the parents a copy of the modified IEP during the resolution period. Allowing the district to unilaterally amend an IEP without sending the parents a copy of it would undermine IDEA notice requirements. According to the court, the confusion caused by the school district emphasized the need for accurate, written IEPs upon which parents could rely. As a result, the parents were entitled to tuition reimbursement. *Board of Educ. of Yorktown Cent. School Dist. v. C.S. & S.S.*, 357 F.Supp.3d 311 (S.D.N.Y. 2019) (2d Cir. appeal filed 1/29/19).

◆   After determining a middle school student with dyslexia and dyscalculia required extended school year (ESY) services, the Hawaii Department of Education (DOE) determined she should have four hours of summer daily special education services. When the parents told their child about the summer placement, she refused to attend. But the parents did not advise the DOE about this. Just before the summer semester, they wrote to the DOE that they intended to make a private placement for their child and would seek public reimbursement for it. They then requested a due process hearing. A hearings officer held equitable considerations did not warrant tuition reimbursement or compensatory education. In response, the parents sued the DOE in a federal court. They argued the hearings officer improperly relied on *T.M. v. Cornwall Cent. School Dist.*, 752 F.3d 145 (2d Cir. 2014), a non-binding Second Circuit decision.

The court held that in order to support a private tuition reimbursement award, the school district must have denied the student a FAPE. Second, the private placement selected by parents must be found appropriate by a hearing officer or court. A court may reduce the amount of reimbursement if the parents do not timely inform the IEP team that they are rejecting an IEP and enrolling their child in a private school. Courts have established that to qualify for an award of tuition reimbursement at public expense, the equities must favor it. In this case, the court held the parents did not timely notify the DOE that they were rejecting the ESY proposal for their child. **As the parents did not provide the student a private school placement during the summer, reimbursement was not warranted.** Even if the student had been denied an appropriate placement for the next school year, the court found the equities did not support full tuition reimbursement. Finding it reasonable for the hearings officer to rely on the *T.M.* case, the court held for the DOE. *W.U. and L.U. v. State of Hawaii, Dep't of Educ.*, No. 18-000197 JAO-RT, 2019 WL 1128754 (D. Haw. 3/12/19).

◆   A New Jersey school board funded an out-of-district private day school placement for a student through grade eight. There, she received an Orton-Gillingham based program with assistive technology and in-class supports. During the student's eighth-grade school year, preparations were made for her to transition to high school. Because the school district served only K-8 students, a representative of a regional high school district attended her child study team meeting. The representative proposed that the student begin grade nine at a public high school in a resource room setting with supplemental instruction, in-class support and modifications. The parent visited the high school, but without giving notice to the district, she signed an enrollment contract with a private school. During the summer before the student entered grade nine, the regional high school district revised its initial IEP draft. Among other things, it reclassified her as a student with an other health impairment.

The parent rejected the proposed IEP and filed a due process complaint, seeking tuition reimbursement for the private placement. An administrative law judge (ALJ) held for the regional high school district. On appeal, a federal court held that **parents who make unilateral private placements without school district consent "do so at their own financial risk."** The IDEA and state laws require parents to give written notice of their intent to enroll their children in private schools at public expense. If they do not provide proper notice, the laws permit a reduction or denial in reimbursement. The court rejected the parent's argument that emotional harm to her child would result because the regional high school district's IEP did not "mirror the exact program" provided to her by the K-8 district. But **the court found the ALJ "short-circuited the equitable analysis" that courts and hearing officers use when reviewing private school tuition reimbursement claims.** It returned the case to the ALJ to determine whether the parent might qualify for any reimbursement and whether the IEP was appropriate. *M.C.I. v. North Hunterdon-Voorhees Regional High School Board of Educ.*, No. 17-1887, 2018 WL 902265 (D.N.J. 2/15/18).

♦ New Jersey parents asked their school district to forward their child's records to a private school for students with language-based learning issues for intake purposes. Although their letter described the private school's program, it did not notify the district of their intent to place their child there. In response, the district declined to send the records to the private school "or any other out of district placement." The parents again submitted a written request to the school district, this time through an attorney, seeking their child's records. The attorney wrote to the district to "again confirm that the parents are seeking, in part, reimbursement and/or placement at the Lewis school." The parents requested a hearing, seeking tuition reimbursement and compensatory education for an unspecified time period in which their child was denied a FAPE. An ALJ dismissed the case, finding the parents failed to timely notify the school district of their intent to remove their child from school and place her in a private school at public expense, as required by the IDEA.

A federal court held the ALJ improperly applied IDEA and state law provisions to categorically bar their claim to reimbursement, instead of as discretionary reasons for reducing or denying reimbursement. In general, the IDEA permits parents who feel a public school placement is not providing a child with a FAPE to make private school placements and then seek tuition reimbursement for the cost from a public agency. The IDEA section relied upon by the ALJ permits a judge to reduce or deny the amount of a tuition reimbursement award "if the equities so warrant." **Parental notice is to be made at an IEP meeting, or in writing 10 business days prior to the removal of the child from a public school.** In this case, the court held the ALJ did not reach the threshold questions of whether the school district denied the student a FAPE and whether the private school placement was appropriate. The court found the ALJ did not explain his reasoning for finding the parents' failure to comply with the IDEA and state law notice requirement "warranted a wholesale denial of the cost of tuition reimbursement, rather than a reduction in tuition reimbursement." The case was returned to the ALJ for consideration of the equities presented in the claim for reimbursement. The ALJ was to also consider the student's entitlement to compensatory education and determine whether the district denied a FAPE. *H.L. & J.L. v. Marlboro Township Board of Educ.*, No. 16-9324 (FLW) (DEA), 2017 WL 5463347 (D.N.J. 11/14/17).

◆ A New Jersey parent signed an enrollment agreement and paid tuition to a private school. He then attended an IEP meeting, where staff members proposed a developmental reading program for his child. The parent requested more specific information about the reading program, but IEP team members only responded that the program would be research-based and focused on phonic skills and comprehension. They also stated it would be instructed by a certified teacher. The parent later claimed his son was denied a free appropriate public education (FAPE) because the team had failed to share basic information about the reading program. When the case reached the U.S. Court of Appeals, Third Circuit, it explained that **the IDEA permits a court or hearing officer to reduce or deny a private school tuition reimbursement claim where parents fail to provide timely written notice of their intention to make a private placement and seek reimbursement for it**. Such notice must be made at least 10 business days prior to a parental removal. A court may deny reimbursement if it finds parental actions were unreasonable and reimbursement is inequitable.

As the lower court and ALJ had found, the parent did not follow IDEA notice requirements. He did not advise the district of his intent to remove the child from district schools at least 10 days prior to placing his child at the private school. The court held the parent did not provide adequate notice to the district when making a private placement. Next, the court upheld the finding that no IDEA procedural violation took place when the school district declined to elaborate on inquiries about methodology to be used in the developmental reading program it had proposed. As the lower court had correctly found the parent was not denied a meaningful opportunity to participate in the IEP process, the judgment for the board was affirmed. *W.D. v. Watchung Hills Regional High School Board of Educ.*, 602 Fed.Appx. 563 (3d Cir. 2015).

◆ A Hawaii parent said school officials did not provide her with a prior notice of placement offer for her autistic child. She challenged an offer for a community-based instruction (CBI) program at a Maui public school. Instead of sending her child to the school, the parent sent him off-island to a residential school and requested an IDEA hearing. A hearing officer denied reimbursement for the off-island placement, finding the state department of education (DOE) made appropriate placement offers for two relevant school years. A federal court affirmed the decision regarding the FAPE issue. The parent then appealed to the U.S. Court of Appeals, Ninth Circuit, where she sought reimbursement for housing expenses and for her visitation costs under the stay-put provision.

The court found no error in the hearing officer's decision to deny the notice claim. **Even if there was a procedural error by the DOE, it did not significantly restrict the parent from participation in the IEP process.** The hearing officer had credited DOE witnesses who were involved with the CBI program. There was no error in the finding that a FAPE was offered to the child. Evidence indicated the DOE paid for weekend visitation expenses for the family and provided weekend support. But the hearing officer had improperly failed to consider a claim to reimbursement for housing expenses as a related service while the student was at the off-island school. Further administrative proceedings were needed to resolve the housing reimbursement issue. *Marcus I. v. Dep't of Educ., State of Hawaii*, 583 Fed.Appx. 753 (9th Cir. 2014).

II. VOUCHER PROGRAMS AND RELIGIOUS SCHOOLS

A. Vouchers and Public Assistance

Arizona, Florida, Georgia, Louisiana, North Carolina, Oklahoma and Utah are among the states with special education voucher programs. Such programs typically require the parents of students wishing to attend a private school through a voucher or scholarship to waive their child's right to a free appropriate public education.

◆   The Missouri Department of Natural Resources denied a church-affiliated preschool and daycare center's application to participate in a program offering reimbursement to nonprofit organizations that purchase playground surfaces made of recycled tires. The department argued that strict exclusion of religious applicants was compelled by Article I, Section 7, of the Missouri Constitution, which directs that "no money shall ever be taken from the public treasury, directly or indirectly, in aid of any church, sect or denomination of religion, or in aid of any priest, preacher, minister or teacher thereof, as such; and that no preference shall be given to nor any discrimination made against any church, sect or creed of religion, or any form of religious faith or worship."

In a federal court, the church sued the department director for violation of the Free Exercise Clause of the First Amendment. The court dismissed the case, and the Eighth Circuit affirmed the decision. On appeal to the U.S. Supreme Court, the department relied on *Locke v. Davey*, 540 U.S. 712 (2004). In *Locke*, the Court upheld the State of Washington's decision not to fund degrees in devotional theology as part of an educational scholarship program. The Court held the Free Exercise Clause protects religious observers against unequal treatment and subjects to the strictest scrutiny laws that target the religious for special disabilities based on religious status. According to the Court, the department's policy discriminated against otherwise eligible recipients by disqualifying them from a public benefit solely because of their religious character. **The Court found the church had to choose "between being a church and receiving a government benefit."** The Court found the state's interest in avoiding Establishment Clause violations amounted to a "policy preference," and it returned the case to a lower court. *Trinity Lutheran Church of Columbia v. Comer*, 137 S.Ct. 2012, 198 L.Ed.2d 551 (U.S. 2017).

◆   An Ohio court held autism service providers could not enforce a claim to over $366,000 for behavioral intervention services they said were provided under Ohio's Autism Scholarship Program. When the providers refused to comply with state requirements to complete new applications for two new sites, the state education department withheld payments. **The case reached the state** court of appeals, which held the state reasonably construed the scholarship law and could withhold the payments. *Silver Lining Group EIC Morrow County v. Ohio Dep't of Educ. Autism Scholarship Program*, 85 N.E.3d 789, 2017 -Ohio- 7834 (Ohio Ct. App. 2017).

In 2018, the Supreme Court of Ohio declined to review the case. *Silver Lining Group EIC Morrow County v. Ohio Dep't of Educ. Autism Scholarship Program*, 152 Ohio St.3d 1424 (Ohio appeal not allowed 3/14/18).

◆   Colorado parents enrolled their child in a charter school under the state's school choice law. Staff members at the school decided the IEP devised by the school district (of which it was a part) was inadequate. Although the student's IEP listed the charter school as his school of attendance, staff members advised the parents that he would not be readmitted the next school year because the school could not implement his IEP. The parents filed a due process complaint, charging the school district with IDEA violations. An administrative law judge (ALJ) denied their request to enroll the child at the charter school, finding they did not show the district could not implement the IEP. In a federal court, the child's mother sought a stay-put order that would require the district to fund a private placement pending the outcome of the proceeding.

The court granted an order requiring the charter school to enroll the child and keep him there for up to 90 days. But it denied a request for public funding of a private placement under the IDEA stay-put provision. When the case came before the Tenth Circuit, it observed that while the student was not attending the charter school at the time of the hearing, the school was listed in his current IEP as his school of attendance. **Since the lower court correctly identified the charter school as the student's stay-put placement, the court held the school district was not required to fund a private school placement.** *Smith v. Cheyenne Mountain School Dist. 12*, 652 Fed.Appx. 697 (10th Cir. 2016).

◆   A Nevada law authorizing public funding for education savings accounts to pay for private school scholarships was struck down in part by the state's highest court. Nevada Legislators authorized the Education Savings Account (ESA) program to allow the transfer of funds from a state Distributive School Account into privately held education savings accounts. The accounts could be used to fund private schooling, tutoring and other education services. Two state court challenges were filed against the ESA program. The cases reached the Supreme Court of Nevada, which held **the use of K–12 public education appropriations to fund education savings accounts undermined state constitutional mandates to fund public education.** Both cases were returned to a lower court for an order halting any K–12 public education appropriations from the State Distributive School Account to fund the education savings accounts. *Schwartz v. Lopez*, 382 P.3d 886 (Nev. 2016).

◆   In 2010, Oklahoma legislators enacted the Lindsey Nicole Henry Scholarships for Students with Disabilities Act to provide money for eligible students with disabilities to offset their tuition costs at participating private schools. Under the program, families decide whether to participate and determine which schools their children will attend. A group of taxpayers filed a state court action, seeking a permanent order to prohibit state officials from using program funds for sectarian schools. They asserted claims under several articles of the Oklahoma Constitution. When the case reached the Supreme Court of Oklahoma, the court found the program is voluntary. **Parents decide which school offers the best learning environment for their children, so that "the circuit between government and religion is broken."** Persuaded by the fact that program funds are paid to parents and not private schools, the court found no violation of the "no aid clause" of the state constitution. It upheld the program. *Oliver v. Hofmeister*, 368 P.3d 1270 (Okla. 2016).

◆   Arizona parents disputed their child's placement and requested a due process hearing. This led to a decision approving a private academy placement they sought for the child. The parents received Arizona Empowerment Scholarships Account (ESA) funds while the case was pending, and they enrolled their child in their school of choice. The school district appealed to a federal court, which found the hearing officer had relied on testimony by an advocate who lacked relevant experience and training. Although the district argued the receipt of ESA funds relieved it of its duty to provide a FAPE to the child, the court found **the ESA program temporarily released the district from its duty to educate the child. But the court held this duty would resume if the family stopped receiving ESA funds.** On appeal, the Ninth Circuit Court of Appeals reversed the lower court's decision. It held the placement proposed by the district called for excessive transitions and jeopardized the child's safety. Evidence indicated the child would have been placed with older students and exposed to a student population with more severe behavioral issues. Testimony established that students at the setting proposed by the district were grouped according to ability, not age. Since the administrative findings were supported by the evidence, the case was returned to a lower court for further proceedings. *Pointe Educational Services v. A.T.*, 610 Fed.Appx. 702 (9th Cir. 2015).

◆   Florida students with disabilities may receive John M. McKay scholarships under a program that provides public funding for private school education. When parents select a private school for an eligible child, the school district must evaluate the child's matrix of services level. The matrix of services information is provided to the state department of education, which notifies the private school of the scholarship amount. For each student, the nature and intensity of the services indicated in the matrix is to be consistent with his or her IEP. The parents of a deaf student claimed their school district understated their child's matrix of services score to reduce the available McKay Scholarship funds he would receive. In a state court, the parents claimed their son's school deliberately miscalculated his matrix score and misled them about services in violation of the Florida Deceptive and Unfair Trade Practices Act (FDUTPA).

The court dismissed the case, and the parents appealed. A state district court of appeal noted they failed to file an administrative complaint objecting to the IEP. It held the parents were not excused from exhausting the administrative process. As for the FDUTPA claim, the court held **the scoring of a matrix under the McKay program was a ministerial act for the department of education to use in allocating state funds for exceptional students**. Scoring was not a "thing of value" under the FDUTPA. As the scoring of a McKay program matrix of services was not "engaging in trade or commerce" as defined by the FDUTPA, the case was properly dismissed. *Montero v. Duval County School Board*, 153 So.3. 407 (Fla. Dist. Ct. App. 2014).

◆ A 2011 Arizona law established the Empowerment Scholarship Accounts (ESA) to provide scholarships to students with disabilities. A group of challengers filed a state court action to block implementation of the program. Grounds for the challenge included violations of the Aid and Religion Clauses of the Arizona Constitution. After the court held for the state superintendent of public instruction, the challengers appealed to the Court of Appeals of Arizona. It held the Religion Clause forbade appropriating public money for any religious worship, exercise or instruction, or the support of any religious establishment. Parents of disabled children who received an ESA voucher had a duty to provide education in reading, grammar, math, social studies and science. Whether this was done at a secular or religious school was a matter of parental choice and did not violate the Religion Clause. The clause is not a blanket prohibition against sending public funds to a religious organization.

The court explained that the Aid Clause of the state constitution prohibited an appropriation of public funds to aid any church, private or sectarian school. In this case, the court found no violation of the Aid Clause, as the "specified object" of the appropriation was the beneficiary families, not schools. Parents could use ESA funds to "customize an education" that met their children's unique educational needs. Since the beneficiary families had discretion about how to spend ESA funds, no program funds were "preordained for a particular destination." **The court held this distinguished the ESA program from other voucher programs that did not meet constitutional requirements.** As the ESA program was religiously neutral, the court held for the superintendent. *Niehaus v. Huppenthal*, 223 Ariz. 195, 310 P.3d 983 (Ariz. Ct. App. 2013).

◆ The Ohio General Assembly adopted the Ohio Pilot Scholarship Program in 1995 in response to a federal court order to remedy problems in the Cleveland School District. The program made vouchers of up to $2,500 available for Cleveland students to attend public or private schools, including schools with religious affiliations. The state supreme court struck down the program on state constitutional grounds in 1999. Legislators cured these deficiencies and reauthorized the program for 1999-2000. A new lawsuit was filed in a federal court, which permanently enjoined the state from administering the program.

The case reached the U.S. Supreme Court, which held the program allowed government aid to reach religious institutions only because of the deliberate choices of the individual recipients. Any incidental advancement of religion, or perceived endorsement of a religious message, was attributable to the individual recipients, not to the government. The New York program struck down in *Committee for Public Educ. and Religious Liberty v. Nyquist*, 413 U.S. 756 (1973), gave benefits exclusively to private schools and the parents of private school enrollees. **Ohio's program offered aid directly to a broad class of individual recipients defined without regard to religion.** *Zelman v. Simmons-Harris*, 536 U.S. 639, 122 S.Ct. 2460, 153 L.Ed.2d 604 (2002).

B. Religious Schools

Public school funding for students with disabilities for private religious education and related services has been held constitutionally permissible, as the benefit to the private school has been characterized as only "attenuated."

◆   A Maryland student with Down syndrome had a low full-scale IQ. His parents asked their school IEP team to place him at a private school with an Orthodox Jewish curriculum. Instead, the team proposed a public school placement. In response, the parents requested a due process hearing, seeking a placement at their school of choice plus tuition costs. They argued their child could not generalize between his home and school environments. The parents sought an IEP including Hebrew literacy, identification of Kosher symbols and other bicultural and bilingual measures. When the case came before a federal court, it rejected their claim that the school had denied the child an appropriate IEP by not allowing him to access the curriculum while remaining a part of his religious community. On appeal, the U.S. Court of Appeals, Fourth Circuit, explained that in *Endrew F. v. Douglas County School Dist. RE-1*, 137 S.Ct. 988 (2017), the Supreme Court disapproved of the "merely more than *de minimis*" FAPE standard formerly relied upon by the Tenth and Fourth Circuit Courts of Appeals. But it found the FAPE duty does not implicate equal educational opportunities for students with disabilities compared to non-disabled peers.

The court held the IDEA does not guarantee any particular level of education or require the maximization of a student's potential. Moreover, the evidence in this case indicated the school district would make reasonable accommodations for the family's religious preferences. The court found the parents' interpretation of the IDEA would impose requirements that are not present in the act. **Federal regulations supported the finding that IDEA funds are not to be used to provide religious and cultural instruction.** While the parents said the ALJ ignored their argument that the IEP had to allow their child to generalize what he learned from one setting to another, the court disagreed. It held they simply argued the religious instruction he received at home should be generalized to a school setting. In sum, the lower court correctly held religious and cultural instruction is not within a school's FAPE duty. In any case, the district stated it would make reasonable accommodations for the student's religious needs. *M.L. v. Smith*, 867 F.3d 487 (4th Cir. 2017).

◆   New Jersey parents claimed a Quaker Friends school expelled their learning disabled child soon after they requested minor accommodations for him. They believed the school then "purposely sabotaged the process" of finding a new school for him. They said the school discriminated against their son by refusing to allow appropriate and reasonable accommodations for his disabilities and by "subjecting him to public humiliation and shaming due to his disabilities." The parents sued the school in a federal court for discrimination in violation of the ADA, Section 504 and the New Jersey Law Against Discrimination (NJLAD).

With regard to the parents' ADA and NJLAD claims, the court found both laws have exemptions for schools with a religious affiliation. Since the school was under control of the Religious Society of Friends, the court dismissed the

ADA and NJLAD claims. **In holding for the school, the court held the ADA exemption of religious organizations is very broad and applied even when a religious entity carries out activities that would otherwise make it a public accommodation.** Since the Section 504 claims were not now before the court, they survived for future consideration. *Sky R. v. Haddonfield Friends School*, No. 14-5730, 2016 WL 1260061 (D.N.J. 3/31/16).

◆   A California student attended public school kindergarten. Her parent became dissatisfied with her progress and placed her in a parochial school. In a due process proceeding, the parent sought an order that the school district violated her child's right to a free appropriate public education over four school years. The parties reached a settlement agreement by which the district agreed to pay the parent $18,000. It further agreed to provide the student a private intensive reading program, as well as speech and language services. The parent agreed to make her child available to the district for assessments at reasonable times and to sign necessary releases so the district could obtain relevant data.

The parties then disputed the terms of an assessment, leading the district to write to the parent of its belief that she did not intend to comply with the agreement. In response, the parent requested a due process hearing. An administrative law judge (ALJ) held for the district on the issue of denial of the parent's request to hold an IEP meeting. But the ALJ held the parent prevailed on the assessment issue, finding the district did not abide by the settlement. Although the parochial school was held inappropriate for the student, the ALJ found she received educational benefits from her instructional aides at the school. The district was ordered to pay her $6,999.25 for their cost. A federal court upheld the ALJ's decision, and appeal reached the U.S. Court of Appeals, Ninth Circuit. It noted the school district did not appeal from the finding that FAPE had been denied during the relevant school year. **Parents were not required to show a private placement furnished every special service needed to maximize a child's potential.** The court held the school provided the child with instructional materials, a curriculum, structure, support and socialization. It also provided her with accommodations under a Section 504 plan. The court held the parent should be reimbursed for $4,010 in tuition costs. It also approved $6,999.25 for the cost of the aides, $2,693 for transportation costs and almost $35,000 of the over $92,000 in attorneys' fees she claimed. *S.L. v. Upland Unified School Dist.*, 747 F.3d 1155 (9th Cir. 2014).

◆   A Maryland religious school student had attention deficit hyperactivity disorder and anxiety. Although he was IDEA-ineligible, his residence school district declared him eligible under Rehabilitation Act Section 504. But the district advised the parents that it could not provide Section 504 services unless he enrolled in a public school. Maryland law did not permit simultaneous dual enrollment in a public and private school. A hearing examiner found the district was not required to provide the student with special education services at his private school. An appeal went to a federal court, which upheld the district's decision. The case then came before the U.S. Court of Appeals, Fourth Circuit.

The court found support for the district's arguments in guidance from the U.S. Department of Education's Office for Civil Rights (OCR). A 1993 OCR letter stated that **a school district was not responsible under Section 504 for the provision of educational services to students not enrolled in a public school based on the choice of the parents**. The court held a requirement that would extend to private school students would conflict with limitations Congress placed on school district responsibilities. A 1997 IDEA amendment clarified that the states only had to allocate a proportionate amount of their federal funds to eligible private school students. The parents' argument would allow all IDEA-eligible students in private schools to claim full services under Section 504. But the court found this interpretation "would create an individual right to special education and related services where none exists." As the district provided the student with access to a free appropriate public education on equal terms with other students, the court held for the district. *D.L. v. Baltimore City Board of School Commissioners*, 706 F.3d 256 (4th Cir. 2013).

◆   A California special education student had significant behavioral problems in the classroom and left the school building at least five times. The district rejected the parents' request to place him in a Tennessee religious school with his older brother and also refused to return him to a county program where he had fewer issues. Rather than address his runaway issues, it proposed removing him from a general education writing class. The parents placed him in the Tennessee school and then sought tuition reimbursement, which a federal court rejected. **Although the district denied the student a FAPE for more than a year, the parents' placement at the religious school had nothing to do with his special needs**, and his behavior problems continued there. *Covington v. Yuba City Unified School Dist.*, 780 F.Supp.2d 1014 (E.D. Cal. 2011).

◆   An Arizona student attended a school for the deaf from grades one through five and then transferred to a public school for grades six through eight. During his public school attendance, the school district furnished him with a sign-language interpreter. His parents enrolled him in a parochial high school for ninth grade and asked the district to continue providing a sign-language interpreter. The district refused, and the student's parents sued. The court ruled for the school district. The Ninth Circuit affirmed, and the U.S. Supreme Court granted the parents' petition for review. On appeal, the school district cited 34 C.F.R. § 76.532(a)(1), an IDEA regulation, as authority for the prohibition against using federal funds for private school sign-language interpreters.

The Court stated that the Establishment Clause did not completely prohibit religious institutions from participating in publicly sponsored benefits. If this were the case, religious groups would not even enjoy police and fire protection or have use of public roads and sidewalks. Government programs that neutrally provide benefits to broad classes of citizens are not subject to Establishment Clause prohibition simply because some religiously affiliated institutions receive "an attenuated financial benefit." Providing a sign-language interpreter under the IDEA was part of a general program for distribution of benefits in a neutral manner to qualified students. The provision of the interpreter provided only an indirect economic benefit to the parochial school and was a neutral service that was part of a general program not "skewed" toward religion. A sign-language interpreter, unlike an instructor or counselor, was ethically bound to transmit everything said in exactly the same way as it was intended. Because **the Establishment Clause did not prevent the district from providing the student with a sign-language interpreter under the IDEA**, the Court reversed the court of appeals' decision. *Zobrest v. Catalina Foothills School Dist.*, 509 U.S. 1, 113 S.Ct. 2462, 125 L.Ed.2d 1 (1993).

◆ A blind student sought vocational rehabilitative services from the Washington Commission for the Blind under a state law making blind persons eligible for educational assistance to enable them to "overcome vocational handicaps and to obtain the maximum degree of self-support and self-care." Because the student intended to pursue a career in the church, the Commission for the Blind denied his request for assistance. The Washington Supreme Court upheld this decision on the ground that the First Amendment prohibited state funding of a student's education at a religious college. The U.S. Supreme Court reversed, finding that Washington's program was such that the commission paid money directly to the student, who would then attend the school of his choice. **The fact that the student chose to attend a religious college did not constitute state support of religion** because the individual, not the state, made the decision to support religious education. The case was returned to the Washington Supreme Court. *Witters v. Washington Dep't of Services for the Blind*, 474 U.S. 481, 106 S.Ct. 748, 88 L.Ed.2d 846 (1986).

On remand, the Washington Supreme Court reconsidered the matter under the Washington Constitution, which more strictly limits expenditures of public funds for religious instruction than the U.S. Constitution. **The court held the disbursement of vocational assistance funds for religious education violated the state constitution** because it would result in the expenditure of public money for religious instruction. *Witters v. State Comm'n for the Blind*, 771 P.2d 1119 (Wash. 1989).

CHAPTER EIGHT

Transition Services and Related Services

I.   TRANSITION SERVICES

Beginning not later than the first IEP to be in effect when a child with a disability is age 16 (and updated annually thereafter), an IEP must include appropriate measurable postsecondary goals based upon age-appropriate transition assessments related to training, education, employment, and (where appropriate) independent living skills. A student's IEP must state the transition services (including courses of study) needed to assist the child in reaching those goals. Beginning not later than one year before the child reaches the age of majority under state law, the IEP must include a statement that the child has been informed of his or her rights. See 20 U.S.C. § 1414(d)(1)(A)(i)(VII).

Federal courts in New York have determined that transition plans are required only for the transition to post-school activities, rather than school transfers. See E. Z.-L. ex. rel. R.L. v. New York City Dep't of Educ., 763 F.Supp.2d 584 (S.D.N.Y. 2011). The IDEA requires "transition services" not when a child transfers between schools, but when a child transitions from school to post-school activities. In A.L. v. New York City Dep't of Educ., 812 F.Supp.2d 492 (S.D.N.Y. 2011), the court held "there is no requirement that an IEP specify a transition plan for a student attending a new school placement."

◆ Claiming their child was denied a free appropriate public education (FAPE), Massachusetts parents filed a due process complaint against their school district to seek reimbursement for a private school placement. When the case reached the U.S. Court of Appeals, First Circuit, it held the lower court properly upheld three IEPs they challenged. It further held First Circuit cases issued prior to *Endrew F. v. Douglas County School Dist. RE-1*, 137 S.Ct. 988 (2017), were still valid. Under both *Endrew F.* and previous First Circuit cases, courts evaluating whether an IEP offers a FAPE must determine whether the IEP was reasonably calculated to confer a meaningful educational benefit in light of the child's circumstances. The court explained that depending on the context, determining whether an IEP was reasonably calculated to offer meaningful progress to a student "may or may not require a sub-inquiry into how challenging the plan is." The lower court correctly followed *Endrew F.* and *Johnson v. Boston Public Schools*, 906 F.3d 182 (1st Cir. 2018).

Despite the student's intellectual disability and serious language deficits, the court held she could be expected to make meaningful progress. Next, the court found the lower court properly relied on prior First Circuit precedents in finding the IEPs did not violate the IDEA's LRE requirement. Contrary to the parents' arguments, the lower court appropriately weighed the LRE and FAPE requirements in affirming the IEPs. Last, the court rejected the parents' claim that the lower court ignored IDEA transition requirements. **In prior cases, the First Circuit found the IDEA "does not require a stand-alone transition plan." Nor is there a particular format for transition assessments.** The court found the transition plans were based on IEP team discussions and extensive educational and psychological evaluations. All three IEPs had "appropriate measurable postsecondary goals based upon age appropriate assessments." As none of the parents' arguments had merit, the court held for the school district. *C.D. v. Natick Public School Dist.*, 924 F.3d 621 (1st Cir. 2019).

♦ A Texas eighth-grader with autism missed over two months of school due to peer bullying. He remained in homebound instruction for most of a semester after the parents provided a physician's note recommending he stay at home. At an admission, review and dismissal (ARD) meeting, ARD committee members rejected a second doctor's note, questioning the integrity of the physician and the sincerity of the note. The committee recommended the student's return to school. After he missed almost a full semester of grade eight, the ARD committee approved his promotion to grade nine. An extended school year (ESY) program was recommended. According to the parents, the summer semester was nearly over when they received formal notice of the recommendation. Upon returning to school for grade nine, the student had inconsistent attendance and fought with peers. He attended full-day counseling programs, and teachers reported he was making "great progress." But the student's parents requested a hearing. They sought an IEP that included the use of applied behavioral analysis (ABA).

A hearing officer held the student received a FAPE, finding his parents refusal to send him to school created his problems. A federal court affirmed the decision, and the parents appealed. The Fifth Circuit found no evidence that the district predetermined an IEP that excluded ABA services. It found no merit to a claim by the parents that the district failed to provide a prior written notice of the recommendation for a summer ESY program. Contrary to their arguments, the district did not fail to timely address peer bullying. The court found the parents admitted their son was willing to return to school, but they failed to follow up with requested paperwork for weeks while keeping him at home. Meanwhile, the district made repeated and reasonable accommodation offers. Last, the court disagreed with the parents' claim that the district offered an unrealistic transition plan describing the student's dreams to become a police officer. **The court found the transition plan included basic transition goals for the student, including part-time work while attending school, attending**

a community college or trade school and gaining independent living skills.
Evidence indicated the district tried to collaborate with the parents in transition
planning. They failed to show their child was denied a FAPE. *Renee J. v.
Houston Independent School Dist.*, 913 F.3d 523 (5th Cir. 2019).

◆   A Michigan parent rejected a community-based inclusion (CBI) program
for her 18-year-old child with autism. School staff placed him in a clinic, then
an empty classroom with no certified teacher for 20 days. The parent said
this placement led to "an autistic meltdown" and a 19-day suspension from
school. After a manifestation determination review, a team found the student's
meltdown was not a manifestation of his autism. Disagreeing with the decision,
the parent requested a due process hearing. An ALJ found the student was
denied a free appropriate public education. Among other things, she held his
IEP did not have measurable goals and lacked an adequate transition plan.
But the ALJ did not award compensatory education, and the student's mother
appealed. A federal court held the transition plan was woefully inadequate.
**There appeared to be no connection between the IEP goals and services.
Staff merely checked relevant boxes for transition considerations.** An adult
living goal in the plan stated the student's ambitions to get married and have his
own home. The court commented that "this transition plan provides nothing."
    Since the transition plan was incomplete and the school failed to adequately
implement the student's IEP, the court held in his favor. Later, the court ordered
the district to provide autism transition planning and 1,200 hours of tutoring
as compensatory education to make up for the district's inadequate transition
plan and failure to properly implement his IEP. The school district appealed the
compensatory award and the award of fees and costs. In 2018, the Sixth Circuit
held the case was not moot, even though the student was now 24 and no longer
attending district schools. It held the lower court did not abuse its discretion by
awarding compensatory education. The district admitted it denied the student
a FAPE by assigning him to a CBI program that was contrary to his IEP. On
the other hand, the court rejected the parent's argument that the 1,200-hour
compensatory education award and year of transition planning was not enough
to remedy her son's loss of benefits. The court rejected a number of alternative
arguments by the district. It found the calculation of the compensatory
education award was not an abuse of discretion. Last, the court found no error in
the decision to award the parent attorneys' fees and costs in excess of $210,000.
Somberg v. Utica Community Schools, 908 F.3d 162 (6th Cir. 2018).

◆   A Massachusetts student with a language-based learning disability attended
a private, out-of-district special education school under IEPs developed by her
school district for grades 3-8. Her grandparents (who served as her guardians)
urged placement in a certain college prep school for grade nine where other
family members had attended. IEP team members expressed concern that the
school did not offer the type of special education curriculum offered at the
student's current school. Later, the district offered to place the student in a
public high school. The grandmother wrote a letter to state officials to complain
about the district's decision. Because of the IEP dispute, the student's current
school became her stay-put placement. But the school announced it could not

meet her needs for grade nine. By this time, the grandparents hired an attorney, who wrote a letter to request the college prep school as the stay-put placement.

The district proposed a placement in a state-approved, private special education school. The grandparents accepted this, and the school became the student's new stay-put placement. Within a short time, she became unhappy with the school 's lack of rigor and her long commute. IEP team members drafted a new IEP that would maintain her stay-put placement while offering a transition plan with the goals of completing high school and advancing to a four-year college. Although the grandmother accepted the IEP, she rejected its implementation at the school designated as the stay-put placement. She notified the district of her intent to place the student at the college prep school and sought reimbursement for her tuition costs. Meanwhile, the district offered the student a new IEP that would place her in a partial inclusion program at a public high school. After rejecting the IEP, the family initiated a due process proceeding. A hearing officer denied the grandparents' request for tuition reimbursement for the college prep school. Further, **the hearing officer found the school district's failure to offer a transition plan for the student during grade nine was cured by later IEPs**. Later, a federal court held that while the district did not provide sufficient transition planning, the student was not denied access to a FAPE. Because of the family's placement decision, she never received the related services specified in the challenged IEPs. The court held the IEPs were reasonably calculated to provide a FAPE. Evidence suggested that the IEP challenge was based on a specific desire to place the student at the college prep school. As substantial evidence supported the hearing officer's decision to deny private tuition reimbursement, the court held for the school district. *Doe v. Belchertown Public Schools*, 347 F.Supp.3d 90 (D. Mass. 2018).

◆   A Hawaii student with autism attended a private autism center. His parent met with representatives of the Hawaii Department of Education (DOE) to discuss his transition from the center to a public-school kindergarten. The parent objected to the IEP and requested a hearing. A hearings officer found the IEP was adequate, as did a federal court. On appeal, the U.S. Court of Appeals, Ninth Circuit, found the IEP did not address the student's transition from the autism center to a public school. It noted some courts have improperly restricted the duty to provide transition services to those who are exiting the public-school system. **Transition services for a student with a disability must ease the transition between institutions or programs – whether public or private.**

The court held that **transition services must be included in the IEP to satisfy the IDEA's supplementary aids and services requirement** when this is necessary for a student to be educated and participate in new academic environments. In this case, the parent planned to move his son to a public school for the first time. Next, the court found vague language in the IEP did not explain the extent to which the student would not participate with nondisabled children in regular classes. The IEP also improperly delegated his placement to teachers outside the IEP process. The DOE placed the student in a mainstream Mandarin class but not mainstream science or social studies classes. Despite finding ABA therapy was critical for the student, the IEP team did not specify it in the IEP. The court held that when a particular methodology plays a critical role for a student, it must be stated in the IEP and not left to a teacher's discretion. Finding the DOE seriously infringed on the parent's opportunity to participate in the IEP process and denied the student a FAPE, the court reversed the judgment and returned the case to the lower court. *R.E.B. v. State of Hawaii Dep't of Educ.*, 870 F.3d 1025 (9th Cir. 2017).

Months later, the three-judge panel of Ninth Circuit judges that wrote the opinion granted the DOE's motion to rehear the case. Although the three-judge panel will rehear the case, it denied the DOE's request for a rehearing before all judges of the Ninth Circuit. *R.E.B. v. State of Hawaii Dep't of Educ.*, No. 14-15895, 2018 WL 1599404, 886 F.3d 1288 (Mem.) (9th Cir. 4/3/18).

◆ Montgomery County Public Schools (MCPS) funded private placements for a student with a history of behavioral, emotional and academic problems. His educational progress during middle school was "minimal," and his behavior problems were of "low frequency, but high intensity." Although the school where the student was placed during middle school was willing to enroll him in its high school program, the parents proposed transitioning him out of a diploma-track program and into a certificate track. A school psychologist found the student in the lower extreme of intellectual ability. Based on these results, the psychologist found the student should be in a program for intellectual disability rather than specific learning disabilities. As the student's private school offered no certificate program, the MCPS referred him to a district IEP team. Team members agreed to place the student in a certificate-track program. At an IEP meeting, team members discussed private school programs and a public school designed for students with significant cognitive disabilities and complex emotional, behavioral or sensory needs. Over the parents' objection, the MCPS placed the student in a public school. In response, the parents placed him in a private school and filed a due process complaint. An administrative law judge (ALJ) held MCPS' placement was reasonably calculated to provide the student a free appropriate public education (FAPE). She rejected arguments by the parents that a public-school placement had been predetermined by MCPS.

On appeal, **a Maryland federal court found the proposed certificate-track program differed significantly from the student's prior placements**. It rejected claims asserting that MCPS improperly labeled the student as emotionally and learning disabled. The ALJ found he was likely happier and performing better because of the switch to a certificate program. This change put the student in a more appropriate environment in view of his cognitive abilities. As the ALJ found the public-school placement would have provided the student a FAPE, it was not error to find his private school progress immaterial. Finding no reason to reverse the ALJ, the court affirmed the judgment for MCPS. *J.R. v. Smith*, No. DKC 16-1633, 2017 WL 3592453 (D. Md. 8/21/17).

◆ The parents of an Arizona private school student with learning disabilities and speech/language impairments disagreed with their school district about the speech therapists who served the student. As a result of the disagreement, the IEP team changed the student's placement to a public high school. The change resulted in the loss of 90 minutes per day of special education math instruction for a full semester. The parents filed a due process complaint, claiming the IEPs did not provide the student necessary transition, speech and math services and extended school year services. An administrative law judge (ALJ) ordered the district to provide the student 40 hours of compensatory special education math instruction. But he denied any other relief. Before a federal court, the parents claimed the ALJ improperly found the transition plans were appropriate and that the IEPs were adequately implemented. The court found the ALJ was entitled to credit a district expert, who was familiar with the student and the district's transition services processes. Next, the court rejected the parents' claim that the plans had several design flaws, noting **the "IDEA does not demand perfection, but rather demands that transition plans be reasonably calculated to confer [the student] with a meaningful benefit."**

The court deferred to the ALJ's findings that the transition plans were adequate. In ruling for the district, the court noted courts in the Ninth Circuit have held a parent is not entitled to his/her choice of service providers. The court held the district was entitled to judgment. *Pangerl v. Peoria Unified School Dist.*, No. CV-14-00836-PHX-JJT, 2017 WL 603834 (D. Ariz. 2/15/17).

◆   An Ohio student with a seizure disorder and other disabilities had severe difficulty with transitions. Her conduct included hitting and scratching. She typically wore a helmet in public settings for safety in case of a seizure, and she was always accompanied by an adult. Even after the student turned 16, she was excluded from IEP meetings where transition services were discussed. It was believed that the meetings would frighten her because they were long and adversarial. The parents filed a due process complaint against the school district just before the student turned 19, asserting the district denied her a free appropriate public education (FAPE) due to the lack of transition services. An independent hearing officer held for the family, and the dispute reached a federal court. It held the school district violated the IDEA by failing to provide the student with adequate transition services. **The court held the student was entitled to transition services regardless of whether she was likely to attain competitive employment or achieve a high level of independence.** It awarded the student some 600 hours of compensatory services. On appeal, the U.S. Court of Appeals, Sixth Circuit, upheld the lower court's finding that the school district violated IDEA requirements relating to the student's transition to post-school outcomes. The district never invited the student to IEP meetings, in violation of an IDEA regulatory mandate to invite students to any IEP meeting when transition is on the agenda. **If a school district does not invite a student to an IEP meeting where transition is discussed, it must take other steps to ensure that the child's preferences and interests are considered.**

Like the lower court, the Sixth Circuit found the team did not ensure that the student's transition interests and preferences were considered when devising her IEP. And the school district did not timely conduct a vocational assessment until she reached age 19. Schools are required to make transition plans for eligible children who have reached age 16, and the court found the school district was in default of its obligation to conduct transition assessments for three full years. The student's IEP for one relevant school year had no postsecondary educational or training goals. Later IEPs had nebulous employment goals and lacked sufficient details about how they would be met. Finding the school district's violations in transition planning caused substantive harm to the student, the court held she was denied a FAPE. *Gibson v. Forest Hills Local School Dist. Board of Educ.*, 655 Fed.Appx. 423 (6th Cir. 2016).

II. RELATED SERVICES

In Renee J. v. Houston Independent School Dist., *913 F.3d 523 (5th Cir. 2019), the Fifth Circuit Court of Appeals cited 34 C.F.R. § 300.43(a), an IDEA regulation requiring schools to provide students with disabilities meaningful transition services to prepare them for adult life to the extent practicable.*

Transition services must include "appropriate measurable postsecondary goals based upon age appropriate transition assessments related to training, education, employment, and, where appropriate, independent living skills; and ... the transition services (including courses of study) needed to assist the child in reaching those goals." 20 U.S.C. § 1414(d)(1)(A)(i)(VIII). Related services include transportation, speech pathology, psychological services, physical and occupational therapy, recreation and medical services that are necessary for the student to receive an educational benefit.

A. Communication Services

◆ A Maine student with autism, cognitive impairments and Landau-Kleffner Syndrome could not speak. After school officials disallowed his parents' request to allow him to wear a recording device school, they filed a due process complaint for denial of a reasonable accommodation. A hearing officer held for the school district. When the parents appealed to a federal court, they added disability discrimination and speech rights claims. But the court held they did not exhaust the IDEA administrative process. Following their appeal to the First Circuit, the parents filed a second due process complaint, arguing the district's refusal to allow a recording device deprived their child of a free appropriate public education. A hearing officer dismissed the second due process case. On appeal, the U.S. Court of Appeals, First Circuit, found the parents filed the second action to comply with the lower court's order. Finding the parents had exhausted all the process required by the IDEA, the court returned the case to the trial court, where they would have an opportunity to present their case.

When the case returned to the trial court, it held the administrative findings precluded the parents from establishing that a recording device was a reasonable accommodation under the ADA or the Rehabilitation Act. **An ADA regulation governing effective communications did not apply to communications between the parents and their child.** After a trial, the court held for the school unit. On appeal, the First Circuit held the hearing officer's findings had a preclusive effect that prohibited the parents from pursuing their ADA claims. It held they could not mount an ADA challenge based on an argument that a device for their son to record his school day would be effective in providing him meaningful access to school benefits. According to the parents, the school unit's special education director agreed to allow them to view video recordings of their child's speech-language therapy sessions, but only if they promised not to use the recordings as a basis for a complaint. **Finding the parents could not show a recording device would benefit their child, the court held for the school unit.** *Pollack v. Regional School Unit 75*, 886 F.3d 75 (1st Cir. 2018).

◆   A Massachusetts student had significant language delays and had a cochlear implant. At age three, he began attending Horace Mann School for the Deaf, which is operated by Boston Public Schools (BPS). Evaluators recommended that the student have instruction in both American Sign Language (ASL) and spoken communication. Despite his progress over the next two school years, the parent resisted the IEP team's recommendations and limited his instruction to sign-supported spoken English. During the student's third year at Horace Mann School, the parent rejected an IEP offering him additional language therapy and other direct services. She removed her child from the school and filed a due process complaint. Although the parties discussed a settlement, their negotiations broke down when BPS insisted on a comprehensive settlement.

A hearing officer found the IEP offered the student a free appropriate public education. The parent sued BPS in a federal court, which held for BPS. On appeal, the U.S. Court of Appeals, First Circuit, rejected her argument that the hearing officer demonstrated bias against her. In the court's opinion, the parent was motivated to place her son privately and she did not base her lawsuit on actual inadequacies in the instruction at Horace Mann School. In sum, the court found the hearing officer based her decision on the quality of education provided to the student and not bias against the parent. According to the First Circuit, its prior cases held that to comply with the IDEA, **an IEP must be reasonably calculated to confer a meaningful educational benefit upon a child, with consideration for the individual child's circumstances**. This complied with *Endrew F. v. Douglas County School Dist. RE-1*, 137 S.Ct. 988 (2017). As the lower court had relied on the correct legal standard, the court found no reason to disturb the decision in favor of the BPS. *Johnson v. Boston Public Schools*, 903 F.3d 182 (1st Cir. 2018).

◆   A Minnesota student's grade-nine IEP called from him to use Braille for all his assignments and instruction. His parents claimed he was not consistently provided accessible, accurate and timely Braille instructional materials. They filed a due process complaint against the district. After a hearing, the ALJ found the "provisions in the IEP were largely, although not perfectly implemented." Evidence indicated the student was progressing in his regular education and honors classes, and "met, and often exceeded, the ability to communicate with the proficiency of his peers." After the ALJ held for the school district, the parents appealed. Later, a federal court upheld the decision for the school district. Appeal then reached the U.S. Court of Appeals, Eighth Circuit.

In reviewing findings that the district may not have perfectly complied with the IEP, the court held "the IDEA does not require perfection." Evidence indicated that the district took steps to timely provide the student with accessible instructional materials. His grades indicated he received educational benefits. According to the student, higher standards imposed by state law may be enforced in an IDEA case. Instead, the court found no heightened standard was placed on the school district so as to create an absolute obligation to guarantee all blind students used Braille instruction to attain a specific level of instruction. Instead, **the IDEA does not guarantee a particular level of education or any particular educational outcome**. This standard was recently discussed in *Endrew F. v. Douglas County School Dist. RE-1*, this chapter. The court found the district complied with an IDEA regulation at 34 C.F.R. Part 300.172 by taking reasonable steps to provide instructional materials in accessible formats. **Prior IDEA cases have found an IEP need not maximize a student's potential or provide the best possible education.** *I.Z.M. v. Rosemount-Apple Valley-Eagan Public Schools*, 863 F.3d 966 (8th Cir. 2017).

◆   Florida parents filed a due process challenge against their child's school board, claiming her school used an unqualified speech-language pathologist. An administrative law judge upheld the IEP. On appeal to a federal court, the parents added discrimination and retaliation claims. According to the parents, their child received no speech therapy. They said the speech-language pathologist employed by the board was improperly certified because the board did not submit a plan required by the state department of education. The court found this technical defect did not affect the student's education. Florida law allows school districts qualifying for a sparsity supplement to use "speech-language associates" instead of certified or licensed speech-language pathologists in certain cases. Nothing indicated the board failed to submit the required plan. In any event, **the professional who provided the student's speech-language services met state requirements for a speech-language associate**. In the court's view, the ALJ's decision was fully supported by the evidence and had to be affirmed. *S.M. and L.C. v. Hendry County School Board*, No. 2:14-cv-237-FtM-38CM, 2017 WL 4417070 (M.D. Fla. 10/5/17).

◆   The parent of a nonverbal Tennessee student filed a federal court complaint charging a school district with allowing the student's IEP goals to remain static for years rather than to modify them. It was asserted that the district used the stagnation of goals as a justification for eliminating or reducing related services. Next, the complaint claimed the district had a policy of understaffing service providers illegally to deprive eligible students of related services to save money. **The court found no support for a claim that the school district intentionally created understaffing to justify the denial of related services.** The complaint did not identify specific instances of a district policy to deny related services. The complaint asserted the student's levels of direct related services had been gradually removed and replaced with inadequate consultative services. In dismissing the case, the court found no basis for avoiding administrative exhaustion. The complaint did not identify any law prohibiting IEP goals from remaining static. Nothing required that related services be provided via direct services rather than consultative ones, if consultative services met a student's needs. As the court found no IDEA violation and the parent did not exhaust her administrative remedies, the case was dismissed. *T.D. v. Rutherford County Board of Educ.*, No. 3:16-cv-14888, 2017 WL 77114 (M.D. Tenn. 1/9/17).

◆   For about six years, a child was a residential student at the Utah Schools for the Deaf and Blind (USDB). Her parent became dissatisfied with a USDB evaluation and her child's slow rate of progress. After testing revealed the child had bilateral hearing loss, her IEP was modified to add a classroom frequency modulated (FM) system. An IEP meeting was held, but no agreement was reached. Because the IEP was not signed, staff members became confused about whether to implement the proposal or the prior year's IEP. As a result, the FM system was not used for a full school year. The USDB agreed to fund an independent educational evaluation (IEE) and used the IEE for its reevaluation. The parent sought to place the child at a Massachusetts school for students with blindness. After a facilitated IEP meeting broke down, the parent requested a due process hearing. At a later IEP meeting, the USDB denied the Massachusetts placement and instead approved a Utah public school placement.

A hearing officer found the USDB had predetermined certain services for the child outside of an IEP meeting. The USDB was ordered to provide direct speech-language-pathology services as compensatory education. **The hearing officer disapproved of a public school placement and held that the child was denied a FAPE because no FM system was used for a full year.** A federal court found multiple failures by USDB to implement the child's IEP. Instead of resolving the issue of placement, the court returned the case to the IEP team. On appeal, the U.S. Court of Appeals, Tenth Circuit, held the lower court improperly delegated the question of the child's placement to the IEP team. USDB staff members steadfastly maintained that a public placement was appropriate. When the case returned to the lower court, it would have to determine the child's placement, including whether she should attend the Massachusetts school. The court would also have to recalculate the attorneys' fees award, with the placement decision playing the biggest factor in an award. *M.S. v. Utah Schools for the Deaf and Blind*, 822 F.3d 1128 (10th Cir. 2016).

◆   A California student with profound hearing loss was able to attend general education classes. She had cochlear implants, but an audiologist concluded she heard only about 52% of what was said. At an IEP meeting to discuss the transition from middle to high school, her parents requested Communication Access Real-Time Translation (CART) transcription services. Although the school district offered the student a number of accommodations, it refused to provide her CART services. In response, she requested a hearing, asserting she had to concentrate intently to understand, leading to fatigue and headaches after her school day. An administrative law judge ordered the school district to provide the student CART services in four classes. When the case reached a federal court, it declined to rule on it until the Ninth Circuit issued an opinion in *K.M. v. Tustin Unified School Dist.*, this chapter. By the time the court was ready to rule on the IDEA claim, the student had graduated from high school.

ADA regulations require a school to furnish appropriate auxiliary aids and services where necessary to afford individuals with disabilities an equal opportunity to participate in and enjoy the benefits of a service, program or activity of the public entity. An ADA regulation requires schools to ensure that communications with students with disabilities were as effective as with others. By contrast, a public entity was not required to take any action that would result in a fundamental alteration in a service, program or activity, or to undergo an undue burden. The court held it could not award judgment on the

ADA or state law claims without further consideration. *Poway Unified School Dist. v. K.C.*, No. 10CV897-GPC (DHU), 2014 WL 129086 (S.D. Cal. 1/14/14).

◆   Two California students with hearing impairments sought word-for-word transcription services. In separate cases, administrative law judges rejected their claim that decisions by their school districts to deny Communication Access Real-Time Translation (CART) services violated the IDEA. On appeal, a federal court affirmed the decisions, also ruling for the districts on discrimination claims under Section 504 of the Rehabilitation Act and Title II of the ADA. When the case reached the U.S. Court of Appeals, Ninth Circuit, it stated that a federal ADA Title II regulation, found at 28 C.F.R. Part 35.160, required public entities to furnish appropriate services where necessary to provide equal opportunities for individuals with disabilities to participate in services and benefits. The regulation required public entities providing auxiliary aids and services to give primary consideration to the requests of disabled individuals. The Ninth Circuit found this did not necessarily mean that a valid IEP also satisfied ADA Title II. **Title II regulations established independent obligations on the part of public schools.** According to the court, the IDEA's FAPE requirement was significantly different from Title II communication requirements. In some situations, **the ADA might require schools to provide different services to hearing-impaired students than what they had to provide under the IDEA**. As a result, the court returned the case to the district court for it to determine whether the school districts had violated ADA Title II. Both districts would have the opportunity to use Title II defenses such as undue burden and fundamental alteration of their educational programs. *K.M. v. Tustin Unified School Dist.*, 725 F.3d 1088 (9th Cir. 2013).

◆   An Ohio school district provided a student several different augmentative and alternative communication (AAC) devices to address her communication and developmental delays. She had little success with the devices. When the student was in seventh grade, her teachers noticed the quality of her school work was poor, but the work she did at home was "perfect or near perfect." Staff grew concerned that the parents' use of a physical support technique was in fact "facilitated communication" and was the cause of this discrepancy. A dispute arose about the student's grade-nine IEP. According to the district, the student had a full scale IQ score of 33. It was estimated that her reading level was near grade one, and testing indicated she had significant adaptive behavior delays. An impartial hearing officer (IHO) found the IEP proposed by the district was designed to offer a FAPE. According to the IHO, the student was receiving little or no educational benefit in a regular education setting, and her IEP needed to be modified. She held the district had to provide an AAC device along with intensive training to allow her to independently communicate.

The case reached a federal court, which noted the IHO had relied on the opinions of two experts hired by the parents to support their argument that the child could perform grade-level work with physical support. It was improper for the IHO to rely on parentally obtained evaluations completed months after the IEP was proposed. There was evidence that the evaluations were unreliable. One of the parents' evaluators improperly allowed the use of physical support that was considered a form of "facilitated communication." This rendered the tests nonstandard. **The student could not effectively communicate the extent of her cognitive abilities**, and her parents had already rejected the AAC devices. Since the district's evaluation was valid and the IEP provided the child a FAPE, the court held for the district. *T.J. v. Winton Woods City School Dist.*, No. 1:10-cv-847, 2013 WL 1090465 (S.D. Ohio 3/15/13).

◆   An Arizona school district furnished a sign-language interpreter to a student with hearing impairments who attended public schools. When the student's parents enrolled him in a parochial school, they requested that the school district continue providing the sign-language interpreter. The district refused to provide this service on Establishment Clause grounds, and the parents sued. Appeal reached the U.S. Supreme Court, which held that **the provision of a sign-language interpreter is a religiously neutral distribution of IDEA benefits that provides only an indirect financial benefit to a parochial school**. The Court held that the Establishment Clause did not prohibit the school district from sending the sign-language interpreter to the parochial school for the student's benefit. *Zobrest v. Catalina Foothills School Dist.*, 509 U.S. 1, 113 S.Ct. 2462, 125 L.Ed.2d 1 (1993).

B. Assistive Technology

Illinois law requires written notices that IEP teams must consider whether a child needs assistive technology in order to receive free, appropriate public education. Another provision requires Chicago schools to provide parents with draft IEPs at least five days before an IEP meeting. The amended law requires teams to provide parents written notices that the team must consider whether a child needs assistive technology in order to receive free, appropriate public education. Notices must provide contact info for the state's assistive technology program. One-Hundredth Illinois General Assembly, P.A. 100-993. S.B. 454; 105 ILCS 5/14–8.02, 105 ILCS 5/14–8.02f.

◆   A Texas child with autism, speech and orthopedic impairments, an intellectual disability, childhood apraxia of speech and dysarthria used signs and assistive technology to communicate with school staff members. She demonstrated success when utilizing a high technology device, and her preferred mode of communication was an iPod touch. The ARD committee informed the student's parents that it recommended discontinuing her sign-language interpreter because she had not increased her use of signs over the past year and relied on assistive technology to communicate. In ARD committee meetings, the mother expressed concern about her child's assistive communication goals and questioned the credentials of some of the ARD committee members. A committee meeting ended in non-consensus and the parents filed a due process complaint against the school district. A special education hearing officer found the school district provided the student a free appropriate public education (FAPE). On appeal, a federal court affirmed the hearing officer's decision, finding the IEP satisfied the factors from the Fifth Circuit's decision in *Cypress-Fairbanks Independent School Dist. v. Michael F.*, 118 F.3d 245 (5th Cir. 1997).

The parents appealed to the U.S. Court of Appeals, Fifth Circuit, where they argued their child would not receive a FAPE because the district discontinued her sign language interpreter assistance. They further objected to the lack of an articulation goal. Based on its review of the record, the court found no error in the trial court's decision. As the lower court found, the student "had not and was unlikely to make meaningful progress in articulating sounds." In addition, **the court found the student did not use her sign-language interpreter and instead communicated primarily and relatively successfully through assistive technology**. In the court's opinion, the lower court faithfully applied the *Michael F.* factors, and it affirmed the judgment for the school district. *E.M. v. Lewisville Independent School Dist.*, 763 Fed.Appx. 361 (5th Cir. 2019).

◆ A seven-year-old, non-verbal Maryland student had an autism spectrum disorder and a rare genetic disorder. She had "complex, challenging, disruptive behaviors such as hyperactivity and aggression." As the student prepared to enter grade one, an IEP team conducted a functional behavioral assessment and created a behavior intervention plan (BIP) that focused on her interfering behaviors. The BIP provided a NovaChat device for communication, a consistent daily routine, a visual schedule, short verbal supports, a token reinforcement system and social stories throughout the day. IEP team members proposed an IEP with 13 goals to address the student's academic, behavioral, physical, speech and language needs. Although her weekly schedule specified just under 17 hours in special education and 14 hours, 35 minutes in general education, her teacher began deviating from this in response to her daily needs. A new IEP was created midway through the student's first-grade year, increasing her time outside general education to 29 hours per week. Seeking a private placement for their child, the parents requested a due process hearing. An administrative law judge (ALJ) held for the school district and a federal court affirmed the decision.

On appeal, the Fourth Circuit Court of Appeals, noted the student's primary problem behavior was biting. As the ALJ found, the skills in her BIP could be generalized to other behaviors. **The IEP had behavior strategies that were reasonably calculated to enable the student to make progress and did not deny her a free appropriate public education.** The parents misconstrued the IDEA's least restrictive environment requirement by arguing their child would spend more time with nondisabled peers in a private school. While she did not progress on all of her IEP goals, her paraprofessional was working with her to determine how she could do so. Given that she could not progress in the general education curriculum, the court upheld the IEP, finding it stated reasonably ambitious goals that were focused on the student's circumstances. *R.F. v. Cecil County Public Schools*, 919 F.3d 237 (4th Cir. 2019).

◆ A California student had autistic-like behavior, an intellectual disability and a speech/language impairment. His IEP specified placement in an intensive applied behavior analysis (ABA) day class with weekly therapy. Near the end of the student's kindergarten year, IEP team members chose not to assess his AT needs. They felt an AT device would not be beneficial, and again proposed an intensive ABA day class. When the parents sought the assignment of a 1:1 aide to their child, the team disagreed. They filed a due process complaint. An administrative law judge (ALJ) held a hearing and found the parents did not show the IEPs were improper. The district was ordered to provide AT services. But the ALJ denied other relief sought by the parents. A federal court held for the school district, and they appealed to the Ninth Circuit. A day after the court held for the parents, the Supreme Court released its opinion in *Endrew F. v. Douglas County School Dist. RE-1*, 137 S.Ct. 988 (2017). Arguing the new case would change the outcome of their lawsuit, the parents appealed to the Supreme Court.

In a brief opinion, the Supreme Court vacated the decision and returned the case to the Ninth Circuit for further consideration in light of *Endrew F.* Several months later, the Ninth Circuit issued a new decision in which it again held for the school district. **According to the Ninth Circuit, *Endrew F.* did not change, but simply clarified, the existing FAPE standard under *Board of Educ. of Hendrick Hudson Cent. School Dist., Westchester County v. Rowley*, 458 U.S. 176 (1982).** Prior Ninth Circuit decisions interpreting the FAPE requirement used the terms "educational benefit," "some educational benefit," or "meaningful educational benefit." The Ninth Circuit held its standard complied with the *Endrew F.* Court's clarification of *Rowley*. The court held the ALJ's decision withstood scrutiny under *Endrew F.* The IEPs were reasonably calculated to enable the student to receive educational benefits and make appropriate progress in light of the circumstances. The ALJ's decision recognized the district had failed to assess the student for a high-tech AT device for a one-year period. But the student made progress on his speech and language goals with non-electronic AT devices. **There was evidence that children with autistic-like behaviors may begin using electronic AT devices as early as age three, but the court held for the district on the ADA and Section 504 claims.** While the district should have assessed the student for a high-tech AT device at an earlier point, the court found its decision not to do so was the result of thorough and good-faith evaluations of the student's skills. *E.F. v. Newport Mesa Unified School Dist.*, 726 Fed.Appx. 535 (9th Cir. 2018).

◆   The parent of a California student with blindness and developmental delays did not believe his IEP would provide him a free appropriate public education. She filed a due process hearing complaint. During the due process case, the school district admitted the IEP incorrectly offered the student 240 minutes of monthly TVI (teacher of the visually impaired) services. According to the district, it unilaterally amended the IEP a month after the IEP meeting to change the offer of TVI services to 240 minutes per week. But it did not inform the mother about this. At the hearing, school witnesses testified that the student was offered 300 minutes of weekly TVI services. An administrative law judge found no IDEA violation based on the unilateral amendment of the IEP.

A federal court affirmed the decision for the school district. On appeal, the U.S. Court of Appeals, Ninth Circuit, held the district interfered with the parent's participation in the IEP process. The court found an IEP is a contract that embodies a binding commitment. The school district is obligated to notify the parent and seek her consent for an IEP amendment. Without consent from the parent, the school district was bound by the IEP as written, unless it sought to re-open the IEP process and propose a new one. Because the district failed to do so, the IEP in force at the time of the hearing was the one signed by the parties. **Since the unilateral amendment to the TVI minutes and failure to identify the assistive technology to be provided infringed upon the parent's participation opportunities, the court held in her favor.** The lower court would have to consider whether the district had offered an appropriate IEP. *M.C. v. Antelope Valley Union High School Dist.*, 852 F.3d 840 (9th Cir. 2017).

C.   Voluntarily Enrolled Private School Students

In Jasa v. Millard Public School Dist. No. 17, *206 F.3d 813 (8th Cir. 2000), the court held local education agencies are not required to pay the cost of a private school education if they have offered a FAPE to the student and the parents nonetheless make a voluntary private school placement.*

◆   A Connecticut child attended a private school at his school district's expense. His parent later grew dissatisfied with his progress and placed him in a private religious school outside the district that provided no special education. The parent paid the school's tuition while the district paid for related services. School officials discontinued the agreement at the end of the year and suggested placement in a public school in the district. But the parent rejected this and filed a due process complaint. A hearing officer held for the school board. The private school was found an inappropriate setting as it provided the child no special education. The parent appealed to a federal court, which held the IEP offered the child a FAPE. But the court held the board violated the stay-put provision by refusing to fund the related services described in the IEP. Appeal reached the U.S. Court of Appeals, Second Circuit. After rejecting the parent's claim that the IEP denied her child a FAPE, the court found her participation rights had not been violated. Throughout the dispute, the student was a resident of the district and the board violated the IDEA by not offering him an IEP.

There was no merit to the board's argument that once a child was enrolled at a school outside the district, any IDEA obligations ended. But the court held the religious school was an inappropriate placement. It offered no special education and did not modify its curriculum to accommodate the student. In the court's view, the board violated the stay-put provision by discontinuing related services at the private school, because **the stay-put provision applies to related services.** As the parent argued, she was entitled to the full value of services which the board was required to fund from the time of the due process request until the end of the proceeding. *Doe v. East Lyme Board of Educ.*, 790 F.3d 440 (2d Cir. 2015).

After the case returned to the lower court, it held a trial, then ordered the board to reimburse the parent for her expenses plus interest. This totaled $127,302.90, of which the board had paid $97,445. Transportation reimbursement was also due, making the total award $36,556, plus interest to be determined by the court. Next, the board was ordered the to place $203,478 into an escrow account for the student as a compensatory education award equivalent to the value of related services that were never provided. The parent appealed to the Second Circuit, which found the lower court had yet to complete its calculation of damages. As there was no final judgment, the appeal was dismissed. *Doe v. East Lyme Board of Educ.*, 747 Fed.Appx. 30 (2d Cir. 2019).

◆ After a student was diagnosed with an autism spectrum disorder, the New York City Department of Education (DOE) agreed to fund his placement at a private center for students with special needs. He made progress there, but the DOE recommended a public school placement for his fourth grade school year. At his committee on special education (CSE) meeting, a center report was discussed. CSE members discussed the related services from a prior IEP and no one objected to this. At the meeting, the parent was consulted on many topics and the CSE recommended a community school placement. A final notice of recommendation described occupational therapy, speech and counseling, but did not detail the frequency, duration or group size for these services. When the parent toured the school where the IEP was to be implemented, she rejected it as too noisy. Noting the IEP did not include specific recommendations for related services, she re-enrolled her child in the center. In a due process proceeding, an impartial hearing officer found the DOE excluded related services recommendations from the IEP. The services were offered without consideration for the child's levels of performance and sufficient parental input.

A federal court later held that while the absence of any representative from the private center from the CSE meeting was an IDEA violation, it did not impede the parent's participation. The center's progress report was considered at the meeting. **The parent actively participated in the CSE's discussion.** The inadvertent omission of a related services program from the IEP was not as significant as the parent argued. The court held a failure to include the related services in a properly designated space did not make the IEP inadequate, since it was discussed in other areas of the IEP. Rejecting all of the parent's arguments, the court held for the DOE. *C.K. v. New York City Dep't of Educ.,* No. 14-cv-836 (RJS), 2015 WL 1808602 (S.D.N.Y. 4/9/15).

D. Other Services

New Hampshire law allows children with disabilities to use audio or video recording devices in their classrooms. Under former law, no school could record a classroom in any way without school board approval after a public hearing. Former law also required the written consent of the teacher and the parent or guardian of each affected student to allow classroom recording.

Under the amended law, nothing precludes the use of audio or video recordings by (or with) a child with a disability, or the child's teacher or service provider when the child's IEP or accommodation plan includes recording as part of the child's special education, related services, assistive technology service or methodology. Audio or video recordings must be made, used and maintained in accordance with the Family Education Rights and Privacy Act (FERPA), 20 U.S.C. § 1232g, and state law. New Hampshire 2016 Regular Session, Ch. 87 (H.B. 1372). New Hampshire Statutes NH ST § 189:68.

◆ Due to autism and complex motor and speech disabilities, a North Carolina student had developmental delays. Her parents became disenchanted with her IEP and requested a due process hearing. An administrative law judge (ALJ) agreed with the school board on every issue in dispute. But the ALJ held the school did not provide the child necessary speech therapy for several months.

The board was ordered to reimburse the parents for 64 hours of speech therapy and related transportation expenses. The board appealed to a review officer, who reversed the speech therapy ruling. The parents never appealed the ALJ's adverse rulings to the review officer. But they sued the school board in a federal court, claiming the board should have provided their child direct, intensive, one-on-one applied behavior analysis. The court held for the board, as the parents did not exhaust their administrative remedies. As for the speech therapy question, the court held for the board. In addition, the court rejected the parents' claim that North Carolina's two-tier due process procedure violated the IDEA.

On appeal, the U.S. Court of Appeals, Fourth Circuit, held the state satisfied IDEA requirements for administrative review to immediately precede any civil action. The IEP called for daily sessions of speech therapy in the "total school environment," as part of the "embedded, inclusive model" of instruction. According to this model, therapists worked with students directly in their regular classrooms when other instruction was taking place. It appeared that the ALJ had ruled against the board primarily on the basis of the speech therapist's decision to shred her personal therapy notes for the relevant times. **The court found the evidence did not show the school district denied the child appropriate therapy.** Her IEP specified a total school environment, not isolated, one-on-one instruction. Since the court found the child received the speech therapy specified in her IEP, it held for the board. *E.L. v. Chapel Hill-Carrboro Board of Educ.*, 773 F.3d 509 (4th Cir. 2014).

◆ A disabled North Carolina student engaged in aggressive, self-injurious behavior and was hyperactive. A service dog was trained to help him redirect some of his problem behaviors. The dog was able to provide deep pressure therapy through physical contact with the student, as well as other techniques for redirecting him. But **school officials rejected the parents' request to permit the student's full-time use of the dog at school** and also questioned whether the dog was a service animal. The IEP team found the dog was not necessary. Instead of challenging that determination, the parents sued for discrimination. A federal court dismissed the case, holding that the parents should have exhausted their administrative remedies before suing. *A.S. v. Catawba County Board of Educ.*, No. 5:11CV27-RLV, 2011 WL 3438881 (W.D.N.C. 8/5/11).

◆ An Illinois autistic student had daily tantrums, an eating disorder and episodes of running on impulse. A doctor prescribed a service dog, which the family obtained two years later. This calmed the student greatly. However, at a preschool IEP meeting, district officials told the mother the service dog could not accompany him to school because even though the dog was hypoallergenic, another student was highly allergic to dogs. The family then sought an order defining the dog as a "service animal" that would allow it to accompany the student to school. The Appellate Court of Illinois found that **the dog met the state's definition of a "service animal"** even though the commands to assist the student came from staff members and not the student himself. The student could bring the dog to school. *K.D. v. Villa Grove Community Unit School Dist. No. 302*, 936 N.E.2d 690 (Ill. App. Ct. 2010).

III. MEDICAL SERVICES

The IDEA specifically excludes medical services from its definition of related services, unless they are provided for diagnostic or evaluative purposes. In determining whether a service is an excluded medical service, courts tend to focus on who has to provide the service and the nature of the service being provided to determine whether it is part of the school district's obligation.

In 1984, the U.S. Supreme Court issued Irving Independent School Dist. v. Tatro, *468 U.S. 883, 104 S.Ct. 3371, 82 L.Ed.2d 664 (1984), which has become the definitive case in distinguishing between an excluded "medical service" and a "related service" that a district must provide under the IDEA.*

To be entitled to related services, a child must be disabled so as to require special education. Only those services necessary to aid a child with disabilities to benefit from special education must be provided, regardless of how easily a school nurse or layperson could furnish them. IDEA regulations state that school nursing services must be performed by a nurse or other qualified person, not by a physician. In Tatro, *the Court found the parents were seeking only the services of a qualified person at the school. They were not asking the school to provide equipment. The Court held clean intermittent catheterization is a related service that is not subject to the IDEA's "medical service" exclusion.*

◆ A Washington student was expelled after a series of behavior incidents culminating with a physical confrontation involving his school's dean of students. A slingshot and other contraband items were found in his backpack. The school found the incident was not a manifestation of a disability. No changes were made to the student's goals and his IEP did not specify time with a 1:1 aide and behavior specialist. During his 45-day exclusion from school, he ran away from home and was put in juvenile detention. A psychologist evaluated the student and found he had prodromal schizophrenia. She recommended placing him in a residential setting. After the suspension, the district placed him in an alternative school on a part-time basis. Over the next seven months, the student was again placed in juvenile detention. He used illegal drugs, ran away from home and was placed in a psychiatric hospital. His parents researched residential placements. After a 28-day elopement, the student was readmitted to a hospital. The parents notified the district of their intention to place him in a residential facility and to seek reimbursement. They enrolled the student in a Utah residential facility with a locked campus and a structured environment.

After a due process hearing, an administrative law judge held for the parents. On appeal, a federal court found the dispute centered on whether the residential placement was a service related to the student's education, or an excluded "medical service." After examining IDEA definitions of "special education" and "related services," the court found the placement was not an excluded "medical service." It rejected the district's theory that any support the student received there was aimed at medical issues. **The court found the residential school provided "related services" and/or the type of services that would be offered in a school nurse's office. These included psychological services, therapeutic recreation, social work services, medication management and counseling.** Further, the court found evidence that the student had to receive the services in a structured residential setting. This was due to his tendency to elope and his truancy resulting from the "perfect storm of his disabilities." In the court's view, the IEP offered by the district was not reasonably calculated to enable the student to progress. His impulsiveness, hallucinations and cognitive disorganization made it unlikely that he would attend school in the absence of constant monitoring. Finding the parents established violations of the IDEA that warranted tuition reimbursement, the court held in their favor. *Edmonds School Dist. v. A.T.*, No. C16-1500RSL, 2017 WL 5157941 (W.D. Wash. 11/7/17).

◆   The parents of a California child with severe disabilities disputed the level of occupational therapy (OT) he needed. State law made a division of the state department of Health Care Services responsible for providing medically necessary OT "by reason of medical diagnosis and when contained in the child's individualized education program." State law also made the department responsible for determining whether a student needed medically necessary OT. The parents filed a due process hearing request, which went before an administrative law judge (ALJ). They settled their claims against two school districts and agreed to pursue claims against the department for additional hours of OT. The ALJ found the department did not offer adequate OT for two school years. It was also held that the department should have followed the state Education Code. The ALJ ordered the department to provide the child additional weekly OT, including compensatory therapy services. A federal court later held for the department, and the parents appealed. The U.S. Court of Appeals, Ninth Circuit, found **the OT services in an IEP were deemed "related services," regardless of whether they were medically or educationally necessary**.

Next, the court found the legislature could not have intended the department to insulate itself from review by implementing its own appeal process. Since the medically necessary occupational therapy services in the student's IEP were needed for him to benefit from special education, the court found the ALJ also had the authority to approve an award of compensatory therapy. The court held the parents were entitled to a stay-put order issued by the ALJ. In addition, the ALJ had authority to order reimbursement to the parents for the cost of independent assessments they obtained. *Douglas v. California Office of Administrative Hearings*, 650 Fed.Appx. 312 (9th Cir. 2016).

◆   A private Pennsylvania school provided medical services to children through the partial hospitalization program (PHP). The PHP is federally subsidized under the Medicaid Act. PHP medical services were integrated into the school's academic program throughout the school day. To settle a dispute, a school district paid some of the costs of educational and medical services for children attending the school. After voluntarily extending the agreement for four years, the district stopped paying tuition subsidies for PHP services. In a federal court, the private school sued the school district. It claimed to represent students at the school who were enrolled by parents for the purpose of receiving medical services in the PHP.

A federal court found the school and parents lacked standing under the Medicaid Act. Alternatively, the school did not state a valid claim. Appeal reached the U.S. Court of Appeals, Third Circuit, which held the parents lacked standing. Since the parents were able to select the school as a provider of partial hospitalization medical services, the court found they did not assert any injury. Their lack of standing was held fatal to the school's claim of representational standing. **No federal law required a school district to subsidize private education provided in conjunction with a medical program at the school.** An equal protection claim on behalf of the students was not timely raised, and the court affirmed the judgment for the school district. *Community Country Day School v. Erie School Dist.*, 618 Fed.Appx. 89 (3d Cir. 2015).

◆ Nursing organizations challenged a California Education Department advisory on students with diabetes in public schools. The advisory authorized student insulin administrations in schools by several groups of persons, including school employees who were adequately trained to administer insulin (pursuant to a treating physician's orders) under a Section 504 plan or IEP. According to the nurses, the advisory condoned the unauthorized practice of nursing. The case reached the Supreme Court of California, which found a long-term shortage of school nurses had led to a previous federal court class action suit. A settlement ended the class action, which led to the advisory at issue. Under it, trained school staff who were not licensed healthcare providers could administer insulin under medical orders, where no nurse was available.

Public school students with diabetes who could not self-administer insulin were entitled to no-cost administration under the IDEA, Section 504 and other federal laws. But the court found some school nurses refused to train unlicensed staff members to administer insulin out of concern for discipline by the nursing board. The advisory concluded it was unlawful for a school district to have a general practice asserting it need not comply with student IDEA or Section 504 rights to have insulin administered at school in the absence of a licensed professional. State Education Code Section 49423 declared that any student required to take prescribed medication during the school day may be assisted by the school nurse or other designated school personnel. **The court rejected the claims and held Section 49423 permitted unlicensed school personnel to administer prescription medications.** *American Nurses Ass'n v. Torlakson*, 57 Cal.4th 570, 304 P.3d 1038 (Cal. 2013).

◆ In 1999, the Supreme Court decided another case involving the extent of a school district's obligation to provide medical services, adopting a bright-line, physician/non-physician test to determine whether a requested service is a related service or a medical service. An Iowa student suffered a spinal cord injury that left him quadriplegic and ventilator dependent. For several years, his family provided him with personal attendant services at school. When the student entered grade five, his mother asserted that the district should provide him with continuous one-on-one nursing services. The district refused. A due process hearing officer determined that the school district had to reimburse the family for nursing costs in the current school year and provide the services in the future. A federal court ruled for the family, and the U.S. Court of Appeals, Eighth Circuit, found the services were related services as defined by the IDEA that were necessary to enable him to benefit from special education.

The court rejected the district's argument that the services were medical services excluded under the IDEA and state law. On appeal, the U.S. Supreme Court held the requested services were not medical services. The Court based its decision on the IDEA definition of related services, the *Tatro* decision, and the purpose of the IDEA to make special education available to all disabled students. **Adopting a bright-line, physician/non-physician standard, the court held that since the disputed services could be performed by someone other than a physician, the district had to provide them.** The district's assertion that a multi-factor standard that includes cost as a consideration was appropriate was rejected. *Cedar Rapids Community School Dist. v. Garret F.,* 526 U.S. 66, 119 S.Ct. 992, 143 L.Ed.2d 154 (1999).

◆ A Michigan school district's insurer sued the district in the state court system to enforce its rights under state law with respect to the provision of nursing services to a student with disabilities. It sought reimbursement for services it believed the district was providing and it was paying for. However, when the case reached the state court of appeals, it noted that the student's IEPs did not specify the services in dispute and that **the services being provided by the district were not being paid for by the insurer**. Further, the court held the insurer had no right to try to determine, through a lawsuit, whether the school district should be providing nursing services to the student. *Progressive Michigan Insurance Co. v. Calhoun Intermediate School Dist.,* No. 290564, 2010 WL 2680112 (Mich. Ct. App. 7/6/10).

IV. TRANSPORTATION

The IDEA requires school districts to provide students with disabilities necessary transportation as a related service. School districts must also furnish transportation to disabled students attending private schools, if this is necessary for the student to receive a FAPE. Transportation includes travel to and from school and between schools, as well as travel in and around school buildings. It also includes any specialized equipment that might be needed.

◆ The families of Tennessee elementary school students with prescriptions to Diastat (an anti-seizure medication) claimed their children were required to transfer to schools with a full-time nurse if their zoned school did not have one. Transfers were required because a board policy stated that only nurses could administer Diastat. The families initiated due process complaints against the board of education and the Tennessee Department of Education (TDOE). In addition to claiming IDEA, Section 504 and Americans with Disabilities Act (ADA) violations, the families said the board and TDOE violated a state law that prohibits the assignment of a student with a seizure disorder to a school other than the student's zoned school based on the seizure disorder.

No due process hearing was held because the parties agreed the case did not implicate a FAPE. The parents sued the board of education, county and TDOE in a federal court. In pretrial activity, the court noted that unless the IEP requires otherwise, a child with a disability is to be educated in the school he/she would have attended if not for a disability. **Both Section 504 and the**

ADA prohibit covered agencies from providing different or separate aids, benefits or services to persons or classes of persons with a disability, unless this is "necessary" to provide the aids, benefits, or services. As a threshold matter, the court denied the TDOE's argument that it could only be held liable for failing to provide the students a FAPE. It held the TDOE, as the responsible state authority, had to ensure the provisions of the IDEA were carried out. Finding there were material issues of fact regarding whether the TDOE carried out its oversight duties, the court denied the TDOE's request for pretrial judgment. Next, the court found material issues of fact regarding the board's official policy and how it was administered. Evidence indicated both families were advised that a transfer was necessary because the children were prescribed Diastat. This appeared to be contrary to Tenn. Code Ann. § 49-5-1602(g)(7), which prohibits the assignment of a student with a seizure disorder to a school other than his/her zoned school based on the disorder. As a result, the court held the case should proceed to a trial. *S.P. v. Knox County Board of Educ.*, 329 F.Supp.3d 584 (E.D. Tenn. 2018; reconsideration denied 5/14/19).

◆   Due to emotional and behavioral disorders, a Minnesota student had an IEP. Her school district of residence placed her in an out-of-district school for grades three and four so she could receive special education services. While the student was attending the out-of-district school, an IEP was created for her that included transportation "individually to and from school" due to her struggles with other students who vocalized while in close proximity to her. Consistent with her IEP, the parents drove their child to and from school and obtained reimbursement from their district of residence for their mileage. The parents later applied for their child to attend school in another district under the state's open enrollment law. After the district accepted the open enrollment application, it agreed with the parents to place the student in an education center in a different district for special education. Although the open-enrollment district agreed to reimburse the parents for mileage between the district's boundary and the education center, it rejected their request for reimbursement for full mileage between their home and the education center. Because of the transportation disagreement, the parties did not update the IEP for the next school year. This meant the provisions of the prior year's IEP remained in effect, including those governing transportation. The case came before an administrative law judge (ALJ), who found the stay-put IEP included transportation between home and school as a necessary related service. As a result, the parents were entitled to receive the full mileage they sought. In a federal court, the open-enrollment district sued the parents, seeking an order that the placement had been voluntary. The court found the overriding concern in IDEA cases is to ensure that a child has access to a free appropriate public education (FAPE). In reviewing the relevant terms, **the court found "related services" includes transportation and such developmental, corrective and other supportive services as may be required to assist a child with a disability to benefit from special education**.

Rejecting the district's claim that the parents simply made a placement based on their preference, the court found the case implicated the district's FAPE obligation. In this case, the operative, stay-put IEP specified that the student needed individualized transportation to and from school. As the open-enrollment district was responsible for providing the student a FAPE, the court found it was necessarily responsible for providing her with the specialized transportation specified in her IEP. Once the student's open-enrollment application was accepted, the open-enrollment district became solely responsible for providing a FAPE. At the time of the student's enrollment, the open-enrollment district had a blanket policy against providing out-of-district transportation to open-enrolled students with IEPs containing specialized transportation provisions. As the state education department found, **the blanket policy violated the IDEA because it failed to determine individual student transportation needs on a case-by-case basis**. As the ALJ correctly held the open-enrollment district responsible for providing the student with transportation as described in her IEP, the court held for the parents. *Osseo Area Schools, Independent School Dist. No. 279 v. M.N.B.*, No. 17-2068 (DSD/HB), 2018 WL 4603279 (D. Minn. 9/25/18, Eighth Circuit appeal filed 10/23/18).

◆   A Georgia parent said her child was entitled to an aide to administer seizure medication called Diastat on his bus to and from school. But the school denied her request and after efforts to resolve the dispute, the parent filed a due process request. An administrative law judge (ALJ) held the district violated the IDEA by failing to staff an IEP meeting with a person having authority to commit district resources or someone who had knowledge of the district's transportation and emergency response capabilities. The ALJ found the administration of Diastat in the event of a prolonged seizure was necessary to enable the child to receive a free appropriate public education. As a remedy, she ordered the school district to reimburse the parent for her driving expenses from the date of the due process request until the district provided a Diastat-trained aide for the child's daily bus ride. But the ALJ found the parties had both acted unreasonably.

The parent was denied 50% of her daily driving costs because she denied the district access to medical information. The IEP was to be amended to provide for a Diastat-trained aide on the bus. When the case reached a federal court, it held the child was denied a FAPE because his IEP did not include adequate health services on the school bus. The ALJ's remedy required a trained aide on the bus who would be ready to administer Diastat if the bus did not reach the child's home or school within five minutes of a seizure. Should the parent decide she wanted the child to receive Diastat without having the bus try to reach home or school, she would have to sign the doctor release form. If the bus could not reach home or school within five minutes, a trained aide could prevent an unreasonable risk. **Since the parties shared the blame for derailing the collaborative IEP process, the court found the ALJ was justified in ordering an amended Diastat procedure and reducing the reimbursement of transportation costs**. *Oconee County School Dist. v. A.B.*, No. 3:14-CV-72, 2015 WL 4041297 (M.D. Ga. 7/1/15, 11th Cir. appeal dismissed 8/31/15).

◆   An Alabama child had a seizure disorder and other serious disabilities. Her school district had no nurse to accompany her on the school bus, so her parent transported her to and from school each day. When the family moved to California, a school district there devised an IEP addressing her transportation needs. Days before the start of the school year, the family returned to Alabama. After the parent reenrolled the child in the school she previously attended, the principal asked the parent to temporarily provide transportation. Since the child was deemed an out-of-state transfer, an IEP meeting was not held immediately. Transportation became burdensome to the parent, and she declined the school district's demand for a transportation reimbursement contract. She claimed she should be paid hourly wages in addition to reimbursement. The district then hired a nurse to accompany the child on her bus and drafted a new IEP to specify bus transportation with medical support. But the parent requested a due process hearing, seeking compensatory education, hourly wages and reimbursement for her costs. A hearing officer denied all relief, and the parent appealed to a federal court.

The court held the school district satisfied the IDEA by offering services in accordance with the California IEP. It found the district never refused to provide transportation and offered an interim arrangement that replicated the terms of the California IEP. **A school receiving a transfer student from another state generally must provide services in a preexisting IEP until an evaluation can be held.** The parent was entitled to reimbursement for her costs, but not for hourly wages. Last, the court held for the board on a Section 504 claim, finding no discrimination. *Ruby J. v. Jefferson County Board of Educ.*, 122 F.Supp.3d 1288 (N.D. Ala. 2015).

CHAPTER NINE

School Liability

I. LIABILITY FOR NEGLIGENCE

Negligence is the failure to use reasonable or ordinary care under the circumstances. In order for a school district to be held liable for negligence, it must have a duty to the person claiming negligence. If a reasonably prudent person cannot foresee any danger of direct injury, there is no duty, and thus no negligence. A school district may be held liable for the acts or omissions of a negligent employee. A pattern of negligence showing a conscious disregard for safety may be "willful or wanton misconduct"– a form of intentional conduct.

The elements of a negligence claim are: 1) the existence of a legal duty to conform one's conduct to the relevant standard of care established by law, 2) a breach of that duty of care that is 3) the direct cause of the injury, and 4) damages or injury. Foreseeability of harm is also a prerequisite to liability in negligence cases. In A.W. v. Lancaster County School Dist. 0001, *784 N.W.2d 907 (Neb. 2010), the Supreme Court of Nebraska held that foreseeability questions are generally for juries, not judges, to determine.*

A. Compliance with IEP Provisions

◆   A Tennessee kindergarten student with autism injured her arm at school but could not explain the cause of injury. At the time, her IEP included goals for her to demonstrate "increased compliance in the school environment with following directives." In a state court, the student's parents sued the school district and its board for negligence. While acknowledging the precise cause of injury was unknown, they argued there was a presumption of negligence by the school district under state law. The parents further argued the most probable explanation was that their child was injured while in the area of her teacher's desk and that the teacher's actions or inactions most likely caused her arm injury. After a year of court activity, the court granted the school district's pretrial judgment motion. It held the parents could not rely on a state-law presumption of negligence and rejected two other liability theories. Months later, the parents sought to amend their complaint by arguing the student had been injured on the school playground. They said she had gone down a slide improperly and that the school district was liable for her injuries. The court agreed with the district that the new theory of injury should not be allowed.

The parents appealed to the Court of Appeals of Tennessee, which reviewed the trial court's finding that they could not show any school employee breached a duty of care owned to them or their child. A trial court has discretion to deny an amended complaint based on several factors. Among these are prejudice, undue delay, lack of notice, bad faith and failure to cure deficiencies by previous amendments. In this case, the trial court denied the parents' request to add the playground injury theory because they had already amended their complaint three times. They did not raise the playground injury theory until the case was over two years old. The appeals court agreed with the lower court that the parents engaged in undue delay. Allowing a fourth amended complaint would have been unfair to the district. Next, **the court found no evidence that any action or inaction by teachers or other school employees may have caused the student's injury**. The court dismissed the parents' remaining arguments, finding they simply reiterated arguments that had already been rejected. The court held for the board, finding no evidence showed how the student injured her arm or what precautions could have been used to prevent injury. *Webster v. Metropolitan Government of Nashville and Davidson County, Tennessee,* No. M2018-00106-COA-R3-CV, 2019 WL 169137 (Tenn. Ct. App. 1/11/19).

◆   A Wyoming student slipped and fell on an icy school playground, causing injuries including a fractured femur. In a state court, her grandparents sued the school district under the Wyoming Governmental Claims Act. According to the grandparents, the act did not bar their suit because the IEP was a contract. The court found the IEP could not be a considered a contract, and it held that no other exception to immunity applied. On appeal, the Supreme Court of Wyoming explained that **a school district and its employees have**

governmental immunity under state law so long as the employees act within the scope of their duties. An exception to immunity exists for actions based on a contract. According to the grandparents, the IEP was a contract providing for "adult supervision throughout the school day." But the court instead found the IEP was not supported by "consideration." Moreover, the school district was obligated to provide the student a free appropriate public education. Even accepting the argument that supervision was a critical part of the IEP, the court found no consideration. The state constitution requires the legislature to provide a free public education for all children in the state. Similarly, federal special education law requires the states to assure that all children with disabilities have a free appropriate public education available to them. **Next, the court found an IEP is not a contract but is a statement produced by a school through a collaborative process to define the appropriate services for a student.**

As the implementation of an IEP is a school obligation provided at no cost to parents, the court found the IEP in this case could not be considered a contract. As no contract existed, the exception to state law immunity did not apply. *SH v. Campbell County School Dist.*, 409 P.3d 1231 (Wyo. 2018).

◆   An Alabama student with cognitive and physical disabilities used a walker or wheelchair. An aide assigned to help him at school began taking him to the weight room to do his classwork. At least two other staff members saw the student and aide there at various times. A classmate reported to a parent that the aide kicked the student's wheelchair and failed to pick up a pencil he had dropped and could not retrieve. When the student's parents learned of this, they put a recording device in his wheelchair. After listening to the recordings, the parents felt they had proof that the aide and a teacher yelled at their child. They reported their suspicions, and both employees were placed on leave. The aide resigned, and the teacher's contract was not renewed. The parents sued the board in a federal court. After some of the issues were settled, the court dismissed the claims under Section 504 and ADA due to failure to administratively exhaust them. The parents filed a due process action, which was resolved. The ADA and Section 504 claims were then refiled. The court held they could not show school officials had actual knowledge of any verbal or physical abuse by the aide or the teacher. There was no evidence of any abusive behavior toward other students by the employees. The court disagreed that taking the child to the weight room in violation of his IEP was disability discrimination. **More than noncompliance with the child's IEP had to be shown to create liability under federal law.**

As the family did not show that a departure from the IEP amounted to gross misjudgment, and there was no showing of intentional discrimination under the ADA or Section 504, the court held for the board of education. *J.S. v. Houston County Board of Educ.*, 120 F.Supp.3d 1287 (M.D. Ala. 2015).

◆   A New York sixth-grader crossed a busy highway to try to catch her school bus after the driver forgot to stop at her house. She was struck by a vehicle and seriously injured. A state court negligence action was filed on the student's behalf and eventually reached the New York Court of Appeals. It held a school district breaches a duty of care if it releases a child without further supervision into "a foreseeably hazardous setting it had a hand in creating." But the court rejected all three of the parent's theories of district liability. It held the injury did not take place "during the act of busing." Evidence showed the student walked onto the highway and there was also no merit to a claim that the district created a hazard. The student was not in the school district's physical custody at the time of the injury. Her mother was at home when the accident occurred.

Finally, the court found **no special duty was owed to the student by virtue of her IEP**. In fact, the IEP only directed the school district to transport her to and from school, providing her the same busing services required for all K-8 students living more than two miles from their schools. Rejecting the parent's other arguments, the court held for the school district. *Williams v. Weatherstone*, 23 N.Y. 384, 15 N.E.3d 792 (N.Y. 2014).

◆   A severely disabled Indiana student did not always chew her food and had a safety plan and a dining plan. Although the dining plan stated that the child's food had to be cut up, a paraprofessional who was assigned to her was unaware of the safety and dining plans. She did not cut up the food, and the child choked. Nobody attempted the Heimlich maneuver or tried to administer CPR. The school nurse was called, but since nobody told her the child was choking, it took her 10 minutes to arrive. Emergency responders arrived in a few minutes and restored the student's airway before taking her to a hospital. Later, school administrators visited the hospital. The student's mother said she asked the assistant principal how long the child had been without oxygen and that he responded "it was a very short period of time." The child died three days after the incident. About nine months later, a school cafeteria worker contacted the parents and said "things were not done properly." The parents filed a notice of tort claim and sued the school district in a state court for negligence, wrongful death and civil rights violations. During the pretrial fact-finding process known as discovery, the parents sought an order preserving video evidence of the incident. The court held for the district and its insurer.

On appeal, the Supreme Court of Indiana found enough evidence of possible fraudulent concealment to allow the tort claims against the district to proceed. While the parents said the assistant principal told them the child was without oxygen for "a very short period of time," there was evidence she may have been without oxygen for as long as 20 minutes. In addition, school officials did not preserve video records from the day of the incident. There was evidence that the cafeteria worker who contacted the parents was threatened with retaliation. **Since a jury might find fraudulent concealment, the parents could pursue their state tort claims.** But the court dismissed their federal civil rights claims. It returned the case to the trial court with instructions for the jury. *Lyons v. Richmond Community School Corp.*, 19 N.E.3d 254 (Ind. 2014).

◆   A 15-year-old Louisiana student was hearing impaired, nonverbal and visually impaired. Because he ate too fast and often did not chew his food, his IEP required staff members to closely supervise him as he ate. While eating his breakfast at school, the student choked. A substitute teacher and an aide tried to assist him, and the school's adaptive physical education teacher also tried to help. Paramedics were unable to intubate the student because of large amounts of food in his airway. They took him to a hospital, where he later died. In a state court, the student's estate sued the school board for negligent supervision. The court found the board negligent and awarded the estate more than $330,000 in damages. On appeal, the state court of appeal found that **a school board may be held liable for failing to adequately supervise students if there is proof of negligence**. In this case, the student's IEP said he had to be monitored to prevent him from eating too fast and swallowing food without chewing. His food was to be cut up into bite-size pieces. In the court's view, the testimony supported the estate. A paramedic stated that unchewed food had been suctioned from the student's airway. **The evidence regarding the death implicated exactly what the IEP sought to prevent.** As a result, the court affirmed the judgment for the estate. *Robertson v. East Baton Rouge Parish School Board*, No. 2012 CA 2039, 2013 WL 3947124 (La. Ct. App. 7/29/13).

The state's highest court later refused to review the decision. *Robertson v. East Baton Rouge Parish School Board*, 126 So.2d 472 (La. 2013).

B. Student Injuries

In Doe v. New Haven Board of Educ., *No. NNHCV 1050 33148S, 2015 WL 6144099 (Conn. Super. Ct. 9/18/15), the court held that for a negligence case to survive dismissal, there must be evidence that a legal duty exists which was breached. Next, the injured party must have suffered an injury that was caused by the allegedly negligent party. If a duty exists, the injured party must show the other party did not exercise reasonable care under the circumstances. It must further be shown that in the absence of the negligence, the injury would not have occurred and that the defending party's conduct was more likely than not the cause of the injury. A threshold inquiry is whether the specific harm alleged by the injured party was foreseeable. Negligence is established if a reasonable person would foresee that injuries of the same general kind would be likely to happen in the absence of adequate safeguards.*

◆   A New York court allowed a parent to pursue an action against a school district for leaving a seven-year-old child with autism on a school bus on a hot day. On a July day when the temperature reached 87 degrees, a school employee found the student wandering in a neighborhood, some 45 minutes after she was due home. It was determined that the child was left unattended on a school bus parked on school property. School officials, including the district superintendent, met with the student and parent, and the superintendent reviewed video evidence of the incident during the next few days. About a month later, the school board president emailed the parent regarding the incident. Over a year later, the parent petitioned a state court for permission to serve a late notice of claim on the district. He asserted that the student had developed signs of psychological and emotional injury. The court granted the petition, and the district appealed.

A state appellate division court noted that all the relevant circumstances must be considered in determining whether to grant a petition for leave to serve a late notice of claim. This includes whether the entity has acquired actual knowledge of the essential facts constituting the claim within 90 days after the claim arose, or a reasonable time thereafter. Other factors include the claimant's reasonable excuse for failure to serve a timely notice and whether the delay would substantially prejudice a defense by the public entity. As a final factor, the court must consider whether the claimant is a minor or is incapacitated. In this case, **the court found the district officials knew about the essential facts constituting the claim within 90 days after it arose, or a reasonable time thereafter**. School officials responded promptly and directly to the parent, even meeting him at the scene. In view of the district's actual knowledge of the essential facts of the case, the court found school officials would not be harmed in maintaining a defense. As a result, the case would proceed. *John P. v. Plainedge Union Free School Dist.*, 165 A.D.3d 1263 (N.Y. App. Div. 2018).

◆   A Pennsylvania seventh-grade student with autism was struck and killed by a vehicle while trying to walk home from school. His IEP did not specify transportation. The student normally walked to and from school with his sister, but she did not do so on the day of his death. No crossing guard was stationed on the route. In a federal court, his estate sued the district for constitutional violations and discrimination. The court rejected the district's argument that claims under Section 504 of the Rehabilitation Act and the Americans with Disabilities Act had to first be presented to a hearing officer. Third Circuit decisions have established that a student's death excuses administrative exhaustion of claims that might otherwise be resolved in a due process hearing.

   The court held the estate properly asserted a claim for liability based on a state-created danger. It held the student's death was foreseeable to the district as a fairly direct result of assigning him to walk along a dangerous road. **If true, the complaint indicated that the district should have known that requiring a child with autism and other disabilities to walk to and from school and cross a dangerous road could result in harm.** After finding the complaint presented sufficient facts to show the harm to the student was foreseeable and fairly direct, the court held the estate was not barred from arguing that the district had a custom and practice of failing to train its employees and that this failure was the moving force behind the constitutional violations. Last, the court held the due process rights in this case were clearly established and a reasonable person would have been aware of them. As a result, the school employees were not entitled to immunity. *Weiser v. Elizabethtown Area School Dist.*, No. 17-625, 2018 WL 1071929 (E.D. Pa. 2/27/18).

◆   A New Jersey student with emotional disturbance became agitated on a school minibus en route to a program operated by a county board. She jumped from the moving bus and was fatally injured. In a federal court action against the school district, bus company, county board and various individuals, her parents said the board acted in reckless disregard for her health, safety and welfare by transporting her on the minibus. No federal claims were brought against the county board. The complaint asserted the school district was on notice that a minibus was inappropriate for the student. There was evidence that the county board recommended separate transportation for her, and that she had engaged in dangerous behavior such as leaving the school grounds and walking in traffic. Evidence was presented that the student hated riding the minibus and refused to board it at the county program site. The court found that while any duty of care in this case most directly belonged to the bus staff, the exercise of that duty "surely required input from the educational professionals most familiar with [the student's] disability and the precautions that it would require." **In the court's view, the complaint adequately stated the existence of a duty of care, breach of that duty, actual and legal causation, and damages.** Rejecting a claim to immunity under the New Jersey Tort Claims Act, the court refused to dismiss the claims against the board. *Williams v. Board of Educ. of Paterson*, No. 15-0765 (KM), 2017 WL 3131974 (D.N.J. 7/21/17).

◆   A 14-year-old Alabama student could not proceed with claims based on injuries from a fall that occurred during a bus evacuation drill at his school. The student has cytomegalovirus, cerebral palsy, asthma, osteopenia and arthritis. A federal court rejected a claim that the school board violated the student's substantive due process rights. **He was not in a custodial relationship with the board.** After rejecting the federal claims, the court declined to exercise supplemental jurisdiction over the remaining state-law claims, which could be refiled in a state court. *McKenzie v. Talladega Board of Educ.*, 242 F.Supp.3d 1244 (N.D. Ala. 2017, 11th Cir. appeal dismissed 8/8/17).

◆   According to a Florida parent's federal court complaint, her child has autism and emotional disabilities. She claimed school bus employees left her child asleep on locked buses after their routes on two occasions. The complaint recited that the child rode a bus for children with special needs that was staffed by an attendant as well as a driver. The parent stated that on the first occasion, the driver parked the bus after completing the route, disembarked with the attendant and left the child sleeping on the bus. She said surveillance video showed the attendant walking past her child prior to exiting. Next, the parent said her child awoke and climbed out an emergency window, causing him to fall to the ground. She said he then walked and hitchhiked some 30 miles home.

A similar series of events took place the next week, according to the parent. After the second incident, the parent filed a federal lawsuit, bringing state-law claims such as negligence, false imprisonment and infliction of emotional distress, but only one constitutional claim. The federal claim arose under 42 U.S.C. § 1983 and asserted the board and school violated the child's constitutional rights. **The court held the parent made conclusory statements that the board failed to adequately train the driver and attendant.** She identified no other similar incidents and did not claim the board knew of and deliberately disregarded a pattern of leaving children with special needs on school buses. Since the complaint did not state a plausible case for constitutional violations, the case was dismissed. *Riha v. Polk County School Dist.*, No. 8:17-cv-787-T-33AAS, 2017 WL 2986227 (M.D. Fla. 7/13/17).

◆   Washington's Court of Appeals held a lower court would have to reconsider a case filed by a student who sought to hold his school district liable for injuries he suffered after being punched by a disabled student. The court explained that **school districts owe a duty to protect students in their custody from reasonably anticipated dangers, including foreseeable misconduct by their peers**. Well-established principles of state law declare that when students are in school, the protective custody of teachers is substituted for that of their parents.

There is a duty to protect students in school from reasonably anticipated dangers. There is a special relationship between students and schools when the protective custody of teachers is substituted for that of the parents. Moreover, there is a legal duty on school districts to take precautions to protect students in their custody from reasonably anticipated dangers. Finding the trial court had improperly instructed the jury, the court returned the case for a new trial. The trial court would have to decide whether to instruct jurors that state and federal laws require schools to educate disabled students in the general education environment, to the maximum extent appropriate. The lower court would also have to consider the issue of contributory negligence by the student. *Hopkins v. Seattle Public School Dist. No. 1*, 195 Wash.App. 96 (Wash. Ct. App. 2016).

The state supreme court then upheld the decision ordering a new trial in the case. *Hopkins v. Seattle Public School Dist. No. 1*, No. 93492-4, 2016 WL 7166715 (Wash. review denied 12/7/16).

◆   A California student who used a breathing machine had a doctor's order requiring her to avoid direct sunlight. According to her mother, the student had to attend a field trip at an outdoor recreation camp. Before the trip, the parent worked with school staff to create a written care plan. She showed a teacher how to operate the breathing machine and provided the physician's order to avoid direct sunlight. After the trip, the parent charged school staff members with forcing her child to stay in direct sunlight for 9.5 hours, even though the child protested and was crying hysterically. The parent said that as a result of the conduct by staff members during the field trip, her child suffered second-degree skin burns, heat exhaustion, heat stroke, permanent damage to her internal organs, emotional distress and post-traumatic stress syndrome.

In a federal court, the parent sued the school district, outdoor recreation area and a county entity, asserting claims for discrimination in violation of Section 504 of the Rehabilitation Act, negligent supervision, intentional infliction of emotional distress and violation of her state constitutional right to attend a safe school. **The court found the parent stated enough facts to proceed under the theory that the district breached a duty of care to her child during the field trip.** Although the court allowed the parent to proceed with the negligent supervision claim and an emotional distress claim on her child's behalf, it held the state constitution does not impose any obligation on the state that may be enforced in a private lawsuit. In addition to dismissing the state constitutional claim, the court held the parent could not pursue an emotional distress claim on her own behalf. *J.M. v. Pleasant Ridge Union School Dist.*, Civ. No. 2:16-00897 WBS CKD, 2016 WL 5930636 (E.D. Cal. 10/11/16).

◆   A Utah student who was pushed down twice by peers before transferring out of a school system was unable to show negligence by her former school district. In a federal court, she brought claims under various legal theories, asserting she was forced to leave her school system after twice being pushed down. She said that the school district failed to reasonably accommodate her health problems resulting from the incidents. Moreover, the student said at least three school employees made degrading remarks about her, including calling her "cripple" and saying she appeared to be drunk. After she withdrew from the school system, she sued the school district, asserting theories of negligence and infliction of emotional distress. She also alleged violations of the Constitution, the Americans with Disabilities Act and Rehabilitation Act Section 504.

Initially, the court rejected the student's claim that the school district violated her due process rights. It held **inaction by school officials is not enough to trigger liability for a constitutional violation**. Next, the court dismissed disability-related claims under Section 504 and the ADA. These claims asserted the school district failed to accommodate the student' disability or offer her a specialized educational program. Finding the claims were education-related, the court held she had to exhaust her administrative remedies under the IDEA before filing them in court. Since the court dismissed all of the federal claims, it declined to consider the negligence and emotional distress claims, which could go before a state court for resolution. *Harper v. Carbon County School Dist.*, 105 F.Supp.3d 1317 (D. Utah 2015).

◆ Connecticut parents sued their school district in the state court system, claiming his teacher repeatedly chose a certain classmate to accompany their child during lavatory breaks. They claimed the classmate sexually assaulted their child on more than one occasion and charged the school district with negligence. According to the parents, allowing special education students to leave a classroom unattended was unsafe and the teacher ignored their child's request that the classmate not go with him during lavatory visits. After three years of pretrial activity, the school officials sought a judgment in the case.

Finding reasonable minds could find the harm in this case was foreseeable to the school officials, the court denied pretrial judgment on the foreseeability question. Although the teacher claimed state law immunity on the theory that her decisions involved discretion and judgment, the court found the evidence was disputed. It was possible that she would not have immunity for her actions, which could be deemed "ministerial" and not protected by immunity. While the duty to supervise students or provide adequate security to protect students from classmates has generally been considered a discretionary government activity in Connecticut, exceptions apply. **Testimony by the school principal indicated she was not aware of any lavatory policy in the building and she stated there was no mandated or prescribed manner for teachers to supervise and monitor students.** As a fact issue existed regarding whether there was a school policy or directive in place creating a ministerial duty, the court denied the officials' claim to immunity. *Doe v. New Haven Board of Educ.*, No. NNHCV 1050 33148S, 2015 WL 6144099 (Conn. Super. Ct. 9/18/15).

◆ A federal court dismissed claims filed by a 21-year-old former Texas student-athlete who said school staff members overlooked his numerous sports injuries, including concussions and dehydration. The court held Section 504 of the Rehabilitation Act "does not create general tort liability for educational malpractice." Despite voluminous evidence presented by the student, the court found nothing indicating any bad faith or gross professional misjudgment by the school district. His doctors annually cleared him to play football without imposing restrictions. There was evidence that coaches never sent the student back onto the field during a game when he suffered an injury. The only time he actually told the staff about a concussion, he avoided treatment in an attempt to stay competitive for a college football scholarship. **As there was no evidence of intentional discrimination, bad faith or gross professional misjudgment by the school district, the Section 504 claims were dismissed.** *Ripple v. Marble Falls Independent School Dist.*, 99 F.Supp.3d 662 (W.D. Tex. 2015).

◆   In the hallway of his high school, a Washington student was fatally shot by a student with disabilities. In a state court, the student's family said the disabled student's behavior and medical records indicated he was at risk for harming others. Evidence was produced that the disabled student was diagnosed with paranoid schizophrenia after attempting suicide two years earlier. After being hospitalized, he underwent 11 months of outpatient care and was prescribed anti-psychotic medication. There was evidence that the disabled student had transferred often and attended at least four different high schools. But there was no evidence he had committed any assaults. During the year of his suicide attempt, the disabled student was categorized as emotionally behaviorally disabled. In pretrial activity, the court rejected the estate's theories of liability.

The case went before the Court of Appeals of Washington. It held school districts must exercise reasonable care when supervising students. But the duty to exercise reasonable care extends only to foreseeable risks of harm. Although the court agreed with the estate that foreseeability is normally a jury question, it pointed out that a trial judge has authority to make the decision if "reasonable minds cannot differ." **As nothing in school or medical records indicated the disabled student presented a risk of harm to anyone at school, the court found the shooting was not foreseeable.** The court found the estate's arguments ignored state and federal antidiscrimination laws and obligations requiring schools to provide appropriate educational opportunities to students with disabilities. As it was not foreseeable to the school district that the student would act violently, the court affirmed the judgment for the district. *Kok v. Tacoma School Dist. No. 10*, 177 Wash.App. 1016 (Wash. Ct. App. 2013). (Wash. review denied), 180 Wash.2d 1016, 327 P.3d 55 (Wash. 2014).

◆   Because of a rare, progressive neurological condition, a New Mexico student was unable to walk, talk or take care of himself. He also had severe osteoporosis. On a morning at his elementary school, the student began crying and his aide removed him from class. She later stated that his leg was "swollen like a balloon." At a medical center, it was determined that the student had a spiral fracture of the femur. He died nine months after breaking his leg.

The student's parents sued the school system in a state court for negligence. The court found the school system owed the student a duty of care to handle him in a way that minimized the stress upon his bones. But due to his weak bones, the student was subject to a fracture (including a spiral fracture) from virtually any routine and non-negligent handling. Finding the school did not breach its duty to the student, the court held for the school system. The parents appealed to the Supreme Court of New Mexico. It noted expert testimony indicated the injury could have resulted from a minimal force. Even the parents' expert had stated a fracture could be the result of any care maneuver, such as putting on clothes, turning over in bed or bathing. Her statements supported a finding that the student could have suffered a fracture from virtually any non-negligent handling. **As the trial court had found, due to the very weak state of his bones the injury could have been caused either by negligent or non-negligent handling.** Since the parents did not show their child's injury could not have occurred in the absence of a negligent act by the school, the court affirmed the judgment for the school system. *Nez v. Gallup-McKinley Public Schools*, No. 31,728, 2014 WL 1314937 (N.M. 2/17/14).

C. Allergies, Asthma and Other Medical Conditions

◆   An Ohio student with cognitive disabilities had an IEP and a Section 504 plan for his severe peanut allergy. When he was in grade three, school employees accidentally put sealed peanut butter containers on breakfast carts brought to his classroom. A food server noticed the mistake and told the teacher, who brought the student to the nurse's office. Although staff observed no signs of an allergic reaction, his mother became greatly upset, and the principal took him to an emergency room. A few weeks later, the parent signed off on a new IEP without objection, but she soon removed her son from the school and filed a due process complaint. After a hearing, the board of education prevailed. A state review officer affirmed the decision, and the parent appealed.

A federal court held for the board and the parent appealed to the Sixth Circuit Court of Appeals. It found no merit to her claim that the board deprived her of a meaningful opportunity to participate in the IEP process. She did not identify any substantive harm from the many wrongs she asserted. One of the claims asserted that the school segregated him from classmates during school transportation. But the court found the parent insisted on driving her son to and from field trip sites. She could not blame the board for her decision. Next, the parent argued her son's IEP was not sufficiently ambitious or specific. But the court found the IEP had goals tailored to his weaknesses in five categories and had detailed academic objectives. According to the parent, her son's IEP should have addressed peer bullying. But the court found she never told the school about bullying or explained how staff should have identified a severe problem. **Although the parent complained that the student's IEP did not address his allergy, the court found a separate medical plan covered this.** After dismissing her remaining arguments, the court held for the board. *Barney v. Akron Board of Educ.*, 763 Fed.Appx. 528 (6th Cir. 2019).

◆   A Utah student attended school with a dog for a few days before being told that a school district policy prohibited her from doing so. After a hearing, a school panel issued an opinion affirming the decision to exclude the dog. The parent sued the district in a federal court, seeking a declaration that the dog was a "service animal" as defined by the Americans with Disabilities Act (ADA) and state law. At some point after filing suit, the family moved outside the school's boundaries. According to the parent, the exclusion of the service animal violated her civil rights. But the court held she did not state a plausible federal claim and dismissed the ADA claim. As for the parent's state-law claim, the court noted the family's move made this question moot. But it also found that even if the matter was not moot, it would still rule in the school district's favor.

Utah law provided that a non-disabled person has a right to be accompanied by an animal in training in a variety of private and public locations, but not schools. **A "service animal" as defined by state law excluded an animal used solely to provide emotional support, well-being, comfort or companionship.** The court found state law did not require a school district to allow a service animal in training that accompanied a non-disabled student into a high school classroom. State law did not extend ADA accommodation requirements to non-disabled students. As the Utah statute did not require accommodations for non-disabled people with service animals in training to the same extent as required by the ADA, the court held for the district. *Naegle v. Canyons School Dist.*, No. 2:17-cv-23-DB, 2018 WL 2376336 (D. Utah 5/23/18).

◆   Due to chronic sinusitis, allergic rhinitis and intermittent asthma, a New Jersey student had a Section 504 plan for grade nine. According to his parents, the plan required him to "teach himself the curriculum and try to identify and understand assignments that had been explained when he was absent." They said he continued to fall behind his peers and accumulated absences. Despite his many absences, the student passed his classes and was promoted to grade ten. During his tenth-grade year, the school board enacted a new attendance policy requiring the retention of students with over 33 absences in a school year. This policy applied regardless of whether absences were excused, approved or unexcused.

During grade ten, the student had 37 medically excused absences, which would trigger grade retention under the new policy. Asserting the policy targeted their son and was discriminatory, the parents sued the board for violating the Rehabilitation Act and the Americans with Disabilities Act. The parties reached a settlement by which the student was allowed to advance to grade eleven. But the parents decided to pursue their case, adding claims for compensatory education, damages and punitive damages. A federal court dismissed the case based on failure to exhaust IDEA administrative remedies. On appeal, the U.S. Court of Appeals, Third Circuit, affirmed the judgment. Months later, the Supreme Court vacated the judgment and returned the case to the Third Circuit for review in light of its recent decision in *Fry v. Napoleon Community Schools*, 137 S.Ct. 743 (U.S. 2017). When the case returned to the Third Circuit, it found the discrimination claims raised questions about whether the student's Section 504 plan addressed his educational needs. **As the complaint emphasized charges that the board failed to provide for the student's educational needs arising from his disability, the court held the parents had to exhaust their claims through the IDEA administrative process before filing a lawsuit.** *S.D. v. Haddon Heights Board of Educ.*, 722 Fed.Appx. 119 (3d Cir. 2018).

◆   An 18-year-old Illinois student fell out of his desk during an English class and began to convulse. The teacher ran to help him and told two students to get the nurse, whose office was located on the other side of the building. He did not call 911 or tell anyone else to do so, despite a school policy requiring this in life-and-death situations. A school nurse arrived in the classroom about seven minutes after the student's collapse, and the head nurse arrived and called 911 several minutes later. Although the nurses and emergency responders tried to revive the student, they could not. According to his autopsy report, the cause of his death was asthma. Later, the family sued the school district, alleging the teacher and school officials acted willfully and wantonly. A jury heard evidence that the student's asthma was noted in his IEP. Although the teacher said he did not know this, a nurse testified that this information was provided to him.

After the trial, the jury returned a $2.5 million verdict for the estate. The court denied post-trial motions by the district for a new trial and other relief. Before the Appellate Court of Illinois, the school district argued it should have had a new trial based on insufficient evidence of willful and wanton conduct. The district argued the lower court issued a jury instruction that was not supported by the evidence, and that immunity should have been granted. The court refused to overturn the verdict. It disagreed with the district's arguments and found the jury was entitled to consider the teacher's delay in calling 911. Failure to call 911 (or tell someone else to call) violated a school policy. The jury was entitled to note the conflict in testimony about the teacher' knowledge of the student's asthma. **Since the teacher pursued a course of action that he must have known would result in the delay of professional medical help, the court let the verdict stand.** *In re Estate of Stewart*, 60 N.E.3d 896, 2016 IL App (2d) 151117 (Ill. App. Ct. 2016).

◆   A federal court held the New York City Department of Education (DOE) did not improperly place a student with allergies and autism in a public school setting. Although the parents argued the IEP proposal did not sufficiently describe their child's allergies and said the school could not accommodate her allergies, the court noted the student was not currently on allergy medications. She had not been hospitalized for at least three years, and the court held the IEP sufficiently addressed her allergies and did not deny her right to a FAPE.

For similar reasons, the court rejected the claim that the assigned school could not accommodate the child's allergies. Evidence indicated the school was willing to make reasonable accommodations for her. **Since the court found the IEP adequately addressed the student's allergies, the DOE did not have to take the additional steps her parents requested.** While the parents claimed some specific sensory management techniques were omitted from the IEP, the court held any such omissions did not deny her a FAPE. Nor was the court swayed by the parents' insistence that the DOE employ the methodology used by their child's private school. There was evidence that she had also progressed through the use of another method. As a result, the court held the DOE offered the student an adequate IEP. *N.B. and C.B. v. New York City Dep't of Educ.*, No. 15 Civ. 4948 (AT), 2016 WL 5816925 (E.D.N.Y. 9/29/16).

◆   A Florida court agreed with a student who had at least six critical medical conditions that she was improperly denied an expedited hearing to consider her request for an exemption from statewide standardized testing. The student's parent sought a permanent exemption. She submitted a letter from a doctor declaring that any of the critical medical conditions could be considered so serious as to warrant consideration for exemption. But the state department of education denied the request without comment or explanation. After some unsuccessful tries to get a hearing, the parent filed a state court petition for an order to compel a hearing. **The court characterized the department's response to the petition as "a confession of error." It granted the family's petition and directed the department to afford a hearing.** *Drew v. Florida Dep't of Educ.*, 202 So.3d 951 (Fla. Dist. Ct. App. 2016).

◆   A Washington student with diabetes and hearing loss had to undergo blood sugar testing every two or three hours. Her mother and grandmother came to school to monitor her blood sugar levels throughout the school day. Later, the mother said the district failed to develop a plan for diabetic care. She demanded that the school district provide her child blood sugar monitoring throughout the day by a licensed health care provider. In response, the district stated that within a few days, the child would be transferred to another school. The parent objected, finding the abrupt transition would jeopardize her child's education.

Near this time, the parent said the voice amplification systems provided to her child did not work. In response, the school seated a paraeducator next to the student to help with class instructions. But the parent believed this contravened provisions of the IEP which required the student to become more independent. By mid-year, the parent withdrew her child from school and requested a due process hearing. An administrative law judge found the district failed to provide the student a free appropriate public education and awarded her 520 hours of private tutoring. **A federal court held a reasonable jury could find the offer to transfer the child on only two days' notice amounted to deliberate indifference to her known disabilities.** This led the court to deny the school district's request for pretrial judgment. Given the child's IEP goal of increasing her independent development, the court found the parent raised a valid issue regarding accommodations for her hearing loss. Since the parent's arguments under state law resembled her successful federal claims, the court held those claims should also proceed. *Snell v. North Thurston School Dist.*, No. C13-5786 RBL, 2015 WL 6396092 (W.D. Wash. 10/21/15).

◆   A Colorado student with hypoglycemia, asthma and a muscular/skeletal weakness claimed her charter school required her to participate in a "human pyramid" and delayed providing necessary nutrition. She said she became dizzy and fell while standing on the backs of two classmates and was injured because no mat or other protection was there. According to the student, classmates verbally and physically harassed her over several months. She said she reported this, but school officials took no action. Largely due to bullying, the student withdrew from the school. In a federal court, the student's parent sued the charter school and the school district in which it was located for negligence, disability discrimination and constitutional rights violations.

The court dismissed the claims against the charter school, finding it could not be sued as an entity separate from the school district. The court then granted the school district immunity from any liability for the human pyramid incident under the state Governmental Immunity Act. It found the exception to state law immunity sought by the student applies only to injuries arising from dangerous conditions in public buildings. But the court held the disability discrimination claims failed because **the student did not allege that the bullying was based**

solely upon a disability. It was not alleged that the human pyramid and snack deprivation incidents related to a disability. In the court's view, the conduct was not shocking to the conscience and no "state-created danger" existed. *Dorsey v. Pueblo School Dist. 60*, 140 F.Supp.3d 1102 (D. Colo. 2015).

◆ A sixth-grade Philadelphia student died from an asthma attack. According to a complaint against her school district, her teacher, principal and other staff knew of her chronic asthma. On the morning of the student's death, she told her teacher she was having trouble breathing. The teacher responded that no nurse was on duty and that she "should be calm." Although her condition worsened, the complaint alleged that nobody contacted emergency medical aid or took her to the hospital. Instead, it was asserted that she was kept at school despite having reported that she could not breathe. Later in the day, the student was driven home and then immediately taken to a hospital. On the way, she suffered a respiratory arrest. Emergency workers and hospital staff were unable to revive the student. Later, a medical examiner declared her cause of death to be acute exacerbation of asthma. In pretrial activity, the court refused to dismiss claims against the school district. As an intentional violation of rights was asserted, the district's request for a pretrial ruling was denied. A claim for deprivation of life and liberty was also not dismissed at the present time, as facts were alleged to support a state-created danger claim. **Since willful misconduct was alleged, the court denied the district's request for immunity under state law.** *Estate of Massey v. City of Philadelphia*, 118 F.Supp.3d 679 (E.D. Pa. 2015).

◆ The Ohio Court of Appeals affirmed the dismissal of a case against a private school accused of feeding a student dairy products and peanuts, despite being told of his dietary restrictions. According to a parent, the student vomited on himself and the school staff refused to help him clean up. She stated that the school then made a false report to a truancy officer and also made a false report of abuse to county family authorities. Based on statements by school staff, a trial court dismissed the case. **The court of appeals disagreed with the parent's claim that the lower court had disregarded her testimony and evidence.** *Morrow v. Sacred Heart School*, No. 2015CA0004, 2015 -Ohio- 5321 (Ohio Ct. App. 12/18/15).

◆ A Pennsylvania student with a severe nut allergy was deemed at risk of life-threatening allergic reactions. Although at least four meetings were held to develop a Section 504 accommodation plan, no agreement was reached. Although the district offered new Section 504 plan proposals, the parents rejected each of them – even one that had been approved by the student's doctor. A hearing officer found the district did not discriminate against the student or deny him a free appropriate public education. Appeal reached the U.S. Court of Appeals, Third Circuit. It found a Section 504 plan relating to food allergies had to be accessible and understandable to staff in the event of an emergency. District teachers and staff were trained to identify symptoms of anaphylaxis and to administer epinephrine. The court held the failure to include each requested accommodation and detail requested by the parents was not a Section 504 violation. **There was evidence that the district worked diligently with**

the parents to ensure their child participated in school activities and had access. Since the parents did not show their child was denied program benefits or subjected to discrimination, the court held for the school district. *T.F. v. Fox Chapel Area School Dist.*, 589 Fed.Appx. 594 (3d Cir. 2014).

◆   A Washington child had asthma and life-threatening allergies. After arriving at school, she had trouble breathing. Staff members felt she was having an asthma attack. They did not consider that she might be having an allergic reaction and did not use epinephrine. A call was made to 911, but no one used CPR or followed an emergency healthcare plan prepared by the school nurse. By the time emergency responders arrived, the child had stopped breathing and lost consciousness. The child died while being transported to a hospital. In a state court, her parents sued the school district, health clerk and school nurse for negligence. A medical examiner attributed the child's death to asthma. By contrast, the family's expert stated she had more likely died of anaphylaxia.

After a long and contentious trial, jurors found the district, clerk and nurse negligent, but found any negligence did not cause the death. A series of post-trial motions seeking a new trial was rejected, and the family appealed to the state court of appeals. In the court's view, there was no inconsistency in the jury verdict with regard to causation of death. **It was not inconsistent to find staff negligence did not cause death, if there was evidence that death would have occurred without regard to staff members' actions.** *Mears v. Bethel School Dist. No. 403*, 332 P.3d 1077 (Wash. Ct. App. 2014).

D. Injuries to Nonstudents

◆   Due to transverse myelitis, an Indiana parent cannot walk and uses a motorized wheelchair. Her child attended a public elementary school and participated in an after-school extracurricular choir for which he received no credit. The choir performed at several public events annually, including two concerts held at the school. During consecutive school years, the student's choir performed at a Christmas concert sponsored by a local historical museum. The museum was housed in a building built in 1901 with no access ramps or elevators. Because the museum was inaccessible, the parent could not attend the concerts. She sued the school district for disability discrimination under the Americans with Disabilities Act and Section 504 of the Rehabilitation Act.

A federal court held the concerts were not considered a "service, program or activity" of the school district, but were instead hosted by the museum. The parent appealed to the Seventh Circuit Court of Appeals. After reviewing the parties' arguments and the views of the U.S. Department of Education, the court found the concerts were "provided or made available" by the museum, rather than the school district. While a public entity cannot avoid its responsibilities by engaging in a "joint endeavor" with a private entity, the court rejected the argument that the concerts were a joint activity. In this case, the court found the concerts were part of the museum's programming. Students who sang at the concerts "were simply invitees of the museum." Further, **the court found the school district's only responsibilities upon accepting the invitation from**

the museum were to arrange for the students to attend the concert and present the music. All other planning, public notices and details were handled by the museum. Finding the museum organized, sponsored and maintained the concerts, the court held the district was not liable under federal disability laws. *Ashby v. Warrick County School Corp.*, 908 F.3d 225 (7th Cir. 2018).

◆   In agreement with the law in many states, the Supreme Court of Oklahoma held a party seeking emotional distress damages must be a "direct victim" of injury rather than a mere "bystander" to an accident. For this reason, the court held the parents and siblings of a child who was injured after getting off a school bus could not recover damages in a personal injury lawsuit. As they were bystanders and not direct victims of the incident, a lower court had properly dismissed their emotional distress claims. Next, the court agreed with the parents that at this stage of the case, they asserted viable claims for wrongful, careless and negligent operation of the school bus. They also alleged failure to properly train and supervise the driver. **While it remained to be seen whether the driver was negligent and whether any breach of the duty to provide reasonable care to the child was foreseeable, the court held the case should proceed.** *Ridings v. Maze*, 414 P.3d 835 (Okla. 2018).

◆   **A North Carolina court held a school board had immunity in a case filed by a wheelchair-bound school visitor who claimed she was injured due to a fall caused by unsafe conditions.** The Court of Appeals of North Carolina held a recent state supreme court decision clarified that immunity applies to acts performed pursuant to a "governmental" function. State law vests school boards with ownership and control of school property. Since the conduct was "governmental" in nature, the board had immunity from any liability. *Bellows v. Asheville City Board of Educ.*, 777 S.E.2d 522 (N.C. Ct. App. 2015).

◆   A nurse slipped and fell on urine in a lavatory while assisting a student who had a seizure. She sued the district for negligence. A state court held for the school district, but an appellate court reversed, finding **issues of fact as to whether the district had notice of the hazardous condition** and sufficient time to clean up the floor. *Goodyear v. Putnam/Norther Westchester Board of Cooperative Educ. Services*, 927 N.Y.S.2d 373 (N.Y. App. Div. 2011).

◆   A New York child with severe autism hit and kicked an occupational therapist, who then sued the child's parents and the district for negligence. An appellate court upheld a ruling against the therapist because the parents had no ability to control their child in school. They had **no duty to warn the therapist because the therapist knew of the student's condition**, and it could also be readily observed. *Johnson v. Cantie*, 905 N.Y.S.2d 384 (N.Y. App. Div. 2010).

◆   A New York City special education teacher initiated a Type Three referral to remove an aggressive student from her class and contemplated quitting because of his behavior. Her supervisors told her to "hang in there" because a Type Three referral could take up to 60 days. Forty-one days after the referral was initiated, the student attacked another child, and the teacher intervened. She was hurt while attempting to protect the other child from the aggressor. She then sued the city for negligence, alleging that a "special relationship" supported her claim. A jury awarded her more than $512,000, but the New York Court of Appeals struck down the award. It noted that **the teacher had no rational basis for relying on the assurances of the board of education**. She was not lulled into a false sense of security that justified a finding of liability against the board. *DiNardo v. City of New York*, 921 N.E. 2d 585 (N.Y. 2009).

E. Suicide

Suicide has been viewed as an intervening act by the victim that breaks any chain of legal causation in a negligence action against a party such as a school district. Many courts have held a student suicide could not have been foreseen by school officials. Suicide cases are typically decided on the basis of state tort law, but some present constitutional and disability rights theories.

◆ Due to anxiety and depression, a New York student was hospitalized multiple times. According to her state-court complaint, her school district represented that she would have therapeutic support while she was at school. Without the school's knowledge, the student left school during a school day and went home. While at home, she tried to commit suicide. Over a year later, the family sued the school district in the state court system, asserting negligence, negligent supervision and negligent hiring, training and retention of school employees. The family sought damages from the district for psychological trauma, pain and suffering, loss of reputation and physical harm to the student.

During pretrial activity, the school district filed a motion for dismissal, arguing the complaint asserted a failure to provide adequate educational services under the IDEA. Under the district's theory, the family had to exhaust available IDEA administrative remedies prior to filing a lawsuit. The court agreed and dismissed the case. On appeal, a New York Appellate Division Court explained that the IDEA has elaborate procedures for resolving disputes. IDEA procedures must be used for claims under other federal laws when seeking relief that is available under the IDEA. However, **the claims in this case did not seek IDEA remedies but instead asserted common-law claims for the recovery of damages. These included negligence and negligent supervision.** Because the family was not seeking relief that could be obtained under the IDEA, the court held there was no requirement to exhaust IDEA administrative remedies before filing suit. Since the lower court should have denied the school district's motion for dismissal, the court reversed the judgment. *P.S. v. Pleasantville Union Free School Dist.*, 91 N.Y.S.3d 242 (N.Y. App. Div. 2019).

◆ Arkansas parents claimed school officials were liable for failing to protect their 16-year-old student with autism from bullying, which they alleged led her to commit suicide. In a federal court, they sued the district superintendent for discrimination in violation of Section 504 of the Rehabilitation Act. Finding insufficient evidence to support the action, the court held for the superintendent. The parents appealed to the Eighth Circuit, where they argued the district did not adequately address their bullying and harassment charges. **The court explained that in the context of education, a Section 504 claim requires a party to show school officials acted in bad faith or with gross misjudgment by departing substantially from accepted professional judgment, practice or standards.** The court found no evidence that school officials knew of specific bullying incidents before the student's death. In the court's view, any failure to address "such inchoate worries falls well short of establishing the level of bad faith or gross misjudgment needed to support a § 504 claim."

Further, the court held Section 504 "does not create general tort liability or educational malpractice." Even if it imported the "deliberate indifference" liability standard for sexual harassment claims under Title IX, it would not find district liability. There was no evidence that the student was the target of anything more than the kind of teasing and name-calling that the Supreme Court has held is not actionable. Last, the family cited no authority for the proposition that a school district can discriminate against a student after his death by failing to investigate harassment that might have occurred before he died. *Estate of Barnwell v. Watson*, 880 F.3d 998 (8th Cir. 2018).

◆   In a state court, the estate of a deceased California student claimed he ran from his third-period class because of peer bullying. He then gained access to the school roof and jumped off, killing himself. It was claimed that the suicide was caused by an uncontrollable impulse and that the school was on notice of daily harassment and bullying by peers. Further, the estate claimed the school used only "weak investigation techniques and took little or no action to curtail the abuse." In pretrial activity, the school district introduced evidence that the student had been fighting with a former girlfriend he had broken up with.

The school district argued there was no evidence of any bullying or harassment in the months prior to the student's suicide. A teacher testified that she observed nothing unusual about the student on the day of his death. The court held in the school district's favor. When the case reached the state court of appeal, it explained that **California law permits a finding of liability for a party whose negligent acts cause a person to have an uncontrollable suicidal impulse**. But if the suicidal person makes an independent decision to end his or her life, there is no liability for negligence. As the lower court found, the estate failed to show the student had an uncontrollable impulse to commit suicide. Since the estate could not show the student had an uncontrollable impulse to commit suicide, the court held the school district could not be held liable for his death. *Ferraro v. Glendale Unified School Dist.*, No. B262428, 2016 WL 2944268 (Cal. Ct. App. 5/17/16).

◆   New York parents could pursue discrimination claims against a school district based on the suicide death of a 17-year-old student, following a federal appeals court decision in their favor. **The court found the student's learning disability, which prompted a need for special education, constituted a substantial limitation on his major life activities.** As a result, it held the complaint stated sufficient facts to permit the estate to pursue discrimination claims under Section 504 and the ADA. Although the lower court's decision on the federal discrimination claims had to be reversed, the Second Circuit held the complaint did not establish any constitutional rights violations or any district-wide policy or custom of due process violations. Nor did the court find school officials were deliberately indifferent to peer harassment. *Spring v. Allegany-Limestone Cent. School Dist.*, 655 Fed.Appx. 25 (2d Cir. 2016).

◆ A 10-year-old Illinois student was found hanging by his shirt collar on the back of a school restroom stall door. He died the next day. A medical examiner ruled his death a suicide. In a state court, the student's mother sued the school district for negligence and willful and wanton conduct. The court dismissed the case, finding the district was entitled to immunity. But the mother was given permission to file a new complaint. After the court dismissed the case, she was allowed to file a third complaint. Unlike the first two complaints, the mother now claimed students at the school played a "hanging game" in the lavatory. She said police investigators found evidence that the game was being played in the stall where her son had been found hanging. The court held the mother again failed to show any evidence that the death was foreseeable to the school district. Regardless of whether the death was caused by suicide or a hanging game, the parent did not show any connection between the death and the district's actions.

On appeal, the Appellate Court of Illinois held no facts showed any special duty to the student or negligence in failing to alert teachers about his mental health history. No negligence regarding a hanging game was asserted. **Under Illinois law, a party may not recover in a tort case for suicide, because the act of suicide is an intervening event that is not foreseeable.** Even if the court had found the claims sufficient to proceed, the district would have immunity under the Illinois Tort Immunity Act. *Marshall v. Evanston Skokie School Dist. 65*, No. 1-13-1654, 2015 IL App (1st) 131654-U (Ill. Ct. App. 3/27/15).

◆ Alabama parents of a 15-year-old student with disabilities who committed suicide sought to impose federal law liability on school officials. They claimed the officials knew about peer harassment and bullying but failed to address it. A federal court rejected the parents' theory that any school employee named in the lawsuit had authority to take corrective action to end peer harassment. While the bullying alleged in this case was severe, the court rejected the family's claim that the bullying was so open and obvious that anyone at the school would know it was taking place. **Only actual knowledge of peer harassment could trigger school liability under Title IX of the 1972 Education Amendments.** Since the parents could not show an "appropriate person" with the authority to act to end the bullying had actual knowledge of any misconduct, the court held for the board of education. *Moore v. Chilton County Board of Educ.*, 1 F.Supp.3d 1281 (M.D. Ala. 2014).

◆ A Delaware teacher told an intervention specialist who contracted with her school district that a student was contemplating suicide. The specialist met with the student for four hours, decided he was feeling better and sent him back to class. Although the specialist emailed the student's teacher, an administrator and school counselors about the meeting, she did not advise the student's grandmother, who was his guardian. That evening, the student hanged himself at home. In a state court, his estate sued the school district under the state wrongful death statute. The court held for the district. On appeal, the Supreme Court of Delaware held the lower court had properly held for the school district on the wrongful death statute claim, as the district had no duty of care to prevent a suicide. No Delaware case suggested there could be liability for an injury to a high school student based on failure to alert medical professionals or parents.

Moreover, the suicide took place while he was at home and out of the school's custody. But the district maintained guidelines for handling suicidal ideation, and school counselors, nurses and psychologists had to follow them. The court found that the school protocol was created to comply with a state regulation requiring emergency preparedness guidelines for each school. The regulation called for schools to immediately contact the parents or guardians of a child who was clearly dangerous to himself or others. In the court's view, **failure to follow the mandated procedures of the protocol amounted to negligence per se**. The court reversed the judgment and returned the case to the lower court. *Rogers v. Christina School Dist.*, 73 A.3d 1 (Del. 2013).

II. LIABILITY FOR INTENTIONAL CONDUCT

Defamation, assault, battery and false imprisonment are some of the intentional tort theories of liability advanced in court actions against school districts and their employees. Courts have rejected constitutional claims based on intentional conduct except where a "special relationship" exists between the victim and school district and there is proof of an official policy of deliberate indifference to the victim's clearly established constitutional rights.

A. School Employees

◆   According to the parents of a child with autism spectrum disorder, the child came home from his elementary school with injuries such as bruising, abrasions and contusions over a two-year period. They said they had to take him to a hospital for treatment of his school injuries. When the parents reported the injuries to school officials, a school employee repeatedly speculated that the injuries were self-inflicted or caused by other students. Ultimately, the employee admitted injuring the student. In a federal court, the parents sued the school district and employee for a variety of causes, including assault, infliction of emotional distress, disability discrimination in violation of the Americans with Disabilities Act (ADA) and constitutional rights violations.

The court granted qualified immunity to the employee and school district on the constitutional claims asserted under 42 U.S.C. § 1983. It found the parents only asserted vague, conclusory allegations. As a result, this part of the complaint was dismissed. Turning to the tort claim for infliction of emotional distress, the court held **the employee properly invoked a Texas law barring claims against employees of a governmental unit by a party who has already filed suit against the employing governmental unit regarding the same subject matter based on election of remedies**. Next, the court agreed with the school district that the assault claim was an intentional tort for which state sovereign immunity had not been waived. As the Supreme Court of Texas has clearly held that all tort theories against a state governmental unit arise under the Texas Tort Claims Act, the court dismissed the assault claim. Last, the court agreed with the school district that the ADA claim sought relief that was also available under the IDEA. Since the parents did not exhaust their IDEA administrative remedies, the ADA claim was dismissed. As none of the claims survived, the court dismissed the case. *Colin v. Fort Worth Independent School Dist.*, No. 4:18-CV-330-A, 2018 WL 4078272 (N.D. Tex. 8/27/18).

◆   Washington parents filed an action seeking reimbursement for educational expenses, private school placement, private tutoring, transportation costs, legal fees and related costs. In addition to naming the school district as a party, they sought to hold school district officials liable for these costs in their individual capacities. A federal court held the officials had no liability for the claims. In the court's view, the right to reimbursement originates from a school district's failure to provide appropriate education, not the actions of employees. **Given the language and intent of the IDEA, the court found the appropriate redress for IDEA violations is against a school district.** Over a year after the district court issued its decision, the court again denied judgment to the parents, who then appealed to the U.S. Court of Appeals, Ninth Circuit. *Crofts v. Issaquah School Dist.*, No. C17-1365RAJ, 2018 WL 1517671 (W.D. Wash. 3/28/18; 9th Cir. appeal filed 6/3/19).

◆   The parent of a nonverbal child with autism claimed a school bus monitor assaulted the child on a school bus. The complaint stated that the monitor hit the child with a rolled-up folder. Then, less than a week later, the monitor allegedly hit the child with a seat belt buckle. The complaint included claims against the bus monitor and the school district for constitutional violations. Among the charges against the district were failure to hire competent personnel and the failure to adequately train, educate, supervise or control its employees with respect to nonverbal students with disabilities. The court held the parent did not show harm resulted from some official custom or policy attributable to the district. As the parent did not show the bus monitor's acts resulted from a district policy and asserted no pattern of prior incidents, the court held the district was entitled to dismissal of the claims against it. An equal protection claim against the bus monitor failed because the parent did not show her child was treated differently from other similarly situated students in the district.

As for the claim against the bus monitor, the court found the incident involving bodily contact with a rolled-up folder did not amount to conduct that shocks the conscience. On the other hand, the assertion that the bus monitor hit the child with a belt buckle required further development of the facts. The parent was allowed 10 days to file papers asserting specific facts that might substantiate a due process violation by the monitor. **In order to prevail, she would have to allege specific facts that would show the bus monitor violated her son's right to bodily integrity through actions that were objectively unreasonable in view of clearly established law.** *Saldana v. Angleton Independent School Dist.*, No. 3:16-CV-159, 2017 WL 749292 (S.D. Tex. 2/27/17).

◆   An Indiana parent claimed his sixth-grade child with special needs was illegally disciplined at school. She said her son's teacher choked him, hit his head against a wall and dragged him down a hallway by the neck after a confrontation with another student. After learning of the incident from a school therapist, she protested to staff and police. Later, the parent sued the school district and its superintendent in a federal court. She asserted a state disciplinary code provision is unconstitutional under the Indiana Constitution and requested both monetary damages and injunctive relief. She added other claims, including liability in tort for the teacher's actions. After dismissing the superintendent from the case, the court found state law provides that in all matters relating to student conduct and discipline, school personnel stand in the relation of parents to students.

Staff members have immunity for reasonable disciplinary action taken in good faith. **Indiana's highest court has found state law creates no explicit civil remedy for constitutional violations by individual officers or governmental entities.** Indiana courts have held there is no state constitutional action for damages, when existing tort law amply protects rights assured by the Indiana Constitution. For this reason, the court found the student's damage claim had to be dismissed. Nor could he pursue an action for injunctive relief seeking to enjoin enforcement of the statute. Next, the court held the federal constitutional claims against the school district had to be dismissed. Although the student claimed the district was liable for failure to train its employees in relevant aspects in a manner that showed deliberate indifference to his rights, the court found this to be a conclusory argument. In the court's view, the complaint did not include facts which would plausibly suggest a federal constitutional violation. Last, the court dismissed the student's claims for assault, battery, false imprisonment and infliction of emotional distress. *Orr v. Ferebee*, No. 1:16-cv-02610-RLY-DML, 2017 WL 1509309 (S.D. Ind. 4/27/17).

◆   A Texas student used a wheelchair and had limited verbal and cognitive skills. During his early teen years, he was repeatedly mistreated by a special education teacher at his public school. Because he could not tell his parents about it, they did not complain until they noticed physical injuries such as a broken thumb, a dislocated knee and skull contusions. When the parents reported their concerns, they learned a classroom aide had reported misconduct by the teacher years earlier, but that nothing was done to remove the teacher.

The parents sued the school district in a federal court, asserting claims under the Americans with Disabilities Act (ADA) and Section 504. They added claims for their medical costs and physical and mental injuries on their son's behalf, and for mental suffering on their behalf. After an eight-day jury trial, a verdict of $850,000 was awarded to the student. The verdict included an award to the parents of $150,000 for mental anguish under Section 504 and the ADA. After the trial, the school district learned that a bank served as the student's guardian as the result of a trust set up during his early childhood. The court granted the district's request to dismiss the case, finding that as the bank was the student's guardian, the parents lacked standing to bring an action on his behalf. On appeal, the Fifth Circuit Court of Appeals held the school district's arguments did not go to the issue of standing. It found the parents suffered an economic injury. Despite the existence of the trust, the parents received the medical bills related to this case and the mother was the obligated party on them. The fact that the student had a trust based on injuries during his infancy was a "fortuity." As the parents made an understandable mistake, the lower court should have avoided forfeiture of the verdict by allowing the bank to ratify their action. **But the court held the parents could not recover the damages for their own mental anguish, as neither the ADA nor Section 504 authorize such claims.** *Rideau v. Keller Independent School Dist.,* 819 F.3d 155 (5th Cir. 2016).

◆   An openly gay Oregon student with disabilities said a teacher told him "shut up, I'll kill you," then threatened to throw him down stairs. The student claimed school district employees had previously subjected him to hostile and discriminatory conduct. He said the dean of students called him a "girl" and another teacher called him "diva" and "priss." Further, the student said the school principal refused to speak to him about these incidents and failed to enforce relevant school policies. The student said he was removed from school because of the incidents and denied a public education. In pretrial activity before a federal court, the student voluntarily dismissed some of the individual school employees from the lawsuit. The court then considered a few of the remaining constitutional claims against school staff members.

Based on the student's assertion that failure to train and supervise school staff violated the First Amendment, the court denied pretrial motions for dismissal by the teacher, the district superintendent and school principal. Next, the court held he could pursue his equal protection claims against the principal and the superintendent. In doing so, **the court found this claim was based on a theory that the district removed the student from school based on his homosexuality**. But the equal protection claims against the teacher and another staff member accused of discriminating against the student were dismissed. The court found the complaint did not assert that their improper actions deprived the student of his equal protection rights. *J.D. v. Hillsboro School Dist.,* No. 3:15-cv-02328-SI, 2016 WL 3085900 (D. Or. 5/31/16).

◆   New York parents said a school bus monitor physically and mentally abused their severely disabled child on a school bus. Asserting the school district knew of the monitor's propensity for misconduct, the parents sued her and the school district in a state court for negligence, assault and battery. After the court held for the bus monitor and the district, the parents appealed. A New York Appellate Division Court recited the general rule that **schools have a duty to adequately supervise students in their care and may be held liable for foreseeable injuries related to the absence of adequate supervision**. In this case, there was evidence that the school received prior complaints of the bus driver's misbehavior toward children on the school bus. As a result, the court reversed the judgment on the claim for negligent supervision of the child.

Similarly, the court held the claims for negligent supervision and training of the monitor should not have been dismissed. It held the parents had to show the district knew (or should have known) of the monitor's propensity for the conduct causing injury. Since the school district failed to prove it had no specific knowledge of the monitor's propensity to engage in misconduct, the negligent supervision and training claim would also return to the trial court. As the parents had established a preliminary case for assault, the case was returned to the lower court for reconsideration. *Timothy Mc. v. Beacon City School Dist.*, 127 A.D.3d 826, 7 N.Y.S.3d 348 (N.Y. App. Div. 2015).

B. Abuse and Sexual Abuse Reporting

In Walker v. State of Maryland, *432 Md. 587, 69 A.3d 1066 (Md. 2013), Maryland's highest court held that intimate though not sexually explicit letters from a paraeducator to an eight-year-old student with disabilities supported a sexual abuse conviction. In affirming the paraeducator's prison sentence of 13 years, the court held "sexual abuse" was not limited to specified acts of incest, rape, sexual offense, sodomy and other practices listed in the statute.*

◆   A Colorado teacher learned her husband was abusing of their daughter, but did not report it. She also allowed him to continue giving private music lessons to children in their home. A parent of one of the daughter's friends reported the abuse, prompting the teacher to respond: "Why are you trying to ruin my life?" In later court proceedings, the teacher pleaded guilty to a misdemeanor abuse charge. When she applied to renew her teacher's license, the state board of education denied it, based on "immoral conduct and unethical behavior regarding her failure to report the abuse of her daughter." Before an administrative law judge (ALJ), the teacher claimed she had battered woman syndrome and was trying to keep her family together. Among other things, the ALJ found the teacher engaged in unethical behavior that offended the morals of the community. Moreover, her failure to report jeopardized the children who received private music lessons from her husband. In an order denying her license application, the state board adopted the ALJ's findings. A state court later upheld the order.

On appeal, the state court of appeals found the state board of education could deny a license application based on incompetent or unethical behavior. Finding no requirement that a law must include a range of sanctions to satisfy due process, the court rejected the teacher's constitutional arguments. Next, the teacher argued her conviction had been improper because the mandatory reporting law did not list parents as individuals who have a duty to report child abuse. The court rejected her arguments, holding **that Colorado teachers are required to report any known or suspected child abuse or neglect without limit to whether the knowledge or suspicion occurs in a professional capacity**. Finding substantial evidence supported denying the teacher's application, the court affirmed the board's decision. *Heotis v. Colorado State Board of Educ.*, No. 18CA0057, 2019 COA 35 (Colo. Ct. App. 3/7/19).

◆   A New York teacher called a parent to report her child was being defiant and had falsely accused her of hurting her. The parent came to school and took the child home. While at home, the parent struck the child with her hand and a belt. She then returned the child to school. The child told the teacher that her parent had struck her. When the school social worker was advised of the incident, she stated that a report should be made to Child Protection Services

(CPS). After calling CPS, school staff reported physical abuse and the fact that counseling had been recommended for the child. Following an investigation, the CPS closed the case as unfounded. The parent sued the school district, principal and social worker in a federal court. In pretrial activity, the court dismissed the parent's claims based on violation of due process rights to intimate association, infliction of emotional distress and municipal liability.

Months later, the district and officials sought to dismiss the retaliation and defamation claims. The court found the parent produced no evidence of an improper motive by school officials. In their roles as mandatory reporters, school officials have immunity from liability whenever they make a report in good faith. Given the difficult role imposed upon educators, the court gave unusual deference to their reporting decisions. It found the principal and social worker had reasonable cause to suspect the parent may have abused the student. No evidence indicated they called the CPS to retaliate against the parent for voicing complaints. Since the parent's complaint was too attenuated to support a claim for retaliation, the court dismissed the case. **On appeal, the U.S. Court of Appeals, Second Circuit, held school administrators are given deference in their decisions to report reasonably suspected abuse and neglect.** It found the report was non-retaliatory. Rejecting the parent's remaining arguments, the court affirmed the judgment for the school district. *Maco v. Baldwin Union Free School Dist.*, 726 Fed.Appx. 37 (2d Cir. 2018).

◆   A Kentucky student had 13 unexcused absences. Rather than face a petition for educational neglect, his parents withdrew him from school and placed him in a private school. The next school year, they returned him to a public school, where he resumed his pattern of poor attendance. After he reached seven unexcused absences or tardies, the county board of education petitioned a family court for educational neglect. In family court proceedings, the parents explained that most of their son's absences and tardies were due to sleeping in and/or behavior issues. They argued the case actually fell under the state's compulsory attendance laws, as it sought to adjudicate their child's status. School officials argued his unexcused absences and tardies supported a finding of educational neglect. The family court agreed with the officials and held the petition supported educational neglect findings. The parents appealed to the Court of Appeals of Kentucky, where they argued the action was an attempt to enforce the compulsory attendance law. Rejecting this argument, the court found **Kentucky statutes do not create a single, specific action for the enforcement of compulsory school attendance**. Evidence indicated a pattern of unexcused school absences and tardies, which the parents did not justify. **The family court could reasonably find they neglected their child's educational needs.** *M.B. and K.B. v. Comwlth. of Kentucky*, No. 2016-CA-001761-ME, 2018 WL 1773515 (Ky. Ct. App. 4/13/18).

◆   A New Jersey student with disabilities lived with his grandparents and uncle. At an IEP meeting, school staff brought up the student's hygiene and body odor. The family members acknowledged that his grooming habits were inadequate, and the uncle told staff he had gotten into the shower with the student three times to show him how to wash. Two staff members called the state Division of Youth and Family Services (DYFS) and reported the shared showers. According to the family, the student's case worker told the DYFS that the uncle cohabitated with a male partner and is gay. A DYFS phone screener told the school staff that the information did not constitute abuse. But the case worker and a school social worker later called the DYFS back and questioned the decision not to take further action. The DYFS investigated, then concluded nothing improper had taken place. Later, the student reported bullying at school. Although the family said peers called him "gay," a school investigation did not corroborate this. The grandmother filed an emergency petition for home services, leading to a private school placement. The family sued the school district and officials in a federal court. They raised claims under the Americans with Disabilities Act, Rehabilitation Act Section 504 and the New Jersey Law Against Discrimination (NJLAD). The court held the retaliation claims failed.

In the court's view, the calls to DYFS were made based on a good-faith belief that the student was abused or improperly supervised. The family admitted the student's hygiene problems and an audiotape confirmed the uncle's statement that he had gotten into the shower to show him how to wash. The court found no issue of the staff members' legitimate child welfare concerns. In ruling for the school district and staff, **the court commented that schools are required to notify law enforcement and child protection authorities when potential child abuse is detected**. The court held staff should not be penalized for taking a short time to reflect on the appropriateness of the decision to call the DYFS. The court found no school liability under the NJLAD and federal antidiscrimination laws. As a reasonable jury could not find the district failed to act reasonably to end sexual orientation harassment, the court held in its favor. *D.V. v. Pennsauken School Dist.*, 247 F.Supp.3d 464 (D.N.J. 2017).

◆ A federal court refused to dismiss constitutional claims by the parents of an Oklahoma child with autism who charged a school district with retaliating against them for their advocacy on his behalf. The parents sued the district and several employees in a federal court for multiple violations of federal law. The court refused to dismiss a First Amendment retaliation claim against the district and three employees. **In future proceedings, the court would consider the validity of the parents' claims that school employees contacted child protection authorities after the parents advocated on behalf of a new IEP for their child.** But the court agreed with the district that the parents could not proceed with a state constitutional claim based on excessive force. *Roe v. Doe*, No. CIV-16-695-M, 2016 WL 7116194 (W.D. Okla. 12/6/16).

◆ An Ohio preschool teacher noticed a three-year-old child had a bloodshot eye. When she asked what happened, he gave conflicting answers. The teacher brought the child under the light and noticed red marks on his face. She told the lead teacher, who lifted the child's shirt and noticed more injuries. After some prodding, the child identified his mother's boyfriend as the perpetrator. One of the teachers called a child protection hotline to report suspected abuse. When the boyfriend arrived at school to pick up the child, he denied responsibility for the injuries and quickly left with the child. The next day, a social worker took the child and his 18-month old sister from their grandparent's home. A doctor discovered injuries suggesting child abuse. The child had a black eye, belt marks and bruises. His sister had black eyes, a swollen hand, a large burn, and two of her pigtails had been ripped out at the roots. At the boyfriend's criminal trial, the court allowed the child's statements to his teachers to come into evidence. In doing so, the court denied the boyfriend's attempt to exclude the statements from evidence under the Confrontation Clause of the Constitution.

A jury found the boyfriend guilty on all but one of the counts, and he was sentenced to 28 years in prison. But he obtained reversal by higher courts in the Ohio court system, which held the child's statements were "testimonial" and geared toward gathering evidence, not in response to an emergency. On appeal, the Supreme Court noted the state court's view that the teachers acted as state agents under a mandatory reporting law, implicating the Confrontation Clause of the Sixth Amendment to the U.S. Constitution. In the Court's view, **the child's statements took place in the context of an ongoing emergency involving suspected child abuse and were not made with the primary purpose of creating evidence** for the prosecution. Use of his statements did not violate the Confrontation Clause. When teachers noticed the injuries, they "rightly became worried" that the child was a victim of serious violence. They needed to know whether it was safe to release him to his guardian and to find the source of his injuries. The teachers were not sure who had abused the child and how to secure his safety. Since the teachers' questioning was primarily aimed at identifying and ending the threat of harm to the child, the Court held for the state. *Ohio v. Clark*, 135 S.Ct. 2173, 192 L.E.2d 306 (U.S. 2015).

◆   An Ohio school administrator told teachers to document comments by a 17-year-old student. One of the teachers noted that during a classroom discussion about menstruation and hygiene, the student said her "dad puts her tampons in her and it really hurts her." The teacher also noted the student said "sometimes she and her dad lick each other on the faces and necks" and "her whole family hangs around the house naked sometimes." In addition, the teacher wrote the child told her "her Dad put her cream on her vagina for her."

Despite knowledge of the parent's strange comments, the administrator told the teachers not to report them. When she finally made a report to child protection authorities, she added irrelevant information about the father, describing him as "unkempt," "creepy" and obsessed about a boyfriend for his daughter. A criminal investigation of the father was dropped, and he sued several officials in a federal court. When the case reached the U.S. Court of Appeals, Sixth Circuit, it agreed with the parent that the administrator's report was motivated at least in part by his protected conduct. **A child abuse report that was made for a partly retaliatory motive could be grounds for liability,** even if there was some evidence of a reasonable basis to suspect child abuse or neglect. The court held the administrator would not be entitled to immunity in the case. *Wenk v. O'Reilly*, 783 F.3d 585 (6th Cir. 2015).

◆   Georgia parents of a child with severe disabilities claimed her teacher was abusive to the special needs students in her classroom. They sued the teacher, principal and school district in a federal court. In response, the principal filed a counterclaim against the student and crossclaims against the school district and several members of the board of education. She argued the district had to provide her legal defense. The court noted that after an investigation into the charges, the principal and district had entered into a settlement agreement.

Although the principal argued the agreement bound the district to provide her defense, the court found the agreement provided the board with discretion on the issue. Georgia law provided school boards with discretion to pay such expenses in a civil case against an employee for their acts or omissions. In sum, **the court found the district and board were not obligated to provide the principal a legal defense in the abuse case**. Rejecting the principal's other arguments, the court held for the school district and board members. *Persadi v. Fulton County School Dist.*, 24 F.Supp.3d 1249 (N.D. Ga. 2014).

C. Parents and Other Third Parties

◆ The parents of two students who died on the day of the mass shooting at Sandy Hook Elementary School sued the board of education in a state court for negligence. The court reviewed evidence that an intruder shot out the glass by the door of the school and entered the building at about 9:35 a.m. on a school day. Upon hearing the shots, the principal and a school psychologist left a planning and placement team meeting to investigate. They were almost immediately shot to death. A teacher was shot but was able to crawl back to the room. A parent called 911, believing the shooter was still outside the room.

In their state court action, the parents claimed the board had a ministerial (non-discretionary) duty to create, enforce and abide by rules and regulations for school management, safety and emergency responses. According to the parents, the school was unable to implement required safety protocols on the day of the shooting, even though harm was "imminent and apparent," resulting in the deaths of their children. The court held the parents did not counter the board's claim to governmental immunity for the discretionary acts of the employees. A ministerial act is one to be performed in a prescribed manner without the exercise of discretion or judgment. By contrast, a discretionary act requires the exercise of judgment. As the school board argued, the statutes cited by the parents did not impose a ministerial duty. State law deems student supervision a discretionary duty. **Since emergencies are by nature sudden and based on rapidly evolving events, "a response can never be one hundred percent scripted and directed." The court found school officials were entitled to the same broad discretion as are police.** *Lewis v. Newtown Board of Educ.*, No. CV 15607650S, 2018 WL 2419001 (Conn. Super. Ct. 5/7/18).

◆ A Montana parent said a high school teacher "got physical" with his child due to a disability issue. When attempting to visit the school principal about the incident, the parent said "the volume of his voice increased" due to his "documented disability." He was deemed no longer welcome at the school and would be charged as a trespasser if he returned. But the parent later returned to school to deliver a list of accommodations for his child. A school resource officer met him at the door and told him he could not go on school property. He was given a written notice that he was excluded from school property and that his child was suspended from school. The parent claimed the principal's act of excluding him from the school, and the use of the resource officer as an intermediary constituted unlawful intimidation or coercion. He claimed these actions denied him access to participation in his son's education, as well as retaliation. In a federal court, the parent sued the school district, principal and a special education supervisor for violating the Americans with Disabilities Act (ADA). In addition to seeking to vindicate his own rights, the parent sought reasonable accommodations for his child, and an order allowing him on school grounds. **The court held that at this stage of the case, the parent stated an ADA claim and could pursue his case.** *Lagervall v. Missoula County Public Schools*, No. CV 16-57-M-DLC-JCL, 2016 WL 3282194 (D. Mont. 6/14/16).

A federal court approved the report and recommendation of the magistrate judge, agreeing that the school district did not violate the parents' rights. *Lagervall v. Missoula County Public Schools*, No. CV 16-57-M-DLC-JCL, 2017 WL 4896103 (D. Mont. 10/30/17).

◆   A California parent accused the principal of his children's elementary school of making racist comments. Claiming student and staff safety concerns, the district posted a deputy outside the school. The parent came to the district office and told an official that the principal "should stay away from his children because [she] had made racist slurs to them." The official said the parent then said if the principal did not stay away from his children "it will be a bad day."

Next, the parent distributed flyers at the school containing a racial epithet and criticism of the principal that caused some parents to remove their children from the school. The school district obtained a temporary restraining order from a state court that required the parent to remain 100 yards away from the principal and her two daughters. Later, the court denied a request for an order that would keep the parent off all school property and issued an order protecting the principal for three years. On appeal, the Court of Appeal of California stated that **employers in the state may obtain workplace restraining orders for an employee who has "suffered unlawful violence or a credible threat of violence from any individual, that can reasonably be construed to be carried out or to have been carried out at the workplace."** The lower court was entitled to rely on events that took place prior to the current school year. While some of the parent's conduct was protected, there was evidence that his threatening behavior caused staff members to reasonably fear him. The court affirmed the lower court's order for workplace protection, as well as the judgment against the parent on his speech rights claim. *Poway Unified School Dist. v. Garnier*, No. D067571, 2016 WL 6247683 (Cal. Ct. App. 10/26/16).

◆   An Oklahoma parent claimed his child's school district repeatedly denied services to his son and retaliated against him by filing a false report with a state agency. He claimed the false report by school authorities led to a juvenile proceeding against his son based on a fabricated incident. In a federal court, the parent sued the school district and two school officials for constitutional rights violations. He did so without the assistance of an attorney, bringing some claims on his own behalf and others on behalf of his son. In his complaint, the parent stated his son was suspended from school for about half of a school year. He said school officials lied under oath at the hearing. As for relief, the parent sought a declaration that school officials violated his First Amendment rights. He asked for an order prohibiting school officials from their course of conduct, plus an award of monetary damages. After explaining that the parent was entitled to pursue claims on his own behalf, the court held he could not pursue claims on behalf of his son without an attorney. It dismissed the claims on behalf of the student, which could be revived with the assistance of counsel.

In the court's view, **none of the actions attributed to school officials could be linked to any constitutionally protected activity by the parent**. Any alleged retaliation was directed solely at the student. At most, the parent could show that two school officials lied under oath at the hearing. Since there was no claim that officials acted with the intent to retaliate against the parent or student, the court found the claims should be dismissed. But the parent could refile the claims on behalf of his son if he hired an attorney. *Wright v. Tanner*, No. 16-CV-117-CVE-PJC, 2016 WL 4991619 (N.D. Okla. 9/16/2016).

D. Corporal Punishment

Mississippi law prohibits public school teachers, assistant teachers, principals, assistant principals or other school personnel from using corporal punishment on any student with a disability. In addition to prohibiting school personnel from corporally punishing students with disabilities, the amended law removes any immunity from liability for the use of corporal punishment on a student with a disability. "Student with a disability" is defined as a student who has an IEP or a Section 504 plan under the Rehabilitation Act. Mississippi 2019 Session Laws, H.B. 1182, Mississippi Statutes § 37–11–57.

Arkansas law prohibits school districts from using corporal punishment on a child who is intellectually disabled, non-ambulatory, non-verbal, or autistic. Districts are forbidden from including student discipline policy provisions that allow the use of corporal punishment on a child who is intellectually disabled, non-ambulatory, non-verbal, or autistic. A teacher or administrator is not immune from civil liability if the teacher or administrator uses corporal punishment on a child who is intellectually disabled, non-ambulatory, non-verbal, or autistic. A similar provision applies to employees and volunteers. Ninety-Second Arkansas General Assembly, 2019 Arkansas Laws Act 557. S.B. 381. Arkansas Code §§ 6–17–112, 6–17–1113, 6–18–503, 6–18–505.

Louisiana legislators acted to prohibit all forms of corporal punishment to a student with an exceptionality, excluding gifted and talented students. Students with IEPs or Section 504 plans are not to be corporally punished in schools. Corporal punishment means "using physical force to discipline a student, with or without an object." This includes hitting, paddling, striking, spanking, slapping or other physical force to cause pain or discomfort, but does not include reasonable and necessary restraint to protect a student or others from bodily harm or to disarm a student. The definition of corporal punishment excludes the use of restraint and seclusion under state law. Louisiana 2017 Regular Session, Act 266, H.B. No. 79. Louisiana R.S. §§ 17:223, 17:416.1.

In Miller v. Monroe School Dist., *this chapter, a federal court rejected a constitutional challenge to a school district's use of aversive procedures on an eight-year-old student with autism. Citing Ninth Circuit authority, the court held "there is no statutory requirement of perfect adherence to the IEP, nor any reason rooted in the statutory text to view minor implementation failures as denials of a free appropriate public education." See* Van Duyn v. Baker School Dist. 5J, *502 F.3d 811 (9th Cir. 2007).*

◆   A Michigan teacher grabbed a moderately disabled preschooler by the head and jerked it back aggressively while yelling in his face. When she was called into a meeting with school administrators, the teacher denied grabbing or yelling and maintained she was only redirecting the student after he made a mess. Finding the teacher's explanation plausible, the administrators sent her back to her classroom. Later in the month, a paraprofessional in the teacher's classroom was accused of spanking a child in the classroom. After an investigation, the school district placed both the teacher and paraprofessional on leave. Later, the teacher was dismissed. The student's parent sued the school district, administrators and teacher in a federal court. The court held for the district, administrators and teacher. On appeal, the U.S. Court of Appeals, Sixth Circuit, found the teacher had a pedagogical justification for her actions.

Requiring a child to clean up a mess he made reflected a common-sense understanding of what teachers typically do and also complied with the expectations of his IEP. Even if the teacher used excessive force, the court found a due process analysis favored the teacher and school district. While grabbing a student and yelling in his face might have been inappropriate and insensitive, it did not shock the conscience in a manner that would create liability under the Due Process Clause. Next, the court found the parent did not show the teacher, school district or administrators violated federal anti-discrimination laws as she did not show intentional discrimination or produce enough evidence for a reasonable jury to show her son was denied participation in (or a benefit of) his educational program solely by reason of a disability. Evidence showed the student was progressing in his IEP goals and his behavior was improving. As no reasonable jury could find discrimination by reason of a disability or any constitutional violation, the lower court had correctly disposed of the federal claims. *Gohl v. Livonia Public Schools School Dist.,* 836 F.3d 672 (6th Cir. 2016).

Without opinion, the Supreme Court refused to review the decision. *Gohl v. Livonia Public Schools,* 138 S.Ct. 56 (U.S. cert. denied 10/2/17).

The case returned to the trial court, which dismissed some of the claims but granted the parent's motion for reconsideration. Although a new appeal was made to the Sixth Circuit, the parties agreed to dismiss the case. *Doe v. Livonia Public Schools,* No. 18-2306, 2019 WL 2056683 (6th Cir. 4/3/19).

◆   An Iowa fifth-grader with "a multitude of behavioral issues" left his class without permission. When a teacher found him in a hallway, he falsely told her he had permission to be there. The student's mother was called, and she came to the school. At the school, the student made no comment about being grabbed or hurt. But on the way home, he told his mother the teacher hurt him. Two days later, the mother said she observed fingerprint-shaped bruises on the student's arm. She did not mention an injury until her child had another behavior incident at school five days later. The principal suspended the teacher for making physical contact with the student. After a hearing, an administrative law judge (ALJ) found the teacher injured the student. Despite finding the incident was an "isolated mistake" in an otherwise spotless teaching career, the ALJ found a one-year suspension was justified. The state board of educational examiners upheld the ALJ's decision, with some modifications. A state court affirmed the suspension, and the teacher appealed to the Court of Appeals of Iowa. **Based on concern about the use of suggestive, leading questions, the student's reputation for lying and failure of the nurse and principal to independently investigate the charges, the court held there was no substantial evidence to support the suspension.** *Babe v. Iowa Board of Educational Examiners*, No. 17-0213, 2018 WL 1098923, 913 N.W.2d 275 (Table) (Iowa Ct. App. 2/21/18).

◆   A group of California parents claimed a teacher taped their children's hands to their desks using painter's tape and sat on them to restrain them. In a federal court, the families alleged excessive force and deliberate indifference to the use of force, and claimed school officials violated their due process rights by intentionally interfering with their familial relationships. The court held the due process claims should proceed. According to the parents, their children were "hit, dragged, manhandled, screamed at and improperly restrained — including use of rubber bungee cords and painter's tape to hold their legs and arms to their desks." Moreover, the parents said their children were routinely subjected to the teacher's cruelty. Since the children were young, vulnerable and had significant disabilities, they could not communicate to their parents about the abuse taking place at school. Finding **the charges were shocking to the conscience under both the Fourth and Fourteenth Amendments to the Constitution**, the court refused to dismiss the case. *Hugunin v. Rocklin Unified School Dist.,* No. 2:15-cv-00939-MCE-DB, 2017 WL 202536 (E.D. Cal. 1/17/17).

◆   A Washington child's IEP included an aversive intervention plan (AIP) and a behavior intervention plan (BIP) authorizing the use of restraint and seclusion. Crisis management strategies in the child's BIP grew progressively more restrictive if his behavior became unsafe, culminating with seclusion in a room with a closed door. Only six days into his third-grade school year, his parent removed him from school because he had been subjected to aversive interventions 10 times. After the state superintendent of public instruction found the district did not comply with the student's plans, the parties agreed that the child should attend a structured learning classroom. But the child was subjected to aversive interventions three times in his first five days at his new school. The parent again removed him from school and notified the district of her intent to provide homebound services. The parent filed a due process complaint against the school district, challenging the use of aversive interventions. She filed a separate federal case against the district, its board and staff for federal disability law and constitutional rights violations. In federal court activity, the court found no constitutional rights violations, since **the child's AIP permitted properly conducted holds and seclusion. But the court found sufficient evidence for the parent to proceed with federal disability discrimination claims.** A jury would have to decide whether teachers acted with deliberate indifference to the student's rights and whether the district's failure to intervene was deliberately indifferent. Claims under the Washington Law Against Discrimination – as well as negligence and related claims – would also go forward. Meanwhile, a state administrative law judge resolved the due process hearing in the district's favor.

The parent appealed to a federal court, claiming the use of aversive interventions denied her child a free appropriate public education. The court explained that the child was never truly placed in "isolation," as a teacher or paraeducator was always with him in his quiet room. Since the child was never left alone, he was not isolated as defined by state law. In addition, the court found no violation of any IEP provisions. And while the child was sometimes kept in his quiet room for more than 20 minutes, the court found he asked for more time to calm down on at least one occasion. **Exceeding the 20-minute limit was found a "technical violation" that did not harm the student.** Since the aversive interventions did not materially violate the IDEA, the court affirmed the ALJ's decision for the school district. *Miller v. Monroe School Dist.*, No. C15-1323-JCC, 2016 WL 4061582 (W.D. Wash. 7/29/16).

E. Restraint and Seclusion

◆   An Ohio teacher and school administrators were held not liable in a civil rights action by the parent of a student with autism who suffered injuries after he fell while wearing a gown referred to as a "body sock" that was used to calm him down. Although the student's IEP called for occupational therapy to address his sensory processing needs, it did not specify the use of a body sock. In a federal court, the student's parent sued the teacher, board of education, school district and others. After the court held for the board, the parent appealed to the U.S. Court of Appeals, Sixth Circuit. **It found there was a pedagogical justification for the use of the body sock and no excessive force.** *Crochran v. Columbus City Schools*, 748 Fed.Appx. 682 (6th Cir. 2018).

◆   A Kentucky in-school security employee restrained a sixth-grader while trying to remove him from a classroom. He tried to use a safe crisis management maneuver to bring the student under control. The student said the employee pressed his knee to the floor while restraining his hands behind his back, causing an injury. Later, the student sued the employee, the county board of education, the principal and district superintendent in a state court. According to the student, the board, superintendent and principal failed to prevent his injuries by negligently hiring, supervising, retaining and training the employee. The student added negligence and infliction of emotional distress claims against the employee. During pretrial activity, the court found the board, principal and superintendent had immunity under state law. The principal and superintendent had immunity under the federal Coverdell Teacher Liability Protection Act.

While the court dismissed the infliction of emotional distress claim against the security employee, it denied pretrial judgment on the negligence claim against him. The court found the employee's possible violations of law, if proven, would not be afforded immunity under federal law. As a result, the court denied his request to dismiss the negligence claim and the assault and battery claim. On appeal, the employee argued he was entitled to immunity under the Coverdell Act because the student did not prove he violated state, federal or local laws and he was not guilty of gross negligence, criminal misconduct or reckless misconduct. **The Court of Appeals of Kentucky held the Coverdell Act affords teachers and other educators immunity from liability, not immunity from suit.** In the court's view, the Coverdell Act does not guarantee that a trial will not occur. As the act provides only an exemption from liability and not complete immunity from suit, the court dismissed the employee's appeal. *Steffan v. Smyzer*, 540 S.W.3d 387 (Ky. Ct. App. 2018).

◆ A Colorado student with Down syndrome and other disabilities, who had been born addicted to cocaine, was sometimes placed in a wrap-around desk at her school that prevented her from pushing the chair out. She could escape by sliding under the restraining bar or crawling over the table. Her mother, concerned about her lack of progress and the belief that the school district was using the wrap-around desk more than for disciplinary reasons, revoked her consent for use of the desk. School staff continued using the desk until the student went home with a broken arm one day. Although the Tenth Circuit Court of Appeals rejected the student's constitutional claims in 2012, it held her federal disability discrimination claims should proceed to a trial. In 2013, the U.S. Supreme Court refused to consider the case, and the dispute later came before a jury. After the jury reached a verdict for the student, **the trial court entered a final judgment in her favor for $2.2 million plus post-judgment interest**. The trial court later granted the school district's motion to stay execution of the judgment pending appeal. *Ebonie S. v. Pueblo School Dist. 60*, Civ. No. 09-cv-00858-WJM-MEH, 2015 WL 4245831 (D. Colo. 7/14/15).

In a later order, the court approved an award of $977,900 in attorneys' fees plus additional expenses of $123,460.22. *Ebonie S. v. Pueblo School Dist. 60*, Civ. No. 09-cv-00858-WJM-MEH, 2016 WL 1110442 (D. Colo. 3/22/16).

◆ The mother of a New Jersey student filed a due process challenge to their school district's failure to provide an aide. She claimed her son was disciplined for behavior that was a manifestation of his disabilities. She became frustrated with the district's use of restraints and kept him home for the last six weeks of the school year. The parties were unable to agree on a placement, and the family later moved to Georgia. The mother sought compensatory education for the improper restraints, and the district claimed that the action was mooted by the move out of the district. The Third Circuit Court of Appeals ultimately ruled that **the claim for compensatory education was not mooted by the family's move**. Otherwise, school districts could simply stop providing services until a family gave up and moved away. The lawsuit could proceed. *D.F. v. Collingswood Borough Board of Educ.*, 694 F.3d 488 (3d Cir. 2012).

When the case returned to the district court, it found no merit to the parent's argument that the administrative decision disrupted the child's stay-put placement and denied him a free appropriate public education. As for the claim that the child had been improperly restrained, the court held the hearing officer had correctly found the parent did not put the school district on sufficient notice of the nature of the problem. *D.F. v. Collingswood*

Public Schools, No. 10-594 (JEI/JS), 2013 WL 103589 (D.N.J. 1/8/13).
In 2015, the parent appealed again to the Third Circuit, which found her
arguments were without merit. In the court's view, **the lower court's opinion
clearly and convincingly showed the improper restraint claim was deficient**.
Next, the court held the claim for compensatory education had been properly
resolved. As a result, it held for the board of education. *D.F. v. Collingswood
Borough Board of Educ.*, 595 Fed.Appx. 49 (3d Cir. 2015).

III. AWARDS AND DAMAGES

A. Attorneys' Fees

*The IDEA allows parents to recover their attorneys' fees where they prevail
in "any action or proceeding" under the IDEA. Many courts have held that
prevailing party status requires a change in the legal relationship of the parties
due to a judgment on the merits of the case or a court-ordered consent decree.
School districts may seek their attorneys' fees from parents, or the attorneys of
parents, if a due process action or court case is found frivolous, unreasonable
or without foundation, or if the parents filed a case for an improper purpose.*

*Parents must succeed on a significant issue in litigation that achieves some
of the benefit sought in filing the action to be deemed "prevailing parties" who
may be entitled to an award of attorneys' fees and costs under the IDEA.*

1. Administrative Proceedings

◆   A federal court ordered a California school district to pay the parents of
a student with disabilities $399,011.78 in attorneys' fees in an IDEA case
that was limited to one school year and netted the student only 106 hours in
compensatory services. The school district admitted liability but claimed the
appropriate amount of fees was no more than $86,490. While the parents'
attorneys charged hourly rates of $650 and $700, the district claimed their
rates should not exceed $450 per hour. **The court explained that parents
must succeed on a significant issue in litigation that achieves some of the
benefit sought in filing the action to be deemed "prevailing parties" who
may be entitled to an award of attorneys' fees and costs under the IDEA.**
To calculate fees, courts determine the reasonable number of hours spent
on the case, then multiply the hours by a reasonable hourly rate. While an
award may be reduced if a parent or attorney unreasonably protracts litigation,
there was no such issue in this case. Although the school district challenged the
quantity of hours billed by the parents' attorneys and argued there was some
duplication of their time, the court largely upheld the amount requested by the
parents. It deducted $10,000 from their fee request to reflect unnecessary time
spent on a question of evidence that was either improper or duplicative. Noting
the parents obtained only one quarter of the amount of compensatory education
they sought, the court reduced their fee request by 5%. Evidence indicated the
hourly rate for federal proceedings of a similar nature in Los Angeles was as

high as $750. For the purposes of the fees award, the court approved an hourly rate of about $650 for the attorneys. After reducing the hourly rates, deducting $10,000 for duplicate work and applying an overall reduction of 5%, the court awarded the parents $399,011.78. *E.S. v. Conejo Valley School Dist.*, No. CV 17-2629 SS, 2019 WL 1598756 (C.D. Cal. 3/27/19).

◆   The U.S. Supreme Court decided not to hear an appeal by Louisiana parents from a lower court decision denying their request for attorneys' fees in an IDEA dispute. After the parents obtained a stay-put order in a due process proceeding against their school district, a mediated settlement was reached. A U.S. district court granted the parents an award of attorneys' fees as prevailing parties. But the U.S. Court of Appeals, Fifth Circuit held **stay-put relief does not resolve the merits of a dispute and thus did not confer prevailing party status on the parents**. *Tina M. v. St. Tammany Parish School Board*, No. 15-1438, 137 S.Ct. 371 (U.S. cert. denied 10/31/16).

◆   A California school district conducted a triennial assessment of a child with multiple disabilities. An occupational therapist conducted the assessment and issued a report that did not indicate whether the child needed occupational therapy (OT). The parent objected to an IEP without OT that only provided for discussions between a teacher and OT therapist. She requested an independent educational evaluation (IEE), but the school district denied payment for it. An administrative law judge (ALJ) upheld the OT assessment. The parent's attorney wrote a letter to the school district offering a settlement. The district's attorney charged the parent with a pattern of litigating and threats to litigate nonexistent claims. The school attorney threatened to seek sanctions against the parent and her attorney should there be any further appeal. The parent appealed the ALJ's decision to a federal court, adding retaliation and discrimination claims. The court affirmed the ALJ's decision and awarded the school district $94,602.34 in attorneys' fees and costs. It found the parents' claims were frivolous, unreasonable, without foundation and brought for improper purposes.

On appeal, the U.S. Court of Appeals, Ninth Circuit, explained that **school districts may recover fees from parents and their attorneys "when a complaint is found frivolous, unreasonable or without foundation, or when a claim is filed for an improper purpose."** While the parent did not prevail on her IDEA claims, the court held they were not frivolous and she did not improperly continue to litigate the case. But the court agreed with the school district that three retaliation-based claims were frivolous, as were claims for monetary damages and injunctive relief. In the court's view, the letter from the parent's attorney was not an attempt to improperly "extort funds" from the district. The court returned the case to the lower court with instructions to determine which fees were attributable solely to litigating the frivolous claims. The school district would only be entitled to attorneys' fees for those claims. *C.W. v. Capistrano Unified School Dist.*, 784 F.3d 1237 (9th Cir. 2015).

◆   Ohio parents filed an administrative complaint against their child's school district, asserting denial of a free appropriate public education (FAPE) for three years. An independent hearing officer (IHO) held a 20-day hearing and then held the district had denied the student a FAPE for two years. The district was ordered to provide him 240 hours of compensatory education in both reading and math. Finding the parents bore at least some of the responsibility for the difficulties in creating an IEP and providing services, the IHO denied the parents prevailing party status, which would defeat a claim for attorneys' fees.

A state review officer affirmed the IHO's decision in part. Meanwhile, the district filed a separate suit, claiming the review officer committed errors in the compensatory education awards for reading and math. The court dismissed the district's claim because the district had not appealed the compensatory education issue to the review officer. Turning to the parents' appeal, the court affirmed the review officer's decision in part but held the district violated the IDEA by not providing adequate transition services. The court then considered the parents' claim for more than $800,000 in attorneys' fees. It held the hourly rates sought by the parents' attorneys were reasonable. But it held an across-the-board reduction in fees was appropriate due to the parents' limited success on the merits of the claim. The student had ultimately won 240 hours of both reading and math instruction as well as about 500 hours of transition services. As a result, the court cut the attorneys' fees award to $300,000. On appeal, the U.S. Court of Appeals, Sixth Circuit, held **binding authority required the district court to more clearly explain its decision to reduce the award of attorneys' fees**. It returned the case to the lower court. *Gibson v. Forest Hills Local School Dist. Board of Educ.*, 655 Fed.Appx. 423 (6th Cir. 2016).

◆   A federal district court held a Florida school board was not entitled to the $661,000 in attorneys' fees it claimed from the parents of a child with a disability who filed an unsuccessful administrative action against the board. After an administrative law judge issued a 191-page opinion in the board's favor, it sought fees under the IDEA and other federal laws. The court explained that **the IDEA allows a local educational agency to recover attorneys' fees from parents who file a claim for an improper purpose**. The IDEA also permits a local educational agency to recover fees from the attorney of a parent who has filed a claim that is found frivolous or unreasonable. The court held the board did not support its claim that the parents' attorney had made a frivolous claim or that the parents filed the action for an improper purpose. As a result, the court held for the parents. *A.L. v. Jackson County School Board*, No. 13-15071, 2015 WL 74999 (N.D. Fla. 1/6/15).

◆   California parents asked their child's school district to provide her with Communication Access Realtime Translation services beginning in grade nine. The district refused, instead offering an alternative transcription technology called TypeWell. A hearing officer held a seven-day hearing before finding the district complied with its IDEA obligations. A federal court upheld the ALJ's decision, and the U.S. Court of Appeals, Ninth Circuit, issued a decision for the parents on their Americans with Disabilities Act (ADA) claim. The parties then reached a settlement by which the district paid the parents $197,500. The parents petitioned the court for over $458,000 in attorneys' fees and costs. It found a "prevailing party" in an IDEA action is one who effects a material alteration of the parties' legal relationship though an enforceable judgment, a consent decree or settlement.

The court explained that while the parents did not prevail on their IDEA claim, the IDEA and ADA claims were intertwined. Litigating the IDEA claim at all levels was necessary for the development and success of their ADA claim. Courts consider many factors in awarding attorneys' fees. **The court held the most critical factor is the degree of success obtained.** Even if a specific claim failed, the time spent on it might still be compensable, if it contributed to success on other claims. The court held the parents were entitled to 50% of the fees they claimed at the administrative level. For the proceedings before the district court, they were entitled to 75% of their claimed attorneys' fees. As the parents prevailed on their Ninth Circuit appeal, they were entitled to 100% of the fees for the district's appeal and subsequent proceedings. In all, the court approved an award of attorneys' fees and costs of almost $385,000. *K.M. v. Tustin Unified School Dist.*, No. SA CV 10-1011-DOC (MLGx), 2015 WL 3465757 (C.D. Cal. 6/1/15).

◆   During elementary school, the parent of a Connecticut student claimed he had to miss significant school time due to respiratory issues. Before the student advanced to grade six, the mother asked the school district to declare him eligible for special education under the other health impairment (OHI) category due to his asthma and allergies. The district only offered to place him in another district school. The mother instead placed him in a private school that lacked a state-approved special education program for grade six. In a due process action, the parent claimed the district failed to identify the student as requiring special education and related services under the OHI category for four years. A hearing officer generally held for the school district, finding that the case involved only a child find issue. The parent then sued the school district in a federal court.

The court found the school district did not abide by its responsibility to hold planning and placement team (PPT) meetings and develop IEPs after the parents made a private placement. On the other hand, the court found the student did not need special education during the years at issue. As he was not IDEA-eligible, the court found no merit to the claims for tuition reimbursement. Finally, the court considered the parent's claim to more than $176,000 in attorneys' fees. It explained that **a party will be deemed to "prevail" if he changes the legal relationship of the parties through a judgment or a legally enforceable settlement**. Under the circumstances, the parent received $55,950 in attorneys' fees. *M.A. v. Torrington Board of Educ.*, 980 F.Supp.2d 279 (D. Conn. 2014).

2. Court Proceedings

◆   A federal court ordered the Dallas Independent School District (DISD) to pay the family of a student with disabilities over $93,000 in attorneys' fees and costs arising from an IDEA proceeding that yielded damages of only $3,575.60 for the family. The court rejected the DISD's argument to exclude expert testimony in support of the attorneys' fees claim. It upheld the amount charged by the attorneys as reasonable, noting the lead attorney had over 20 years of litigation experience. While the total amount of fees and costs claimed by the parent's attorney amounted to $208,550.60, the court agreed with the DISD that a significant reduction was in order. But instead of a 75% reduction, the court found the full award was subject to a 50% reduction. As the DISD argued, the parent prevailed on only two of the four issues in dispute. Despite obtaining an original award of over $25,000 in tuition reimbursement, she was denied her costs for psychiatric medical management and compensatory counseling.

Next, **the court found the parent's success at the due process hearing was progressively "whittled away" as the case went through the court system**. She netted only $3,575.60 in tuition reimbursement and was entirely denied a request for transportation costs. In addition to imposing a 50% across-the-board fee reduction, the court found an additional 5% reduction was due based on billing errors by the parent's attorneys. As a result, the court awarded the parent attorneys' fees of $93,847.88. *Dallas Independent School Dist. v. Woody*, No. 3:15-CV-1961, 2018 WL 6304401 (N.D. Tex. 11/30/18).

♦   After prevailing in a due process proceeding, Georgia parents asked a federal court to approve their request for $420,000 in attorneys' fees. The court instead awarded them $283,372.86. Dissatisfied, the parents appealed to the U.S. Court of Appeals, Eleventh Circuit. It noted an IDEA provision at 20 U.S.C. § 1415 (i)(3)(B) generally provides a court with authority to award "reasonable attorneys' fees to a prevailing party who is the parent of a child with a disability." If a court finds the parent unreasonably protracted the litigation, or if a parent's attorney charges an excessive rate or spends excessive time on a proceeding, the award is to be reduced. Another IDEA provision states that if a district unreasonably protracts litigation or violates 20 U.S.C. § 1415, the fee reduction provision does not apply. The parents said the district unreasonably protracted the litigation or violated 20 U.S.C. § 1415 by denying timely access to their child's records. As the lower court found, the general IDEA rule is that a court may only award reasonable attorneys' fees, in its discretion. **The court found no support for the theory that the lower court could not make any fee reduction.** There was also no error by the lower court in reducing the hourly rate claimed by one attorney from $650 to $500, and a finding that eight days of preparation for a one-day hearing was excessive. Finding no support for the parents' arguments, the court affirmed the decision reducing the award of fees. *Williams v. Fulton County School Dist.*, 717 Fed.Appx. 913 (11th Cir. 2017).

♦   An Ohio charter school attorney obtained the reversal of a federal court order that awarded the parent of a disabled child her attorney's fees as a sanction for filing frivolous or harassing actions. After a lower court found the attorney made a frivolous argument and filed confidential documents as exhibits, it awarded the parent $7,500 from the attorney. When the case reached the U.S. Court of Appeals, Sixth Circuit, it held **the case had "needlessly devolved" into a dispute over fees and unjustified sanctions**. The court found none of the attorney's actions were unreasonable and it reversed the lower court's order. *Oakstone Community School v. Williams*, 615 Fed.Appx. 284 (6th Cir. 2015).

♦   In a case that reached the U.S. Court of Appeals, Sixth Circuit, a Michigan student obtained 768 hours of 1:1 compensatory education by a teacher certified to teach students with autism. Later, the parents claimed district evaluations of their child were inappropriate and that they were entitled to reimbursement for the cost of an independent educational evaluation (IEE). The district filed a federal case against the parents and their attorney, seeking attorneys' fees and costs for prolonging the litigation and pursuing claims for improper purposes. In addition, the school district sought an order allowing the release of documents that the administrative law judge (ALJ) had reviewed in private during the IEE hearing. At the hearing, the ALJ had denied the district's request to access these documents. The court agreed with the parents' attorney that as the administrative action was over, the IEE issue was moot. The school district was the prevailing party, and **the district stated a plausible claim for attorneys' fees against the parents and their attorney.** As the court found enough facts were stated to support the claim for fees against the parents and their attorney, it denied their motions for dismissal. *Northport Public School v. Woods,* No. 1:11-cv-982, 2014 WL 1920429 (W.D. Mich. 5/14/14).

3. Settlement

◆   A federal district court approved a $550,000 settlement between a California school district and a student with a history of significant behavior issues based on multiple incidents of abuse by a staff member that caused injury. Citing many incidents of physical abuse of her child by the staff member, the student's mother sued the school district in a federal court for constitutional violations, disability discrimination and failure to provide reasonable accommodations. During pretrial activity, the parties reached a settlement that avoided the need for a trial. **When the parties presented their settlement agreement to the court for approval, it explained that courts must determine whether a settlement serves the child's best interests.** After conducting an independent inquiry into the agreement, the court noted a special needs trust would be set up for the student. Testimony indicated $435,000 would be placed in the trust for his benefit and that the remaining $115,000 would go to his lawyers.

The court found the amount allocated to the special needs trust would be more than sufficient to cover expected costs of care as well as compensatory services the student needed as a result of the multiple incidents forming the basis for the lawsuit. The trust proceeds would cover applied behavior analysis therapy or therapeutic interventions if the student needed them. Witnesses stated the amount would cover two to four years of private schooling or residential treatment. The court found the amount compared favorably with settlement agreements approved by courts in similar cases. Finding the settlement served the student's best interests, the court approved the agreement and directed the parties to request dismissal of the case. *P.R. v. Fresno Unified School Dist.,* No. 1:19-cv-00220-DAD-BAM, 2019 WL 1651267 (E.D. Cal. 4/16/19).

◆   A parent filed a due process hearing request against the Chicago Board of Education and her child's charter school, charging educators with impeding her child's right to a free appropriate public education. A hearing officer ordered the school to provide the child additional services. Later, a federal court dismissed the case. It held the parent could not pursue the action on behalf of her child without hiring an attorney. In addition, the court found she failed to state a claim. The parent did not show she was "aggrieved" by a decision under the IDEA, and could not pursue punitive damages, which are unavailable in an IDEA case. In 2015, appeal reached the Seventh Circuit. It upheld the dismissal of the claims brought on behalf of the child, but found the parent could proceed in her own right under the IDEA. She could pursue relief not ordered by the hearing officer, including reimbursement for her out-of-pocket expenses.

When the case returned to the district court, the parent obtained counsel and began negotiations with the board. A federal magistrate judge held a settlement conference. According to a settlement checklist, the board agreed to pay the parent $8,100 in return for releasing her claims. A week after the settlement was reached, the parent asked the court to clarify the scope of the settlement. She felt she had only settled the IDEA claim for out-of-pocket expenses. At a hearing, the parent's attorney stated that there had been an oral agreement reached and that she had reviewed this with the parent before signing the checklist on her behalf. But the parent said that she did not authorize the attorney to sign the checklist. She sought to continue with claims under the IDEA and 42 U.S.C. § 1983, as well as punitive damages. The court adopted the magistrate judge's recommendation to enforce the settlement agreement. Next, the parent asked the district court for relief, claiming the court committed fraud by ignoring her Section 1983 claim and enforcing the settlement. The court denied the motion, and the parent appealed to the Seventh Circuit again. The court found she had agreed to settle the case based on objective evidence, including her own testimony. **The parent's subjective intent was irrelevant as her objective conduct reflected an intent to be bound by the agreement.** *Foster v. Board of Educ. of City of Chicago*, 611 Fed.Appx. 874 (7th Cir. 2017).

◆ A federal court agreed to the dismissal of two cases by an Arizona parent who charged her son's school with denying him a free appropriate public education and denying her IEP participation opportunities. **The court found none of the violations identified by the parent deprived her of participation rights or denied her son a FAPE.** While the school did not hold an IEP meeting she had requested to discuss a home-based program, not all the team members could be present at the time. In light of the agreement, the Ninth Circuit held the actions were properly dismissed. *LMH v. Deer Valley Unified School Dist.*, Nos. 16–16467, No. 17–16642, 2018 WL 994127 (9th Cir. 2/16/18).

◆ A California student's parents disputed gastrostomy tube feeding services provided to their son at school. They removed him from district schools for significant time periods for home instruction. They rejected a school district offer to pay them $75,000 annually for a home program and rejected a counter offer of $150,000 per year. The parents said their annual home school costs were $157,000. When the district rejected a parental demand of $250,000 per year for the home program, the parties requested due process hearings. An administrative law judge (ALJ) consolidated the cases and held for the district on 12 of 15 claims, including those involving the provision of a free appropriate public education. But the court refused to dismiss claims under the Americans with Disabilities Act (ADA) and Section 504. The parents sought almost $1.4 million in attorneys' fees and costs, but the court instead awarded them about $55,000. On appeal, the U.S. Court of Appeals, Ninth Circuit, held gastrostomy tube feeding is a specialized physical health care service that must be described in an IEP. State law went beyond the federal minimum by defining a required accommodation, and this accommodation was enforceable in court.

In the court's opinion, **the school district failed to provide a required accommodation by not identifying the category of employee who would assist the child with gastrostomy tube feedings**. But since the evidence did not show the district was deliberately indifferent to the student's rights under the ADA and Rehabilitation, the court found no liability on these claims. The family was entitled to reconsideration of a claim that the district did not comply with an administrative ruling requiring that a school nurse personally assist the student with tube feedings. The court found the school district's offer to pay the parents $150,000 per year for their educational costs was less than the $157,000 in annual costs they claimed for the home program. The Ninth Circuit ordered the lower court to reconsider the claim based on compliance with the ALJ's order that a school nurse personally assist the child with gastrostomy tube feedings. It also returned the claim for attorneys' fees to the lower court. Later, the U.S. Supreme Court denied the school district's appeal. *San Diego Unified School Dist. v. T.B.*, No. 15-1059, 136 S.Ct. 1679 (U.S. cert. denied, 4/18/16).

◆   A federal lawsuit led to an agreement by Connecticut officials in 2002 to increase the participation rate of students with intellectual disabilities in general education classes and take measures to reduce the discriminatory identification of such students. The agreement stated five goals to encourage compliance with the IDEA, including an increase in the percent of students with intellectual disabilities in regular classes, a reduction in discriminatory identification of such students, and an increase in the share of the school day students would spend with their non-disabled peers. The agreement sought to increase the placement of students with intellectual disabilities in neighborhood schools, and to increase their extra-curricular participation rates. In 2009, representatives of the students asserted the state was out of compliance with the agreement.

Appeal reached the U.S. Court of Appeals, Second Circuit, which found the agreement operated as a consent decree, giving the lower court continuing authority to supervise it. There was no showing of "substantial noncompliance" with the agreement. The essential purposes of the agreement were limited to five identified areas. The court found nothing in the agreement covered the quality of education. **Evidence indicated students made significant progress toward the goals of the agreement, including a reduction in the discriminatory identification of students.** It appeared to the court that the state was trying to implement the agreement even after it was no longer bound to do so. As it was not shown that the state failed to comply with the agreement, the court held for the state. *P.J. v. Connecticut Board of Educ.*, 550 Fed.Appx. 20 (2d Cir. 2013).

◆   Pennsylvania parents prepared to file a due process action against a school district. Attorneys for the parties negotiated an agreement to resolve their complaint. About three weeks later, the parents reviewed an agreement reducing the terms to writing. They changed some of the terms and sent the agreement to their lawyer, who made the changes and returned a draft to them. The draft contained terms that were explicitly rejected by the school district during the settlement negotiations. Without notifying their own attorney, the parents signed the draft document and hand-delivered it to the school district's office. School officials did not closely review the draft and forwarded it to the superintendent.

Unaware of any revisions, the school board voted to approve the draft agreement without any discussion. Later, the parents submitted costs to the district for educational services. The district denied payment, noting that it had rejected responsibility for the service during settlement talks. School officials then realized they had approved the parents' draft rather than the agreement their attorneys created. The district rescinded the agreement and filed a complaint with the state office of dispute resolution. The case reached the Commonwealth Court of Pennsylvania, which held **failure by the school district to read or have the agreement reviewed by its attorneys was no defense.** As a result, the court held the draft was valid. As there was no basis for rescission and any failure to read the contract before signing it was no defense, the court held for the parents. *A.S. and R.S. v. Office for Dispute Resolution,* 88 A.3d 256 (Pa. Commw. Ct. 2014).

B. Compensatory Education

Compensatory education is a judge-made remedy calling for the belated provision of necessary educational services by a school district to a student with a disability. It is intended to provide a child with the educational benefits that likely would have accrued from services that should have been provided, but were not. Courts award compensatory education even after a student has reached age 21 to remedy the denial of FAPE during time periods when the student was still IDEA-eligible. In M.W. v. New York City Dep't of Educ., *a federal court explained that compensatory education may be available to students over age 21, based on "gross procedural violations."*

In Artichoker v. Todd County School Dist., *3:15-CV-03021-RAL, 2016 WL 7489033 (D.S.D. 12/29/16), a federal court upheld administrative findings that **an award of compensatory education would not be appropriate for a student who had not yet been declared eligible for special education.** Although her guardian had requested an evaluation, compensatory education would be inappropriate before there was an eligibility determination. See Chapter Two, Section II.G. for a full summary of the case.*

1. Generally

◆   A District of Columbia student with a learning disability had IEPs calling for 27.5 hours of weekly specialized instruction outside general education. When he entered high school, the district placed him in a school it identified as having the programming to meet his needs. But during his first year and one-half at the school, the district never provided him 27.5 hours of weekly specialized instruction outside of general education as required by his IEPs.

The district reduced the student's special education requirement to 20 hours per week because that was all the school could provide. According to the parent, she was not told about the IEP modification. She filed a due process complaint.

After a hearing, a hearing officer found the school district denied the student a free appropriate public education. But the hearing officer found the time missed by the student was not material. He also found the IEP reducing the student's special education hours was appropriate, and he awarded the student 50 hours of compensatory education. The parent appealed to a federal court, which rejected the hearing officer's finding that the student's lack of academic progress was due to his social maladjustment and not his disability. Evidence indicated that the school never fulfilled the student's IEP requirements. **It appeared that the school could not provide specialized support to students with 20 or more hours of specialized instruction outside general education.** The court held the district denied the student a FAPE during the period up to its reduction in special education hours, as well as the period after the reduction in hours. Unlike the hearing officer, the court found the failure to provide IEP hours was not inconsequential. It also held 50 hours of compensatory education did not make up for the 542 hours of specialized education denied to the student during this time. The court ordered the parties to discuss an appropriate compensatory education remedy. Rejecting the district's argument that the student was to blame for his lack of progress as a result of his poor attendance, the court held the IDEA placed the responsibility on the school district to appropriately place him and implement his IEP. *Wade v. District of Columbia*, 322 F.Supp.3d 123 (D.D.C. 2018).

◆   A federal court ordered a Delaware charter school to provide compensatory education to a student who was frequently absent from school and was denied special education for three school years. Although she had a 504 plan providing classroom accommodations, it did not address her frequent absences due to health problems. **The court held a child who has been deprived of a FAPE is entitled to compensatory education in an amount of time equal to the educational deprivation, but excluding time reasonably required for the school district to rectify the problem.** Evidence indicated the student was very sick on some of her days of absence and would not have been able to work with a home instructor for long time periods. Due to the relative intensity of home instruction, she was awarded only 2.5 hours for each day of instruction she missed. On the other hand, the court awarded the student seven hours of compensatory education for each day she attended the charter school over the three-year period. The school was directed to fund the compensatory award at $75 per hour and to place the funding for it into a third-party trust. *Rayna P. v. Campus Community School*, No 16-63, 2018 WL 3825893 (D. Del. 8/10/18).

◆   A New York parent challenged an IEP offered to his child, stating it provided insufficient Applied Behavior Analysis (ABA) therapy. The IEP recommended 10 hours of weekly ABA therapy for the child, but the parent sought 15 hours of this weekly therapy. After losing his impartial hearing challenge at the administrative levels, the parent appealed to a federal court. The New York City Department of Education (DOE) sought dismissal, arguing that a resolution agreement had been reached in conjunction with a different IEP that provided the child with 15 hours of weekly ABA. In response, the parent argued the DOE might again seek to reduce the hours of weekly ABA therapy. He asked for 1,000 hours of compensatory ABA therapy. A federal magistrate judge agreed with the DOE that the case was moot. Over the parent's objection, the federal court adopted a report and recommendation by the magistrate judge.

The parent appealed to the Second Circuit Court of Appeals, which noted a new DOE proposal omitted any ABA therapy. The new IEP was found relevant and would be considered on appeal. In this case, the magistrate judge and trial court found "speculative" the risk that the DOE would issue the student a new IEP decreasing his ABA therapy. But the new IEP established that the parent's fears were not speculative. **As the DOE issued a new IEP without any ABA therapy, the court held the case was no longer moot. It held the lower court would have to consider the parent's claim for compensatory education.** *Toth v. City of New York, Dep't of Educ.*, 720 Fed.Appx. 48 (2d Cir. 2018).

◆   An evaluation of a Pennsylvania preschool student led to a finding by his school district that he was a child with an emotional disturbance. He was then evaluated by a psychologist at his parents' request. After finding he had symptoms of ADHD, the psychologist recommended a placement in a partial hospitalization program. The district modified his IEP, adding weekly consultation, physical therapy and speech/language therapy. Near the end of the school year, the student was diagnosed with an autism spectrum disorder. The next fall, his parents rejected developmental preschool placements suggested by the school district. A third school did not accept the student, who continued receiving home services and did not enroll in school.

The parties agreed on a developmental preschool placement with a focus on speech/language therapy. A neuropsychologist diagnosed the student with autism, and the district changed his eligibility classification to autism. A district report indicated he was making great progress in language and social skills in the district's language classroom. But the parents filed a due process complaint against the district. A hearing officer held the district violated the student's procedural rights by improperly classifying him as emotionally disturbed. He found the district denied the student a FAPE for about 17 months and awarded him 1,350 hours of services. This amounted to five hours of compensatory services for each day FAPE was denied. The school district appealed to a federal court, which explained that school districts must offer services based on needs, not classification. **No evidence linked the district's incorrect classification to any substantive harm to the student.** To the contrary, the evidence indicated he was making progress in the language classroom, was actively participating in preschool activities, independently greeting peers, making eye contact and showing motivation. **The court upheld the compensatory education award, which sought to place the student in the same position he would occupy if not for the district's violation.** *Montgomery County Intermediate Unit No. 23 v. C.M.*, No. 17-1523, 2017 WL 4548022 (E.D. Pa. 10/12/17).

◆   Utah parents became dissatisfied with their child's slow progress at the Utah Schools for the Deaf and Blind (USDB), where she was a residential student.

After testing revealed the child had mild to moderate bilateral hearing loss, her IEP was modified to add a classroom frequency modulated (FM) system. The parents refused to sign a new IEP. For some time, staff members were unsure whether to implement the proposed IEP or the prior year's IEP. As a result, the FM system was not used in the classroom for a full school year. The USDB agreed to fund an independent educational evaluation (IEE) at a Massachusetts school. Although USDB agreed to use the IEE, it refused to reimburse the parent for her transportation to Massachusetts. After a facilitated IEP meeting was cut short, the parent filed a due process hearing request. USDB rejected the Massachusetts placement and approved a public school placement. A hearing officer found USDB predetermined services for the child. USDB was ordered to provide speech-language-pathology services as compensatory education.

The hearing officer held the child was denied a free appropriate public education (FAPE). The FM system was not used for a year, without approval by the team or notice to the parent. A federal court found USDB did not properly implement the IEP. After approving of an award of compensatory education, the court returned the case to the IEP team to "determine placement at an appropriate residential school that will provide her with the services ordered." On appeal, the U.S. Court of Appeals, Tenth Circuit, held the lower court had improperly delegated to the IEP team the question of the child's appropriate placement. The IDEA does not allow such a delegation. **Finding that the lower court order would allow the agency that failed to provide the child a FAPE to determine the remedy for its own violation, the Tenth Circuit vacated the judgment.** When the case returned to the lower court, it would have to determine the child's placement and recalculate the attorneys' fees award. *M.S. v. Utah Schools for the Deaf and Blind*, 822 F.3d 1128 (10th Cir. 2016).

◆ A District of Columbia student had behavioral problems early in his school career and was evaluated for attention deficit disorder and similar disabilities. Before anything came of the evaluation, the parent filed an administrative complaint against the school district, asserting failure to comply with the IDEA's child find obligation despite its knowledge that her child had a suspected disability. A hearing officer ruled against the parent, finding the child's performance and behavior had improved and he was able to keep up with his classmates. No compensatory education was awarded. Noting that the hearing officer did not address the child's future special education needs, the parent made a formal request for a special education evaluation. When the district did not act, she asked for relief from a federal court. Before the court issued a ruling, the school district completed a comprehensive evaluation of the child. There was no provision in the IEP for compensatory education for his K-1 school years. After the court held the school district's IEP offer made the case moot, the parent appealed. The U.S. Court of Appeals, District of Columbia Circuit, found the parent was now demanding compensatory education, not just a special education evaluation. **The district's decision to provide an IEP for the child did not moot the parent's request for compensatory education.** Since the action was not moot, the case would return to the trial court for consideration of a compensatory education award. *Boose v. District of Columbia*, 786 F.3d 1054 (D.C. Cir. 2015).

◆   California parents said their school district tried to remove their child from general education classes so he could be "warehoused" with severely disabled children. The school district filed a due process hearing request, but while the case was pending the parents filed five state complaint resolution proceeding (CRP) complaints against the district. They asserted non-compliance with state and federal law. After the student was removed from school, the district dismissed the due process case. For this reason, there was no final administrative ruling in that matter. The parents sued the school district and the state education department, seeking compensatory education and damages.

A federal court held the IDEA administrative exhaustion requirement applies when a party "seeks a remedy under the IDEA or its functional equivalent." This includes a party seeking to alter an IEP or a child's placement, or a claim for denial of a FAPE. Ninth Circuit authority clarified that the exhaustion rule is a "claims processing provision" that can be excused if administrative remedies would be futile or if a government agency acts contrary to law. In this case, the parents said the education department did not monitor, investigate and enforce the IDEA. The court held it could not yet determine whether the department failed to investigate the claims or otherwise stymie attempts to obtain district compliance. **Prior Ninth Circuit cases held CRPs can suffice for exhaustion purposes and had found the CRP and due process hearing procedures to be simply alternative means of addressing an IDEA complaint.** As a result, the parents could pursue their IDEA and Rehabilitation Act claims. *Everett H. v. Dry Creek Joint Elementary School Dist.*, 5 F.Supp.3d 1184 (E.D. Cal. 2014).

◆   A Pennsylvania student had violent tendencies and developmental delays. He had bipolar disorder and a serious emotional disturbance. Before the student entered district schools, he attended a partial hospitalization program (PHP). Although the IEP team located a private school, the parents soon expressed dissatisfaction and sought another placement. The team did not change the placement, and it recommended an ESY program. The private school informed the parents that it would no longer provide transportation for their child due to his violent behavior. He had threatened to bring a gun on a bus and kill people. Asserting denial of a FAPE, the parents requested a due process hearing. During the hearing, the school district conceded it owed the student compensatory occupational and physical therapy services that it had failed to provide during his kindergarten school year. But a hearing officer awarded the student only 17 hours of compensatory education for occupational and physical therapy.

A state appeals panel increased the award of compensatory education to 24.5 hours, and the case reached a federal court. Although a psychologist stated the student was the most violent child he had evaluated during his 30-year career, the court found the student's teachers stated he was making social and academic progress. Like the hearing officer, the court found the placement did not deny the student a FAPE. It appeared that the student had received only one hour of instruction while attending the PHP. **A school district remained responsible for IDEA services while a student was placed in a private setting such as the PHP.** As a result, the court held the child was entitled to full days of compensatory education. Finding he had been denied 28 hours of weekly IEP services during a 15-week period, the court awarded him 420 hours of compensatory education. This would be added to awards made for the denial of services during the school year and summer, for a total of 439.5 hours. *Tyler W. v. Upper Perkiomen School Dist.*, 963 F.Supp.2d 427 (E.D. Pa. 2013).

◆ An Alaska school district wanted to change the setting for a student's special education writing instruction to a resource room because the student's teacher was taking family leave. The district failed to provide prior notice to his parents. The student's mother learned of the change at an IEP meeting. After the teacher returned from leave, the district kept the student in the resource room for writing instruction. The student's mother sought to move the student's writing instruction back to the general education classroom. A hearing officer ruled that the district violated the IDEA by keeping the student in the resource room after the teacher returned from leave and awarded 15 hours of compensatory writing instruction in the general education classroom. The Supreme Court of Alaska upheld that award. **The failure to return the student to the general education classroom after his teacher returned from leave justified the award.** *Madeline P. v. Anchorage School Dist.*, 265 P.3d 308 (Alaska 2011).

2. Beyond Age 21

In Somberg v. Utica Community Schools, *the court declined to apply* Endrew F. v. Douglas County School Dist. RE-1, *137 S.Ct. 988 (2017), in considering a compensatory education award. It held the* Endrew F. *standard applied to the assessment of an IEP, not to awards of compensatory education.*

◆ A Michigan school district did not comply with the IEP of a student with autism who was expected to graduate. After his parent objected, the school provided him instruction in the principal's office, where he was segregated from peers. The parent filed a due process complaint, asserting the district denied him a free appropriate public education (FAPE). She withdrew her son from the district and placed him privately. An administrative law judge (ALJ) held the district denied the student a FAPE. On appeal, a federal court affirmed the ALJ's findings of multiple FAPE deficiencies. But unlike the ALJ, the court held the student was entitled to an award of compensatory education.

After additional proceedings, including an appeal to the Sixth Circuit, the court held the school district should pay the student for 1,200 hours of tutoring. A special master appointed to oversee the compensatory award ordered the district to pay the family over $210,000 in attorneys' fees and litigation costs. The case eventually returned to the Sixth Circuit, which held the case was not moot, even though the student was now 24 and no longer attending district schools. It held the lower court did not abuse its discretion by awarding compensatory education. **As the district admitted, it denied the student a FAPE by assigning him to a program that was contrary to his IEP.** But the court rejected the parent's argument that the 1,200-hour compensatory education award and year of transition planning was not enough to remedy her son's loss of benefits. As a result, the compensatory education award was affirmed. *Somberg v. Utica Community Schools*, 908 F.3d 162 (6th Cir. 2018).

◆ A Pennsylvania student with Asperger's Disorder had IEPs addressing his learning deficits in reading comprehension and written and oral expression. A dispute arose between his school district and his parents regarding reimbursement for extended school year services and an independent educational evaluation. Both parties filed due process hearing requests, which went before a hearing officer. The hearing officer found the district failed to administer appropriate educational services and awarded him 990 hours of compensatory education. The order permitted the parents to determine the appropriate instruction. Over the next three years, the parties were unable to agree on specific services. After graduating, the student earned an associate's degree, then enrolled in a bachelor's degree program. Two years later, he asked the school district to use the compensatory education award to pay for his college tuition and expenses.

The parties discussed the student's request for months. When an impasse was reached, he sued the school district in a federal court. In pretrial activity, the court considered the student's claim for over $84,000 in tuition and expenses for his collegiate programs. The court held neither the IDEA nor the hearing officer's order contemplated an unrestricted right to college tuition reimbursement. **The student identified no other court decision approving of college tuition reimbursement in lieu of compensatory education.** A compensatory education award must be reasonably tailored to address the educational deficit that resulted from a denial of FAPE. Compensatory education "is a surrogate" for the education a student missed when FAPE was denied. Finding a payment for college tuition reimbursement based on a prior award of compensatory education was not contemplated by the hearing officer's decision or the IDEA, the court held for the district. *Stapleton v. Penns Valley Area School Dist.*, No. 4:15-cv-2323, 2017 WL 6336611 (M.D. Pa. 12/12/17).

◆ A Pennsylvania school district evaluated a student for speech and language therapy. His first IEP had only speech and language goals, and he did not perform at grade level. After repeating his kindergarten year, the student began to have behavior problems. Evaluations obtained by the parents indicated he had bipolar disorder, extreme visual and motor skills problems and "borderline retardation." But the district did not evaluate his cognitive abilities. At some point, the district mistakenly identified the student as having mental retardation. He remained in the life skills program for grades three and four. When the student's mother realized the district had improperly identified her son as mentally retarded, she withdrew him from the program.

When the student was in grade eight, the family moved out of the district and asked for a hearing. A hearing officer found the district denied the student appropriate services in all eight years he was in district schools. An hour of compensatory education was awarded for each hour of each school day he had attended school in the district. Later, the parents charged the district with failure to comply with the order. They sued the district in a federal court to recover the monetary equivalent of nearly 10,000 hours of compensatory education. The court dismissed the case, and appeal reached the U.S. Court of Appeals, Third Circuit. It held that while the district misdiagnosed or misclassified the student, this did not demonstrate deliberate indifference to his rights. Since the parents could not show intentional conduct or deliberate indifference by the school district, the court held for the district on the Section 504 and ADA claims. But unlike the lower court, the Third Circuit held the IDEA claims should not be dismissed. The award envisioned a fund for the parents to draw upon, but the district had refused to set one up. The district's claim that the fund was optional would have placed all the responsibility on the parents to remedy its past failures. **This was contrary to the IDEA, which requires a remedy for those who are denied appropriate services.** As a result, the IDEA claims were not dismissed. *D.E. v. Cent. Dauphin School Dist.*, 765 F.3d 260 (3d Cir. 2014).

◆ A federal court held an Ohio school district violated the IDEA by failing to provide a student who had a seizure disorder and other disabilities with adequate transition services. It was clear to the court that the district violated an IDEA mandate to invite the 16-year-old student to IEP team meetings to discuss her postsecondary goals. In addition, the district did not offer her age-appropriate assessments for postsecondary goals. After finding this conduct resulted in a denial of FAPE, the court held a conference with the parties to discuss an appropriate remedy. The parties were unable to agree, and the court provided them an opportunity to propose remedies. In reviewing Sixth Circuit authority, the court noted reservations about basing compensatory education awards on "rote hour-by-hour" calculations. While such awards are not per se inappropriate, the Sixth Circuit has warned against awards that appear punitive.

Even though the student had reached age 22, the parties agreed that the court was authorized to order compensatory services. In the court's view, neither of the parties had proposed an appropriate remedy. The student was entitled to transition services regardless of whether she was likely to attain competitive employment or achieve a high level of independence. The remedy proposed by the parents' expert appeared likely to provide her more than the district could have provided her during her high school career. As a result, the court adopted an employment goal recommended by an expert and an assessment by Goodwill Industries. The student was entitled to an award of some 600 hours of compensatory services. *Gibson v. Forest Hills School Dist. Board of Educ.*, No. 1:11-cv-329, 2014 WL 533392 (S.D. Ohio 2/11/14).

C. Monetary Damages

In Lewis v. Scott County Public Schools Board of Educ., *a federal court held West Virginia parents could not base a tort-like claim for monetary damages on a violation of the IDEA. In* Sellers v. School Board of Manassas, Virginia, *141 F.3d 524 (4th Cir. 1998), the Fourth Circuit Court of Appeals held that* **tort-like damages are inconsistent with IDEA purposes.**

◆ A Vermont parent said a classmate verbally and physically abused one of her sons. She said her other son witnessed the misconduct and that she reported bullying to the principal on a daily basis. The parent claimed the only action taken by the principal and school was to have one of her sons sign a safety contract. Next, the parent claimed the classmate's father and the school nurse accused her of trying to physically remove the classmate from a classroom.

The parent said the classmate's father abused his professional authority as a police officer by engaging in intimidation and threats against her, including threats to arrest her. The parent removed her children from school and began homeschooling them. She claimed they began to suffer from post-traumatic stress disorder from "years of bullying." School officials charged the parent with truancy. When the truancy charges reached a state court, the judge ordered both boys to reside with their father pending the outcome of the case.

After the truancy charges were dismissed, the parent said she lost custody of the boys. Seeking an award of some $1.5 million in damages, she sued the principal, school district, classmate's parents and others in a federal court. Among other things, the parent said the principal made false statements to protect herself from charges that she violated Vermont's anti-bullying law and the IDEA. First, the court dismissed the claims filed by the parent on behalf of her children. A non-attorney cannot represent another person in a federal court. The court found the remaining claims did not involve federal law. **Federal courts have powers to hear only cases involving federal questions or disputes in excess of $75,000 among people residing in different states.** While the parent asserted additional violations of federal law, the court found no federal right was implicated in connection with her malicious prosecution and abuse of process claims. The court dismissed the complaint. *Amanna v. Dummerston School*, No. 5:17-cv-118, 2018 WL 1363838 (D. Vt. 3/13/18).

◆   A Virginia student said school staff members yelled at him after he spilled his lunch tray. He said they forced him to clean up the accident and that the school's assistant principal then yelled at him, grabbed him around the neck, pulled him to the floor, and forced him into a chair. After being restrained, the student was then forced to continue the cleanup on his hands and knees. He said a resource officer then took him to the floor and pulled his hands above his head when taking him to the office. In a federal court, the student and his parent sued the school district and officials for violating the IDEA. They added state law negligence claims, asserting school officials were negligent in resolving his behavior problems. In reviewing a motion for dismissal by the district and school officials, **the court noted the only federal claim stated that there were IDEA violations justifying monetary damages**. But the Fourth Circuit decided years ago that the IDEA does not create a private cause for damages.

In addition, **the Supreme Court has not approved of compensatory or punitive damage awards for an IDEA violation**. Otherwise, the IDEA would be transformed into a remedy for tort-like damages that would conflict with the law's intent. Next, the court agreed with the school board that it had immunity for the negligence claims filed against it. As the negligence claims against the individual school officials failed to include sufficient facts, all the negligence claims were dismissed. *Lewis v. Scott County Public Schools Board of Educ.*, No. 2:15CV00030, 2016 WL 1611384 (W.D. Va. 4/21/16).

◆   The mother of an Oregon student claimed that after she filed administrative charges, claiming numerous procedural and substantive IEP deficiencies, the school district and its in-house attorney "went into litigation mode." After an administrative law judge ordered the district to provide compensatory education, but before a spot opened up with an outside service provider, the student graduated. The mother sued, but a federal court dismissed all but the retaliation charges. It awarded the mother $1 in nominal damages for the attorney's actions in trying to dissuade her from exercising her rights under the IDEA. However, the Ninth Circuit reversed, noting that **the IDEA does not permit the awarding of nominal damages**. The court held the parents of graduated students did not have standing to pursue prospective IDEA claims. *C.O. v. Portland Public Schools*, 679 F.3d 1162 (9th Cir. 2012).

IV. GOVERNMENTAL IMMUNITY

Governmental immunity prohibits lawsuits against the government and its officials. Eleventh Amendment immunity protects states against lawsuits in federal court for money damages, not from prospective relief, like injunctions.

In the 1990 amendments to the IDEA, Congress authorized lawsuits against the states for violations of the IDEA. Generally, the Eleventh Amendment protects states or state officials in their official capacities from (a) federal court lawsuits (b) brought by individuals (c) seeking money damages.

A. Federal Law

◆   Connecticut parents failed to convince the Second Circuit Court of Appeals that a municipal police officer should be held liable for constitutional violations arising from the use of a Taser on their deaf child. **The court explained that qualified immunity protects officials from liability for civil damages as long as their conduct does not violate clearly established rights of which a reasonable person would have known.** A right is clearly established if its contours are sufficiently clear that a reasonable official would understand that what he is doing violates that right. Prior case law clearly established that police officers cannot tase a compliant or non-threatening suspect. In this case, the student argued his clearly established right not to be tased was violated because he did not understand the officer's instructions and warnings.

The court disagreed with the student, finding it was objectively reasonable to the officer that he complied with clearly established law. Only after the student apparently ignored the officer's second warning was a taser deployed. Faced with a noncompliant 12-year-old who had already fled the school and harmed a teacher, the officer had a reasonable belief that the student was a harm to himself and others. He also had to consider the risk that the student would flee. Moreover, the court found the officer had a reasonable basis for believing a teacher signaled his warnings to the student, who then ignored them. Under the circumstances, the court refused to find the officer acted unreasonably. *Muschette v. Gionfriddo*, 910 F.3d 65 (2d Cir. 2018).

◆   The Kansas Supreme Court refused to review a lower court decision which held the federal Paul D. Coverdell Teacher Protection Act is not available as a defense for a school district in a negligence action by a student who reported that peers bullied him due to his "lazy eye" and height. After a classmate hit the student and fractured his jaw, his mother removed him from school. The family sued the school district, the bullies and their parents in the state court system. In pretrial activity, the principal obtained judgment based on the Coverdell Act. On appeal, the Court of Appeals of Kansas noted the Coverdell Act is a No Child Left Behind Act provision that immunizes teachers and other educators from liability when they take "reasonable actions to maintain order, discipline, and an appropriate educational environment" at school. **The court held the Coverdell Act immunizes teachers, administrators and other school employees, but not school districts.** There was no basis for granting immunity because the trial court made no findings about negligence. After the court returned the case to the trial court to consider the district's potential liability, the state supreme court denied further review. *Sanchez v. Unified School Dist. 469*, 339 P.3d 399 (Kan. Ct. App. 2014, Kansas review denied 7/22/15).

♦ A Georgia paraprofessional reportedly sprayed a special needs student with water for acting out during a class. Based on a school police officer's investigation, the principal made a child abuse complaint against the paraprofessional. A school police officer appeared before a magistrate judge to obtain an arrest warrant. According to the paraprofessional, she did this without revealing exculpatory information and falsely stated that he had admitted to the abuse. The paraprofessional was arrested and charged with simple battery and cruelty to children in the third degree. He was then fired by the school district.

In a federal court, the paraprofessional sued the school district, officer and principal for civil rights violations. The court held the officer was entitled to qualified immunity, finding there would have been probable cause for an arrest even if the exculpatory information had been included. There was probable cause for the simple battery charge, rendering the arrest valid. On appeal, the U.S. Court of Appeals, Eleventh Circuit, explained **that qualified immunity protects government officials who are engaged in discretionary functions when they are sued in their individual capacities**. Like the lower court, the Eleventh Circuit held that even if the officer omitted material evidence, there would still be probable cause to support the simple battery charge. The officer was entitled to immunity, since an arrest did not require probable cause with respect to each charge. The court held the officer did not have to resolve legal questions or investigate possible defenses. The officer had reason to doubt the paraprofessional was acting in good faith, and the court held for the officer. *Elmore v. Fulton County School Dist.*, 605 Fed.Appx. 906 (11th Cir. 2015).

♦ A severely autistic, nonverbal seven-year-old Texas student began to repeatedly slide a compact disc across a table. According to his parent, an aide grabbed the child from behind, shoved him and repeatedly kicked him. Criminal court proceedings were brought against the aide, who was placed on leave and had to surrender her teaching certificate. In a separate federal case, the parent sued the aide, principal and school district for civil rights violations. She added assault and battery claims against the aide, and negligence and emotional distress claims against the aide and principal. In pretrial activity, the court held the parent stated a plausible claim for constitutional rights violations. Finding the right of a student to be free from assault by a school official was clearly established at the time of the incident, the court denied the aide immunity.

The court also held the parent made out viable civil rights claims against the school district and principal. The aide appealed to the U.S. Court of Appeals, Fifth Circuit. On appeal, **the court held qualified immunity shields a government official from liability in a federal civil rights action if the official's actions were objectively reasonable in light of clearly established law**. Corporal punishment in schools is a constitutional violation only when it is arbitrary, capricious or unrelated to the goal of maintaining an atmosphere conducive to learning. In this case, the court found the aide was acting to discipline the student. State civil and criminal remedies were available to redress the conduct. In fact, the aide was charged with criminal assault causing bodily harm. She was also placed on leave and required to surrender her license. As a result, the court held the aide was entitled to immunity. The judgment was reversed. *Marquez v. Garnett*, 567 Fed.Appx. 214 (5th Cir. 2014).

◆   A Minnesota charter school special education coordinator and a teacher at the school said the charter entity knowingly submitted false documents and records to the U.S. and the state to obtain funding it was not entitled to receive. They said the charter entity manipulated school attendance and enrollment reports and overstated the special education services it provided. Although the special education coordinator spoke to school officials about the discrepancies, she said her concerns were dismissed. She said her contract was not renewed based on charges that she violated student privacy laws. In a federal court, the former special education coordinator and teacher sued the charter entity under the federal False Claim Act (FCA) and its Minnesota counterpart. In its defense, the charter entity claimed to be an arm of the state that was entitled to immunity. The court found state law defined "charter schools" as "school districts" for the purposes of tort liability. As a result, **the charter school entity was not entitled to immunity in this case**. The court held the complaint omitted specific facts such as the time, place and content of the false representations. Since the employees might be able to cure these deficiencies by adding specific or clearer allegations, the court granted them permission to refile their complaint. *U.S. v. Minnesota Transitions Charter Schools*, 50 F.Supp.3d 1106 (D. Minn. 2014).

◆   In 1989, the U.S. Supreme Court, in *Dellmuth v. Muth*, 491 U.S. 223, 109 S.Ct. 2397, 105 L.Ed.2d 181 (1989), ruled that while school districts could be sued under the IDEA, states had Eleventh Amendment immunity in IDEA cases. Congress passed the Education of the Handicapped Act Amendments of 1990 – known as the Individuals with Disabilities Education Act, and included section 20 U.S.C. § 1403, which abrogates a state's Eleventh Amendment immunity to suit in federal court for violations of the IDEA.

◆   In 1974, a Pennsylvania state school and hospital resident brought a class action suit against the school and its officials, as well as various state and local mental health administrators. The resident claimed that conditions at the institution violated Section 504 of the Rehabilitation Act, the Developmentally Disabled Assistance and Bill of Rights Act, 42 U.S.C. §§ 6001-6081

(DDABRA), Pennsylvania mental health legislation, and the Eighth and Fourteenth Amendments to the U.S. Constitution. When the case reached the U.S. Supreme Court, it reversed a decision by the Third Circuit, holding that the DDABRA created no substantive rights. *Pennhurst State School and Hospital v. Halderman*, 451 U.S. 1, 101 S.Ct. 1531, 67 L.Ed.2d 694 (1981).

When the case returned to the Third Circuit Court of Appeals, it affirmed its previous decision. The U.S. Supreme Court again reversed and remanded the case. **The Supreme Court held the Eleventh Amendment prohibits federal courts from ordering state officials to conform their conduct to state laws.** *Pennhurst State School and Hospital v. Halderman*, 465 U.S. 89, 104 S.Ct. 900, 79 L.Ed.2d 67 (1984).

◆   A Missouri student with a learning disability tried to bring a knife to his charter school. He was arrested and admitted to a psychiatric hospital. After the school expelled him, his mother enrolled him in a public school. The superintendent knew of the knife incident and his hospitalization, but didn't inform staff members, and the IEP did not refer to the knife incident. About a year later, the student attacked a classmate with a box cutter and sliced his neck open. The victim sued the superintendent for negligence, but the Supreme Court of Missouri granted him immunity under the Coverdell Act – a provision of NCLB. **The superintendent did not have to provide notice of the student's criminal conduct because the student wasn't attending district schools at the time of the incident.** Moreover, the court found the student's IEP made no mention of potentially violent behavior. The superintendent was entitled to judgment. *Dydell v. Taylor*, 332 S.W.3d 848 (Mo. 2011).

B. State Statutory Immunity

In Kinderdine v. Mahoning County Board of Developmental Disabilities, *this chapter, the Court of Appeals of Ohio explained that immunity is a doctrine that provides government agencies and their staff members a complete defense to a tort action. In Ohio, an exception to immunity applies if a negligent act involves a "physical defect" on the grounds of a political subdivision, such as a school district.*

◆   The parents of a six-year-old Wyoming student claimed he was improperly restrained by a teacher when he ran into a school hallway. They claimed a school employee pushed a service tray at him, kicked an object at him and dumped items on his head. The parents said the employee showed a confidential recording of their child at the school. They advanced a group of claims in a state court based on these incidents and others at a special services building where they said two employees restrained and hurt him, then carried out a plan to have him taken into protective custody. The parents said an employee called law enforcement officers and told them the student was suicidal and a danger to himself and others. The student was then taken into protective custody. For each count, the parents claimed a school employee was acting in an "official capacity" and within his/her scope of employment. They charged the district with negligence, violation of its policies and failure to train and supervise its employees. After a hearing, the court dismissed the case, holding the employees had immunity under the Wyoming Governmental Claims Act (WGCA).

Appeal reached the Supreme Court of Wyoming, which explained that the WGCA confers immunity from liability for torts upon government entities and public employees "while acting within the scope of duties," unless an exception applies. In this case, the complaint referenced conduct by school employees who were acting within the scope of their employment. **Since all the claims stated that one or more school employees acted within the scope of their employment, the court held the claims were barred by the WGCA.** Further, the court rejected the parents' argument that any exception to WGCA immunity applied. *Whitham v. Feller*, 415 P.3d 1264 (Wyo. 2018).

◆   A Texas student with disabilities had little control over his body, and his wheelchair was locked in place during transportation. A bus driver and an attendant noticed he was in distress and stopped the bus. But they did not take him to a nearby emergency room, and neither employee tried to resuscitate him. About one hour after getting onto the bus, he died. The parents sued the school district in a state court for wrongful death, claiming the driver negligently drove the bus at an unsafe speed. They said their child was "thrown around in his wheelchair," and that the employees failed to use available cameras and other equipment to protect him during the bus ride. Last, they claimed the locks on the chair and restraints were unsafe. During pretrial activity, the parents claimed video footage from a bus camera showed the student slid in his chair. The court dismissed the case, and they appealed to the state court of appeals.

The court found that state law generally grants immunity to government entities, but waives immunity for injuries that arise from the operation or use of motor vehicles. It held the waiver based on negligent use or operation of a motor vehicle does not extend to student restraints and wheelchairs. The district had immunity for any claims arising from negligent use of those items. The allegations of failure to use the bus cameras, mirrors and other devices to monitor and protect the student amounted to negligent supervision claims that were also subject to immunity. Next, **the court found no evidence that the driver operated the bus at an unsafe speed or engaged in unsafe maneuvers**. Further, it found the decisions not to take the student to the hospital or try to resuscitate him were unrelated to the operation or use of the bus. In sum, the court held the case had been properly dismissed on immunity grounds. *Delameter v. Beaumont Independent School Dist.*, No. 09-17-00045-CV, 2018 WL 651268 (Tex. Ct. App. 2/1/18; petition for review filed 3/16/18).

◆   A Michigan teaching assistant (TA) claimed co-workers moved a student with Tourette syndrome from a classroom for students with serious cognitive impairments into a classroom for students with moderate cognitive impairments. She said she fell against a cement wall and suffered a traumatic brain injury when she tried to restrain him. In a state court complaint, the TA claimed the co-workers caused her injuries by moving the student to the less restrictive setting and assigning her to serve as his 1:1 aide despite her lack of qualifications.

The co-workers sought immunity under the Michigan Governmental Tort

Liability Act. The court denied immunity to the co-workers, and they appealed. The state court of appeals held they were school employees acting within the course and scope of their employment at the relevant time. State law provides for immunity from liability for any injury caused by a governmental employee acting in the scope of his/her employment, unless the conduct is grossly negligent and is the "direct cause" of an injury. While the TA asserted that the co-workers should have known assigning the student to a less restrictive setting would cause her to be injured, she did not explain how they should have known this. Nor did she show his Tourette syndrome and frequent tantrums created such a risk of injury that the co-workers acted recklessly or in willful disregard for safety or substantial risks. **The decision to change the student's placement took place before the TA acted to restrain him.** Since the TA failed to show the co-workers had no immunity and did not prove they were the most direct cause of her injuries, the court reversed the trial court's judgment. *Kostaroff v. Wyandotte Public Schools*, Nos. 330472, 330505, 2017 WL 2200617 (Mich. Ct. App. 5/18/17).

◆   Michigan school officials earned immunity in a defamation case filed by a substitute teacher who was not rehired after she stated she was having problems with black students. According to the substitute, a school principal told her she would receive no further assignments at the school as the result of her comment. In a state court action against the school district and two principals, the substitute asserted defamation. The court awarded immunity to the district and principals. Later, **the state court of appeals held that staffing teachers in public schools and monitoring their performance is a governmental function**. As such, the lower court properly granted the district and principals immunity. *Carter v. Warren Consolidated School Dist.*, No. 332706, 2017 WL 4518682 (Mich. Ct. App. 10/10/17).

◆   Shortly after enrolling in a new school, a Connecticut student with a history of sexual misconduct sexually assaulted a child on their bus for special needs children. In a state court action against a social worker, the state Department of Children and Families (DCF) and the school board, the parents claimed the social worker failed to notify school officials about the student's history. In considering the social worker's dismissal motion, the court explained that sovereign immunity is a legal doctrine that protects government employees and officials from lawsuits resulting from the performance of their duties.

The court held the social worker correctly argued that the complaint related to conduct that she took (or failed to take) while performing her official duties as a DCF employee. As the damages sought by the parents were premised on the social worker's job duties for the DCF and not actions she might have taken in her individual capacity, the claim was effectively an action against the state. After finding the social worker was protected by immunity in her official capacity, the court also held she was entitled to state statutory immunity. It held the parents did not show she acted recklessly, wantonly, maliciously, or beyond the scope of her employment. **In order to defeat the social worker's claim to statutory immunity, the court found the parents had to show "highly unreasonable conduct, involving an extreme departure from ordinary**

care, in a situation where a high degree of danger is apparent." The court
found the parents did not create a reasonable inference that the social worker
intentionally or maliciously failed to provide information about the student
upon his enrollment at their child's school. As the social worker was protected
by immunity, the court held the parents could not further pursue the lawsuit.
Doe v. East Hartford Board of Educ., No. CV165041837S, 2018 WL 632279
(Conn. Super. Ct. 1/2/18).

◆   A Mississippi student reported bullying and intimidation by a group of
students. Her mother reported the bullying and asked administrators at the
school for their help. The school suspended one of the bullies from riding the
school bus for five days. Despite the bus suspension, the principal placed the
suspended bully on the same bus the next day. While on the bus, the bully and
others attacked the student and beat her into unconsciousness with a metal belt
buckle. Later, the bully was expelled from school. The student's family sued the
school district in a state court for negligence under the Mississippi Torts Claims
Act (MTCA). The court held the school district was entitled to discretionary
immunity, and the student appealed to the Supreme Court of Mississippi. On
appeal, the court explained that the MTCA is the exclusive civil remedy in
the state for acts or omissions by a governmental entity. Sovereign immunity
protects entities such as school districts (and their employees who act within the
course and scope of their duties) in specific situations described in the MTCA.
    Under state case law precedent, the court held **the school district had a
duty to hold the bully and her accomplices to a strict account for their
conduct. State antibullying laws place a ministerial duty on schools to
prevent bullying.** But the lower court did not address either Section 37-9-69
or the state's antibullying laws. The court held these laws did not convert the
school's duty to prevent bullying into a discretionary one. In returning the
case to the lower court, the supreme court ordered a trial to determine whether
the school district used ordinary care under a state law provision regarding
discretionary function immunity. Finding the school district had a ministerial
state law duty to provide a safe environment, the court reversed the judgment.
Smith v. Leake County School Dist., 195 So.3d 771 (Miss. 2016).

◆   A seven-year-old Ohio child with autism wandered away from his summer
enrichment program and drowned in a school pool. According to his parents,
he left the gym through a door with a faulty latch mechanism. They said he
was then able to enter a swimming pool because a motorized pool cover had
not been placed over the pool after the last group used it. The parents sued the
school district in the state court system for negligence. A trial court denied
governmental immunity to two county agencies named in the suit, but it
awarded pretrial judgment to a lifeguard who worked at the pool but was not
present at the time of the drowning. Appeal went before the Court of Appeals
of Ohio, which held the county agencies and employees should have immunity.
    **A provision of state law confers immunity on those performing
governmental and discretionary functions.** An exception to immunity allows
for liability caused by the negligence of employees involving physical defects
within or on the grounds of buildings used in connection with the performance

of a governmental function. The court found the failure to use an available safety device does not constitute a "physical defect" for the purposes of the immunity exception. This defeated the parents' claim that failure to use a pool cover was a physical defect that precluded government immunity. Next, the court reversed the lower court's decision that a defect in the door latch mechanism qualified for the exception to government immunity. Despite evidence that the latch stuck or did not work properly, the court noted that the door did not cause the death. The student was not hit or trapped by the door. As a result, the lower court had improperly granted immunity on that issue. *Kinderdine v. Mahoning County Board of Developmental Disabilities*, 69 N.E.3d 49 (Ohio Ct. App. 2016).

◆ New Jersey's Supreme Court held a board of education and school nurse were not liable for failing to report the results of an eye examination to a student who later developed amblyopia (lazy eye). Under the relevant state law, the court found neither a public entity nor a public employee is liable for failing to make an examination, unless the exam or diagnosis is for treatment. In this case, the visual acuity tests involved routine screening, not treatment. The court found the testing constituted a "physical examination" under state law. It held a complete physical examination includes the communication of test results to the patient. The court found the reporting of test results is an integral component of a complete eye examination. **Since reporting the results of an eye examination are included within the definition of a "physical examination," the court held the reporting of examinations deserved state law immunity.** Failure to extend immunity for inadequately communicating test results would have a chilling effect on public health examinations. Application of state law immunity required a decision for the board and nurse. *Parsons v. Mullica Township Board of Educ.*, 226 N.J. 297, 142 A.3d 715 (N.J. 2016).

◆ According to a state court complaint filed by a group of Ohio families, an alternative school student fired 10 rounds of ammunition at a high school, killing three students, paralyzing another and injuring two more. The families said the shooter was mentally unstable and had previously committed violent acts, making him at high risk for more violence. During pretrial activity, the court held for the school district, high school, members of the board, alternative school and the county educational service center. While the court granted immunity to a group of employees and administrators for negligence claims, it denied immunity for claims based on recklessness, maliciousness, conscious disregard for safety, and for willful and wanton misconduct. On appeal, the Court of Appeals of Ohio explained that state law generally creates immunity for public employees, unless an exception applies. Among the exceptions is a provision declaring that a political subdivision is not immune from liability for negligence on grounds or buildings used for a governmental function "due to physical defects." According to the families, the board and its employees negligently failed to remedy a hazardous condition on school grounds. But the court found the complaint did not identify any unreasonable board policies. **Since the shooter was the sole, direct cause of the injuries, the court held the board and employees could not be stripped of immunity on the**

theory that they created a "physical defect" on school grounds. The court rejected the families' argument that the individual board members acted with conscious disregard and malice, as well as willfully and wantonly, by failing to warn victims and secure school grounds. Despite the very general allegations by the families, the court found the complaint was sufficient to deny the employees' and administrators' present claim to immunity. *Parmertor v. Chardon Local Schools*, 47 N.E.3d 942 (Ohio Ct. App. 2016).

◆   A Georgia paraprofessional responsible for assisting a kindergartner with her wheelchair earned immunity in a tort action for damages. According to the state court of appeals, she was using her discretion when she let go of the wheelchair to restrain another child. After the paraprofessional took her hands off the wheelchair, it rolled away and flipped over. Later, the child's parents filed a state court action against the paraprofessional. When the case reached the court of appeals, it explained that **official immunity extends to discretionary actions taken in the scope of official authority**. Finding the actions of the paraprofessional were discretionary, the court held she was entitled to immunity. *Postell v. Anderson*, 797 S.E.2d 397 (Ga. Ct. App. 2015).

◆   Arizona parents said a school employee took pornographic photos of their non-verbal special needs child. In their state court lawsuit, the school district successfully argued it did not know the employee had a prior record of inappropriate conduct. The Court of Appeals of Arizona reversed the lower court's ruling on immunity. It held immunity would not apply only if the school district had actual knowledge (rather than "constructive knowledge") of a propensity for misconduct. The trial court then issued a ruling for the school district, and the parents appealed. When the case returned to the state court of appeals, it held state law insulated a public entity from any liability for a loss caused by an employee's felony acts. The court rejected the parents' argument that "constructive knowledge" of the employee's propensity for misconduct was sufficient to apply an exception to the rule of immunity. Immunity applied unless the public entity actually knew of the propensity for misconduct. **As the parents did not suggest the school district had any actual knowledge of the employee's misconduct when he was a health care employee, the court held immunity had been properly granted.** In addition, the district was entitled to its costs for defending the appeal. *Gallagher v. Tucson Unified School Dist.*, No. 2 CA-CV 2014-124, 2015 WL 2221657 (Ariz. Ct. App. 5/12/15).

◆   Arizona parents claimed a school employee sexually abused and exploited their child. They said he took pornographic pictures of her while she was at school. The parents sought to hold the school district liable for negligent hiring and supervision of the employee. They urged the court that a previous employer could have told the school district about the circumstances of his termination from employment. Although the district moved the court for state law immunity, the court denied it. Appeal went to the Court of Appeals of Arizona. **The court stated that Arizona law immunizes public entities for losses arising out of (and directly attributable to) a felony by a public employee.** Immunity protects an employer "unless the public entity knew of the public employee's propensity for that action." According to the parents, the immunity from this state law applied even if the public entity had only "constructive knowledge" of an employee felony. But the court said the law referred only to "knowledge." It found the legislature could have said "constructive knowledge" had it wished to apply that standard. Since nothing indicated the district had actual knowledge of the employee's propensity for felonious conduct, the court held the district was entitled to immunity. It declined to resolve the merits of the claim based on "negligent failure to investigate," allowing the lower court to consider this. *Tucson Unified School Dist. v. Borek*, 322 P.3d 171 (Ariz. Ct. App. 2014).

♦   A Delaware parent said her autistic child fell down stairs at school while under the supervision of her teachers and paraprofessionals. She claimed the school staff should be liable for "gross, willful and wanton negligence" that caused her child to suffer serious and permanent injuries to her legs, hips and head. In her state court complaint, the parent said the school failed to properly and reasonably supervise the student, failed to provide her with an environment free from danger, hired incompetent and improperly trained and supervised staff, and did not meet the applicable standards of care. While the parent argued that the student's status as a special needs child should cause a "heightened standard of care," a state court held her complaint did not indicate facts that might show previous falls on the steps or any known safety hazards.

According to the court, there were no facts in the complaint to adequately state a claim for gross or wanton negligence. **And while the parent asserted there had been negligent hiring and supervision by the district, these decisions were discretionary and protected by immunity.** Since she was unable to overcome the district's defense of state law immunity, the case was dismissed. *Tews v. Cape Henlopen School Dist.*, C.A. No. 12C-08158 JRJ, 2013 WL 1087580 (Del. Super. Ct. 2/14/13).

♦   A six-year-old student with autism, who was nonverbal, somehow lost the tip of his finger while riding a tricycle during adapted physical education. **Two teachers and two paraeducators were present at the time of the injury, but no one witnessed the incident.** Doctors reattached the fingertip, but the student missed the rest of the semester because of complications that required multiple surgeries. When the student's parent sued the district for negligence, it claimed immunity under the Delaware State Tort Claims Act. The superior court denied immunity to the district because there was a question as to whether district employees acted with gross negligence. *Smith v. Christina School Dist.*, No. N10C-06-208 JRJ, 2011 WL 5924393 (Del. Super. Ct. 11/28/11).

CHAPTER TEN

Student Civil Rights

I. BULLYING AND HARASSMENT

A. Bullying

Although state anti-bullying laws and school district policies require schools to address bullying, they do not create causes of action for private lawsuits. For this reason, bullying cases are decided on tort and constitutional theories, as well as state and federal disability and anti-discrimination laws.

◆   A Texas student with an autism spectrum disorder had a learning disability and a speech impediment. As a ninth-grader, he was of small stature and had bleached blonde hair. According to the student, teachers made comments about his appearance and did not intervene when classmates bullied him. Some of the incidents alleged by the student involved homophobic slurs. He said a student on his school bus told him, "You're autistic, you're gay, and you can't sit here." Another student yelled "faggot" during a class. He said a student assistant who was supposed to help him with classroom tasks called him "bitch boy." According to the student, he reported this to a teacher, who simply responded, "Too bad." The student claimed he was the frequent victim of insults and bullying in school hallways, where others shoved, kicked and knocked things from his hands, but administrators did nothing about it. His parents filed a complaint with the state education agency. They said their son had post-traumatic stress disorder and lived in constant fear of repercussions from the bullying and harassment. The parents filed a due process complaint against the school district. The parties settled the claims regarding special education services. After the hearing officer dismissed the IDEA claims, the parents sued the school district in a federal court, asserting many non-IDEA claims. In pretrial activity, the claims were voluntarily dismissed except one arising under Title IX of the Education Amendments of 1972. The court referred the case to a federal magistrate judge, who found the Title IX claim charged the district with failing to provide a non-hostile educational environment. As the family did not assert a denial of FAPE, there was no need for an IDEA due process hearing.

The magistrate judge recommended that the Title IX claim should proceed. In addition to asserting the student was bullied by peers, the parents claimed he was harassed by teachers and that the school remained deliberately indifferent to this. **Sexual harassment "can encompass a wide range of maltreatment," including the use of sex-specific terms like "bitch" and comments about appearance.** Finding the complaint met the elements of a Title IX claim, the magistrate recommended against dismissal. *Prendergast v. Wylie Independent School Dist.*, No. 4:18-cv-00020-ALM-KPJ, 2018 WL 6710034 (E.D. Tex. 12/4/18).

Within days, the court adopted the magistrate's recommendation, allowing the Title IX claim to proceed. *Prendergast v. Wylie Independent School Dist.*, No. 4:18-cv-20, 2018 WL 6705536 (E.D. Tex. 12/20/18).

◆ A North Carolina elementary student with a severe nut allergy said a classmate told him to "watch out" because he was going to bring nuts to school the next day. The school agreed to treat the remarks as a violation of the code of conduct, and an emergency plan was created for the student. After the student and his mother reported other incidents that they considered bullying, a new plan was made. Although the school increased its supervision of students, he continued to report bullying and the family asked the school to step up its response. The student said the principal called him into his office and told him he was "accountable for the bullying and the bullying situation would improve" if he "was nicer" to the classmate. After viewing school surveillance footage that corroborated a bullying incident, the principal told the student and classmate he was "hitting the reset button and that they were to start over." School officials created a Section 504 plan that separated the two at lunch and recess, but the student reported further bullying. He said the classmate enlisted friends to join the bullying. After the classmate was suspended for misconduct, an administrator tried to persuade the mother to transfer the student and his sister. The mother reported that a classmate assaulted her daughter but was not disciplined. In response to her report, the district superintendent informed the family that "the only option left was to transfer RM and KM to another school."

When the student was diagnosed with Post Traumatic Stress Disorder, the parents removed him from school and sued the board of education in a federal court. In pretrial activity, the court held many of the claims were barred by state law immunity. **To impose tort liability, state law requires claimants to show a government agency has agreed to waive its liability.** The board in this case had not done so. The school officials named in the action enjoyed discretionary immunity. There was no showing that they acted maliciously, corruptly or outside their authority. **The complaint admitted school officials tried to**

address the bullying through meetings, a safety plan, new class schedules and a Section 504 plan. Claims for infliction of emotional distress failed to meet the high threshold required to impose liability, and there were no grounds for constitutional liability. Last, the court rejected disability discrimination claims under state and federal law. There was no showing of intentional discrimination by the board or any facts indicating officials acted in bad faith or with gross misjudgment. *RM v. Charlotte-Mecklenburg County Board of Educ.*, No. 3:16-CV-00528-GCM, 2017 WL 2115108 (N.D.N.C. 5/15/17).

◆   A New Jersey court held a teacher who was accused of bullying a student with disabilities at a wrestling camp had a right to a hearing. Twice during the camp, the teacher told the student that he hoped the student "did not have access to any weapons or keys to the gun closet." After an investigation, the school found the teacher's comments violated the New Jersey Anti-Bullying Bill of Rights. The district's board voted to suspend the teacher from his coaching activities. **When the case reached the Superior Court of New Jersey, it held the teacher was entitled to the procedural protections of the Anti-Bullying Act.** In the court's view, school staff members are entitled to the same procedural rights as students under the act. *S.G. v. Board of Educ. of Hunterdon Cent. Regional School Dist., Hunterdon County*, No. A-5199-15T3, 2018 WL 1095324 (N.J. Super. Ct. App. Div. 3/1/18).

◆   An Oklahoma middle school student's IEP allowed him to leave class early to avoid bullying in school hallways. His parent claimed a math teacher harassed him in his class, refused to follow his IEP and assigned him to sit next to students who bullied him. In addition, the parent said that when her son reported bullying to other teachers and the principal, he was told to disregard it or "deal with it." Next, the parent said that due to bullying and the teacher's failure to follow the IEP, her son cried in class, suffered emotional breakdowns and had falling grades. She sued the school district in a federal court under negligence theories, breach of an implied contract based on the student handbook, retaliation, state-created danger and equal protection violations.

First, the court found the case was filed outside the 180-day limitations period of the Oklahoma Governmental Tort Claims Act. This disposed of the negligence claims. **Although the parent claimed the district breached a contract based on the student handbook, the court refused to recognize this theory.** A claim under the Due Process Clause of the Fourteenth Amendment fell short of the relevant standard of liability and the parent abandoned the equal protection claim. Punitive damages were unavailable. As the parent did not first exhaust her administrative remedies by requesting a due process hearing, the court dismissed the IDEA claims. *Hale v. Independent School Dist. No. 45, Kay County, Oklahoma*, No. CIV-16-1279, 2017 WL 239391 (W.D. Okla. 1/19/17).

◆   A Maryland student had attention deficit hyperactivity disorder, weak visual-spatial ability and a nonverbal learning disability. His parents said he was often bullied, sexually harassed and physically threatened by classmates. In one episode, the student called African-American students a racial epithet after they called him names. The student's mother and stepfather both worked for the school district. They attended a hearing to consider discipline of the student for using the racial epithet. The stepfather claimed the school retaliated against him by not hiring him to teach a summer P.E. class he had previously taught.

Later, the parents sued the school board in a federal court. But the court found "absolutely no evidence" that the board discriminated against the student. Nor was there evidence of a link between the stepfather's advocacy and any board action. After the court dismissed the case, the family appealed to the U.S. Court of Appeals, Fourth Circuit. Noting the student's bullying claims were filed under Section 504 of the Rehabilitation Act, the court observed that Section 504 language closely resembles that of Title IX of the Education Amendments of 1972. The court applied the Title IX sexual harassment liability standard to the disability-based bullying claim and held there could be no school liability. It was not proven that any bullying was based on a disability. In fact, the student's evidence strongly suggested he was both a victim and perpetrator of race-based bullying and slurs. There was evidence that the school responded to every reported instance of bullying. **In ruling for the board, the court noted federal law does not require schools to eradicate each instance of harassment.** Instead, schools are held liable for known student-on-student harassment only when their response (or lack of a response) is clearly unreasonable. The court found no merit to the stepfather's claim that he was not hired for summer work based on his advocacy. As a result, the court held for the board. *S.B. v. Board of Educ. of Harford County*, 819 F.3d 69 (4th Cir. 2016).

◆ New York parents said their third-grade daughter was bullied at school almost daily and that staff members did not confront the bullies. When the parents sought to raise the issue of bullying with the committee on special education, they said the principal "flatly refused to discuss the issue with them."

The parents said team members told them bullying was "an inappropriate topic to consider" during an IEP meeting. They placed their child in a private school for students with learning disabilities and filed an action against the New York City Department of Education (DOE) for private school tuition reimbursement. An impartial hearing officer (IHO) held for the department, and a review officer affirmed the decision. A federal court held for the parents, ruling that **significant, unremedied peer bullying may deny a disabled child a free appropriate public education (FAPE).** After additional proceedings, the case reached the U.S. Court of Appeals, Second Circuit. It found the DOE denied the student a FAPE by refusing to discuss bullying with her parents, despite their reasonable concerns. Staff members confirmed that the student was constantly teased, excluded from groups and subjected to a hostile environment. Since the DOE's persistent refusal to discuss bullying in the IEP process significantly impeded the parents' participation rights, the court found a denial of FAPE that justified the award of private school tuition reimbursement. *T.K. and S.K. v. New York City Dep't of Educ.*, 810 F.3d 869 (2d Cir. 2016).

◆ A Texas student endured years of bullying at school. His parents said that when they reported bullying, it often led to more misconduct and did more harm than good. By fifth grade, the student said peers assaulted him in the locker room and lavatory. He said they took his clothes from his locker and poured soap on them. Later, the student said peers took his shoes, threw them in a toilet and urinated on them. He said a student punched him while he had tics, saying "he was trying to fix them." Nothing was done because he did not report this until the next day. Later, he reported being sprayed in the face with cleaner by a student. In seventh grade, the student was involved in a locker room fight in which he said another student slammed his head against a wall. But the school determined he started the fight. After the student had "tear-away" pants ripped from him, he said the school's response was telling him "not to wear those pants anymore." After this incident, the parents removed their son from school and sued the school district for peer harassment. A federal court held the parents did not show the harassment was based on a disability and also failed to show the district was deliberately indifferent to any harassment.

Appeal reached the U.S. Court of Appeals, Fifth Circuit, which held for the school district. **The court found the family could not prevail under the highly deferential standard for peer harassment cases.** *Nevills v. Mart Independent School Dist.*, 608 Fed.Appx. 217 (5th Cir. 2015).

B. Peer Harassment and Sexual Assault

In peer sexual harassment cases arising under Title IX of the Education Amendments of 1972, the courts apply the "deliberate indifference" standard from Davis v. Monroe County Board of Educ., 526 U.S. 629 (1999). In Davis, *the Supreme Court held that school districts may be held liable under Title IX for student-on-student harassment, where school officials have actual knowledge of peer harassment, but their response is found clearly unreasonable.*

To establish school liability under Davis, *students must show 1) sexual harassment by peers; 2) deliberate indifference by school officials who have actual knowledge of the peer harassment; and 3) harassment that is so severe, pervasive and objectively offensive it deprives the student of access to educational opportunities. Federal courts have held a teacher's knowledge of peer harassment may create "actual knowledge" that triggers Title IX liability.*

◆   A California student with disabilities claimed three male students bullied her, leading her to attempt suicide. She said a relationship with another student turned abusive and that he raped her multiple times. According to the student, the abusive student videotaped a rape incident. She said some incidents took place on campus and that images of her without clothing on were circulated at her school. Further, the student claimed the school's principal ignored her reports in order to protect a student with whom she had a family connection.

In a federal court, the student sued the school district and officials for violating Title IX of the Education Amendments of 1972, the Americans with Disabilities Act (ADA), Section 504 of the Rehabilitation Act and California's Unruh Civil Rights Act. In pretrial activity, the district and principal sought dismissal of the state-law claim. The court found the Unruh Act guarantees all persons in the state equal accommodations, advantages, facilities, privileges, or services in all business establishments of every kind. Although the district argued it could not be a "business establishment," the court found state supreme court precedent held the term is to be construed in the broadest sense. Other federal courts have found school districts are covered by the Unruh Act, which declares that a violation of the ADA is also a state-law violation. Like the ADA, the Unruh Act is concerned with equal access to public accommodations. **Rejecting the principal's arguments, the court held the student stated a valid preliminary claim under the Unruh Act against the school district and employees.** *Yates v. East Side Union High School Dist.*, No. 18-cv-02966-JD, 2019 WL 721313 (N.D. Cal. 2/20/19).

◆   A Florida student with disabilities was susceptible to peer pressure. When he was 11 years old, he attended an alternative school for students with behavioral problems. According to a federal complaint filed on his behalf, the student was in an in-school suspension room with a "seventeen-year-old known sexual predator" who had harmed other students. The complaint stated that the 17-year-old classmate convinced the student to leave school grounds with him and that three school employees saw them leaving the room together. Next, the complaint stated that the classmate sexually assaulted the student off campus.

The classmate later pleaded guilty to criminal charges and was incarcerated. Following the assault, the student suffered anxiety and flashbacks. The complaint recited that he was civilly committed twice. In pretrial activity, the court held the student could not pursue constitutional theories of liability. It held he produced no facts showing his injuries resulted from a board policy or custom. The court found no liability based on a charge that the board did not adequately train suspension room monitors to supervise students with disabilities. Nothing in the complaint showed the board knew that the classmate caused injuries to others due to ineffective supervision. **The court held that to impose liability on the board for disability discrimination, the student had to show discrimination resulting from bad faith or gross misjudgment.** It held he did not show his current placement met this standard. Although the student included a bullying claim, the court found he did not show any peer bullying based on a disability. Having rejected his federal claims, the court refused to hear his state-law claims. *L.C. v. Pinellas County School Board*, No. 8:18-cv-1066-T-23AAS, 2018 WL 6601868 (M.D. Fla. 12/17/18).

◆   A federal court held a Texas school district should not be held liable for injuries to a student with disabilities arising from a sexual assault in an elementary school lavatory. On appeal, the U.S. Court of Appeals, Fifth Circuit, held liability under the U.S. Constitution through 42 U.S.C. § 1983 requires proof of a deprivation of rights by a person acting under color of state law. The Due Process Clause does not require states to protect citizens from private actors such as the assailant in this case. **The student did not assert abuse by a state actor or a specific deficiency by the district that allowed abuse to occur.** The claims were not based on private conduct by the assailant but on the district's shortcomings in monitoring students, training teachers and reporting sexual assault. As a result, the court held the constitutional claims were properly dismissed. Title IX liability requires actual knowledge by a school district of sexual harassment by a harasser who is under the district's control, among other things. **Yet the student admitted he did**

not tell his teacher about the incident, and he begged his mother not to reveal it. Since ADA and Section 504 liability also depend on proof of actual knowledge by a school district, these claims failed. Rejecting all the claims, the court held for the district. *Doe v. Columbia-Brazoria Independent School Dist.*, 855 F.3d 681 (5th Cir. 2017).

◆   A federal appeals court upheld the dismissal of a sexual harassment case filed by a Georgia high school student with disabilities who initially claimed she was gang-raped in a school lavatory, but later changed her story. The court held for the school district, and the case reached the U.S. Court of Appeals, Eleventh Circuit. It noted that **liability in Title IX peer harassment cases requires proof that a federal funding recipient acted with deliberate indifference to known acts of sufficiently severe harassment or discrimination**. The Eleventh Circuit disagreed with the family that two prior incidents in the school district involving different students in 2002 and 2008 created "actual notice" sufficient to trigger Title IX liability. The court held the circumstances surrounding the prior cases were not sufficiently similar to those of this case. One involved an after-school sexual assault to a non-disabled student, while the other involved an attack on a student left unattended in a classroom. After finding neither the 2002 or 2008 incident would alert a responsible school official to the possibility of the assault, the court upheld a lower court's findings that the district response was not deliberately indifferent to the rights of the student. The court found the district's actions following the incident were not clearly unreasonable.

Despite the parent's arguments, a campus police investigation was deemed adequate and thorough. The court found no merit to the parent's claim that there was a political reason for turning the investigation over to the county police department. Nothing indicated the county police investigation was intended to subvert the prior investigation by campus police. Next, the court found the student was not singled out for discipline during a manifestation determination. Finding no reasonable jury would find the school district's response was clearly unreasonable, the court held for the district. *Doe, I v. Bibb County School Dist.*, 688 Fed.Appx. 791 (11th Cir. 2017).

◆   A New Hampshire student with autism, emotional disturbance and an other health impairment underwent a series of psychiatric hospitalizations after engaging in aggressive, sexualized behavior. He remained in a residential treatment facility for over a year, then transferred to the center's day program. While in the day program, a girl began interacting in a sexual manner with the student. He said she made sexual taunts, hugged him, breathed heavily on his neck and followed him around school. A school IEP team met three times during this period but did not discuss the girl's conduct or tell the parents about it. A decision was made to change the student's placement. Several months after the student left the center, he sexually assaulted his younger sister. He was hospitalized and later released to live with his grandparents in another state. When the parents requested his records, they learned about the girl's misconduct. After making a report to the state department of children, youth and families, the parents placed their son in a residential school for students with sexualized behaviors. They sued the school district, education center and various officials in a federal court for negligence and violations of Title IX.

The court granted a motion to dismiss the negligence claims against the education center and school district. It noted the state supreme court has limited any duty involving a special relationship between students and their schools to risks that are reasonably foreseeable at times when parental protection is compromised. **The court rejected the parents' claim that schools owe a duty to students to inform their parents of events occurring when the student is in school custody.** Such a duty would be grounded in a special relationship that has not been recognized by New Hampshire courts. Although the court granted motions to dismiss most of the negligence claims, it denied a motion by the district's director of student services. It also allowed the federal claims to proceed against the residential center. *Ashley M. and Kevin M. v. Spaulding Youth Center*, Civil No. 16-cv-37-JL, 2016 WL 5477574 (D. N.H. 9/29/16).

◆   According to papers filed on behalf of an intellectually disabled Missouri student, her school district negligently allowed her to be raped by another student in an unsupervised area of her school. The student's complaint said she spoke in "baby talk," could not perceive danger and was susceptible to suggestion. Moreover, she had a tendency to wander away when she became frustrated. It was further alleged that the student was relentlessly bullied and harassed by peers. Her complaint stated that she was sexually assaulted at least three times by a student in an area of the school building that was supposed to be locked. After the third incident, her parents sued the school district and school officials in a state court for premises liability and related claims.

Asserting that the claims arose under federal law, the school district removed the action to a federal court. It successfully argued that the student's complaint made references to her IEP, and that the claims amounted to a "repackaged" federal claim arising under the IDEA. Although she sought to return the case to the state court system, the federal court denied this and dismissed the case. When the case reached the U.S. Court of Appeals, Eighth Circuit, it found the case did not concern educational placement. The IEP was mentioned solely to show the district knew of the conditions making the student vulnerable to an assault. The complaint was characterized as a state law action for damages based on the student's brutal injuries from repeated sexual assault while under school supervision. Further, the state claims did not rely on any federal laws. **Since the case did not involve issues of educational placement, and there was no effort to seek IDEA relief, the case was returned to a state court.** *Moore v. Kansas City Public Schools*, 828 F.3d 687 (8th Cir. 2016).

◆   A North Carolina student with disabilities experienced harassment and bullying in district schools. In a federal court action against the board of education, school principal and district superintendent, her parents asserted that she experienced harassment and threats which they repeatedly reported to teachers and administrators, including the principal. The family said the school failed to take corrective action or discipline peers who harassed the student and did not properly investigate reports. The court found state law sets a high standard of proof in negligent supervision cases. To prove her case, the student had to show the board knew of (or had reason to know) school administrators were incompetent. The court found the family did not make this showing.

The family did not state that complaints were made to the board or that it heard of the harassment. Significantly, **the court rejected a claim that the duration, severity and volume of the complaints put the board on notice of a need to train and further supervise employees about responding to harassment and bullying.** While the parents advanced the theory that the board had "constructive notice" of the bullying, the court found this was insufficient to support the claim. As the family produced no facts suggesting the board should have known administrators were ill-prepared to handle harassment and bullying, the claim failed. The court dismissed a negligent supervision claim, and a claim under the state constitution. *M.H. v. Onslow County Board of Educ.*, No. 7:16-CV-00069-FL, 2016 WL 5678402 (E.D.N.C. 9/30/16).

◆   A Connecticut student with a learning disability said coaches and other high school staff tolerated and encouraged bullying by peers. In a federal court, he filed a 14-count complaint asserting violations of state and federal laws. In pretrial activity, the court considered claims that teammates called the student names and harassed him daily. He said they called him vulgar and demeaning names, threw him down, threw rocks at him and caused him to swallow a rock. Although the student claimed he reported many incidents, he said these reports only led to escalating harassment. He became afraid to attend school and missed significant school time. Some of the bullying involved sexual contact, which was investigated by police. The student said he was sexually assaulted by a student in the presence of several others, but he did not feel safe reporting it. School officials denied learning of any bullying, harassment or retaliation.

The court dismissed the due process, equal protection and disability discrimination claims, along with a harassment claim under Title IX of the Education Amendments of 1972 and the state law claims. But the court allowed the student to amend his complaint to present newly discovered evidence about the head coach from interviews conducted by the Department of Children and Families. The new evidence supported a claim that the coach violated the student's due process rights. **Since the court found statements from the department's investigation supported a claim that the head coach sent players a message of approval about their misconduct, the student could proceed with a due process claim against him.** *Doe v. Torrington Board of Educ.*, No. 3:15-cv-00452 (MPS), 2016 WL 6821061 (D. Conn. 11/17/16).

◆   A disabled student who was led from her classroom then raped in a school closet by a non-disabled student was unable to convince a federal court that her school district should be held liable for her injuries. **Placement in a restrictive setting did not create a custodial relationship that would trigger a constitutional duty to protect her.** The court found no showing that the student was assaulted because of her cognitive disabilities or was likely to be harassed due to her disabilities. No evidence showed her attacker was a threat or had a prior history of sexual assault. While the federal claims were all dismissed, the court held the student's remaining state claims could be refiled in a state court. *Martin v. East St. Louis School Dist. #189*, No. 14-cv-1393-MJR-SWC, 2016 WL 1718332 (S.D. Ill. 4/29/16).

◆ A Texas parent complained that a student with a disability who had previously sexually assaulted a girl and spent time in an alternative education program would soon be returning to his child's middle school. Although the parent insisted that the student with a disability go to another school, officials reassured him that other children would be protected. Midway through the school year, the disabled student and another male were accused of "T-bagging everybody." The child of the parent who complained said he had been subjected to this misconduct, and that the disabled student teased and taunted him many other times. Administrators investigated and placed the disabled student and his friend on in-school suspension. After interviewing over 50 students, administrators recommended sending the disabled student and his friend to a disciplinary alternative educational placement. Although the disabled student was transferred, the child's parent withdrew his son from the school district.

In a federal court, the parent sued the district for sexual harassment in violation of Title IX. After the court dismissed the case, he appealed to the Fifth Circuit Court of Appeals. It held that **liability under Title IX for peer-to peer sexual harassment requires proof that the school district had actual knowledge of the harassment**. But the lower court found the district had no knowledge of the harassment until the T-bagging incidents were reported. When administrators learned of the problem, they took prompt investigative and remedial action. Since the court found the school district responded promptly once it learned of the harassment, there was no Title IX violation. *Kelly v. Allen Independent School Dist.*, 602 Fed.Appx. 949 (5th Cir. 2015).

◆ A Nevada student said a classmate approached her from behind, put one hand under her chin and the other on her forehead, then pulled her head straight back, causing injuries. In a federal court, the student sued the school district for disability discrimination and negligence. The court analyzed the peer harassment claim under the liability standard from *Davis v. Monroe County Board of Educ.*, 526 U.S. 629 (1999). The court found the student's own statements prevented any finding that the classmate was harassing her on the basis of a disability. She did not show the school was deliberately indifferent to any misconduct. While she felt bullied by the classmate, she never reported anything to the school. **Since there was no evidence that the school knew of any discriminatory treatment of the student based on a disability, her discrimination claim failed.** *Visnovits v. White Pine County School Dist.*, No. 3:14-CV-00182, 2015 WL 1806299 (D. Nev. 4/21/15).

◆ A New Jersey student with disabilities reported being sexually assaulted at school by a male student. Although she said a similar incident took place two years earlier, an investigation of that case found any sexual contact had been consensual. The parents provided the school a psychological evaluation report describing a history of taunting by peers and repeated episodes in which peers touched the student or tried to have sex with her. They sued the school board, an assistant principal and a substitute teacher who let the students in the room where the assault took place. After dismissing IDEA, Section 504, Americans with Disabilities Act and state law against discrimination claims, the family said the first incident should have put the school on notice that the student was at a heightened risk to be sexually victimized by peers. But the court held **the Constitution does not impose a duty on the states to protect individuals from harm inflicted by private actors, such as the male student in this case**. While the student would have a heavy burden at trial to meet the Title IX standard, the court refused to dismiss the Title IX claim. *Lockhart v. Willingboro High School*, 170 F.Supp.3d 722 (D.N.J. 2015).

C. Sexual Assault by School Staff Members

The U.S. Supreme Court has recognized the potential for school liability under Title IX where a student is harassed by peers or staff members. In Gebser v. Lago Vista Independent School Dist., *524 U.S. 274, 118 S.Ct. 1989, 141 L.Ed.2d 277 (1998), the Supreme Court held school districts may be held liable for sexual harassment of students by teachers and other staff under Title IX.*

Damages are inappropriate in a Title IX case unless an official with the authority to address the discrimination fails to act despite actual knowledge of it, in a manner amounting to deliberate indifference.

◆   A Pennsylvania high school freshman had sexual relations with a teacher's aide. He dropped out of school the following year, and the aide became pregnant as the result of their relationship. Some 12 years after their child was born, the student sued the school district, aide and others in a federal court. Ruling that no reasonable jury could find the officials had actual notice that the aide presented a substantial danger to students, the court held for the district and officials. The student appealed the Title IX ruling to the Third Circuit Court of Appeals.

In the court's view, substantial facts were at issue that made pretrial judgment inappropriate on the student's Title IX claim. **To prevail on his Title IX claim, the student had to show that an "appropriate person" at the school had "actual notice" of discriminatory conduct but was deliberately indifferent to it.** There was no dispute that "appropriate persons" were present at a meeting who had authority to address discrimination and institute corrective measures for the district. As the evidence could support the claim that these persons had actual knowledge of the danger to students posed by the aide, the court held pretrial judgment was improper. If true, the student's claims suggested the officials made no serious effort to stop the aide's inappropriate conduct. As a result, the case was returned to the lower court for more fact-finding on the Title IX claim. *C.K. v. Wrye*, 751 Fed.Appx. 179 (3d Cir. 2018).

◆   A Nevada student claimed he attempted suicide as the result of sexual harassment by one of his teachers. In a federal court action against his school district, a teacher and the school principal, the student claimed he exchanged explicit text messages with his English teacher. He said the teacher eventually engaged him in a sexual relationship during his freshman year of high school. When the misconduct was reported, he said he was questioned in a school office where other students saw him and realized he was having a relationship with the teacher. The student said peers harassed him in person and on social media. He said the principal retaliated against him and that his Section 504 plan was not implemented. A federal court considered his case and found insufficient facts to support a substantive due process claim. The court found insufficient facts to show the school did not implement or modify his Section 504 plan and allowed teachers and students to harass him. **There was no merit to a constitutional claim based on the principal's decision to hire the English teacher despite knowledge that she had previously flirted with another male student.** As for the harassment claim, the court found it was not shown that the principal acted with deliberate indifference. She was entitled to qualified immunity, as the court found nothing made her aware of previous inappropriate conduct by the teacher.

The court held the student could pursue his Section 1983 claim based on the manner in which school police questioned him while visible to others in an open school office. Otherwise, the constitutional claims failed. Once the improper relationship was discovered, the district investigated and fired the teacher, who was criminally charged. The student could pursue claims based on infliction of emotional distress arising from his suicide attempt. *Doe v. Clark County School Dist.*, No. 2:15-cv-00793-APG-GWF, 2017 WL 1483428 (D. Nev. 4/21/17).

◆   A Pennsylvania student with disabilities said an assistant principal (AP) at her school repeatedly sexually assaulted her. According to the student, her peers accused her of having sex with the AP and called her names such as "whore" and "home-wrecker." When a teacher reported the suspected relationship of the AP and student, administrators interviewed several students but found the report was not substantiated. According to the student, peers continued to harass her. Nothing was officially reported to the police until the following school year, when a school resource officer reported the relationship to municipal police.

After a brief investigation, the AP was arrested. The student transferred to another district and filed a federal case against the AP, school district and other officials. In the court's view, the constitutional claims were not viable since no violation was the result of a municipal custom, practice or policy. A "failure to intervene" claim against school administrators was dismissed, as the court held it was not shown they were deliberately indifferent to constitutional violations by the AP. **The court held the notice requirement was not satisfied based on claims of unsubstantiated rumors at the school.** It also dismissed the claims based on constitutional theories of failure to train, negligent hiring, negligent retention and failure to discipline the AP. On the other hand, the court held the student made out a valid preliminary Title IX case against the school district. As she claimed officials knew a hostile environment was created but did not respond to it, her Title IX claim was held viable. *M.S. v. Susquehanna Township School Dist.*, 43 F.Supp.3d 412 (M.D. Pa. 2014).

◆   A Massachusetts high school student was sexually harassed by her school soccer coach, but she did not reveal this for months. When her parents approached the school for help with her emotional problems, they were advised to file a child in need of services petition with a juvenile court. When the student finally told a friend she had been assaulted, her mother reported it. Another report involving the coach then surfaced. He was fired and later pled guilty to criminal charges. It was learned that throughout the fall and winter, the coach verbally harassed the student, texted her pictures of his penis, and asked for nude photos of her. After his arrest, the school held a class-wide assembly to discuss the incident and arrest. According to the parents, the student's absence was noted at the assembly, leading to speculation that she was the victim. After being admitted to a hospital, the student was evaluated for special education. Her parents placed her in a residential therapeutic school for which they sought reimbursement from the school system. After the school district found her eligible for special education, it agreed to pay for a residential placement.

The student ran away from the residential school, and the team could find no other placement for her. After a due process hearing, the parents filed a federal court case. The court held constitutional claims based on sexual abuse could proceed. **Further evidence would be heard regarding whether the school was deliberately indifferent to earlier reports of sexual relations between the coach and other students.** There was no merit to an IDEA claim, but the family raised enough evidence to avoid pretrial dismissal of their claims under Section 504 and the ADA. The court refused to dismiss a negligence claim based on failure to dismiss the coach after a reported sexual relationship. *Doe v. Bradshaw*, No. 11-11593-DPW, 2013 WL 5236110 (D. Mass. 9/16/13).

II. REASONABLE ACCOMMODATION

Rehabilitation Act Section 504 states that no otherwise qualified individual with a disability shall, "solely by reason of her or his disability," be excluded from participation in, denied the benefits of, or be subjected to discrimination under any program or activity receiving federal assistance.

In school settings, a viable Section 504 claim is stated when it is alleged that a school has denied reasonable accommodations that are necessary for a disabled student to receive the full benefits of the school program.

The Americans with Disabilities Act of 1990 (ADA) is based upon the anti-discrimination principles of Section 504 and covers public and private entities without regard to their receipt of federal funding.

A. Generally

Under the ADA and the Rehabilitation Act, educational facilities, as well as many other entities, are required to make reasonable accommodations for disabled individuals. This entails the reasonable modification of policies, practices or procedures when such modifications are necessary for disabled individuals to participate in programs or to benefit from services. However, modifications that would fundamentally alter the schools' programs or services, or that would result in an undue burden or hardship, are not required.

◆ A Pennsylvania charter school student had attention deficit/hyperactivity disorder. His parents requested teaching and testing accommodations for him while he attended the school. According to the parents, the school agreed to make accommodations when it admitted the student for grade nine. But they later said the school either could not or would not provide the accommodations. Charging the school with failing to reasonably accommodate his disability in violation of the Americans with Disabilities Act (ADA), the parents filed a lawsuit seeking injunctive relief on behalf of the student and all similarly situated charter school students and applicants. In addition to the ADA claim, the family asserted state-law claims against the school including breach of contract and infliction of emotional distress. During pretrial activity, the student graduated from high school and enrolled in a university. Noting the student's graduation, the court dismissed the case for lack of standing and mootness. It declined to hear the state-law claims, which went to a state court. On appeal, the U.S. Court of Appeals, Third Circuit, explained that the U.S. Constitution allows federal courts to consider "actual cases and controversies only, not moot ones."

A case is moot if the suing party no longer has a personal stake in the case or the court can no longer grant the requested relief. **Graduation may eliminate a personal stake in the outcome of a case, and it typically moots a claim for an injunction or a declaration.** In this case, the student's graduation meant he would never again be subjected to the school's teaching methods. As the case was mooted by his graduation, the court held he could not "rescue" the ADA claim via any existing exception to the mootness doctrine. Next, the court rejected an invitation to recognize a new exception to mootness based on the student's "constructive expulsion" from the charter school. He could not obtain relief for any "residual reputational or psychological trauma" under the ADA, but he could continue seeking damages in a state court. As the lower court had correctly found the case moot, the court held for the charter school. *Mirabella v. William Penn Charter School*, No. 752 Fed.Appx. 131 (3d Cir. 2018).

◆ A West Virginia student with diabetes wore an insulin pump. She had a Section 504 plan stating she would not be penalized for medical absences. After she accumulated five absences, truancy notices were sent to the student and her father. The student then accumulated 14 additional absences, which the board considered unexcused. Without further notice to the student or her father, the board of education filed a truancy complaint. A few weeks later, the student's father identified dates that the student was absent due to her diabetes and the truancy complaint was dismissed. Later, the student sued the board in a state court for failure to accommodate her. In her action, the student added claims for malicious prosecution and reckless infliction of emotional distress.

In awarding judgment to the board, the judge found probable cause to file a truancy case. The student appealed to the Supreme Court of Appeals of West Virginia, which found the lower court had complied with state rules and code provisions on school attendance. **Despite the board's concession that it did not meet quarterly to review her absences, the student did not show how the board failed to reasonably accommodate her illness.** As the lower court found, the student did not show any extreme or outrageous conduct by the board that would support a claim for reckless infliction of emotional distress. She did not show the filing of the truancy complaint was malicious. There was probable cause to file the complaint, as the student had accrued 14 additional unexcused absences beyond the five that triggered the initial notice from the assistant principal. As a result, the court held for the board of education. *C.D. v. Grant County Board of Educ.*, No. 16-1035, 2017 WL 4711425 (W. Va. 10/20/17).

◆   A Massachusetts student said his school's Wi-Fi signal triggered symptoms of Electromagnetic Hypersensitivity Syndrome (EHS). His parents claimed that when they asked the school to replace the classroom Wi-Fi with ethernet access, the school refused, saying it already complied with federal safety limits. But the school also offered to keep the student at least eight feet from Wi-Fi sources and let him connect to the internet via ethernet. The family sued the school for failure to make a reasonable accommodation in violation of the Americans with Disabilities Act (ADA). In addition, the family asserted retaliation in violation of the ADA, negligence, misrepresentation and breach of contract.

A federal court excluded testimony and opinion from a physician who proposed to declare that the student's symptoms were evidence of specific causation. In the court's view, the doctor failed to articulate a scientifically reliable basis linking the student's symptoms with the school Wi-Fi. She failed to describe her efforts to identify other environmental factors that might cause or contribute to his symptoms. Although a pediatric neurosurgeon offered evidence of causation based on her experience and education, the court found insufficient evidence that the student suffered EHS caused by the school's Wi-Fi. **In the court's view, the student's symptoms could have been caused by many factors. Since the evidence did not show a causal link between his symptoms and the school Wi-Fi, the negligence and ADA reasonable accommodation claims failed.** On the other hand, the family's ADA retaliation claim had to be further considered. This was primarily because the school did not explain why it disallowed the student's participation in school athletics and excluded his brother from a graduation program. *G v. Fay School*, 282 F.Supp.3d 381 (D. Mass. 2017).

◆   An Arizona student attended a program for gifted students with at least one disability. After a few months, she refused to go to class, destroyed property, threatened to harm herself, acted aggressively, caused disruption and was noncompliant. During one incident, the student did not cooperate with a school resource officer and hit her. The school suspended the student, held an IEP meeting and transferred her to a school for students with emotional disturbances. On her second day there, the student had to be escorted to an intervention room. She kicked a paraprofessional in the face, and a municipal police officer arrested her for aggravated assault and criminal damage. About six weeks later, a teacher called the same officer to escort the student to the intervention room. The officer tried to handcuff the student, but the student resisted and scratched her, requiring backup. As a result, the student was again arrested for aggravated assault. This time, she was placed in juvenile detention.

Juvenile charges from both incidents were dismissed, and the student was moved to a private psychiatric school. After pursuing a due process complaint, the parents sued the district, municipality and municipal officer. They settled their claims against the officer and municipality and reached an agreement with the district regarding the IDEA claims. But claims arising under Section 504 of the Rehabilitation Act and Title II of the Americans with Disabilities Act (ADA) went forward, as did several tort claims. Appeal reached the U.S. Court of Appeals, Ninth Circuit, where the parents argued the district discriminated against their child by failing to provide her with reasonable accommodations, including a behavior intervention plan and a functional behavioral assessment. The court held **the Section 504 and ADA claims should go forward for denial of meaningful access to educational opportunities and reasonable accommodations**. Evidence indicated that placement in the school for students with emotional disturbances denied the student meaningful access to art, music and gifted education programming. The lower court would have to reconsider whether accommodations would have helped her keep her original placement. *A.G. v. Paradise Valley Unified School Dist.*, 815 F.3d 1195 (9th Cir. 2016).

◆   Kentucky parents insisted that their diabetic child attend his neighborhood school. Their school district refused because no school nurse worked at the site. Although full-time nurses worked at two other district schools, the parents rejected both sites. School nurses believed he needed assistance from a nurse and that insulin injections were a nursing function. The district again denied enrollment at the neighborhood school, and the child began attending a district school staffed by a nurse. His parents sued the school board in a federal court for violations of the ADA, Section 504 and the Kentucky Civil Rights Act.

In ruling for the board and superintendent, the court found the student had no right under Section 504 to attend a neighborhood school. In 2012, the U.S. Court of Appeals, Sixth Circuit, returned the case to the trial court for further proceedings. The court again held for the board, and the case returned to the Sixth Circuit. It noted a recent change to Kentucky law barred a school from excluding students on the sole basis that it does not have a full-time nurse. Since state law forbade the actions which the student sought to enjoin, his request was now moot. Next, the court found no merit to the student's claims for damages under the ADA, Section 504 and state law. It found no evidence that the board knew it would likely violate the student's rights. Kentucky Civil Right Act claims are treated like federal claims, so the state law claim also failed. *R.K. v. Board of Educ. of Scott County, Kentucky,* 637 Fed.Appx. 922 (6th Cir. 2016).

◆   Due to Klinefelter Syndrome and ADHD, a California student was eligible for Section 504 accommodations. He enrolled in an advanced placement (AP) calculus course, where he struggled and suffered from anxiety and weight loss. His mother asked for permission to drop the class, but was told the three-day window for dropping classes had passed. An assistant principal told her no exceptions could be made to the school policy. A hearing officer denied the parent's request for an order requiring the district to pay for a Section 504 evaluation and remove a failing AP calculus grade from the student's records.

A federal court held the student was prohibited from dropping the AP class under a general rule of the district, not because of a disability. But it held **the student had a plausible claim against administrators regarding a timeline and procedure for proposing and conducting evaluations for students who might need Section 504 accommodations**. The student could refile this claim to allege he was denied a service or benefit solely due to a disability. But he could not show any deprivation of a protected interest in not being allowed to drop his AP course. A due process right is only implicated when exclusion from the entire educational process is at stake. *S.M. v. San Jose Unified School Dist.*, No. 14-CV-03613, 2015 WL 1737535 (N.D. Cal. 4/13/15).

B. Service Animals

In Fry v. Napoleon Community Schools, *137 S.Ct. 743 (U.S. 2017), the Supreme Court held a Michigan student deserved another chance to pursue disability discrimination claims arising from a decision by school administrators to disallow her service dog from school. The Court held she should have an opportunity to show she did not have to bring an IDEA due process proceeding prior to filing suit.*

◆ A Michigan student with severe cerebral palsy had a service dog trained to help her with mobility and activities such as opening doors, turning on and off lights and transferring on and off a toilet. Her parents asked school officials to allow the dog to accompany their child to school. After a brief trial period, the dog was not allowed at school. In response, the parents removed their child from school and began homeschooling her. They filed a federal agency complaint, charging the school district with violating the ADA and Section 504 of the Rehabilitation Act. The agency held the district did not comply with the ADA and Section 504, even if a 1:1 aide provided the student a FAPE. School officials allowed the dog to accompany the student to school. But the parents felt the administration would resist their child's return to school, so they placed her in another district, where the dog and student were welcomed. The parents sued the school district and a regional school district in a federal court.

The court dismissed the case because the parents did not first file an IDEA due process complaint. The case reached the U.S. Supreme Court, which held a party cannot escape the exhaustion requirement by simply filing an action under a law other than the IDEA. If the action seeks a remedy that implicates a FAPE, exhaustion is required. This is because the only relief an IDEA hearing officer can order is relief from the denial of a FAPE. **Courts should review the substance of a complaint when determining whether the FAPE obligation is implicated.** To illustrate its decision, the Court offered two considerations. A court should examine whether the same claim could be brought if the alleged conduct took place at a public facility other than a school. Next, a reviewing court should examine whether an employee or visitor to a school could have brought the same kind of grievance. If the family could have filed a similar claim against a non-school entity, or a similar action could have been filed by an employee or a school visitor, the complaint would be unlikely to involve a FAPE. If a complaint appeared to involve the FAPE duty, a court should still examine the history of the proceedings to determine whether the family has previously invoked IDEA procedures. *Fry v. Napoleon Community Schools,* 137 S.Ct. 743, 197 L.Ed.2d 46 (U.S. 2017).

When the case returned to the Sixth Circuit, it found important information was missing about the proceedings prior to the filing of the lawsuit. It sent the case to the trial court to address the deficiency of information about this time period. When the case returned to the trial court in 2018, it permitted the parties to engage in discovery, then considered and denied their motions for pretrial judgment. Months later, the parents again moved for pretrial judgment. This time, the court found no evidence indicating they sued under the ADA and Section 504 "as a strategic calculation to maximize the prospect of a remedy for the denial of a FAPE." The parents did not request any relief for the denial of a FAPE, or even any relief relating to an IEP. In fact, **the student no longer attended an elementary school**. In sum, the court held the action was not subject to the IDEA's exhaustion rule. *Fry v. Napoleon Community Schools*, 371 F.Supp.3d 387 (E.D. Mich. 2019).

♦   A Utah student attended school with a dog for a few days before being told that a school district policy prohibited her from doing so. After a hearing, a school panel issued an opinion affirming the decision to exclude the dog. The parent sued the district in a federal court, seeking a declaration that the dog was a "service animal" as defined by the Americans with Disabilities Act (ADA) and state law. At some point after filing suit, the family moved outside the school's boundaries. According to the parent, the exclusion of the service animal violated her civil rights. But the court found she did not clarify "what those civil rights might be." It held she did not state a plausible federal claim and dismissed the ADA claim. As for the parent's state-law claim, the court noted the family's move made this question moot. But it also found that even if the matter was not moot, it would still rule in the school district's favor.

Utah law provided that a non-disabled person has a right to be accompanied by an animal in training in a variety of private and public locations, but not schools. **A "service animal" as defined by state law excluded an animal used solely to provide emotional support, well-being, comfort or companionship**. The court found state law did not require a school district to allow a service animal in training that accompanied a non-disabled student into a high school classroom. State law did not extend ADA accommodation requirements to non-disabled students. As the Utah statute did not require accommodations for non-disabled people with service animals in training to the same extent as required by the ADA, the court held for the district. *Naegle v. Canyons School Dist.*, No. 2:17-cv-23-DB, 2018 WL 2376336 (D. Utah 5/23/18).

♦   A federal court dismissed a case by New Hampshire parents who sought to compel their school district to provide a handler for their child's service dog. As explained by the Supreme Court in *Fry v. Napoleon Community Schools*, 137 S.Ct. 743 (U.S. 2017), IDEA administrative remedies must be exhausted before a lawsuit is brought under federal laws seeking relief that is available under the IDEA. As the parties noted, **the dog was not educationally necessary for the student, as it did not assist him in achieving his IEP goals.** In the court's view, the complaint disclosed dissatisfaction by the parents with the level of services being provided to the student. Applying the *Fry* analysis, the court held they could not have stated a similar claim for relief under the ADA or Rehabilitation Act against a non-school entity. Nor could an adult state a claim against the district based on refusal to provide a dog handler. The court found the rights claimed by the parents were unique to the student's effort to obtain a FAPE. Last, the relationship of the parties suggested the parents were seeking relief relating to their child's education. As they failed to exhaust their administrative remedies, the court dismissed the case. *A.R. v. School Administrative Unit #23*, No. 15-cv-152-SM, 2017 WL 4621587 (D.N.H. 10/12/17).

◆   A Florida child had cerebral palsy, a seizure disorder and other disabilities that required her to have daily living support. Her mother obtained a service dog that was trained to perform life-saving duties and to alert responders in case of a medical crisis. The school board required the mother to provide a handler for the dog, provide proof of liability insurance and proof of vaccinations mirroring those for Florida dog breeders. A health care plan was devised to address the board's responsibilities in the event that the student had a seizure, but neither the plan nor the student's IEP specified the use of a service dog. In a federal court, the mother sued the board for violating federal disability protection laws.

The court relied on 28 C.F.R. Part 35.136, a federal regulation that generally requires public entities to modify their policies so disabled persons may use their service animals. **Unless an entity could show a requested modification would fundamentally alter its program, the modification was deemed necessary to avoid discrimination.** The board did not argue that allowing the student to attend school with the service dog would fundamentally alter its program. The court held the policies requiring additional insurance and vaccinations amounted to impermissible discrimination. It also found that since the dog would be tethered to the student's wheelchair and was fully trained, there was no need for a separate handler. *Alboniga v. School Board of Broward County Florida*, 87 F.Supp.3d 1319 (S.D. Fla. 2015).

III. FEDERAL CIVIL RIGHTS REMEDIES

Section 1983 of Title 42 of the U.S. Code (42 U.S.C. § 1983) is a federal statute that creates no rights itself, but is used to enforce rights created by federal laws and the Constitution. Section 1983 imposes liability on a school district or other government entity that has a policy or custom of violating constitutional rights. It also creates individual liability for school officials who violate clearly established constitutional rights. The IDEA expressly allows disabled students to cumulate all their available remedies under federal law.

◆   A Texas student said he was improperly disciplined and denied privileges while attending a Texas high school. He said he was subjected to a variety of improper and unconstitutional actions by school officials and a municipal police officer. He said the officer put him in a choke hold and violently attacked him following a hallway incident with a classmate. After he graduated from high school, he sued the school district and the municipal police officer in a federal court for numerous federal law violations. In pretrial activity, the court assessed the claims that were unrelated to the student's arrest.

Although the student asserted constitutional claims under 42 U.S.C. § 1983, the court found they were not viable. He did not show other similarly situated students were treated differently than he was, defeating an equal protection claim. A due process claim failed because the student did not show the school did not provide the constitutional minimum notice and an opportunity to be heard regarding any of his disciplinary incidents. The court held he did not show any civil rights violation based on his arrest by the municipal officer.

Liability under 42 U.S.C. § 1983 requires proof of a violation resulting from a municipal policy or custom, which the student in this case did not allege. *Clinton v. Dallas Independent School Dist.*, No. 3:17-CV-2981-S, 2019 WL 1411474 (N.D. Tex. 3/27/19).

◆   A New York student said her parent emailed one of her teachers to suggest that he remove a video from his Facebook page that students were viewing. In the parent's opinion, the video showed the teacher in an intoxicated state. Later, the student said she had a panic attack when she learned the teacher posted the email from her parent. Her parent reported the posting, and the school suspended the teacher for a week. According to the student, classmates confronted her and blamed her for the teacher's suspension. The student filed a federal civil rights lawsuit against the school district for denial of a free appropriate public education in violation of Section 504 of the Rehabilitation Act and the Americans with Disabilities Act (ADA). She claimed the school district should have provided her an English tutor rather than making her choose between staying in the teacher's class or transferring to another tenth-grade English class.

The student added state-law negligence claims based on the failure to provide her a tutor, negligent infliction of emotional harm, and negligent hiring and supervision of the teacher. They also included civil rights claims arising under 42 U.S.C. § 1983 based on Section 504 and ADA violations. **The court found the IDEA exhaustion requirement applies to ADA and Section 504 claims involving the education of a child with a disability.** It disagreed with the family's claim to be excused from the exhaustion requirement based on lack of procedural protection notices from the district. Although the student claimed the school district refused to provide a tutor, she did not ask for one until well after the teacher's return to school. The court found the Section 1983 claims duplicated the Section 504 and ADA claims and were subject to administrative exhaustion. As a result, the court dismissed all the federal claims. *Parent and Student v. Pittsford Cent. School Dist.*, 237 F.Supp.3d 82 (W.D.N.Y. 2017).

◆   A Pennsylvania substitute teacher's class became unruly, and she repeatedly asked for quiet. A student began recording the classroom on his phone. The substitute told him "shut up," and said "it's day 13 and I can't stand you already." Among other things, she asked if he "had a problem" and whether he "suffered from Tourette's." After the student's parents learned of the incident, they asked for an investigation. An independent investigator found no violation of the state school code. But the superintendent reprimanded the substitute and required that she acknowledge her inappropriate conduct and enroll in a remedial course.

When the school board decided not to dismiss the substitute, the parents sued the school district, superintendent and substitute. A federal court held for the district and appeal went before the U.S. Court of Appeals, Third Circuit. It held the family's due process claim failed because it did not assert any affirmative action that created a danger to the student. Instead, the parents only claimed the substitute "inflicted cruel and unusual treatment" on their child through her verbal abuse. **Prior Third Circuit cases have found verbal abuse is not a constitutional violation.** While telling the student to "shut up" and asking if he had Tourette's Syndrome was found "disturbing," the court found it did not rise to the level of a constitutional rights violation. Next, the court held the state law claims had been properly dismissed. It was not shown that the superintendent engaged in any willful misconduct. The matter was referred to an independent investigator for review. This led to a report that there was no state code violation by the substitute. In addition, the substitute had to acknowledge her wrongful conduct and attend a remedial course. As the family's arguments lacked merit, the court held for the school district. *L.H. v. Pittston Area School Dist.*, 666 Fed.Appx. 212 (3d Cir. 2016).

IV. DISCRIMINATION

In J.S., III v. Houston County Board of Educ., *this chapter, the U.S. Court of Appeals, Eleventh Circuit, found the alleged exclusion and isolation of a student from peers on the basis of his disability went beyond the scope of an IDEA claim for misdiagnosis or failure to provide appropriate academic work. The court relied on* Olmstead v. L.C. ex rel. Zimring, *527 U.S. 581 (1999), in which the U.S. Supreme Court held that* **unjustified institutional isolation of a person with a disability is a form of disability discrimination under the ADA**.

◆   An Iowa student suffered a traumatic brain injury as an infant and was later diagnosed with ADHD, dysgraphia and a nonverbal learning disorder. Due to these disabilities, he had a Section 504 plan allowing extra time for assignments and tests. While scoring in the 99th and 97th percentile for verbal comprehension and working memory, the student's processing speed index was found to be in the ninth percentile. As a high school freshman in a public school, he was found eligible for special education. A team developed an IEP for him and met to modify it multiple times over the next 18 months. Unhappy with their son's progress, the parents placed him in a private Pennsylvania academy. During the next summer, the IEP team met and agreed to incorporate changes and updates to the IEP based on the parents' suggestions. The results of a private evaluation were also considered. After the parents filed a due process complaint, an administrative law judge held a hearing. He then dismissed the case, finding the student was not an Iowa resident and that the district had no obligation to him.

In a federal court, the parents sued the school district for disability discrimination. The court found that in K-12 education cases filed under Section 504 and the ADA, a party must prove more than non-compliance with the laws. Rather, they must show school officials acted in bad faith or with gross misjudgment. To make this showing, **a party must show a substantial departure from accepted professional judgment, practice or standards**. Moreover, **the courts have found Congress did not intend to create Section 504 and ADA liability in the absence of a gross departure from accepted professional standards**. In this case, the court found the parents did not allege the school district acted in bad faith. They simply argued the IEP was inappropriate. The court held noncompliance with the IDEA alone is not bad faith or gross misjudgment. As the district argued, the parents failed to show gross misjudgment or bad faith under Section 504 and the ADA. No evidence suggested anything more than a disagreement between the district and the parents. On appeal, the Eighth Circuit found the lower court properly held for the school district. It held the parents did not show the district acted in bad faith or with gross misjudgment when offering the IEP. *Doe v. Pleasant Valley School Dist.*, 745 Fed.Appx. 658 (8th Cir. 2018).

◆ A Hawaii parent said her son's preschool teacher occasionally seated him in a Rifton chair even though this was not stated in his IEP or behavior plan. She further asserted this conduct violated a Section 504 regulation found at 34 C.F.R. Part 104.33(b)(1)(i) that requires educational aids and services to be designed to meet a child's individual educational needs. A federal court held a jury trial and found no violation of Section 504 of the Rehabilitation Act. On appeal, the Ninth Circuit Court of Appeals noted that implementing an IEP is one means of ensuring compliance with Section 504 requirements. It held the parent incorrectly argued the use of a Rifton chair not specified in an IEP necessarily violated Section 504 regulations requiring the provision of a free appropriate public education (FAPE). Further, the court found disputed facts regarding the chair that made a trial appropriate on the Section 504 issues. Next, the court held the lower court did not commit error in dismissing the state-law claims of assault and battery and negligent infliction of emotional distress.

The court found the evidence was insufficient to show any employee demonstrated the level of malice required to overcome the qualified privilege defense. The lower court did not commit error in formulating instructions for the jury. In fact, it properly drew a careful distinction between a claim for denial of a FAPE under the IDEA and a claim for disability discrimination based on denial of meaningful access to education under Section 504. **To prevail on a claim for monetary damages under Section 504, the parent had to show intentional discrimination by school employees.** As the parent failed to show any error by the lower court, the Ninth Circuit affirmed the judgment. *Ricks v. State of Hawaii Dep't of Educ.*, 752 Fed.Appx. 518 (9th Cir. 2019).

◆ The parents of an 18-year-old Virginia student with Down syndrome claimed his school tried to prevent him from graduating with a regular high school diploma. They said his IEPs had included rigorous goals since he was in grade two and the ultimate goal for him was to graduate with a standard diploma. But the parents claimed that shortly after their son entered high school, he was denied services specified in his IEP. They accused certain teachers and specialists of choosing not to work with him on some IEP goals. According to the parents, their child was allowed to avoid academic participation and watched videos on YouTube instead. Next, they claimed special educators at the school began suggesting new IEPs that did not contain the rigor shown in prior IEPs. They refused to consent to the IEPs and filed a due process complaint.

A hearing officer held the school district provided the child a FAPE. Later, the parents challenged the decision in federal court. They added claims against the district for disability discrimination and retaliation against them in violation of Section 504 of the Rehabilitation Act and the Americans with Disabilities Act (ADA). **The court held that students with disabilities must show either bad faith or gross misjudgment by school officials to prevail on an ADA or Section 504 claim.** In the context of education, a party must assert more than simple failure to provide a FAPE under the IDEA. In this case, the court found a sufficient showing of bad faith or gross misjudgment by district staff to allow the discrimination and retaliation claims to proceed. *B.D. v. Fairfax County School Board*, No. 1:18-cv-1425, 2019 WL 692804 (E.D. Va. 2/19/19).

◆ A New York preschool student had an autism spectrum disorder and other disabilities. For three school years, he did not achieve annual goals in several areas and developed behaviors that interfered with his learning. Although the parents requested applied behavioral analysis (ABA) for him, the district declined. They obtained private services during the summer in an autism program. During one school year, the district did not provide the student with a special education teacher on many days and did not provide a certified teacher on 47 school days. Next, the parents said their son was not provided with appropriate speech therapy and was not placed in his least restrictive environment. Despite the student's increasing behavior problems, the district did not conduct a functional behavioral analysis, offer mental health services or ABA therapy. The parents filed a due process complaint against the school district, asserting the denial of a free appropriate public education (FAPE) for three school years.

After dismissing many of the claims as untimely, a hearing officer upheld the other claims. Neither party appealed, but the parents sued the school district in a federal court under Section 504 of the Rehabilitation Act. **The court explained that as Section 504 requires proof of discrimination, a Section 504 claim must assert more than a faulty IEP. A Section 504 complaint must show some level of intentional discrimination.** In the court's opinion, the complaint asserted gross negligence or reckless indifference sufficient to support a Section 504 claim. In particular, the district did not provide a certified teacher for 47 days. As the parents raised their FAPE claims before the hearing officer, the case was not dismissed. *Robert F. v. North Syracuse Cent. School Dist.*, No. 5:18-CV-0594 (LEK/ATB), 2019 WL 1173457 (N.D.N.Y. 3/13/19).

◆ Due to severe physical disabilities and cognitive impairments, an Alabama student used a walker and a wheelchair. A paraprofessional who was assigned to assist him began taking him out of his regular classroom to the school's weight room. He said the student disrupted the classroom and could do physical therapy and use a private restroom in the weight room. A classmate told her parents she saw the paraprofessional kick the student's wheelchair, berate him and refuse to pick up his pencil. The classmate's parents then told the student's parents about this. They placed an audio recorder in the child's wheelchair, which captured verbal abuse by the paraprofessional and a special education teacher. They also felt the recorder captured evidence of physical abuse. After learning about the recording, the school district placed the paraprofessional and the teacher on leave. The paraprofessional resigned and the teacher's contract was not renewed. In a federal court, the parents sued the school board, paraprofessional, teacher and other school employees. After the claims against the paraprofessional and teacher were settled, the court held for the board.

On appeal, the U.S. Court of Appeals, Eleventh Circuit, found the family was alleging exclusion and isolation of the student on the basis of his disability. Employing the liability standard used by courts in harassment cases under Title

IX, the court sought to determine whether school officials were "deliberately indifferent" in their response to known misconduct by staff members. **Title IX liability is predicated upon notice to an "appropriate person" with the authority to remedy a violation.** In this case, the court held further fact-finding was needed to determine whether the principal and the student's teachers were "appropriate persons" for imposing liability. While the teachers lacked supervisory authority over the paraprofessional, they had authority to ensure the IEP was implemented. One teacher served as the student's case manager. As a reasonable jury could find school employees were deliberately indifferent to the student's removal from his regular classes, the discrimination claim could go forward. But the court found no reasonable jury would find the paraprofessional's conduct put school officials on notice of possible abuse. *J.S., III v. Houston County Board of Educ.*, 877 F.3d 979 (11th Cir. 2017).

◆   A Pennsylvania student was the only African-American in his second-grade class. His parent expressed concerns that his teacher was treating him unfairly. In response, the teacher said no other student had such frequent or intense behavior incidents. The parent rejected a proposal for her son to join a behavior group, stating he was being targeted due to race discrimination. The teacher believed the student's oppositional behavior was intensifying. At the same time, the parent became increasingly vocal about the treatment of her son. When she told the teacher she would no longer speak to him about her son, the teacher began to keep a reflection journal to record the student's behavior and responses. After the parent threatened a lawsuit, a community agency employee was enlisted to address the problem. He met with the parent and proposed a Response to Instruction and Intervention (RTII) behavior plan for the student.

The parent rejected the plan and sued the school district and school officials in a federal court for race discrimination and retaliation. The court found she did not establish a case under either theory. On appeal, the U.S. Court of Appeals, Third Circuit, found no evidence that any Caucasian students had behavior issues as frequent or intense as the student. It also found no evidence to support a claim that the teacher had deliberately destroyed notes that would show classmates engaged in similar conduct. Although the parent said the teacher retaliated against her by keeping detailed notes of her son's conduct, the court found no evidence of a link between his note-taking and any retaliation. In fact, it was understandable that the teacher would keep better notes, given that the parent said she would no longer speak to him. **Finding no link between the parent's threats of litigation and the imposition of an RTII plan, the court held for the school district and officials.** *Davis v. Quaker Valley School Dist.*, 693 Fed.Appx. 131 (3d Cir. 2017).

◆   An Ohio board of education voted down a request to allow a transgender student with an eating disorder and other disabilities to continue using school restrooms according to her gender identity. As her fourth-grade school year approached, she attempted suicide based on fears that teachers and peers would harass and bully her. Upon her return to school, she used a staff restroom with a staff escort. According to the student, teachers and other students continued calling her a boy (or told her to act like one). She said some teachers called her by her birth name. By contrast, school officials maintained they took prompt action to revise school records to reflect the name change. The district sued the U.S. government in a federal court, seeking an order to block federal enforcement of Title IX in a manner permitting the use of school lavatories based on gender identity. In denying the school district's request for relief, the court held the student was entitled to preliminary relief. This meant she was to be treated and referred to as a girl, and could use the girls' lavatory at school.

According to the court, Title IX regulations (found at 34 C.F.R. Part 106.33) are ambiguous as to how to define "sex" with regard to student access to sex-segregated restrooms. This led the court to find the agency's interpretation not clearly inconsistent with law. In issuing an order for the student, the court held transgender status is protected by the Equal Protection Clause. On appeal, the U.S. Court of Appeals, Sixth Circuit, held discrimination based on transgender status is prohibited by federal civil rights statutes. There was evidence that the student is a vulnerable 11-year-old with special needs who will suffer irreparable harm if excluded from girls' restrooms. **Exclusion of the student from girls' restrooms had already caused substantial and immediate adverse effects on her daily life, leading to multiple suicide attempts.** Since the relevant factors weighed in her favor, the court denied the school district's request for a stay. *Dodds v. U.S. Dep't of Educ.*, 845 F.3d 217 (6th Cir. 2016).

◆ After enrolling their child in a school district, Washington parents withdrew their consent to his special education program. They said his teacher and a co-principal blamed their child for classroom incidents in which a classmate made cruel racial remarks. The parents said the school blamed their child for other incidents and improperly decided not to question important student witnesses. When the child wrote two "disturbing essays" describing incidents in which the classmate was violently harmed, nobody told the parents about them. When the district investigated, information about one of the essays appeared in the report. As soon as the parents saw it, they asked for an immediate transfer of their son. They sued the district, and their case reached the state court of appeals. It held the school district did not follow proper investigation procedures because they did not interview all the students in the work group.

The co-principal could not explain her feeling that the child's condition would affect his ability to hear a racial epithet. The essays were not shared with the parents, and the school did not take into account the discrepancy between his grades in social studies class and his other classes. In fact, the court found the school refused to consider any scenario in which the child was not to blame for conflicts with the classmate. The school district did not appropriately discipline the classmate, despite his history of serious behavior problems. The court found the parents showed harassment that was severe, pervasive and objectively offensive and deprived their child of access to educational opportunities or benefits. In ruling for the student, **the court held school districts have a duty to promptly investigate harassment and take prompt and effective steps calculated to end it**. It held there was a violation of state law. *Mercer Island School Dist. v. Office of Superintendent of Public Instruction*, 186 Wash.App. 939, 347 P.3d 924 (Wash. Ct. App. 2015).

◆   African-American students and their parents accused a Pennsylvania school district of intentional race discrimination in placement decisions. They claimed the district violated the IDEA in its identification and placement decisions. Some claimed they were denied opportunities to take challenging classes to prepare for college and said their classes amounted to "baby work." The court noted **Title VI of the Civil Rights Act of 1964 requires proof of intentional discrimination**. It held the statistical evidence was insufficient to prove a Title VI violation and nothing supported the discrimination claims except subjective belief. As there was no evidence of intentional discrimination by the district, the court found no Title VI violation. For similar reasons, the court found no merit to the constitutional claims. On appeal, the Third Circuit held the Rehabilitation Act, ADA, IDEA and Title VI claims based on discrimination were properly dismissed. With the exception of one family, these claims were properly dismissed due to the failure to exhaust IDEA administrative remedies.

The claims of some students had already been resolved in a companion case – *S.H. v. Lower Merion School Dist.*, 729 F.3d 248 (3d Cir. 2013). In *S.H.*, the court held students who were misidentified but not eligible for IDEA services could not bring IDEA claims. As for a student who had graduated, her IDEA claims were time-barred by an IDEA limitations period. Claims against the state department of education were barred by the settlement of a separate federal case. As for claims under Title VI and the Equal Protection Clause of the Fourteenth Amendment, the students said the disproportionate placement of African-Americans in remedial classes had a discriminatory purpose based on racial bias. But the court found insufficient evidence of intentional discrimination. **Despite statistics showing minority students were overrepresented in the district's low-achievement classes, no evidence of intentional discrimination was found.** Although the students raised many arguments about the use of evidence by the lower court, the court held for the school district. *Blunt v. Lower Merion School Dist.*, 767 F.3d 247 (3d Cir. 2014).

V. POLICE INVOLVEMENT

Excessive force and false arrest claims by disabled students against school districts, school administrators, municipal police and school resource officers (SROs) continue to occupy federal court dockets. Jennifer A. Sughrue, Ph.D., a professor from Southeastern Louisiana University, recommends that school IEP teams consider counseling SROs in advance about students with emotional behavioral disturbance (EBD) or aggressive tendencies. Dr. Sughrue also recommends that for any student with a behavior intervention plan, the student's IEP team should include SROs in IEP team meetings.

◆   The Ninth Circuit Court of Appeals held two California school resource officers (SROs) who arrested and handcuffed a group of middle school girls to teach them a lesson and command their respect clearly violated their Fourth Amendment rights. In the court's view, the actual motivation of the arresting SRO was clear. He told the students he was arresting them to prove a point and to teach them a lesson. The court held the arrest of a middle school student could not be justified as a scare tactic, a lesson, or as punishment for disrespect. Next, the court held the arrest, handcuffing and transportation of the students was a disproportionate response to the school's needs. The SROs faced a room of seven seated, mostly quiet middle school girls, and only generalized allegations of fighting and conflict amongst them. **The court explained that qualified immunity insulates an officer from liability unless precedent places a legal issue beyond debate.** At the time of the arrests, it was clearly established that a police seizure at the request of a school official must be reasonably related to its purposes, and not excessively intrusive under the circumstances. The court held no officer could have reasonably believed the law authorized the arrest of middle school students in order to prove a point. Last, the court rejected the officers' claims that probable cause existed to arrest the students under a state law. *Scott v. County of San Bernardino*, 903 F.3d 943 (9th Cir. 2018).

◆   Despite finding a Maryland school resource officer (SRO) used excessive force by handcuffing a calm and compliant 10-year-old student, the Fourth Circuit Court of Appeals held the SRO should have immunity in the student's lawsuit, since no case law clearly defined her conduct as a constitutional violation. The case involved a calm, compliant 10-year-old who was handcuffed several days after hitting another child. At most, she committed a misdemeanor assault. Contrary to the SRO's statements, the court found she could not have reasonably believed the student presented any risk of harm to anyone. She had no prior behavior incidents or involvement with law enforcement. The court found the use of force intruded upon the student's Fourth Amendment rights.

    In finding a constitutional violation, the court commented that even a child with a history of attacking school officials should not be handcuffed if, at the time of the handcuffing, she did not present a danger. As the student presented no such risk, the court held the handcuffing was unjustified. Next, the court commented that officers should use restraint when dealing with student misconduct. Handcuffing was counterproductive to the mission of the schools. But the court found no case law put the SRO on notice that she was violating the student's rights by handcuffing her. In fact, criminal case law suggested that the use of handcuffs would rarely be excessive force, if there was probable cause for an arrest. The SRO was thus entitled to qualified immunity in the case. **In future cases, the court's holding made it clear to a reasonable officer that handcuffing a student under similar circumstances would give rise to a violation.** *E.W. v. Dolgos*, 884 F.3d 172 (4th Cir. 2018).

◆   A New Mexico child with autism disrupted his class and did not respond to interventions. After locking himself in the school nurse's lavatory, he ran out and into the cafeteria. A school security officer was then dispatched to the school. When the child saw her, he again ran. She blocked a door and he kicked and swung his arms. After the student pulled computer cables out of their wall sockets, a social worker tried intervening, but he tried to hit her and then kicked her. The child's mother arrived at school, but while waiting for her, he started playing with a rubber band and shot the officer with it. He then started to kick her. After the student disregarded her instructions, she handcuffed him. When the handcuffs were removed, the child had welts and scratches on his wrists. The mother withdrew the child from school and sued the school district for violating the ADA. Finding no intentional discrimination or denial of a reasonable accommodation, the court held for the school district.

On appeal, the U.S. Court of Appeals, Tenth Circuit, found no evidence of any action against the child on the basis of his disability. **There was no showing that simply because the child had a BIP, his conduct manifested a disability.** There was no authority suggesting a 15-minute interference with a disabled child's education could be deemed a denial of benefits. The court held no liability could be found in this case based on a failure-to-train theory. No similar incidents took place in the district, and it did not appear that the district knew a lack of training would make injury to the child substantially likely. The parents did not show they requested a reasonable accommodation or an obvious need for one existed. As all the claims failed, the court held for the district. *J.V. & M.Q. Albuquerque Public Schools,* 813 F.3d 1289 (10th Cir. 2016).

◆   After teasing by peers, a Maryland student had a behavior outburst. A school resource officer (SRO) came to the class, as did an assistant principal (AP) and another employee who was familiar with the student. When confronted by the SRO, AP and employee, the student remained upset and lifted a desk, tipping it over near the AP. The student also said he was going to harm himself. The SRO told the student he was going to place him in handcuffs and take him to the hospital for an evaluation. The student pulled away from the SRO and continued to struggle while being handcuffed. Next, the student kicked the SRO in the upper thigh. The SRO lifted his arm up, causing the student significant pain in one hand. At the hospital, a splint was placed on the student's wrist. Although clinicians recommended inpatient psychiatric treatment, his parents took him home. In a federal court, the student's family sued the SRO, school board and police department for use of excessive force and related claims. The court found no evidence that the officer used objectively unreasonable force.

The student admitted he flipped over a desk and continued to struggle and kick the SRO. As a result, the court found the SRO acted reasonably by lifting the student's arm to gain control of him. Since the excessive force claim failed, the court found the remaining claims also failed. On appeal, the U.S. Court of Appeals, Fourth Circuit, found that **evaluating an officer's conduct requires careful balancing of the intrusion on an individual's Fourth Amendment interests against the government interests at stake**. Like the lower court, the Fourth Circuit found the SRO's conduct was reasonable. Since the student actively resisted the SRO, the court found the force he used was reasonable. *J.W. v. Corporal Carrier,* 645 Fed.Appx. 263 (4th Cir. 2016).

◆   A Pennsylvania student claimed school administrators questioned him about a rumor that he had a knife at school. He denied this and emptied his pockets to show them he had no knife. The administrators then told him to go to his classroom and retrieve a binder from his classroom so it could be searched. The student returned to the office with the binder, where the administrators told him to empty his pockets and lift his shirt. According to the student, a school resource officer searched him and slammed him to the floor, causing serious injuries, including a fractured kneecap. Asserting a variety of physical and emotional injuries, the student sued the school district, resource officer and administrators in a federal court. In the court's view, the student stated sufficient facts to establish that the school acted unreasonably. It found there was a claim of unreasonable grabbing and touching by the resource officer. If true, this would support a constitutional claim for an unlawful search.

There was evidence that the administrators told the student they believed he had no knife prior to the resource officer's involvement. Further, he said they told him they believed his statement that the rumor was false. The student was allowed to walk to the office alone, then return to his classroom. He sat unsupervised while waiting to be interviewed. **The court found these actions belied the district's claim that there was serious concern that the student actually had a knife.** As a result, the court allowed his Fourth Amendment claim to proceed. He also could pursue his state law claims for intentional conduct, assault, battery and false imprisonment. *Salyer v. Hollidaysburg Area School Dist.,* Civ. No. 3:16-57, 2016 WL 5376218 (W.D. Pa. 9/26/16).

◆ A New Mexico school resource officer (SRO) arrested and handcuffed an 11-year-old student with an emotional disturbance after she attacked a classmate and hit, scratched and kicked her teacher. The student's mother sued the SRO and county in a federal court for constitutional rights violations. Among other things, the mother argued the state Delinquency Act required the SRO to consider her child's age and mental disability before arresting her. She claimed the SRO willfully ignored state law when making the arrest. The court stated that police officers are required to investigate easily accessible evidence. But if probable cause is established, an officer is generally not required to continue searching for more evidence before an arrest. As the student had attacked a classmate and a teacher, the court held the SRO had probable cause to arrest her. The court found he had no duty to investigate whether a disability prevented her from forming criminal intent. **The court said the student's IEP did not indicate her disability prevented her from engaging in intentional conduct.** As the SRO made a lawful arrest, no Fourth Amendment violation was found. The mother then appealed to the Tenth Circuit Court of Appeals.

On appeal, the court found the SRO had probable cause to arrest the child after seeing her commit the crime of battery on a school official. It also held she did not use excessive force. In the absence of a constitutional violation by the SRO, the county could not be held liable for failing to train its officers. Even if there was a cause of action for a disabled arrestee under the ADA, the court held it would not apply in this case. The case did not involve a request for a reasonable accommodation. **The SRO observed criminal conduct and there was no "wrongful arrest," as the mother claimed.** As a result, the county prevailed. *J.H. v. Bernalillo County,* 806 F.3d 1255 (10th Cir. 2015).

◆ A federal court held the parents of a child with autism showed his school committed many IDEA errors, including improper notice of a change in placement after a school meltdown. The court found the student was "on high alert because he is afraid of what is going to happen to him. Police involvement, restraints and seclusion can be frightening for any student, but more so for a student with disabilities." **Because the school district did not properly** implement his IEP, the court held he should remain in general education settings, but with proper support. State law claims against the school district alleging emotional distress and negligence were dismissed. The same was true of a claim against the school district for punitive damages. *Troy School Dist. v. K.M.*, No. 12-CV-15413, 2015 WL 1495334 (E.D. Mich. 3/31/15).

VI. SCHOOL ATHLETICS

In PGA Tour v. Martin, *532 U.S. 661 (2001), the Supreme Court held the Americans with Disabilities Act (ADA) requires an individualized inquiry to determine whether a modification is reasonable and necessary for an individual and whether it would fundamentally alter the nature of the competition.*

◆   After attending high school in Virginia for two years, a student-athlete with physical and learning disabilities moved to Florida. He repeated grade ten in compliance with an assessment by his new school. For grades 10-11, the student participated on the school football, basketball and lacrosse teams. By the end of his eleventh-grade year, the student had competed in interscholastic athletics for four consecutive years of high school. As a result, he became ineligible for interscholastic participation under a Florida High School Athletic Association (FHSAA) bylaw. As a twelfth-grader, the student asked the FHSAA for a waiver from its bylaw to allow him an additional year of interscholastic sports eligibility. After two hearings, the FHSAA denied his request for a waiver.

Two days before the lacrosse season began, the student petitioned a federal court for a preliminary injunction allowing him to participate on his school team. The court found that by delaying his application until immediately before the season, the student undercut his argument that the denial of injunctive relief would cause him an irreparable injury. In fact, the court found the student created the "emergency" nature of the case by delaying his request for relief. It held he could not show he was adversely affected by the FHSAA bylaw on the sole basis of a disability. Instead, **the student was excluded from competition based on his completion of four consecutive years of interscholastic athletics**. Rejecting the student's claim that the FHSAA did not reasonably accommodate his disabilities, the court denied his request for relief. *Pritchard v. Florida High School Athletic Ass'n*, 371 F.Supp.3d 1081 (M.D. Fla. 2019).

◆   An Illinois student with spastic quadriplegia related to cerebral palsy represented his school as a para-athlete in three sports. During his junior year of high school, he sought accommodations from the Illinois High School Association (IHSA), including the creation of a separate division with different time standards for para-ambulatory runners in state sectional and championship meets. The IHSA denied this request as well as his request for a new para-ambulatory division in an annual 5K Road Race. After an IHSA board affirmed the denial of the accommodations, the student sought a federal court order that would require the creation of an IHSA division for para-ambulatory athletes in sectional and state meets as well as the 5K Road Race. The court held for the

IHSA, and the student appealed to the U.S. Court of Appeals, Seventh Circuit.

As the IHSA argued, the creation of a division for para-ambulatory runners in state track and field meets and the 5K Road Race would fundamentally alter the nature of competition by guaranteeing the student's participation and success. According to the court, lowered qualifying time standards resulting from the para-ambulatory division requested by the student would undermine the competitiveness of the state championship and road race events. **The Supreme Court has recognized that the lowering of a program's eligibility or qualifying requirements is unreasonable. Section 504 does not require a school to substantially modify its program to accommodate a student.** Since IHSA qualifying times ensured a certain level of competition and maintained "a necessary scarcity of opportunity," the court found the creation of a new division would fundamentally alter the nature of IHSA state meets and the 5K Road Race. As the accommodation was unreasonable, the court held for the IHSA. *A.H. v. Illinois High School Ass'n*, 881 F.3d 587 (7th Cir. 2018).

◆   A California student had an emotional disturbance, which manifested in emotional outbursts, anger, defiance, yelling and swearing. Despite being one of his school's best junior varsity basketball players, he said coaches kept him off varsity teams at three different schools in the district. The student claimed one coach told him he had "a bad attitude and would be trouble." The student's IEP team acknowledged the importance of basketball to his school progress. He asserted multiple school transfers and rejections from varsity teams affected his academic performance and emotional health. In defense of its actions, the district argued the student "simply was not Varsity material given his emotional state." It was asserted that he was given opportunities to participate on varsity teams, but "the coaches could not ignore his blatant behavioral issues." **In pretrial activity, the court held the student stated plausible claims for disability discrimination and failure to accommodate his disability.** While further development of the facts might prove his behavioral outbursts prevented him from playing varsity basketball, the court found he satisfied the elements of the claims. It was sufficient for the student to assert that his disability motivated the coaches to exclude him. *Brown v. Elk Grove Unified School Dist.*, No. 2:17-CV-00396-KJM-DB, 2018 WL 953162 (E.D. Cal. 2/20/18).

◆   A federal magistrate judge allowed a New Hampshire student who said she suffered permanent disabilities during her high school athletic career to proceed with many of her claims against a school district. The magistrate judge found the student and her parent could pursue disability discrimination and harassment claims under the Americans with Disabilities Act (ADA) and Section 504 of the Rehabilitation Act as they pertained to her academy and school district. The magistrate judge noted the student claimed she was excluded from participation in – and denied the benefits of – services, programs and activities offered by the academy and school district. However, as there is no individual liability under Section 504 and the ADA, the claims against the individual educators in their personal capacities could not proceed. The magistrate judge found nothing supported the parent's remaining claim for disability discrimination. She found sufficient support for the student's retaliation claim based on her assertion that the academy reduced her playing time and refused to intervene when she complained of peer bullying and harassment by the school athletic director. Sexual harassment claims under Title IX of the Education Amendments could proceed against the academy and school district.

The magistrate judge observed that there is no individual liability under Title IX. While the facts were found "minimally sufficient to allow" an equal protection claim by the student, her mother could not purse an equal protection claim. A due process claim based on claimed violations of the student's special education rights could proceed. *Tveter v. Derry Cooperative School Dist. SAU # 10*, Case No. 16-cv-329-PB, 2017 WL 2062944 (D.N.H. 4/25/17).

A few weeks later, a federal court approved of the magistrate judge's report and recommendations. *Tveter v. Derry Cooperative School Dist. SAU # 10*, Case No. 16-cv-329-PB, 2017 WL 2062855 (D.N.H. 5/12/17).

◆   A Kentucky student with ADHD and auditory processing issues attended a school for learning disabilities in Ohio. When he entered high school, his parents selected an Ohio school because of its support program, technology platform and superior college placement and resource programs. As a freshman, the student wanted to play soccer for the high school. An Ohio High School Athletic Association (OHSAA) bylaw prohibited student-athletes whose parents do not live in Ohio from playing interscholastic sports. After the OHSAA denied a request for a waiver, the student obtained a federal court order to enjoin the OHSAA from enforcing its residency bylaw against him.

Near the end of the school year, the parents sought a permanent order to block the OHSAA from enforcing its residency bylaw. But the court found the OHSAA bylaw did not bar him on the basis of a disability. **There was no connection between the student's disability and the reason for his ineligibility – his parents' residency.** The services provided by the Ohio school were not unique and were available at other schools in Kentucky and Ohio. Since the parents showed no connection between their child's disability and the bylaw, and they sent him to the Ohio school for reasons unrelated to a disability, the court denied their request for an order. *C.S. v. Ohio High School Athletic Ass'n*, No. 1:14-cv-525, 2015 WL 4575217 (S.D. Ohio 7/29/15).

CHAPTER ELEVEN

Employment

I. DISCIPLINE AND DISCHARGE

A. Misconduct

State laws establish the permissible grounds for disciplinary action against a teacher. Two frequently stated grounds for discipline are neglect of duty and conduct unbecoming a teacher. Courts that review employee suspension and discharge actions must analyze each case under applicable state laws, collective bargaining agreements, and relevant school board policies.

In Moberg v. Monterey Peninsula Unified School Dist. Board of Educ., *No. H037865, 2013 WL 140374 (Cal. Ct. App. 1/11/13), a judge found a teacher who sent abusive and disrespectful emails to colleagues undercut basic program goals. She wrote: "Special education is an area where a team approach is not only desirable, but essential." Frequent emails by the teacher to colleagues indicated his inability to become a member of the special education team.*

In Horn v. Board of Educ. of Cahokia School Dist. No. 187, *this chapter, the court relied on an Illinois Supreme Court test for determining whether a teacher can remediate or not. In* Gilliland v. Board of Education of Pleasant

355

View Consolidated School Dist. No. 622, *67 Ill. 2d 143 (1977), the court considered whether irremediable conduct (1) caused damage to a student, faculty, or the school and (2) a warning would not have corrected the conduct.*

◆   A New York court upheld the dismissal of a teacher based on evidence that she violated a school protocol by leaving a student who was having a crisis, then taunted her by sending a package of get well cards and a home-school application to her home. In the court's view, it was reasonable for the board to find the teacher abdicated her responsibilities, then caused unwelcome confusion in the student's home. Prior New York decisions established that imposing severe consequences on an employee is not unfair or shocking to the conscience unless it is obviously disproportionate to the misconduct and a violation of public policy or the public interest. In this case, **the court upheld the dismissal, finding the teacher's poor judgment, failure to take responsibility for her actions and lack of remorse indicated her inappropriate behavior was unlikely to change**. *Denicolo v. Board of Educ. of City of New York*, 171 A.D.3d 565 (N.Y. App. Div. Ct. 2019).

◆   A New Jersey board of education brought tenure charges against a special education teacher for unbecoming conduct. Among the 18 charges were lying under oath, violating state and federal regulations, directing that a student be found ineligible for special education without an evaluation and making unilateral placement decisions. The teacher was charged with failing to work collaboratively with school representatives and attorneys and violating school district policies. The board certified tenure charges, suspended the teacher and forwarded the tenure charges to the state commissioner of education. In the resulting arbitration proceeding, she sought to disqualify the board's attorneys from testifying against her and representing the board. The arbitrator denied these requests, and the attorneys presented testimony. **After a hearing, the arbitrator issued an award terminating the teacher's employment. He found her testimony not credible and held the tenure charges were proven.**

A state court affirmed the arbitration award. On appeal, a New Jersey appellate division court held the participation of the board's attorneys in the tenure proceedings did not create a conflict of interest and their testimony was properly allowed. According to the teacher, the arbitration award was obtained through fraud, corruption and/or undue means. But she did not raise this argument previously and the issue did not implicate the public interest. The court affirmed the arbitration award terminating the teacher's employment for unbecoming conduct. *Tobia v. Board of Educ. of Lakewood Township*, No. A-5336-15T1, 2018 WL 1247426 (N.J. Super Ct. App. Div. 3/12/18).

◆   A Louisiana principal observed a teacher was tardy on multiple occasions and placed her on "electronic sign-in status." During the next 45 days, the teacher was tardy 40 times. Several months later, she was not present at the start of an in-service training, and she had another teacher sign in for her. When questioned about the in-service incident, the teacher first denied having another teacher sign in for her. Upon further questioning, she stated that she was ill and had to leave the session to use the lavatory several times. Surveillance cameras did not confirm this account. After a hearing, the district superintendent notified the teacher of her employment termination. At the end of the tenure panel proceeding, the superintendent confirmed the termination of employment and the teacher appealed. A trial court held the statute upon which the board had relied was unconstitutional. **The Supreme Court of Louisiana found there is no due process guarantee under the state or federal constitutions requiring a full evidentiary hearing prior to employment termination.** *LaPointe v. Vermilion Parish School Board*, 173 So.3d 1152 (La. 2015).

After further review, the trial court held the decision refusing to reinstate the teacher following her tenure hearing was not arbitrary or capricious. The case returned to the Court of Appeal of Louisiana, which found **the electronic sign-in was a lesser punishment and not a rule that had to be published as specified in the relevant collective bargaining agreement**. The court noted the teacher remained habitually tardy, even after receiving her "wake up call." Further, there was no merit to her claim that her punishment did not conform with the board's progressive discipline policy. The court upheld the termination decision, finding it was not arbitrary and capricious. *LaPointe v. Vermilion Parish School Board*, No. CA 17-713, 2018 WL 903429 (La. Ct. App. 2/15/18).

◆   An Illinois special education teacher was on an employment "awareness phase" for IEP issues. He then falsified the signature of a local education agency (LEA) designee on a student's IEP. The school district was on a state action plan based on issues involving the accuracy of IEPs. Finding the forgery inexcusable, the district superintendent felt the conduct constituted fraud and showed moral indifference to what one would expect from a teacher. Moreover, he deemed the conduct a breach of the teacher's duties to faculty and students, and felt the department lost confidence and trust in the teacher. After a hearing, a hearing officer found that since the teacher received no written warning before the dismissal, the board had to prove his conduct was irremediable. The hearing officer found no evidence of harm such that a warning could not have corrected the teacher. The board rejected this and found his conduct was irremediable and showed moral indifference to the community and the intent to commit fraud.

After the board voted to dismiss the teacher, a state circuit court affirmed the decision. On appeal, the Appellate Court of Illinois found the teacher had signed the LEA designee's name without her knowledge on a legally binding IEP. This act did not comply with the expectations for a teacher. The court found the teacher's conduct was harmful to the district. There was a significant lack of trust, and harm was done to the faculty and the department. **The court held the board could reasonably find the teacher's conduct was sufficiently immoral and/or criminal to warrant dismissal.** He forged the signature to avoid consequences and put the school district and the student at risk for personal gain. *Horn v. Board of Educ. of Cahokia School Dist. No. 187*, No. 14-MR-468, 2017 IL App (5th) 150405-U (Ill. App. Ct. 4/3/17).

◆   An Ohio intervention specialist worked for a school board for 15 years, teaching students with special needs. In 2013-14, she had to use the Ohio Teacher Evaluation System (OTES) for the first time. The OTES is used for teacher evaluation and assessing student academic progress. The specialist was required to devise and administer a student learning objective (SLO) test at both the start and end of the school year. She used the San Diego Quick Assessment (SDQA) as her special needs students' SLO test. The SDQA consists of a list of 10 words for each grade level, which the students are to read aloud until three errors are made. After administering the SDQA to special needs students in Fall 2013, the specialist printed out lists of words for her students to bring home and study. For the Spring 2014 SDQA administration, she gave some students the same words. Based on the assessment results, all her students met or exceeded expectations for a full grade level. Soon after the spring SDQA administration, the district superintendent placed the specialist on unpaid administrative leave.

After a hearing, an impartial hearing referee found the board failed to show the specialist committed academic fraud. Rejecting the hearing referee's recommendation, the board discharged the specialist. A state court affirmed this decision, and the result was affirmed by the state court of appeals. *Routson-Gim-Belluardo v. Jefferson Township Local School Board of Educ.*, 61 N.E.3d 914 (Ohio Ct. App. 2016) (Appeal not allowed, 146 Ohio St.3d 1490, 8/31/16).

While the specialist's dismissal case was proceeding, the Ohio Department of Education (ODE) began an action to suspend or revoke her teaching license. The ODE based its action on charges of inappropriately administering the SLO test to give students an advantage and falsifying a SLO score for a student suspected of not taking the year-end test. A hearing officer found the ODE proved the specialist engaged in conduct unbecoming an educator. Although the hearing officer held the specialist's license should be revoked, she could reapply for a license in two years. Appeal reached the Court of Appeals of Ohio. It found no merit to the specialist's claim that she did not intend to give her students an advantage. The board did not have to prove intent before taking action against an educator for conduct unbecoming to a person's position.

While intent is irrelevant to the conduct unbecoming inquiry, the hearing officer noted it could not be conclusively determined whether the specialist intended to improve her own OTES score. This was deemed a mitigating factor in reducing the recommended suspension from five years to two. In affirming the two-year license suspension, **the court found "conduct unbecoming" encompasses a wide variety of conduct, including misconduct that negatively reflects upon the teaching profession**. *Routson-Gim-Belluardo v. Ohio Dep't of Educ.*, 90 N.E.3d 180, 2017 -Ohio- 2611 (Ohio Ct. App. 2017).

◆   A West Virginia special education teacher reportedly slapped a disabled student and withheld food from him. The school district immediately suspended her and the state Department of Health and Human Resources investigated. It was found that child abuse had occurred and that the teacher had used hot sauce as a form of discipline. She filed a grievance against the board of education to contest the recommendation to dismiss her. After a hearing held by the state department of education, the teacher was fired. She pursued a grievance based on due process denials. Meanwhile, the county prosecutor brought multiple criminal charges against the teacher. Prior to a hearing on her grievance, she entered into a pretrial disposition of the criminal matters.

Under a plea agreement, the teacher agreed to voluntarily dismiss her grievance and remain "permanently terminated from employment with Mingo

County Schools." In return, the state dismissed the criminal case. Almost two years later, the teacher sought to rescind her decision to withdraw the grievance, saying it had been "induced by gross unethical, if not illegal, conduct" by the former county prosecutor and his wife, who worked in the school district. A state grievance board denied the teacher's request, and this decision was affirmed by a state circuit court. **On appeal, the Supreme Judicial Court of West Virginia found no error in the lower court's decision and it affirmed the judgment for the board of education.** *Grace v. Mingo County Board of Educ.*, No. 15-0525, 2016 WL 870597 (W. Va. 3/7/16).

◆ West Virginia's highest court held a newly hired sign-language interpreter could be ordered to undergo drug testing based on observation of her glassy eyes, rambling speech, exaggerated politeness and erratic body movements while at school. A grievance board upheld the non-renewal of the sign-language interpreter's contract. **The case reached the West Virginia Supreme Court of Appeals, which found the principal knew about the interpreter's demeanor and could find she might have been under the influence of drugs or alcohol based on her observations.** The court rejected the sign-language interpreter's defense that there were "non-impaired" reasons for her conduct. There was ample support for suspending and later not rehiring her. *Layne v. Kanawha County Board of Educ.*, No. 16-0407, 2017 WL 657002 (W.Va. 2/17/17).

◆ A New York Appellate Division Court held invalid an unsatisfactory rating that was assigned to a special education teacher based on her argument with another teacher. After forfeiting tenure in another job to obtain the special education teaching position, the teacher had a satisfactory job performance review in her first year. But she was later placed on a four-day suspension without pay after she loudly argued with a colleague in front of students. The two argued about whether students with disabilities should share space with other students in an art cluster. When the case reached the Appellate Division, it found **the incident was insufficient to support a finding of unprofessional conduct.** Moreover, the teacher's failure to admit that the conversation was an "argument" was not evidence of insubordination. Finding no rational basis for an unsatisfactory rating, the court held for the teacher. *Mendez v. New York City Dep't of Educ.*, 132 A.D.3d 533 (N.Y. App. Div. 2015).

◆ A North Carolina assistant principal (AP) and a social worker met with other school staff members and a hospital/homebound (HH) instructor to discuss a high school student who was suicidal and failing her classes. Neither the student's parent nor any special education teacher attended the meeting. Although the HH instructor said the meeting would have to be reconvened with the rest of the team present, the AP said he could drop the student from two classes so she could participate in HH programs. Believing that the mother and student attended the meeting, the chair of the exceptional children's department told a special education teacher to document placing the student in an HH program. The social worker created IEP meeting notes indicating the parent and student had attended the meeting. When the HH instructor visited the student's home, the parent learned of the action to remove her child from classes and begin an HH program. After an investigation and hearing, the board suspended the AP for three days without pay and the social worker for one day.

Among the board's findings was that the AP knew (or should have known) there had to be a "proper IEP team meeting" in order to change the student's schedule and that the social worker intentionally falsified his meeting notes. When the case reached the state court of appeals, it noted testimony indicating the AP had firsthand knowledge that the student had an IEP and had even attended one of her prior IEP meetings. **Instead of assembling the IEP team, the AP had simply dropped two of the student's classes and placed her in the HH program.** As the board found, the social worker falsified his notes to make it look like an actual IEP meeting had taken place. The employees were not entitled to a hearing before an independent hearing officer. Finding the board's decision was supported by evidence and not arbitrary, capricious or an abuse of discretion, the court of appeals held for the board. *Marisco v. New Hanover County Board of Educ.*, 776 S.E.2d 364 (Table) (N.C. Ct. App. 7/21/15; N.C. review denied, 12/15/15).

B. Incompetence

In Little Lake City School Dist. v. Comm'n on Professional Competence, *2013 WL 6182625 (Cal. Ct. App. 11/26/13), and* Terkosky v. Indiana Dep't of Educ., *996 N.E.2d 832 (Ind. Ct. App. 2013) the courts relied in part on* Morrison v. State Board of Educ., *1 Cal.3d 214 (Cal. 1969). In* Morrison, *the California Supreme Court offered a nonexclusive list of factors to assess a teacher's fitness to teach. First among them was the likelihood that a teacher's conduct has adversely affected students or colleagues. Other factors include the degree of adversity, the likelihood of a recurrence of the conduct and its timing.*

◆ An Illinois teacher's evaluations indicated deficiencies in planning and preparation, classroom environment, instruction and professional responsibility. She was placed on a remediation plan but received two more unsatisfactory ratings. The teacher took a medical leave. When she returned to work two years later, the remediation plan was modified to accommodate her medical restrictions. But she received a third unsatisfactory rating and was dismissed. At a hearing before the Illinois State Board of Education, the school district claimed the teacher did not show progress in her remediation plan upon returning from leave, even with accommodations. She argued her remediation plan was "not achievable" and that she was overworked and stressed.

The hearing officer upheld the dismissal, finding the teacher did not correct the performance deficiencies identified by the district. After losing at the administrative level, she appealed to a state court. She sought to supplement the record with over 400 documents that were not introduced at her hearing. Much of the documentation consisted of her lesson plans, which she felt would prove compliance with the remediation plan. But the court refused to grant the teacher's request for a new hearing, rejecting her claim that illness prevented her from full participation in the hearing. **She appealed to the Appellate Court of Illinois, which held it was clear that she did not satisfy her remediation**

plan. She had the opportunity to introduce her lesson plans at her administrative hearing, but failed to do so. A new hearing was held unnecessary, and the court held for the school district. *Johansson v. Naperville Community Unit School Dist. 203*, No. 2-16-0436, 2017 IL App (2d) 160436-U (Ill. App. Ct. 2/23/17).

◆ In her first year of work for a Massachusetts school district, a special education teacher had the highest number of disciplinary referrals among non-tenured teachers at her school. According to the school committee, she overused the disciplinary referral process by sending students to administrators without first trying to control classes herself. An initial evaluation of the teacher rated her "focus for growth" in the areas of effective classroom environment and effective instruction. Near the end of the school year, she was laid off due to budgetary reasons, along with many other employees. She was 64 years old.

During the summer months, the budget was restored. But the teacher did not receive a reinstatement notice. After the teacher's union became involved in her case, the school committee issued new employment evaluations that removed references to "do not recommend for reappointment." As part of a settlement between the union and school committee, poor marks were removed from her evaluations. After not being rehired, the teacher sued the school committee for age discrimination. A state court held for the school committee, and she appealed. **On appeal, the Appellate Court of Massachusetts found credible evidence that the teacher's contract was not renewed due to performance issues.** The court found the school committee's evidence effectively contradicted that of the teacher and did not mask any discriminatory intent. No evidence indicated the school committee was motivated by discriminatory intent. As the teacher could not prove age discrimination simply by asserting that a younger person replaced her, the court held for the school committee. *Perry v. Franklin Public Schools*, 89 Mass.App.Ct. 1115 (Mass. App. Ct. 3/29/16).

◆ A California alternative education administrator acknowledged making the "terrible mistake" of using a special education student in an on-campus drug sting. She marked a $5 bill and then observed the student purchase marijuana from another student at school during a lunch period. Even though she acknowledged her error in judgment, the school district notified her of its intent to dismiss her. Prior to a hearing, the district identified several grounds for employment termination, including immoral or unprofessional conduct, evident unfitness for service and refusal to obey relevant California laws and reasonable school regulations. Before the state Commission on Professional Competence, the administrator expressed contrition, stated she had learned from the experience and promised to handle things differently in the future.

Next, the administrator said she was focused on getting drugs off campus. She claimed to be unaware that she had to report a drug sale to police. After the hearing, the commission found the decision not to stop the drug sale was immoral conduct under state law. It found that although statutory grounds for termination existed, her conduct did not demonstrate such unfitness to teach as to warrant termination. The commission reversed the district's decision to dismiss the administrator and ordered her reinstatement with lost wages and benefits. When the case reached the Court of Appeal of California, it held the commission's selection of a penalty was subject to a deferential "abuse of discretion" standard. While the district argued the commission had to uphold a termination decision once it made a finding of unfitness to teach, **the court explained that the commission could determine whether dismissal was appropriate**. Despite the troubling facts and the placement of students in danger, the court refused to substitute its judgment for that of the commission. As the commission found, it was unlikely that the administrator would engage in similar misconduct. *Bellflower Unified School Dist. v. Comm'n on Professional Competence*, No. B262523, 2016 WL 1706727 (Cal. Ct. App. 4/26/16).

◆   The U.S. Supreme Court denied a petition to review a New York court decision upholding a teacher's dismissal based on his inability to control the same group of special needs children for three years. Before being assigned to a self-contained classroom, the teacher had satisfactory employment ratings for 18 years in schools operated by the New York City Department of Education. Based on his performance in the self-contained classroom, the teacher was eventually subjected to a disciplinary hearing. A hearing officer then upheld the charges for dismissal. **Although a state appellate court found the termination shocking, the Court of Appeals of New York later dismissed the case.** It did not find the termination "shocks the judicial conscience." *Russo v. New York City Dep't of Educ.*, 25 N.Y.3d 946, 29 N.E.3d 896 (N.Y. 2015). Without opinion, the Supreme Court refused to hear the case. *Russo v. New York City Dep't of Educ.*, No. 14-299, 136 S.Ct. 416 (cert. denied 11/2/15).

◆   A teacher accused of striking two students while she worked at a school on Chicago's South Side received another opportunity for review of a decision dismissing her from her job. In 2012, a state appeals court reversed an action dismissing the teacher, finding the board ignored factors used to determine whether a teacher's conduct was irremediable. One of the students had ADHD, and his testimony could be reexamined. When the case returned to the board, it again justified the dismissal, finding the student's testimony was more credible than that of the teacher. But when the case returned to the state appellate court, it found **the board again failed to determine whether the teacher's conduct was irremediable**. It returned the case to the board with directions to comply with its orders. *Rule v. Illinois State Board of Educ.*, No. 1-13-3685, 2015 IL App (1st) 133685-U (Ill. App. Ct. 9/15/15).

◆   A Washington special education teacher co-taught a curriculum known as Connected Mathematics Program Part 2 (CMP2) in a blended (special and general education) classroom. After the principal ended use of the blended model, she assigned the teacher to a special education math class. At a midyear review, an assistant principal rated the teacher's performance unsatisfactory in instructional skill and knowledge of subject matter. He was placed on probation under a performance improvement plan. After three observations of the teacher, the assistant principal found he did not show adequate improvement in his areas of deficiency. After the district provided the teacher notice of its intent to nonrenew his contract for failure to remediate his teaching deficiencies, a hearing officer found sufficient cause to nonrenew his employment contract.

A state superior court upheld the decision. On appeal, the Court of Appeals of Washington held **the teacher had no standing to challenge his non-renewal based on IDEA violations. He was unable to show any authority preventing a school from requiring teachers to follow a certain curriculum.** The court found no authority for his claims and held for the district. *Cummings v. Seattle School Dist. No. 1*, 178 Wash.App. 1027 (Wash. Ct. App. 12/23/13).

◆ A California special education teacher was cited for unprofessionalism and failing to collaborate with teachers about student IEP goals. She was charged with frequent tardiness and performance issues. After threats of employment termination, she was placed on a 90-day improvement plan. At the conclusion of the plan, the teacher's performance was found deficient, and the school district placed her on leave pending dismissal. After a hearing, the state Commission on Professional Competence found no cause for dismissal. A state superior court affirmed the decision, and the district appealed. On appeal, the Court of Appeal of California found the teacher instructed a large number of students. Due to her heavy workload, she could not meet with general education teachers during the school day. She was never offered a substitute on collaboration dates. The court found no testimony to support the claims of failure to collaborate and communicate with general education teachers. The court found many of the criticisms in her performance evaluations were baseless. There was no evidence that the school district offered to help the teacher, and it did not show she failed to communicate with others or was frequently tardy. **The court upheld the commissioner's decision, finding the performance improvement plan was unreasonable and "virtually ensured [her] failure by increasing her duties."** *Little Lake City School Dist. v. Comm'n on Professional Competence*, No. B244991, 2013 WL 6182625 (Cal. Ct. App. 11/26/13).

C. Speech Rights and Retaliation

1. Speech Rights

Under Garcetti v. Ceballos, *547 U.S. 410 (2006), public employees who speak pursuant to their official duties do not "speak as citizens" under the First Amendment. Public employees do not have First Amendment protection when they speak about their job duties, regardless of any possible public concern.*

◆ Illinois law required public employees to pay an agency fee to the union representing all bargaining unit employees. The agency fee amounted to a portion of dues attributable to activities germane to the union's duties as collective bargaining representative. Excluded from agency fees were union expenditures in support of political candidates. Under the law, the unions did not have to obtain employee consent before deducting agency fees. A state employee objected to the union representing employees in his bargaining unit. He did not join the union and sued it for violating his First Amendment rights.

Finding the employee's arguments were foreclosed by *Abood v. Detroit Board of Educ.*, 431 U.S. 209, 97 S.Ct. 1782, 52 L.Ed.2d 261 (1977), the court upheld the law. After the Seventh Circuit affirmed the judgment, the Supreme

Court held the designation of a union as an employee's exclusive representative "substantially restricts the rights of individual employees." Prior decisions recognized a significant infringement upon First Amendment rights occurs when public employees are required to support a union. The Court found any burden imposed on unions could be eliminated by significantly less restrictive means than agency fees. In overruling *Abood*, the Court rejected a claim that the inability to collect agency fees would cripple public employee unions and impair efficient government operations. **The Supreme Court held no agency fee or other payment to a union could be deducted from nonmember wages unless the employee affirmatively consented.** *Janus v. American Federation of State, County, and Municipal Employees, Council 31*, 138 S.Ct. 2448, 201 L.Ed.2d 924 (U.S. 2018).

◆ A Louisiana school nurse claimed her relationship with school administrators deteriorated after a student committed suicide. She claimed she was transferred to another school and that this amounted to a demotion. She could no longer work at the school her children attended, and she had "a list of concerns regarding the facilities at her new school." Although the nurse filed two grievances, the board of education took no formal action. She said she was issued a false evaluation in which she was accused of excessive absences. Within months, the nurse resigned and sued the board in a federal court. After the court held for the board, the nurse appealed to the U.S. Court of Appeals, Fifth Circuit. Applying the standard used in Title VII employment discrimination cases, the court held the nurse did not show her transfer was a demotion. **Reprimands did not change the nurse's employment status. There was no evidence that she lost any pay, benefits or job responsibilities.** After finding any changes presented by the job transfer did not amount to a demotion, the court upheld the decision to dismiss the nurse's state-law whistleblower claim. Since did not speak as a citizen on a matter of public concern, her First Amendment claim failed.

The court found no support for the nurse's due process claim based on a loss of her liberty and reputational interests. According to the court, she did not show any extreme or outrageous conduct that would support a claim for intentional infliction of emotional distress. Finding all the claims had been properly dismissed, the court held for the board of education. *Rayborn v. Bossier Parish School Board*, 881 F.3d 409 (5th Cir. 2018).

◆ A Washington special education teacher felt some of her students were ready for mainstream classes but were being held out of them due to impermissible financial reasons. She emailed her concerns about improper placements to her union representative and the school district human resources department. After administrators learned of her concerns, the teacher said her relationship with them began to deteriorate. The next school year, more EBD students were moved into mainstream academic classes in a concerted effort to move the EBD program from a self-contained to an inclusive model. The teacher complained about the policy change and emailed her objections to the administration. This time, she was transferred to another school. Prior to the first day of the new school year, she collapsed in a hallway, "sobbing uncontrollably." Although the teacher was allowed a medical leave, she decided not to return to work.

Asserting she had been "constructively discharged," the teacher resigned and sued the school district and administrators for wrongful discharge and speech rights violations. A federal court held for the district and officials, and she appealed to the U.S. Court of Appeals, Ninth Circuit. The court held the teacher's communications to supervisors and parents about the treatment of students in the EBD program related to the public concern. Her job duties included communicating with administrators and parents about the progress of EBD students, as well as pointing out any failure to comply with IEPs. **Speech "up the chain of command" was made pursuant to her official duties and was not protected by** *Garcetti v. Ceballos*, **547 U.S. 410 (2006).** Speaking with parents was also part of the teacher's job description. Since her communications came in her role as a public employee, her First Amendment claim failed. The state law claims were returned to the lower court for further consideration. *Coomes v. Edmonds School Dist. No. 15*, 816 F.3d 1255 (9th Cir. 2016).

◆ An Indiana family support specialist claimed a school security guard arrested her when she tried to intervene on behalf of a special education student. According to the guard, the specialist saw the student in handcuffs and entered a school security office without any authority. The specialist said she received permission to enter. She believed any charges against the student had been dropped because a manifestation hearing had reached the conclusion that the student's conduct was manifestation of his disability. According to the security guard, the family specialist became loud and aggressive, and was repeatedly asked to leave. The family specialist said that as she was leaving, she told the security guard she would speak with her attorney. She said he then pushed her face into a concrete wall and handcuffed her so tightly it bruised her. The family specialist sued the school district, security guard, the colleague and their municipal employer in a federal court. Among the family specialist's claims was that the school district did not properly train employees regarding arrest and interactions with students in public schools. Finding the municipality to be a separate entity from the school district, the court dismissed the municipality.

Next, the court found no evidence to support a claim based on improper training. The fact that the arrest took place at a school was incidental. Moreover, the specialist did not show improper training resulted from a school district custom or practice. For this reason, the district could not be held liable. **A retaliation claim based on the First Amendment was held not viable, since there was no evidence that the security guards acted in response to the family specialist's speech.** Instead, they both said she was arrested due to her unruly behavior. But the court declined to dismiss the false arrest and excessive force claims against the security guards. *Grimes v. Gary Community School Corp.*, No. 2:13-cv-36-PPS-APR, 2016 WL 1162370 (N.D. Ind. 3/23/16).

◆ A federal court held an Ohio elementary school intervention specialist had no First Amendment protection when she complained to her supervisors about lack of adequate support required for her students as required in their IEPs. According to the intervention specialist, she said she was asked to backdate information about a student's IEP, but refused to do so. She said this led to her placement on leave and her contract non-renewal. Although the specialist sued the school district, a federal court held she could not pursue her case. It held that **staff complaints to supervisors about their work conditions are unprotected by the First Amendment.** *Williams v. Trotwood Madison City Schools*, No. 3:16-CV-00207, 2016 WL 7117392 (S.D. Ohio 12/716).

◆ A Georgia special education teacher complained to her principal about the services being provided to a student. She believed a date on an IEP document was forged, and she challenged a colleague's qualifications. The teacher said her principal retaliated against her by threatening to place her on a performance development plan (PDP). She felt compelled to quit because of this threat and other conduct she claimed was retaliatory. In a federal court, the teacher asserted speech rights violations and retaliation under state law. The court held for the school district, and she appealed. The U.S. Court of Appeals, Eleventh Circuit, held that to prevail on a claim for retaliation by a government employer based on protected speech, an employee must show the speech involves the public concern. Next, the employee's interest in free speech must outweigh the employer's interest in efficient operations. **Recent Supreme Court cases have emphasized that a public employee's speech is not protected when the statements are made pursuant to official duties.** Under Eleventh Circuit case law, an employee cannot transform a personal grievance into a matter of public concern by invoking the public's interest in how a public institution is run.

In this case, the teacher did not show a serious and material change in her employment terms or conditions. She was never placed on a PDP. Although she said she was forced to quit due to her supervisor's disagreement with a change to an IEP, the court held this and other matters that she complained about did not create conditions that would force a reasonable person to resign. **The teacher did not raise these issues as a public concern, but to address issues that personally affected her work.** The court held for the school district, determining that no reasonable jury could find her speech was protected. *Lamar v. Clayton County School Dist.*, 605 Fed.Appx. 804 (11th Cir. 2015).

2. Retaliation

In Baker v. Benton Area School Dist., *this chapter, a New York court noted that mere criticism, false accusations or verbal reprimands of a public employee generally do not support a First Amendment claim.*

◆ A Pennsylvania school counselor learned that a student made a video in a school restroom and posted it on social media. The video depicted two students with disabilities and a background of vulgar, explicit music. The counselor claimed administrators said parents should not be told about the incident and that it should not be reported to child protection authorities. She said the principal and the director of special education made fun of the video. The counselor said she wrote a letter to the superintendent and the board of education about the video. She criticized the district's "misuse of special education law" to allow unqualified students to graduate. During a school investigation, the counselor said administrators told her that some of her evaluations "were so extremely negative" that they had no choice but to dismiss her. In a federal court, she sued the school district and three administrators for violating her constitutional rights.

The court dismissed the counselor's due process and speech rights claims against the school district, noting that she did not assert any official policy or custom leading to injury. On the other hand, the court refused to dismiss a conspiracy claim. Many courts have held criticism or reprimands are insufficient to advance a First Amendment claim. The counselor asserted her poor evaluations were part of a scheme to engineer her dismissal. She learned she would be losing her job only five days after reporting suspected legal violations. The court dismissed the First Amendment retaliation claims against the school district, but it allowed these claims to go forward against the administrators. The counselor could proceed with Whistleblower Law claims, but her defamation and due process claims were dismissed. *Baker v. Benton Area School Dist.*, No. 4:16-CV-02311, 2017 WL 3701722 (M.D. Pa. 8/28/17).

◆   The Rhode Island Supreme Court held school officials did not retaliate against a teacher by filing truancy charges against her child with disabilities, who attended school in the district in which she worked. The teacher claimed her peers and her principal created a hostile work environment for her. She said the special education department often called her during her workday to deal with issues regarding her child. The school department twice filed truancy charges regarding the child's attendance. Later, the teacher sued the department in a state court. It held the school department had legal grounds to bring the truancy charges based on the child's school absences. **On appeal, the Rhode Island Supreme Court held the teacher did not present sufficient evidence to prove the school department retaliated against her for advocating on behalf of her son.** *Azar v. Town of Lincoln*, 173 A.3d 862 (R.I. 2017).

◆   A Colorado teacher emailed her district superintendent about "the horrific state of special education" in the school district and questioned the legality of the district's Pragmatic Learning and Executive Functioning (PLEX) program. She also posted criticisms of the program on her Facebook page. After further emails, an assistant principal advised her she should stop criticizing the PLEX program and the district's special education practices. The assistant principal said the teacher should cancel a meeting she had scheduled with parents to discuss her complaints and should stop communicating with them so much.

About a month after meeting with the assistant principal, the teacher was warned she would be temporarily removed from her classroom since she lacked "highly qualified" teacher status under the No Child Left Behind Act. She was not removed, but the next school year, she complained about a PLEX student who assaulted a classmate and made a death threat. The school district suspended the student for one day. Believing this discipline was inadequate, the teacher asked for a change in the student's placement and threatened not to report to work. After the district said it would issue a letter of reprimand to the teacher if she did not report to work, she resigned. She sued the district for retaliation and speech rights violations. A federal court found the teacher did not suffer any "adverse employment action" that could serve as the basis for a retaliation claim. **Unrealized threats of discipline and mere inconvenience**

do not amount to "adverse employment action" sufficient to trigger liability for retaliation. No consequences were attached to the directive that the teacher not criticize the PLEX program. Finding she did not allege any injury from the district's directives, the court held she could not pursue a claim for prior restraint of her speech. As all of her claims failed, the court dismissed the case. *Carpenter v. School Dist. No. 1, City and County of Denver, Colorado,* No. 16-cv-01706-RBJ, 2017 WL 1407041 (D. Colo. 4/20/17).

◆   Two Texas school administrators were members of an elementary school Section 504 committee. The committee found a student with a disability should have an accommodation on a state test. A proctor was to read him questions during the test. Shortly after this decision, a school district Section 504 coordinator found the student lacked supporting documentation to qualify for the accommodation and denied it. Based on findings that the administrators illegally classified ineligible students as eligible for accommodations, the district suspended them. Their grievances were denied and the school board voted to dismiss them. A state court denied the district's motion for pretrial judgment in a lawsuit by the administrators under the Texas Whistleblower Act. Appeal reached the Court of Appeals of Texas, which rejected arguments by the school district that immunity applied. First, the court found the action had been timely filed based on the act's 30-day filing period. Next, the court found evidence that the administrators made a good-faith report to the Texas Education Agency (TEA) about suspected Section 504 violations. The school district presented no valid arguments that the TEA was not an appropriate law enforcement authority under the Whistleblower Act. Last, **the court rejected an argument by the district that the administrators were not reporting an actual violation of law, but sought only to validate their actions to protect their jobs**. The court affirmed the denial of judgment to the district. *Powers v. Northside Independent School Dist.,* 662 Fed.Appx. 306 (5th Cir. 2016).

◆   A Maryland teacher worked at the same school attended by her disabled son. Conflict arose when the principal discontinued her son's medically recommended, gluten-free diet. The teacher objected and said there had been an IEP violation. She pressed school officials to evaluate the child's needs but said the principal began retaliating against her for advocating on behalf of her son. At a meeting, the teacher was warned that her refusal to obey the principal was "borderline insubordination." She was also sent a reprimand letter. The teacher was transferred to a different school, where she continued asking about her son.

According to the teacher, retaliation against her continued at the transfer school. She claimed she received critical, inaccurate and degrading evaluations. The district transferred the teacher to a different site, where she noticed closer supervision. She removed her child from the district and sued the board of education in a federal court. In her complaint, the teacher said the school district interfered with the IEP process, denied her access to school records, launched an investigation about her residency and helped the child's father in his quest for child custody. Some of the claims related to employment grievances. The court held the IDEA and federal disability discrimination claims related to the son's education and were subject to administrative exhaustion. Any interference by the board in the evaluation of the student could have been addressed at a due process hearing. **But the court noted that the employment claims alleged retaliatory acts directed toward the teacher as a professional.** She alleged injuries that were professional in nature and irrelevant to any IDEA dispute. So the teacher could proceed with her employment retaliation claims. *Southard v. Wicomico County Board of Educ.*, 79 F.Supp.3d 552 (D. Md. 2015).

◆   After 20 years of service as a special education teacher in Massachusetts, a teacher developed post-traumatic stress disorder (PTSD) from repeated assaults by a violent special needs student. She said special needs students were being improperly removed from general education classes to receive IEP services. According to the teacher, some were not properly served due to scheduling conflicts created because students were being pulled out of their classes. The teacher requested reasonable accommodations for her PTSD. Within four days, the district notified her that her performance did not meet expectations. She resubmitted a reasonable accommodation request for a mentor, additional training and a "clear schedule." After citing the principal for harassing acts, being critical and giving contradictory instructions, the teacher resigned. In a federal court, she sued the school district and town, asserting discrimination and retaliation under Section 504 and the Americans with Disabilities Act.

   The court held advocacy on behalf of disabled students who were not receiving IEP services could be deemed "protected activity" under federal law. At this early stage of the case, the court found the teacher's claim that she was "constructively discharged" to be plausible. She would be allowed to demonstrate that her advocacy resulted in adverse employment action. She also stated a claim for denial of reasonable accommodations. *Smith v. Public Schools of Northborough-Southborough*, 133 F.Supp.3d 289 (D. Mass. 2015).

◆   The U.S. Court of Appeals, Fifth Circuit, upheld a lower court ruling against a Texas special education teacher who alleged violations of the Family and Medical Leave Act (FMLA). While taking medical leave, the school district notified the teacher of her employment termination. The court noted she received her full medical leave and was paid through the end of her probationary contract. As the lower court found, the district justified the action based on performance concerns about the teacher and her use of school time to conduct a private for-profit business. **No connection was made between the employment action and the exercise of her FMLA rights.** *Henderson v. Grand Prairie Independent School Dist.*, 559 Fed.Appx. 403 (5th Cir. 2014).

◆   Two Connecticut special education paraprofessionals worked with non-verbal autistic children who were not toilet trained and were identified as "runners." The paraprofessionals voiced concerns to the school principal about the lack of a changing table. They also questioned safety issues related to the unfenced school playground, the failure of special education teachers to instruct the children in sign language and other matters. Both the principal and director of special education told the paraprofessionals to respect the special education teachers' expertise. An administrator said the paraprofessionals had created a "toxic environment." The paraprofessionals again raised their concerns about the students' safety issues and educational goals in response to a survey. The paraprofessionals said they were dismissed a few weeks later. Asserting they had been dismissed in retaliation for raising their concerns about students, they sued the school district. **A state court found they were not engaged in protected activity under the IDEA and did not state claims for wrongful discharge in violation of a public policy.** Regardless of whether any conduct by school administrators was considered intentional, the school district would have immunity for discretionary actions. *Bonaguide v. Regional School Dist. 6*, No. CV126007409S, 2015 WL 493455 (Conn. Super. Ct. 1/8/15).

II. EMPLOYMENT DISCRIMINATION

Congress enacted the Americans with Disabilities Act (ADA) in 1991 to extend disability protection to most employees who work for employers with at least 15 employees. The ADA Amendments Act of 2008 expanded the ADA's definition of "major life activity" to include a non-exhaustive list of physical activities. It clarified that an episodic impairment or one in remission is deemed a "disability" if it substantially limits a major life activity when active. "Mitigating measures," such as medications, are not considered when determining if a person is substantially limited in a major life activity.

A federal regulation interpreting the FMLA (found at 29 C.F.R. Part 825.220(b)) prohibits an employer from discouraging an employee from taking leave. But another FMLA regulation allows employers to verify a claimed medical condition, assess how long an employee might be out of work, and best accommodate his or her return to work. See 29 C.F.R. Part 825.307.

A. Age and Disability Discrimination

◆ The Seventh Circuit Court of Appeals affirmed a lower court judgment finding a Chicago teacher who was absent or tardy without excuse 130 times over a two-year period could not claim disability status in a federal discrimination lawsuit against the Chicago Board of Education. The lower court held the teacher's frequent absences prevented her from performing essential job functions. As such, **she was not a "qualified individual with a disability" under the Americans with Disabilities Act**. On appeal, the court found no reason to disturb the judgment. It noted the teacher received six time extensions for her appeal, made inadequate filings and violated court rules. *Moore-Fotso v. Board of Educ. of City of Chicago*, 755 Fed. Appx. 587 (7th Cir. 2019).

◆ A Kentucky certified special education teacher applied to an education board for employment in any open position. Instead of posting a job vacancy, the board issued an emergency certificate to another candidate and hired her to teach. The teacher claimed this violated the board's hiring practices and amounted to age discrimination. In a state court, the teacher sued the board for using improper employment practices. After the court dismissed the action, he added a claim for age discrimination. This claim was also dismissed, and the teacher appealed to the Court of Appeals of Kentucky. On appeal, the teacher said the board's decision to issue an emergency certificate to the candidate instead of posting the position created sufficient grounds to present his case to a jury. The court noted he did not cite any relevant law on age discrimination.

Although the teacher argued the board acted to avoid hiring him on the basis of his age, the court found no evidence of discrimination. He claimed only that a jury could make a reasonable inference of discrimination based on false statements made by the board and its improper issuance of an emergency certificate. **In pretrial statements, the teacher admitted he might be less qualified for the job than the candidate who was hired for the job.** The lower court found the board had reasons other than age to hire a younger person than the teacher for the position. He only argued that the emergency certificate was evidence of age discrimination. Since it did not appear that the teacher could show the board intended to engage in age discrimination, the court held for the board of education. *Hicks v. Pike County Board of Educ.*, No. 2015-CA-001973-MR, 2018 WL 672285 (Ky. Ct. App. 2/2/18).

◆   A Wisconsin assistant principal (AP) took an extended leave due to injuries from a student assault. Her doctor found she could not be "in the vicinity of potentially unruly students." Finding "virtually all students are 'potentially' unruly," the school district said this restriction barred virtually all student contact. The AP took a three-year leave. Upon her return, the district tried to find a replacement position for her. All but one position would have required the AP to be in the vicinity of potentially unruly students. After a federal court held for the school district, the AP appealed to the Seventh Circuit Court of Appeals.

The court held employers must make reasonable accommodations that will allow a qualified individual with a disability to perform the essential functions of a job under the ADA. **Reassigning an employee to a vacant position is a reasonable accommodation, if the employee can perform the job. The court found the ADA does not require employers to promote employees in order to accommodate them.** Further, the identification of reasonable accommodations for a disabled employee requires both the employer and employee to engage in a flexible, interactive process. Both parties are responsible for the process. It was repeatedly stated during the AP's leave that she needed to avoid "the vicinity of potentially unruly students." After her leave, the district identified available positions and identified some lateral moves for her. As the district argued, the AP did not have to be promoted into a position for which she was not the most qualified candidate. As a result, the school district prevailed. *Brown v. Milwaukee Board of School Directors*, 855 F.3d 818 (7th Cir. 2017).

◆   An Illinois special education teacher said she engaged in protected activity by refusing to change her teaching methods following a negative performance evaluation. In awarding judgment to the school district, a federal court found no evidence that she engaged in any activity protected by Section 504. On appeal, the U.S. Court of Appeals, Seventh Circuit, explained that Section 504 is "a sister statute to the Americans with Disabilities Act" (ADA). Both laws prohibit discrimination based on disability and employ the same liability standards. **Under the ADA's anti-interference provision, it is unlawful to coerce, intimidate, threaten or interfere with any individual on the account** of his/her having aided or encouraged any other in the exercise of his/her ADA rights. The teacher said she engaged in protected activity by refusing to change her teaching methods following her negative performance evaluation.

But the court found no evidence that the teacher's opposition to her evaluation was an assertion of rights on behalf of her students. Even if the evaluation was faulty or her supervisor lacked qualifications as an evaluator, the court found nothing to indicate the teacher's teaching style had protection under federal disability laws. In holding for the district, the court observed "the law protects assertions of rights, not teaching methods." The fact that the teacher instructed students with disabilities did not render her teaching a "protected activity." *Frakes v. Peoria School Dist. No. 150*, 872 F.3d 545 (7th Cir. 2017).

◆ A Texas school bus monitor asked the bus driver to stop at a gas station so he could use the lavatory. Although the only student on the bus had been dropped off, the driver declined the request. After the driver told the monitor to wait until the next scheduled stop, the monitor involuntarily urinated in his pants. He concealed himself behind the bus doors to finish urinating into a bottle. The monitor's pants were wet but he did not wet his seat or anything else.

After the monitor was fired for engaging in unprofessional conduct and failing to protect students from exposure to bodily fluids, he sued the school district for discharging him based on a disability. At the conclusion of a six-day trial, jurors found the monitor's urinary incontinence was a motivating factor in his dismissal. The court upheld a verdict of $41,292 in back wages plus $125,000 in compensatory damages. **Appeal reached the Supreme Court of Texas, which agreed with the monitor that urinary incontinence caused by a diuretic medication for his congestive heart failure might allow him to gain the protection of disability law.** It held the state appeals court committed an error by finding the monitor's only disability was his heart condition. Urinary incontinence would also qualify as a disability if it substantially limited his bladder function or ability to perform work-related functions. As the jury could have found the monitor's incontinence was a disability, the court reversed the judgment. *Green v. Dallas County Schools*, 537 S.W.3d 501 (Tex. 2017).

◆ An Illinois teacher claimed her relationship with her principal deteriorated due to her history of post-traumatic stress disorder (PTSD). Near the end of a school year, the teacher took a leave of absence. When she returned to work, the school district reassigned her to a school where she taught students with severe emotional and behavioral disorders. A student in her classroom broke away from a police officer and ran into her, causing a concussion and neck injury. A psychologist notified the district that the event "retriggered" the teacher's PTSD, necessitating leave. Although leave was allowed, the district refused to allow the teacher to transfer into another classroom. She returned to her job the next fall, but tensions increased and she earned the first "unsatisfactory" evaluation in her 14-year career. The poor rating led to her layoff and discharge.

In a federal court, the teacher claimed the district violated the Americans with Disabilities Act (ADA) and Section 504 of the Rehabilitation Act. After the court held for the district, she appealed. The U.S. Court of Appeals, Seventh Circuit, found **the ADA and Section 504 make employers and employees**

responsible for engaging in an interactive process to find a reasonable accommodation for a disability. Both parties must make good-faith efforts to identify reasonable accommodations. The court found evidence that the district refused to engage in the interactive process after learning of the teacher's need for a transfer. Moreover, the district "simply sat on its hands" instead of seeking more information. Had the district inquired about her condition, it would have learned that many of the problems cited in her evaluation were likely caused by her PTSD. There was evidence that the teacher's request for a transfer could have been accommodated, as at least seven special education teaching jobs were available in district schools. In the court's opinion, the teacher deserved a trial. *Lawler v. Peoria School Dist. No. 150,* 837 F.3d 779 (7th Cir. 2016).

◆ A Washington teacher accused a co-worker of circumventing IEP protocols and singling out minority students for different treatment. Although their union tried to mediate their dispute, the effort failed. According to the teacher, the mediation session traumatized her and forced her to take a six-week medical leave. During negotiations for her return to work, she sought a full-time job with only non-teaching duties. But the district stated it lacked the resources for this and redistributed her students and caseload among other teachers. When the teacher abruptly sought to return to work prior to her expected return date, the district offered her substitute work. But she insisted upon a non-teaching position, refused to return to work and sued the school district in a state court.

After the teacher dropped some of her claims, the court dismissed the remaining ones. On appeal, the state court of appeals found no evidence that the co-worker was motivated by race, gender or any other protected class. Nor could the teacher show "associational discrimination," since she did not show any adverse actions based on advocacy for, or association with students of color. **The court rejected the teacher's claim that the district retaliated against her, demoted her and forced her from her job based on her complaints.** Her complaints about the co-worker amounted to disagreements over student assignments and style of communication. She did not show any racial remarks or complaints by parents or students about the co-worker. As the lower court found, the teacher's attempt to return to work prior to the date she was expected to return (and upon her own terms) caught the district by surprise. The court found no evidence indicated any adverse employment action against her. *Bailey v. Kent School Dist.,* 194 Wash.App. 1002 (Wash. Ct. App. 2016).

◆ A Wisconsin teacher with diabetes and depression claimed her school's failure to move her from special education classrooms to general education classes exacerbated her disabilities to the point of a breakdown. Although the school district offered to reassign her, she believed the offers were "not made unconditionally" and that one position was not even for full-time work. Twice, an administrator rejected her requests for reassignment to a general education classroom. Eventually, the teacher's thoughts of hopelessness and suicide peaked, and she had to go to an emergency room. She sued the district for failure to accommodate her disabilities and retaliation. A federal court explained that parties seeking reasonable accommodations under federal disability laws must make their employers aware of any non-obvious, medically necessary accommodations. Once an employee discloses a disability, the employer must engage in an interactive process to determine appropriate accommodations.

Failure to engage in the interactive process may create employer liability if it prevents the identification of an appropriate accommodation for a qualified individual. **An employer's duty to reasonably accommodate an employee does not assure that an employee receives a preferred or requested accommodation.** Instead, the law only requires "some reasonable accommodation." In this case, the court found a significant number of disputed facts that made pretrial judgment impossible. Among these was whether the district was aware of the specific accommodations being requested and the teacher's reasons for requesting them. Questions such as the availability of general education positions in the district were unresolved. Since many factual issues still had to be resolved, the court held the teacher could pursue her case. *Cole v. Kenosha Unified School Dist. Board of Educ.*, No. 14-CV-1546-JPS, 2016 WL 1430028 (E.D. Wis. 4/11/16).

◆ A Maryland student accused a middle school assistant principal (AP) of grabbing her arms, shaking her and pinning her against a wall. Child Protective Services conducted a child abuse investigation. The school system began an employment investigation and reassigned the AP. He took leave based on a medical opinion that he had stress, anxiety and high blood pressure. After a few days, the AP returned to school. But he said the school principal berated him, causing a panic attack. After a week of leave, the AP returned to school but again took medical leave after being reprimanded by the principal. This time, the AP was diagnosed with acute stress disorder. A pre-disciplinary conference was held while the AP was still on leave. Two weeks later, the board presented him with a formal reprimand for engaging in physical contact with the student.

During the summer break, the AP was cleared for work. In conformity with instructions by a medical professional, he was reassigned to a special academy for children with behavioral issues. The AP sued the board for violations of the FMLA and ADA. A federal court dismissed the case. On appeal, the U.S. Court of Appeals, Fourth Circuit, found the board did not interfere with the AP's FMLA leave by scheduling a pre-disciplinary conference while he was still on leave. This was a legitimate part of an ongoing investigation. **FMLA regulations permit an employer to obtain a second medical opinion (and even a third, if the first two conflict).** Reprimands did not qualify as "adverse employment action" as they did not lead to more discipline. And the transfer to the specialized school was not retaliatory. In fact, the AP's medical professional recommended a transfer to a less stressful school. Finding the AP could not show the board denied requested accommodations, committed retaliatory action or violated the FMLA, the court held for the school system. *Adams v. Anne Arundel County Public Schools*, 789 F.3d 422 (4th Cir. 2015).

◆ A Florida elementary teacher was discharged because of the continued recurrence of tuberculosis. She sued her school board in a federal court. The case reached the U.S. Supreme Court, which held tuberculosis is a disability under Section 504 because it affects the respiratory system and the ability to work, which is a "major life activity." The Court reasoned the teacher's contagion and physical impairment resulted from tuberculosis. It would be unfair to allow employers to distinguish between a disease's potential effect on others and its effect on the employee to justify discriminatory treatment. **Discrimination based on the contagious effects of a physical impairment would be inconsistent with the purpose of Section 504.** The case was returned to a lower court to determine whether the teacher was otherwise qualified for her job and if the board could reasonably accommodate her. *School Board of Nassau County v. Arline*, 480 U.S. 273, 107 S. Ct. 1123, 94 L.Ed.2d 307 (1987).

The district court then held the teacher was "otherwise qualified," as she posed no threat of transmitting tuberculosis to others. The court ordered her reinstatement or $768,724 in wages, representing her earnings until retirement. *Arline v. School Board of Nassau County*, 692 F.Supp. 1286 (M.D. Fla. 1988).

In *Bragdon v. Abbott*, 524 U.S. 624, 118 S.Ct. 2196, 141 L.Ed.2d 540 (1998), the Supreme Court held an individual with HIV was entitled to the protections of the ADA, despite the fact that she was not yet symptomatic.

B. Title VII and Related State Laws

State and federal anti-discrimination laws prohibit specific forms of employment discrimination. Title VII of the Civil Rights Act of 1964 is the primary federal law prohibiting discrimination on grounds including race, sex, national origin and religion. State civil rights acts are based upon Title VII, often directly incorporating its language and standards. Many other state and federal acts prohibit employment discrimination on the basis of other grounds.

1. Sex Discrimination

◆ An Indiana school administrator was promoted to serve as an elementary school principal in 2002. She remained in the position until the end of the 2013-14 school year, when the school was closed due to declining enrollment. The school board reassigned the administrator to serve as an assistant principal at another elementary school. Near this time, the board advertised a principal position at still another elementary school. Although the administrator applied for the job and was ranked first by an interview committee, the board hired a male who had been working at the school for the past two years as an interim principal. At the end of the school year, the administrator retired after learning she would not have her contract renewed. She filed a federal discrimination charge, then a lawsuit for discrimination and retaliation. Appeal reached the Seventh Circuit Court of Appeals, which found reason to doubt the existence of adverse employment action against the administrator. The court noted many of the job duties and skills for principals and assistant principals were the same.

In any event, the administrator did not show she was reassigned as a pretext for discrimination. Further, the court agreed with the school district that the reason it chose the male administrator for a promotion was not sex-based. There was evidence that he was chosen because of his experience working at the elementary school. **Although the administrator contended that the district retaliated against her for filing a discrimination complaint, the court found**

no evidence of retaliation. Last, the court rejected a claim for violation of the Equal Pay Act, finding the administrator's salary was frozen as part of a district response to its financial crisis. Any pay differences among various district employees was the result of historical differences in pay, not sex discrimination. *Terry v. Gary Community School Corp.*, 910 F.3d 1000 (7th Cir. 2018).

◆ A Connecticut special education teacher estimated she spent about two-thirds of her time instructing potentially aggressive students. She asked to be excused from "restraining activities" for the students, presenting her employer a note from her doctor. The school honored the request. Six months later, while the teacher was pregnant, she asked to be excused from working closely with or having 1:1 contact with her students. This time, the request was denied, as the employer believed it involved the elimination of an essential function of her job. Soon, the employer placed the teacher on Family and Medical Leave Act (FMLA) leave. When she declined to return to work after the expiration of this 12-week leave, the employer dismissed her. According to the teacher, the employer committed pregnancy discrimination and retaliation for seeking an extension of her leave to care for her children. In a federal court, she asserted violations of state law, the Americans with Disabilities Act (ADA), the FMLA and Title VII of the Civil Rights Act of 1964. The court held for the employer, and the teacher appealed. The U.S. Court of Appeals, Second Circuit, rejected the pregnancy discrimination claim. Neither of her two ADA disability claims was viable. **Since working closely with students was an essential job function, the employer was not required to excuse the teacher from this aspect of her job.** As there was a neutral, non-discriminatory explanation for her dismissal, the teacher's claims failed. *Turner v. Eastconn Regional Educ. Service Center*, 588 Fed.Appx. 41 (2d Cir. 2014).

◆ New York's highest court held a school aide introduced enough evidence to avoid pretrial dismissal of her discrimination and retaliation case. In the court's view, there was sufficient evidence that her former principal's stated reason for firing her was only a pretext for discrimination. According to the court, the aide came forward with evidence that the former principal directed repeated homophobic remarks at her and reported her for misconduct in an after-school program that he did not supervise. **There was evidence that the aide did not engage in any misconduct worthy of reporting.** *Sandiford v. City of New York Dep't of Educ.*, 22 N.Y.3d 914, 999 N.E.2d 1144 (N.Y. 2013).

◆ Before telling her principal that she was pregnant, a Tennessee teacher had good employment evaluations. Four months later, she was laid off. She was told the district would soon need fewer special education teachers. Asserting pregnancy discrimination and breach of her employment contract, the teacher sued the board of education in a federal court. In response, the board claimed it should prevail because her performance was poor and she did not hold an appropriate teaching license. The court found several reasons to deny the board's request for pretrial judgment. The teacher's evaluations at the relevant time were good. She had a waiver from teaching license requirements during the school year and could have obtained one for another year. In fact, the teacher said the principal had evaluated her as meeting required competency levels for all designated domains and had recommended that she advance to a professional license. Her employment evaluations rated her "satisfactory." But four months after announcing her pregnancy, the teacher was dismissed.

The court found evidence that the teacher was given at least three different explanations for the action on various occasions. And the principal misinformed her about how much maternity leave she could take. Finally, the court noted evidence that **the teacher's eventual replacement lacked full teaching certification and was no more qualified than she was**. Since she raised enough evidence to avoid pretrial dismissal of her discrimination and contract claims, the court denied judgment to the board. *Poling v. Cheatham County Board of Educ.*, No. 3-11-1100, 2014 WL 3697880 (M.D. Tenn. 7/24/14).

◆ A Nevada school employee said she was transferred to another position 20 months after being harassed during a meeting by two male coworkers. When her case reached the Supreme Court, it held no reasonable person could believe that the incident leading to the lawsuit violated Title VII. **Sexual harassment is actionable only if it is so severe or pervasive as to alter the conditions of the victim's employment** and create an abusive working environment. It found there was only "an isolated incident" that could not be considered serious. The Court found no causality between the job transfer proposed by the school district and the employee's complaint 20 months earlier. *Clark County School Dist. v. Breeden*, 532 U.S. 268, 121 S.Ct. 1508, 149 L.Ed.2d 509 (2001).

2. Race Discrimination and Affirmative Action

◆ An African-American teacher was unable to show discrimination by an Alabama board of education because she was unable to show an applicant of another race was treated more favorably than she was. After hiring the teacher, the board learned she was not yet certified to teach in Alabama. Although the board advised her to register for state-required certification tests, she did not timely register for them. As a result, a recommendation to hire the teacher was canceled. She later sued the board for race discrimination. When the case reached the U.S. Court of Appeals, Eleventh Circuit, it found the board had relied on the same pre-employment procedures for applicants of various races. **Since the teacher did not show she was treated differently than others based on her race, the court held for the board of education.** *Bolton v. Baldwin County Public Schools*, 627 Fed.Appx. 800 (11th Cir. 2015).

◆ A California special education teacher of South African origin worked for Los Angeles Unified School District (LAUSD) for about five years before having conflicts with her principal. According to the teacher, the principal falsely said she misbehaved at IEP meetings and ordered her to submit IEPs to him four days before meetings, in violation of LAUSD policy. She said he yelled at her and fabricated student complaints about her. In a state court complaint against LAUSD and the principal, the teacher claimed he threatened her, wrote up a false report and required her to submit lesson plans. When she submitted two lesson plans in her native Zulu, she said he called it "gibberish."

After a state superior court held for LAUSD, the teacher appealed. When the case reached the Court of Appeal of California, it found that no LAUSD employee had ever disparaged the teacher's national origin or native language. It appeared that the principal did not know the lesson plan was written in Zulu.

There was evidence that the reprimands were related to performance or absences. It appeared that the teacher had taunted the principal in her lesson plans and wrote a plan in Zulu after being told to use English. Although the teacher claimed LAUSD and the principal committed unlawful discrimination, the court found evidence that the principal's conduct was directed at her deficiencies. **As LAUSD stated non-discriminatory reasons for documenting the teacher's employment deficiencies, the court held the national origin discrimination and retaliation claims were properly dismissed.** *Mnyandu v. Los Angeles Unified School Dist.*, No. B239104, 2013 WL 1820810 (Cal. Ct. App. 5/1/13).

◆   After receiving unsatisfactory performance ratings for three years, a Maryland special education teacher resigned and filed a complaint with the EEOC, alleging race discrimination, harassment and retaliation for her internal complaints of discrimination. When she later sued, a federal court ruled against her. **The performance evaluations she endured could not be construed as harassment**, and she failed to show that they were a pretext for discrimination or that they were used in retaliation for protected conduct. *Austin v. Board of Educ. of Howard County*, 2011 WL 6736724 (D. Md. 12/21/11).

III.   LABOR RELATIONS

Since collective bargaining agreements typically refer employment disputes to an arbitrator, court review of arbitration awards is sharply limited. Court review is generally limited to whether a dispute was properly before an arbitrator. Many courts employ an "essence test" to determine if an arbitration award was rationally derived from the relevant collective bargaining agreement. Absent a violation of law or public policy, courts may not disturb an award that "draws its essence" from the collective bargaining agreement.

A.   Collective Bargaining and Arbitration

◆   **Colorado's highest court agreed with Denver teachers that a collective bargaining agreement (CBA) provision could be interpreted as requiring their school district to pay them for attending English Learning Acquisition (ELA) program training.** Each CBA required payment for "extra duty," including "in-service education." As two lower courts found, the CBAs could be interpreted to require pay for ELA training. The court held the CBAs were not silent on compensation for training and education, and the district did not retain authority under a management rights clause to decide whether to pay the teachers for ELA training. In sum, a trial court had correctly found the CBAs were ambiguous and a jury trial was needed. *School Dist. No. 1, County of Denver v. Denver Classroom Teachers Ass'n*, 433 P.3d 38 (Colo. 2019).

◆   Three New York students said a teacher helped some of their classmates on a standardized test. Although the teacher did not alter answers or give students correct answers, she pointed out that certain answers "might be wrong," and she "suggested they take another look at them." The case came before an arbitrator, who issued an award terminating the teacher's employment for misconduct. She appealed to a state court, which granted her request to vacate the arbitration award. On appeal, the New York Supreme Court, Appellate Division, held the findings of misconduct were supported by adequate evidence and not irrational. But the court found that under the circumstances, the penalty of termination "shocks our sense of fairness." In modifying the lower court's judgment, the court found a result is "shocking to one's sense of fairness" if the sanction is so grave in its impact on the individual that it is disproportionate to the misconduct. Further, the court found the teacher's behavior demonstrated only a lapse in judgment and was only "a one-time mistake." Prior to the misconduct, she had worked for the New York City Department of Education (DOE) for 11 years, had an unblemished record and was considered to be a good teacher. Last, the court found nothing to suggest the teacher could not remedy her behavior.

The case was returned to the lower court for it to impose a lesser penalty. The DOE appealed to the New York Court of Appeals, which consolidated the case with those of two other teachers who were fired despite compiling good teaching records over long time periods. One of the cases involved a teacher who made inappropriate comments to students. The other involved a special education teacher who falsified time sheets that inaccurately indicated she had provided home instruction to a disabled student over a two-month period. In all three cases, an appellate division court found the penalty of employment termination was disproportionate and shocking to its sense of fairness. On appeal, the court held the lower court decisions had to be reversed. It found **the fact that reasonable minds might disagree over a penalty was not a proper basis for vacating an arbitration award or refashioning the penalty**. Finding the lower courts had exceeded their authority by reweighing the evidence, the court reversed the judgments in all three cases. *Bolt v. New York City Dep't of Educ.*, 30 N.Y.3d 1065, 91 N.E.3d 1234, 69 N.Y.S.3d 255 (N.Y. 2018).

◆   A Pennsylvania school district employee was responsible for accompanying a special education student to his classes and monitoring him. An adapted English teacher complained that the employee stopped accompanying the student to class. She said he arrived at her classroom several minutes early without the student. When class was over, the employee would stay after the student left. Finding the employee's presence in her classroom during her prep time distracting, the teacher complained to the district special education coordinator. An assistant principal admonished the employee to stay with the student. For a short time, the employee stopped arriving early in the teacher's classroom and staying after class. But he soon resumed doing this, which he justified as a way to increase the student's independence. The teacher emailed the special education coordinator that the employee's conduct was "really getting annoying and starting to creep her out." She then noticed two drawings that were supposed to have been submitted by the student appeared to have been drawn by someone else. At a meeting with administrators, the employee admitted drawing the pictures, which depicted the strangulation of a figure resembling the teacher. Administrators suspended the employee without pay, and he filed a grievance. After a board hearing, the employee was discharged.

An arbitrator then found just cause to suspend but not to discharge him. According to the arbitrator, the district had to a provide written notice and a meeting for each incident, and also interview each party involved in the conflict. Appeal went before the Commonwealth Court of Pennsylvania. It found nothing in the CBA required the school district to take the additional steps specified by the arbitrator. **Since no CBA provisions required the district to afford the teacher additional written notices, meetings and interviews with witnesses in order to support a just cause dismissal, the court vacated the arbitration award.** *Rose Tree Media School Dist. v. Rose Tree Media Secretaries and Educ. Support Personnel Ass'n-ESPA, PSEA-NEA*, 157 A.3d 558 (Pa. Commw. Ct. 2017).

◆ A Massachusetts court held a teacher who took two maternity leaves during her first five years of employment with a school district could arbitrate the question of whether she had tenure. Over five consecutive school years, the teacher worked for the school district. She took maternity leave during her first and fourth years of work. At the end of the teacher's fifth year, the district notified her of her non-renewal. After her union petitioned for arbitration, the school committee filed a state court action. **The state court of appeals held arbitration is the state's sole remedy for teacher dismissals.** As a result, the case was to be arbitrated. *Plymouth Public Schools v. Educ. Ass'n of Plymouth & Carver*, 89 Mass.App.Ct. 643 (Mass. App. Ct. 2016).

◆ An Ohio school intervention specialist who was charged with assaulting a wheelchair-bound student was allowed to challenge an adverse arbitration matter in a state court. After reportedly hitting the student because his wheelchair was blocking the way of another child, the specialist was dismissed. A jury then found her guilty of felony assault. After lower court activity, **the Supreme Court of Ohio held the board did not show the specialist was served with a copy of the arbitration award**. Since her appeal was timely, she could pursue her case. *Cox v. Dayton Public Schools Board of Educ.*, 147 Ohio St.3d 298, 64 N.E.3d 977 (Ohio 2016).

◆ A Vermont principal saw an instructional assistant "yank" the arm of a child with challenging behaviors. Later in the day, the principal called the assistant into his office and placed him on leave. The instructional assistant and a union representative met with the principal, who advised him that he would recommend employment termination. He then wrote a letter declaring the intent to recommend terminating the instructional assistant's employment. The instructional assistant sued the school system in a state court. The court held his sole remedy was to pursue a grievance and binding arbitration under the terms of the relevant collective bargaining agreement (CBA). On appeal, the Supreme Court of Vermont held the general rule is that employees subject to a CBA must exhaust their available CBA remedies before resorting to a lawsuit. According to the employee, he was not obligated to follow the CBA grievance policy. He accused the school system of preventing him from using the grievance policy.

But the court found the principal had formally advised the employee of his employment termination. In addition, **the principal had observed the conduct leading to discipline and the employee received a fair chance to confront him and rebut the charges**. Instead of filing a grievance, he asked to be reassigned. Not even the employee believed a grievance was filed, and the school was not responsible for his decision to forgo a grievance. Contrary to his argument, the school system did not repudiate the grievance process or prevent him from using it. As the employee knew of the terms of the CBA yet did not file a grievance, the school system prevailed. *Kingston v. Montpelier Public School System,* No. 2014-406, 2015 WL 1086184 (Vt. 3/6/15).

◆   A New Jersey teacher was supposed to provide home instruction to a special needs student no less than three times weekly. But the student's mother reported the teacher only came to the home five times during a school year. This prompted an investigation, which concluded that the teacher engaged in a pattern of falsifying district home inspection forms and failing to appear at the house to provide instruction. At a board meeting, the board voted to withhold her salary increments from a later school year based on findings that she falsified forms and engaged in conduct unbecoming a teacher. The teacher was also prohibited from providing home instruction services and declared ineligible from participating in extracurricular activities for one year. The board notice stated that it would serve as a letter of reprimand to be placed in the teacher's personnel file. Although the employee association representing teachers in the school district filed a grievance on the teacher's behalf, the board denied it.

The New Jersey Public Employment Relations Commission (PERC) held the salary increment withholding and letter of reprimand were predominantly disciplinary (and not evaluative) in nature. As a result, the PERC held the matter should proceed to arbitration. A New Jersey appeals court observed that the charges against the teacher did not require specialized educational expertise to resolve. Charges of leaving work early, falsifying time sheets and missing work are disciplinary in nature. The court agreed with the PERC that the notice to the teacher was a letter of reprimand that was disciplinary in nature. **Rejecting the board's claim that the action was evaluative in nature, the court held the PERC had correctly held the case should proceed to binding arbitration.** *Atlantic City Board of Educ. v. Atlantic City Educ. Ass'n,* 2015 WL 463342 (N.J. Super. Ct. App. Div. 2/5/15).

◆   A Pennsylvania special education classroom assistant who worked with emotionally disturbed students was found unconscious in a school lavatory. She admitted wearing a Fentanyl patch that she had obtained from a friend. As she did not have a prescription for it, her use of the patch was a misdemeanor. After providing notice, the classroom assistant's intermediate unit fired her for using and possessing a controlled substance for which she had no prescription. But an arbitrator conditionally reinstated her, finding no just cause for discharge under the state school code. He also cited her previously unblemished 23-year career.

On appeal, the Supreme Court of Pennsylvania found the arbitration award was rationally derived from the collective bargaining agreement. It returned the case to a lower court so it could decide whether the arbitration award was precluded by a public policy. When the case returned to the lower court, it found the assistant had an extensive history of abusing pain pills. In the court's opinion, immediate reinstatement to the classroom violated public policy. By the time the employee's union appealed, the state supreme court was considering another case involving public policy considerations. The state supreme court instructed the Commonwealth Court of Pennsylvania to reconsider the classroom assistant's case in view of the other case. When the classroom assistant's case returned to the lower court, it held **compelling public policies existed to educate children about the dangers of illegal drugs and the need to protect them from drugs and drug abuse**. As the award violated public policy, it could not be enforced. *Westmoreland Intermediate Unit #7 v. Westmoreland Intermediate Unit #7 Classroom Assistants Educ. Support Personnel Ass'n, PSEA/NEA*, 72 A.3d 755 (Pa. Commw. Ct. 2013). Further appeal was denied by the state supreme court in 2014.

B. Unfair Labor Practices

New Jersey's supreme court held the receipt of notice of a funding cut did not allow a school board to require all its teachers to take a three-day unpaid leave in violation of the relevant collective bargaining agreement. **Allowing the board to claim a need for a management prerogative in tight budgetary times "would eviscerate the durability of collective negotiated agreements."** In the Matter of Robbinsville Township Board of Educ. v. Washington Township Educ. Ass'n, *227 N.J. 192, 149 A.3d 1283 (N.J. 2016)*.

◆ **Union officials committed an unfair labor practice by trying to enforce a collective bargaining agreement (CBA) clause requiring a non-union teacher to pay a fair-share fee in violation of a state "Right to Work" provision**, according to the Court of Appeals of Michigan. A 2013 state law prohibited unions from restraining public employees in the exercise of rights in agreements, contracts and practices taking effect, extended or renewed after March 28, 2013. According to the union, a "grandfather provision" applied to an agency shop clause in its CBA because it was agreed on and signed before March 28, 2013. But the court disagreed, finding no grandfather clause in the relevant section of the amended law that would allow the enforcement of unlawful contract provisions. Instead, the court found the union was attempting to compel the teacher to financially support the union in violation of the 2013 state-law amendment. As this was a restraint or coercion of his rights, the court agreed with the MERC that the union committed an unfair labor practice. As a result, the judgment for the teacher was affirmed, and the court held a $500 fine could be imposed on the union. *Clarkston Educ. Ass'n v. Conwell*, No. 340470, 2019 WL 165563 (Mich. Ct. App. 1/10/19).

◆ Under the collective bargaining agreement (CBA) between a teacher's union and an Illinois school board, teachers had 64 minutes of continuous preparation time each day. Further, a CBA provision allowed teachers release time for completing IEPs. A teacher said she was forced to work additional hours at home in order to prepare for her classes and work on IEPs, in violation of the CBA. She filed a state-court action against the board, seeking some $18,000 in overtime pay under the federal Fair Labor Standards Act (FLSA) and provisions of Illinois law. Agreeing with the school board, the court held the teacher was required to exhaust her remedies under the CBA. In an amended complaint, the teacher claimed she was not seeking overtime pay but "wages earned, contracted for and unpaid" under the FLSA, the Illinois Wage Payment and Collection Act and the Illinois Minimum Wage Act. Again, the court dismissed the case for failure to use the CBA procedures.

Appeal reached the Appellate Court of Illinois, which considered the FLSA and state minimum wage law claims. It held the teacher could not assert a valid claim under either law. The court found a Minimum Wage Law claim was contingent upon establishing a violation of the FLSA. **A provision of the FLSA at 29 U.S.C. § 213(a)(1) states that the act does not apply to employees in executive, administrative or professional jobs, or to elementary and secondary school teachers.** As the teacher conceded she taught at a Chicago elementary school, the court held she was excluded from asserting an FLSA claim under 29 U.S.C. § 213(a)(1). Since the teacher could not assert an FLSA claim, her minimum wage law claim also failed. Given her failure to state claims under the FLSA and the minimum wage law, the court affirmed the judgment for the board. *Marshall v. Chicago Board of Educ.*, No. 1-17-0314, 2018 IL App (1st) 170314-U (Ill. App. Ct. 2/26/18).

◆   A Nebraska professional employees union represented paraprofessionals, office personnel, and operations employees. Although the collective bargaining agreements (CBAs) for these employees described the vacation time to which each employee was entitled, the CBAs did not describe how vacation time was to accrue. Each of the CBAs allowed the school district to change its policies at any time. Near the end of the 2010-11 school year, the district's board voted to change the vacation accrual policy so that vacation time would accrue over the school year instead of being granted as a lump sum at the start of a school year.

The union local asked the district not to implement the change, and two meetings were held to discuss it. At the time, contracts for the next school year were being negotiated. But the union did not propose any changes to the accrual policy. After CBAs for 2011-12 were signed with no changes to the policy, the union petitioned the state commission of industrial relations (CIR), asserting bad faith bargaining and unilateral action by the district. The CIR held the union had a duty to bargain over any changes to the policy and had waived its rights regarding what was otherwise a mandatory subject of collective bargaining. Appeal reached the Supreme Court of Nebraska. It held the school district acted within its authority to amend the policy and adopt a new one. The union failed to request negotiations over the subject. **Federal labor law cases indicated that a union waived its right to bargain by failing to request bargaining or otherwise not informing an employer that its employees wished to bargain.** Finding a clear waiver by the union to bargain, the court held for the district. *Service Employees Int'l Union (AFL-CIO) Local 226 v. Douglas County School Dist. 001*, 286 Neb. 755, 839 N.W.2d 290 (Neb. 2013).

◆   A veteran Wisconsin special education teacher was charged with using excessive force on students. Her union filed a grievance, arguing there was no just cause for dismissal and seeking her reinstatement. Before the arbitrator issued a decision, Wisconsin legislators enacted 2011 Act 10, which took away many collective bargaining rights of public school employees. The act went into effect for employees covered by existing collective bargaining agreements on the day an agreement expired. After a hearing, the arbitrator found the district did not have just cause to dismiss the teacher. He ordered her to be reinstated with lost wages and benefits, reduced by an amount equal to a 30-day suspension.

Among the findings was that many charges of inappropriate conduct were not credible and that most of the contact between the teacher and students was "incidental and permissible." In response, the school district filed a state court action to vacate the arbitration award. The court found the arbitration award did not disregard either state law or any public policy. On appeal, the Court of Appeals of Wisconsin held Act 10 had no effect until the expiration of current labor agreements. Under the agreement in effect at the time of the teacher's dismissal, she had a right not to be discharged without just cause. As Act 10 took effect after the relevant facts of this case took place, the court dismissed the school district's first argument. **There was no authority for the district's claim that the use of incidental contact not authorized or required by an IEP required dismissal.** As the teacher had engaged in mostly permissible contact, the court upheld the arbitration award. *School Dist. of Kewaskum v. Kewaskum Educ. Ass'n*, 351 Wis.2d 527, 840 N.W.2d 179 (Wis. Ct. App. 2013).

IV. TENURE, DUE PROCESS AND OTHER RIGHTS

State tenure laws protect qualified school employees by establishing minimum procedural protections for adverse employment actions proposed by an education agency. These protections, in conjunction with existing contract rights and constitutional rights to notice and an opportunity to be heard, are referred to as due process rights.

In Richardson v. New York City Board of Educ., *this chapter, the Second Circuit Court of Appeals held an employee cannot "short-circuit" due process by resigning, then claim to have been denied procedural rights. An employee's resignation ends any contractual and tenure rights.*

A. Tenure and Due Process Rights

◆   A tenured New Jersey special education teacher accepted assignments from her school board to teach English to special education students in an alternative education program. She did not need any additional certification for her work at the alternative school and was paid an hourly wage for the assignment. After the teacher worked in the alternative program for several years, the board assigned her duties to another teacher. The teacher claimed she was tenured in the alternative assignment, and she filed an administrative complaint against the board. When the case came before an administrative law judge (ALJ), she found the term "extracurricular" applied to programs such as the alternative assignment.

Further, she held the board had the authority to assign teachers to "extracurricular duties" as it saw fit. As the alternative school assignment was extracurricular and the teacher did not require additional certification beyond what she already held, the ALJ found she was not entitled to tenure in the alternative program. Following a decision by the state commissioner of education that adopted the ALJ's order, the teacher appealed to a New Jersey Appellate Division Court.

The court explained that many New Jersey cases have held a teacher who is tenured cannot acquire separate tenure in an extracurricular assignment, if the teacher is not required to possess another certificate besides the one held for the tenured position. In a previous case, the commissioner held a board may assign teachers to extracurricular duties in addition to regular classroom assignments without conferring tenure status, if the teacher receives reasonable remuneration. In this case, the teacher was performing "extracurricular duties" when she worked at the alternative program. She was paid a separate wage for the assignment that was not an integral portion of her salary for her tenured position. **As the alternative school assignment was voluntary and not a part of the teacher's primary tenured position, the court held she did not have tenure rights in the assignment.** The Supreme Court of New Jersey later accepted the teacher's petition for review. *Melnyk v. Board of Educ. of Delsea Regional High School Dist. Gloucester County*, No. C-861 September Term 2018082354, 2019 WL 2166817 (Table) (N.J. cert. granted 5/14/19).

◆ The New York City Department of Education (DOE) investigated a parent's complaint that an administrator falsely documented her telephonic participation in an IEP review. A DOE investigation was begun. After the end of the school year, the administrator retired before any disciplinary charges were brought against her. A DOE director approved an investigative report's recommendation to place her on an ineligible list for future DOE employment. Three years after retiring, the administrator became aware of her placement on the ineligible list. As a result of a previous DOE investigation report, she was denied a DOE security clearance. In a federal court, the administrator sued the DOE, its board and the City of New York for violating her due process rights.

The case reached the U.S. Court of Appeals, Second Circuit, which found **the administrator's voluntary retirement foreclosed her from seeking protections as a tenured employee. State tenure protections did not extend beyond retirement.** The administrator identified no statutory or contractual authority providing a retired employee with a protected property interest in future DOE employment. Prior Second Circuit decisions have held that prospective government employment is not a protected property interest. At the time of her resignation, the administrator relinquished her state-law tenure protections. She retained no due process rights under state law, board regulations or the relevant collective bargaining agreement. *Richardson v. New York City Board of Educ.*, 711 Fed.Appx. 11 (2d Cir. 2017).

◆ Three Oklahoma teachers had temporary contracts that would expire at the end of the school year. They received excellent evaluations, and their principals recommended rehiring them. A week before the board met to consider whether to renew their contracts, a board member asked the superintendent to remove the teachers' names from the list of teachers who were to be rehired. According to the teacher, the board member accused her of being late to work each day. She said the board member told her she would not vote to rehire the other teachers because one "did not care about special education," and the other was "disorganized." Another teacher claimed the board members retaliated against her for speaking out in favor of a bond issue. After the board did not rehire the teachers, they sued members of the board in a federal court. The court held for the board members. On appeal, the U.S. Court of Appeals, Tenth Circuit, held the lower court should not have dismissed certain claims based on the collective bargaining agreement (CBA). The board members breached several CBA provisions that did not implicate the state Teacher Due Process Act (TDPA).

Even if the teachers had temporary contracts and no state tenure law protection, the court found they were covered by the CBA. According to the teachers, the board members conducted their own employment evaluations, interfered with school administration and discussed board business prior to a meeting in violation of the Open Meeting Act. These charges were unrelated to the TDPA, defeating the board members' claim that their action failed because of their temporary teaching status. Moreover, the court held the teacher who claimed the board members retaliated against her for speaking out in favor of a bond issue could pursue her First Amendment claims. But the court rejected the teachers' due process claim. **Oklahoma law does not grant due process rights to temporary contract teachers.** In addition, the teachers did not show they had property rights under their contracts based on the custom and practice of the board. State courts have held that temporary contract teachers are not afforded the due process protections granted to career teachers. In sum, the court held the teachers presented a sufficient claim under the evaluation provision of the CBA and a CBA provision requiring the board to comply with state laws unrelated to the TDPA. *Utter v. Colclazier*, 714 Fed.Appx. 872 (10th Cir. 2017).

◆ Five student witnesses claimed that a New York teacher took a knife from the desk in his classroom and waved it around to get control of the class. A student and a paraprofessional stated that on the same day, the teacher pulled a stool out from under a student. An arbitration hearing was held to consider the teacher's employment termination case. At the conclusion of the proceeding, the arbitrator found the teacher's employment should be terminated. A state court denied the teacher's petition to vacate the arbitration award, and he appealed to the New York Supreme Court, Appellate Division. It held the award was rational and not arbitrary and capricious. The teacher did not present clear and convincing evidence that the arbitrator was biased against him.

Ample testimony supported the events of the day leading up to his employment termination. **The court found the teacher's due process rights were not violated when the arbitrator denied his late requests for further fact-finding and to call "dozens of vaguely identified witnesses."** He was given more time to arrange for another attorney when his counsel withdrew. Although the teacher raised other arguments, the court rejected them without comment and affirmed the arbitrator's decision. *Grassel v. Dep't of Educ. of City of New York*, 158 A.D.3d 501, 73 N.Y.S.3d 130 (N.Y. App. Div. 2018).

◆ A North Carolina special education teacher found a new school schedule was increasing student behavior problems. She went over her principal's head and complained to the district director of exceptional children. Later, the teacher said she was not rehired due to classroom management problems and insubordinate behavior. The teacher sued the board, principal and others in a federal court. In holding for the board, the court found Title VII prohibits retaliation by employers against employees who have opposed any practice made unlawful by Title VII. Since Title VII does not prohibit disability discrimination, the claim failed. Next, the court rejected the teacher's equal protection claim.

In the court's opinion, **the teacher had no protected due process interest in employment**. State law governed her probationary employment terms. While she claimed an administrator gave her verbal assurances of reemployment, this did not create a property interest. Since the teacher did not earn a proficient rating in all five of the state's professional teaching standards, she did not meet state requirements for a continuing teaching license. As a result, she had no property interest in her licensure. Rejecting the teacher's remaining arguments, the court dismissed the action. The teacher appealed to the Fourth Circuit. In a brief opinion, the appeals court affirmed the judgment for the board. *Harmon v. Cumberland County Board of Educ. A/K/A Cumberland County School Dist. North Carolina*, 669 Fed.Appx. 174 (4th Cir. 2016).

◆ Illinois legislators amended the state School Code in 2011 to make teacher performance evaluation ratings a focus in rehiring decisions following layoffs. To determine the order of layoffs, the law put teachers into four groups. Group one was made up of untenured teachers who had not received performance evaluations. Group two teachers had a performance evaluation of "needs improvement" or "unsatisfactory" in one of their last two evaluations. Group three and four teachers had some combination of "satisfactory," "proficient" or "excellent" performance evaluations in their most recent evaluations. Two special education teachers who had been classified within group two were laid off by their employer. When the case reached the Appellate Court of Illinois, it held the amended law only permitted the recall of teachers who were in groups three and four. In fact, **the district was prohibited from recalling teachers classified in groups one and two**. The court rejected the teachers' argument that a school board might subvert the rights of all tenured teachers by giving them unsatisfactory ratings. Due process protection was provided in the form of committee appointments and public hearings. The court held the school district had complied with Section 24-12. Rejecting all the teachers' arguments, the court held for the district. *Pioli v. North Chicago Community Unit School Dist. No. 187*, No. 2-13-0512, 2014 IL App. (2d) 130512-U (Ill. App. Ct. 1/13/14).

After the court issued its decision, the Supreme Court of Illinois denied a petition by the teachers to review the case. *Pioli v. North Chicago Community Unit School Dist. No. 187*, 3 N.E.3d 1053 (Table) (Ill. 2014).

◆ A Pennsylvania state university police officer was charged with felony counts related to marijuana possession. State police notified the university about the charges, and the university immediately suspended the officer without pay pursuant to a state executive order requiring such action where a state employee is formally charged with a felony. University officials demoted the officer but did not inform him that they had obtained his confession from police records. He sued university officials contesting his suspension without pay. The U.S. Supreme Court agreed to hear the case and **held that the university did not have to suspend the officer with pay pending a hearing**. The criminal complaint established an independent basis for believing that he had committed a felony, and the suspension did not violate his due process rights. *Gilbert v. Homar*, 520 U.S. 924, 117 S.Ct. 1807, 138 L.Ed.2d 120 (1997).

B. Certification Issues

In Routson-Gim-Belluardo v. Ohio Dep't of Educ., *90 N.E.3d 180, 2017-Ohio- 2611 (Ohio Ct. App. 2017), this chapter, the Ohio Department of Education upheld the two-year license suspension of a specialist for conduct unbecoming a teacher. A state court later affirmed the decision, finding that "conduct unbecoming" encompasses a wide variety of conduct, including misconduct that negatively reflects upon the teaching profession.*

Many courts considering whether a teacher remains fit to teach consider some or all of the factors first noted by the Supreme Court of California in Morrison v. State Board of Educ., *1 Cal.32 214, 82 Cal.Rptr. 175, 461 P.2d 375 (Cal. 1969). These include: 1) whether it is likely that the conduct at issue will be repeated; 2) any extenuating or aggravating circumstances; 3) any effects of notoriety or publicity; 4) any impairment of teacher-student relationships; 5) any disruption of the educational process; 6) the teacher's motive; and 7) the proximity or remoteness in time of the conduct.*

◆   A Colorado teacher learned her husband was abusing their daughter, but she did not report it. She also allowed him to continue giving private music lessons to children in their home. A parent of one of the daughter's friends reported the abuse, prompting the teacher to respond: "Why are you trying to ruin my life?" In later court proceedings, the teacher pleaded guilty to a misdemeanor abuse charge. When she applied to renew her teacher's license, the state board of education denied it, based on "immoral conduct and unethical behavior regarding her failure to report the abuse of her daughter." Before an administrative law judge (ALJ), the teacher claimed she had battered woman syndrome and was trying to keep her family together. Among other things, the ALJ found the teacher engaged in unethical behavior that offended the morals of the community and jeopardized children. In an order denying her license application, the state board adopted the ALJ's findings. A state court later upheld the order.

On appeal, **the state court of appeals found the state board of education could deny a license application based on incompetent or unethical behavior**. According to the court, "unethical behavior" is "immoral conduct that affects the health, safety, or welfare of children," or conduct that offends the morals of the community. The court rejected the teacher's argument that her conviction was improper because parents are not listed in the mandatory reporting law as individuals who have a duty to report child abuse. It held the mandatory reporting duty is not limited to the circumstances under which a reporter learns of suspected abuse or neglect. Further, the court found the law did not limit a teacher's reporting duty to knowledge gained or first suspected during employment. **In sum, the court found Colorado public school teachers are required to report any known or suspected child abuse or neglect without limit to whether the knowledge or suspicion occurs in a professional capacity.** As substantial evidence supported denying the teacher's application, the court affirmed the state board's decision. *Heotis v. Colorado State Board of Educ.*, No. 18CA0057, 2019 COA 35 (Colo. Ct. App. 3/7/19).

◆ An Iowa court reversed the suspension and temporary license revocation of a teacher charged with abusing a child with disabilities, finding hearsay statements by the child's parent were not substantial evidence of abuse. According to the Court of Appeals of Iowa, the decision to suspend the teacher's license was not supported by substantial evidence. **The student never identified the teacher as the source of bruising on his arm.** No eyewitnesses saw any contact. In addition, the court found the board relied on hearsay testimony by the parent. While hearsay may be admitted in an administrative proceeding, the court found "the hearsay essentially comes through the filter of a parent" in this case. As the parent acknowledged, the student was not always truthful. The principal accepted the parent's statements at face value without questioning the student. An investigator acknowledged that the student did not mention physical contact in an interview. The court found the student's later account was obtained through the use of leading questions.

Based on concern about the use of suggestive, leading questions, the student's reputation for lying and failure of the nurse and principal to independently investigate, the court found no substantial evidence supported the suspension. The court found the only one who felt the student's bruises matched the fingerprints of an adult hand was his mother. The evidence did not eliminate other possible causes, such as medical procedures, caretakers or classmates. Finding no basis for sanctions, the court reversed the judgment and instructed the lower court to return the case to the Iowa Board of Educational Examiners for of dismissal. *Babe v. Iowa Board of Educ. Examiners*, No. 17-0213, 2018 WL 1098923 (Iowa Ct. App. 2/21/18).

◆ An Ohio court upheld the revocation of the teaching license of an intervention specialist for conduct unbecoming a teacher, including charges of inappropriate physical contact with students. The Court of Appeals of Ohio rejected the specialist's claim that the board did not use a specific definition when charging her with "conduct unbecoming a teacher." It found the hearing officer properly relied on the state administrative code's definition of the term.

Next, the court rejected the specialist's claim that she was denied due process. It found the department's notices described the charges against her and that she was provided a full and fair opportunity to be heard. As the board argued, a lower court abused its discretion in reversing the board's decision. It appeared to the court that the lower court made a "sweeping generalization" about the testimony of three education department witnesses who were found to have a personality conflict with the specialist. In addition, the court of appeals found the lower court was dismissive of other parts of the board's decision, focusing instead on the testimony of the three department witnesses. After a review of the record, the court found the lower court abused its discretion. **Noting the specialist acknowledged her inappropriate conduct, the court found her misconduct reflected negatively on the teaching profession,** and it reinstated the board's decision. *Langdon v. Ohio Dep't of Educ.*, 87 N.E.3d 1276 (Ohio Ct. App. 2017).

◆ A West Virginia school board terminated a special education aide's employment based on lack of need. When doing so, the board placed her name on its preferred recall list. Over the summer, the board advertised a job vacancy for an ECCAT/kindergarten aide position. It did not provide the employee any notice about the position, and she did not apply for it. An applicant who held ECCAT certification was hired for the job. At the time, the employee lacked ECCAT certification. She filed a grievance over the decision, claiming the board was required by state law to provide her notice of the vacancy. After a hearing, the board denied the grievance, on grounds that any failure to provide notice was a harmless error. **Even with notice, the selected applicant would have been appointed due to her superior qualifications.**

After a series of unsuccessful appeals, the employee appealed to the Supreme Court of Appeals of West Virginia. There, she argued the board had hired a less-senior aide for the vacancy. In the court's view, the employee's seniority as a special education aide did not count as seniority as an ECCAT. **An applicant in the classification title of employment has the first opportunity for promotion and vacancies.** State law defines "aides" and "ECCATs" differently and establishes separate qualifications for these positions. As the employee did not hold an ECCAT classification title, the court held she was not qualified for the job vacancy in this case. *Mayle v. Barbour County Board of Educ.*, No. 17-0204, 2018 WL 317375 (W.Va. 1/8/18).

◆ Arizona's state board of education board denied a special education teaching certificate to an applicant based on findings of his unprofessional conduct. The board cited his criminal convictions for driving under the influence, disorderly conduct, unlawful possession of a firearm and phone harassment. Although he filed an appeal in a state superior court, it was dismissed after he failed to timely file papers despite several time extensions. In 2009, the applicant mailed his substitute teaching certificate to the state education department, stating that he no longer wished to possess it and requesting that it expire immediately. In 2010, the state board filed a disciplinary complaint against the applicant, based on the same grounds it used in denying his application for a special education teaching certificate. After a hearing which the applicant did not attend, a board committee recommended the revocation of his substitute teaching certificate. The board adopted the recommendation and revoked the applicant's certificate.

A state court affirmed the decision. On appeal, the state court of appeals cited a state law authorizing the board to proceed with disciplinary action against a certificate-holder after the suspension, expiration or surrender of a certificate. It rejected the applicant's argument that the law only permitted the board to continue a disciplinary action, not to initiate a new one, after the surrender of a certificate. Even if the certificate expired in 2009 and the applicant chose not to renew it, the court held the board could still file a disciplinary complaint against him. **Although the applicant argued the board denied him due process by not allowing him to be heard at the committee hearing, the court rejected this claim.** The committee allowed him ample opportunity to participate in the hearing process and repeatedly rescheduled the hearing at his request over a period of five months. Since there was no violation of due process and the applicant's other arguments lacked merit, the court affirmed the revocation action. *Houston v. Arizona State Board of Educ.*, No. 1 CA-CV-0706, 2017 WL 56700 (Ariz. Ct. App. 1/5/17).

◆ An Ohio teacher with 25 years of experience in the same district restrained a preschool student who would not get on his school bus. As it was a Friday, her report was not given to the principal until the following Monday. The Ohio Department of Education initiated an action to permanently revoke the teacher's license for conduct unbecoming to the teaching profession. A hearing officer recommended permanent revocation, and the state board of education resolved to permanently revoke her license. Appeal reached the Court of Appeals of Ohio, which returned the case to a hearing officer. This resulted in a decision to suspend the teacher for 39 months. When the case returned to the court of appeals, it held the board was entitled to use standards from the state administrative code and the Licensure Code of Professional Conduct for Ohio Educators when interpreting the term "conduct unbecoming."

The Licensure Code included acts of cruelty to children and acts of child endangerment in defining "conduct unbecoming." The court held it was reasonable and consistent with its 2012 decision for the board to find the conduct at issue was unbecoming. Moreover, the court found the board's resolution had been supported by reliable and substantial evidence. Finally, **the court held the penalty imposed on the teacher was appropriate and in accordance with law.** *Orth v. State of Ohio, Dep't of Educ.*, No. 14AP-19, 2014-Ohio- 5353 (Ohio Ct. App. 12/4/14).

◆ A Massachusetts teacher with six continuous years of service in district schools had professional status and a right to seek a personal leave of absence of up to two years under the relevant collective bargaining agreement (CBA). Following what was described as "a great deal of miscommunication" among the teacher, state education department officials and a school district secretary, the teacher believed his application for a preliminary special education license had been denied. He received waivers from the state for the next two years and was able to continue teaching special education. The state denied the teacher's request for a third waiver from licensing requirements. This time, the district superintendent declared him ineligible for work. Although the teacher requested a year of leave to obtain a proper license, the school committee claimed it no longer had an employment relationship with him.

An arbitrator found the lack of a license or waiver did not extinguish his professional status or his rights under the CBA. Noting that the CBA provided the teacher a right to unpaid leaves of up to two years for personal reasons, the arbitrator held in his favor. On appeal, the state court of appeals noted the school committee took no steps to terminate the teacher's employment relationship in accordance with his contract, relevant state law or the CBA. Like the arbitrator,

the court held the teacher's unlicensed status did not automatically eliminate his rights. He was still entitled to the termination processes of the teacher termination law, as well as his CBA rights. Significantly, the teacher had professional teacher status and could not be dismissed for reasons other than those listed in the termination statute. In the absence of proper proceedings under the termination statute, the employment relationship continued. Finding the arbitrator did not exceed her powers, the court held the teacher had been wrongfully denied leave to obtain a proper license. *School Committee of Marshfield v. Marshfield Educ. Ass'n*, 3 N.E.3d 602 (Mass. App. Ct. 2014).

◆   An Idaho special education teacher with a history of depression and bipolar disorder experienced a bout of severe depression that left her unable to take the classes necessary to prevent her teaching certification from expiring. She sought provisional certification from the school board, but it discharged her because of her lack of action over the previous five years. When she sued for disability discrimination, a federal court and the Ninth Circuit ruled against her. **She failed to show that the school board's compliance with state law certification requirements was discriminatory** in effect. She wasn't qualified within the meaning of the ADA. *Johnson v. Board of Trustees of Boundary County School Dist. No. 101*, 666 F.3d 561 (9th Cir. 2011).

C. Workers' Compensation and Other Cases

Typically, employees must resort to the workers' compensation system when they are injured in the workplace, even if a co-worker causes the injury. An exception to workers' compensation exclusivity exists when an employer intends to injure an employee or intentionally creates a dangerous condition that made employee injuries substantially certain.

In Binkowski v. Board of Educ. of City of New Haven, *180 Conn.App. 580 (Conn. Ct. App. 2018), Connecticut school administrators convinced the state appellate court that they did not act intentionally or seek to injure a teacher who claimed their failure to discipline students led to an assault.*

◆   A Connecticut teacher claimed administrators at her elementary school had a policy of not involving themselves in any issues related to student discipline. She said they refused to allow teachers to send disruptive students out of classrooms and did not intervene, even in cases of disruption or violence. Further, the teacher said administrators refused to let teachers summon help under any circumstances and refused to provide protection to teachers facing disruptive or violent students in their classrooms. According to the teacher, school violence escalated. She said two students assaulted her in her classroom, causing a severe sprain of her left knee and ankle. She said school administrators failed to send security, call 911 or respond to her calls for help in any way. Claiming the administrators acted willfully and maliciously, the teacher sued the school board in a state court. But the court held her case was barred by the exclusivity provisions of the state workers' compensation act.

The teacher appealed to the Connecticut Appellate Court. Like the lower court, it found her case did not fall within an exception to the exclusivity provisions of the workers' compensation act. In fact, **the teacher was unable to show any intentional conduct by the school administrators**. To prove intent, the teacher had to show that intentional conduct by the administrators was designed to cause her injury. She did not show the administrators had a "conscious purpose" of causing her injury and did not show they directed or authorized the students to assault her. Since the teacher only asserted that the administrators condoned the assault, the court found no exception to workers' compensation exclusivity applied. It held for the board. *Binkowski v. Board of Educ. of City of New Haven*,180 Conn.App. 580 (Conn. App. Ct. 2018).

◆   The Louisiana Supreme Court declined to hear an appeal by a special education teacher who challenged a lower court decision finding she cannot pursue a Family and Medical Leave Act (FMLA) claim because the state has not waived immunity in FMLA cases. When the teacher was in her first year of work for the state department of education, she sought medical leave before she had accrued any leave time. She was eventually granted provisional FMLA leave but was later dismissed. The teacher sued the department for race, sex, disability and age discrimination, libel and violations of the FMLA. **Finding the state has never waived its immunity regarding the FMLA's self-care provision, the state court of appeal held for the department.** *Nugent v. McNease,* 209 So.3d 99 (La. 2016).

◆   Utah's highest court held more consideration was due a special education teacher's unemployment compensation application after she quit because she felt she would be fired if her performance did not improve. The court explained that a worker is ineligible for unemployment benefits if he or she quits without good cause. **A worker may show good cause where the unemployment is caused by pressures so compelling that a reasonably prudent person would be justified in quitting.** In this case, the teacher consistently asserted she had quit because she feared she would fail an evaluation. During administrative proceedings, a hearing officer did not consider the reasonableness of the teacher's fears, instead finding it was possible she could have passed another evaluation if she had simply gone through with it. The question of whether there was good cause to quit depended upon whether a reasonable person would consider resignation the only reasonable option. Since the state Department of Workforce Services had incorrectly held the teacher might have retained her job, the court returned the case to that agency for further consideration. *Sawyer v. Dep't of Workforce Services*, 345 P.3d 1253 (Utah 2015).

◆   A Minnesota school bus driver was dismissed for twice failing to assure all special needs students exited her bus. She sought unemployment benefits. A state agency denied her request, finding she was discharged for employment misconduct. On appeal, the state court of appeals rejected her claim that she had good reason to believe others would ensure that all children had exited the bus. In the court's view, **failure by the driver to complete walk-throughs of the bus violated reasonable instructions from her supervisor**. In addition, the conduct of co-workers was not a valid defense to her misconduct. As the driver's conduct demonstrated deliberate disregard for her employer's interests and could have endangered the safety of children on her bus, the court upheld the decision that she had committed employment misconduct and was not entitled to benefits. *Johnson v. Minneapolis Special School Dist. #001*, No. A14-0778, 2015 WL 1013646 (Minn. Ct. App. 3/9/15).

◆ A North Carolina teacher was kicked at work by an aggressive student with autism. She missed work for part of the school year due to knee surgery. At the start of the next school year, the teacher returned as a resource teacher for K-2 students. Less than halfway through the school year, she had severe pain and swelling in her knee and underwent another surgery. The doctor permanently restricted her from handling or assisting students. The school district offered the teacher a position as a resource teacher for the next year, but her doctor stated that the position was not within her work restrictions. Several months later, a digital job analysis of the resource teacher position was completed.

When the findings of the analysis were presented to the doctor, he found the position was "very safe" for the teacher. But there was no evidence that the district ever offered her the position. After consideration by the North Carolina Industrial Commission, the teacher was awarded disability benefits for temporary total disability until she returned to work, with ongoing medical treatment and benefits for post-traumatic stress, depression and anxiety. On appeal, the Court of Appeals of North Carolina rejected the district's arguments that the teacher had unjustifiably refused suitable employment. **No evidence showed the district had ever offered the teacher another job.** Evidence supported the findings that her post-traumatic stress disorder, depression and anxiety were related to her work injury. It was not unreasonable for the teacher to turn down resource room work until her doctor reviewed the digital job analysis, and the court held in her favor. *Tatum v. Cumberland County Schools*, 758 S.E.2d 707 (N.C. Ct. App. 2014).

◆ A Louisiana special education teacher was repeatedly punched by a 200-pound student with autism. A few weeks later, she was bitten on the hand. A week after that, she was placed on disability leave for neck pain, for which she was eligible for "assault pay" under a state law. When she tried to return to work seven months later, she was sent home with very high blood pressure. She remained on disability leave for the next four years and then sued the school board under the ADA. The teacher claimed she suffered from PTSD and that the school board had refused to accommodate her. **A federal court ruled against her, finding that she was not disabled under the ADA because she never informed the board of her PTSD** and because she continued to receive "assault pay," which was inconsistent with her assertion that she could return to work. In a brief order, the U.S. Court of Appeals, Fifth Circuit, affirmed the judgment for the school board. *Whetstone v. Jefferson Parish Public School Board*, 529 Fed.Appx. 394 (5th Cir. 2013).

CHAPTER TWELVE

School District Operations

I.   BUDGET AND FINANCE

In 2017, New York's highest court affirmed the dismissal of most of the claims brought by two groups of parents who sought to revive decades-old litigation contesting state school financing equity issues.

A. State and Local Educational Funding

◆   In 2009, a group of students, parents and citizen organizations sued Florida officials and the state board of education in a state court, seeking a declaration that Florida's K-12 public education system was being maintained in violation of the state constitution. Among other things, the complaint claimed the state's educational accountability policy, "misuse" of standardized test results, low graduation rates and low test scores denied students a "high quality education" as required by the state constitution. The complaint stated that these and other failings had a disproportionate impact on minority students, low income students and those with disabilities. After a trial, the court dismissed the complaint.

After a state district court of appeal affirmed the judgment, appeal reached the Supreme Court of Florida. In the court's view, K-12 education funding in the state was at the highest level in state history. Florida was addressing graduation rates and closing the achievement gap at a higher rate than other states. Further, the court held the challengers did not establish a causal relationship between student performance and a lack of resources. **State school choice programs, including one providing scholarships for eligible students with disabilities, had no negative effect on the uniformity or efficiency of the state system of public schools.** As the court held in a previous case, the state legislature is vested with "enormous discretion" to comply with its duty to make provision for an adequate and uniform system of free public schools. Although the challengers submitted additional arguments, the court rejected them, finding they were inviting the court to intrude into the legislature's power. *Citizens for Strong Schools v. Florida State Board of Educ.*, 262 So.3d 127 (Fla. 2019).

◆ Ruling that state education funding is a duty of the state and not local education agencies, the Supreme Court of North Carolina held a challenge to a local board's financial decisions was properly dismissed. In the court's opinion, **the "general and uniform system of free public schools," assured by the state constitution imposed a duty on the General Assembly, not on local boards.** No provision of the constitution required county commissioners to provide for educational rights. In *Hoke County Board of Educ. v. State*, 358 N.C. 605, 599 S.E.2d 365 (2004), the court held the state had the ultimate responsibility for the actions or inactions of a local school board. Since it was the state's duty to correct the actions or inactions of a county board, the court held the students and their representatives who filed the lawsuit could not assert constitutional claims against the county commissioners. They were free to assert claims against the state and could join the ongoing state educational finance litigation in *Leandro v. State*, 346 N.C. 336, 488 S.E.2d 249 (1997). *Silver v. Halifax County Board of Commissioners*, 821 S.E.2d 755 (N.C. 2018).

◆ The Supreme Court of Mississippi held the governor did not violate constitutional principles by cutting state agency budgets, including a $19.8 million reduction to the Mississippi Adequate Education Program in 2017. The court denied a challenge to the budget cuts filed by two state legislators who claimed a state law allowing the executive branch to make appropriations decisions violated the separation-of-powers doctrine. In the court's opinion, the case did not implicate the doctrine because the governor was exercising his core powers of budget control. **The court upheld the law by which the budgets were reduced, finding it did not affect legislative appropriations and did not permit budget-making (as opposed to budget control) by the governor.** *Clark v. Bryant*, 253 So.3d 297 (Miss. 2018).

◆ Kansas' highest court has issued five school finance decisions in recent years involving litigation over Article 6 of the Kansas Constitution. The article imposes a duty on the legislature to "make suitable provision for finance of the educational interests of the state." A group of challengers filed suit in 2010 asserting that the State violated this constitutional requirement by inequitable and inadequate funding of K–12 public education. In the first of two decisions in 2017, the court held the Classroom Learning Assuring Student Success (CLASS) Act of 2015 was unconstitutional. The act operated as a block grant to school districts, freezing K–12 funding levels for fiscal years 2016 and 2017 at 2015 levels until the Act expired on June 30, 2017. In the court's view, the

CLASS Act did not meet the structure requirement contained in the test it outlined in a 2014 opinion. Significantly, the court found the CLASS Act was minimally responsive to changing conditions such as increased enrollment. Next, the court held the CLASS Act did not meet the implementation requirements for constitutional adequacy it described in 2014. Evidence revealed that the state failed to provide the basic skills of math and reading for a quarter of all public school K-12 students, and was leaving significant groups of harder-to-educate students further behind. The court found evidence that student achievement rose when funding increased after its decision in *Montoy v. State*, 282 Kan. 9, 138 P.3d 755 (2006), but fell when education funding began to decrease in 2009.

Finding a correlation between funding and student achievement, the court held that falling student achievement was caused by underfunding. The court held the state's public education financing system was not reasonably calculated so that all Kansas public school students could meet or exceed the minimum standards of adequacy. The court retained jurisdiction to allow the legislature to bring the education financing system into compliance with Article 6. *Gannon v. State of Kansas*, 305 Kan. 850, 390 P.3d 461 (Kan. 2017).

After the Kansas Legislature passed Senate Bill 19 of 2017, the state supreme court held **the state did not meet its burden of showing Senate Bill 19 met the adequacy and equity requirements of Article 6 of the Kansas Constitution.** Although the bill made positive strides, the court held the state's public education financing system still was not reasonably calculated for all Kansas students to meet or exceed the standards set out in *Rose v. Council for Better Educ.*, 790 S.W.2d 186 (Ky. 1989), and contained in Kansas law. The system was not providing districts "reasonably equal access to substantially similar educational opportunity through similar tax effort." The court retained jurisdiction and stayed its mandate to provide the legislature another chance to bring the education financing system into compliance with the state constitution. *Gannon v. State of Kansas*, 306 Kan. 1170, 402 P.3d 513 (Kan. 2017).

◆   From 1995 to 2006, the New York Court of Appeals issued three decisions in what became known as the Campaign for Fiscal Equity (CFE) litigation, culminating with *Campaign for Fiscal Equity v. State of New York*, 8 N.Y.3d 14 (N.Y. 2006). The CFE decisions established that there is a constitutional floor for educational adequacy and that the courts are responsible for deciding the nature of the duty to provide a sound basic education in the state. In one of the CFE cases, the court held "unevenness of educational opportunity" does not render the school financing system unconstitutionally infirm unless it can be shown that the system's funding inequities resulted in the deprivation of a "sound basic education." Years after the CFE cases were closed, two new challenges were filed in the state court system against the governor and other state officials and entities, asserting claims that students were not being provided with a sound basic education in violation of state law. Following lower court activity, the cases came before the New York Court of Appeals.

Summarizing its CFE decisions, the court held that to proceed with a state funding challenge, facts must be stated regarding each district and assert some failure to meet the constitutional minimum. In this case, the challengers admitted many districts were not deficient in funding. They only made specific pleadings involving New York City and Syracuse schools. **In future activity, the challengers would need to present evidence that the state breached its constitutional duty to provide a sound basic education to students.** Next, the court rejected claims that the state had to increase its spending annually under 2007 legislation. Claims asserting noncompliance with orders from the CFE litigation were not viable, as that litigation is over. Claims for failure to comply with legislation and a $290 million withholding from New York City schools did not amount to constitutional violations. Apart from the New York City and Syracuse claims, the complaints were properly dismissed. *Aristy-Farer v. State of New York*, 29 N.Y.3d 501, 81 N.E.3d 360, 58 N.Y.S.3d 877 (N.Y. 2017).

◆   An Ohio court held autism service providers could not enforce a claim to over $366,000 for behavioral intervention services they said were provided under Ohio's Autism Scholarship Program. When the providers refused to comply with state requirements to complete new applications for two new sites, the state education department withheld payments. **The case reached the state court of appeals, which held the state reasonably construed the scholarship law and could withhold the payments.** In 2018, the Supreme Court of Ohio declined to review the case. *Silver Lining Group EIC Morrow County v. Ohio Dep't of Educ. Autism Scholarship Program*, 152 Ohio St.3d 1424 (Ohio appeal not allowed 3/14/18).

◆   South Carolina's highest court imposed deadlines on state officials to respond to a 2014 decision finding the state's public school funding scheme as a whole violated the South Carolina Constitution. **The court held school districts must work with the state to address the violation with proposals for a House task force and a Senate special subcommittee.** The state is to submit a written statement to the court after the 2016 legislative session detailing efforts to implement a constitutional education system. The court is then to review the state's efforts and issue an order. *Abbeville County School Dist. v. State of South Carolina*, 415 S.C. 19 (S.C. 2015).

◆   A group of disabled students asserted Pennsylvania's special education funding method resulted in inequities that violated the IDEA and other federal laws. In a federal district court, they claimed an inequitable distribution of special education funding. The court reviewed a state law section specifying the apportioning of base supplement funds to school districts based on the daily membership of students in each district from the prior school year. The section made the assumption that 16% of the students in each district had a disability. According to the students, they attended school in districts where the special needs population was 17% or greater, and the market value/personal income ratio of taxpayers was a certain level. By contrast, most students in the state attended schools in districts where disabled students made up 15% or less of the student population. State special education subsidies averaged $3,326 per special education student in districts represented by the class, while the average special education subsidy in non-class districts was $4,108. An expert for the students said "IEP students" in the school districts within the class had lower math and reading scores and lower graduation rates than their counterparts in the non-class districts. But the expert did not provide evidence of any relationship between the funding disparities and any denial of a FAPE.

In ruling for the state, the court found no evidence that any student's IEP was affected by a lack of funding, or that any student was denied a FAPE by the funding formula. Any denial of FAPE was found to be related to problems with the IEPs, rather than systemic violations. On appeal, the U.S. Court of Appeals, Third Circuit, found that to prevail, the students had to prove they were treated differently than others based on a disability. But the court held they did not show they were deprived of a benefit or opportunity provided to some other group of students. **As the district court had found, the students did not show the funding formula deprived them of any program, benefit or service provided to disabled students who attended school in the non-class districts.** *CG v. Pennsylvania Dep't of Educ.*, 734 F.3d 229 (3d Cir. 2013).

◆ After the New York Court of Appeals held that school districts had to make special education services available to all students residing within district boundaries even if they were attending private schools, the New York legislature enacted a statute that created a new school district whose boundaries were coterminous with a Hasidic community. Residents demanded education of their children in accordance with their tradition of segregating the sexes in school. Taxpayers and an association representing New York school districts sued the state for a declaration that the statute was unconstitutional.

The case reached the U.S. Supreme Court, which held that a state may not delegate authority to a group chosen by religion. Although the statute did not expressly identify the Hasidic community as a recipient of governmental authority, it had clearly been passed to benefit them. The Court held the result was a purposeful and forbidden fusion of governmental and religious functions. **The creation of a school district for the religious community violated the Establishment Clause.** The legislation extended a special franchise to the Hasidic community that violated the constitutional requirement of religious neutrality by the government. The statute crossed "the line from permissible accommodation to impermissible establishment." Thus, the statute was held unconstitutional. *Board of Educ. of Kiryas Joel Village School Dist. v. Grumet,* 512 U.S. 687, 114 S.Ct. 2481, 129 L.Ed.2d 546 (1994).

◆ The New York legislature abolished the Kiryas Joel Village School District, passing two statutes that provided a mechanism for the organization of new school districts. The laws authorized school districts consisting of the entire territory of a municipality coterminous with preexisting school districts when the educational interests of the community required such action, and where certain student enrollment and property tax requirements were satisfied. The taxpayers sought a declaration that the new statutes were unconstitutional. After a lower court agreed with the taxpayers, the Court of Appeals of New York agreed to review the case. It held that despite the apparently neutral criteria in the amendments, **the Hasidic village was the only municipality that could ever avail itself of the statutory mechanism.** The legislation impermissibly favored that group. The court affirmed the judgment for the taxpayers. *Grumet v. Cuomo,* 90 N.Y.2d 57, 659 N.Y.S.2d 173, 681 N.E.2d 340 (N.Y. 1997).

In 1997, the legislature passed another law, but broadened its applicability to municipalities that were as yet unformed. A school district for Kiryas Joel was reconstituted under the new act, and a new challenge was mounted. The court of appeals held that while the 1997 law was facially neutral with respect to religion, its actual effect benefited only Kiryas Joel, and its potential benefit extended to only one other district in the state. Thus, the law was not neutral in effect. The law violated the Establishment Clause by preferring one religion to others. *Grumet v. Pataki*, 93 N.Y.2d 677, 720 N.E.2d 66 (N.Y. 1999).

B. Federal Funding Issues

◆   As a condition for receiving funds under the Individuals with Disabilities Education Act (IDEA), states must comply with the "maintenance of state financial support" (MFS) clause of the law. The MFS clause prohibits states from reducing the amount of state support for special education and related services below the amount from the previous fiscal year. If a state reduces its financial support for special education and related services, the U.S. Secretary of Education may withhold funding by a corresponding amount. For fiscal year 2012, Texas reduced its special education funding by about $33.3 million from the amount for fiscal year 2011. In response, the secretary issued a proposed determination that the state of Texas was ineligible for $33.3 million in future grants. The state petitioned the U.S. Court of Appeals, Fifth Circuit, for review. According to the state, it complied with the MFS clause by applying a weighted-student model. The court disagreed, finding the weighted-student model contradicted the plain language of the MFS clause. Further, **the law required the states to maintain the same level of funding without regard to fluctuation in student needs**. As Texas appropriated about $33.3 million less for special education and related services in 2012 than in 2011, the court found it did not make funds "available in any practical way." Texas' weighted-student model circumvented the federal waiver process by allowing the state to reduce its funding if it decided the needs of students were met. The court found the weighted-student model created a perverse incentive for states to escape their financial obligations by minimizing student special education needs. Last, the court found Spending Clause legislation such as the IDEA permits Congress to condition the receipt of federal money upon compliance by the recipient with federal laws and rules. Finding Texas had clear notice that its interpretation of the MFS clause was incompatible with the law, the court held for the secretary. *Texas Educ. Agency v. U.S. Dep't of Educ.*, 908 F.3d 127 (5th Cir. 2018).

◆   Rhode Island students with disabilities sued the state board of education, claiming they would qualify for a free appropriate public education (FAPE) under the federal Individuals with Disabilities Education Act (IDEA) if not for a state law and regulation that allows local education boards to terminate their eligibility at age 21. The court found "children with disabilities are entitled to receive FAPE services up to the day they turn 22, but only if this does not conflict with state law or practice." Rhode Island's compulsory education statute generally required school attendance up to 18, giving local boards discretion to impose age limitations. The court found the state obligation to make a FAPE available to all children with disabilities aged 18-21 did not apply if it conflicted with the state's provision of public education to non-disabled, general education students of the same age. The court held public education for non-disabled general education students over the age of 18 was not a legal right.

After the court held for the state board of education, appeal reached the U.S. Court of Appeals, First Circuit. It rejected the lower court's conclusion that the state's adult education programs for non-disabled students beyond the age of 21 were not "public education" within the meaning of the IDEA. **The court held the IDEA's requirement that the states provide appropriate services to students until their twenty-second birthdays was not inconsistent with state law and practice "respecting the provision of public education."** It returned the case to the lower court for entry of a judgment in favor of the student. The lower court was instructed to work with the parties to develop appropriate remedies in accordance with the First Circuit's decision. *K.L. v. Rhode Island Bd. of Educ.*, 907 F.3d 639 (1st Cir. 2018).

◆ The Federal Impact Aid Program provides financial assistance to local school districts whose ability to finance public school education is adversely affected by a federal presence – e.g., where a significant amount of federal land is exempt from local property taxes. The statute prohibits a state from offsetting this federal aid by reducing state aid to a local district. To avoid unreasonably interfering with a state program that seeks to equalize per-pupil expenditures, the statute contains an exception permitting a state to reduce its own local funding on account of the federal aid where the Secretary of Education finds that the state program "equalizes expenditures" among local school districts. Two New Mexico school districts disputed certain calculations under the act, and the case reached the U.S. Supreme Court, which held that the Secretary of Education could identify the school districts that should be "disregarded" by looking to the number of a district's pupils as well as to the size of the district's expenditures per pupil. Thus, **the state could factor in the receipt of federal Impact Aid funds when making its own distributions of educational aid to its school districts.** *Zuni Public School Dist. No. 89 v. Dep't of Educ.*, 550 U.S. 81, 127 S.Ct. 1534, 167 L.Ed.2d 449 (2007).

◆ A group of Louisiana citizens sued the Jefferson Parish School Board for violating the First Amendment, alleging that the board improperly provided Chapter Two funds to parochial schools for the purpose of acquiring library materials and media equipment. A federal court agreed that the funding failed the *Lemon* test from *Lemon v. Kurtzman*, 403 U.S. 602 (1971). It also found that the loan of materials to sectarian schools constituted impermissible direct government aid to the schools. Two years later, the court reversed itself in post-judgment activity, citing an intervening Supreme Court decision holding that a state could provide a sign-language interpreter on site at a parochial school. The citizens appealed to the Fifth Circuit, which held the Chapter Two grants were unconstitutional. The U.S. Supreme Court found that the use of the funds by private schools did not result in government indoctrination of religion, because eligibility was determined on a neutral basis and through private choices made by parents. Chapter Two had no impermissible content and did not define its recipients by reference to religion. Chapter Two funding in the school district did not create an improper incentive for parents to select religious schools. **The Court found the program was neutral with regard to religion, and private decision-making controlled the allocation of funds to private schools.**

The Court held students who attended schools receiving Chapter Two funds were the ultimate beneficiaries of the assistance, even though the schools used them to purchase computers, software, books and other equipment. The Court upheld the board's use of Chapter Two funding. The parish did not need to exclude religious schools from the program. *Mitchell v. Helms*, 530 U.S. 793, 120 S.Ct. 2530, 147 L.Ed.2d 660 (2000).

◆   Title I of the Elementary and Secondary Education Act of 1965 provides federal funding through states to local educational agencies to provide remedial education, guidance and job counseling to at-risk students and students residing in low-income areas. Title I requires that funding be made available for all eligible students, including those attending private schools. The New York City Board of Education attempted to implement Title I programs at parochial schools by allowing public employees to instruct students on private school grounds during school hours. The U.S. Supreme Court agreed with a group of taxpayers that this violated the Establishment Clause in *Aguilar v. Felton*, 473 U.S. 402 (1985). In response to *Aguilar*, local education boards modified Title I programs by moving classes to remote sites, including mobile instructional units parked near sectarian schools. However, a new group of parents and parochial school students sued New York school officials in federal court.

The case reached the U.S. Supreme Court, which held that **it would no longer presume that the presence of a public school teacher on parochial school grounds creates a symbolic union between church and state.** The provision of Title I services at parochial schools resembled the provision of a sign-language interpreter under the IDEA. New York City's Title I program was constitutionally permissible because it did not result in government indoctrination, define funding recipients by reference to religion, or create excessive entanglement between education officials and religious schools. *Agostini v. Felton*, 521 U.S. 203, 138 L.Ed.2d 391, 117 S.Ct. 1997 (1997).

C. Residency Disputes

In A.P. v. Lower Merion School Dist.*, this chapter, a federal court held a due process hearing officer will have to resolve a residency question before a parent can proceed with an IDEA dispute against a Pennsylvania school district where her child formerly attended school.*

◆   Wisconsin's open-enrollment law allowed students to transfer from their school districts of residence to nonresident districts that had the available space. Provisions of the law distinguished between regular education and special education students. If a student with a disability required special education, a nonresident district could deny an application if it could not provide necessary services or lacked space. Among the factors for approving an application were whether the district offered the services in a student's IEP, whether space was available for the special education and services in the IEP, class-size limits, pupil-teacher ratios and enrollment projections. Three families submitted open-enrollment applications to nonresident school districts on behalf of children with disabilities. Each of the families asserted that the school districts denied their applications. In a federal court, they sued the state superintendent of public instruction and three school districts. After the court held for the state and local entities, the families appealed to the U.S. Court of Appeals, Seventh Circuit.

The court held nonresident school districts could not reject open-enrollment applicants based on the mere fact of having a disability. But the open-enrollment law "allows nonresident districts to realistically assess whether they have the capacity and resources to comply with a transfer student's IEP." Transfer decisions were based on student special needs and hinged on attributes of students' disabilities rather than on mere stereotypes. The court found the open-enrollment program sought to maximize school choice to the extent that excess capacity existed in a nonresident district. Instead of considering the mere fact of a disability, the open-enrollment program considered the capacity of a nonresident district to meet an applicant's needs based on an IEP. The court held for the state and local entities, as requiring nonresident districts to accept transfer students without regard to capacity would amount fundamentally alter the open-enrollment program. *P.F. v. Taylor*, 914 F.3d 467 (7th Cir. 2019).

◆   The Eighth Circuit Court of Appeals declined to hear discrimination claims against an Iowa school district that denied an open enrollment application by an Iowa teenager with polycystic ovarian syndrome and depression. She was first required to exhaust her IDEA administrative remedies. The court found the student's claim that her district of residence had mishandled the open enrollment application essentially stated that free appropriate public education (FAPE) had been denied. It was claimed that the district of residence was unable to meet the student's educational needs and failed to make reasonable accommodations to enable her to receive a FAPE. The court rejected the parents' claim that any exception to the administrative exhaustion rule applied. Moreover, it found a complaint to the state board was separate and distinct from the claims they now asserted and did not exempt them from IDEA exhaustion. The court found the fact that the parents sought monetary damages in the present action did not preclude them from filing a due process complaint. They could have filed a due process challenge against the district for failing to identify their child and to provide her with a FAPE. **In sum, the court dismissed the case due to failure by the parents to exhaust available IDEA administrative remedies.** *Nelson v. Charles City Community School Dist.*, 900 F.3d 587 (8th Cir. 2018).

◆   Dissatisfied with a Pennsylvania school district's implementation of her child's IEP, a parent enrolled him in a private Maryland school. She then moved to Maryland and enrolled her other children in public schools. The parent filed a due process complaint against the Pennsylvania district, seeking reimbursement for private school tuition. The district agreed to reimburse her tuition costs for a full school year. Later, the parent tried to re-enroll the child in the Pennsylvania school he formerly attended, seeking more private tuition reimbursement. The school district advised her that residency is a prerequisite for enrollment. The parent filed a due process complaint with a state agency, asserting the district failed to offer her child a free appropriate public education (FAPE). A hearing officer dismissed the case, finding he lacked authority to resolve the residency question. The parent appealed to a federal court, where she sought a ruling on the question of residency and an award of private school tuition reimbursement.

Under Pennsylvania law, a child who resides in a school district is entitled to attend a public school there. **A child's district of residence is the district in which his parent or guardian resides.** According to the parent, she remained a resident in the Pennsylvania district. The court found the residency issue was intertwined with the FAPE dispute and thus had to be addressed in a due process hearing. The IDEA requires exhaustion of administrative remedies before a lawsuit may be filed to seek relief available under the IDEA. In this case, the parent had raised the residency issue during the due process hearing. But the hearing officer did not decide it, finding it was beyond his authority. **Since the hearing officer had an obligation to resolve the residency dispute as a part of the due process hearing, the case was returned to the hearing officer.** *A.P. v. Lower Merion School Dist.*, 294 F.Supp.3d 406 (E.D. Pa. 2018).

◆   **A federal court held a Florida parent could not pursue claims that a Florida school district failed to provide a free appropriate public education (FAPE) to his child with autism because the family moved from the district after he filed suit.** In response to the student's "664 incidents of unsafe behavior" that were "gravely impeding his ability to receive a FAPE," the district placed him in a school where he would have a full continuum of autism supports. Claiming the school board denied his son a FAPE, the parent filed a due process complaint. An administrative law judge denied the complaint. After appealing to a federal court, the parent relocated to Virginia. The court held the possibility that the family would return to Florida did not overcome the board's arguments that the case was moot. *Burke v. Hillsborough County School Board*, No. 8:17-cv-993-T-33JSS, 2018 WL 1139064 (M.D. Fla. 3/2/18, 11th Cir. appeal filed 3/29/18).

◆   A California charter school student exhibited provoking and attention-seeking behavior. His family moved outside the school's attendance zone but remained within the school district's boundaries. After the move, the student was readmitted by the charter school as an intra-district transfer student. His parents accused the school of improper disciplinary action. Relations among school staff and the parents deteriorated to the point that the principal sent the parents a letter advising them that if staff members felt unsafe, they could call the police. The parents were told that since they now lived outside the school's attendance zone, an application for grade two should be submitted to the child's school district of residence. The family reapplied, but enrollment at the charter school was denied because the second-grade class was full. In a federal court, the parents sued the school district, charter school, principal and superintendent.

In pretrial activity, the court dismissed most of the claims based on Eleventh Amendment immunity. The charter school was a "conversion" school, not a "start up" school. For this reason, the court upheld the admission priority for resident second-graders. In the court's view, disability discrimination laws did not apply to the student. He was "not qualified to enroll" at the charter school because he resided outside the school's attendance boundaries. On appeal, the U.S. Court of Appeals, Ninth Circuit, found no evidence to show the admission decision was motivated by disability discrimination. **Evidence showed the student was denied admission pursuant to a valid admissions policy.** *J.C. v. Cambrian School Dist.*, 648 Fed.Appx. 652 (9th Cir. 2016).

II. STUDENT RECORDS AND PRIVACY

In R.F. v. Cecil County Public Schools, *910 F.3d 237 (4th Cir. 2019), the Fourth Circuit Court of Appeals rejected a claim by Maryland parents that there was any legal significance to the destruction of daily data collected by their child's teacher. In the court's opinion, **the IDEA does not specify how often a school district should collect data or how long it should be maintained**.*

The federal Family Educational Rights and Privacy Act (FERPA) prohibits the unauthorized release by an educational agency of personally identifiable student information without prior parental consent. State laws also impose obligations upon local educational agencies to protect student privacy. These laws occasionally come into conflict with public information disclosure acts.

The Supreme Court has held FERPA creates no personal enforcement rights. Federal guidance permits health care providers to disclose protected student health information to school nurses, physicians or other health care providers for treatment purposes, without authorization. See http://www2.ed.gov/policy/gen/guid/fpco/doc/ferpa-hipaa-guidance.pdf.

A New Hampshire law provides that unless requested by a student's parents at the time of graduation, local education agencies must destroy a student's records and final IEP within a reasonable time after his or her 26th birthday. Further, the law states that all such records must be destroyed by a student's 30th birthday. Upon a student's graduation from high school, his or her parents may request to have the student's records and final IEP destroyed or retained until the student's 26th birthday. The parents may, at any time prior to the student's 26th birthday, request, in writing, that the records be retained until the student's 30th birthday. New Hampshire 2018 Session Laws, Ch. 76, H.B. New Hampshire 1551. Revised Statutes § 186–C:10–a.

In K.C. v. Fulton County School Dist., *No. 1:03-CV-3501-TWT, 2006 WL 1868348 (N.D. Ga. 6/30/06), a federal court held writing samples, daily work and teachers' private notes did not constitute "educational records" under either FERPA or the IDEA. For this reason, the court denied a request by Georgia parents for some 700 pages of their son's school records.*

◆ A federal appeals court reviewed a claim by California parents that their child's school district violated FERPA by failing to turn over emails that were not maintained in a physical file. The court found that FERPA regulations declare that **"education records" are those containing information directly relating to a student that are "maintained by an educational agency" or a person acting for the agency**. The term "maintained" has been construed by courts to mean "kept in a filing cabinet in a records room at the school or on a permanent secure database." As the district in this case turned over emails it "maintained as part of the student's educational records," the court found there was no FERPA violation. *Burnett v. San Mateo Foster City School Dist.*, 739 Fed.Appx. 870 (9th Cir. 2018).

◆ A Pennsylvania media entity asked a school district for access to security video footage depicting an incident on a school bus of a teacher disciplining an elementary student. A trial court ordered school officials to disclose the video, finding images of students on the bus were "not directly relevant to those students." It held **the images were directly relevant to the teacher's performance and thus not "education records" under the Family Educational Rights and Privacy Act (FERPA)**. An intermediate court affirmed the judgment for the media entity and the school district appealed to the state supreme court, which agreed to review the case. On appeal, the court will consider whether the footage may be disclosed under FERPA. *Easton Area School Dist. v. Mille*r, No. 530 MAL 2018, 2019 WL 42256 (Pa. petition allowed 2/4/19).

◆ The U.S. Court of Appeals, Fourth Circuit, disagreed with an argument by Maryland parents who claimed there was legal significance in the destruction of daily data collected by their child's teacher. In the court's view, **the IDEA does not specify how often a school district should collect data or how long it should be maintained**. The court found no significant infringement of the parents' rights in this case. They still had access to their child's data in her quarterly reports and did not suffer any significant infringement in their participation rights. Although the parents claimed the IEP was inadequate, the court upheld it. *R.F. v. Cecil County Public Schools*, 919 F.3 237 (4th Cir. 2019).

◆ Audits of approved preschool special education programs in New York revealed widespread fraud and abuse in cost reporting. State legislators responded by amending the law to increase financial oversight and permit municipalities to recover overpayments. The amendments required the department to provide guidelines for fiscal audits. The department then amended its regulations to require municipalities to submit detailed plans for certain audits. A private individual sought disclosure by the department of any and all audit standards in the department's possession. After the department denied the request, the individual filed a state court lawsuit to compel disclosure of the records. The department released 55 pages of documents in response to his state Freedom of Information Law (FOIL) request. These included audit plans for two school systems, including New York City, with some records redacted (blocked).

The court largely held for the department, and the case eventually came before the New York Court of Appeals. At issue in this case was an exception contained in state law that allows for the denial of public access to records compiled for law enforcement purposes, which if disclosed would reveal investigative techniques or procedures (except routine techniques and procedures). The court held the term "law enforcement" in the relevant statute is not limited to the enforcement of criminal laws. Courts interpreting the federal FOIL have exempted materials compiled for both civil and criminal enforcement matters. Next, the court found the audits at issue in this case were not simply routine fiscal audits. Instead, the court found they were specifically targeted at ferreting out improper and potentially illegal fraudulent reporting of costs by preschool special education providers. **The court agreed with the department that the blocking of parts of the records was necessary to prevent interference with a law enforcement investigation.** Although the court affirmed the part of the judgment which held the records were properly redacted, it returned the case to a lower court to determine an award of attorneys' fees for the individual. *Madeiros v. New York State Educ. Dep't*, 30 N.Y.3d 67, 86 N.E.3d 527, 64 N.Y.S.3d 635 (N.Y. 2017).

◆ A citizen requested standardized test results for students from a Virginia school system. He was told that the Virginia Department of Education (VDOE) was the custodian of the information. But the VDOE denied having the reports and claimed they were "scholastic records" that were exempt from disclosure. The individual sought a state court order requiring the disclosure. The court held the data being sought was subject to disclosure and declined to shield it under a state law provision covering "scholastic records" as well as corresponding federal law requirements under the FERPA. The court held for the individual and awarded him attorneys' fees. It agreed with his claim that the local school board did not actually use student growth percentile (SGP) data as a teacher performance indicator. As a result, the VDOE was ordered to produce the information. The VDOE, Virginia Education Association and the local board appealed to the Supreme Court of Virginia. At the time of the lower court proceedings, Section 22.1–295.1(C) of the Virginia Code stated that "Teacher performance indicators, or other data used by the local school board to judge the performance or quality of a teacher, maintained in a teacher's personnel file or otherwise shall be confidential," subject to disclosure by a court order, for the purposes of a grievance proceeding involving a teacher, or as otherwise required by law.

Disagreeing with the lower court, the Supreme Court of Virginia held SGP data are "teacher performance indicators," even if they are not actually used to evaluate a teacher. In construing the law, the court found no ambiguity and no requirement that teacher performance indicators actually be used to remain confidential. As the SGP data would disclose individual teacher names and license numbers, the court held the requested data was confidential. The award of attorneys' fees and costs was returned to the lower court for reconsideration. *Virginia Educ. Ass'n v. Davison*, 803 S.E.2d 320 (Va. 2017).

◆ A Pennsylvania student with a history of sexual misconduct graduated from a treatment program for troubled male youths. He enrolled in a public high school and was found eligible for special education and related services. He was also placed in a foster home, under the nonprofit organization's supervision and treatment. Late in the student's senior year of high school, he sexually assaulted another student with a disability as they sat in their English class. An assistant principal learned of the incident and told the victimized student's parents. They reported the assault and the student later submitted pleas to charges of indecent assault and exposure. In a federal court, the victim's parents sued the school district, school officials, the nonprofit organization and several employees for violating Section 504 and Title IX. They added claims for negligence and due process violations, claiming the school and organization knew the student was a sexual predator, yet placed him in a position where he could harm their child.

When the case reached the U.S. Court of Appeals, Third Circuit, it rejected a claim that the student waived any privilege by agreeing to testify and disclose some 94 pages of documents during pretrial activity. Next, the court found a lower court decision to protect all the documents from disclosure under state law had to be reconsidered. **Federal courts recognize a psychotherapist-patient privilege that protects from disclosure any confidential communications between a licensed psychotherapist and a patient in the course of diagnosis.** But the lower court improperly held it must prohibit disclosure of documents on the basis of state law. A federal court may give a state law persuasive or controlling effect, but the final analysis of privilege turns on federal, not state law. The lower court should have considered whether Pennsylvania law promoted sufficiently important interests to outweigh the family's need for the evidence. The case was returned to the lower court. *Swanger v. Warrior Run School Dist.*, 659 Fed.Appx. 120 (3d Cir. 2016).

◆ A Utah court held school officials correctly denied a parent unrestricted access to surveillance video of a fight involving his son and other students. A lower court held the parent could have a copy of the video records with the images of other students blocked out. But the parent appealed instead. The state court of appeals held a surveillance recording was an "education record" under FERPA. Unless there is written consent by parents, FERPA prohibits the release of education records maintained by a school. **FERPA guidance indicated that if student education records contained information on multiple students, the parent requesting access had a right to inspect and review only the records related to his or her own child.** If another student was depicted, the parent would not have the right to inspect and review such records. Since FERPA applied, the court held the school district correctly insisted that the parent obtain consent from all the other parents of children depicted in the records before releasing them. *Bryner v. Canyons School Dist.*, 351 P.3d 852 (Utah Ct. App. 2015; U.S. cert. denied 10/3/16).

◆ New York parents agreed with members of their school's committee on special education on a new IEP for their son placing him in an out-of-district program. The school district's director of pupil personal services sought the parents' signatures on a consent form to forward their son's records to five schools where possible placements had been identified. But they refused to provide their consent and requested further information about the schools. Within days, the school district informed them it would send referral packets to the schools containing the student's psychiatric and special education records.

The parents sued the school district and the director of pupil personal services for constitutional rights and state law violations. A federal court noted that the referral packets included draft IEPs, the student's social history, daily attendance records, report cards, teacher updates and psychological evaluation reports. In the court's view, these records contained highly confidential and personally traceable information. Courts have recognized a due process right to privacy protecting individuals from disclosure of personal matters. The court held the complaint stated a viable privacy interest. **Information about a person's psychiatric health and medical data is considered very intimate.** Next, the court denied the director's claim to qualified immunity, as **there is a clearly established right of privacy in medical and special education records.** Although the director had no immunity for the due process claim, the court found the school district could not be held liable for any of the claimed privacy violations. Courts have routinely held there can be no school district liability for constitutional rights violations, unless the violations result from a district policy or custom. The court dismissed an equal protection claim because the parents did not show their son was treated differently from his peers. While the state law claims against the district were dismissed, the parents could amend their complaint to pursue them. *W.A. and M.S. v. Hendrick Hudson Cent. School Dist.*, No. 14-CV-8093 (KMK), 2016 WL 1274587 (S.D.N.Y. 3/31/16).

◆ A Massachusetts resident sought copies of agreements between a school district and the parents of disabled students regarding certain out-of-district placements. The request was denied due to the belief that this would disclose student records in violation of FERPA and state student records regulations. A state court then held the records had to be released, after the name of each child and any description of a disability was blocked out. On appeal, the Supreme Judicial Court of Massachusetts explained that any disclosure of information about a public school student is governed in part by FERPA and in part by state law. Disclosure of information on special education students is further protected by special education laws and regulations. FERPA has a two-part definition of "education records" and applies to records that "(i) contain information directly related to a student; and (ii) are maintained by an educational agency or institution or by a person acting for such agency or institution." In the court's view, the agreements contained information that was directly related to the students and maintained by the district. But a school may disclose an education record after removing personally identifiable information about a student.

In this case, the agreements might link student names to information about their services, programming, progress, needs, and type of disability. This information was highly personal and exempt from disclosure. But the financial terms of out-of-district placements would not cause an unwarranted invasion of privacy. In fact, the court held the public had a right to know the financial terms of the agreements. The case was returned to the trial court to review evidence about action needed to remove personally identifiable information from any records that were subject to disclosure. *Champa v. Weston Public Schools*, 39 N.E.3d 435 (Mass. 2015).

◆ The parents of a Connecticut child with autism believed his school had videotapes from a school bus security camera that were likely to show two other boys bullying him. Claiming the school district took no precautionary measures to protect him and did not discipline the other students, the parent sought the video records from the company which operated the bus. The district denied the request, as other students on the bus were identifiable. The parents filed a state court action to compel disclosure of the video records. The court held **the** videos constituted "education records" within the meaning of FERPA.

The court noted that in *Ragusa v. Malverne Union Free School Dist.*, 549 F.Supp.2d 288 (E.D.N.Y. 2002), a New York federal court held **a party seeking the disclosure of FERPA records must demonstrate that the need for the information outweighs the privacy interest of the other students**. FERPA required the school district to oppose the student's record request in this case, until FERPA requirements found at 20 U.S.C. § 1232g(b)(2)(B) were satisfied. While a FERPA exception permitted the release of education records pursuant to a court order, such an order could only result from a petition such as the one in this case. Parents and students who might be affected by the release of the records had to be notified in advance. *Goldberg v. Regional School Dist. #18*, No. KNL-CV-146020037S, 2014 WL 6476823 (Conn. Super. Ct. 10/20/14).

◆ A lawsuit arose under the Health Insurance Portability and Accountability Act (HIPAA) over whether Wyoming's Protection and Advocacy (P&A) System could access records without the authorization of the individuals to investigate abuse and neglect allegations. A federal court held HIPAA's privacy rule did not bar the state hospital and training school from disclosing protected information without the authorization of the individual so long as the disclosure was mandated by another federal law. It held the purpose of all the laws could be met by **allowing the P&A system to access incident reports with names withheld** to make probable cause determinations. If probable cause was found, the P&A system could then seek more information. *Protection and Advocacy System v. Freudenthal*, 412 F.Supp.2d 1211 (D. Wyo. 2006).

◆ The U.S. Supreme Court held an "education record" under FERPA is one that is "maintained by an educational agency or institution or by a person acting for such agency or institution." According to the court, student papers are not "maintained" within the meaning of FERPA when students correct them or call out grades. **The word "maintain" suggested that FERPA records were kept in files or cabinets in a "records room at the school or on a permanent secure database."** The momentary handling of assignments by students who scored the papers of classmates, then called out scores did not conform to this definition. Because Congress did not intend to intervene in drastic fashion with traditional state functions by exercising minute control over teaching methods, the Court reversed and remanded the case. *Owasso Independent School Dist. No. I-011 v. Falvo*, 534 U.S. 426, 122 S.Ct. 934, 151 L.Ed.2d 896 (2002).

◆ In *Gonzaga Univ. v. Doe*, 536 U.S. 273, 122 S.Ct. 2268, 153 L.Ed.2d 309 (2002), **the U.S. Supreme Court held FERPA creates no personal rights that can be enforced in a court under 42 U.S.C. § 1983**. It held Congress enacted FERPA to force schools to respect students' privacy with respect to education records. It did not confer enforceable rights upon students. As a result, the Court reversed a state court jury award of over $1 million in damages for a Gonzaga University student who asserted FERPA violations by the university based on the disclosure of his education records to a state agency.

III. GIFTED STUDENT PROGRAMS

The IDEA does not create rights or entitlements for gifted and exceptional students. State laws may establish gifted student programs and requirements, but generally do not confer a property interest in gifted student program participation. But in B.C. v. Penn Manor School Dist., *906 A.2d 642 (Pa. Commw. Ct. 2006), the court awarded a gifted student one hour of compensatory education for each school day he was denied appropriate educational services.*

◆ A federal court held a Pennsylvania school district violated IDEA evaluation requirements by failing to appropriately assess for special education eligibility a gifted student who received almost all A grades. In the court's opinion, the school district discounted an assessment of the student indicating she had an emotional disturbance without sufficient reason. It found **a student who is classified as "mentally gifted may nonetheless meet IDEA eligibility criteria."** The court cautioned that "when evaluating a child with above average cognition and academic performance, a school district must take care to ensure it is not distracted from focusing upon the child's disability-related educational needs." While the court found the district conducted an adequate assessment for a specific learning disability, it found the district failed to adequately assess the student for an OHI or an emotional disturbance. Finding the district "seemingly made no effort to explore a causal relationship between M.J.'s emotional functioning and her attendance, which the District itself points out was adversely impacting her educational performance," the court held the district had to fund an independent educational evaluation. *Rose Tree Media School Dist. v. M.J.*, No. 18-cv-1063, 2019 WL 1062487 (E.D. Pa. 3/6/19).

◆ Arkansas school officials assumed a gifted student with an autism spectrum disorder and ADHD could not qualify for special education due to his academic success. Because of his trouble with social skills, his parent sought three times to obtain special education services, including speech therapy. But the school district found the students' academic needs were adequately met by his Section 504 plan. In addition to finding him ineligible for special education, the district found his behavior at school was acceptable and did not hinder his learning. The parent filed a due process hearing complaint. A hearing officer held the district denied the student a free appropriate public education by failing to adequately evaluate him for special education. The district was ordered to hire a behavioral analyst, conduct a functional behavioral assessment and evaluate his language and behavior deficits. Further, the district was to hire a health care aide, develop an IEP and allow mental health professionals to observe him if necessary.

On appeal, a federal district court held further evaluation of the student was needed. As the hearing officer found, all prior efforts to evaluate him had been defective. **The court found the school district had taken the erroneous position that a student without academic deficits could not qualify for special education.** Evidence did not clearly indicate that the district's evaluations complied with IDEA procedures. At the last evaluation conference, a decision was made to simply not test the student. District staff felt a student must have academic deficits in order qualify for special education and an IEP. Since a "twice-exceptional" or "2E" child with average (or above) academic performance may qualify for special education, the court held the hearing officer correctly ordered additional testing of the student. But the court found no intentional discrimination by the district, requiring dismissal of his non-IDEA claims. *Lawrence County School Dist. v. McDaniel*, No. 3:17-CV-00004 BSM, 2018 WL 1569484 (E.D. Ark. 3/30/18).

◆   A New Jersey school district offered honors classes, advanced placement (AP) classes, college prep enriched (CPE) classes and college prep (CP) classes. CP and CPE classes had the same weight for student GPA calculations. But additional weight was assigned for honors and AP class grades. Enrollment in honors and AP classes required a recommendation from a teacher or a parent's signed waiver acknowledging the demands of advanced coursework and reciting that "no accommodations or curricular adjustments will be made." School transcripts did not designate or distinguish between CP and CPE courses, but they noted AP and honors classes. The families of two students with learning disabilities sued the school district in a federal court, claiming the policies excluded them from AP and honors classes and devalued CPE classes.

In assessing the case, the court considered the argument that CPE classes are more rigorous than CP classes and deserved the same recognition as honors and AP classes. It observed that another group of parents in the district had threatened a new lawsuit to challenge a retroactive change in the district policy. The school district had already decided to change the designation for CPE classes in transcripts beginning with the 2017-18 school year. The fact that another group of parents was threatening to sue the district could put the district "in an impossible position" if a preliminary order was issued in this case. In addition, the court found the students were never excluded from AP or honors classes. **No IEP accommodations were denied in any AP or honors classes. Because none of the factors justified preliminary relief, the court held for the school district.** *Leddy v. Northern Valley Regional High School Dist.*, Civ. No. 17-5245 (KM) (JBC), 2017 WL 3923291 (D.N.J. 9/6/17).

◆   A South Carolina parent said her child's school district violated the state gifted and talented statute. The court dismissed the case, and the family's lawyer received permission to withdraw from the case. Without the assistance of counsel, the parent appealed to the Court of Appeals of South Carolina. First, **the court found no right of action existed under the gifted and talented statute, which requires schools to provide programs for gifted and talented students to develop their unique talents**. In so ruling, the court held the law was neither enacted for the special benefit of a private party nor written to protect against a particular kind of harm. Similarly, no right of action existed under the state Parental Involvement in Their Children's Education Act. Next, the court held an equal protection claim had been properly dismissed.

The student did not claim he or other gifted and talented students at his school had been treated differently than similar students at other schools. According to the student, his due process rights were violated when his request to transfer to a different school was denied. But the court held the claim failed because he had no right to attend a specific school. In addition, he received an opportunity to be heard. Last, the court held the parent could not advance her child's case without counsel. In an IDEA case, the U.S. Supreme Court declined to rule on whether non-attorney parents could litigate claims on behalf of their children. Other courts, including the Fourth Circuit, have held non-attorney parents cannot litigate the claims of their minor children. As a result, the district prevailed. *Doe v. Board of Trustees, Richland School Dist. 2*, No. 2013-002436, 2015 WL 3885922 (S.C. Ct. App. 6/24/15).

IV. STATE REGULATORY AUTHORITY

A. State and School District Authority

A recent amendment requires the Virginia Board of Education to establish a program to train school bus drivers, aides and other board employees who assist in transporting students on school buses about autism spectrum disorders (ASDs). The training program is to cover characteristics of ASDs, strategies for interacting with students with ASDs, and ways to collaborate with other employees who assist in transporting students on school buses. Virginia Regular Session, Ch. 586, S.B. 229. Code of Virginia, § 22.1-298.3. 2.

◆   A Vermont school committee met with the district teachers association to go over ground rules for negotiations. The association sought to keep the meetings in executive session. But the committee claimed the negotiations should be held in public as a "meeting" under the state Open Meetings law. The committee filed a complaint, seeking a declaration that it was required to hold a meeting in public unless "premature general public knowledge would clearly place the public body or a person involved at a substantial disadvantage." A state court dismissed the case, finding the dispute was for the Vermont Labor Relations Board. The committee appealed to the Supreme Court of Vermont, which held **collective bargaining negotiations are not "meetings" under the Vermont Open Meetings Law**. This reflected the legislature's intent for negotiations between school boards and teachers associations to be "conducted on a level playing field." *Negotiations Committee of Caledonia Cent. Supervisory Union v. Caledonia Cent. Educ. Ass'n*, 184 A.3d 236 (Vt. 2018).

◆   A New York City Health Code provision required children ages six to 59 months to receive annual influenza vaccinations when attending city-regulated child care or school-based programs. Child care providers or schools faced fines if they did not maintain documentation showing each child was vaccinated or was exempt from the requirement. Exemptions were granted based on a doctor's certification or a parent's religious beliefs. Objecting parents sued city health agencies and officials in a state court for an order prohibiting enforcement of the influenza vaccine requirement. A trial court held in the parents' favor, as did a state appellate division court. Appeal reached the Court of Appeals of New York, which found the agencies had lawfully amended the city code to require influenza vaccination after a public hearing and comment period. It found a direct connection between the flu vaccine rules and the preservation of health and safety. While acknowledging that the rules necessarily infringed upon personal choice, the court held the rules did not relate only to personal health choices. They ensured increased public safety and health for all.

The court found the state had historically delegated significant power to the city board to promulgate health regulations. As the board argued, the flu vaccine rules were supported by research indicating children have the highest rates of flu and that vaccination programs produce "herd immunity" in the general population. **In sum, the court found the flu vaccine rules were within the board's regulatory authority and did not constitute impermissible policy-making.** *Garcia v. New York City Dep't of Health and Mental Hygiene*, 31 N.Y.3d 601, 106 N.E.3d 1187 (N.Y. 2018).

◆   California Senate Bill No. 277 eliminated the "personal beliefs" exemption from a state law requirement that students receive vaccines for specified infectious diseases before being admitted to schools or daycares. A medical exemption remained part of the law and students with IEPs were allowed access to required services. A state superior court dismissed the case and the parents appealed to the Court of Appeal of California. It noted many federal and state cases have upheld laws requiring immunization, including U.S. Supreme Court decisions in 1905 and 1944. The court found the parents' 38-page complaint consisted principally of argument. In rejecting their arguments, the court found that since *Jacobson v. Massachusetts*, 197 U.S. 11 (1905), it has been settled law that compulsory vaccination is within a state's police power. The court found no support for the parents' claim based on free exercise of religion. Relying on *Phillips v. City of New York*, 775 F.3d 538 (2d Cir. 2015), the court held mandatory vaccination as a condition for school admission does not violate the Free Exercise Clause.

In *Prince v. Massachusetts*, 321 U.S. 158 (1944), the Supreme Court held the right to freely practice religion does not include liberty to expose a community or a child to disease. Citing *Prince*, **the court found a parent's free exercise rights are subject to limitation if it appears parental decisions will jeopardize the health or safety of a child**. The court rejected the parents' remaining arguments, finding Senate Bill No. 277 did not violate any rights. It held the law was justified due to the compelling interest in fighting contagious diseases. *Brown v. Smith*, 24 Cal.App.5th 1135 (Cal. Ct. App. 2018).

◆   A Minnesota student attended a Catholic school from kindergarten until grade five. She struggled in her classes and her parents obtained an evaluation from the Minneapolis Public Schools (MPS), which found she needed special education and related services. MPS then began busing the student from her private school to a public school for special education services. The parents grew dissatisfied with MPS and filed a complaint requesting an impartial due process hearing. An administrative law judge found the MPS had denied the student a free appropriate public education (FAPE). The MPS appealed to a federal court, which rejected the argument that private school students in the state do not have individual rights to a FAPE or a due process hearing.

On appeal, the Eighth Circuit Court of Appeals found state law prohibited the denial of special instruction and services to a student "on a shared time basis because of attendance at a nonpublic school." **While federal law assures private school students a "proportionate share of funds only, without any individual entitlement to the provision of special education services," Minnesota law does not discuss proportionality.** For this reason, the court held private school students have a state-law right to a FAPE on a shared-time basis. Minnesota's shared-time statute required a district to provide appropriate services for the part of the regular school day when the student is in attendance. Finding state law granted students in nonpublic schools rights to a FAPE and due process hearings, the court held for the parents. *Special School Dist. No. 1, Minneapolis Public Schools v. R.M.M.*, 861 F.3d 769 (8th Cir. 2017).

◆ A New York court held a school district could not obtain court relief in a dispute over a finding by the state that its dispute resolution practices were not in compliance with state and federal law requirements. The IDEA conditions funding upon submission by local educational agencies of a plan providing assurances to the state that its provision of services to students with disabilities complied with state policies and procedures. Nothing in the IDEA confers a private right of action to contest state regulatory and enforcement action. In the court's view, the delegation of IDEA regulatory and enforcement power to the U.S. Secretary of Education and the states (but not local educational agencies) suggested Congress intended to deny local agencies a right to challenge state compliance with the IDEA. **Since Congress did not intend to grant school districts a private right of action to challenge a state's enforcement of state and federal special education laws and regulations, the court held for the state education department.** In 2017, the state's highest court affirmed the judgment, finding the school district failed to exhaust its administrative remedies. The court also found the district did not articulate an actual, concrete injury. *East Ramapo Cent. School Dist. v. King*, 29 N.Y.3d 938, 73 N.E.3d 342, 51 N.Y.S.3d 2 (N.Y. 2017).

◆ The parent of a student who did not qualify for extended school year (ESY) services complained to the Minnesota Department of Education (MDE) that her child's school district limited ESY services to students who showed academic regression throughout the year. She said her child qualified for ESY services under a state rule recognizing eligibility where "services are necessary for the pupil to attain and maintain self-sufficiency because of the critical nature of the skill." The MDE requested district records and identified seven employees it wished to interview. On the day of the scheduled onsite interviews, an MDE investigator reported feeling "unsafe" and canceled the interviews because the district's superintendent wanted to tape the interviews and was "very antagonistic." Although the MDE never interviewed the remaining district staff members, it found the district did not comply with state ESY rules.

Further, the MDE found the district failed to ensure that each IEP team decided whether ESY services were necessary. The MDE ordered corrective actions and ordered the district to revise its eligibility process to comply with state rules. The district was ordered to provide staff with training on ESY eligibility processes and to hold IEP meetings for five students. On appeal, the state court of appeals found ample support for the MDE's conclusion that the school district improperly trained staff for assessing whether students qualified for ESY services. District training materials applied the wrong standard, stating that students could not be eligible for services unless they had a "unique need." While the court upheld the MDE's order, it found problems with the investigation. After determining to conduct additional interviews "on paper," the MDE did not follow through. The court found the reasons expressed by the MDE for not conducting the interviews were not credible. But it did not reverse the order, as **the MDE's errors in its review of the case were unrelated to the corrective action it ordered**. As a result, the court affirmed the MDE's decision. *In re Complaint Brought on Behalf of Student 1*, No. 241 A17-0085, 2017 WL 4341799 (Minn. Ct. App. 10/2/17).

B. Compulsory Attendance and Delinquency

State compulsory attendance and delinquency laws impose obligations on students that may be impacted by juvenile court orders. Many states have acted to create alternative placements for students who would otherwise be suspended or expelled for violation of state laws.

◆ A Texas student missed 40 school days during her first two years of high school due to a severe respiratory condition. Based on her absences, the school principal initiated a truancy proceeding against her. According to the student's parent, the principal said that if the student "did not plead guilty, the matter would be for a grand jury to decide." She said that when she reported concerns about the principal and filed a bullying complaint against him, he began retaliating against the student. The parent said her daughter became depressed and attempted suicide after transferring to another school. She filed a due process proceeding against the school district. The parties agreed to dismiss the action under a written stipulation declaring "there are no issues related to the [IDEA] or concerns that the student did or did not receive a Free Appropriate Public Education." The parent sued the district and the principal in a federal court for retaliation in violation of Section 504 the Rehabilitation Act and the ADA. Claims were also filed for civil rights violations under 42 U.S.C. § 1983.

According to the school district, the Section 504 and ADA claims were simply repackaged IDEA claims and the principal had immunity from the Section 1983 claims. But the court held the district stipulated that no IDEA issues were in dispute, and it refused to dismiss the ADA and Section 504 claims. However, the Section 1983 claims against the district had to be dismissed. **The complaint did not assert that any injury resulted from an official district policy or custom.** Last, the court held the Section 1983 claims against the principal had to be dismissed because the family did not produce concrete evidence of a constitutional injury. *Boggs v. Krum Independent School Dist.*, 376 F.Supp.3d 714 (E.D. Tex. 2019).

◆ During the 2014-15 school year, a Kentucky student had 13 unexcused absences. Rather than face a petition for educational neglect, his parents withdrew him from school and placed him in a private school. The next school year, they returned him to a public school, where he resumed his pattern of poor attendance. After he reached seven unexcused absences or tardies, the county board of education petitioned a family court for educational neglect. In family court proceedings, the parents explained that most of their son's absences and tardies were due to sleeping in and/or behavior issues. They argued the case actually fell under the state's compulsory attendance laws, as it sought to adjudicate their child's status. School officials argued his unexcused absences and tardies supported a finding of educational neglect. The family court agreed with them and held the petition supported a finding of educational neglect.

The parents appealed to the Court of Appeals of Kentucky, where they argued the action was properly viewed as one to enforce the compulsory attendance law. This required the school district to perform certain duties in advance of any petition for habitual truancy. Rejecting the parents' argument, the court explained that **Kentucky statutes do not create a single, specific action for the enforcement of compulsory school attendance**. It found "one of the legislative purposes of the dependency, neglect and abuse statutes is to protect a child's fundamental right to educational instruction." Next, the court explained that while the compulsory attendance law was not directly applicable in a petition for educational neglect, the dependency, neglect and abuse statutes incorporated the term "habitual truant." Evidence indicated a pattern of unexcused school absences and tardies, which the parents did not justify. The family court could reasonably conclude they neglected their child's education needs. *M.B. and K.B. v. Comwlth. of Kentucky,* No. 2016-CA-001761-ME, 2018 WL 1773515 (Ky. Ct. App. 4/13/18).

◆   A Kentucky student was disciplined 26 times for bullying, defiance and misconduct. School employees investigated his parent's reports of harassment but could not verify them. Relations between the family and school district deteriorated after a teacher reported the student told him he would "burn in hell." A school therapist said the parent threatened her. The superintendent wrote to the parent to request that all communications with staff go through the school office. She requested a Section 504 hearing, claiming the district failed to identify a disability and provide her son a free appropriate public education. Up until then, the parent never told the district about a disability diagnosis. Within a few weeks, the school disciplined the student twice for misconduct.

After the second incident, the school required the student to complete a threat assessment. The superintendent then wrote the parent a letter directing her not to come to school without his permission. The student did not complete a threat assessment for over two months and did not attend school for over three months. Meanwhile, the superintendent filed a criminal trespass complaint against the parent after she appeared on campus. Although the parent's daughter was not subject to discipline, she did not attend school during the student's absence. This led to the filing of a truancy charge against the parent. She sued the school board and officials in a federal court. **In pretrial proceedings, the court held Section 504 and the ADA do not create individual liability.** For this reason, the claims against the school employees had to be dismissed. The state civil rights act claims against them were also dismissed. The claims seeking relief for the denial of a FAPE were subject to IDEA exhaustion and had to be dismissed. The court found the board disciplined the student for legitimate, non-discriminatory reasons. It rejected claims that the board retaliated against the parent by banning her from school grounds and prosecuting her for criminal trespass and truancy. **The trespass complaint resulted from the parent's disregard of the letter, not the hearing request.** The court found no support for the claim that the truancy charges were retaliatory. As the student did not show he was denied adequate procedures, the court dismissed his due process claim. The board and officials were entitled to immunity for the remaining claims. *H.C. and R.D.C. v. Fleming County Board of Educ.*, No. 5:16-235-DCR, 2017 WL 4249546 (E.D. Ky. 9/27/17). (6th Cir. appeal filed 10/27/17).

◆   **Wyoming's highest court held school officials have no duty to counsel a parent prior to a charge of educational neglect.** In lower court proceedings, a parent argued a state juvenile court had improperly applied child protection laws. She invoked compulsory attendance laws that required schools to provide notices and counseling to students and parents, and to investigate truancy causes. But the court held the compulsory education laws did not apply in this neglect case. Instead, the case arose under the state's child protective services statutes. The court upheld the parent's neglect conviction, finding school compliance with the compulsory attendance statutes had no bearing on the case. *In re JM*, 334 P.3d 568 (Wyo. 2014).

◆   The Supreme Court of Nebraska upheld a truancy petition despite a student's claim that her school district did not offer her services required by the state compulsory attendance law. The court rejected a claim that juvenile court authority required school compliance with Nebraska compulsory attendance statutes. **State compulsory attendance laws imposed no preconditions on juvenile court jurisdiction, so a school district did not have to comply with services described in the laws before a proceeding was initiated.** *In re Interest of Samantha C.*, 287 Neb. 644, 843 N.W.2d 665 (Neb. App. 2014).

◆   An Alabama school handbook provided for referral to an "early warning program" conducted by the county juvenile court system where a student had three unexcused absences in a semester. After a student accumulated a tenth tardy in a single semester (for a total of 40 minutes), her principal reported her to the school truant officer. The principal did not refer her to the early warning program or contact her parents, as specified in the handbook. A court adjudicated the student a child in need of supervision and placed her on probation for the rest of the school year. She appealed to the Alabama Court of Civil Appeals, admitting to being tardy on 10 occasions, but asserting that a medical condition had made it difficult for her to be on time for school. And after receiving prescription medication, she was not late for school again. The court upheld the lower court's ruling, noting that **nothing in state law required the principal to investigate the causes of the student's tardiness.** Also, the principal did not violate the student's due process rights by failing to follow the handbook's progressive discipline procedures. The handbook placed a duty on the student to provide a timely excuse for her absences. *S.H. v. State of Alabama*, 868 So.2d 1110 (Ala. Civ. App. 2003).

V. STUDENTS AND JUVENILE JUSTICE

In Comwlth. of Massachusetts v. Nathaniel N., *764 N.E.2d 883 (Mass. App. Ct. 2002), the court explained that **the IDEA does not prevent state law enforcement and judicial authorities from exercising their responsibilities when students with disabilities commit crimes**.*

Section 1412(a)(1)(B)(ii) of the IDEA provides that a FAPE need not be provided to children with disabilities "aged 18 through 21 to the extent that State law does not require that special education and related services under this part be provided to children with disabilities who, in the educational placement prior to their incarceration in an adult correctional facility," were not identified as a child with a disability or did not have an IEP.

Section 1412(a)(11)(C) allows states discretion as to whether they will provide services to students with disabilities who are convicted as adults under state law and subsequently incarcerated in adult prisons. As a result of these provisions, cases have arisen over exactly what obligations states have to incarcerated students with disabilities, primarily under state law. In Los Angeles Unified School Dist. v. Garcia, *this chapter, the Supreme Court of California held a parent's district of residence had the responsibility to serve the special education needs of an IDEA-eligible incarcerated adult student.*

Virginia law allows students with disabilities to introduce their IEPs, Section 504 plans, behavior intervention plans and functional behavioral assessments into juvenile proceedings in order to show whether they acted intentionally or willfully. The provision applies to acts committed during school hours, during school-related or school-sponsored activities on the property of a public or private school, daycare center or school bus. Virginia Laws 2016, Ch. 726. H.B. 1213. Code of Virginia § 16.1-274.2.

A Tennessee law requires the state department of education to develop rules to ensure students incarcerated in detention centers are provided educational services by a local education agency serving the county in which the center is located. The department will be required to monitor the educational services provided to students incarcerated in detention centers. Tennessee Code Title 37, Ch. 5, Part 1; Title 37, Ch. 5, Part 5 and Title 49, Ch. 6, Part 30.

◆ A 17-year-old California student had experienced emotional trauma since at least the age of four, when she witnessed her mother's death from a brain aneurysm. After the death of her mother, the student began living with her maternal grandparents. At the age of 11, she was removed from her grandparents' care and became a ward of the Los Angeles County Department of Children and Family Services (DCFS). Because the student had a severe emotional disturbance, she qualified for special education. She experienced five mental health hospitalizations with episodes of violence toward others. At the age of 12, the student was again hospitalized and had been in eight different out-of-home placements. These included residential placements and a locked treatment facility. While in the facility, the student assaulted a staff member and broke a peer's nose, leading to her arrest and a seven-month juvenile hall detention. After a DCFS emergency placement in a temporary facility, she was placed in a level-12 residential facility within the Los Angeles Unified School

District (LAUSD). While the student was in the temporary facility, her guardian filed a due process complaint, asserting she was denied a free appropriate public education (FAPE). Her placement at the time was a locked residential treatment facility with a rate classification level of 14. An administrative law judge (ALJ) held for the LAUSD, and the guardian appealed. According to the guardian, the ALJ improperly held LAUSD's failure to consider a residential placement was not a denial of FAPE. The court agreed and reversed the judgment. On appeal, the Ninth Circuit Court of Appeals found the lower court correctly held the student was denied a FAPE because the LAUSD had to consider whether a residential placement should be offered for educational purposes as part of her IEP. The court found the LAUSD was bound to consider a residential placement offer even though the county DCFS had placed her in a residential setting for mental health treatment under state law and pursuant to a juvenile court order. In the court's view, **the LAUSD "had an independent obligation to ensure that a continuum of alternative placements was available" to meet the student's educational needs**. As a result, the Ninth Circuit held for the student. *M.S. v. Los Angeles Unified School Dist.*, 913 F.3d 1119 (9th Cir. 2019).

◆   The Second Circuit Court of Appeals held a Connecticut city police officer did not have to pay damages for constitutional violations arising from the use of a Taser on a deaf child who claimed he did not understand the officer's warnings. A lower court held the officer violated a clearly established right not to be tased. On appeal, the Second Circuit noted the officer gave the student two warnings before deploying his taser. School staff members translated the officer's warnings to the student, but he did not respond. **The court refused to find the officer acted unreasonably, and held he was entitled to qualified immunity.** *Muschette v. Gionfriddo*, 910 F.3d 65 (2d Cir. 2018).

◆   A Massachusetts student who had autism, an anxiety disorder, obsessive-compulsive disorder and post-traumatic stress disorder had a bladder condition. She had a great deal of trouble toileting and had to use the lavatory frequently, sometimes for hours at a time. The student fixated on "obsessive rituals and rigidities that control[led] every aspect of her daily life." She was intolerant of busy and unpredictable settings and could not use public restrooms. Although the student briefly participated in an online school, her parents placed her in a public school so she could receive special education. Even with a shortened school day and home-based services, she was absent often enough to trigger provisions of the state Children Requiring Assistance (CRA) law. A few months after the student enrolled in school, the school district filed a CRA petition asserting she was habitually truant. A judge adjudicated her a child requiring assistance. On appeal, the Supreme Judicial Court of Massachusetts explained that the CRA statute creates "status offenses." A child who repeatedly runs away from home, disobeys lawful and reasonable parental commands or fails to obey lawful and reasonable school regulations is "habitually truant."

A CRA proceeding may be initiated when a student "willfully fails to attend school for more than eight school days in a quarter." The court said a child may be found to be habitually truant under the statute when the petition is proven "beyond a reasonable doubt." In reviewing a truancy case, a court may consider making changes to a student's custody arrangements and may impose conditions on the student. However, it cannot impose penalties for criminal contempt. **After reviewing the law and definitions of the term "willful," the court found the CRA statute's habitual truancy provision requires "purposeful conduct by the child."** In this case, the court said the evidence did not support finding that the student willfully failed to attend school. Nothing suggested that the student had tendencies that could lead to juvenile delinquency. In fact, the juvenile court judge acknowledged that she wanted to go to school and was saddened by her inability to do so. Since the record did not support a finding that the student willfully failed to attend school, the court returned the case to the juvenile court for an order dismissing the CRA petition. *Millis Public Schools v. M.P.*, 478 Mass. 767, 89 N.E.3d 1170 (Mass. 2018).

◆ A California student pleaded guilty to misdemeanor theft and marijuana charges and was placed on probation. Within four months, he was charged with five sexual offenses against his nine-year-old niece. The student's probation was revoked, and he admitted to one count of lewd conduct. The next year, he was found unsupervised in the presence of children under 13. After admitting failure to enter a treatment program, the student was ordered to juvenile detention for 77 days and then to his mother's custody under supervision. But his probation was revoked due to absences or tardiness at school and other counts. Following revocation of his probation, the student was ordered into a "level A" placement.

On appeal, the Court of Appeal of California held the student had forfeited his claim that he had special needs because he failed to produce evidence of an IEP. While a report regarding his sexual crimes stated he had once had an IEP, his mother said he received passing grades and was "not a special education student." While there was evidence that the student had a specific learning disability, a later study reported his only identified educational need was English as a Second Language. At the conclusion of his juvenile disposition, the court found no IEP had been established. As a result, **the court had found the student was not an individual with special needs**. But the student correctly argued that the juvenile court should not have ordered him to pay $20 for each drug test. The costs of required testing cannot be made a condition of probation. *In re Jose G.*, No. C076503, 2015 WL 3814292 (Cal. Ct. App. 6/19/15).

◆ Due to specific learning deficiencies and speech and language impairments, a 15-year-old Los Angeles charter school student was eligible for special education. Before turning 16, he was charged with felonies and held in a Los Angeles juvenile facility. He received special education from the Los Angeles County Office of Education while awaiting trial. When he turned 18, he was transferred to the Los Angeles County Jail. A due process hearing was filed on behalf of the student and others like him, asserting denial of a free appropriate public education (FAPE). It was argued that no special education system existed for eligible inmates incarcerated in the Los Angeles County Jail.

Applying state Education Code Section 56041, an administrative law judge (ALJ) held the school districts of residence of the parents of 18- to 22-year-old eligible students bore the responsibility of providing a FAPE. A federal district court affirmed the ALJ's order and held Los Angeles Unified School

District (LAUSD) was responsible for providing the student special education. While appeal was pending before the U.S. Court of Appeals, Ninth Circuit, the student pleaded guilty to several charges and was sentenced to 12 years in a state prison. Since there was no provision in state law concerning who bore the responsibility for educating a student in an adult jail, the LAUSD claimed the state had to pay for it. **The Ninth Circuit thought it likely that LAUSD would have to pay, since it was the student's last district of residence. It referred the case to the California Supreme Court for a more definitive answer.** *Los Angeles Unified School Dist. v. Garcia*, 669 F.3d 956 (9th Cir. 2012).

After accepting the question, the state supreme court noted that state and federal law generally require a state to provide FAPE to eligible students until age 22. Of the various Education Code sections regarding allocation of special education services, the court found only Section 56041 expressly referred to students ages 18 through 22. **The court found it consistent with state obligations under the IDEA to allocate the responsibility for special education to the district of residence of the parents of eligible students who were incarcerated in county jails.** In response to the Ninth Circuit's question, the court held a parent's district of residence had to serve the class of students identified in the case. *Los Angeles Unified School Dist. v. Garcia*, 58 Cal.4th 175, 314 P.3d 767 (Cal. 2013).

The case returned to the Ninth Circuit, which affirmed a district court decision that LAUSD was responsible for providing special education to the adult student. It rejected LAUSD's claim that the county in which the jail is located should pay for the costs of special education for such adult students. *Los Angeles Unified School Dist. v. Garcia*, 741 F.3d 956 (9th Cir. 2014).

VI. EVERY STUDENT SUCCEEDS AND OTHER FEDERAL LAWS

On December 7, 2016, the U.S. Department of Education published final regulations interpreting the Every Student Succeeds Act (ESSA). The ESSA is a 2015 amendment to the Elementary and Secondary Education Act (ESEA) of 1965 which alters or deletes parts of the No Child Left Behind (NCLB) Act. See the Department of Education's website for links to the final ESSA regulations and interpretive guidance at https://ed.gov/policy/elsec/leg/essa/index.html.

ESSA provisions are intended to relieve state and local educational agencies "from the more onerous provisions" of the NCLB Act. Instead of requiring states to make "adequate yearly progress," federal law will now rely upon comprehensive state-designed systems to improve the capacity of states to identify and support their struggling schools. ESSA provisions require school districts to use evidence-based models to support whole-school interventions in the lowest-performing five percent of schools. In schools where subgroups of students are persistently underperforming, school districts will be required to make targeted interventions and supports to narrow student achievement gaps.

The ESSA prohibits the U.S. government from using mandates or incentives such as the Common Core to require particular standards. ESSA incentives aim at establishing or expanding access to high-quality, state-funded preschool education for children from low and moderate income families. Incentives are to close the achievement gap, as are expanded incentives for teacher and administrator preparation and more resources for high-poverty neighborhoods.

As under the NCLB Act, students will participate in statewide assessments in grades 3-8 and once during high school. Testing in science is to occur three times for students in grades 3-12. States can use other indicators of student achievement and school quality to report progress such as student engagement, access to and completion of advanced coursework and school climate and safety. States will be required to improve student learning in the lowest five percent of schools and schools in which any group consistently underperforms.

An ESSA school expenditure reporting requirement is intended to reveal funding distributions for each school. In all, the ESSA will provide states over $15 billion per year in formula funding, with more funds for competitive grants. ESSA provisions end School Improvement Acts as described in the NCLB Act.

A provision of the ESSA strikes the term "teachers who are highly qualified" and inserts the term "teachers who meet the applicable State certification and licensure requirements." State agency Title I plans must be submitted to the education department with meaningful, timely consultation with stakeholders.

Statewide accountability systems must include subgroups for economically disadvantaged students, students from major racial and ethnic groups and English learners. Data will be disaggregated for English language learners, migrant and homeless students, children in foster care and military-connected children and children with disabilities. As under the NCLB Act, up to one percent of students with the most significant cognitive disabilities may take alternative assessments aligned to alternate academic achievement standards.

The ESSA authorized the Jacob K. Javits Gifted and Talented Students Education Program to build and enhance the ability of schools to identify gifted and talented students and meet their needs. A PDF file containing the full text of the Every Student Succeeds Act (114th Congress, S-1177, H.B. 5) may be found at https://www.gpo.gov/fdsys/pkg/BILLS-114s1177enr/pdf/BILLS-114s1177enr. pdf. The U.S. Department of Education has promised periodic guidance on its interpretation of the ESSA at http://www.ed.gov/ESSA.

Several federal courts have held there is no private right of action to enforce the NCLB Act. Instead, states that failed to meet the Act's requirements were subject to the withholding of funds by the U.S. Department of Education. Newark Parents Ass'n v. Newark Public Schools, *547 F.3d 199 (3d Cir. 2008).*

◆   A student began attending a Tennessee high school in 2014, when he and his mother were staying at a domestic violence shelter. He had ADHD, autism, asthma and migraines, but was ineligible for special education. The family relocated seven times in a year. In early 2016, the family moved to a domestic abuse shelter in Georgia. Claiming the district refused to enroll her son for the 2016-17 school year, the parent filed a federal action asserting violations of the McKinney-Vento Homeless Assistance Act. After the parties settled the case, the student returned to the same high school. His mother disputed a school special education eligibility decision and requested an independent evaluation.

A psychologist found the student "may be eligible for special services" with an autism spectrum disorder. Meanwhile, he turned 18. When the student met with school staff to consider the evaluator's report, he said he did not need special education and remained in the general education curriculum. He earned at least three As in advanced placement classes and graduated with a regular diploma. In a federal court, the mother sued the school board for discrimination and violations of the IDEA, the 14th Amendment and the McKinney-Vento Act. After dismissing the discrimination and constitutional claims, the court held that **when a child turns 18, all IDEA rights of a parent transfer to the child. The student's decision to decline special education overcame his mother's preference.** She could not revive her McKinney-Vento claim, as it was dismissed by stipulation. Although the parent sought to advance new legal theories, the court dismissed the case. *Harris v. Cleveland City Board of Educ.*, No. 1:17-cv-00121 REEVES/LEE, 2018 WL 1124961 (E.D. Tenn. 3/1/18).

◆   An Indiana parent claimed school administrators ignored her requests to evaluate her son's special education needs and her request for a due process hearing. In a federal court, she asserted violations of the IDEA and the No Child Left Behind Act. **The court held there is no private right of action to enforce the No Child Left Behind Act.** *Hudson-Harris v. Board of School Commissioners of City of Indianapolis*, No. 1:16-cv-00245-TWP-DML, 2017 WL 605177 (S.D. Ind. 2/15/17).

◆   Because some of its special education teachers had not attained designation as "highly qualified teachers" (HQTs), Pittsburgh's Board of Public Education laid off teachers without regard to seniority in 2012. The Pittsburgh Federation of Teachers filed a grievance on behalf of the teachers, arguing the board violated the relevant collective bargaining agreement (CBA) by failing to comply with system-seniority order. An arbitrator held for the federation, finding the board violated the relevant CBA. After a state trial court upheld the arbitrator's decision, appeal went to the Commonwealth Court of Pennsylvania.

On appeal, the court held the arbitrator correctly found the layoff of non-HQTs out of system-seniority violated the CBA. **Next, the court found the award did not violate either the No Child Left Behind (NCLB) Act or the IDEA.** In finding the layoff of special education teachers out of system-seniority order was premature, the arbitrator had noted there was no NCLB Act penalty for noncompliance by teachers, such as forfeiture of seniority rights. The court explained that a school district is not penalized by the NCLB Act until it fails to achieve adequate yearly progress for three consecutive years. Since the district had achieved adequate yearly progress status the previous school year, it did not face sanctions for not having 100% HQTs. The layoffs were governed solely by the CBA. As no law or public policy required teachers to have HQT status at the time of the layoff, the court upheld the arbitration award. *Pittsburgh Board of Public Educ. v. Pittsburgh Federation of Teachers*, 105 A.3d 847 (Pa. Commw. Ct. 2014).

APPENDIX A

The statutory text of the Individuals with Disabilities Education Act, as amended through December 10, 2015, is reproduced below.

TITLE I—AMENDMENTS TO THE INDIVIDUALS WITH DISABILITIES EDUCATION ACT

PART A—GENERAL PROVISIONS

SEC. 601. SHORT TITLE; TABLE OF CONTENTS; FINDINGS; PURPOSES.

(a) SHORT TITLE – This title may be cited as the 'Individuals with Disabilities Education Act'.

(b) TABLE OF CONTENTS – The table of contents for this title is as follows:

SUBPART 3—SUPPORTS TO IMPROVE RESULTS FOR CHILDREN WITH DISABILITIES

SUBPART 4—GENERAL PROVISIONS

SEC. 602. DEFINITIONS.

Except as otherwise provided, in this chapter:

(1) Assistive technology device

(A) In general

The term "assistive technology device" means any item, piece of equipment, or product system, whether acquired commercially off the shelf, modified, or customized, that is used to increase, maintain, or improve functional capabilities of a child with a disability.

(B) Exception

The term does not include a medical device that is surgically implanted, or the replacement of such device.

(2) Assistive technology service

The term "assistive technology service" means any service that directly assists a child with a disability in the selection, acquisition, or use of an assistive technology device. Such term includes--

(A) the evaluation of the needs of such child, including a functional evaluation of the child in the child's customary environment;

(B) purchasing, leasing, or otherwise providing for the acquisition of assistive technology devices by such child;

(C) selecting, designing, fitting, customizing, adapting, applying, maintaining, repairing, or replacing assistive technology devices;

(D) coordinating and using other therapies, interventions, or services with assistive technology devices, such as those associated with existing education and rehabilitation plans and programs;

(E) training or technical assistance for such child, or, where appropriate, the family of such child; and

(F) training or technical assistance for professionals (including individuals providing education and rehabilitation services), employers, or other individuals who provide services to, employ, or are otherwise substantially involved in the major life functions of such child.

(3) Child with a disability

(A) In general

The term "child with a disability" means a child--

(i) with intellectual disabilities, hearing impairments (including deafness), speech or language impairments, visual impairments (including blindness), serious emotional disturbance (referred to in this chapter as "emotional disturbance"), orthopedic impairments, autism, traumatic brain injury, other health impairments, or specific learning disabilities; and

(ii) who, by reason thereof, needs special education and related services.

(B) Child aged 3 through 9

The term "child with a disability" for a child aged 3 through 9 (or any subset of that age range, including ages 3 through 5), may, at the discretion of the State and the local educational agency, include a child--

(i) experiencing developmental delays, as defined by the State and as measured by appropriate diagnostic instruments and procedures, in 1 or more of the following areas: physical development; cognitive development; communication development; social or emotional development; or adaptive development; and

(ii) who, by reason thereof, needs special education and related services.

(4) Repealed. Pub.L. 114-95, Title IX, §

9215(ss)(1)(A), Dec. 10, 2015, 129 Stat. 2181

(5) Educational service agency

The term "educational service agency"--

(A) means a regional public multiservice agency--

(i) authorized by State law to develop, manage, and provide services or programs to local educational agencies; and

(ii) recognized as an administrative agency for purposes of the provision of special education and related services provided within public elementary schools and secondary schools of the State; and

(B) includes any other public institution or agency having administrative control and direction over a public elementary school or secondary school.

(6) Elementary school

The term "elementary school" means a nonprofit institutional day or residential school, including a public elementary charter school, that provides elementary education, as determined under State law.

(7) Equipment

The term "equipment" includes--

(A) machinery, utilities, and built-in equipment, and any necessary enclosures or structures to house such machinery, utilities, or equipment; and

(B) all other items necessary for the functioning of a particular facility as a facility for the provision of educational services, including items such as instructional equipment and necessary furniture; printed, published, and audio-visual instructional materials; telecommunications, sensory, and other technological aids and devices; and books, periodicals, documents, and other related materials.

(8) Excess costs

The term "excess costs" means those costs that are in excess of the average annual per-student expenditure in a local educational agency during the preceding school year for an elementary school or secondary school student, as may be appropriate, and which shall be computed after deducting--

(A) amounts received--

(i) under subchapter II;

(ii) under part A of title I of the Elementary and Secondary Education Act of 1965; and

(iii) under part A of title III of that Act; and

(B) any State or local funds expended for programs that would qualify for assistance under any of those parts.

(9) Free appropriate public education

The term "free appropriate public education" means special education and related services that--

(A) have been provided at public expense, under public supervision and direction, and without charge;

(B) meet the standards of the State educational agency;

(C) include an appropriate preschool, elementary school, or secondary school education in the State involved; and

(D) are provided in conformity with the individualized education program required under section 1414(d) of this title.

(10) Repealed. Pub.L. 114-95, Title IX, § 9214(d)(1), Dec. 10, 2015, 129 Stat. 2164

(11) Homeless children

The term "homeless children" has the meaning given the term "homeless children and youths" in section 11434a of Title 42.

(12) Indian

The term "Indian" means an individual who is a member of an Indian tribe.

(13) Indian tribe

The term "Indian tribe" means any Federal or State Indian tribe, band, rancheria, pueblo, colony, or community, including any Alaska Native village or regional village corporation (as defined in or established under the Alaska Native Claims Settlement Act (43 U.S.C. 1601 et seq.)).

(14) Individualized education program; IEP

The term "individualized education program" or "IEP" means a written statement for each child with a disability that is developed, reviewed, and revised in accordance with section 1414(d) of this title.

(15) Individualized family service plan

The term "individualized family service plan" has the meaning given the term in section 1436 of this title.

(16) Infant or toddler with a disability

The term "infant or toddler with a disability" has the meaning given the term in section 1432 of this title.

(17) Institution of higher education

The term "institution of higher education"--

(A) has the meaning given the term in section 1001 of this title; and

(B) also includes any college or university receiving funding from the Secretary of the Interior under the Tribally Controlled Colleges and Universities Assistance Act of 1978.

(18) Limited English proficient

The term "limited English proficient" has the meaning given the term "English learner" in section 8101 of the Elementary and Secondary Education Act of 1965.

(19) Local educational agency

(A) In general

The term "local educational agency" means a public board of education or other public authority legally constituted within a State for either administrative control or direction of, or to perform a service function for, public elementary schools or secondary schools in a city, county, township, school district, or other political subdivision of a State, or for such combination of school districts or counties as are recognized in a State as an administrative agency for its public elementary schools or secondary schools.

(B) Educational service agencies and other public institutions or agencies

The term includes--

(i) an educational service agency; and

(ii) any other public institution or agency having administrative control and direction of a public elementary school or secondary school.

(C) BIA funded schools

The term includes an elementary school or secondary school funded by the Bureau of Indian Affairs, but only to the extent that such inclusion makes the school eligible for programs for which specific eligibility is not provided to the school in another provision of law and the school does not have a student population that is smaller than the student population of the local educational agency receiving assistance under this chapter with the smallest student population, except that the school shall not be subject to the jurisdiction of any State educational agency other than the Bureau of Indian Affairs.

(20) Native language

The term "native language", when used with respect to an individual who is limited English proficient, means the language normally used by the individual or, in the case of a child, the language normally used by the parents of the child.

(21) Nonprofit

The term "nonprofit", as applied to a school, agency, organization, or institution, means a school, agency, organization, or institution owned and operated by 1 or more nonprofit corporations or associations no part of the net earnings of which inures, or may lawfully inure, to the benefit of any private shareholder or individual.

(22) Outlying area

The term "outlying area" means the United States Virgin Islands, Guam, American Samoa, and the Commonwealth of the Northern Mariana Islands.

(23) Parent

The term "parent" means--

(A) a natural, adoptive, or foster parent of a child (unless a foster parent is prohibited by State law from serving as a parent);

(B) a guardian (but not the State if the child is a ward of the State);

(C) an individual acting in the place of a natural or adoptive parent (including a grandparent, stepparent, or other relative) with whom the child lives, or an individual who is legally responsible for the child's welfare; or

(D) except as used in sections 1415(b)(2) and 1439(a)(5) of this title, an individual assigned under either of those sections to be a surrogate parent.

(24) Parent organization

The term "parent organization" has the meaning given the term in section 1471(g) of this title.

(25) Parent training and information center

The term "parent training and information center" means a center assisted under section 1471 or 1472 of this title.

(26) Related services

(A) In general

The term "related services" means transportation, and such developmental, corrective, and other supportive services (including speech-language pathology and audiology services, interpreting services, psychological services, physical and occupational therapy, recreation, including therapeutic recreation, social work services, school nurse services designed to enable a child with a disability to receive a free appropriate public education as described in the individualized education program of the child, counseling services, including rehabilitation counseling, orientation and mobility services, and medical services, except that such medical services shall be for diagnostic and evaluation purposes only) as may be required to assist a child with a disability to benefit from special education, and includes the early identification and assessment of disabling conditions in children.

(B) Exception

The term does not include a medical device that is surgically implanted, or the replacement of such device.

(27) Secondary school

The term "secondary school" means a nonprofit institutional day or residential school, including a public secondary charter school, that provides secondary education, as determined under State law, except that it does not include any education beyond grade 12.

(28) Secretary

The term "Secretary" means the Secretary of Education.

(29) Special education

The term "special education" means specially designed instruction, at no cost to parents, to meet the unique needs of a child with a disability, including--

(A) instruction conducted in the classroom, in the home, in hospitals and institutions, and in other settings; and

(B) instruction in physical education.

(30) Specific learning disability

(A) In general

The term "specific learning disability" means a disorder in 1 or more of the basic psychological processes involved in understanding or in using language, spoken or written, which disorder may manifest itself in the imperfect ability to listen, think, speak, read, write, spell, or do mathematical calculations.

(B) Disorders included

Such term includes such conditions as perceptual disabilities, brain injury, minimal brain dysfunction, dyslexia, and developmental aphasia.

(C) Disorders not included

Such term does not include a learning problem that is primarily the result of visual, hearing, or motor disabilities, of intellectual disabilities, of emotional disturbance, or of environmental, cultural, or economic disadvantage.

(31) State

The term "State" means each of the 50 States, the District of Columbia, the Commonwealth of Puerto Rico, and each of the outlying areas.

(32) State educational agency

The term "State educational agency" means the State board of education or other agency or officer primarily responsible for the State supervision of public elementary schools and secondary schools, or, if there is no such officer or agency, an officer or agency designated by the Governor or by State law.

(33) Supplementary aids and services

The term "supplementary aids and services" means aids, services, and other supports that are provided in regular education classes or other education-related settings to enable children with disabilities to be educated with nondisabled children to the maximum extent appropriate in accordance with section 1412(a)(5) of this title.

(34) Transition services

The term "transition services" means a coordinated set of activities for a child with a disability that--

(A) is designed to be within a results-oriented process, that is focused on improving the academic and functional achievement of the child with a disability to facilitate the child's movement from school to post-school activities, including post-secondary education, vocational education, integrated employment (including supported employment), continuing and adult education, adult services, independent living, or community participation;

(B) is based on the individual child's needs, taking into account the child's strengths, preferences, and interests; and

(C) includes instruction, related services, community experiences, the development of employment and other post-school adult living objectives, and, when appropriate, acquisition of daily living skills and functional vocational evaluation.

(35) Universal design

The term "universal design" has the meaning given the term in section 3002 of Title 29.

(36) Ward of the State

(A) In general

The term "ward of the State" means a child who, as determined by the State where the child resides, is a foster child, is a ward of the State, or is in the custody of a public child welfare agency.

(B) Exception

The term does not include a foster child who has a foster parent who meets the definition of a parent in paragraph (23).

SEC. 603. OFFICE OF SPECIAL EDUCATION PROGRAMS.

(a) ESTABLISHMENT- There shall be, within the Office of Special Education and Rehabilitative Services in the Department of Education, an Office of Special Education Programs, which shall be the principal agency in the Department for administering and carrying out this title and other programs and activities concerning the education of children with disabilities.

(b) DIRECTOR- The Office established under subsection (a) shall be headed by a Director who shall be selected by the Secretary and shall report directly to the Assistant Secretary for Special Education and Rehabilitative Services.

(c) VOLUNTARY AND UNCOMPENSATED SERVICES- Notwithstanding section 1342 of title 31, United States Code, the Secretary is authorized to accept voluntary and uncompensated services in furtherance of the purposes of this title.

SEC. 604. ABROGATION OF STATE SOVEREIGN IMMUNITY.

(a) IN GENERAL- A State shall not be immune under the 11th amendment to the Constitution of the United States from suit in Federal court for a violation of this title.

(b) REMEDIES- In a suit against a State for a violation of this title, remedies (including remedies both at law and in equity) are available for such a violation to the same extent as those remedies are available for such a violation in the suit against any public entity other than a State.

(c) EFFECTIVE DATE- Subsections (a) and (b) apply with respect to violations that occur in whole or part after the date of enactment of the Education of the Handicapped Act Amendments of 1990.

SEC. 605. ACQUISITION OF EQUIPMENT; CONSTRUCTION OR ALTERATION OF FACILITIES.

(a) IN GENERAL- If the Secretary determines that a program authorized under this title will be improved by permitting program funds to be used to acquire appropriate equipment, or to construct new facilities or alter existing facilities, the Secretary is authorized to allow the use of those funds for those purposes.

(b) COMPLIANCE WITH CERTAIN REGULATIONS- Any construction of new facilities or alteration of existing facilities under subsection (a) shall comply with the requirements of—

(1) appendix A of part 36 of title 28, Code of Federal Regulations (commonly known as the 'Americans with Disabilities Accessibility Guidelines for Buildings and Facilities'); or

(2) appendix A of subpart 101-19.6 of title 41, Code of Federal Regulations (commonly known as the 'Uniform Federal Accessibility Standards').

SEC. 606. EMPLOYMENT OF INDIVIDUALS WITH DISABILITIES.

The Secretary shall ensure that each recipient of assistance under this title makes positive efforts to employ and advance in employment qualified individuals with disabilities in programs assisted under this title.

SEC. 607. REQUIREMENTS FOR PRESCRIBING REGULATIONS.

(a) IN GENERAL- In carrying out the provisions of this title, the Secretary shall issue regulations under this title only to the extent that such regulations are necessary to ensure that there is compliance with the specific requirements of this title.

(b) PROTECTIONS PROVIDED TO CHILDREN- The Secretary may not implement, or publish in final form, any regulation prescribed pursuant to this title that—

(1) violates or contradicts any provision of this title; or

(2) procedurally or substantively lessens the protections provided to children with disabilities under this title, as embodied in regulations in effect on July 20, 1983 (particularly as such protections related to parental consent to initial evaluation or initial placement in special education, least restrictive environment, related services, timelines, attendance of evaluation personnel at individualized education program meetings, or qualifications of personnel), except to the extent that such regulation reflects the clear and unequivocal intent of Congress in legislation.

(c) PUBLIC COMMENT PERIOD- The Secretary shall provide a public comment period of not less than 75 days on any regulation proposed under part B or part C on which an opportunity for public comment is otherwise required by law.

(d) POLICY LETTERS AND STATEMENTS- The Secretary may not issue policy letters or other statements (including letters or statements regarding issues of national significance) that—

(1) violate or contradict any provision of this title; or

(2) establish a rule that is required for compliance with, and eligibility under, this title without following the requirements of section 553 of title 5, United States Code.

(e) EXPLANATION AND ASSURANCES- Any written response by the Secretary under subsection (d) regarding a policy, question, or interpretation under part B shall include an explanation in the written response that—

(1) such response is provided as informal guidance and is not legally binding;

(2) when required, such response is issued in compliance with the requirements of section 553 of title 5, United States Code; and

(3) such response represents the interpretation by the Department of Education of the applicable statutory or regulatory requirements in the context of the specific facts presented.

(f) CORRESPONDENCE FROM

DEPARTMENT OF EDUCATION DESCRIBING INTERPRETATIONS OF THIS TITLE-

(1) IN GENERAL- The Secretary shall, on a quarterly basis, publish in the Federal Register, and widely disseminate to interested entities through various additional forms of communication, a list of correspondence from the Department of Education received by individuals during the previous quarter that describes the interpretations of the Department of Education of this title or the regulations implemented pursuant to this title.

(2) ADDITIONAL INFORMATION- For each item of correspondence published in a list under paragraph (1), the Secretary shall—

(A) identify the topic addressed by the correspondence and shall include such other summary information as the Secretary determines to be appropriate; and

(B) ensure that all such correspondence is issued, where applicable, in compliance with the requirements of section 553 of title 5, United States Code.

SEC. 608. STATE ADMINISTRATION.

(a) RULEMAKING- Each State that receives funds under this title shall—

(1) ensure that any State rules, regulations, and policies relating to this title conform to the purposes of this title;

(2) identify in writing to local educational agencies located in the State and the Secretary any such rule, regulation, or policy as a State-imposed requirement that is not required by this title and Federal regulations; and

(3) minimize the number of rules, regulations, and policies to which the local educational agencies and schools located in the State are subject under this title.

(b) SUPPORT AND FACILITATION- State rules, regulations, and policies under this title shall support and facilitate local educational agency and school-level system improvement designed to enable children with disabilities to meet the challenging State student academic achievement standards.

SEC. 609. PAPERWORK REDUCTION.

(a) PILOT PROGRAM-

(1) PURPOSE- The purpose of this section is to provide an opportunity for States to identify ways to reduce paperwork burdens and other administrative duties that are directly associated with the requirements of this title, in order to increase the time and resources available for instruction and other activities aimed at improving educational and functional results for children with disabilities.

(2) AUTHORIZATION-

(A) IN GENERAL- In order to carry out the purpose of this section, the Secretary is authorized to grant waivers of statutory requirements of, or regulatory requirements relating to, part B for a period of time not to exceed 4 years with respect to not more than 15 States based on proposals submitted by States to reduce excessive paperwork and noninstructional time burdens that do not assist in improving educational and functional results for children with disabilities.

(B) EXCEPTION- The Secretary shall not waive under this section any statutory requirements of, or regulatory requirements relating to, applicable civil rights requirements.

(C) RULE OF CONSTRUCTION- Nothing in this section shall be construed to—

(i) affect the right of a child with a disability to receive a free appropriate public education under part B; and

(ii) permit a State or local educational agency to waive procedural safeguards under section 615.

(3) PROPOSAL-

(A) IN GENERAL- A State desiring to participate in the program under this section shall submit a proposal to the Secretary at such time and in such manner as the Secretary may reasonably require.

(B) CONTENT- The proposal shall include—

(i) a list of any statutory requirements of, or regulatory requirements relating to, part B that the State desires the Secretary to waive, in whole or in part; and

(ii) a list of any State requirements that the State proposes to waive or change, in whole or in part, to carry out a waiver granted to the State by the Secretary.

(4) TERMINATION OF WAIVER- The Secretary shall terminate a State's waiver under this section if the Secretary determines that the State—

(A) needs assistance under section 616(d)(2)(A)(ii) and that the waiver has contributed to or caused such need for assistance;

(B) needs intervention under section 616(d)(2)(A)(iii) or needs substantial intervention under section 616(d)(2)(A)(iv); or

(C) failed to appropriately implement its waiver.

(b) REPORT- Beginning 2 years after the date of enactment of the Individuals with Disabilities Education Improvement Act of 2004, the Secretary shall include in the annual report to Congress submitted pursuant to section 426 of the Department of Education Organization Act information related to the effectiveness of waivers granted under subsection (a), including any specific recommendations for broader implementation of such waivers, in—

(1) reducing—

(A) the paperwork burden on teachers, principals, administrators, and related service providers; and

(B) noninstructional time spent by teachers in complying with part B;

(2) enhancing longer-term educational planning;

(3) improving positive outcomes for children with disabilities;

(4) promoting collaboration between IEP Team members; and

(5) ensuring satisfaction of family members.

SEC. 610. FREELY ASSOCIATED STATES.

The Republic of the Marshall Islands, the Federated States of Micronesia, and the Republic of Palau shall continue to be eligible for competitive grants administered by the Secretary under this title to the extent that such grants continue to be available to States and local educational agencies under this title.

PART B—ASSISTANCE FOR EDUCATION OF ALL CHILDREN WITH DISABILITIES

SEC. 611. AUTHORIZATION; ALLOTMENT; USE OF FUNDS; AUTHORIZATION OF APPROPRIATIONS.

(a) Grants to States

(1) Purpose of grants

The Secretary shall make grants to States, outlying areas, and freely associated States, and provide funds to the Secretary of the Interior, to assist them to provide special education and related services to children with disabilities in accordance with this subchapter.

(2) Maximum amount

The maximum amount of the grant a State may receive under this section—

(A) for fiscal years 2005 and 2006 is—

(i) the number of children with disabilities in the State who are receiving special education and related services—

(I) aged 3 through 5 if the State is eligible for a grant under section 1419 of this title; and

(II) aged 6 through 21; multiplied by

(ii) 40 percent of the average per-pupil expenditure in public elementary schools and secondary schools in the United States; and

(B) for fiscal year 2007 and subsequent fiscal years is—

(i) the number of children with disabilities in the 2004-2005 school year in the State who received special education and related services—

(I) aged 3 through 5 if the State is eligible for a grant under section 1419 of this title; and

(II) aged 6 through 21; multiplied by

(ii) 40 percent of the average per-pupil expenditure in public elementary schools and secondary schools in the United States; adjusted by

(iii) the rate of annual change in the sum of—

(I) 85 percent of such State's population described in subsection (d)(3)(A)(i)(II); and

(II) 15 percent of such State's population described in subsection (d)(3)(A)(i)(III).

(b) Outlying areas and freely associated States; Secretary of the Interior

(1) Outlying areas and freely associated States

(A) Funds reserved

From the amount appropriated for any fiscal year under subsection (i), the Secretary shall reserve not more than 1 percent, which shall be used—

(i) to provide assistance to the outlying areas in accordance with their respective populations of individuals aged 3 through 21; and

(ii) to provide each freely associated State a grant in the amount that such freely associated State received for fiscal year 2003 under this subchapter, but only if the freely associated State meets the applicable requirements of this subchapter, as well as the requirements of section 1411(b)(2)(C) of this title as such section was in effect on the day before December 3, 2004.

(B) Special rule

The provisions of Public Law 95-134, permitting the consolidation of grants by the outlying areas, shall not apply to funds provided to the outlying areas or the freely associated States under this section.

(C) Definition

In this paragraph, the term "freely associated States" means the Republic of the Marshall Islands, the Federated States of Micronesia, and the Republic of Palau.

(2) Secretary of the Interior

From the amount appropriated for any fiscal year under subsection (i), the Secretary shall reserve 1.226 percent to provide assistance to the Secretary of the Interior in accordance with subsection (h).

(c) Technical assistance

(1) In general

The Secretary may reserve not more than ½ of 1 percent of the amounts appropriated under this subchapter for each fiscal year to provide technical assistance activities authorized under section 1416(i) of this title.

(2) Maximum amount

The maximum amount the Secretary may reserve under paragraph (1) for any fiscal year is $25,000,000, cumulatively adjusted by the rate of inflation as measured by the percentage increase, if any, from the preceding fiscal year in the Consumer Price Index For All Urban Consumers, published by the Bureau of Labor Statistics of the Department of Labor.

(d) Allocations to States

(1) In general

After reserving funds for technical assistance, and for payments to the outlying areas, the freely associated States, and the Secretary of the Interior under subsections (b) and (c) for a fiscal year, the Secretary shall allocate the remaining amount among the States in accordance with this subsection.

(2) Special rule for use of fiscal year 1999 amount

If a State received any funds under this section for fiscal year 1999 on the basis of children aged 3 through 5, but does not make a free appropriate public education available to all children with disabilities aged 3 through 5 in the State in any subsequent fiscal year, the Secretary shall compute the State's amount for fiscal year 1999, solely for the purpose of calculating the State's allocation in that subsequent year under paragraph (3) or (4), by subtracting the amount allocated to the State for fiscal year 1999 on the basis of those children.

(3) Increase in funds

If the amount available for allocations to States under paragraph (1) for a fiscal year is equal to or greater than the amount allocated to the States under this paragraph for the preceding fiscal year, those allocations shall be calculated as follows:

(A) Allocation of increase

(i) In general

Except as provided in subparagraph (B), the Secretary shall allocate for the fiscal year--

(I) to each State the amount the State received under this section for fiscal year 1999;

(II) 85 percent of any remaining funds to States on the basis of the States' relative populations of children aged 3 through 21 who are of the same age as children with disabilities for whom the State ensures the availability of a free appropriate public education under this subchapter; and

(III) 15 percent of those remaining funds to States on the basis of the States' relative populations of children described in subclause (II) who are living in poverty.

(ii) Data

For the purpose of making grants under this paragraph, the Secretary shall use the most recent population data, including data on children living in poverty, that are available and satisfactory to the Secretary.

(B) Limitations

Notwithstanding subparagraph (A), allocations under this paragraph shall be subject to the following:

(i) Preceding year allocation

No State's allocation shall be less than its allocation under this section for the preceding fiscal year.

(ii) Minimum

No State's allocation shall be less than the greatest of--

(I) the sum of--

(aa) the amount the State received under this section for fiscal year 1999; and

(bb) 1/3 of 1 percent of the amount by which the amount appropriated under subsection (i) for the fiscal year exceeds the amount appropriated for this section for fiscal year 1999;

(II) the sum of--

(aa) the amount the State received under this section for the preceding fiscal year; and

(bb) that amount multiplied by the percentage by which the increase in the funds appropriated for this section from the preceding fiscal year exceeds 1.5 percent; or

(III) the sum of--

(aa) the amount the State received under this section for the preceding fiscal year; and

(bb) that amount multiplied by 90 percent of the percentage increase in the amount appropriated for this section from the preceding fiscal year.

(iii) Maximum

Notwithstanding clause (ii), no State's allocation under this paragraph shall exceed the sum of--

(I) the amount the State received under this section for the preceding fiscal year; and

(II) that amount multiplied by the sum of 1.5 percent and the percentage increase in the amount appropriated under this section from the preceding fiscal year.

(C) Ratable reduction

If the amount available for allocations under this paragraph is insufficient to pay those allocations in full, those allocations shall be ratably reduced, subject to subparagraph (B)(i).

(4) Decrease in funds

If the amount available for allocations to States under paragraph (1) for a fiscal year is less than the amount allocated to the States under this section for the preceding fiscal year, those allocations shall be calculated as follows:

(A) Amounts greater than fiscal year 1999 allocations

If the amount available for allocations is greater than the amount allocated to the States for fiscal year 1999, each State shall be allocated the sum of--

(i) the amount the State received under this section for fiscal year 1999; and

(ii) an amount that bears the same relation to any remaining funds as the increase the State received under this section for the preceding fiscal year over fiscal year 1999 bears to the total of all such increases for all States.

(B) Amounts equal to or less than fiscal year 1999 allocations

(i) In general

If the amount available for allocations under this paragraph is equal to or less than the amount allocated to the States for fiscal year 1999, each State shall be allocated the amount the State received for fiscal year 1999.

(ii) Ratable reduction

If the amount available for allocations under this paragraph is insufficient to make the allocations described in clause (i), those allocations shall be ratably reduced.

(e) State-level activities

(1) State administration

(A) In general

For the purpose of administering this subchapter, including paragraph (3), section 1419 of this title, and the coordination of activities under this subchapter with, and providing technical assistance to, other programs that provide services to children with disabilities--

(i) each State may reserve for each fiscal year not more than the maximum amount the State was eligible to reserve for State administration under this section for fiscal year 2004 or $800,000 (adjusted in accordance with subparagraph (B)), whichever is greater; and

(ii) each outlying area may reserve for each fiscal year not more than 5 percent of the amount the outlying area receives under

subsection (b)(1) for the fiscal year or $35,000, whichever is greater.

(B) Cumulative annual adjustments

For each fiscal year beginning with fiscal year 2005, the Secretary shall cumulatively adjust--

(i) the maximum amount the State was eligible to reserve for State administration under this subchapter for fiscal year 2004; and

(ii) $800,000,

by the rate of inflation as measured by the percentage increase, if any, from the preceding fiscal year in the Consumer Price Index For All Urban Consumers, published by the Bureau of Labor Statistics of the Department of Labor.

(C) Certification

Prior to expenditure of funds under this paragraph, the State shall certify to the Secretary that the arrangements to establish responsibility for services pursuant to section 1412(a)(12)(A) of this title are current.

(D) Subchapter III

Funds reserved under subparagraph (A) may be used for the administration of subchapter III, if the State educational agency is the lead agency for the State under such subchapter.

(2) Other State-level activities

(A) State-level activities

(i) In general

Except as provided in clause (iii), for the purpose of carrying out State-level activities, each State may reserve for each of the fiscal years 2005 and 2006 not more than 10 percent from the amount of the State's allocation under subsection (d) for each of the fiscal years 2005 and 2006, respectively. For fiscal year 2007 and each subsequent fiscal year, the State may reserve the maximum amount the State was eligible to reserve under the preceding sentence for fiscal year 2006 (cumulatively adjusted by the rate of inflation as measured by the percentage increase, if any, from the preceding fiscal year in the Consumer Price Index For All Urban Consumers, published by the Bureau of Labor Statistics of the Department of Labor).

(ii) Small State adjustment

Notwithstanding clause (i) and except as provided in clause (iii), in the case of a State for which the maximum amount reserved for State administration is not greater than $850,000, the State may reserve for the purpose of carrying out State-level activities for each of the fiscal years 2005 and 2006, not more than 10.5 percent from the amount of the State's allocation under subsection (d) for each of the fiscal years 2005 and 2006, respectively. For fiscal year 2007 and each subsequent fiscal year, such State may reserve the maximum amount the State was eligible to reserve under the preceding sentence for fiscal year 2006 (cumulatively adjusted by the rate of inflation as measured by the percentage increase, if any, from the preceding fiscal year in the Consumer Price Index For All Urban Consumers, published by the Bureau of Labor Statistics of the Department of Labor).

(iii) Exception

If a State does not reserve funds under paragraph (3) for a fiscal year, then--

(I) in the case of a State that is not described in clause (ii), for fiscal year 2005 or 2006, clause (i) shall be applied by substituting "9.0 percent" for "10 percent"; and

(II) in the case of a State that is described in clause (ii), for fiscal year 2005 or 2006, clause (ii) shall be applied by substituting "9.5 percent" for "10.5 percent".

(B) Required activities

Funds reserved under subparagraph (A) shall be used to carry out the following activities:

(i) For monitoring, enforcement, and complaint investigation.

(ii) To establish and implement the mediation process required by section 1415(e) of this title, including providing for the cost of mediators and support personnel.

(C) Authorized activities

Funds reserved under subparagraph (A) may be used to carry out the following activities:

(i) For support and direct services, including technical assistance, personnel preparation, and professional development and training.

(ii) To support paperwork reduction activities, including expanding the use of technology in the IEP process.

(iii) To assist local educational agencies in providing positive behavioral interventions and supports and appropriate mental health services for children with disabilities.

(iv) To improve the use of technology in the classroom by children with disabilities to enhance learning.

(v) To support the use of technology, including technology with universal design principles and assistive technology devices, to maximize accessibility to the general education curriculum for children with disabilities.

(vi) Development and implementation of transition programs, including coordination of services with agencies involved in supporting the transition of children with disabilities to postsecondary activities.

(vii) To assist local educational agencies in meeting personnel shortages.

(viii) To support capacity building activities and improve the delivery of services by local educational agencies to improve results for children with disabilities.

(ix) Alternative programming for children with disabilities who have been expelled from school, and services for children with disabilities in correctional facilities, children enrolled in State-operated or State-supported schools, and children with disabilities in charter schools.

(x) To support the development and provision of appropriate accommodations for children with disabilities, or the development and provision of alternate assessments that are valid and reliable for assessing the performance of children with disabilities, in accordance with sections 6311(b) and 6361 of this title.

(xi) To provide technical assistance to schools and local educational agencies, and direct services, including direct student services described in section 6303b(c)(3) of this title to children with disabilities, to schools or local educational agencies implementing comprehensive support and improvement activities or targeted support and improvement activities under section 6311(d) of this title on the basis of consistent underperformance of the disaggregated subgroup of children with disabilities, including providing professional development to special and regular education teachers, who teach children with disabilities, based on scientifically based research to improve educational instruction, in order to improve academic achievement based on the challenging academic standards described in section 6311(b)(1) of this title.

(3) Local educational agency risk pool

(A) In general

(i) Reservation of funds

For the purpose of assisting local educational agencies (including a charter school that is a local educational agency or a consortium of local educational agencies) in addressing the needs of high need children with disabilities, each State shall have the option to reserve for each fiscal year 10 percent of the amount of funds the State reserves for State-level activities under paragraph (2)(A)--

(I) to establish and make disbursements from the high cost fund to local educational agencies in accordance with this paragraph during the first and succeeding fiscal years of the high cost fund; and

(II) to support innovative and effective ways of cost sharing by the State, by a local educational agency, or among a consortium of local educational agencies, as determined by the State in coordination with representatives from local educational agencies, subject to subparagraph (B)(ii).

(ii) Definition of local educational agency

In this paragraph the term "local educational agency" includes a charter school that is a local educational agency, or a consortium of local educational agencies.

(B) Limitation on uses of funds

(i) Establishment of high cost fund

A State shall not use any of the funds the State reserves pursuant to subparagraph (A)(i), but may use the funds the State reserves under paragraph (1), to establish and support the high cost fund.

(ii) Innovative and effective cost sharing

A State shall not use more than 5 percent of the funds the State reserves pursuant to subparagraph (A)(i) for each fiscal year to support innovative and effective ways of cost sharing among consortia of local educational agencies.

(C) State plan for high cost fund

(i) Definition

The State educational agency shall establish the State's definition of a high need child with a disability, which definition shall be developed in consultation with local educational agencies.

(ii) State plan

The State educational agency shall develop, not later than 90 days after the State reserves funds under this paragraph, annually review, and amend as necessary, a State plan for the high cost fund. Such State plan shall--

(I) establish, in coordination with representatives from local educational agencies, a definition of a high need child with a disability that, at a minimum--

(aa) addresses the financial impact a high need child with a disability has on the budget of the child's local educational agency; and

(bb) ensures that the cost of the high need child with a disability is greater than 3 times the average per pupil expenditure (as defined in section 7801 of this title) in that State;

(II) establish eligibility criteria for the participation of a local educational agency that, at a minimum, takes into account the number and percentage of high need children with disabilities served by a local educational agency;

(III) develop a funding mechanism that provides distributions each fiscal year to local educational agencies that meet the criteria developed by the State under subclause (II); and

(IV) establish an annual schedule by which the State educational agency shall make its distributions from the high cost fund each fiscal year.

(iii) Public availability

The State shall make its final State plan publicly available not less than 30 days before the beginning of the school year, including dissemination of such information on the State website.

(D) Disbursements from the high cost fund

(i) In general

Each State educational agency shall make all annual disbursements from the high cost fund established under subparagraph (A)(i) in accordance with the State plan published pursuant to subparagraph (C).

(ii) Use of disbursements

Each State educational agency shall make annual disbursements to eligible local educational agencies in accordance with its State plan under subparagraph (C)(ii).

(iii) Appropriate costs

The costs associated with educating a high need child with a disability under subparagraph (C)(i) are only those costs associated with providing direct special education and related services to such child that are identified in such child's IEP.

(E) Legal fees

The disbursements under subparagraph (D) shall not support legal fees, court costs, or other costs associated with a cause of action brought on behalf of a child with a disability to ensure a free appropriate public education for such child.

(F) Assurance of a free appropriate public education

Nothing in this paragraph shall be construed--

(i) to limit or condition the right of a child with a disability who is assisted under this subchapter to receive a free appropriate public education pursuant to section 1412(a)(1) of this title in the least restrictive environment pursuant to section 1412(a)(5) of this title; or

(ii) to authorize a State educational agency or local educational agency to establish a limit on what may be spent on the education of a child with a disability.

(G) Special rule for risk pool and high need assistance programs in effect as of January 1, 2004

Notwithstanding the provisions of subparagraphs (A) through (F), a State may use funds reserved pursuant to this paragraph for implementing a placement neutral cost sharing and reimbursement program of high need, low incidence, catastrophic, or extraordinary aid to local educational agencies that provides services to high need students based on eligibility criteria for such programs that were created not later than January 1, 2004, and are currently in operation, if such program serves children that meet the requirement of the definition of a high need child with a disability as described in subparagraph (C)(ii)(I).

(H) Medicaid services not affected

Disbursements provided under this paragraph shall not be used to pay costs that otherwise would be reimbursed as medical assistance for a child with a disability under the State medicaid program under title XIX of the Social Security Act.

(I) Remaining funds

Funds reserved under subparagraph (A) in any fiscal year but not expended in that fiscal year pursuant to subparagraph (D) shall be allocated to local educational agencies for the succeeding fiscal year in the same manner as funds are allocated to local educational agencies under subsection (f) for the succeeding fiscal year.

(4) Inapplicability of certain prohibitions

A State may use funds the State reserves under paragraphs (1) and (2) without regard to--

(A) the prohibition on commingling of funds in section 1412(a)(17)(B) of this title; and

(B) the prohibition on supplanting other funds in section 1412(a)(17)(C) of this title.

(5) Report on use of funds

As part of the information required to be submitted to the Secretary under section 1412 of this title, each State shall annually describe how amounts under this section--

(A) will be used to meet the requirements of this chapter; and

(B) will be allocated among the activities described in this section to meet State priorities based on input from local educational agencies.

(6) Special rule for increased funds

A State may use funds the State reserves under paragraph (1)(A) as a result of inflationary increases under paragraph (1)(B) to carry out activities authorized under clause (i), (iii), (vii), or (viii) of paragraph (2)(C).

(7) Flexibility in using funds for subchapter III

Any State eligible to receive a grant under section 1419 of this title may use funds made available under paragraph (1)(A), subsection (f)(3), or section 1419(f)(5) of this title to develop and implement a State policy jointly with the lead agency under subchapter III and the State educational agency to provide early intervention services (which shall include an educational component that promotes school readiness and incorporates preliteracy, language, and numeracy skills) in accordance with subchapter III to children with disabilities who are eligible for services under section 1419 of this title and who previously received services under subchapter III until such children enter, or are eligible under State law to enter, kindergarten, or elementary school as appropriate.

(f) Subgrants to local educational agencies

(1) Subgrants required

Each State that receives a grant under this section for any fiscal year shall distribute any funds the State does not reserve under subsection (e) to local educational agencies (including public charter schools that operate as local educational agencies) in the State that have established their eligibility under section 1413 of this title for use in accordance with this subchapter.

(2) Procedure for allocations to local educational agencies

For each fiscal year for which funds are allocated to States under subsection (d), each State shall allocate funds under paragraph (1) as follows:

(A) Base payments

The State shall first award each local educational agency described in paragraph (1) the amount the local educational agency would have received under this section for fiscal year 1999, if the State had distributed 75 percent of its grant for that year under section 1411(d) of this title as section 1411(d) was then in effect.

(B) Allocation of remaining funds

After making allocations under subparagraph (A), the State shall--

(i) allocate 85 percent of any remaining funds to those local educational agencies on the basis of the relative numbers of children enrolled in public and private elementary schools and secondary schools within the local educational agency's jurisdiction; and

(ii) allocate 15 percent of those remaining funds to those local educational agencies in accordance with their relative numbers of children living in poverty, as determined by the State educational agency.

(3) Reallocation of funds

If a State educational agency determines that a local educational agency is adequately providing a free appropriate public education to all children with disabilities residing in the area served by that local educational agency with State and local funds, the State educational agency may reallocate any portion of the funds under this subchapter that are not needed by that local educational agency to provide a free appropriate public education to other local educational agencies in the State that are not adequately providing special education and related services to all children with disabilities residing in the areas served by those other local educational agencies.

(g) Definitions

In this section:

(1) Average per-pupil expenditure in public elementary schools and secondary schools in the United States

The term "average per-pupil expenditure in public elementary schools and secondary schools in the United States" means--

(A) without regard to the source of funds--

(i) the aggregate current expenditures, during the second fiscal year preceding the fiscal year for which the determination is made (or, if satisfactory data for that year are not available, during the most recent preceding fiscal year for which satisfactory data are available) of all local educational agencies in the 50 States and the District of Columbia; plus

(ii) any direct expenditures by the State for the operation of those agencies; divided by

(B) the aggregate number of children in average daily attendance to whom those agencies provided free public education during that preceding year.

(2) State

The term "State" means each of the 50 States, the District of Columbia, and the Commonwealth of Puerto Rico.

(h) Use of amounts by Secretary of the Interior

(1) Provision of amounts for assistance

(A) In general

The Secretary of Education shall provide amounts to the Secretary of the Interior to meet the need for assistance for the education of children with disabilities on reservations aged 5 to 21, inclusive, enrolled in elementary schools and secondary schools for Indian children operated or funded by the Secretary of the Interior. The amount of such payment for any fiscal year shall be equal to 80 percent of the amount allotted under subsection (b)(2) for that fiscal year. Of the amount described in the preceding sentence--

(i) 80 percent shall be allocated to such schools by July 1 of that fiscal year; and

(ii) 20 percent shall be allocated to such schools by September 30 of that fiscal year.

(B) Calculation of number of children

In the case of Indian students aged 3 to 5, inclusive, who are enrolled in programs affiliated with the Bureau of Indian Affairs (referred to in this subsection as the "BIA") schools and that are required by the States in which such schools are located to attain or maintain State accreditation, and which schools have such accreditation prior to October 7, 1991, the school shall be allowed to count those children for the purpose of distribution of the funds provided under this paragraph to the Secretary of the Interior. The Secretary of the Interior shall be responsible for meeting all of the requirements of this subchapter for those children, in accordance with paragraph (2).

(C) Additional requirement

With respect to all other children aged 3 to 21, inclusive, on reservations, the State educational agency shall be responsible for ensuring that all of the requirements of this subchapter are implemented.

(2) Submission of information

The Secretary of Education may provide the Secretary of the Interior amounts under paragraph (1) for a fiscal year only if the Secretary of the Interior submits to the Secretary of Education information that--

(A) demonstrates that the Department of the Interior meets the appropriate requirements, as determined by the Secretary of Education, of sections 1412 of this title (including monitoring and evaluation activities) and 1413 of this title;

(B) includes a description of how the Secretary of the Interior will coordinate the provision of services under this subchapter with local educational agencies, tribes and tribal organizations, and other private and Federal service providers;

(C) includes an assurance that there are public hearings, adequate notice of such hearings, and an opportunity for comment afforded to members of tribes, tribal governing bodies, and affected local school boards before the adoption of the policies, programs, and procedures related to the requirements described in subparagraph (A);

(D) includes an assurance that the Secretary of the Interior will provide such information as the Secretary of Education may require to comply with section 1418 of this title;

(E) includes an assurance that the Secretary of the Interior and the Secretary of Health and Human Services have entered into a memorandum of agreement, to be provided to the Secretary of Education, for the coordination of services, resources, and personnel between their respective Federal, State, and local offices and with State and local educational agencies and other entities to facilitate the provision of services to Indian children with disabilities residing on or near reservations (such agreement shall provide for the apportionment of responsibilities and costs, including child find, evaluation, diagnosis, remediation or therapeutic measures, and (where appropriate) equipment and medical or personal supplies as needed for a child to remain in school or a program); and

(F) includes an assurance that the Department of the Interior will cooperate with the Department of Education in its exercise of monitoring and oversight of this application, and any agreements entered into between the Secretary of the Interior and other entities under this subchapter, and will fulfill its duties under this subchapter.

(3) Applicability

The Secretary shall withhold payments under this subsection with respect to the information described in paragraph (2) in the same manner as the Secretary withholds payments under section 1416(e)(6) of this title.

(4) Payments for education and services for Indian children with disabilities aged 3 through 5

(A) In general

With funds appropriated under subsection (i), the Secretary of Education shall make payments to the Secretary of the Interior to be distributed to tribes or tribal organizations (as defined under section 5304 of Title 25) or consortia of tribes or tribal organizations to provide for the coordination of assistance for special education and related services for children with disabilities aged 3 through 5 on reservations served by elementary schools and secondary schools for Indian children operated or funded by the Department of the Interior. The amount of such payments under subparagraph (B) for any fiscal year shall be equal to 20 percent of the amount allotted under subsection (b)(2).

(B) Distribution of funds

The Secretary of the Interior shall distribute the total amount of the payment under subparagraph (A) by allocating to each tribe, tribal organization, or consortium an amount based on the number of children with disabilities aged 3 through 5 residing on reservations as reported annually, divided by the total of those children served by all tribes or tribal organizations.

(C) Submission of information

To receive a payment under this paragraph, the tribe or tribal organization shall submit such figures to the Secretary of the Interior as required to determine the amounts to be allocated under subparagraph (B). This information shall be compiled and submitted to the Secretary of Education.

(D) Use of funds

The funds received by a tribe or tribal organization shall be used to assist in child find, screening, and other procedures for the early identification of children aged 3 through 5, parent training, and the provision of direct services. These activities may be carried out directly or through contracts or cooperative agreements with the BIA, local educational agencies, and other public or private nonprofit organizations. The tribe or tribal organization is encouraged to involve Indian parents in the development and implementation of these activities. The tribe or tribal organization shall, as appropriate, make referrals to local, State, or Federal entities for the provision of services or further diagnosis.

(E) Biennial report

To be eligible to receive a grant pursuant to subparagraph (A), the tribe or tribal organization shall provide to the Secretary of the Interior a biennial report of activities undertaken under this paragraph, including the number of contracts and cooperative agreements entered into, the number of children contacted and receiving services for each year, and the estimated number of children needing services during the 2 years following the year in which the report is made. The Secretary of the Interior shall include a summary of this information on a biennial basis in the report to the Secretary of Education required under this subsection. The Secretary of Education may require any additional information from the Secretary of the Interior.

(F) Prohibitions

None of the funds allocated under this paragraph may be used by the Secretary of the Interior for administrative purposes, including child count and the provision of technical assistance.

(5) Plan for coordination of services

The Secretary of the Interior shall develop and implement a plan for the coordination of services for all Indian children with disabilities residing on reservations covered under this chapter. Such plan shall provide for the coordination of services benefiting those children from whatever source, including tribes, the Indian Health Service, other BIA divisions, and other Federal agencies. In developing the plan, the Secretary of the Interior shall consult with all interested and involved parties. The plan shall be based on the needs of the children and the system best suited for meeting those needs, and may involve the establishment of cooperative agreements between the BIA, other Federal agencies, and other entities. The plan shall also be distributed upon request to States, State educational agencies and local educational agencies, and other agencies providing services to infants, toddlers, and children with disabilities, to tribes, and to other interested parties.

(6) Establishment of advisory board

To meet the requirements of section 1412(a)

(21) of this title, the Secretary of the Interior shall establish, under the BIA, an advisory board composed of individuals involved in or concerned with the education and provision of services to Indian infants, toddlers, children, and youth with disabilities, including Indians with disabilities, Indian parents or guardians of such children, teachers, service providers, State and local educational officials, representatives of tribes or tribal organizations, representatives from State Interagency Coordinating Councils under section 1441 of this title in States having reservations, and other members representing the various divisions and entities of the BIA. The chairperson shall be selected by the Secretary of the Interior. The advisory board shall--

(A) assist in the coordination of services within the BIA and with other local, State, and Federal agencies in the provision of education for infants, toddlers, and children with disabilities;

(B) advise and assist the Secretary of the Interior in the performance of the Secretary of the Interior's responsibilities described in this subsection;

(C) develop and recommend policies concerning effective inter- and intra-agency collaboration, including modifications to regulations, and the elimination of barriers to inter- and intra-agency programs and activities;

(D) provide assistance and disseminate information on best practices, effective program coordination strategies, and recommendations for improved early intervention services or educational programming for Indian infants, toddlers, and children with disabilities; and

(E) provide assistance in the preparation of information required under paragraph (2)(D).

(7) Annual reports

(A) In general

The advisory board established under paragraph (6) shall prepare and submit to the Secretary of the Interior and to Congress an annual report containing a description of the activities of the advisory board for the preceding year.

(B) Availability

The Secretary of the Interior shall make available to the Secretary of Education the report described in subparagraph (A).

(i) Authorization of appropriations

For the purpose of carrying out this subchapter, other than section 1419 of this title, there are authorized to be appropriated--

(1) $12,358,376,571 for fiscal year 2005;

(2) $14,648,647,143 for fiscal year 2006;

(3) $16,938,917,714 for fiscal year 2007;

(4) $19,229,188,286 for fiscal year 2008;

(5) $21,519,458,857 for fiscal year 2009;

(6) $23,809,729,429 for fiscal year 2010;

(7) $26,100,000,000 for fiscal year 2011; and

(8) such sums as may be necessary for fiscal year 2012 and each succeeding fiscal year.

SEC. 612. STATE ELIGIBILITY.

(a) In general

A State is eligible for assistance under this subchapter for a fiscal year if the State submits a plan that provides assurances to the Secretary that the State has in effect policies and procedures to ensure that the State meets each of the following conditions:

(1) Free appropriate public education

(A) In general

A free appropriate public education is available to all children with disabilities residing in the State between the ages of 3 and 21, inclusive, including children with disabilities who have been suspended or expelled from school.

(B) Limitation

The obligation to make a free appropriate public education available to all children with disabilities does not apply with respect to children--

(i) aged 3 through 5 and 18 through 21 in a State to the extent that its application to those children would be inconsistent with State law or practice, or the order of any court, respecting the provision of public education to children in those age ranges; and

(ii) aged 18 through 21 to the extent that State law does not require that special education and related services under this subchapter be provided to children with disabilities who, in the educational placement prior to their incarceration in an adult correctional facility--

(I) were not actually identified as being a child with a disability under section 1401 of this title; or

(II) did not have an individualized education program under this subchapter.

(C) State flexibility

A State that provides early intervention services in accordance with subchapter III to a child who is eligible for services under section 1419 of this title, is not required to provide such child with a free appropriate public education.

(2) Full educational opportunity goal

The State has established a goal of providing full educational opportunity to all children with disabilities and a detailed timetable for accomplishing that goal.

(3) Child find

(A) In general

All children with disabilities residing in the State, including children with disabilities who are homeless children or are wards of the State and children with disabilities attending private schools, regardless of the severity of their disabilities, and who are in need of special education and related services, are identified, located, and evaluated and a practical method is developed and implemented to determine which children with disabilities are currently receiving needed special education and related services.

(B) Construction

Nothing in this chapter requires that children be classified by their disability so long as each child who has a disability listed in section 1401 of this title and who, by reason of that disability, needs special education and related services is regarded as a child with a disability under this subchapter.

(4) Individualized education program

An individualized education program, or an individualized family service plan that meets the requirements of section 1436(d) of this title, is developed, reviewed, and revised for each child with a disability in accordance with section 1414(d) of this title.

(5) Least restrictive environment

(A) In general

To the maximum extent appropriate, children with disabilities, including children in public or private institutions or other care facilities, are educated with children who are not disabled, and special classes, separate schooling, or other removal of children with disabilities from the regular educational environment occurs only when the nature or severity of the disability of a child is such that education in regular classes with the use of supplementary aids and services cannot be achieved satisfactorily.

(B) Additional requirement

(i) In general

A State funding mechanism shall not result in placements that violate the requirements of subparagraph (A), and a State shall not use a funding mechanism by which the State distributes funds on the basis of the type of setting in which a child is served that will result in the failure to provide a child with a disability a free appropriate public education according to the unique needs of the child as described in the child's IEP.

(ii) Assurance

If the State does not have policies and procedures to ensure compliance with clause (i), the State shall provide the Secretary an assurance that the State will revise the funding mechanism as soon as feasible to ensure that such mechanism does not result in such placements.

(6) Procedural safeguards

(A) In general

Children with disabilities and their parents are afforded the procedural safeguards required by section 1415 of this title.

(B) Additional procedural safeguards

Procedures to ensure that testing and evaluation materials and procedures utilized for the purposes of evaluation and placement of children with disabilities for services under this chapter will be selected and administered so as not to be racially or culturally discriminatory. Such materials or procedures shall be provided and administered in the child's native language or mode of communication, unless it clearly is not feasible to do so, and no single procedure shall be the sole criterion for determining an appropriate educational program for a child.

(7) Evaluation

Children with disabilities are evaluated in accordance with subsections (a) through (c) of section 1414 of this title.

(8) Confidentiality

Agencies in the State comply with section 1417(c) of this title (relating to the confidentiality of records and information).

(9) Transition from subchapter III to preschool programs

Children participating in early intervention programs assisted under subchapter III, and who will participate in preschool programs assisted under this subchapter, experience a smooth and effective transition to those preschool programs in a manner consistent with section 1437(a)(9) of this title. By the third birthday of such a child, an individualized education program or, if consistent with sections 1414(d)(2)(B) and 1436(d) of this title, an individualized family service plan, has been developed and is being implemented for the child. The local educational agency will participate in transition planning conferences arranged by the designated lead agency under section 1435(a)(10) of this title.

(10) Children in private schools

(A) Children enrolled in private schools by their parents

(i) In general

To the extent consistent with the number and location of children with disabilities in the State who are enrolled by their parents in private elementary schools and secondary schools in the school district served by a local educational agency, provision is made for the participation of those children in the program assisted or carried out under this subchapter by providing for such children special education and related services in accordance with the following requirements, unless the Secretary has arranged for services to those children under subsection (f):

(I) Amounts to be expended for the provision of those services (including direct services to parentally placed private school children) by the local educational agency shall be equal to a proportionate amount of Federal funds made available under this subchapter.

(II) In calculating the proportionate amount of Federal funds, the local educational agency, after timely and meaningful consultation with representatives of private schools as described in clause (iii), shall conduct a thorough and complete child find process to determine the number of parentally placed children with disabilities attending private schools located in the local educational agency.

(III) Such services to parentally placed private school children with disabilities may be provided to the children on the premises of private, including religious, schools, to the extent consistent with law.

(IV) State and local funds may supplement and in no case shall supplant the proportionate amount of Federal funds required to be expended under this subparagraph.

(V) Each local educational agency shall maintain in its records and provide to the State educational agency the number of children evaluated under this subparagraph, the number of children determined to be children with disabilities under this paragraph, and the number of children served under this paragraph.

(ii) Child find requirement

(I) In general

The requirements of paragraph (3) (relating to child find) shall apply with respect to children with disabilities in the State who are enrolled in private, including religious, elementary schools and secondary schools.

(II) Equitable participation

The child find process shall be designed to ensure the equitable participation of parentally placed private school children with disabilities and an accurate count of such children.

(III) Activities

In carrying out this clause, the local educational agency, or where applicable, the State educational agency, shall undertake activities similar to those activities undertaken for the agency's public school children.

(IV) Cost

The cost of carrying out this clause, including individual evaluations, may not be considered in determining whether a local educational agency has met its obligations under clause (i).

(V) Completion period

Such child find process shall be completed in a time period comparable to that for other students attending public schools in the local educational agency.

(iii) Consultation

To ensure timely and meaningful consultation, a local educational agency, or where appropriate, a State educational agency, shall consult with private school representatives and representatives of parents of parentally placed private school children with disabilities during the design and development of special education and related services for the children, including regarding--

(I) the child find process and how parentally placed private school children suspected of having a disability can participate equitably, including how parents, teachers, and private school officials will be informed of the process;

(II) the determination of the proportionate amount of Federal funds available to serve parentally placed private school children with disabilities under this subparagraph, including the determination of how the amount was calculated;

(III) the consultation process among the local educational agency, private school officials, and representatives of parents of parentally placed private school children with disabilities, including how such process will operate throughout the school year to ensure that parentally placed private school children with disabilities identified through the child find process can meaningfully participate in special education and related services;

(IV) how, where, and by whom special education and related services will be provided for parentally placed private school children with disabilities, including a discussion of types of services, including direct services and alternate service delivery mechanisms, how such services will be apportioned if funds are insufficient to serve all children, and how and when these decisions will be made; and

(V) how, if the local educational agency disagrees with the views of the private school officials on the provision of services or the types of services, whether provided directly or through a contract, the local educational agency shall provide to the private school officials a written explanation of the reasons why the local educational agency chose not to provide services directly or through a contract.

(iv) Written affirmation

When timely and meaningful consultation as required by clause (iii) has occurred, the local educational agency shall obtain a written affirmation signed by the representatives of participating private schools, and if such representatives do not provide such affirmation within a reasonable period of time, the local educational agency shall forward the documentation of the consultation process to the State educational agency.

(v) Compliance

(I) In general

A private school official shall have the right to submit a complaint to the State educational agency that the local educational agency did not engage in consultation that was meaningful and timely, or did not give due consideration to the views of the private school official.

(II) Procedure

If the private school official wishes to submit a complaint, the official shall provide the basis of the noncompliance with this subparagraph by the local educational agency to the State educational agency, and the local educational agency shall forward the appropriate documentation to the State educational agency. If the private school official is dissatisfied with the decision of the State educational agency, such official may submit a complaint to the Secretary by providing the basis of the noncompliance with this subparagraph by the local educational agency to the Secretary, and the State educational agency shall forward the appropriate documentation to the Secretary.

(vi) Provision of equitable services

(I) Directly or through contracts

The provision of services pursuant to this subparagraph shall be provided--

(aa) by employees of a public agency; or

(bb) through contract by the public agency with an individual, association, agency, organization, or other entity.

(II) Secular, neutral, nonideological

Special education and related services provided to parentally placed private school children with disabilities, including materials and equipment, shall be secular, neutral, and nonideological.

(vii) Public control of funds

The control of funds used to provide special education and related services under this subparagraph, and title to materials, equipment, and property purchased with those funds, shall be in a public agency for the uses and purposes provided in this chapter, and a public agency shall administer the funds and property.

(B) Children placed in, or referred to, private schools by public agencies

(i) In general

Children with disabilities in private schools and facilities are provided special education and related services, in accordance with an individualized education program, at no cost to their parents, if such children are placed in, or referred to, such schools or facilities by the State or appropriate local educational agency as the means of carrying out the requirements of this subchapter or any other applicable law requiring the provision of special education and related services to all children with disabilities within such State.

(ii) Standards

In all cases described in clause (i), the State educational agency shall determine whether such schools and facilities meet standards that apply to State educational agencies and local educational agencies and that children so served have all the rights the children would have if served by such agencies.

(C) Payment for education of children enrolled in private schools without consent of or referral by the public agency

(i) In general

Subject to subparagraph (A), this subchapter does not require a local educational agency to pay for the cost of education, including special education and related services, of a child with a disability at a private school or facility if that agency made a free appropriate public education available to the child and the parents elected to place the child in such private school or facility.

(ii) Reimbursement for private school placement

If the parents of a child with a disability, who previously received special education and related services under the authority of a public agency, enroll the child in a private elementary school or secondary school without the consent of or referral by the public agency, a court or a hearing officer may require the agency to reimburse the parents for the cost of that enrollment if the court or hearing officer finds that the agency had not made a free appropriate public education available to the child in a timely manner prior to that enrollment.

(iii) Limitation on reimbursement

The cost of reimbursement described in clause (ii) may be reduced or denied--

(I) if--

(aa) at the most recent IEP meeting that the parents attended prior to removal of the child from the public school, the parents did not inform the IEP Team that they were rejecting the placement proposed by the public agency to provide a free appropriate public education to their child, including stating their concerns and their intent to enroll their child in a private school at public expense; or

(bb) 10 business days (including any

holidays that occur on a business day) prior to the removal of the child from the public school, the parents did not give written notice to the public agency of the information described in item (aa);

(II) if, prior to the parents' removal of the child from the public school, the public agency informed the parents, through the notice requirements described in section 1415(b)(3) of this title, of its intent to evaluate the child (including a statement of the purpose of the evaluation that was appropriate and reasonable), but the parents did not make the child available for such evaluation; or

(III) upon a judicial finding of unreasonableness with respect to actions taken by the parents.

(iv) Exception

Notwithstanding the notice requirement in clause (iii)(I), the cost of reimbursement--

(I) shall not be reduced or denied for failure to provide such notice if--

(aa) the school prevented the parent from providing such notice;

(bb) the parents had not received notice, pursuant to section 1415 of this title, of the notice requirement in clause (iii)(I); or

(cc) compliance with clause (iii)(I) would likely result in physical harm to the child; and

(II) may, in the discretion of a court or a hearing officer, not be reduced or denied for failure to provide such notice if--

(aa) the parent is illiterate or cannot write in English; or

(bb) compliance with clause (iii)(I) would likely result in serious emotional harm to the child.

(11) State educational agency responsible for general supervision

(A) In general

The State educational agency is responsible for ensuring that--

(i) the requirements of this subchapter are met;

(ii) all educational programs for children with disabilities in the State, including all such programs administered by any other State agency or local agency--

(I) are under the general supervision of individuals in the State who are responsible for educational programs for children with disabilities; and

(II) meet the educational standards of the State educational agency; and

(iii) in carrying out this subchapter with respect to homeless children, the requirements of subtitle B of title VII of the McKinney-Vento Homeless Assistance Act (42 U.S.C. 11431 et seq.) are met.

(B) Limitation

Subparagraph (A) shall not limit the responsibility of agencies in the State other than the State educational agency to provide, or pay for some or all of the costs of, a free appropriate public education for any child with a disability in the State.

(C) Exception

Notwithstanding subparagraphs (A) and (B), the Governor (or another individual pursuant to State law), consistent with State law, may assign to any public agency in the State the responsibility of ensuring that the requirements of this subchapter are met with respect to children with disabilities who are convicted as adults under State law and incarcerated in adult prisons.

(12) Obligations related to and methods of ensuring services

(A) Establishing responsibility for services

The Chief Executive Officer of a State or designee of the officer shall ensure that an interagency agreement or other mechanism for interagency coordination is in effect between each public agency described in subparagraph (B) and the State educational agency, in order to ensure that all services described in subparagraph (B)(i) that are needed to ensure a free appropriate public education are provided, including the provision of such services during the pendency of any dispute under clause (iii). Such agreement or mechanism shall include the following:

(i) Agency financial responsibility

An identification of, or a method for defining, the financial responsibility of each agency for providing services described in subparagraph (B)(i) to ensure a free appropriate public education to children with disabilities, provided that the financial responsibility of each public agency described in subparagraph (B), including the State medicaid agency and other public insurers of children with disabilities, shall precede the financial responsibility of the local educational agency (or the State agency responsible for developing the child's IEP).

(ii) Conditions and terms of reimbursement

The conditions, terms, and procedures under which a local educational agency shall be reimbursed by other agencies.

(iii) Interagency disputes

Procedures for resolving interagency disputes (including procedures under which local educational agencies may initiate proceedings) under the agreement or other mechanism to secure reimbursement from other agencies or otherwise implement the provisions of the agreement or mechanism.

(iv) Coordination of services procedures

Policies and procedures for agencies to determine and identify the interagency coordination responsibilities of each agency to promote the coordination and timely and appropriate delivery of services described in subparagraph (B)(i).

(B) Obligation of public agency

(i) In general

If any public agency other than an educational agency is otherwise obligated under Federal or State law, or assigned responsibility under State policy pursuant to subparagraph (A), to provide or pay for any services that are also considered special education or related services (such as, but not limited to, services described in section 1401(1) relating to assistive technology devices, 1401(2) relating to assistive technology services, 1401(26) relating to related services, 1401(33) relating to supplementary aids and services, and 1401(34) of this title relating to transition services) that are necessary for ensuring a free appropriate public education to children with disabilities within the State, such public agency shall fulfill that obligation or responsibility, either directly or through contract or other arrangement pursuant to subparagraph (A) or an agreement pursuant to subparagraph (C).

(ii) Reimbursement for services by public agency

If a public agency other than an educational agency fails to provide or pay for the special education and related services described in clause (i), the local educational agency (or State agency responsible for developing the child's IEP) shall provide or pay for such services to the child. Such local educational agency or State agency is authorized to claim reimbursement for the services from the public agency that failed to provide or pay for such services and such public agency shall reimburse the local educational agency or State agency pursuant to the terms of the interagency agreement or other mechanism described in subparagraph (A)(i) according to the procedures established in such agreement pursuant to subparagraph (A)(ii).

(C) Special rule

The requirements of subparagraph (A) may be met through--

(i) State statute or regulation;

(ii) signed agreements between respective agency officials that clearly identify the responsibilities of each agency relating to the provision of services; or

(iii) other appropriate written methods as determined by the Chief Executive Officer of the State or designee of the officer and approved by the Secretary.

(13) Procedural requirements relating to local educational agency eligibility

The State educational agency will not make a final determination that a local educational agency is not eligible for assistance under this subchapter without first affording that agency reasonable notice and an opportunity for a hearing.

(14) Personnel qualifications

(A) In general

The State educational agency has established and maintains qualifications to ensure that personnel necessary to carry out this subchapter are appropriately and adequately prepared and trained, including that those personnel have the content knowledge and skills to serve children with disabilities.

(B) Related services personnel and paraprofessionals

The qualifications under subparagraph (A) include qualifications for related services personnel and paraprofessionals that--

(i) are consistent with any State-approved or State-recognized certification, licensing, registration, or other comparable requirements that apply to the professional discipline in which those personnel are providing special education or related services;

(ii) ensure that related services personnel who deliver services in their discipline or profession meet the requirements of clause (i) and have not had certification or licensure requirements waived on an emergency, temporary, or provisional basis; and

(iii) allow paraprofessionals and assistants who are appropriately trained and supervised, in accordance with State law, regulation, or written policy, in meeting the requirements of this subchapter to be used to assist in the provision of special education and related services under this subchapter to children with disabilities.

(C) Qualifications for special education teachers

The qualifications described in subparagraph (A) shall ensure that each person employed as a special education teacher in the State who teaches elementary school, middle school, or secondary school--

(i) has obtained full State certification as a special education teacher (including participating in an alternate route to certification as a special educator, if such alternate route meets minimum requirements described in section 2005.56(a)(2)(ii) of title 34, Code of Federal Regulations, as such section was in effect on November 28, 2008), or passed the State special education teacher licensing examination, and holds a license to teach in the State as a special education teacher, except with respect to any teacher teaching in a public charter school who shall meet the requirements set forth in the State's public charter school law;

(ii) has not had special education certification or licensure requirements waived on an emergency, temporary, or provisional basis; and

(iii) holds at least a bachelor's degree..1

(D) Policy

In implementing this section, a State shall adopt a policy that includes a requirement that local educational agencies in the State take measurable steps to recruit, hire, train, and retain personnel who meet the applicable requirements described in this paragraph to provide special education and related services under this subchapter to children with disabilities.

(E) Rule of construction

Notwithstanding any other individual right of action that a parent or student may maintain under this subchapter, nothing in this paragraph shall be construed to create a right of action on behalf of an individual student for the failure of a particular State educational agency or local educational agency staff person to meet the applicable requirements described in this paragraph, or to prevent a parent from filing a complaint about staff qualifications with the State educational agency as provided for under this subchapter.

(15) Performance goals and indicators

The State--

(A) has established goals for the performance of children with disabilities in the State that--

(i) promote the purposes of this chapter, as stated in section 1400(d) of this title;

(ii) are the same as the State's long-term goals and measurements of interim progress for children with disabilities under section 6311(c)(4)(A)(i) of this title;

(iii) address graduation rates and dropout rates, as well as such other factors as the State may determine; and

(iv) are consistent, to the extent appropriate, with any other goals and standards for children established by the State;

(B) has established performance indicators the State will use to assess progress toward achieving the goals described in subparagraph (A), including measurements of interim progress for children with disabilities under section 6311(c)(4)(A)(i) of this title; and

(C) will annually report to the Secretary and the public on the progress of the State, and of children with disabilities in the State,

toward meeting the goals established under subparagraph (A), which may include elements of the reports required under section 6311(h) of this title.

(16) Participation in assessments

(A) In general

All children with disabilities are included in all general State and districtwide assessment programs, including assessments described under section 6311 of this title, with appropriate accommodations and alternate assessments where necessary and as indicated in their respective individualized education programs.

(B) Accommodation guidelines

The State (or, in the case of a districtwide assessment, the local educational agency) has developed guidelines for the provision of appropriate accommodations.

(C) Alternate assessments

(i) In general

The State (or, in the case of a districtwide assessment, the local educational agency) has developed and implemented guidelines for the participation of children with disabilities in alternate assessments for those children who cannot participate in regular assessments under subparagraph (A) with accommodations as indicated in their respective individualized education programs.

(ii) Requirements for alternate assessments

The guidelines under clause (i) shall provide for alternate assessments that--

(I) are aligned with the challenging State academic content standards under section 6311(b)(1) of this title and alternate academic achievement standards under section 6311(b)(1)(E) of this title; and

(II) if the State has adopted alternate academic achievement standards permitted under section 6311(b)(1)(E) of this title, measure the achievement of children with disabilities against those standards.

(iii) Conduct of alternate assessments

The State conducts the alternate assessments described in this subparagraph.

(D) Reports

The State educational agency (or, in the case of a districtwide assessment, the local educational agency) makes available to the public, and reports to the public with the same frequency and in the same detail as it reports on the assessment of nondisabled children, the following:

(i) The number of children with disabilities participating in regular assessments, and the number of those children who were provided accommodations in order to participate in those assessments.

(ii) The number of children with disabilities

participating in alternate assessments described in subparagraph (C)(ii)(I).

(iii) The number of children with disabilities participating in alternate assessments described in subparagraph (C)(ii)(II).

(iv) The performance of children with disabilities on regular assessments and on alternate assessments (if the number of children with disabilities participating in those assessments is sufficient to yield statistically reliable information and reporting that information will not reveal personally identifiable information about an individual student), compared with the achievement of all children, including children with disabilities, on those assessments.

(E) Universal design

The State educational agency (or, in the case of a districtwide assessment, the local educational agency) shall, to the extent feasible, use universal design principles in developing and administering any assessments under this paragraph.

(17) Supplementation of State, local, and other Federal funds

(A) Expenditures

Funds paid to a State under this subchapter will be expended in accordance with all the provisions of this subchapter.

(B) Prohibition against commingling

Funds paid to a State under this subchapter will not be commingled with State funds.

(C) Prohibition against supplantation and conditions for waiver by Secretary

Except as provided in section 1413 of this title, funds paid to a State under this subchapter will be used to supplement the level of Federal, State, and local funds (including funds that are not under the direct control of State or local educational agencies) expended for special education and related services provided to children with disabilities under this subchapter and in no case to supplant such Federal, State, and local funds, except that, where the State provides clear and convincing evidence that all children with disabilities have available to them a free appropriate public education, the Secretary may waive, in whole or in part, the requirements of this subparagraph if the Secretary concurs with the evidence provided by the State.

(18) Maintenance of State financial support

(A) In general

The State does not reduce the amount of State financial support for special education and related services for children with disabilities, or otherwise made available because of the excess costs of educating those children, below the amount of that support for the preceding fiscal year.

(B) Reduction of funds for failure to maintain support

The Secretary shall reduce the allocation of funds under section 1411 of this title for any fiscal year following the fiscal year in which the State fails to comply with the requirement of subparagraph (A) by the same amount by which the State fails to meet the requirement.

(C) Waivers for exceptional or uncontrollable circumstances

The Secretary may waive the requirement of subparagraph (A) for a State, for 1 fiscal year at a time, if the Secretary determines that--

(i) granting a waiver would be equitable due to exceptional or uncontrollable circumstances such as a natural disaster or a precipitous and unforeseen decline in the financial resources of the State; or

(ii) the State meets the standard in paragraph (17)(C) for a waiver of the requirement to supplement, and not to supplant, funds received under this subchapter.

(D) Subsequent years

If, for any year, a State fails to meet the requirement of subparagraph (A), including any year for which the State is granted a waiver under subparagraph (C), the financial support required of the State in future years under subparagraph (A) shall be the amount that would have been required in the absence of that failure and not the reduced level of the State's support.

(19) Public participation

Prior to the adoption of any policies and procedures needed to comply with this section (including any amendments to such policies and procedures), the State ensures that there are public hearings, adequate notice of the hearings, and an opportunity for comment available to the general public, including individuals with disabilities and parents of children with disabilities.

(20) Rule of construction

In complying with paragraphs (17) and (18), a State may not use funds paid to it under this subchapter to satisfy State-law mandated funding obligations to local educational agencies, including funding based on student attendance or enrollment, or inflation.

(21) State advisory panel

(A) In general

The State has established and maintains an advisory panel for the purpose of providing policy guidance with respect to special education and related services for children with disabilities in the State.

(B) Membership

Such advisory panel shall consist of

members appointed by the Governor, or any other official authorized under State law to make such appointments, be representative of the State population, and be composed of individuals involved in, or concerned with, the education of children with disabilities, including--

(i) parents of children with disabilities (ages birth through 26);

(ii) individuals with disabilities;

(iii) teachers;

(iv) representatives of institutions of higher education that prepare special education and related services personnel;

(v) State and local education officials, including officials who carry out activities under subtitle B of title VII of the McKinney-Vento Homeless Assistance Act (42 U.S.C. 11431 et seq.);

(vi) administrators of programs for children with disabilities;

(vii) representatives of other State agencies involved in the financing or delivery of related services to children with disabilities;

(viii) representatives of private schools and public charter schools;

(ix) not less than 1 representative of a vocational, community, or business organization concerned with the provision of transition services to children with disabilities;

(x) a representative from the State child welfare agency responsible for foster care; and

(xi) representatives from the State juvenile and adult corrections agencies.

(C) Special rule

A majority of the members of the panel shall be individuals with disabilities or parents of children with disabilities (ages birth through 26).

(D) Duties

The advisory panel shall--

(i) advise the State educational agency of unmet needs within the State in the education of children with disabilities;

(ii) comment publicly on any rules or regulations proposed by the State regarding the education of children with disabilities;

(iii) advise the State educational agency in developing evaluations and reporting on data to the Secretary under section 1418 of this title;

(iv) advise the State educational agency in developing corrective action plans to address findings identified in Federal monitoring reports under this subchapter; and

(v) advise the State educational agency in developing and implementing policies relating to the coordination of services for children with disabilities.

(22) Suspension and expulsion rates

(A) In general

The State educational agency examines data, including data disaggregated by race and ethnicity, to determine if significant discrepancies are occurring in the rate of long-term suspensions and expulsions of children with disabilities--

(i) among local educational agencies in the State; or

(ii) compared to such rates for nondisabled children within such agencies.

(B) Review and revision of policies

If such discrepancies are occurring, the State educational agency reviews and, if appropriate, revises (or requires the affected State or local educational agency to revise) its policies, procedures, and practices relating to the development and implementation of IEPs, the use of positive behavioral interventions and supports, and procedural safeguards, to ensure that such policies, procedures, and practices comply with this chapter.

(23) Access to instructional materials

(A) In general

The State adopts the National Instructional Materials Accessibility Standard for the purposes of providing instructional materials to blind persons or other persons with print disabilities, in a timely manner after the publication of the National Instructional Materials Accessibility Standard in the Federal Register.

(B) Rights of State educational agency

Nothing in this paragraph shall be construed to require any State educational agency to coordinate with the National Instructional Materials Access Center. If a State educational agency chooses not to coordinate with the National Instructional Materials Access Center, such agency shall provide an assurance to the Secretary that the agency will provide instructional materials to blind persons or other persons with print disabilities in a timely manner.

(C) Preparation and delivery of files

If a State educational agency chooses to coordinate with the National Instructional Materials Access Center, not later than 2 years after December 3, 2004, the agency, as part of any print instructional materials adoption process, procurement contract, or other practice or instrument used for purchase of print instructional materials, shall enter into a written contract with the publisher of the print instructional materials to--

(i) require the publisher to prepare and, on or before delivery of the print instructional materials, provide to the National Instructional Materials Access Center electronic files containing the contents of the print instructional materials using the National Instructional Materials Accessibility Standard; or

(ii) purchase instructional materials from the publisher that are produced in, or may be rendered in, specialized formats.

(D) Assistive technology

In carrying out this paragraph, the State educational agency, to the maximum extent possible, shall work collaboratively with the State agency responsible for assistive technology programs.

(E) Definitions

In this paragraph:

(i) National Instructional Materials Access Center

The term "National Instructional Materials Access Center" means the center established pursuant to section 1474(e) of this title.

(ii) National Instructional Materials Accessibility Standard

The term "National Instructional Materials Accessibility Standard" has the meaning given the term in section 1474(e)(3)(A) of this title.

(iii) Specialized formats

The term "specialized formats" has the meaning given the term in section 1474(e)(3)(D) of this title.

(24)   Overidentification   and disproportionality

The State has in effect, consistent with the purposes of this chapter and with section 1418(d) of this title, policies and procedures designed to prevent the inappropriate overidentification or disproportionate representation by race and ethnicity of children as children with disabilities, including children with disabilities with a particular impairment described in section 1401 of this title.

(25) Prohibition on mandatory medication

(A) In general

The State educational agency shall prohibit State and local educational agency personnel from requiring a child to obtain a prescription for a substance covered by the Controlled Substances Act (21 U.S.C. 801 et seq.) as a condition of attending school, receiving an evaluation under subsection (a) or (c) of section 1414 of this title, or receiving services under this chapter.

(B) Rule of construction

Nothing in subparagraph (A) shall be construed to create a Federal prohibition against teachers and other school personnel consulting or sharing classroom-based observations with parents or guardians regarding a student's academic and functional performance, or behavior in the classroom or school, or regarding the need for evaluation for special education or related services under paragraph (3).

(b) State educational agency as provider of free appropriate public education or direct services

If the State educational agency provides free appropriate public education to children with disabilities, or provides direct services to such children, such agency--

(1) shall comply with any additional requirements of section 1413(a) of this title, as if such agency were a local educational agency; and

(2) may use amounts that are otherwise available to such agency under this subchapter to serve those children without regard to section 1413(a)(2)(A)(i) of this title (relating to excess costs).

(c) Exception for prior State plans

(1) In general

If a State has on file with the Secretary policies and procedures that demonstrate that such State meets any requirement of subsection (a), including any policies and procedures filed under this subchapter as in effect before the effective date of the Individuals with Disabilities Education Improvement Act of 2004, the Secretary shall consider such State to have met such requirement for purposes of receiving a grant under this subchapter.

(2) Modifications made by State

Subject to paragraph (3), an application submitted by a State in accordance with this section shall remain in effect until the State submits to the Secretary such modifications as the State determines necessary. This section shall apply to a modification to an application to the same extent and in the same manner as this section applies to the original plan.

(3) Modifications required by the Secretary

If, after the effective date of the Individuals with Disabilities Education Improvement Act of 2004, the provisions of this chapter are amended (or the regulations developed to carry out this chapter are amended), there is a new interpretation of this chapter by a Federal court or a State's highest court, or there is an official finding of noncompliance with Federal law or regulations, then the Secretary may require a State to modify its application only to the extent necessary to ensure the State's compliance with this subchapter.

(d) Approval by the Secretary

(1) In general

If the Secretary determines that a State is eligible to receive a grant under this subchapter, the Secretary shall notify the State of that determination.

(2) Notice and hearing

The Secretary shall not make a final determination that a State is not eligible to receive a grant under this subchapter until after providing the State--

(A) with reasonable notice; and

(B) with an opportunity for a hearing.

(e) Assistance under other Federal programs

Nothing in this chapter permits a State to reduce medical and other assistance available, or to alter eligibility, under titles V and XIX of the Social Security Act with respect to the provision of a free appropriate public education for children with disabilities in the State.

(f) By-pass for children in private schools

(1) In general

If, on December 2, 1983, a State educational agency was prohibited by law from providing for the equitable participation in special programs of children with disabilities enrolled in private elementary schools and secondary schools as required by subsection (a)(10)(A), or if the Secretary determines that a State educational agency, local educational agency, or other entity has substantially failed or is unwilling to provide for such equitable participation, then the Secretary shall, notwithstanding such provision of law, arrange for the provision of services to such children through arrangements that shall be subject to the requirements of such subsection.

(2) Payments

(A) Determination of amounts

If the Secretary arranges for services pursuant to this subsection, the Secretary, after consultation with the appropriate public and private school officials, shall pay to the provider of such services for a fiscal year an amount per child that does not exceed the amount determined by dividing--

(i) the total amount received by the State under this subchapter for such fiscal year; by

(ii) the number of children with disabilities served in the prior year, as reported to the Secretary by the State under section 1418 of this title.

(B) Withholding of certain amounts

Pending final resolution of any investigation or complaint that may result in a determination under this subsection, the Secretary may withhold from the allocation of the affected State educational agency the amount the Secretary estimates will be necessary to pay the cost of services described in subparagraph (A).

(C) Period of payments

The period under which payments are made under subparagraph (A) shall continue until the Secretary determines that there will no longer be any failure or inability on the part of the State educational agency to meet the requirements of subsection (a)(10)(A).

(3) Notice and hearing

(A) In general

The Secretary shall not take any final action under this subsection until the State educational agency affected by such action has had an opportunity, for not less than 45 days after receiving written notice thereof, to submit written objections and to appear before the Secretary or the Secretary's designee to show cause why such action should not be taken.

(B) Review of action

If a State educational agency is dissatisfied with the Secretary's final action after a proceeding under subparagraph (A), such agency may, not later than 60 days after notice of such action, file with the United States court of appeals for the circuit in which such State is located a petition for review of that action. A copy of the petition shall be forthwith transmitted by the clerk of the court to the Secretary. The Secretary thereupon shall file in the court the record of the proceedings on which the Secretary based the Secretary's action, as provided in section 2112 of Title 28.

(C) Review of findings of fact

The findings of fact by the Secretary, if supported by substantial evidence, shall be conclusive, but the court, for good cause shown, may remand the case to the Secretary to take further evidence, and the Secretary may thereupon make new or modified findings of fact and may modify the Secretary's previous action, and shall file in the court the record of the further proceedings. Such new or modified findings of fact shall likewise be conclusive if supported by substantial evidence.

(D) Jurisdiction of court of appeals; review by United States Supreme Court

Upon the filing of a petition under subparagraph (B), the United States court of appeals shall have jurisdiction to affirm the action of the Secretary or to set it aside, in whole or in part. The judgment of the court shall be subject to review by the Supreme Court of the United States upon certiorari or certification as provided in section 1254 of Title 28.

SEC. 613. LOCAL EDUCATIONAL AGENCY ELIGIBILITY.

(a) In general

A local educational agency is eligible for assistance under this subchapter for a fiscal year if such agency submits a plan that provides assurances to the State educational agency that the local educational agency meets each of the following conditions:

(1) Consistency with State policies

The local educational agency, in providing for the education of children with disabilities within its jurisdiction, has in effect policies, procedures, and programs that are consistent with the State policies and procedures established under section 1412 of this title.

(2) Use of amounts

(A) In general

Amounts provided to the local educational agency under this subchapter shall be expended in accordance with the applicable provisions of this subchapter and--

(i) shall be used only to pay the excess costs of providing special education and related services to children with disabilities;

(ii) shall be used to supplement State, local, and other Federal funds and not to supplant such funds; and

(iii) shall not be used, except as provided in subparagraphs (B) and (C), to reduce the level of expenditures for the education of children with disabilities made by the local educational agency from local funds below the level of those expenditures for the preceding fiscal year.

(B) Exception

Notwithstanding the restriction in subparagraph (A)(iii), a local educational agency may reduce the level of expenditures where such reduction is attributable to--

(i) the voluntary departure, by retirement or otherwise, or departure for just cause, of special education personnel;

(ii) a decrease in the enrollment of children with disabilities;

(iii) the termination of the obligation of the agency, consistent with this subchapter, to provide a program of special education to a particular child with a disability that is an exceptionally costly program, as determined by the State educational agency, because the child--

(I) has left the jurisdiction of the agency;

(II) has reached the age at which the obligation of the agency to provide a free appropriate public education to the child has terminated; or

(III) no longer needs such program of special education; or

(iv) the termination of costly expenditures for long-term purchases, such as the acquisition of equipment or the construction of school facilities.

(C) Adjustment to local fiscal effort in certain fiscal years

(i) Amounts in excess

Notwithstanding clauses (ii) and (iii) of subparagraph (A), for any fiscal year for which the allocation received by a local educational agency under section 1411(f) of this title exceeds the amount the local educational agency received for the previous fiscal year, the local educational agency may reduce the level of expenditures otherwise required by subparagraph (A)(iii) by not more than 50 percent of the amount of such excess.

(ii) Use of amounts to carry out activities under ESEA

If a local educational agency exercises the authority under clause (i), the agency shall use an amount of local funds equal to the reduction in expenditures under clause (i) to carry out activities authorized under the Elementary and Secondary Education Act of 1965.

(iii) State prohibition

Notwithstanding clause (i), if a State educational agency determines that a local educational agency is unable to establish and maintain programs of free appropriate public education that meet the requirements of subsection (a) or the State educational agency has taken action against the local educational agency under section 1416 of this title, the State educational agency shall prohibit the local educational agency from reducing the level of expenditures under clause (i) for that fiscal year.

(iv) Special rule

The amount of funds expended by a local educational agency under subsection (f) shall count toward the maximum amount of expenditures such local educational agency may reduce under clause (i).

(D) Schoolwide programs under title I of the ESEA

Notwithstanding subparagraph (A) or any other provision of this subchapter, a local educational agency may use funds received under this subchapter for any fiscal year to carry out a schoolwide program under section 1114 of the Elementary and Secondary Education Act of 1965, except that the amount so used in any such program shall not exceed--

(i) the number of children with disabilities participating in the schoolwide program; multiplied by

(ii)(I) the amount received by the local educational agency under this subchapter for that fiscal year; divided by

(II) the number of children with disabilities in the jurisdiction of that agency.

(3) Personnel development

The local educational agency shall ensure that all personnel necessary to carry out this subchapter are appropriately and adequately prepared, subject to the requirements of section 1412(a)(14) of this title and section 2102(b) of the Elementary and Secondary Education Act of 1965.

(4) Permissive use of funds

(A) Uses

Notwithstanding paragraph (2)(A) or section 1412(a)(17)(B) of this title (relating to commingled funds), funds provided to the local educational agency under this subchapter may be used for the following activities:

(i) Services and aids that also benefit nondisabled children

For the costs of special education and related services, and supplementary aids and services, provided in a regular class or other education-related setting to a child with a disability in accordance with the individualized education program of the child, even if 1 or more nondisabled children benefit from such services.

(ii) Early intervening services

To develop and implement coordinated, early intervening educational services in accordance with subsection (f).

(iii) High cost education and related services

To establish and implement cost or risk sharing funds, consortia, or cooperatives for the local educational agency itself, or for local educational agencies working in a consortium of which the local educational agency is a part, to pay for high cost special education and related services.

(B) Administrative case management

A local educational agency may use funds received under this subchapter to purchase appropriate technology for recordkeeping, data collection, and related case management activities of teachers and related services personnel providing services described in the individualized education program of children with disabilities, that is needed for the implementation of such case management activities.

(5) Treatment of charter schools and their students

In carrying out this subchapter with respect to charter schools that are public schools of the local educational agency, the local educational agency--

(A) serves children with disabilities attending those charter schools in the same manner as the local educational agency serves children with disabilities in its other schools, including providing supplementary and related services on site at the charter school to the same extent to which the local educational agency has a policy or practice of providing such services on the site to its other public schools; and

(B) provides funds under this subchapter to those charter schools--

(i) on the same basis as the local educational agency provides funds to the local educational agency's other public schools, including proportional distribution based on relative enrollment of children with disabilities; and

(ii) at the same time as the agency distributes other Federal funds to the agency's other public schools, consistent with the State's charter school law.

(6) Purchase of instructional materials

(A) In general

Not later than 2 years after December 3, 2004, a local educational agency that chooses to coordinate with the National Instructional Materials Access Center, when purchasing print instructional materials, shall acquire the print instructional materials in the same manner and subject to the same conditions as a State educational agency acquires print instructional materials under section 1412(a)(23) of this title.

(B) Rights of local educational agency

Nothing in this paragraph shall be construed to require a local educational agency to coordinate with the National Instructional Materials Access Center. If a local educational agency chooses not to coordinate with the National Instructional Materials Access Center, the local educational agency shall provide an assurance to the State educational agency that the local educational agency will provide instructional materials to blind persons or other persons with print disabilities in a timely manner.

(7) Information for State educational agency

The local educational agency shall provide the State educational agency with information necessary to enable the State educational agency to carry out its duties under this subchapter, including, with respect to paragraphs (15) and (16) of section 1412(a) of this title, information relating to the performance of children with disabilities participating in programs carried out under this subchapter.

(8) Public information

The local educational agency shall make available to parents of children with disabilities and to the general public all documents relating to the eligibility of such agency under this subchapter.

(9) Records regarding migratory children with disabilities

The local educational agency shall cooperate in the Secretary's efforts under section 1308 of the Elementary and Secondary Education Act of

1965 to ensure the linkage of records pertaining to migratory children with a disability for the purpose of electronically exchanging, among the States, health and educational information regarding such children.

(b) Exception for prior local plans

(1) In general

If a local educational agency or State agency has on file with the State educational agency policies and procedures that demonstrate that such local educational agency, or such State agency, as the case may be, meets any requirement of subsection (a), including any policies and procedures filed under this subchapter as in effect before the effective date of the Individuals with Disabilities Education Improvement Act of 2004, the State educational agency shall consider such local educational agency or State agency, as the case may be, to have met such requirement for purposes of receiving assistance under this subchapter.

(2) Modification made by local educational agency

Subject to paragraph (3), an application submitted by a local educational agency in accordance with this section shall remain in effect until the local educational agency submits to the State educational agency such modifications as the local educational agency determines necessary.

(3) Modifications required by State educational agency

If, after the effective date of the Individuals with Disabilities Education Improvement Act of 2004, the provisions of this chapter are amended (or the regulations developed to carry out this chapter are amended), there is a new interpretation of this chapter by Federal or State courts, or there is an official finding of noncompliance with Federal or State law or regulations, then the State educational agency may require a local educational agency to modify its application only to the extent necessary to ensure the local educational agency's compliance with this subchapter or State law.

(c) Notification of local educational agency or State agency in case of ineligibility

If the State educational agency determines that a local educational agency or State agency is not eligible under this section, then the State educational agency shall notify the local educational agency or State agency, as the case may be, of that determination and shall provide such local educational agency or State agency with reasonable notice and an opportunity for a hearing.

(d) Local educational agency compliance

(1) In general

If the State educational agency, after reasonable notice and an opportunity for a hearing, finds that a local educational agency or State agency that has been determined to be eligible under this section is failing to comply with any requirement described in subsection (a), the State educational agency shall reduce or shall not provide any further payments to the local educational agency or State agency until the State educational agency is satisfied that the local educational agency or State agency, as the case may be, is complying with that requirement.

(2) Additional requirement

Any State agency or local educational agency in receipt of a notice described in paragraph (1) shall, by means of public notice, take such measures as may be necessary to bring the pendency of an action pursuant to this subsection to the attention of the public within the jurisdiction of such agency.

(3) Consideration

In carrying out its responsibilities under paragraph (1), the State educational agency shall consider any decision made in a hearing held under section 1415 of this title that is adverse to the local educational agency or State agency involved in that decision.

(e) Joint establishment of eligibility

(1) Joint establishment

(A) In general

A State educational agency may require a local educational agency to establish its eligibility jointly with another local educational agency if the State educational agency determines that the local educational agency will be ineligible under this section because the local educational agency will not be able to establish and maintain programs of sufficient size and scope to effectively meet the needs of children with disabilities.

(B) Charter school exception

A State educational agency may not require a charter school that is a local educational agency to jointly establish its eligibility under subparagraph (A) unless the charter school is explicitly permitted to do so under the State's charter school law.

(2) Amount of payments

If a State educational agency requires the joint establishment of eligibility under paragraph (1), the total amount of funds made available to the affected local educational agencies shall be equal to the sum of the payments that each such local educational agency would have received under section 1411(f) of this title if such agencies were eligible for such payments.

(3) Requirements

Local educational agencies that establish joint eligibility under this subsection shall--

(A) adopt policies and procedures that are consistent with the State's policies and procedures under section 1412(a) of this title; and

(B) be jointly responsible for implementing programs that receive assistance under this subchapter.

(4) Requirements for educational service agencies

(A) In general

If an educational service agency is required by State law to carry out programs under this subchapter, the joint responsibilities given to local educational agencies under this subsection shall--

(i) not apply to the administration and disbursement of any payments received by that educational service agency; and

(ii) be carried out only by that educational service agency.

(B) Additional requirement

Notwithstanding any other provision of this subsection, an educational service agency shall provide for the education of children with disabilities in the least restrictive environment, as required by section 1412(a)(5) of this title.

(f) Early intervening services

(1) In general

A local educational agency may not use more than 15 percent of the amount such agency receives under this subchapter for any fiscal year, less any amount reduced by the agency pursuant to subsection (a)(2)(C), if any, in combination with other amounts (which may include amounts other than education funds), to develop and implement coordinated, early intervening services, which may include interagency financing structures, for students in kindergarten through grade 12 (with a particular emphasis on students in kindergarten through grade 3) who have not been identified as needing special education or related services but who need additional academic and behavioral support to succeed in a general education environment.

(2) Activities

In implementing coordinated, early intervening services under this subsection, a local educational agency may carry out activities that include--

(A) professional development (which may be provided by entities other than local educational agencies) for teachers and other school staff to enable such personnel to deliver scientifically based academic instruction and behavioral interventions, including scientifically based literacy instruction, and, where appropriate, instruction on the use of adaptive and instructional software; and

(B) providing educational and behavioral evaluations, services, and supports, including scientifically based literacy instruction.

(3) Construction

Nothing in this subsection shall be construed to limit or create a right to a free appropriate public education under this subchapter.

(4) Reporting

Each local educational agency that develops and maintains coordinated, early intervening services under this subsection shall annually report to the State educational agency on--

(A) the number of students served under this subsection; and

(B) the number of students served under this subsection who subsequently receive special education and related services under this chapter during the preceding 2-year period.

(5) Coordination with Elementary and Secondary Education Act of 1965

Funds made available to carry out this subsection may be used to carry out coordinated, early intervening services aligned with activities funded by, and carried out under, the Elementary and Secondary Education Act of 1965 if such funds are used to supplement, and not supplant, funds made available under the Elementary and Secondary Education Act of 1965 for the activities and services assisted under this subsection.

(g) Direct services by the State educational agency

(1) In general

A State educational agency shall use the payments that would otherwise have been available to a local educational agency or to a State agency to provide special education and related services directly to children with disabilities residing in the area served by that local educational agency, or for whom that State agency is responsible, if the State educational agency determines that the local educational agency or State agency, as the case may be--

(A) has not provided the information needed to establish the eligibility of such local educational agency or State agency under this section;

(B) is unable to establish and maintain programs of free appropriate public education that meet the requirements of subsection (a);

(C) is unable or unwilling to be consolidated with 1 or more local educational agencies in order to establish and maintain such programs; or

(D) has 1 or more children with disabilities who can best be served by a regional or State program or service delivery system designed to meet the needs of such children.

(2) Manner and location of education and services

The State educational agency may provide special education and related services under paragraph (1) in such manner and at such locations (including regional or State centers) as the State educational agency considers appropriate. Such education and services shall be provided in accordance with this subchapter.

(h) State agency eligibility

Any State agency that desires to receive a subgrant for any fiscal year under section 1411(f) of this title shall demonstrate to the satisfaction of the State educational agency that--

(1) all children with disabilities who are participating in programs and projects funded under this subchapter receive a free appropriate public education, and that those children and their parents are provided all the rights and procedural safeguards described in this subchapter; and

(2) the agency meets such other conditions of this section as the Secretary determines to be appropriate.

(i) Disciplinary information

The State may require that a local educational agency include in the records of a child with a disability a statement of any current or previous disciplinary action that has been taken against the child and transmit such statement to the same extent that such disciplinary information is included in, and transmitted with, the student records of nondisabled children. The statement may include a description of any behavior engaged in by the child that required disciplinary action, a description of the disciplinary action taken, and any other information that is relevant to the safety of the child and other individuals involved with the child. If the State adopts such a policy, and the child transfers from 1 school to another, the transmission of any of the child's records shall include both the child's current individualized education program and any such statement of current or previous disciplinary action that has been taken against the child.

(j) State agency flexibility

(1) Adjustment to State fiscal effort in certain fiscal years

For any fiscal year for which the allotment received by a State under section 1411 of this title exceeds the amount the State received for the previous fiscal year and if the State in school year 2003-2004 or any subsequent school year pays or reimburses all local educational agencies within the State from State revenue 100 percent of the non-Federal share of the costs of special education and related services, the State educational agency, notwithstanding paragraphs (17) and (18) of section 1412(a) of this title and section 1412(b) of this title, may reduce the level of expenditures from State sources for the education of children with disabilities by not more than 50 percent of the amount of such excess.

(2) Prohibition

Notwithstanding paragraph (1), if the Secretary determines that a State educational agency is unable to establish, maintain, or oversee programs of free appropriate public education that meet the requirements of this subchapter, or that the State needs assistance, intervention, or substantial intervention under section 1416(d)(2)(A) of this title, the Secretary shall prohibit the State educational agency from exercising the authority in paragraph (1).

(3) Education activities

If a State educational agency exercises the authority under paragraph (1), the agency shall use funds from State sources, in an amount equal to the amount of the reduction under paragraph (1), to support activities authorized under the Elementary and Secondary Education Act of 1965 or to support need based student or teacher higher education programs.

(4) Report

For each fiscal year for which a State educational agency exercises the authority under paragraph (1), the State educational agency shall report to the Secretary the amount of expenditures reduced pursuant to such paragraph and the activities that were funded pursuant to paragraph (3).

(5) Limitation

Notwithstanding paragraph (1), a State educational agency may not reduce the level of expenditures described in paragraph (1) if any local educational agency in the State would, as a result of such reduction, receive less than 100 percent of the amount necessary to ensure that all children with disabilities served by the local educational agency receive a free appropriate public education from the combination of Federal funds received under this chapter and State funds received from the State educational agency.

SEC. 614. EVALUATIONS, ELIGIBILITY DETERMINATIONS, INDIVIDUALIZED EDUCATION PROGRAMS, AND EDUCATIONAL PLACEMENTS.

(a) Evaluations, parental consent, and reevaluations

(1) Initial evaluations

(A) In general

A State educational agency, other State agency, or local educational agency shall conduct a full and individual initial evaluation in accordance with this paragraph and subsection (b), before the initial provision of special education and related services to a child with a disability under this subchapter.

(B) Request for initial evaluation

Consistent with subparagraph (D), either a parent of a child, or a State educational agency, other State agency, or local educational agency may initiate a request for an initial evaluation to determine if the child is a child with a disability.

(C) Procedures

(i) In general

Such initial evaluation shall consist of procedures--

(I) to determine whether a child is a child with a disability (as defined in section 1401 of this title) within 60 days of receiving parental consent for the evaluation, or, if the State establishes a timeframe within which the evaluation must be conducted, within such timeframe; and

(II) to determine the educational needs of such child.

(ii) Exception

The relevant timeframe in clause (i)(I) shall not apply to a local educational agency if--

(I) a child enrolls in a school served by the local educational agency after the relevant timeframe in clause (i)(I) has begun and prior to a determination by the child's previous local educational agency as to whether the child is a child with a disability (as defined in section 1401 of this title), but only if the subsequent local educational agency is making sufficient progress to ensure a prompt completion of the evaluation, and the parent and subsequent local educational agency agree to a specific time when the evaluation will be completed; or

(II) the parent of a child repeatedly fails or refuses to produce the child for the evaluation.

(D) Parental consent

(i) In general

(I) Consent for initial evaluation

The agency proposing to conduct an initial evaluation to determine if the child qualifies as a child with a disability as defined in section 1401 of this title shall obtain informed consent from the parent of such child before conducting the evaluation. Parental consent for evaluation shall not be construed as consent for placement for receipt of special education and related services.

(II) Consent for services

An agency that is responsible for making a free appropriate public education available to a child with a disability under this subchapter shall seek to obtain informed consent from the parent of such child before providing special education and related services to the child.

(ii) Absence of consent

(I) For initial evaluation

If the parent of such child does not provide consent for an initial evaluation under clause (i)(I), or the parent fails to respond to a request to provide the consent, the local educational agency may pursue the initial evaluation of the child by utilizing the procedures described in section 1415 of this title, except to the extent inconsistent with State law relating to such parental consent.

(II) For services

If the parent of such child refuses to consent to services under clause (i)(II), the local educational agency shall not provide special education and related services to the child by utilizing the procedures described in section 1415 of this title.

(III) Effect on agency obligations

If the parent of such child refuses to consent to the receipt of special education and related services, or the parent fails to respond to a request to provide such consent--

(aa) the local educational agency shall not be considered to be in violation of the requirement to make available a free appropriate public education to the child for the failure to provide such child with the special education and related services for which the local educational agency requests such consent; and

(bb) the local educational agency shall not be required to convene an IEP meeting or develop an IEP under this section for the child for the special education and related services for which the local educational agency requests such consent.

(iii) Consent for wards of the State

(I) In general

If the child is a ward of the State and is not residing with the child's parent, the agency shall make reasonable efforts to obtain the informed consent from the parent (as defined in section 1401 of this title) of the child for an initial evaluation to determine whether the child is a child with a disability.

(II) Exception

The agency shall not be required to obtain informed consent from the parent of a child for an initial evaluation to determine whether the child is a child with a disability if--

(aa) despite reasonable efforts to do so, the agency cannot discover the whereabouts of the parent of the child;

(bb) the rights of the parents of the child have been terminated in accordance with State law; or

(cc) the rights of the parent to make educational decisions have been subrogated by a judge in accordance with State law and consent for an initial evaluation has been given by an individual appointed by the judge to represent the child.

(E) Rule of construction

The screening of a student by a teacher or specialist to determine appropriate instructional strategies for curriculum implementation shall not be considered to be an evaluation for eligibility for special education and related services.

(2) Reevaluations

(A) In general

A local educational agency shall ensure that a reevaluation of each child with a disability is conducted in accordance with subsections (b) and (c)--

(i) if the local educational agency determines that the educational or related services needs, including improved academic achievement and functional performance, of the child warrant a reevaluation; or

(ii) if the child's parents or teacher requests a reevaluation.

(B) Limitation

A reevaluation conducted under subparagraph (A) shall occur--

(i) not more frequently than once a year, unless the parent and the local educational agency agree otherwise; and

(ii) at least once every 3 years, unless the parent and the local educational agency agree that a reevaluation is unnecessary.

(b) Evaluation procedures

(1) Notice

The local educational agency shall provide notice to the parents of a child with a disability, in accordance with subsections (b)(3), (b) (4), and (c) of section 1415 of this title, that describes any evaluation procedures such agency proposes to conduct.

(2) Conduct of evaluation

In conducting the evaluation, the local educational agency shall--

(A) use a variety of assessment tools and strategies to gather relevant functional, developmental, and academic information, including information provided by the parent, that may assist in determining--

(i) whether the child is a child with a disability; and

(ii) the content of the child's individualized education program, including information related to enabling the child to be involved in and progress in the general education curriculum, or, for preschool children, to participate in appropriate activities;

(B) not use any single measure or assessment as the sole criterion for determining whether a child is a child with a disability or determining an appropriate educational program for the child; and

(C) use technically sound instruments that may assess the relative contribution of cognitive and behavioral factors, in addition to physical or developmental factors.

(3) Additional requirements

Each local educational agency shall ensure that--

(A) assessments and other evaluation materials used to assess a child under this section--

(i) are selected and administered so as not to be discriminatory on a racial or cultural basis;

(ii) are provided and administered in the language and form most likely to yield accurate information on what the child knows and can do academically, developmentally, and functionally, unless it is not feasible to so provide or administer;

(iii) are used for purposes for which the assessments or measures are valid and reliable;

(iv) are administered by trained and knowledgeable personnel; and

(v) are administered in accordance with any instructions provided by the producer of such assessments;

(B) the child is assessed in all areas of suspected disability;

(C) assessment tools and strategies that provide relevant information that directly assists persons in determining the educational needs of the child are provided; and

(D) assessments of children with disabilities who transfer from 1 school district to another school district in the same academic year are coordinated with such children's prior and subsequent schools, as necessary and as expeditiously as possible, to ensure prompt completion of full evaluations.

(4) Determination of eligibility and educational need

Upon completion of the administration of

assessments and other evaluation measures--

(A) the determination of whether the child is a child with a disability as defined in section 1401(3) of this title and the educational needs of the child shall be made by a team of qualified professionals and the parent of the child in accordance with paragraph (5); and

(B) a copy of the evaluation report and the documentation of determination of eligibility shall be given to the parent.

(5) Special rule for eligibility determination

In making a determination of eligibility under paragraph (4)(A), a child shall not be determined to be a child with a disability if the determinant factor for such determination is--

(A) lack of appropriate instruction in reading, including in the essential components of reading instruction (as defined in section 6368(3) of this title, as such section was in effect on the day before December 10, 2015);

(B) lack of instruction in math; or

(C) limited English proficiency.

(6) Specific learning disabilities

(A) In general

Notwithstanding section 1406(b) of this title, when determining whether a child has a specific learning disability as defined in section 1401 of this title, a local educational agency shall not be required to take into consideration whether a child has a severe discrepancy between achievement and intellectual ability in oral expression, listening comprehension, written expression, basic reading skill, reading comprehension, mathematical calculation, or mathematical reasoning.

(B) Additional authority

In determining whether a child has a specific learning disability, a local educational agency may use a process that determines if the child responds to scientific, research-based intervention as a part of the evaluation procedures described in paragraphs (2) and (3).

(c) Additional requirements for evaluation and reevaluations

(1) Review of existing evaluation data

As part of an initial evaluation (if appropriate) and as part of any reevaluation under this section, the IEP Team and other qualified professionals, as appropriate, shall--

(A) review existing evaluation data on the child, including--

(i) evaluations and information provided by the parents of the child;

(ii) current classroom-based, local, or State assessments, and classroom-based observations; and

(iii) observations by teachers and related services providers; and

(B) on the basis of that review, and input from the child's parents, identify what additional data, if any, are needed to determine--

(i) whether the child is a child with a disability as defined in section 1401(3) of this title, and the educational needs of the child, or, in case of a reevaluation of a child, whether the child continues to have such a disability and such educational needs;

(ii) the present levels of academic achievement and related developmental needs of the child;

(iii) whether the child needs special education and related services, or in the case of a reevaluation of a child, whether the child continues to need special education and related services; and

(iv) whether any additions or modifications to the special education and related services are needed to enable the child to meet the measurable annual goals set out in the individualized education program of the child and to participate, as appropriate, in the general education curriculum.

(2) Source of data

The local educational agency shall administer such assessments and other evaluation measures as may be needed to produce the data identified by the IEP Team under paragraph (1)(B).

(3) Parental consent

Each local educational agency shall obtain informed parental consent, in accordance with subsection (a)(1)(D), prior to conducting any reevaluation of a child with a disability, except that such informed parental consent need not be obtained if the local educational agency can demonstrate that it had taken reasonable measures to obtain such consent and the child's parent has failed to respond.

(4) Requirements if additional data are not needed

If the IEP Team and other qualified professionals, as appropriate, determine that no additional data are needed to determine whether the child continues to be a child with a disability and to determine the child's educational needs, the local educational agency--

(A) shall notify the child's parents of--

(i) that determination and the reasons for the determination; and

(ii) the right of such parents to request an assessment to determine whether the child continues to be a child with a disability and to determine the child's educational needs; and

(B) shall not be required to conduct such an

assessment unless requested to by the child's parents.

(5) Evaluations before change in eligibility

(A) In general

Except as provided in subparagraph (B), a local educational agency shall evaluate a child with a disability in accordance with this section before determining that the child is no longer a child with a disability.

(B) Exception

(i) In general

The evaluation described in subparagraph (A) shall not be required before the termination of a child's eligibility under this subchapter due to graduation from secondary school with a regular diploma, or due to exceeding the age eligibility for a free appropriate public education under State law.

(ii) Summary of performance

For a child whose eligibility under this subchapter terminates under circumstances described in clause (i), a local educational agency shall provide the child with a summary of the child's academic achievement and functional performance, which shall include recommendations on how to assist the child in meeting the child's postsecondary goals.

(d) Individualized education programs

(1) Definitions

In this chapter:

(A) Individualized education program

(i) In general

The term "individualized education program" or "IEP" means a written statement for each child with a disability that is developed, reviewed, and revised in accordance with this section and that includes--

(I) a statement of the child's present levels of academic achievement and functional performance, including--

(aa) how the child's disability affects the child's involvement and progress in the general education curriculum;

(bb) for preschool children, as appropriate, how the disability affects the child's participation in appropriate activities; and

(cc) for children with disabilities who take alternate assessments aligned to alternate achievement standards, a description of benchmarks or short-term objectives;

(II) a statement of measurable annual goals, including academic and functional goals, designed to--

(aa) meet the child's needs that result from the child's disability to enable the child to be involved in and make progress in the general education curriculum; and

(bb) meet each of the child's other educational needs that result from the child's disability;

(III) a description of how the child's progress toward meeting the annual goals described in subclause (II) will be measured and when periodic reports on the progress the child is making toward meeting the annual goals (such as through the use of quarterly or other periodic reports, concurrent with the issuance of report cards) will be provided;

(IV) a statement of the special education and related services and supplementary aids and services, based on peer-reviewed research to the extent practicable, to be provided to the child, or on behalf of the child, and a statement of the program modifications or supports for school personnel that will be provided for the child--

(aa) to advance appropriately toward attaining the annual goals;

(bb) to be involved in and make progress in the general education curriculum in accordance with subclause (I) and to participate in extracurricular and other nonacademic activities; and

(cc) to be educated and participate with other children with disabilities and nondisabled children in the activities described in this subparagraph;

(V) an explanation of the extent, if any, to which the child will not participate with nondisabled children in the regular class and in the activities described in subclause (IV)(cc);

(VI)(aa) a statement of any individual appropriate accommodations that are necessary to measure the academic achievement and functional performance of the child on State and districtwide assessments consistent with section 1412(a)(16)(A) of this title; and

(bb) if the IEP Team determines that the child shall take an alternate assessment on a particular State or districtwide assessment of student achievement, a statement of why--

(AA) the child cannot participate in the regular assessment; and

(BB) the particular alternate assessment selected is appropriate for the child;

(VII) the projected date for the beginning of the services and modifications described in subclause (IV), and the anticipated frequency, location, and duration of those services and modifications; and

(VIII) beginning not later than the first IEP to be in effect when the child is 16, and updated annually thereafter--

(aa) appropriate measurable postsecondary goals based upon age appropriate transition assessments related to training, education, employment, and, where appropriate, independent living skills;

(bb) the transition services (including courses of study) needed to assist the child in reaching those goals; and

(cc) beginning not later than 1 year before the child reaches the age of majority under State law, a statement that the child has been informed of the child's rights under this chapter, if any, that will transfer to the child on reaching the age of majority under section 1415(m) of this title.

(ii) Rule of construction

Nothing in this section shall be construed to require--

(I) that additional information be included in a child's IEP beyond what is explicitly required in this section; and

(II) the IEP Team to include information under 1 component of a child's IEP that is already contained under another component of such IEP.

(B) Individualized education program team

The term "individualized education program team" or "IEP Team" means a group of individuals composed of--

(i) the parents of a child with a disability;

(ii) not less than 1 regular education teacher of such child (if the child is, or may be, participating in the regular education environment);

(iii) not less than 1 special education teacher, or where appropriate, not less than 1 special education provider of such child;

(iv) a representative of the local educational agency who--

(I) is qualified to provide, or supervise the provision of, specially designed instruction to meet the unique needs of children with disabilities;

(II) is knowledgeable about the general education curriculum; and

(III) is knowledgeable about the availability of resources of the local educational agency;

(v) an individual who can interpret the instructional implications of evaluation results, who may be a member of the team described in clauses (ii) through (vi);

(vi) at the discretion of the parent or the agency, other individuals who have knowledge or special expertise regarding the child, including related services personnel as appropriate; and

(vii) whenever appropriate, the child with a disability.

(C) IEP Team attendance

(i) Attendance not necessary

A member of the IEP Team shall not be required to attend an IEP meeting, in whole or in part, if the parent of a child with a disability and the local educational agency agree that the attendance of such member is not necessary because the member's area of the curriculum or related services is not being modified or discussed in the meeting.

(ii) Excusal

A member of the IEP Team may be excused from attending an IEP meeting, in whole or in part, when the meeting involves a modification to or discussion of the member's area of the curriculum or related services, if--

(I) the parent and the local educational agency consent to the excusal; and

(II) the member submits, in writing to the parent and the IEP Team, input into the development of the IEP prior to the meeting.

(iii) Written agreement and consent required

A parent's agreement under clause (i) and consent under clause (ii) shall be in writing.

(D) IEP Team transition

In the case of a child who was previously served under subchapter III, an invitation to the initial IEP meeting shall, at the request of the parent, be sent to the subchapter III service coordinator or other representatives of the subchapter III system to assist with the smooth transition of services.

(2) Requirement that program be in effect

(A) In general

At the beginning of each school year, each local educational agency, State educational agency, or other State agency, as the case may be, shall have in effect, for each child with a disability in the agency's jurisdiction, an individualized education program, as defined in paragraph (1)(A).

(B) Program for child aged 3 through 5

In the case of a child with a disability aged 3 through 5 (or, at the discretion of the State educational agency, a 2-year-old child with a disability who will turn age 3 during the school year), the IEP Team shall consider the individualized family service plan that contains the material described in section 1436 of this title, and that is developed in accordance with this section, and the individualized family service plan may serve as the IEP of the child if using that plan as the IEP is--

(i) consistent with State policy; and

(ii) agreed to by the agency and the child's parents.

(C) Program for children who transfer school districts

(i) In general

(I) Transfer within the same State

In the case of a child with a disability who transfers school districts within the same academic year, who enrolls in a new school, and who had an IEP that was in effect in the same State, the local educational agency shall provide such child with a free appropriate public education, including services comparable to those described in the previously held IEP, in consultation with the parents until such time as the local educational agency adopts the previously held IEP or develops, adopts, and implements a new IEP that is consistent with Federal and State law.

(II) Transfer outside State

In the case of a child with a disability who transfers school districts within the same academic year, who enrolls in a new school, and who had an IEP that was in effect in another State, the local educational agency shall provide such child with a free appropriate public education, including services comparable to those described in the previously held IEP, in consultation with the parents until such time as the local educational agency conducts an evaluation pursuant to subsection (a)(1), if determined to be necessary by such agency, and develops a new IEP, if appropriate, that is consistent with Federal and State law.

(ii) Transmittal of records

To facilitate the transition for a child described in clause (i)--

(I) the new school in which the child enrolls shall take reasonable steps to promptly obtain the child's records, including the IEP and supporting documents and any other records relating to the provision of special education or related services to the child, from the previous school in which the child was enrolled, pursuant to section 99.31(a)(2) of title 34, Code of Federal Regulations; and

(II) the previous school in which the child was enrolled shall take reasonable steps to promptly respond to such request from the new school.

(3) Development of IEP

(A) In general

In developing each child's IEP, the IEP Team, subject to subparagraph (C), shall consider--

(i) the strengths of the child;

(ii) the concerns of the parents for enhancing the education of their child;

(iii) the results of the initial evaluation or most recent evaluation of the child; and

(iv) the academic, developmental, and functional needs of the child.

(B) Consideration of special factors

The IEP Team shall--

(i) in the case of a child whose behavior impedes the child's learning or that of others, consider the use of positive behavioral interventions and supports, and other strategies, to address that behavior;

(ii) in the case of a child with limited English proficiency, consider the language needs of the child as such needs relate to the child's IEP;

(iii) in the case of a child who is blind or visually impaired, provide for instruction in Braille and the use of Braille unless the IEP Team determines, after an evaluation of the child's reading and writing skills, needs, and appropriate reading and writing media (including an evaluation of the child's future needs for instruction in Braille or the use of Braille), that instruction in Braille or the use of Braille is not appropriate for the child;

(iv) consider the communication needs of the child, and in the case of a child who is deaf or hard of hearing, consider the child's language and communication needs, opportunities for direct communications with peers and professional personnel in the child's language and communication mode, academic level, and full range of needs, including opportunities for direct instruction in the child's language and communication mode; and

(v) consider whether the child needs assistive technology devices and services.

(C) Requirement with respect to regular education teacher

A regular education teacher of the child, as a member of the IEP Team, shall, to the extent appropriate, participate in the development of the IEP of the child, including the determination of appropriate positive behavioral interventions and supports, and other strategies, and the determination of supplementary aids and services, program modifications, and support for school personnel consistent with paragraph (1)(A)(i)(IV).

(D) Agreement

In making changes to a child's IEP after the annual IEP meeting for a school year, the parent of a child with a disability and the local educational agency may agree not to convene an IEP meeting for the purposes of making such changes, and instead may develop a written document to amend or modify the child's current IEP.

(E) Consolidation of IEP Team meetings

To the extent possible, the local educational agency shall encourage the consolidation of reevaluation meetings for the child and other IEP Team meetings for the child.

(F) Amendments

Changes to the IEP may be made either by the entire IEP Team or, as provided in subparagraph (D), by amending the IEP rather than by redrafting the entire IEP. Upon request, a parent shall be provided with a revised copy of the IEP with the amendments incorporated.

(4) Review and revision of IEP

(A) In general

The local educational agency shall ensure that, subject to subparagraph (B), the IEP Team--

(i) reviews the child's IEP periodically, but not less frequently than annually, to determine whether the annual goals for the child are being achieved; and

(ii) revises the IEP as appropriate to address--

(I) any lack of expected progress toward the annual goals and in the general education curriculum, where appropriate;

(II) the results of any reevaluation conducted under this section;

(III) information about the child provided to, or by, the parents, as described in subsection (c)(1)(B);

(IV) the child's anticipated needs; or

(V) other matters.

(B) Requirement with respect to regular education teacher

A regular education teacher of the child, as a member of the IEP Team, shall, consistent with paragraph (1)(C), participate in the review and revision of the IEP of the child.

(5) Multi-year IEP demonstration

(A) Pilot program

(i) Purpose

The purpose of this paragraph is to provide an opportunity for States to allow parents and local educational agencies the opportunity for long-term planning by offering the option of developing a comprehensive multi-year IEP, not to exceed 3 years, that is designed to coincide with the natural transition points for the child.

(ii) Authorization

In order to carry out the purpose of this paragraph, the Secretary is authorized to approve not more than 15 proposals from States to carry out the activity described in clause (i).

(iii) Proposal

(I) In general

A State desiring to participate in the program under this paragraph shall submit a proposal to the Secretary at such time and in such manner as the Secretary may reasonably require.

(II) Content

The proposal shall include--

(aa) assurances that the development of a multi-year IEP under this paragraph is optional for parents;

(bb) assurances that the parent is required to provide informed consent before a comprehensive multi-year IEP is developed;

(cc) a list of required elements for each multi-year IEP, including--

(AA) measurable goals pursuant to paragraph (1)(A)(i)(II), coinciding with natural transition points for the child, that will enable the child to be involved in and make progress in the general education curriculum and that will meet the child's other needs that result from the child's disability; and

(BB) measurable annual goals for determining progress toward meeting the goals described in subitem (AA); and

(dd) a description of the process for the review and revision of each multi-year IEP, including--

(AA) a review by the IEP Team of the child's multi-year IEP at each of the child's natural transition points;

(BB) in years other than a child's natural transition points, an annual review of the child's IEP to determine the child's current levels of progress and whether the annual goals for the child are being achieved, and a requirement to amend the IEP, as appropriate, to enable the child to continue to meet the measurable goals set out in the IEP;

(CC) if the IEP Team determines on the basis of a review that the child is not making sufficient progress toward the goals described in the multi-year IEP, a requirement that the local educational agency shall ensure that the IEP Team carries out a more thorough review of the IEP in accordance with paragraph (4) within 30 calendar days; and

(DD) at the request of the parent, a requirement that the IEP Team shall conduct a review of the child's multi-year IEP rather than or subsequent to an annual review.

(B) Report

Beginning 2 years after December 3, 2004, the Secretary shall submit an annual report to the Committee on Education and the Workforce of the House of Representatives and the Committee on Health, Education, Labor, and Pensions of the Senate regarding the effectiveness of the program under this paragraph and any specific recommendations for broader implementation of such program, including--

(i) reducing--

(I) the paperwork burden on teachers, principals, administrators, and related service providers; and

(II) noninstructional time spent by teachers in complying with this subchapter;

(ii) enhancing longer-term educational planning;

(iii) improving positive outcomes for

children with disabilities;

(iv) promoting collaboration between IEP Team members; and

(v) ensuring satisfaction of family members.

(C) Definition

In this paragraph, the term "natural transition points" means those periods that are close in time to the transition of a child with a disability from preschool to elementary grades, from elementary grades to middle or junior high school grades, from middle or junior high school grades to secondary school grades, and from secondary school grades to post-secondary activities, but in no case a period longer than 3 years.

(6) Failure to meet transition objectives

If a participating agency, other than the local educational agency, fails to provide the transition services described in the IEP in accordance with paragraph (1)(A)(i)(VIII), the local educational agency shall reconvene the IEP Team to identify alternative strategies to meet the transition objectives for the child set out in the IEP.

(7) Children with disabilities in adult prisons

(A) In general

The following requirements shall not apply to children with disabilities who are convicted as adults under State law and incarcerated in adult prisons:

(i) The requirements contained in section 1412(a)(16) of this title and paragraph (1)(A)(i)(VI) (relating to participation of children with disabilities in general assessments).

(ii) The requirements of items (aa) and (bb) of paragraph (1)(A)(i)(VIII) (relating to transition planning and transition services), do not apply with respect to such children whose eligibility under this subchapter will end, because of such children's age, before such children will be released from prison.

(B) Additional requirement

If a child with a disability is convicted as an adult under State law and incarcerated in an adult prison, the child's IEP Team may modify the child's IEP or placement notwithstanding the requirements of sections1 1412(a)(5)(A) of this title and paragraph (1)(A) if the State has demonstrated a bona fide security or compelling penological interest that cannot otherwise be accommodated.

(e) Educational placements

Each local educational agency or State educational agency shall ensure that the parents of each child with a disability are members of any group that makes decisions on the educational placement of their child.

(f) Alternative means of meeting participation

When conducting IEP team2 meetings and placement meetings pursuant to this section, section 1415(e) of this title, and section 1415(f)(1)(B) of this title, and carrying out administrative matters under section 1415 of this title (such as scheduling, exchange of witness lists, and status conferences), the parent of a child with a disability and a local educational agency may agree to use alternative means of meeting participation, such as video conferences and conference calls.

SEC. 615. PROCEDURAL SAFEGUARDS.

(a) ESTABLISHMENT OF PROCEDURES-Any State educational agency, State agency, or local educational agency that receives assistance under this part shall establish and maintain procedures in accordance with this section to ensure that children with disabilities and their parents are guaranteed procedural safeguards with respect to the provision of a free appropriate public education by such agencies.

(b) TYPES OF PROCEDURES- The procedures required by this section shall include the following:

(1) An opportunity for the parents of a child with a disability to examine all records relating to such child and to participate in meetings with respect to the identification, evaluation, and educational placement of the child, and the provision of a free appropriate public education to such child, and to obtain an independent educational evaluation of the child.

(2)(A) Procedures to protect the rights of the child whenever the parents of the child are not known, the agency cannot, after reasonable efforts, locate the parents, or the child is a ward of the State, including the assignment of an individual to act as a surrogate for the parents, which surrogate shall not be an employee of the State educational agency, the local educational agency, or any other agency that is involved in the education or care of the child. In the case of—

(i) a child who is a ward of the State, such surrogate may alternatively be appointed by the judge overseeing the child's care provided that the surrogate meets the requirements of this paragraph; and

(ii) an unaccompanied homeless youth as defined in section 725(6) of the McKinney-Vento Homeless Assistance Act (42 U.S.C.

11434a(6)), the local educational agency shall appoint a surrogate in accordance with this paragraph.

(B) The State shall make reasonable efforts to ensure the assignment of a surrogate not more than 30 days after there is a determination by the agency that the child needs a surrogate.

(3) Written prior notice to the parents of the child, in accordance with subsection (c)(1), whenever the local educational agency—

(A) proposes to initiate or change; or

(B) refuses to initiate or change,the identification, evaluation, or educational placement of the child, or the provision of a free appropriate public education to the child.

(4) Procedures designed to ensure that the notice required by paragraph (3) is in the native language of the parents, unless it clearly is not feasible to do so.

(5) An opportunity for mediation, in accordance with subsection (e).

(6) An opportunity for any party to present a complaint—

(A) with respect to any matter relating to the identification, evaluation, or educational placement of the child, or the provision of a free appropriate public education to such child; and

(B) which sets forth an alleged violation that occurred not more than 2 years before the date the parent or public agency knew or should have known about the alleged action that forms the basis of the complaint, or, if the State has an explicit time limitation for presenting such a complaint under this part, in such time as the State law allows, except that the exceptions to the timeline described in subsection (f)(3)(D) shall apply to the timeline described in this subparagraph.

(7)(A) Procedures that require either party, or the attorney representing a party, to provide due process complaint notice in accordance with subsection (c)(2) (which shall remain confidential)—

(i) to the other party, in the complaint filed under paragraph (6), and forward a copy of such notice to the State educational agency; and

(ii) that shall include—

(I) the name of the child, the address of the residence of the child (or available contact information in the case of a homeless child), and the name of the school the child is attending;

(II) in the case of a homeless child or youth (within the meaning of section 725(2) of the McKinney-Vento Homeless Assistance Act (42 U.S.C. 11434a(2)), available contact information for the child and the name of the school the child is attending;

(III) a description of the nature of the problem of the child relating to such proposed initiation or change, including facts relating to such problem; and

(IV) a proposed resolution of the problem to the extent known and available to the party at the time.

(B) A requirement that a party may not have a due process hearing until the party, or the attorney representing the party, files a notice that meets the requirements of subparagraph (A)(ii).

(8) Procedures that require the State educational agency to develop a model form to assist parents in filing a complaint and due process complaint notice in accordance with paragraphs (6) and (7), respectively.

(c) NOTIFICATION REQUIREMENTS-

(1) CONTENT OF PRIOR WRITTEN NOTICE- The notice required by subsection (b)(3) shall include—

(A) a description of the action proposed or refused by the agency;

(B) an explanation of why the agency proposes or refuses to take the action and a description of each evaluation procedure, assessment, record, or report the agency used as a basis for the proposed or refused action;

(C) a statement that the parents of a child with a disability have protection under the procedural safeguards of this part and, if this notice is not an initial referral for evaluation, the means by which a copy of a description of the procedural safeguards can be obtained;

(D) sources for parents to contact to obtain assistance in understanding the provisions of this part;

(E) a description of other options considered by the IEP Team and the reason why those options were rejected; and

(F) a description of the factors that are relevant to the agency's proposal or refusal.

(2) DUE PROCESS COMPLAINT NOTICE-

(A) COMPLAINT- The due process complaint notice required under subsection (b) (7)(A) shall be deemed to be sufficient unless the party receiving the notice notifies the hearing officer and the other party in writing that the receiving party believes the notice has not met the requirements of subsection (b)(7) (A).

(B) RESPONSE TO COMPLAINT-

(i) LOCAL EDUCATIONAL AGENCY RESPONSE-

(I) IN GENERAL- If the local educational

agency has not sent a prior written notice to the parent regarding the subject matter contained in the parent's due process complaint notice, such local educational agency shall, within 10 days of receiving the complaint, send to the parent a response that shall include—

(aa) an explanation of why the agency proposed or refused to take the action raised in the complaint;

(bb) a description of other options that the IEP Team considered and the reasons why those options were rejected;

(cc) a description of each evaluation procedure, assessment, record, or report the agency used as the basis for the proposed or refused action; and

(dd) a description of the factors that are relevant to the agency's proposal or refusal.

(II) SUFFICIENCY- A response filed by a local educational agency pursuant to subclause (I) shall not be construed to preclude such local educational agency from asserting that the parent's due process complaint notice was insufficient where appropriate.

(ii) OTHER PARTY RESPONSE- Except as provided in clause (i), the non-complaining party shall, within 10 days of receiving the complaint, send to the complaint a response that specifically addresses the issues raised in the complaint.

(C) TIMING- The party providing a hearing officer notification under subparagraph (A) shall provide the notification within 15 days of receiving the complaint.

(D) DETERMINATION- Within 5 days of receipt of the notification provided under subparagraph (C), the hearing officer shall make a determination on the face of the notice of whether the notification meets the requirements of subsection (b)(7)(A), and shall immediately notify the parties in writing of such determination.

(E) AMENDED COMPLAINT NOTICE-

(i) IN GENERAL- A party may amend its due process complaint notice only if—

(I) the other party consents in writing to such amendment and is given the opportunity to resolve the complaint through a meeting held pursuant to subsection (f)(1)(B); or

(II) the hearing officer grants permission, except that the hearing officer may only grant such permission at any time not later than 5 days before a due process hearing occurs.

(ii) APPLICABLE TIMELINE- The applicable timeline for a due process hearing under this part shall recommence at the time the party files an amended notice, including the timeline under subsection (f)(1)(B).

(d) PROCEDURAL SAFEGUARDS NOTICE-

(1) IN GENERAL-

(A) COPY TO PARENTS- A copy of the procedural safeguards available to the parents of a child with a disability shall be given to the parents only 1 time a year, except that a copy also shall be given to the parents—

(i) upon initial referral or parental request for evaluation;

(ii) upon the first occurrence of the filing of a complaint under subsection (b)(6); and

(iii) upon request by a parent.

(B) INTERNET WEBSITE- A local educational agency may place a current copy of the procedural safeguards notice on its Internet website if such website exists.

(2) CONTENTS- The procedural safeguards notice shall include a full explanation of the procedural safeguards, written in the native language of the parents (unless it clearly is not feasible to do so) and written in an easily understandable manner, available under this section and under regulations promulgated by the Secretary relating to—

(A) independent educational evaluation;

(B) prior written notice;

(C) parental consent;

(D) access to educational records;

(E) the opportunity to present and resolve complaints, including—

(i) the time period in which to make a complaint;

(ii) the opportunity for the agency to resolve the complaint; and

(iii) the availability of mediation;

(F) the child's placement during pendency of due process proceedings;

(G) procedures for students who are subject to placement in an interim alternative educational setting;

(H) requirements for unilateral placement by parents of children in private schools at public expense;

(I) due process hearings, including requirements for disclosure of evaluation results and recommendations;

(J) State-level appeals (if applicable in that State);

(K) civil actions, including the time period in which to file such actions; and

(L) attorneys' fees.

(e) MEDIATION-

(1) IN GENERAL- Any State educational agency or local educational agency that receives assistance under this part shall ensure that procedures are established and implemented to allow parties to disputes involving any matter,

including matters arising prior to the filing of a complaint pursuant to subsection (b)(6), to resolve such disputes through a mediation process.

(2) REQUIREMENTS- Such procedures shall meet the following requirements:

(A) The procedures shall ensure that the mediation process—

(i) is voluntary on the part of the parties;

(ii) is not used to deny or delay a parent's right to a due process hearing under subsection (f), or to deny any other rights afforded under this part; and

(iii) is conducted by a qualified and impartial mediator who is trained in effective mediation techniques.

(B) OPPORTUNITY TO MEET WITH A DISINTERESTED PARTY- A local educational agency or a State agency may establish procedures to offer to parents and schools that choose not to use the mediation process, an opportunity to meet, at a time and location convenient to the parents, with a disinterested party who is under contract with—

(i) a parent training and information center or community parent resource center in the State established under section 671 or 672; or

(ii) an appropriate alternative dispute resolution entity, to encourage the use, and explain the benefits, of the mediation process to the parents.

(C) LIST OF QUALIFIED MEDIATORS- The State shall maintain a list of individuals who are qualified mediators and knowledgeable in laws and regulations relating to the provision of special education and related services.

(D) COSTS- The State shall bear the cost of the mediation process, including the costs of meetings described in subparagraph (B).

(E) SCHEDULING AND LOCATION- Each session in the mediation process shall be scheduled in a timely manner and shall be held in a location that is convenient to the parties to the dispute.

(F) WRITTEN AGREEMENT- In the case that a resolution is reached to resolve the complaint through the mediation process, the parties shall execute a legally binding agreement that sets forth such resolution and that—

(i) states that all discussions that occurred during the mediation process shall be confidential and may not be used as evidence in any subsequent due process hearing or civil proceeding;

(ii) is signed by both the parent and a representative of the agency who has the authority to bind such agency; and

(iii) is enforceable in any State court of competent jurisdiction or in a district court of the United States.

(G) MEDIATION DISCUSSIONS- Discussions that occur during the mediation process shall be confidential and may not be used as evidence in any subsequent due process hearing or civil proceeding.

(f) IMPARTIAL DUE PROCESS HEARING-

(1) IN GENERAL-

(A) HEARING- Whenever a complaint has been received under subsection (b)(6) or (k), the parents or the local educational agency involved in such complaint shall have an opportunity for an impartial due process hearing, which shall be conducted by the State educational agency or by the local educational agency, as determined by State law or by the State educational agency.

(B) RESOLUTION SESSION-

(i) PRELIMINARY MEETING- Prior to the opportunity for an impartial due process hearing under subparagraph (A), the local educational agency shall convene a meeting with the parents and the relevant member or members of the IEP Team who have specific knowledge of the facts identified in the complaint—

(I) within 15 days of receiving notice of the parents' complaint;

(II) which shall include a representative of the agency who has decisionmaking authority on behalf of such agency;

(III) which may not include an attorney of the local educational agency unless the parent is accompanied by an attorney; and

(IV) where the parents of the child discuss their complaint, and the facts that form the basis of the complaint, and the local educational agency is provided the opportunity to resolve the complaint, unless the parents and the local educational agency agree in writing to waive such meeting, or agree to use the mediation process described in subsection (e).

(ii) HEARING- If the local educational agency has not resolved the complaint to the satisfaction of the parents within 30 days of the receipt of the complaint, the due process hearing may occur, and all of the applicable timelines for a due process hearing under this part shall commence.

(iii) WRITTEN SETTLEMENT AGREEMENT- In the case that a resolution is reached to resolve the complaint at a meeting described in clause (i), the parties shall execute a legally binding agreement that is—

(I) signed by both the parent and a representative of the agency who has the authority to bind such agency; and

(II) enforceable in any State court of competent jurisdiction or in a district court of the United States.

(iv) REVIEW PERIOD- If the parties execute an agreement pursuant to clause (iii), a party may void such agreement within 3 business days of the agreement's execution.

(2) DISCLOSURE OF EVALUATIONS AND RECOMMENDATIONS-

(A) IN GENERAL- Not less than 5 business days prior to a hearing conducted pursuant to paragraph (1), each party shall disclose to all other parties all evaluations completed by that date, and recommendations based on the offering party's evaluations, that the party intends to use at the hearing.

(B) FAILURE TO DISCLOSE- A hearing officer may bar any party that fails to comply with subparagraph (A) from introducing the relevant evaluation or recommendation at the hearing without the consent of the other party.

(3) LIMITATIONS ON HEARING-

(A) PERSON CONDUCTING HEARING- A hearing officer conducting a hearing pursuant to paragraph (1)(A) shall, at a minimum—

(i) not be—

(I) an employee of the State educational agency or the local educational agency involved in the education or care of the child; or

(II) a person having a personal or professional interest that conflicts with the person's objectivity in the hearing;

(ii) possess knowledge of, and the ability to understand, the provisions of this title, Federal and State regulations pertaining to this title, and legal interpretations of this title by Federal and State courts;

(iii) possess the knowledge and ability to conduct hearings in accordance with appropriate, standard legal practice; and

(iv) possess the knowledge and ability to render and write decisions in accordance with appropriate, standard legal practice.

(B) SUBJECT MATTER OF HEARING- The party requesting the due process hearing shall not be allowed to raise issues at the due process hearing that were not raised in the notice filed under subsection (b)(7), unless the other party agrees otherwise.

(C) TIMELINE FOR REQUESTING HEARING- A parent or agency shall request an impartial due process hearing within 2 years of the date the parent or agency knew or should have known about the alleged action that forms the basis of the complaint, or, if the State has an explicit time limitation for requesting such a hearing under this part, in such time as the State law allows.

(D) EXCEPTIONS TO THE TIMELINE- The timeline described in subparagraph (C) shall not apply to a parent if the parent was prevented from requesting the hearing due to—

(i) specific misrepresentations by the local educational agency that it had resolved the problem forming the basis of the complaint; or

(ii) the local educational agency's withholding of information from the parent that was required under this part to be provided to the parent.

(E) DECISION OF HEARING OFFICER-

(i) IN GENERAL- Subject to clause (ii), a decision made by a hearing officer shall be made on substantive grounds based on a determination of whether the child received a free appropriate public education.

(ii) PROCEDURAL ISSUES- In matters alleging a procedural violation, a hearing officer may find that a child did not receive a free appropriate public education only if the procedural inadequacies—

(I) impeded the child's right to a free appropriate public education;

(II) significantly impeded the parents' opportunity to participate in the decisionmaking process regarding the provision of a free appropriate public education to the parents' child; or

(III) caused a deprivation of educational benefits.

(iii) RULE OF CONSTRUCTION- Nothing in this subparagraph shall be construed to preclude a hearing officer from ordering a local educational agency to comply with procedural requirements under this section.

(F) RULE OF CONSTRUCTION- Nothing in this paragraph shall be construed to affect the right of a parent to file a complaint with the State educational agency.

(g) APPEAL-

(1) IN GENERAL- If the hearing required by subsection (f) is conducted by a local educational agency, any party aggrieved by the findings and decision rendered in such a hearing may appeal such findings and decision to the State educational agency.

(2) IMPARTIAL REVIEW AND INDEPENDENT DECISION- The State educational agency shall conduct an impartial review of the findings and decision appealed under paragraph (1). The officer conducting such review shall make an independent decision upon completion of such review.

(h) SAFEGUARDS- Any party to a hearing conducted pursuant to subsection (f) or (k), or an appeal conducted pursuant to subsection (g), shall be accorded—

(1) the right to be accompanied and advised

by counsel and by individuals with special knowledge or training with respect to the problems of children with disabilities;

(2) the right to present evidence and confront, cross-examine, and compel the attendance of witnesses;

(3) the right to a written, or, at the option of the parents, electronic verbatim record of such hearing; and

(4) the right to written, or, at the option of the parents, electronic findings of fact and decisions, which findings and decisions—

(A) shall be made available to the public consistent with the requirements of section 617(b) (relating to the confidentiality of data, information, and records); and

(B) shall be transmitted to the advisory panel established pursuant to section 612(a)(21).

(i) ADMINISTRATIVE PROCEDURES-

(1) IN GENERAL-

(A) DECISION MADE IN HEARING- A decision made in a hearing conducted pursuant to subsection (f) or (k) shall be final, except that any party involved in such hearing may appeal such decision under the provisions of subsection (g) and paragraph (2).

(B) DECISION MADE AT APPEAL- A decision made under subsection (g) shall be final, except that any party may bring an action under paragraph (2).

(2) RIGHT TO BRING CIVIL ACTION-

(A) IN GENERAL- Any party aggrieved by the findings and decision made under subsection (f) or (k) who does not have the right to an appeal under subsection (g), and any party aggrieved by the findings and decision made under this subsection, shall have the right to bring a civil action with respect to the complaint presented pursuant to this section, which action may be brought in any State court of competent jurisdiction or in a district court of the United States, without regard to the amount in controversy.

(B) LIMITATION- The party bringing the action shall have 90 days from the date of the decision of the hearing officer to bring such an action, or, if the State has an explicit time limitation for bringing such action under this part, in such time as the State law allows.

(C) ADDITIONAL REQUIREMENTS- In any action brought under this paragraph, the court—

(i) shall receive the records of the administrative proceedings;

(ii) shall hear additional evidence at the request of a party; and

(iii) basing its decision on the preponderance of the evidence, shall grant such relief as the court determines is appropriate.

(3) JURISDICTION OF DISTRICT COURTS; ATTORNEYS' FEES-

(A) IN GENERAL- The district courts of the United States shall have jurisdiction of actions brought under this section without regard to the amount in controversy.

(B) AWARD OF ATTORNEYS' FEES-

(i) IN GENERAL- In any action or proceeding brought under this section, the court, in its discretion, may award reasonable attorneys' fees as part of the costs—

(I) to a prevailing party who is the parent of a child with a disability;

(II) to a prevailing party who is a State educational agency or local educational agency against the attorney of a parent who files a complaint or subsequent cause of action that is frivolous, unreasonable, or without foundation, or against the attorney of a parent who continued to litigate after the litigation clearly became frivolous, unreasonable, or without foundation; or

(III) to a prevailing State educational agency or local educational agency against the attorney of a parent, or against the parent, if the parent's complaint or subsequent cause of action was presented for any improper purpose, such as to harass, to cause unnecessary delay, or to needlessly increase the cost of litigation.

(ii) RULE OF CONSTRUCTION- Nothing in this subparagraph shall be construed to affect section 327 of the District of Columbia Appropriations Act, 2005.

(C) DETERMINATION OF AMOUNT OF ATTORNEYS' FEES- Fees awarded under this paragraph shall be based on rates prevailing in the community in which the action or proceeding arose for the kind and quality of services furnished. No bonus or multiplier may be used in calculating the fees awarded under this subsection.

(D) PROHIBITION OF ATTORNEYS' FEES AND RELATED COSTS FOR CERTAIN SERVICES-

(i) IN GENERAL- Attorneys' fees may not be awarded and related costs may not be reimbursed in any action or proceeding under this section for services performed subsequent to the time of a written offer of settlement to a parent if—

(I) the offer is made within the time prescribed by Rule 68 of the Federal Rules of Civil Procedure or, in the case of an administrative proceeding, at any time more than 10 days before the proceeding begins;

(II) the offer is not accepted within 10 days; and

(III) the court or administrative hearing

officer finds that the relief finally obtained by the parents is not more favorable to the parents than the offer of settlement.

(ii) IEP TEAM MEETINGS- Attorneys' fees may not be awarded relating to any meeting of the IEP Team unless such meeting is convened as a result of an administrative proceeding or judicial action, or, at the discretion of the State, for a mediation described in subsection (e).

(iii) OPPORTUNITY TO RESOLVE COMPLAINTS- A meeting conducted pursuant to subsection (f)(1)(B)(i) shall not be considered—

(I) a meeting convened as a result of an administrative hearing or judicial action; or

(II) an administrative hearing or judicial action for purposes of this paragraph.

(E) EXCEPTION TO PROHIBITION ON ATTORNEYS' FEES AND RELATED COSTS- Notwithstanding subparagraph (D), an award of attorneys' fees and related costs may be made to a parent who is the prevailing party and who was substantially justified in rejecting the settlement offer.

(F) REDUCTION IN AMOUNT OF ATTORNEYS' FEES- Except as provided in subparagraph (G), whenever the court finds that—

(i) the parent, or the parent's attorney, during the course of the action or proceeding, unreasonably protracted the final resolution of the controversy;

(ii) the amount of the attorneys' fees otherwise authorized to be awarded unreasonably exceeds the hourly rate prevailing in the community for similar services by attorneys of reasonably comparable skill, reputation, and experience;

(iii) the time spent and legal services furnished were excessive considering the nature of the action or proceeding; or

(iv) the attorney representing the parent did not provide to the local educational agency the appropriate information in the notice of the complaint described in subsection (b)(7) (A), the court shall reduce, accordingly, the amount of the attorneys' fees awarded under this section.

(G) EXCEPTION TO REDUCTION IN AMOUNT OF ATTORNEYS' FEES- The provisions of subparagraph (F) shall not apply in any action or proceeding if the court finds that the State or local educational agency unreasonably protracted the final resolution of the action or proceeding or there was a violation of this section.

(j) MAINTENANCE OF CURRENT EDUCATIONAL PLACEMENT- Except as provided in subsection (k)(4), during the pendency of any proceedings conducted pursuant to this section, unless the State or local educational agency and the parents otherwise agree, the child shall remain in the then-current educational placement of the child, or, if applying for initial admission to a public school, shall, with the consent of the parents, be placed in the public school program until all such proceedings have been completed.

(k) PLACEMENT IN ALTERNATIVE EDUCATIONAL SETTING-

(1) AUTHORITY OF SCHOOL PERSONNEL-

(A) CASE-BY-CASE DETERMINATION- School personnel may consider any unique circumstances on a case-by-case basis when determining whether to order a change in placement for a child with a disability who violates a code of student conduct.

(B) AUTHORITY-. School personnel under this subsection may remove a child with a disability who violates a code of student conduct from their current placement to an appropriate interim alternative educational setting, another setting, or suspension, for not more than 10 school days (to the extent such alternatives are applied to children without disabilities).

(C) ADDITIONAL AUTHORITY- If school personnel seek to order a change in placement that would exceed 10 school days and the behavior that gave rise to the violation of the school code is determined not to be a manifestation of the child's disability pursuant to subparagraph (E), the relevant disciplinary procedures applicable to children without disabilities may be applied to the child in the same manner and for the same duration in which the procedures would be applied to children without disabilities, except as provided in section 612(a)(1) although it may be provided in an interim alternative educational setting.

(D) SERVICES- A child with a disability who is removed from the child's current placement under subparagraph (G) (irrespective of whether the behavior is determined to be a manifestation of the child's disability) or subparagraph (C) shall—

(i) continue to receive educational services, as provided in section 612(a)(1), so as to enable the child to continue to participate in the general education curriculum, although in another setting, and to progress toward meeting the goals set out in the child's IEP; and

(ii) receive, as appropriate, a functional behavioral assessment, behavioral intervention services and modifications, that are designed to address the behavior violation so that it does not recur.

(E) MANIFESTATION DETERMINATION-

(i) IN GENERAL- Except as provided in subparagraph (B), within 10 school days of any decision to change the placement of a child with a disability because of a violation of a code of student conduct, the local educational agency, the parent, and relevant members of the IEP Team (as determined by the parent and the local educational agency) shall review all relevant information in the student's file, including the child's IEP, any teacher observations, and any relevant information provided by the parents to determine—

(I) if the conduct in question was caused by, or had a direct and substantial relationship to, the child's disability; or

(II) if the conduct in question was the direct result of the local educational agency's failure to implement the IEP.

(ii) MANIFESTATION- If the local educational agency, the parent, and relevant members of the IEP Team determine that either subclause (I) or (II) of clause (i) is applicable for the child, the conduct shall be determined to be a manifestation of the child's disability.

(F) DETERMINATION THAT BEHAVIOR WAS A MANIFESTATION- If the local educational agency, the parent, and relevant members of the IEP Team make the determination that the conduct was a manifestation of the child's disability, the IEP Team shall—

(i) conduct a functional behavioral assessment, and implement a behavioral intervention plan for such child, provided that the local educational agency had not conducted such assessment prior to such determination before the behavior that resulted in a change in placement described in subparagraph (C) or (G);

(ii) in the situation where a behavioral intervention plan has been developed, review the behavioral intervention plan if the child already has such a behavioral intervention plan, and modify it, as necessary, to address the behavior; and

(iii) except as provided in subparagraph (G), return the child to the placement from which the child was removed, unless the parent and the local educational agency agree to a change of placement as part of the modification of the behavioral intervention plan.

(G) SPECIAL CIRCUMSTANCES- School personnel may remove a student to an interim alternative educational setting for not more than 45 school days without regard to whether the behavior is determined to be a manifestation of the child's disability, in cases where a child—

(i) carries or possesses a weapon to or at school, on school premises, or to or at a school function under the jurisdiction of a State or local educational agency;

(ii) knowingly possesses or uses illegal drugs, or sells or solicits the sale of a controlled substance, while at school, on school premises, or at a school function under the jurisdiction of a State or local educational agency; or

(iii) has inflicted serious bodily injury upon another person while at school, on school premises, or at a school function under the jurisdiction of a State or local educational agency.

(H) NOTIFICATION- Not later than the date on which the decision to take disciplinary action is made, the local educational agency shall notify the parents of that decision, and of all procedural safeguards accorded under this section.

(2) DETERMINATION OF SETTING- The interim alternative educational setting in subparagraphs (C) and (G) of paragraph (1) shall be determined by the IEP Team.

(3) APPEAL-

(A) IN GENERAL- The parent of a child with a disability who disagrees with any decision regarding placement, or the manifestation determination under this subsection, or a local educational agency that believes that maintaining the current placement of the child is substantially likely to result in injury to the child or to others, may request a hearing.

(B) AUTHORITY OF HEARING OFFICER-

(i) IN GENERAL- A hearing officer shall hear, and make a determination regarding, an appeal requested under subparagraph (A).

(ii) CHANGE OF PLACEMENT ORDER- In making the determination under clause (i), the hearing officer may order a change in placement of a child with a disability. In such situations, the hearing officer may—

(I) return a child with a disability to the placement from which the child was removed; or

(II) order a change in placement of a child with a disability to an appropriate interim alternative educational setting for not more than 45 school days if the hearing officer determines that maintaining the current placement of such child is substantially likely to result in injury to the child or to others.

(4) PLACEMENT DURING APPEALS- When an appeal under paragraph (3) has been

requested by either the parent or the local educational agency—

(A) the child shall remain in the interim alternative educational setting pending the decision of the hearing officer or until the expiration of the time period provided for in paragraph (1)(C), whichever occurs first, unless the parent and the State or local educational agency agree otherwise; and

(B) the State or local educational agency shall arrange for an expedited hearing, which shall occur within 20 school days of the date the hearing is requested and shall result in a determination within 10 school days after the hearing.

(5) PROTECTIONS FOR CHILDREN NOT YET ELIGIBLE FOR SPECIAL EDUCATION AND RELATED SERVICES-

(A) IN GENERAL- A child who has not been determined to be eligible for special education and related services under this part and who has engaged in behavior that violates a code of student conduct, may assert any of the protections provided for in this part if the local educational agency had knowledge (as determined in accordance with this paragraph) that the child was a child with a disability before the behavior that precipitated the disciplinary action occurred.

(B) BASIS OF KNOWLEDGE- A local educational agency shall be deemed to have knowledge that a child is a child with a disability if, before the behavior that precipitated the disciplinary action occurred—

(i) the parent of the child has expressed concern in writing to supervisory or administrative personnel of the appropriate educational agency, or a teacher of the child, that the child is in need of special education and related services;

(ii) the parent of the child has requested an evaluation of the child pursuant to section 614(a)(1)(B); or

(iii) the teacher of the child, or other personnel of the local educational agency, has expressed specific concerns about a pattern of behavior demonstrated by the child, directly to the director of special education of such agency or to other supervisory personnel of the agency.

(C) EXCEPTION- A local educational agency shall not be deemed to have knowledge that the child is a child with a disability if the parent of the child has not allowed an evaluation of the child pursuant to section 614 or has refused services under this part or the child has been evaluated and it was determined that the child was not a child with a disability under this part.

(D) CONDITIONS THAT APPLY IF NO BASIS OF KNOWLEDGE-

(i) IN GENERAL- If a local educational agency does not have knowledge that a child is a child with a disability (in accordance with subparagraph (B) or (C)) prior to taking disciplinary measures against the child, the child may be subjected to disciplinary measures applied to children without disabilities who engaged in comparable behaviors consistent with clause (ii).

(ii) LIMITATIONS- If a request is made for an evaluation of a child during the time period in which the child is subjected to disciplinary measures under this subsection, the evaluation shall be conducted in an expedited manner. If the child is determined to be a child with a disability, taking into consideration information from the evaluation conducted by the agency and information provided by the parents, the agency shall provide special education and related services in accordance with this part, except that, pending the results of the evaluation, the child shall remain in the educational placement determined by school authorities.

(6) REFERRAL TO AND ACTION BY LAW ENFORCEMENT AND JUDICIAL AUTHORITIES-

(A) RULE OF CONSTRUCTION- Nothing in this part shall be construed to prohibit an agency from reporting a crime committed by a child with a disability to appropriate authorities or to prevent State law enforcement and judicial authorities from exercising their responsibilities with regard to the application of Federal and State law to crimes committed by a child with a disability.

(B) TRANSMITTAL OF RECORDS- An agency reporting a crime committed by a child with a disability shall ensure that copies of the special education and disciplinary records of the child are transmitted for consideration by the appropriate authorities to whom the agency reports the crime.

(7) DEFINITIONS- In this subsection:

(A) CONTROLLED SUBSTANCE- The term 'controlled substance' means a drug or other substance identified under schedule I, II, III, IV, or V in section 202(c) of the Controlled Substances Act (21 U.S.C. 812(c)).

(B) ILLEGAL DRUG- The term 'illegal drug' means a controlled substance but does not include a controlled substance that is legally possessed or used under the supervision of a licensed health-care professional or that is legally possessed or used under any other authority under that Act or under any other provision of Federal law.

(C) WEAPON- The term 'weapon' has the

meaning given the term 'dangerous weapon' under section 930(g)(2) of title 18, United States Code.

(D) SERIOUS BODILY INJURY- The term 'serious bodily injury' has the meaning given the term 'serious bodily injury' under paragraph (3) of subsection (h) of section 1365 of title 18, United States Code.

(l) RULE OF CONSTRUCTION- Nothing in this title shall be construed to restrict or limit the rights, procedures, and remedies available under the Constitution, the Americans with Disabilities Act of 1990, title V of the Rehabilitation Act of 1973, or other Federal laws protecting the rights of children with disabilities, except that before the filing of a civil action under such laws seeking relief that is also available under this part, the procedures under subsections (f) and (g) shall be exhausted to the same extent as would be required had the action been brought under this part.

(m) TRANSFER OF PARENTAL RIGHTS AT AGE OF MAJORITY-

(1) IN GENERAL- A State that receives amounts from a grant under this part may provide that, when a child with a disability reaches the age of majority under State law (except for a child with a disability who has been determined to be incompetent under State law)—

(A) the agency shall provide any notice required by this section to both the individual and the parents;

(B) all other rights accorded to parents under this part transfer to the child;

(C) the agency shall notify the individual and the parents of the transfer of rights; and

(D) all rights accorded to parents under this part transfer to children who are incarcerated in an adult or juvenile Federal, State, or local correctional institution.

(2) SPECIAL RULE- If, under State law, a child with a disability who has reached the age of majority under State law, who has not been determined to be incompetent, but who is determined not to have the ability to provide informed consent with respect to the educational program of the child, the State shall establish procedures for appointing the parent of the child, or if the parent is not available, another appropriate individual, to represent the educational interests of the child throughout the period of eligibility of the child under this part.

(n) ELECTRONIC MAIL- A parent of a child with a disability may elect to receive notices required under this section by an electronic mail (e-mail) communication, if the agency makes such option available.

(o) SEPARATE COMPLAINT- Nothing in this section shall be construed to preclude a parent from filing a separate due process complaint on an issue separate from a due process complaint already filed.

SEC. 616. MONITORING, TECHNICAL ASSISTANCE, AND ENFORCEMENT.

(a) FEDERAL AND STATE MONITORING-

(1) IN GENERAL- The Secretary shall—

(A) monitor implementation of this part through—

(i) oversight of the exercise of general supervision by the States, as required in section 612(a)(11); and

(ii) the State performance plans, described in subsection (b);

(B) enforce this part in accordance with subsection (e); and

(C) require States to—

(i) monitor implementation of this part by local educational agencies; and

(ii) enforce this part in accordance with paragraph (3) and subsection (e).

(2) FOCUSED MONITORING- The primary focus of Federal and State monitoring activities described in paragraph (1) shall be on—

(A) improving educational results and functional outcomes for all children with disabilities; and

(B) ensuring that States meet the program requirements under this part, with a particular emphasis on those requirements that are most closely related to improving educational results for children with disabilities.

(3) MONITORING PRIORITIES- The Secretary shall monitor the States, and shall require each State to monitor the local educational agencies located in the State (except the State exercise of general supervisory responsibility), using quantifiable indicators in each of the following priority areas, and using such qualitative indicators as are needed to adequately measure performance in the following priority areas:

(A) Provision of a free appropriate public education in the least restrictive environment.

(B) State exercise of general supervisory authority, including child find, effective monitoring, the use of resolution sessions, mediation, voluntary binding arbitration, and a system of transition services as defined in sections 602(34) and 637(a)(9).

(C) Disproportionate representation of racial and ethnic groups in special education and related services, to the extent the representation is the result of inappropriate identification.

(4) PERMISSIVE AREAS OF REVIEW- The Secretary shall consider other relevant information and data, including data provided by States under section 618.

(b) STATE PERFORMANCE PLANS-

(1) PLAN-

(A) IN GENERAL- Not later than 1 year after the date of enactment of the Individuals with Disabilities Education Improvement Act of 2004, each State shall have in place a performance plan that evaluates that State's efforts to implement the requirements and purposes of this part and describes how the State will improve such implementation.

(B) SUBMISSION FOR APPROVAL- Each State shall submit the State's performance plan to the Secretary for approval in accordance with the approval process described in subsection (c).

(C) REVIEW- Each State shall review its State performance plan at least once every 6 years and submit any amendments to the Secretary.

(2) TARGETS-

(A) IN GENERAL- As a part of the State performance plan described under paragraph (1), each State shall establish measurable and rigorous targets for the indicators established under the priority areas described in subsection (a)(3).

(B) DATA COLLECTION-

(i) IN GENERAL- Each State shall collect valid and reliable information as needed to report annually to the Secretary on the priority areas described in subsection (a)(3).

(ii) RULE OF CONSTRUCTION- Nothing in this title shall be construed to authorize the development of a nationwide database of personally identifiable information on individuals involved in studies or other collections of data under this part.

(C) PUBLIC REPORTING AND PRIVACY-

(i) IN GENERAL- The State shall use the targets established in the plan and priority areas described in subsection (a)(3) to analyze the performance of each local educational agency in the State in implementing this part.

(ii) REPORT-

(I) PUBLIC REPORT- The State shall report annually to the public on the performance of each local educational agency located in the State on the targets in the State's performance plan. The State shall make the State's performance plan available through public means, including by posting on the website

of the State educational agency, distribution to the media, and distribution through public agencies.

(II) STATE PERFORMANCE REPORT- The State shall report annually to the Secretary on the performance of the State under the State's performance plan.

(iii) PRIVACY- The State shall not report to the public or the Secretary any information on performance that would result in the disclosure of personally identifiable information about individual children or where the available data is insufficient to yield statistically reliable information.

(c) APPROVAL PROCESS-

(1) DEEMED APPROVAL- The Secretary shall review (including the specific provisions described in subsection (b)) each performance plan submitted by a State pursuant to subsection (b)(1)(B) and the plan shall be deemed to be approved by the Secretary unless the Secretary makes a written determination, prior to the expiration of the 120-day period beginning on the date on which the Secretary received the plan, that the plan does not meet the requirements of this section, including the specific provisions described in subsection (b).

(2) DISAPPROVAL- The Secretary shall not finally disapprove a performance plan, except after giving the State notice and an opportunity for a hearing.

(3) NOTIFICATION- If the Secretary finds that the plan does not meet the requirements, in whole or in part, of this section, the Secretary shall—

(A) give the State notice and an opportunity for a hearing; and

(B) notify the State of the finding, and in such notification shall—

(i) cite the specific provisions in the plan that do not meet the requirements; and

(ii) request additional information, only as to the provisions not meeting the requirements, needed for the plan to meet the requirements of this section.

(4) RESPONSE- If the State responds to the Secretary's notification described in paragraph (3)(B) during the 30-day period beginning on the date on which the State received the notification, and resubmits the plan with the requested information described in paragraph (3)(B)(ii), the Secretary shall approve or disapprove such plan prior to the later of—

(A) the expiration of the 30-day period beginning on the date on which the plan is resubmitted; or

(B) the expiration of the 120-day period described in paragraph (1).

(5) FAILURE TO RESPOND- If the State does not respond to the Secretary's notification described in paragraph (3)(B) during the 30-day period beginning on the date on which the State received the notification, such plan shall be deemed to be disapproved.

(d) SECRETARY'S REVIEW AND DETERMINATION-

(1) REVIEW- The Secretary shall annually review the State performance report submitted pursuant to subsection (b)(2)(C)(ii)(II) in accordance with this section.

(2) DETERMINATION-

(A) IN GENERAL- Based on the information provided by the State in the State performance report, information obtained through monitoring visits, and any other public information made available, the Secretary shall determine if the State—

(i) meets the requirements and purposes of this part;

(ii) needs assistance in implementing the requirements of this part;

(iii) needs intervention in implementing the requirements of this part; or

(iv) needs substantial intervention in implementing the requirements of this part.

(B) NOTICE AND OPPORTUNITY FOR A HEARING- For determinations made under clause (iii) or (iv) of subparagraph (A), the Secretary shall provide reasonable notice and an opportunity for a hearing on such determination.

(e) ENFORCEMENT-

(1) NEEDS ASSISTANCE- If the Secretary determines, for 2 consecutive years, that a State needs assistance under subsection (d)(2)(A)(ii) in implementing the requirements of this part, the Secretary shall take 1 or more of the following actions:

(A) Advise the State of available sources of technical assistance that may help the State address the areas in which the State needs assistance, which may include assistance from the Office of Special Education Programs, other offices of the Department of Education, other Federal agencies, technical assistance providers approved by the Secretary, and other federally funded nonprofit agencies, and require the State to work with appropriate entities. Such technical assistance may include—

(i) the provision of advice by experts to address the areas in which the State needs assistance, including explicit plans for addressing the area for concern within a specified period of time;

(ii) assistance in identifying and implementing professional development, instructional strategies, and methods of instruction that are based on scientifically based research;

(iii) designating and using distinguished superintendents, principals, special education administrators, special education teachers, and other teachers to provide advice, technical assistance, and support; and

(iv) devising additional approaches to providing technical assistance, such as collaborating with institutions of higher education, educational service agencies, national centers of technical assistance supported under part D, and private providers of scientifically based technical assistance.

(B) Direct the use of State-level funds under section 611(e) on the area or areas in which the State needs assistance.

(C) Identify the State as a high-risk grantee and impose special conditions on the State's grant under this part.

(2) NEEDS INTERVENTION- If the Secretary determines, for 3 or more consecutive years, that a State needs intervention under subsection (d)(2)(A)(iii) in implementing the requirements of this part, the following shall apply:

(A) The Secretary may take any of the actions described in paragraph (1).

(B) The Secretary shall take 1 or more of the following actions:

(i) Require the State to prepare a corrective action plan or improvement plan if the Secretary determines that the State should be able to correct the problem within 1 year.

(ii) Require the State to enter into a compliance agreement under section 457 of the General Education Provisions Act, if the Secretary has reason to believe that the State cannot correct the problem within 1 year.

(iii) For each year of the determination, withhold not less than 20 percent and not more than 50 percent of the State's funds under section 611(e), until the Secretary determines the State has sufficiently addressed the areas in which the State needs intervention.

(iv) Seek to recover funds under section 452 of the General Education Provisions Act.

(v) Withhold, in whole or in part, any further payments to the State under this part pursuant to paragraph (5).

(vi) Refer the matter for appropriate enforcement action, which may include referral to the Department of Justice.

(3) NEEDS SUBSTANTIAL INTERVENTION- Notwithstanding paragraph (1) or (2), at any time that the Secretary determines that a State needs substantial

intervention in implementing the requirements of this part or that there is a substantial failure to comply with any condition of a State educational agency's or local educational agency's eligibility under this part, the Secretary shall take 1 or more of the following actions:

(A) Recover funds under section 452 of the General Education Provisions Act.

(B) Withhold, in whole or in part, any further payments to the State under this part.

(C) Refer the case to the Office of the Inspector General at the Department of Education.

(D) Refer the matter for appropriate enforcement action, which may include referral to the Department of Justice.

(4) OPPORTUNITY FOR HEARING-

(A) WITHHOLDING FUNDS- Prior to withholding any funds under this section, the Secretary shall provide reasonable notice and an opportunity for a hearing to the State educational agency involved.

(B) SUSPENSION- Pending the outcome of any hearing to withhold payments under subsection (b), the Secretary may suspend payments to a recipient, suspend the authority of the recipient to obligate funds under this part, or both, after such recipient has been given reasonable notice and an opportunity to show cause why future payments or authority to obligate funds under this part should not be suspended.

(5) REPORT TO CONGRESS- The Secretary shall report to the Committee on Education and the Workforce of the House of Representatives and the Committee on Health, Education, Labor, and Pensions of the Senate within 30 days of taking enforcement action pursuant to paragraph (1), (2), or (3), on the specific action taken and the reasons why enforcement action was taken.

(6) NATURE OF WITHHOLDING-

(A) LIMITATION- If the Secretary withholds further payments pursuant to paragraph (2) or (3), the Secretary may determine—

(i) that such withholding will be limited to programs or projects, or portions of programs or projects, that affected the Secretary's determination under subsection (d)(2); or

(ii) that the State educational agency shall not make further payments under this part to specified State agencies or local educational agencies that caused or were involved in the Secretary's determination under subsection (d)(2).

(B) WITHHOLDING UNTIL RECTIFIED- Until the Secretary is satisfied that the condition that caused the initial withholding has been substantially rectified—

(i) payments to the State under this part shall be withheld in whole or in part; and

(ii) payments by the State educational agency under this part shall be limited to State agencies and local educational agencies whose actions did not cause or were not involved in the Secretary's determination under subsection (d)(2), as the case may be.

(7) PUBLIC ATTENTION- Any State that has received notice under subsection (d) (2) shall, by means of a public notice, take such measures as may be necessary to bring the pendency of an action pursuant to this subsection to the attention of the public within the State.

(8) JUDICIAL REVIEW-

(A) IN GENERAL- If any State is dissatisfied with the Secretary's action with respect to the eligibility of the State under section 612, such State may, not later than 60 days after notice of such action, file with the United States court of appeals for the circuit in which such State is located a petition for review of that action. A copy of the petition shall be transmitted by the clerk of the court to the Secretary. The Secretary thereupon shall file in the court the record of the proceedings upon which the Secretary's action was based, as provided in section 2112 of title 28, United States Code.

(B) JURISDICTION; REVIEW BY UNITED STATES SUPREME COURT- Upon the filing of such petition, the court shall have jurisdiction to affirm the action of the Secretary or to set it aside, in whole or in part. The judgment of the court shall be subject to review by the Supreme Court of the United States upon certiorari or certification as provided in section 1254 of title 28, United States Code.

(C) STANDARD OF REVIEW- The findings of fact by the Secretary, if supported by substantial evidence, shall be conclusive, but the court, for good cause shown, may remand the case to the Secretary to take further evidence, and the Secretary may thereupon make new or modified findings of fact and may modify the Secretary's previous action, and shall file in the court the record of the further proceedings. Such new or modified findings of fact shall be conclusive if supported by substantial evidence.

(f) STATE ENFORCEMENT- If a State educational agency determines that a local educational agency is not meeting the requirements of this part, including the targets in the State's performance plan, the State educational agency shall prohibit the local educational agency from reducing the local educational agency's maintenance of effort under section 613(a)(2)(C) for any fiscal year.

(g) RULE OF CONSTRUCTION- Nothing in this section shall be construed to restrict the Secretary from utilizing any authority under the General Education Provisions Act to monitor and enforce the requirements of this title.

(h) DIVIDED STATE AGENCY RESPONSIBILITY- For purposes of this section, where responsibility for ensuring that the requirements of this part are met with respect to children with disabilities who are convicted as adults under State law and incarcerated in adult prisons is assigned to a public agency other than the State educational agency pursuant to section 612(a)(11)(C), the Secretary, in instances where the Secretary finds that the failure to comply substantially with the provisions of this part are related to a failure by the public agency, shall take appropriate corrective action to ensure compliance with this part, except that—

(1) any reduction or withholding of payments to the State shall be proportionate to the total funds allotted under section 611 to the State as the number of eligible children with disabilities in adult prisons under the supervision of the other public agency is proportionate to the number of eligible individuals with disabilities in the State under the supervision of the State educational agency; and

(2) any withholding of funds under paragraph (1) shall be limited to the specific agency responsible for the failure to comply with this part.

(i) DATA CAPACITY AND TECHNICAL ASSISTANCE REVIEW- The Secretary shall—

(1) review the data collection and analysis capacity of States to ensure that data and information determined necessary for implementation of this section is collected, analyzed, and accurately reported to the Secretary; and

(2) provide technical assistance (from funds reserved under section 611(c)), where needed, to improve the capacity of States to meet the data collection requirements.

SEC. 617. ADMINISTRATION.

(a) RESPONSIBILITIES OF SECRETARY- The Secretary shall—

(1) cooperate with, and (directly or by grant or contract) furnish technical assistance necessary to, a State in matters relating to—

(A) the education of children with disabilities; and

(B) carrying out this part; and

(2) provide short-term training programs and institutes.

(b) PROHIBITION AGAINST FEDERAL MANDATES, DIRECTION, OR CONTROL- Nothing in this title shall be construed to authorize an officer or employee of the Federal Government to mandate, direct, or control a State, local educational agency, or school's specific instructional content, academic achievement standards and assessments, curriculum, or program of instruction.

(c) CONFIDENTIALITY- The Secretary shall take appropriate action, in accordance with section 444 of the General Education Provisions Act, to ensure the protection of the confidentiality of any personally identifiable data, information, and records collected or maintained by the Secretary and by State educational agencies and local educational agencies pursuant to this part.

(d) PERSONNEL- The Secretary is authorized to hire qualified personnel necessary to carry out the Secretary's duties under subsection (a), under section 618, and under subpart 4 of part D, without regard to the provisions of title 5, United States Code, relating to appointments in the competitive service and without regard to chapter 51 and subchapter III of chapter 53 of such title relating to classification and general schedule pay rates, except that no more than 20 such personnel shall be employed at any time.

(e) MODEL FORMS- Not later than the date that the Secretary publishes final regulations under this title, to implement amendments made by the Individuals with Disabilities Education Improvement Act of 2004, the Secretary shall publish and disseminate widely to States, local educational agencies, and parent and community training and information centers—

(1) a model IEP form;

(2) a model individualized family service plan (IFSP) form;

(3) a model form of the notice of procedural safeguards described in section 615(d); and

(4) a model form of the prior written notice described in subsections (b)(3) and (c)(1) of section 615 that is consistent with the requirements of this part and is sufficient to meet such requirements.

SEC. 618. PROGRAM INFORMATION.

(a) IN GENERAL- Each State that receives assistance under this part, and the Secretary of the Interior, shall provide data each year to the

Secretary of Education and the public on the following:

(1)(A) The number and percentage of children with disabilities, by race, ethnicity, limited English proficiency status, gender, and disability category, who are in each of the following separate categories:

(i) Receiving a free appropriate public education.

(ii) Participating in regular education.

(iii) In separate classes, separate schools or facilities, or public or private residential facilities.

(iv) For each year of age from age 14 through 21, stopped receiving special education and related services because of program completion (including graduation with a regular secondary school diploma), or other reasons, and the reasons why those children stopped receiving special education and related services.

(v)(I) Removed to an interim alternative educational setting under section 615(k)(1).

(II) The acts or items precipitating those removals.

(III) The number of children with disabilities who are subject to long-term suspensions or expulsions.

(B) The number and percentage of children with disabilities, by race, gender, and ethnicity, who are receiving early intervention services.

(C) The number and percentage of children with disabilities, by race, gender, and ethnicity, who, from birth through age 2, stopped receiving early intervention services because of program completion or for other reasons.

(D) The incidence and duration of disciplinary actions by race, ethnicity, limited English proficiency status, gender, and disability category, of children with disabilities, including suspensions of 1 day or more.

(E) The number and percentage of children with disabilities who are removed to alternative educational settings or expelled as compared to children without disabilities who are removed to alternative educational settings or expelled.

(F) The number of due process complaints filed under section 615 and the number of hearings conducted.

(G) The number of hearings requested under section 615(k) and the number of changes in placements ordered as a result of those hearings.

(H) The number of mediations held and the number of settlement agreements reached through such mediations.

(2) The number and percentage of infants and toddlers, by race, and ethnicity, who are at risk of having substantial developmental delays (as defined in section 632), and who are receiving early intervention services under part C.

(3) Any other information that may be required by the Secretary.

(b) DATA REPORTING-

(1) PROTECTION OF IDENTIFIABLE DATA- The data described in subsection (a) shall be publicly reported by each State in a manner that does not result in the disclosure of data identifiable to individual children.

(2) SAMPLING- The Secretary may permit States and the Secretary of the Interior to obtain the data described in subsection (a) through sampling.

(c) TECHNICAL ASSISTANCE- The Secretary may provide technical assistance to States to ensure compliance with the data collection and reporting requirements under this title.

(d) DISPROPORTIONALITY-

(1) IN GENERAL- Each State that receives assistance under this part, and the Secretary of the Interior, shall provide for the collection and examination of data to determine if significant disproportionality based on race and ethnicity is occurring in the State and the local educational agencies of the State with respect to—

(A) the identification of children as children with disabilities, including the identification of children as children with disabilities in accordance with a particular impairment described in section 602(3);

(B) the placement in particular educational settings of such children; and

(C) the incidence, duration, and type of disciplinary actions, including suspensions and expulsions.

(2) REVIEW AND REVISION OF POLICIES, PRACTICES, AND PROCEDURES- In the case of a determination of significant disproportionality with respect to the identification of children as children with disabilities, or the placement in particular educational settings of such children, in accordance with paragraph (1), the State or the Secretary of the Interior, as the case may be, shall—

(A) provide for the review and, if appropriate, revision of the policies, procedures, and practices used in such identification or placement to ensure that such policies, procedures, and practices comply with the requirements of this title;

(B) require any local educational agency identified under paragraph (1) to reserve the maximum amount of funds under section 613(f) to provide comprehensive coordinated early intervening services to serve children in the local educational agency, particularly children in those groups that were significantly overidentified under paragraph (1); and

(C) require the local educational agency to publicly report on the revision of policies, practices, and procedures described under subparagraph (A).

SEC. 619. PRESCHOOL GRANTS.

(a) IN GENERAL- The Secretary shall provide grants under this section to assist States to provide special education and related services, in accordance with this part—

(1) to children with disabilities aged 3 through 5, inclusive; and

(2) at the State's discretion, to 2-year-old children with disabilities who will turn 3 during the school year.

(b) ELIGIBILITY- A State shall be eligible for a grant under this section if such State—

(1) is eligible under section 612 to receive a grant under this part; and

(2) makes a free appropriate public education available to all children with disabilities, aged 3 through 5, residing in the State.

(c) ALLOCATIONS TO STATES-

(1) IN GENERAL- The Secretary shall allocate the amount made available to carry out this section for a fiscal year among the States in accordance with paragraph (2) or (3), as the case may be.

(2) INCREASE IN FUNDS- If the amount available for allocations to States under paragraph (1) for a fiscal year is equal to or greater than the amount allocated to the States under this section for the preceding fiscal year, those allocations shall be calculated as follows:

(A) ALLOCATION-

(i) IN GENERAL- Except as provided in subparagraph (B), the Secretary shall—

(I) allocate to each State the amount the State received under this section for fiscal year 1997;

(II) allocate 85 percent of any remaining funds to States on the basis of the States' relative populations of children aged 3 through 5; and

(III) allocate 15 percent of those remaining funds to States on the basis of the States' relative populations of all children aged 3 through 5 who are living in poverty.

(ii) DATA- For the purpose of making grants under this paragraph, the Secretary shall use the most recent population data, including data on children living in poverty, that are available and satisfactory to the Secretary.

(B) LIMITATIONS- Notwithstanding subparagraph (A), allocations under this paragraph shall be subject to the following:

(i) PRECEDING YEARS- No State's allocation shall be less than its allocation under this section for the preceding fiscal year.

(ii) MINIMUM- No State's allocation shall be less than the greatest of—

(I) the sum of—

(aa) the amount the State received under this section for fiscal year 1997; and

(bb) 1/3 of 1 percent of the amount by which the amount appropriated under subsection (j) for the fiscal year exceeds the amount appropriated for this section for fiscal year 1997;

(II) the sum of—

(aa) the amount the State received under this section for the preceding fiscal year; and

(bb) that amount multiplied by the percentage by which the increase in the funds appropriated under this section from the preceding fiscal year exceeds 1.5 percent; or

(III) the sum of—

(aa) the amount the State received under this section for the preceding fiscal year; and

(bb) that amount multiplied by 90 percent of the percentage increase in the amount appropriated under this section from the preceding fiscal year.

(iii) MAXIMUM- Notwithstanding clause (ii), no State's allocation under this paragraph shall exceed the sum of—

(I) the amount the State received under this section for the preceding fiscal year; and

(II) that amount multiplied by the sum of 1.5 percent and the percentage increase in the amount appropriated under this section from the preceding fiscal year.

(C) RATABLE REDUCTIONS- If the amount available for allocations under this paragraph is insufficient to pay those allocations in full, those allocations shall be ratably reduced, subject to subparagraph (B)(i).

(3) DECREASE IN FUNDS- If the amount available for allocations to States under paragraph (1) for a fiscal year is less than the amount allocated to the States under this section for the preceding fiscal year, those allocations shall be calculated as follows:

(A) ALLOCATIONS- If the amount available for allocations is greater than the amount allocated to the States for fiscal year 1997, each State shall be allocated the sum of—

(i) the amount the State received under this section for fiscal year 1997; and

(ii) an amount that bears the same relation to any remaining funds as the increase the State received under this section for the preceding fiscal year over fiscal year 1997 bears to the total of all such increases for all States.

(B) RATABLE REDUCTIONS- If the amount available for allocations is equal to or less than the amount allocated to the States for fiscal year 1997, each State shall be allocated the amount the State received for fiscal year 1997, ratably reduced, if necessary.

(d) RESERVATION FOR STATE ACTIVITIES-

(1) IN GENERAL- Each State may reserve not more than the amount described in paragraph (2) for administration and other State-level activities in accordance with subsections (e) and (f).

(2) AMOUNT DESCRIBED- For each fiscal year, the Secretary shall determine and report to the State educational agency an amount that is 25 percent of the amount the State received under this section for fiscal year 1997, cumulatively adjusted by the Secretary for each succeeding fiscal year by the lesser of—

(A) the percentage increase, if any, from the preceding fiscal year in the State's allocation under this section; or

(B) the percentage increase, if any, from the preceding fiscal year in the Consumer Price Index For All Urban Consumers published by the Bureau of Labor Statistics of the Department of Labor.

(e) STATE ADMINISTRATION-

(1) IN GENERAL- For the purpose of administering this section (including the coordination of activities under this part with, and providing technical assistance to, other programs that provide services to children with disabilities) a State may use not more than 20 percent of the maximum amount the State may reserve under subsection (d) for any fiscal year.

(2) ADMINISTRATION OF PART C- Funds described in paragraph (1) may also be used for the administration of part C.

(f) OTHER STATE-LEVEL ACTIVITIES- Each State shall use any funds the State reserves under subsection (d) and does not use for administration under subsection (e)—

(1) for support services (including establishing and implementing the mediation process required by section 615(e)), which may benefit children with disabilities younger than 3 or older than 5 as long as those services also benefit children with disabilities aged 3 through 5;

(2) for direct services for children eligible for services under this section;

(3) for activities at the State and local levels to meet the performance goals established by the State under section 612(a)(15);

(4) to supplement other funds used to develop and implement a statewide coordinated services system designed to improve results for children and families, including children with disabilities and their families, but not more than 1 percent of the amount received by the State under this section for a fiscal year;

(5) to provide early intervention services (which shall include an educational component that promotes school readiness and incorporates preliteracy, language, and numeracy skills) in accordance with part C to children with disabilities who are eligible for services under this section and who previously received services under part C until such children enter, or are eligible under State law to enter, kindergarten; or

(6) at the State's discretion, to continue service coordination or case management for families who receive services under part C.

(g) SUBGRANTS TO LOCAL EDUCATIONAL AGENCIES-

(1) SUBGRANTS REQUIRED- Each State that receives a grant under this section for any fiscal year shall distribute all of the grant funds that the State does not reserve under subsection (d) to local educational agencies in the State that have established their eligibility under section 613, as follows:

(A) BASE PAYMENTS- The State shall first award each local educational agency described in paragraph (1) the amount that agency would have received under this section for fiscal year 1997 if the State had distributed 75 percent of its grant for that year under section 619(c)(3), as such section was then in effect.

(B) ALLOCATION OF REMAINING FUNDS- After making allocations under subparagraph (A), the State shall—

(i) allocate 85 percent of any remaining funds to those local educational agencies on the basis of the relative numbers of children enrolled in public and private elementary schools and secondary schools within the local educational agency's jurisdiction; and

(ii) allocate 15 percent of those remaining funds to those local educational agencies in accordance with their relative numbers of children living in poverty, as determined by the State educational agency.

(2) REALLOCATION OF FUNDS- If a State educational agency determines that a local educational agency is adequately providing a free appropriate public education to all children with disabilities aged 3 through 5 residing in the area served by the local educational agency with State and local funds, the State educational agency may reallocate any portion of the funds under this section

that are not needed by that local educational agency to provide a free appropriate public education to other local educational agencies in the State that are not adequately providing special education and related services to all children with disabilities aged 3 through 5 residing in the areas the other local educational agencies serve.

(h) PART C INAPPLICABLE- Part C does not apply to any child with a disability receiving a free appropriate public education, in accordance with this part, with funds received under this section.

(i) STATE DEFINED- In this section, the term 'State' means each of the 50 States, the District of Columbia, and the Commonwealth of Puerto Rico.

(j)   AUTHORIZATION   OF APPROPRIATIONS- There are authorized to be appropriated to carry out this section such sums as may be necessary.

PART C—INFANTS AND TODDLERS WITH DISABILITIES

SEC. 631. FINDINGS AND POLICY.

(a) FINDINGS- Congress finds that there is an urgent and substantial need—

(1) to enhance the development of infants and toddlers with disabilities, to minimize their potential for developmental delay, and to recognize the significant brain development that occurs during a child's first 3 years of life;

(2) to reduce the educational costs to our society, including our Nation's schools, by minimizing the need for special education and related services after infants and toddlers with disabilities reach school age;

(3) to maximize the potential for individuals with disabilities to live independently in society;

(4) to enhance the capacity of families to meet the special needs of their infants and toddlers with disabilities; and

(5) to enhance the capacity of State and local agencies and service providers to identify, evaluate, and meet the needs of all children, particularly minority, low-income, inner city, and rural children, and infants and toddlers in foster care.

(b) POLICY- It is the policy of the United States to provide financial assistance to States—

(1) to develop and implement a statewide, comprehensive, coordinated, multidisciplinary, interagency system that provides early intervention services for infants and toddlers with disabilities and their families;

(2) to facilitate the coordination of payment for early intervention services from Federal, State, local, and private sources (including public and private insurance coverage);

(3) to enhance State capacity to provide quality early intervention services and expand and improve existing early intervention services being provided to infants and toddlers with disabilities and their families; and

(4) to encourage States to expand opportunities for children under 3 years of age who would be at risk of having substantial developmental delay if they did not receive early intervention services.

SEC. 632. DEFINITIONS.

In this part:

(1) AT-RISK INFANT OR TODDLER- The term 'at-risk infant or toddler' means an individual under 3 years of age who would be at risk of experiencing a substantial developmental delay if early intervention services were not provided to the individual.

(2) COUNCIL- The term 'council' means a State interagency coordinating council established under section 641.

(3) DEVELOPMENTAL DELAY- The term 'developmental delay', when used with respect to an individual residing in a State, has the meaning given such term by the State under section 635(a)(1).

(4) EARLY INTERVENTION SERVICES- The term 'early intervention services' means developmental services that—

(A) are provided under public supervision;

(B) are provided at no cost except where Federal or State law provides for a system of payments by families, including a schedule of sliding fees;

(C) are designed to meet the developmental needs of an infant or toddler with a disability, as identified by the individualized family service plan team, in any 1 or more of the following areas:

(i) physical development;

(ii) cognitive development;

(iii) communication development;

(iv) social or emotional development; or

(v) adaptive development;

(D) meet the standards of the State in which the services are provided, including the requirements of this part;

(E) include—

(i) family training, counseling, and home visits;

(ii) special instruction;

(iii) speech-language pathology and audiology services, and sign language and cued language services;

(iv) occupational therapy;

(v) physical therapy;

(vi) psychological services;

(vii) service coordination services;

(viii) medical services only for diagnostic or evaluation purposes;

(ix) early identification, screening, and assessment services;

(x) health services necessary to enable the infant or toddler to benefit from the other early intervention services;

(xi) social work services;

(xii) vision services;

(xiii) assistive technology devices and assistive technology services; and

(xiv) transportation and related costs that are necessary to enable an infant or toddler and the infant's or toddler's family to receive another service described in this paragraph;

(F) are provided by qualified personnel, including—

(i) special educators;

(ii) speech-language pathologists and audiologists;

(iii) occupational therapists;

(iv) physical therapists;

(v) psychologists;

(vi) social workers;

(vii) nurses;

(viii) registered dietitians;

(ix) family therapists;

(x) vision specialists, including ophthalmologists and optometrists;

(xi) orientation and mobility specialists; and

(xii) pediatricians and other physicians;

(G) to the maximum extent appropriate, are provided in natural environments, including the home, and community settings in which children without disabilities participate; and

(H) are provided in conformity with an individualized family service plan adopted in accordance with section 636.

(5) INFANT OR TODDLER WITH A DISABILITY- The term 'infant or toddler with a disability'—

(A) means an individual under 3 years of age who needs early intervention services because the individual—

(i) is experiencing developmental delays, as measured by appropriate diagnostic instruments and procedures in 1 or more of the areas of cognitive development, physical development, communication development, social or emotional development, and adaptive development; or

(ii) has a diagnosed physical or mental condition that has a high probability of resulting in developmental delay; and

(B) may also include, at a State's discretion—

(i) at-risk infants and toddlers; and

(ii) children with disabilities who are eligible for services under section 619 and who previously received services under this part until such children enter, or are eligible under State law to enter, kindergarten or elementary school, as appropriate, provided that any programs under this part serving such children shall include—

(I) an educational component that promotes school readiness and incorporates pre-literacy, language, and numeracy skills; and

(II) a written notification to parents of their rights and responsibilities in determining whether their child will continue to receive services under this part or participate in preschool programs under section 619.

SEC. 633. GENERAL AUTHORITY.

The Secretary shall, in accordance with this part, make grants to States (from their allotments under section 643) to assist each State to maintain and implement a statewide, comprehensive, coordinated, multidisciplinary, interagency system to provide early intervention services for infants and toddlers with disabilities and their families.

SEC. 634. ELIGIBILITY.

In order to be eligible for a grant under section 633, a State shall provide assurances to the Secretary that the State—

(1) has adopted a policy that appropriate early intervention services are available to all infants and toddlers with disabilities in the State and their families, including Indian infants and toddlers with disabilities and their families residing on a reservation geographically located in the State, infants and toddlers with disabilities who are homeless children and their families, and infants and toddlers with disabilities who are wards of the State; and

(2) has in effect a statewide system that meets the requirements of section 635.

SEC. 635. REQUIREMENTS FOR STATEWIDE SYSTEM.

(a) IN GENERAL- A statewide system described in section 633 shall include, at a minimum, the following components:

(1) A rigorous definition of the term 'developmental delay' that will be used by the State in carrying out programs under this part in order to appropriately identify infants and toddlers with disabilities that are in need of services under this part.

(2) A State policy that is in effect and that ensures that appropriate early intervention services based on scientifically based research, to the extent practicable, are available to all infants and toddlers with disabilities and their families, including Indian infants and toddlers with disabilities and their families residing on a reservation geographically located in the State and infants and toddlers with disabilities who are homeless children and their families.

(3) A timely, comprehensive, multidisciplinary evaluation of the functioning of each infant or toddler with a disability in the State, and a family-directed identification of the needs of each family of such an infant or toddler, to assist appropriately in the development of the infant or toddler.

(4) For each infant or toddler with a disability in the State, an individualized family service plan in accordance with section 636, including service coordination services in accordance with such service plan.

(5) A comprehensive child find system, consistent with part B, including a system for making referrals to service providers that includes timelines and provides for participation by primary referral sources and that ensures rigorous standards for appropriately identifying infants and toddlers with disabilities for services under this part that will reduce the need for future services.

(6) A public awareness program focusing on early identification of infants and toddlers with disabilities, including the preparation and dissemination by the lead agency designated or established under paragraph (10) to all primary referral sources, especially hospitals and physicians, of information to be given to parents, especially to inform parents with premature infants, or infants with other physical risk factors associated with learning or developmental complications, on the availability of early intervention services under this part and of services under section 619, and procedures for assisting such sources in disseminating such information to parents of infants and toddlers with disabilities.

(7) A central directory that includes information on early intervention services, resources, and experts available in the State and research and demonstration projects being conducted in the State.

(8) A comprehensive system of personnel development, including the training of paraprofessionals and the training of primary referral sources with respect to the basic components of early intervention services available in the State that—

(A) shall include—

(i) implementing innovative strategies and activities for the recruitment and retention of early education service providers;

(ii) promoting the preparation of early intervention providers who are fully and appropriately qualified to provide early intervention services under this part; and

(iii) training personnel to coordinate transition services for infants and toddlers served under this part from a program providing early intervention services under this part and under part B (other than section 619), to a preschool program receiving funds under section 619, or another appropriate program; and

(B) may include—

(i) training personnel to work in rural and inner-city areas; and

(ii) training personnel in the emotional and social development of young children.

(9) Policies and procedures relating to the establishment and maintenance of qualifications to ensure that personnel necessary to carry out this part are appropriately and adequately prepared and trained, including the establishment and maintenance of qualifications that are consistent with any State-approved or recognized certification, licensing, registration, or other comparable requirements that apply to the area in which such personnel are providing early intervention services, except that nothing in this part (including this paragraph) shall be construed to prohibit the use of paraprofessionals and assistants who are appropriately trained and supervised in accordance with State law, regulation, or written policy, to assist in the provision of early intervention services under this part to infants and toddlers with disabilities.

(10) A single line of responsibility in a lead agency designated or established by the Governor for carrying out—

(A) the general administration and supervision of programs and activities receiving assistance under section 633, and the monitoring of programs and activities used by the State to carry out this part, whether or not such programs or activities are receiving assistance made available under section 633, to ensure that the State complies with this part;

(B) the identification and coordination of all available resources within the State from Federal, State, local, and private sources;

(C) the assignment of financial responsibility in accordance with section 637(a)(2) to the appropriate agencies;

(D) the development of procedures to ensure that services are provided to infants and toddlers with disabilities and their families under this part in a timely manner pending the resolution of any disputes among public agencies or service providers;

(E) the resolution of intra- and interagency disputes; and

(F) the entry into formal interagency agreements that define the financial responsibility of each agency for paying for early intervention services (consistent with State law) and procedures for resolving disputes and that include all additional components necessary to ensure meaningful cooperation and coordination.

(11) A policy pertaining to the contracting or making of other arrangements with service providers to provide early intervention services in the State, consistent with the provisions of this part, including the contents of the application used and the conditions of the contract or other arrangements.

(12) A procedure for securing timely reimbursements of funds used under this part in accordance with section 640(a).

(13) Procedural safeguards with respect to programs under this part, as required by section 639.

(14) A system for compiling data requested by the Secretary under section 618 that relates to this part.

(15) A State interagency coordinating council that meets the requirements of section 641.

(16) Policies and procedures to ensure that, consistent with section 636(d)(5)—

(A) to the maximum extent appropriate, early intervention services are provided in natural environments; and

(B) the provision of early intervention services for any infant or toddler with a disability occurs in a setting other than a natural environment that is most appropriate, as determined by the parent and the individualized family service plan team, only when early intervention cannot be achieved satisfactorily for the infant or toddler in a natural environment.

(b) POLICY- In implementing subsection (a)(9), a State may adopt a policy that includes making ongoing good-faith efforts to recruit and hire appropriately and adequately trained personnel to provide early intervention services to infants and toddlers with disabilities, including, in a geographic area of the State where there is a shortage of such personnel, the most qualified individuals available who are making satisfactory progress toward completing applicable course work necessary to meet the standards described in subsection (a)(9).

(c) Flexibility To Serve Children 3 Years of Age Until Entrance Into Elementary School-

(1) IN GENERAL- A statewide system described in section 633 may include a State policy, developed and implemented jointly by the lead agency and the State educational agency, under which parents of children with disabilities who are eligible for services under section 619 and previously received services under this part, may choose the continuation of early intervention services (which shall include an educational component that promotes school readiness and incorporates preliteracy, language, and numeracy skills) for such children under this part until such children enter, or are eligible under State law to enter, kindergarten.

(2) REQUIREMENTS- If a statewide system includes a State policy described in paragraph (1), the statewide system shall ensure that—

(A) parents of children with disabilities served pursuant to this subsection are provided annual notice that contains—

(i) a description of the rights of such parents to elect to receive services pursuant to this subsection or under part B; and

(ii) an explanation of the differences between services provided pursuant to this subsection and services provided under part B, including—

(I) types of services and the locations at which the services are provided;

(II) applicable procedural safeguards; and

(III) possible costs (including any fees to be charged to families as described in section 632(4)(B)), if any, to parents of infants or toddlers with disabilities;

(B) services provided pursuant to this subsection include an educational component that promotes school readiness and incorporates preliteracy, language, and numeracy skills;

(C) the State policy will not affect the right

of any child served pursuant to this subsection to instead receive a free appropriate public education under part B;

(D) all early intervention services outlined in the child's individualized family service plan under section 636 are continued while any eligibility determination is being made for services under this subsection;

(E) the parents of infants or toddlers with disabilities (as defined in section 632(5)(A)) provide informed written consent to the State, before such infants or toddlers reach 3 years of age, as to whether such parents intend to choose the continuation of early intervention services pursuant to this subsection for such infants or toddlers;

(F) the requirements under section 637(a)(9) shall not apply with respect to a child who is receiving services in accordance with this subsection until not less than 90 days (and at the discretion of the parties to the conference, not more than 9 months) before the time the child will no longer receive those services; and

(G) there will be a referral for evaluation for early intervention services of a child who experiences a substantiated case of trauma due to exposure to family violence (as defined in section 320 of the Family Violence Prevention and Services Act).

(3) REPORTING REQUIREMENT- If a statewide system includes a State policy described in paragraph (1), the State shall submit to the Secretary, in the State's report under section 637(b)(4)(A), a report on the number and percentage of children with disabilities who are eligible for services under section 619 but whose parents choose for such children to continue to receive early intervention services under this part.

(4) AVAILABLE FUNDS- If a statewide system includes a State policy described in paragraph (1), the policy shall describe the funds (including an identification as Federal, State, or local funds) that will be used to ensure that the option described in paragraph (1) is available to eligible children and families who provide the consent described in paragraph (2)(E), including fees (if any) to be charged to families as described in section 632(4)(B).

(5) RULES OF CONSTRUCTION-

(A) SERVICES UNDER PART B- If a statewide system includes a State policy described in paragraph (1), a State that provides services in accordance with this subsection to a child with a disability who is eligible for services under section 619 shall not be required to provide the child with a free appropriate public education under part B for the period of time in which the child is receiving services

under this part.

(B) SERVICES UNDER THIS PART- Nothing in this subsection shall be construed to require a provider of services under this part to provide a child served under this part with a free appropriate public education.

SEC. 636. INDIVIDUALIZED FAMILY SERVICE PLAN.

(a) ASSESSMENT AND PROGRAM DEVELOPMENT- A statewide system described in section 633 shall provide, at a minimum, for each infant or toddler with a disability, and the infant's or toddler's family, to receive—

(1) a multidisciplinary assessment of the unique strengths and needs of the infant or toddler and the identification of services appropriate to meet such needs;

(2) a family-directed assessment of the resources, priorities, and concerns of the family and the identification of the supports and services necessary to enhance the family's capacity to meet the developmental needs of the infant or toddler; and

(3) a written individualized family service plan developed by a multidisciplinary team, including the parents, as required by subsection (e), including a description of the appropriate transition services for the infant or toddler.

(b) PERIODIC REVIEW- The individualized family service plan shall be evaluated once a year and the family shall be provided a review of the plan at 6-month intervals (or more often where appropriate based on infant or toddler and family needs).

(c) PROMPTNESS AFTER ASSESSMENT- The individualized family service plan shall be developed within a reasonable time after the assessment required by subsection (a)(1) is completed. With the parents' consent, early intervention services may commence prior to the completion of the assessment.

(d) CONTENT OF PLAN- The individualized family service plan shall be in writing and contain—

(1) a statement of the infant's or toddler's present levels of physical development, cognitive development, communication development, social or emotional development, and adaptive development, based on objective criteria;

(2) a statement of the family's resources, priorities, and concerns relating to enhancing the development of the family's infant or toddler with a disability;

(3) a statement of the measurable results

or outcomes expected to be achieved for the infant or toddler and the family, including pre-literacy and language skills, as developmentally appropriate for the child, and the criteria, procedures, and timelines used to determine the degree to which progress toward achieving the results or outcomes is being made and whether modifications or revisions of the results or outcomes or services are necessary;

(4) a statement of specific early intervention services based on peer-reviewed research, to the extent practicable, necessary to meet the unique needs of the infant or toddler and the family, including the frequency, intensity, and method of delivering services;

(5) a statement of the natural environments in which early intervention services will appropriately be provided, including a justification of the extent, if any, to which the services will not be provided in a natural environment;

(6) the projected dates for initiation of services and the anticipated length, duration, and frequency of the services;

(7) the identification of the service coordinator from the profession most immediately relevant to the infant's or toddler's or family's needs (or who is otherwise qualified to carry out all applicable responsibilities under this part) who will be responsible for the implementation of the plan and coordination with other agencies and persons, including transition services; and

(8) the steps to be taken to support the transition of the toddler with a disability to preschool or other appropriate services.

(e) PARENTAL CONSENT- The contents of the individualized family service plan shall be fully explained to the parents and informed written consent from the parents shall be obtained prior to the provision of early intervention services described in such plan. If the parents do not provide consent with respect to a particular early intervention service, then only the early intervention services to which consent is obtained shall be provided.

SEC. 637. STATE APPLICATION AND ASSURANCES.

(a) APPLICATION- A State desiring to receive a grant under section 633 shall submit an application to the Secretary at such time and in such manner as the Secretary may reasonably require. The application shall contain—

(1) a designation of the lead agency in the State that will be responsible for the administration of funds provided under section 633;

(2) a certification to the Secretary that the arrangements to establish financial responsibility for services provided under this part pursuant to section 640(b) are current as of the date of submission of the certification;

(3) information demonstrating eligibility of the State under section 634, including—

(A) information demonstrating to the Secretary's satisfaction that the State has in effect the statewide system required by section 633; and

(B) a description of services to be provided to infants and toddlers with disabilities and their families through the system;

(4) if the State provides services to at-risk infants and toddlers through the statewide system, a description of such services;

(5) a description of the uses for which funds will be expended in accordance with this part;

(6) a description of the State policies and procedures that require the referral for early intervention services under this part of a child under the age of 3 who—

(A) is involved in a substantiated case of child abuse or neglect; or

(B) is identified as affected by illegal substance abuse, or withdrawal symptoms resulting from prenatal drug exposure;

(7) a description of the procedure used to ensure that resources are made available under this part for all geographic areas within the State;

(8) a description of State policies and procedures that ensure that, prior to the adoption by the State of any other policy or procedure necessary to meet the requirements of this part, there are public hearings, adequate notice of the hearings, and an opportunity for comment available to the general public, including individuals with disabilities and parents of infants and toddlers with disabilities;

(9) a description of the policies and procedures to be used—

(A) to ensure a smooth transition for toddlers receiving early intervention services under this part (and children receiving those services under section 635(c)) to preschool, school, other appropriate services, or exiting the program, including a description of how—

(i) the families of such toddlers and children will be included in the transition plans required by subparagraph (C); and

(ii) the lead agency designated or established under section 635(a)(10) will—

(I) notify the local educational agency for the area in which such a child resides that the child will shortly reach the age of eligibility for preschool services under part B, as determined in accordance with State law;

(II) in the case of a child who may be eligible for such preschool services, with the approval of the family of the child, convene a conference among the lead agency, the family, and the local educational agency not less than 90 days (and at the discretion of all such parties, not more than 9 months) before the child is eligible for the preschool services, to discuss any such services that the child may receive; and

(III) in the case of a child who may not be eligible for such preschool services, with the approval of the family, make reasonable efforts to convene a conference among the lead agency, the family, and providers of other appropriate services for children who are not eligible for preschool services under part B, to discuss the appropriate services that the child may receive;

(B) to review the child's program options for the period from the child's third birthday through the remainder of the school year; and

(C) to establish a transition plan, including, as appropriate, steps to exit from the program;

(10) a description of State efforts to promote collaboration among Early Head Start programs under section 645A of the Head Start Act, early education and child care programs, and services under part C; and

(11) such other information and assurances as the Secretary may reasonably require.

(b) ASSURANCES- The application described in subsection (a)—

(1) shall provide satisfactory assurance that Federal funds made available under section 643 to the State will be expended in accordance with this part;

(2) shall contain an assurance that the State will comply with the requirements of section 640;

(3) shall provide satisfactory assurance that the control of funds provided under section 643, and title to property derived from those funds, will be in a public agency for the uses and purposes provided in this part and that a public agency will administer such funds and property;

(4) shall provide for—

(A) making such reports in such form and containing such information as the Secretary may require to carry out the Secretary's functions under this part; and

(B) keeping such reports and affording such access to the reports as the Secretary may find necessary to ensure the correctness and verification of those reports and proper disbursement of Federal funds under this part;

(5) provide satisfactory assurance that Federal funds made available under section

643 to the State—

(A) will not be commingled with State funds; and

(B) will be used so as to supplement the level of State and local funds expended for infants and toddlers with disabilities and their families and in no case to supplant those State and local funds;

(6) shall provide satisfactory assurance that such fiscal control and fund accounting procedures will be adopted as may be necessary to ensure proper disbursement of, and accounting for, Federal funds paid under section 643 to the State;

(7) shall provide satisfactory assurance that policies and procedures have been adopted to ensure meaningful involvement of underserved groups, including minority, low-income, homeless, and rural families and children with disabilities who are wards of the State, in the planning and implementation of all the requirements of this part; and

(8) shall contain such other information and assurances as the Secretary may reasonably require by regulation.

(c) STANDARD FOR DISAPPROVAL OF APPLICATION- The Secretary may not disapprove such an application unless the Secretary determines, after notice and opportunity for a hearing, that the application fails to comply with the requirements of this section.

(d) SUBSEQUENT STATE APPLICATION- If a State has on file with the Secretary a policy, procedure, or assurance that demonstrates that the State meets a requirement of this section, including any policy or procedure filed under this part (as in effect before the date of enactment of the Individuals with Disabilities Education Improvement Act of 2004), the Secretary shall consider the State to have met the requirement for purposes of receiving a grant under this part.

(e) MODIFICATION OF APPLICATION- An application submitted by a State in accordance with this section shall remain in effect until the State submits to the Secretary such modifications as the State determines necessary. This section shall apply to a modification of an application to the same extent and in the same manner as this section applies to the original application.

(f) MODIFICATIONS REQUIRED BY THE SECRETARY- The Secretary may require a State to modify its application under this section, but only to the extent necessary to ensure the State's compliance with this part, if—

(1) an amendment is made to this title, or a

Federal regulation issued under this title;

(2) a new interpretation of this title is made by a Federal court or the State's highest court; or

(3) an official finding of noncompliance with Federal law or regulations is made with respect to the State.

SEC. 638. USES OF FUNDS.

In addition to using funds provided under section 633 to maintain and implement the statewide system required by such section, a State may use such funds—

(1) for direct early intervention services for infants and toddlers with disabilities, and their families, under this part that are not otherwise funded through other public or private sources;

(2) to expand and improve on services for infants and toddlers and their families under this part that are otherwise available;

(3) to provide a free appropriate public education, in accordance with part B, to children with disabilities from their third birthday to the beginning of the following school year;

(4) with the written consent of the parents, to continue to provide early intervention services under this part to children with disabilities from their 3rd birthday until such children enter, or are eligible under State law to enter, kindergarten, in lieu of a free appropriate public education provided in accordance with part B; and

(5) in any State that does not provide services for at-risk infants and toddlers under section 637(a)(4), to strengthen the statewide system by initiating, expanding, or improving collaborative efforts related to at-risk infants and toddlers, including establishing linkages with appropriate public or private community-based organizations, services, and personnel for the purposes of—

(A) identifying and evaluating at-risk infants and toddlers;

(B) making referrals of the infants and toddlers identified and evaluated under subparagraph (A); and

(C) conducting periodic follow-up on each such referral to determine if the status of the infant or toddler involved has changed with respect to the eligibility of the infant or toddler for services under this part.

SEC. 639. PROCEDURAL SAFEGUARDS.

(a) MINIMUM PROCEDURES- The procedural safeguards required to be included

in a statewide system under section 635(a)(13) shall provide, at a minimum, the following:

(1) The timely administrative resolution of complaints by parents. Any party aggrieved by the findings and decision regarding an administrative complaint shall have the right to bring a civil action with respect to the complaint in any State court of competent jurisdiction or in a district court of the United States without regard to the amount in controversy. In any action brought under this paragraph, the court shall receive the records of the administrative proceedings, shall hear additional evidence at the request of a party, and, basing its decision on the preponderance of the evidence, shall grant such relief as the court determines is appropriate.

(2) The right to confidentiality of personally identifiable information, including the right of parents to written notice of and written consent to the exchange of such information among agencies consistent with Federal and State law.

(3) The right of the parents to determine whether they, their infant or toddler, or other family members will accept or decline any early intervention service under this part in accordance with State law without jeopardizing other early intervention services under this part.

(4) The opportunity for parents to examine records relating to assessment, screening, eligibility determinations, and the development and implementation of the individualized family service plan.

(5) Procedures to protect the rights of the infant or toddler whenever the parents of the infant or toddler are not known or cannot be found or the infant or toddler is a ward of the State, including the assignment of an individual (who shall not be an employee of the State lead agency, or other State agency, and who shall not be any person, or any employee of a person, providing early intervention services to the infant or toddler or any family member of the infant or toddler) to act as a surrogate for the parents.

(6) Written prior notice to the parents of the infant or toddler with a disability whenever the State agency or service provider proposes to initiate or change, or refuses to initiate or change, the identification, evaluation, or placement of the infant or toddler with a disability, or the provision of appropriate early intervention services to the infant or toddler.

(7) Procedures designed to ensure that the notice required by paragraph (6) fully informs the parents, in the parents' native language, unless it clearly is not feasible to do so, of all

procedures available pursuant to this section.

(8) The right of parents to use mediation in accordance with section 615, except that—

(A) any reference in the section to a State educational agency shall be considered to be a reference to a State's lead agency established or designated under section 635(a)(10);

(B) any reference in the section to a local educational agency shall be considered to be a reference to a local service provider or the State's lead agency under this part, as the case may be; and

(C) any reference in the section to the provision of a free appropriate public education to children with disabilities shall be considered to be a reference to the provision of appropriate early intervention services to infants and toddlers with disabilities.

(b) SERVICES DURING PENDENCY OF PROCEEDINGS- During the pendency of any proceeding or action involving a complaint by the parents of an infant or toddler with a disability, unless the State agency and the parents otherwise agree, the infant or toddler shall continue to receive the appropriate early intervention services currently being provided or, if applying for initial services, shall receive the services not in dispute.

SEC. 640. PAYOR OF LAST RESORT.

(a) NONSUBSTITUTION- Funds provided under section 643 may not be used to satisfy a financial commitment for services that would have been paid for from another public or private source, including any medical program administered by the Secretary of Defense, but for the enactment of this part, except that whenever considered necessary to prevent a delay in the receipt of appropriate early intervention services by an infant, toddler, or family in a timely fashion, funds provided under section 643 may be used to pay the provider of services pending reimbursement from the agency that has ultimate responsibility for the payment.

(b) OBLIGATIONS RELATED TO AND METHODS OF ENSURING SERVICES-

(1) ESTABLISHING FINANCIAL RESPONSIBILITY FOR SERVICES-

(A) IN GENERAL- The Chief Executive Officer of a State or designee of the officer shall ensure that an interagency agreement or other mechanism for interagency coordination is in effect between each public agency and the designated lead agency, in order to ensure—

(i) the provision of, and financial responsibility for, services provided under this part; and

(ii) such services are consistent with the requirements of section 635 and the State's application pursuant to section 637, including the provision of such services during the pendency of any such dispute.

(B) CONSISTENCY BETWEEN AGREEMENTS OR MECHANISMS UNDER PART B- The Chief Executive Officer of a State or designee of the officer shall ensure that the terms and conditions of such agreement or mechanism are consistent with the terms and conditions of the State's agreement or mechanism under section 612(a)(12), where appropriate.

(2) REIMBURSEMENT FOR SERVICES BY PUBLIC AGENCY-

(A) IN GENERAL- If a public agency other than an educational agency fails to provide or pay for the services pursuant to an agreement required under paragraph (1), the local educational agency or State agency (as determined by the Chief Executive Officer or designee) shall provide or pay for the provision of such services to the child.

(B) REIMBURSEMENT- Such local educational agency or State agency is authorized to claim reimbursement for the services from the public agency that failed to provide or pay for such services and such public agency shall reimburse the local educational agency or State agency pursuant to the terms of the interagency agreement or other mechanism required under paragraph (1).

(3) SPECIAL RULE- The requirements of paragraph (1) may be met through—

(A) State statute or regulation;

(B) signed agreements between respective agency officials that clearly identify the responsibilities of each agency relating to the provision of services; or

(C) other appropriate written methods as determined by the Chief Executive Officer of the State or designee of the officer and approved by the Secretary through the review and approval of the State's application pursuant to section 637.

(c) REDUCTION OF OTHER BENEFITS- Nothing in this part shall be construed to permit the State to reduce medical or other assistance available or to alter eligibility under title V of the Social Security Act (relating to maternal and child health) or title XIX of the Social Security Act (relating to medicaid for infants or toddlers with disabilities) within the State.

SEC. 641. STATE INTERAGENCY COORDINATING COUNCIL.

(a) ESTABLISHMENT-

(1) IN GENERAL- A State that desires to receive financial assistance under this part shall establish a State interagency coordinating council.

(2) APPOINTMENT- The council shall be appointed by the Governor. In making appointments to the council, the Governor shall ensure that the membership of the council reasonably represents the population of the State.

(3) CHAIRPERSON- The Governor shall designate a member of the council to serve as the chairperson of the council, or shall require the council to so designate such a member. Any member of the council who is a representative of the lead agency designated under section 635(a)(10) may not serve as the chairperson of the council.

(b) COMPOSITION-

(1) IN GENERAL- The council shall be composed as follows:

(A) PARENTS- Not less than 20 percent of the members shall be parents of infants or toddlers with disabilities or children with disabilities aged 12 or younger, with knowledge of, or experience with, programs for infants and toddlers with disabilities. Not less than 1 such member shall be a parent of an infant or toddler with a disability or a child with a disability aged 6 or younger.

(B) SERVICE PROVIDERS- Not less than 20 percent of the members shall be public or private providers of early intervention services.

(C) STATE LEGISLATURE- Not less than 1 member shall be from the State legislature.

(D) PERSONNEL PREPARATION- Not less than 1 member shall be involved in personnel preparation.

(E) AGENCY FOR EARLY INTERVENTION SERVICES- Not less than 1 member shall be from each of the State agencies involved in the provision of, or payment for, early intervention services to infants and toddlers with disabilities and their families and shall have sufficient authority to engage in policy planning and implementation on behalf of such agencies.

(F) AGENCY FOR PRESCHOOL SERVICES- Not less than 1 member shall be from the State educational agency responsible for preschool services to children with disabilities and shall have sufficient authority to engage in policy planning and implementation on behalf of such agency.

(G) STATE MEDICAID AGENCY- Not less than 1 member shall be from the agency responsible for the State medicaid program.

(H) HEAD START AGENCY- Not less than 1 member shall be a representative from a Head Start agency or program in the State.

(I) CHILD CARE AGENCY- Not less than 1 member shall be a representative from a State agency responsible for child care.

(J) AGENCY FOR HEALTH INSURANCE- Not less than 1 member shall be from the agency responsible for the State regulation of health insurance.

(K) OFFICE OF THE COORDINATOR OF EDUCATION OF HOMELESS CHILDREN AND YOUTH- Not less than 1 member shall be a representative designated by the Office of Coordinator for Education of Homeless Children and Youths.

(L) STATE FOSTER CARE REPRESENTATIVE- Not less than 1 member shall be a representative from the State child welfare agency responsible for foster care.

(M) MENTAL HEALTH AGENCY- Not less than 1 member shall be a representative from the State agency responsible for children's mental health.

(2) OTHER MEMBERS- The council may include other members selected by the Governor, including a representative from the Bureau of Indian Affairs (BIA), or where there is no BIA-operated or BIA-funded school, from the Indian Health Service or the tribe or tribal council.

(c) MEETINGS- The council shall meet, at a minimum, on a quarterly basis, and in such places as the council determines necessary. The meetings shall be publicly announced, and, to the extent appropriate, open and accessible to the general public.

(d) MANAGEMENT AUTHORITY- Subject to the approval of the Governor, the council may prepare and approve a budget using funds under this part to conduct hearings and forums, to reimburse members of the council for reasonable and necessary expenses for attending council meetings and performing council duties (including child care for parent representatives), to pay compensation to a member of the council if the member is not employed or must forfeit wages from other employment when performing official council business, to hire staff, and to obtain the services of such professional, technical, and clerical personnel as may be necessary to carry out its functions under this part.

(e) FUNCTIONS OF COUNCIL-

(1) DUTIES- The council shall—

(A) advise and assist the lead agency designated or established under section 635(a)(10) in the performance of the responsibilities set forth in such section, particularly the identification of the sources of fiscal and other support for services for early intervention programs, assignment of financial responsibility to the appropriate agency, and the promotion of the interagency agreements;

(B) advise and assist the lead agency in the preparation of applications and amendments thereto;

(C) advise and assist the State educational agency regarding the transition of toddlers with disabilities to preschool and other appropriate services; and

(D) prepare and submit an annual report to the Governor and to the Secretary on the status of early intervention programs for infants and toddlers with disabilities and their families operated within the State.

(2) AUTHORIZED ACTIVITY- The council may advise and assist the lead agency and the State educational agency regarding the provision of appropriate services for children from birth through age 5. The council may advise appropriate agencies in the State with respect to the integration of services for infants and toddlers with disabilities and at-risk infants and toddlers and their families, regardless of whether at-risk infants and toddlers are eligible for early intervention services in the State.

(f) CONFLICT OF INTEREST- No member of the council shall cast a vote on any matter that is likely to provide a direct financial benefit to that member or otherwise give the appearance of a conflict of interest under State law.

SEC. 642. FEDERAL ADMINISTRATION.

Sections 616, 617, and 618 shall, to the extent not inconsistent with this part, apply to the program authorized by this part, except that—

(1) any reference in such sections to a State educational agency shall be considered to be a reference to a State's lead agency established or designated under section 635(a)(10);

(2) any reference in such sections to a local educational agency, educational service agency, or a State agency shall be considered to be a reference to an early intervention service provider under this part; and

(3) any reference to the education of children with disabilities or the education of all children with disabilities shall be considered to be a reference to the provision of appropriate early intervention services to infants and toddlers with disabilities.

SEC. 643. ALLOCATION OF FUNDS.

(a) RESERVATION OF FUNDS FOR OUTLYING AREAS-

(1) IN GENERAL- From the sums appropriated to carry out this part for any fiscal year, the Secretary may reserve not more than 1 percent for payments to Guam, American Samoa, the United States Virgin Islands, and the Commonwealth of the Northern Mariana Islands in accordance with their respective needs for assistance under this part.

(2) CONSOLIDATION OF FUNDS- The provisions of Public Law 95-134, permitting the consolidation of grants to the outlying areas, shall not apply to funds those areas receive under this part.

(b) PAYMENTS TO INDIANS-

(1) IN GENERAL- The Secretary shall, subject to this subsection, make payments to the Secretary of the Interior to be distributed to tribes, tribal organizations (as defined under section 4 of the Indian Self-Determination and Education Assistance Act), or consortia of the above entities for the coordination of assistance in the provision of early intervention services by the States to infants and toddlers with disabilities and their families on reservations served by elementary schools and secondary schools for Indian children operated or funded by the Department of the Interior. The amount of such payment for any fiscal year shall be 1.25 percent of the aggregate of the amount available to all States under this part for such fiscal year.

(2) ALLOCATION- For each fiscal year, the Secretary of the Interior shall distribute the entire payment received under paragraph (1) by providing to each tribe, tribal organization, or consortium an amount based on the number of infants and toddlers residing on the reservation, as determined annually, divided by the total of such children served by all tribes, tribal organizations, or consortia.

(3) INFORMATION- To receive a payment under this subsection, the tribe, tribal organization, or consortium shall submit such information to the Secretary of the Interior as is needed to determine the amounts to be distributed under paragraph (2).

(4) USE OF FUNDS- The funds received by a tribe, tribal organization, or consortium shall be used to assist States in child find,

screening, and other procedures for the early identification of Indian children under 3 years of age and for parent training. Such funds may also be used to provide early intervention services in accordance with this part. Such activities may be carried out directly or through contracts or cooperative agreements with the Bureau of Indian Affairs, local educational agencies, and other public or private nonprofit organizations. The tribe, tribal organization, or consortium is encouraged to involve Indian parents in the development and implementation of these activities. The above entities shall, as appropriate, make referrals to local, State, or Federal entities for the provision of services or further diagnosis.

(5) REPORTS- To be eligible to receive a payment under paragraph (2), a tribe, tribal organization, or consortium shall make a biennial report to the Secretary of the Interior of activities undertaken under this subsection, including the number of contracts and cooperative agreements entered into, the number of infants and toddlers contacted and receiving services for each year, and the estimated number of infants and toddlers needing services during the 2 years following the year in which the report is made. The Secretary of the Interior shall include a summary of this information on a biennial basis to the Secretary of Education along with such other information as required under section 611(h)(3)(E). The Secretary of Education may require any additional information from the Secretary of the Interior.

(6) PROHIBITED USES OF FUNDS- None of the funds under this subsection may be used by the Secretary of the Interior for administrative purposes, including child count, and the provision of technical assistance.

(c) STATE ALLOTMENTS-

(1) IN GENERAL- Except as provided in paragraphs (2) and (3), from the funds remaining for each fiscal year after the reservation and payments under subsections (a), (b), and (e), the Secretary shall first allot to each State an amount that bears the same ratio to the amount of such remainder as the number of infants and toddlers in the State bears to the number of infants and toddlers in all States.

(2) MINIMUM ALLOTMENTS- Except as provided in paragraph (3), no State shall receive an amount under this section for any fiscal year that is less than the greater of—

(A) 1/2 of 1 percent of the remaining amount described in paragraph (1); or

(B) $500,000.

(3) RATABLE REDUCTION-

(A) IN GENERAL- If the sums made available under this part for any fiscal year are insufficient to pay the full amounts that all States are eligible to receive under this subsection for such year, the Secretary shall ratably reduce the allotments to such States for such year.

(B) ADDITIONAL FUNDS- If additional funds become available for making payments under this subsection for a fiscal year, allotments that were reduced under subparagraph (A) shall be increased on the same basis the allotments were reduced.

(4) DEFINITIONS- In this subsection—

(A) the terms 'infants' and 'toddlers' mean children under 3 years of age; and

(B) the term 'State' means each of the 50 States, the District of Columbia, and the Commonwealth of Puerto Rico.

(d) REALLOTMENT OF FUNDS- If a State elects not to receive its allotment under subsection (c), the Secretary shall reallot, among the remaining States, amounts from such State in accordance with such subsection.

(e) RESERVATION FOR STATE INCENTIVE GRANTS-

(1) IN GENERAL- For any fiscal year for which the amount appropriated pursuant to the authorization of appropriations under section 644 exceeds $460,000,000, the Secretary shall reserve 15 percent of such appropriated amount to provide grants to States that are carrying out the policy described in section 635(c) in order to facilitate the implementation of such policy.

(2) AMOUNT OF GRANT-

(A) IN GENERAL- Notwithstanding paragraphs (2) and (3) of subsection (c), the Secretary shall provide a grant to each State under paragraph (1) in an amount that bears the same ratio to the amount reserved under such paragraph as the number of infants and toddlers in the State bears to the number of infants and toddlers in all States receiving grants under such paragraph.

(B) MAXIMUM AMOUNT- No State shall receive a grant under paragraph (1) for any fiscal year in an amount that is greater than 20 percent of the amount reserved under such paragraph for the fiscal year.

(3) CARRYOVER OF AMOUNTS-

(A) FIRST SUCCEEDING FISCAL YEAR- Pursuant to section 421(b) of the General Education Provisions Act, amounts under a grant provided under paragraph (1) that are not obligated and expended prior to the beginning of the first fiscal year succeeding the fiscal year for which such amounts were appropriated shall remain available for obligation and expenditure during such first succeeding fiscal year.

(B) SECOND SUCCEEDING FISCAL YEAR- Amounts under a grant provided under paragraph (1) that are not obligated and expended prior to the beginning of the second fiscal year succeeding the fiscal year for which such amounts were appropriated shall be returned to the Secretary and used to make grants to States under section 633 (from their allotments under this section) during such second succeeding fiscal year.

SEC. 644. AUTHORIZATION OF APPROPRIATIONS.

For the purpose of carrying out this part, there are authorized to be appropriated such sums as may be necessary for each of the fiscal years 2005 through 2010.

PART D—NATIONAL ACTIVITIES TO IMPROVE EDUCATION OF CHILDREN WITH DISABILITIES

SEC. 650. FINDINGS.

Congress finds the following:

(1) The Federal Government has an ongoing obligation to support activities that contribute to positive results for children with disabilities, enabling those children to lead productive and independent adult lives.

(2) Systemic change benefiting all students, including children with disabilities, requires the involvement of States, local educational agencies, parents, individuals with disabilities and their families, teachers and other service providers, and other interested individuals and organizations to develop and implement comprehensive strategies that improve educational results for children with disabilities.

(3) State educational agencies, in partnership with local educational agencies, parents of children with disabilities, and other individuals and organizations, are in the best position to improve education for children with disabilities and to address their special needs.

(4) An effective educational system serving students with disabilities should—

(A) maintain high academic achievement standards and clear performance goals for children with disabilities, consistent with the standards and expectations for all students in the educational system, and provide for appropriate and effective strategies and methods to ensure that all children with disabilities have the opportunity to achieve those standards and goals;

(B) clearly define, in objective, measurable terms, the school and post-school results that children with disabilities are expected to achieve; and

(C) promote transition services and coordinate State and local education, social, health, mental health, and other services, in addressing the full range of student needs, particularly the needs of children with disabilities who need significant levels of support to participate and learn in school and the community.

(5) The availability of an adequate number of qualified personnel is critical—

(A) to serve effectively children with disabilities;

(B) to assume leadership positions in administration and direct services;

(C) to provide teacher training; and

(D) to conduct high quality research to improve special education.

(6) High quality, comprehensive professional development programs are essential to ensure that the persons responsible for the education or transition of children with disabilities possess the skills and knowledge necessary to address the educational and related needs of those children.

(7) Models of professional development should be scientifically based and reflect successful practices, including strategies for recruiting, preparing, and retaining personnel.

(8) Continued support is essential for the development and maintenance of a coordinated and high quality program of research to inform successful teaching practices and model curricula for educating children with disabilities.

(9) Training, technical assistance, support, and dissemination activities are necessary to ensure that parts B and C are fully implemented and achieve high quality early intervention, educational, and transitional results for children with disabilities and their families.

(10) Parents, teachers, administrators, and related services personnel need technical assistance and information in a timely, coordinated, and accessible manner in order to improve early intervention, educational, and transitional services and results at the State and local levels for children with disabilities and their families.

(11) Parent training and information activities assist parents of a child with a disability in dealing with the multiple pressures of parenting such a child and are of particular

importance in—

(A) playing a vital role in creating and preserving constructive relationships between parents of children with disabilities and schools by facilitating open communication between the parents and schools; encouraging dispute resolution at the earliest possible point in time; and discouraging the escalation of an adversarial process between the parents and schools;

(B) ensuring the involvement of parents in planning and decisionmaking with respect to early intervention, educational, and transitional services;

(C) achieving high quality early intervention, educational, and transitional results for children with disabilities;

(D) providing such parents information on their rights, protections, and responsibilities under this title to ensure improved early intervention, educational, and transitional results for children with disabilities;

(E) assisting such parents in the development of skills to participate effectively in the education and development of their children and in the transitions described in section 673(b)(6);

(F) supporting the roles of such parents as participants within partnerships seeking to improve early intervention, educational, and transitional services and results for children with disabilities and their families; and

(G) supporting such parents who may have limited access to services and supports, due to economic, cultural, or linguistic barriers.

(12) Support is needed to improve technological resources and integrate technology, including universally designed technologies, into the lives of children with disabilities, parents of children with disabilities, school personnel, and others through curricula, services, and assistive technologies.

Subpart 1—State Personnel Development Grants

SEC. 651. PURPOSE; DEFINITION OF PERSONNEL; PROGRAM AUTHORITY.

(a) Purpose

The purpose of this part is to assist State educational agencies in reforming and improving their systems for personnel preparation and professional development in early intervention, educational, and transition services in order to improve results for children with disabilities.

(b) Definition of personnel

In this part the term "personnel" means special education teachers, regular education teachers, principals, administrators, related services personnel, paraprofessionals, and early intervention personnel serving infants, toddlers, preschoolers, or children with disabilities, except where a particular category of personnel, such as related services personnel, is identified.

(c) Competitive grants

(1) In general

Except as provided in subsection (d), for any fiscal year for which the amount appropriated under section 1455 of this title, that remains after the Secretary reserves funds under subsection (e) for the fiscal year, is less than $100,000,000, the Secretary shall award grants, on a competitive basis, to State educational agencies to carry out the activities described in the State plan submitted under section 1453 of this title.

(2) Priority

In awarding grants under paragraph (1), the Secretary may give priority to State educational agencies that--

(A) are in States with the greatest personnel shortages; or

(B) demonstrate the greatest difficulty meeting the requirements of section 1412(a)(14) of this title.

(3) Minimum amount

The Secretary shall make a grant to each State educational agency selected under paragraph (1) in an amount for each fiscal year that is--

(A) not less than $500,000, nor more than $4,000,000, in the case of the 50 States, the District of Columbia, and the Commonwealth of Puerto Rico; and

(B) not less than $80,000 in the case of an outlying area.

(4) Increase in amount

The Secretary may increase the amounts of grants under paragraph (4) to account for inflation.

(5) Factors

The Secretary shall determine the amount of a grant under paragraph (1) after considering--

(A) the amount of funds available for making the grants;

(B) the relative population of the State or outlying area;

(C) the types of activities proposed by the State or outlying area;

(D) the alignment of proposed activities

with section 1412(a)(14) of this title;

(E) the alignment of proposed activities with the State plans and applications submitted under sections 6311 and 6611(d)1 respectively, of this title; and

(F) the use, as appropriate, of scientifically based research activities.

(d) Formula grants

(1) In general

Except as provided in paragraphs (2) and (3), for the first fiscal year for which the amount appropriated under section 1455 of this title, that remains after the Secretary reserves funds under subsection (e) for the fiscal year, is equal to or greater than $100,000,000, and for each fiscal year thereafter, the Secretary shall allot to each State educational agency, whose application meets the requirements of this part, an amount that bears the same relation to the amount remaining as the amount the State received under section 1411(d) of this title for that fiscal year bears to the amount of funds received by all States (whose applications meet the requirements of this part) under section 1411(d) of this title for that fiscal year.

(2) Minimum allotments for States that received competitive grants

(A) In general

The amount allotted under this subsection to any State educational agency that received a competitive multi-year grant under subsection (c) for which the grant period has not expired shall be not less than the amount specified for that fiscal year in the State educational agency's grant award document under that subsection.

(B) Special rule

Each such State educational agency shall use the minimum amount described in subparagraph (A) for the activities described in the State educational agency's competitive grant award document for that year, unless the Secretary approves a request from the State educational agency to spend the funds on other activities.

(3) Minimum allotment

The amount of any State educational agency's allotment under this subsection for any fiscal year shall not be less than--

(A) the greater of $500,000 or ½ of 1 percent of the total amount available under this subsection for that year, in the case of each of the 50 States, the District of Columbia, and the Commonwealth of Puerto Rico; and

(B) $80,000, in the case of an outlying area.

(4) Direct benefit

In using grant funds allotted under paragraph (1), a State educational agency shall, through grants, contracts, or cooperative agreements, undertake activities that significantly and directly benefit the local educational agencies in the State.

(e) Continuation awards

(1) In general

Notwithstanding any other provision of this part, from funds appropriated under section 1455 of this title for each fiscal year, the Secretary shall reserve the amount that is necessary to make a continuation award to any State educational agency (at the request of the State educational agency) that received a multi-year award under this subchapter (as this subchapter was in effect on the day before December 3, 2004), to enable the State educational agency to carry out activities in accordance with the terms of the multi-year award.

(2) Prohibition

A State educational agency that receives a continuation award under paragraph (1) for any fiscal year may not receive any other award under this part for that fiscal year.

SEC. 652. ELIGIBILITY AND COLLABORATIVE PROCESS.

(a) ELIGIBLE APPLICANTS- A State educational agency may apply for a grant under this subpart for a grant period of not less than 1 year and not more than 5 years.

(b) PARTNERS-

(1) IN GENERAL- In order to be considered for a grant under this subpart, a State educational agency shall establish a partnership with local educational agencies and other State agencies involved in, or concerned with, the education of children with disabilities, including—

(A) not less than 1 institution of higher education; and

(B) the State agencies responsible for administering part C, early education, child care, and vocational rehabilitation programs.

(2) OTHER PARTNERS- In order to be considered for a grant under this subpart, a State educational agency shall work in partnership with other persons and organizations involved in, and concerned with, the education of children with disabilities, which may include—

(A) the Governor;

(B) parents of children with disabilities ages birth through 26;

(C) parents of nondisabled children ages birth through 26;

(D) individuals with disabilities;

(E) parent training and information centers or community parent resource centers funded under sections 671 and 672, respectively;

(F) community based and other nonprofit organizations involved in the education and employment of individuals with disabilities;

(G) personnel as defined in section 651(b);

(H) the State advisory panel established under part B;

(I) the State interagency coordinating council established under part C;

(J) individuals knowledgeable about vocational education;

(K) the State agency for higher education;

(L) public agencies with jurisdiction in the areas of health, mental health, social services, and juvenile justice;

(M) other providers of professional development that work with infants, toddlers, preschoolers, and children with disabilities; and

(N) other individuals.

(3) REQUIRED PARTNER- If State law assigns responsibility for teacher preparation and certification to an individual, entity, or agency other than the State educational agency, the State educational agency shall—

(A) include that individual, entity, or agency as a partner in the partnership under this subsection; and

(B) ensure that any activities the State educational agency will carry out under this subpart that are within that partner's jurisdiction (which may include activities described in section 654(b)) are carried out by that partner.

SEC. 653. APPLICATIONS.

(a) In general

(1) Submission

A State educational agency that desires to receive a grant under this part shall submit to the Secretary an application at such time, in such manner, and including such information as the Secretary may require.

(2) State plan

The application shall include a plan that identifies and addresses the State and local needs for the personnel preparation and professional development of personnel, as well as individuals who provide direct supplementary aids and services to children with disabilities, and that--

(A) is designed to enable the State to meet the requirements of section 1412(a)(14) of this title and section 1435(a)(8) and (9) of this title;

(B) is based on an assessment of State and local needs that identifies critical aspects and areas in need of improvement related to the preparation, ongoing training, and professional

development of personnel who serve infants, toddlers, preschoolers, and children with disabilities within the State, including--

(i) current and anticipated personnel vacancies and shortages; and

(ii) the number of preservice and inservice programs; and

(C) is integrated and aligned, to the maximum extent possible, with State plans and activities under the Elementary and Secondary Education Act of 1965, the Rehabilitation Act of 1973, and the Higher Education Act of 1965.

(3) Requirement

The State application shall contain an assurance that the State educational agency will carry out each of the strategies described in subsection (b)(4).

(b) Elements of State personnel development plan

Each State personnel development plan under subsection (a)(2) shall--

(1) describe a partnership agreement that is in effect for the period of the grant, which agreement shall specify--

(A) the nature and extent of the partnership described in section 1452(b) of this title and the respective roles of each member of the partnership, including the partner described in section 1452(b)(3) of this title if applicable; and

(B) how the State educational agency will work with other persons and organizations involved in, and concerned with, the education of children with disabilities, including the respective roles of each of the persons and organizations;

(2) describe how the strategies and activities described in paragraph (4) will be coordinated with activities supported with other public resources (including part B [subchapter II] and part C [subchapter III] funds retained for use at the State level for personnel and professional development purposes) and private resources;

(3) describe how the State educational agency will align its personnel development plan under this part with the plan and application submitted under sections 1111 and 2101(d), respectively, of the Elementary and Secondary Education Act of 1965;

(4) describe those strategies the State educational agency will use to address the professional development and personnel needs identified under subsection (a)(2) and how such strategies will be implemented, including--

(A) a description of the programs and activities to be supported under this part that will provide personnel with the knowledge and skills to meet the needs of, and improve the performance and achievement of, infants, toddlers, preschoolers, and children with disabilities; and

(B) how such strategies will be integrated, to the maximum extent possible, with other activities supported by grants funded under section 1462 of this title;

(5) provide an assurance that the State educational agency will provide technical assistance to local educational agencies to improve the quality of professional development available to meet the needs of personnel who serve children with disabilities;

(6) provide an assurance that the State educational agency will provide technical assistance to entities that provide services to infants and toddlers with disabilities to improve the quality of professional development available to meet the needs of personnel serving such children;

(7) describe how the State educational agency will recruit and retain teachers who meet the qualifications described in section 1412(a)(14)(C) of this title and other qualified personnel in geographic areas of greatest need;

(8) describe the steps the State educational agency will take to ensure that poor and minority children are not taught at higher rates by teachers who do not meet the qualifications described in section 1412(a)(14)(C) of this title; and

(9) describe how the State educational agency will assess, on a regular basis, the extent to which the strategies implemented under this part have been effective in meeting the performance goals described in section 1412(a)(15) of this title.

(c) Peer review

(1) In general

The Secretary shall use a panel of experts who are competent, by virtue of their training, expertise, or experience, to evaluate applications for grants under section 1451(c)(1) of this title.

(2) Composition of panel

A majority of a panel described in paragraph (1) shall be composed of individuals who are not employees of the Federal Government.

(3) Payment of fees and expenses of certain members

The Secretary may use available funds appropriated to carry out this part to pay the expenses and fees of panel members who are not employees of the Federal Government.

(d) Reporting procedures

Each State educational agency that receives a grant under this part shall submit annual performance reports to the Secretary. The reports shall--

(1) describe the progress of the State

educational agency in implementing its plan;

(2) analyze the effectiveness of the State educational agency's activities under this part and of the State educational agency's strategies for meeting its goals under section 1412(a)(15) of this title; and

(3) identify changes in the strategies used by the State educational agency and described in subsection (b)(4), if any, to improve the State educational agency's performance.

SEC. 654. USE OF FUNDS.

(a) Professional development activities

A State educational agency that receives a grant under this part shall use the grant funds to support activities in accordance with the State's plan described in section 1453 of this title, including 1 or more of the following:

(1) Carrying out programs that provide support to both special education and regular education teachers of children with disabilities and principals, such as programs that--

(A) provide teacher mentoring, team teaching, reduced class schedules and case loads, and intensive professional development;

(B) use standards or assessments for guiding beginning teachers that are consistent with challenging State academic achievement standards and with the requirements for professional development, as defined in section 7801 of this title; and

(C) encourage collaborative and consultative models of providing early intervention, special education, and related services.

(2) Encouraging and supporting the training of special education and regular education teachers and administrators to effectively use and integrate technology--

(A) into curricula and instruction, including training to improve the ability to collect, manage, and analyze data to improve teaching, decisionmaking, school improvement efforts, and accountability;

(B) to enhance learning by children with disabilities; and

(C) to effectively communicate with parents.

(3) Providing professional development activities that--

(A) improve the knowledge of special education and regular education teachers concerning--

(i) the academic and developmental or functional needs of students with disabilities; or

(ii) effective instructional strategies, methods, and skills, and the use of State academic content standards and student academic achievement and functional standards, and State assessments, to improve teaching practices and student academic achievement;

(B) improve the knowledge of special education and regular education teachers and principals and, in appropriate cases, paraprofessionals, concerning effective instructional practices, and that--

(i) provide training in how to teach and address the needs of children with different learning styles and children who are limited English proficient;

(ii) involve collaborative groups of teachers, administrators, and, in appropriate cases, related services personnel;

(iii) provide training in methods of--

(I) positive behavioral interventions and supports to improve student behavior in the classroom;

(II) scientifically based reading instruction, including early literacy instruction;

(III) early and appropriate interventions to identify and help children with disabilities;

(IV) effective instruction for children with low incidence disabilities;

(V) successful transitioning to postsecondary opportunities; and

(VI) using classroom-based techniques to assist children prior to referral for special education;

(iv) provide training to enable personnel to work with and involve parents in their child's education, including parents of low income and limited English proficient children with disabilities;

(v) provide training for special education personnel and regular education personnel in planning, developing, and implementing effective and appropriate IEPs; and

(vi) provide training to meet the needs of students with significant health, mobility, or behavioral needs prior to serving such students;

(C) train administrators, principals, and other relevant school personnel in conducting effective IEP meetings; and

(D) train early intervention, preschool, and related services providers, and other relevant school personnel, in conducting effective individualized family service plan (IFSP) meetings.

(4) Developing and implementing initiatives to promote the recruitment and retention of special education teachers who meet the qualifications described in section 1412(a)(14)(C) of this title, particularly initiatives that have been proven effective in recruiting and retaining teachers, including programs that provide--

(A) teacher mentoring from exemplary special education teachers, principals, or superintendents;

(B) induction and support for special education teachers during their first 3 years of employment as teachers; or

(C) incentives, including financial incentives, to retain special education teachers who have a record of success in helping students with disabilities.

(5) Carrying out programs and activities that are designed to improve the quality of personnel who serve children with disabilities, such as--

(A) innovative professional development programs (which may be provided through partnerships that include institutions of higher education), including programs that train teachers and principals to integrate technology into curricula and instruction to improve teaching, learning, and technology literacy, which professional development shall be consistent with the definition of professional development in section 7801 of this title; and

(B) the development and use of proven, cost effective strategies for the implementation of professional development activities, such as through the use of technology and distance learning.

(6) Carrying out programs and activities that are designed to improve the quality of early intervention personnel, including paraprofessionals and primary referral sources, such as--

(A) professional development programs to improve the delivery of early intervention services;

(B) initiatives to promote the recruitment and retention of early intervention personnel; and

(C) interagency activities to ensure that early intervention personnel are adequately prepared and trained.

(b) Other activities

A State educational agency that receives a grant under this part shall use the grant funds to support activities in accordance with the State's plan described in section 1453 of this title, including 1 or more of the following:

(1) Reforming special education and regular education teacher certification (including recertification) or licensing requirements to ensure that--

(A) special education and regular education teachers have--

(i) the training and information necessary to

address the full range of needs of children with disabilities across disability categories; and

(ii) the necessary subject matter knowledge and teaching skills in the academic subjects that the teachers teach;

(B) special education and regular education teacher certification (including recertification) or licensing requirements are aligned with challenging State academic content standards; and

(C) special education and regular education teachers have the subject matter knowledge and teaching skills, including technology literacy, necessary to help students with disabilities meet challenging State student academic achievement and functional standards.

(2) Programs that establish, expand, or improve alternative routes for State certification of special education teachers for individuals with a baccalaureate or master's degree who meet the qualifications described in section 1412(a)(14)(C) of this title, including mid-career professionals from other occupations, paraprofessionals, and recent college or university graduates with records of academic distinction who demonstrate the potential to become highly effective special education teachers.

(3) Teacher advancement initiatives for special education teachers that promote professional growth and emphasize multiple career paths (such as paths to becoming a career teacher, mentor teacher, or exemplary teacher) and pay differentiation.

(4) Developing and implementing mechanisms to assist local educational agencies and schools in effectively recruiting and retaining special education teachers who meet the qualifications described in section 1412(a)(14)(C) of this title.

(5) Reforming tenure systems, implementing teacher testing for subject matter knowledge, and implementing teacher testing for State certification or licensing, consistent with title II of the Higher Education Act of 1965.

(6) Funding projects to promote reciprocity of teacher certification or licensing between or among States for special education teachers, except that no reciprocity agreement developed under this paragraph or developed using funds provided under this part may lead to the weakening of any State teaching certification or licensing requirement.

(7) Assisting local educational agencies to serve children with disabilities through the development and use of proven, innovative strategies to deliver intensive professional development programs that are both cost effective and easily accessible, such as strategies that involve delivery through the use of technology, peer networks, and distance learning.

(8) Developing, or assisting local educational agencies in developing, merit based performance systems, and strategies that provide differential and bonus pay for special education teachers.

(9) Supporting activities that ensure that teachers are able to use challenging State academic content standards and student academic achievement and functional standards, and State assessments for all children with disabilities, to improve instructional practices and improve the academic achievement of children with disabilities.

(10) When applicable, coordinating with, and expanding centers established under, section 6613(c)(18) of this title (as such section was in effect on the day before December 10, 2015) to benefit special education teachers.

(c) Contracts and subgrants

A State educational agency that receives a grant under this part--

(1) shall award contracts or subgrants to local educational agencies, institutions of higher education, parent training and information centers, or community parent resource centers, as appropriate, to carry out its State plan under this part; and

(2) may award contracts and subgrants to other public and private entities, including the lead agency under subchapter III, to carry out the State plan.

(d) Use of funds for professional development

A State educational agency that receives a grant under this part shall use--

(1) not less than 90 percent of the funds the State educational agency receives under the grant for any fiscal year for activities under subsection (a); and

(2) not more than 10 percent of the funds the State educational agency receives under the grant for any fiscal year for activities under subsection (b).

(e) Grants to outlying areas

Public Law 95-134, permitting the consolidation of grants to the outlying areas, shall not apply to funds received under this part.

SEC. 655. AUTHORIZATION OF APPROPRIATIONS.

There are authorized to be appropriated to carry out this subpart such sums as may be necessary for each of the fiscal years 2005 through 2010.

Subpart 2—Personnel Preparation, Technical Assistance, Model Demonstration Projects, and Dissemination of Information

SEC. 661. PURPOSE; DEFINITION OF ELIGIBLE ENTITY.

(a) PURPOSE- The purpose of this subpart is—

(1) to provide Federal funding for personnel preparation, technical assistance, model demonstration projects, information dissemination, and studies and evaluations, in order to improve early intervention, educational, and transitional results for children with disabilities; and

(2) to assist State educational agencies and local educational agencies in improving their education systems for children with disabilities.

(b) DEFINITION OF ELIGIBLE ENTITY-

(1) IN GENERAL- In this subpart, the term eligible entity' means—

(A) a State educational agency;

(B) a local educational agency;

(C) a public charter school that is a local educational agency under State law;

(D) an institution of higher education;

(E) a public agency not described in subparagraphs (A) through (D);

(F) a private nonprofit organization;

(G) an outlying area;

(H) an Indian tribe or a tribal organization (as defined under section 4 of the Indian Self-Determination and Education Assistance Act); or

(I) a for-profit organization, if the Secretary finds it appropriate in light of the purposes of a particular competition for a grant, contract, or cooperative agreement under this subpart.

(2) SPECIAL RULE- The Secretary may limit which eligible entities described in paragraph (1) are eligible for a grant, contract, or cooperative agreement under this subpart to 1 or more of the categories of eligible entities described in paragraph (1).

SEC. 662. PERSONNEL DEVELOPMENT TO IMPROVE SERVICES AND RESULTS FOR CHILDREN WITH DISABILITIES.

(a) In general

The Secretary, on a competitive basis, shall award grants to, or enter into contracts or cooperative agreements with, eligible entities to carry out 1 or more of the following objectives:

(1) To help address the needs identified in the State plan described in section 1453(a)(2) of this title for personnel, as defined in section 1451(b) of this title, who meet the applicable requirements described in section 1412(a)(14) of this title, to work with infants or toddlers with disabilities, or children with disabilities, consistent with the qualifications described in section 1412(a)(14) of this title.

(2) To ensure that those personnel have the necessary skills and knowledge, derived from practices that have been determined, through scientifically based research, to be successful in serving those children.

(3) To encourage increased focus on academics and core content areas in special education personnel preparation programs.

(4) To ensure that regular education teachers have the necessary skills and knowledge to provide instruction to students with disabilities in the regular education classroom.

(5) To ensure that all special education teachers meet the qualifications described in section 1412(a)(14)(C) of this title.

(6) To ensure that preservice and in-service personnel preparation programs include training in--

(A) the use of new technologies;

(B) the area of early intervention, educational, and transition services;

(C) effectively involving parents; and

(D) positive behavioral supports.

(7) To provide high-quality professional development for principals, superintendents, and other administrators, including training in--

(A) instructional leadership;

(B) behavioral supports in the school and classroom;

(C) paperwork reduction;

(D) promoting improved collaboration between special education and general education teachers;

(E) assessment and accountability;

(F) ensuring effective learning environments; and

(G) fostering positive relationships with parents.

(b) Personnel development; enhanced support for beginning special educators

(1) In general

In carrying out this section, the Secretary shall support activities--

(A) for personnel development, including activities for the preparation of personnel who will serve children with high incidence and low incidence disabilities, to prepare special education and general education teachers, principals, administrators, and related services personnel (and school board members, when appropriate) to meet the diverse and individualized instructional needs of children with disabilities and improve early intervention, educational, and transitional services and results for children with disabilities, consistent with the objectives described in subsection (a); and

(B) for enhanced support for beginning special educators, consistent with the objectives described in subsection (a).

(2) Personnel development

In carrying out paragraph (1)(A), the Secretary shall support not less than 1 of the following activities:

(A) Assisting effective existing, improving existing, or developing new, collaborative personnel preparation activities undertaken by institutions of higher education, local educational agencies, and other local entities that incorporate best practices and scientifically based research, where applicable, in providing special education and general education teachers, principals, administrators, and related services personnel with the knowledge and skills to effectively support students with disabilities, including--

(i) working collaboratively in regular classroom settings;

(ii) using appropriate supports, accommodations, and curriculum modifications;

(iii) implementing effective teaching strategies, classroom-based techniques, and interventions to ensure appropriate identification of students who may be eligible for special education services, and to prevent the misidentification, inappropriate overidentification, or underidentification of children as having a disability, especially minority and limited English proficient children;

(iv) effectively working with and involving parents in the education of their children;

(v) utilizing strategies, including positive behavioral interventions, for addressing the conduct of children with disabilities that impedes their learning and that of others in the classroom;

(vi) effectively constructing IEPs, participating in IEP meetings, and implementing IEPs;

(vii) preparing children with disabilities to participate in statewide assessments (with or without accommodations) and alternate assessments, as appropriate, and to ensure that all children with disabilities are a part of all accountability systems under the Elementary

and Secondary Education Act of 1965; and

(viii) working in high need elementary schools and secondary schools, including urban schools, rural schools, and schools operated by an entity described in section 6113(d)(1)(A)(ii) of the Elementary and Secondary Education Act of 1965, and schools that serve high numbers or percentages of limited English proficient children.

(B) Developing, evaluating, and disseminating innovative models for the recruitment, induction, retention, and assessment of new, special education teachers who meet the qualifications described in section 1412(a)(14)(C) of this title to reduce teacher shortages, especially from groups that are underrepresented in the teaching profession, including individuals with disabilities.

(C) Providing continuous personnel preparation, training, and professional development designed to provide support and ensure retention of special education and general education teachers and personnel who teach and provide related services to children with disabilities.

(D) Developing and improving programs for paraprofessionals to become special education teachers, related services personnel, and early intervention personnel, including interdisciplinary training to enable the paraprofessionals to improve early intervention, educational, and transitional results for children with disabilities.

(E) In the case of principals and superintendents, providing activities to promote instructional leadership and improved collaboration between general educators, special education teachers, and related services personnel.

(F) Supporting institutions of higher education with minority enrollments of not less than 25 percent for the purpose of preparing personnel to work with children with disabilities.

(G) Developing and improving programs to train special education teachers to develop an expertise in autism spectrum disorders.

(H) Providing continuous personnel preparation, training, and professional development designed to provide support and improve the qualifications of personnel who provide related services to children with disabilities, including to enable such personnel to obtain advanced degrees.

(3) Enhanced support for beginning special educators

In carrying out paragraph (1)(B), the Secretary shall support not less than 1 of the following activities:

(A) Enhancing and restructuring existing programs or developing preservice teacher education programs to prepare special education teachers, at colleges or departments of education within institutions of higher education, by incorporating an extended (such as an additional 5th year) clinical learning opportunity, field experience, or supervised practicum into such programs.

(B) Creating or supporting teacher-faculty partnerships (such as professional development schools) that--

(i) consist of not less than--

(I) 1 or more institutions of higher education with special education personnel preparation programs;

(II) 1 or more local educational agencies that serve high numbers or percentages of low-income students; or

(III) 1 or more elementary schools or secondary schools, particularly schools that have failed to make adequate yearly progress on the basis, in whole and in part, of the assessment results of the disaggregated subgroup of students with disabilities;

(ii) may include other entities eligible for assistance under this subchapter; and

(iii) provide--

(I) high-quality mentoring and induction opportunities with ongoing support for beginning special education teachers; or

(II) inservice professional development to beginning and veteran special education teachers through the ongoing exchange of information and instructional strategies with faculty.

(c) Low incidence disabilities; authorized activities

(1) In general

In carrying out this section, the Secretary shall support activities, consistent with the objectives described in subsection (a), that benefit children with low incidence disabilities.

(2) Authorized activities

Activities that may be carried out under this subsection include activities such as the following:

(A) Preparing persons who--

(i) have prior training in educational and other related service fields; and

(ii) are studying to obtain degrees, certificates, or licensure that will enable the persons to assist children with low incidence disabilities to achieve the objectives set out in their individualized education programs described in section 1414(d) of this title, or to assist infants and toddlers with low incidence disabilities to achieve the outcomes described in their individualized family service plans

described in section 1436 of this title.

(B) Providing personnel from various disciplines with interdisciplinary training that will contribute to improvement in early intervention, educational, and transitional results for children with low incidence disabilities.

(C) Preparing personnel in the innovative uses and application of technology, including universally designed technologies, assistive technology devices, and assistive technology services--

(i) to enhance learning by children with low incidence disabilities through early intervention, educational, and transitional services; and

(ii) to improve communication with parents.

(D) Preparing personnel who provide services to visually impaired or blind children to teach and use Braille in the provision of services to such children.

(E) Preparing personnel to be qualified educational interpreters, to assist children with low incidence disabilities, particularly deaf and hard of hearing children in school and school related activities, and deaf and hard of hearing infants and toddlers and preschool children in early intervention and preschool programs.

(F) Preparing personnel who provide services to children with significant cognitive disabilities and children with multiple disabilities.

(G) Preparing personnel who provide services to children with low incidence disabilities and limited English proficient children.

(3) Definition

In this section, the term "low incidence disability" means--

(A) a visual or hearing impairment, or simultaneous visual and hearing impairments;

(B) a significant cognitive impairment; or

(C) any impairment for which a small number of personnel with highly specialized skills and knowledge are needed in order for children with that impairment to receive early intervention services or a free appropriate public education.

(4) Selection of recipients

In selecting eligible entities for assistance under this subsection, the Secretary may give preference to eligible entities submitting applications that include 1 or more of the following:

(A) A proposal to prepare personnel in more than 1 low incidence disability, such as deafness and blindness.

(B) A demonstration of an effective collaboration between an eligible entity and a local educational agency that promotes recruitment and subsequent retention of personnel who meet the applicable requirements described in section 1412(a)(14) of this title to serve children with low incidence disabilities.

(5) Preparation in use of braille

The Secretary shall ensure that all recipients of awards under this subsection who will use that assistance to visually impaired or blind children that can appropriately be provided in Braille, will prepare those individuals to provide those services in Braille.

(d) Leadership preparation; authorized activities

(1) In general

In carrying out this section, the Secretary shall support leadership preparation activities that are consistent with the objectives described in subsection (a).

(2) Authorized activities

Activities that may be carried out under this subsection include activities such as the following:

(A) Preparing personnel at the graduate, doctoral, and postdoctoral levels of training to administer, enhance, or provide services to improve results for children with disabilities.

(B) Providing interdisciplinary training for various types of leadership personnel, including teacher preparation faculty, related services faculty, administrators, researchers, supervisors, principals, and other persons whose work affects early intervention, educational, and transitional services for children with disabilities, including children with disabilities who are limited English proficient children.

(e) Applications

(1) In general

An eligible entity that wishes to receive a grant, or enter into a contract or cooperative agreement, under this section shall submit an application to the Secretary at such time, in such manner, and containing such information as the Secretary may require.

(2) Identified State needs

(A) Requirement to address identified needs

An application for assistance under subsection (b), (c), or (d) shall include information demonstrating to the satisfaction of the Secretary that the activities described in the application will address needs identified by the State or States the eligible entity proposes to serve.

(B) Cooperation with State educational agencies

An eligible entity that is not a local educational agency or a State educational agency shall include in the eligible entity's application information demonstrating to the satisfaction of the Secretary that the eligible entity and 1 or more State educational agencies or local educational agencies will cooperate in carrying out and monitoring the proposed project.

(3) Acceptance by States of personnel preparation requirements

The Secretary may require eligible entities to provide in the eligible entities' applications assurances from 1 or more States that such States intend to accept successful completion of the proposed personnel preparation program as meeting State personnel standards or other requirements in State law or regulation for serving children with disabilities or serving infants and toddlers with disabilities.

(f) Selection of recipients

(1) Impact of project

In selecting eligible entities for assistance under this section, the Secretary shall consider the impact of the proposed project described in the application in meeting the need for personnel identified by the States.

(2) Requirement for eligible entities to meet State and professional qualifications

The Secretary shall make grants and enter into contracts and cooperative agreements under this section only to eligible entities that meet State and professionally recognized qualifications for the preparation of special education and related services personnel, if the purpose of the project is to assist personnel in obtaining degrees.

(3) Preferences

In selecting eligible entities for assistance under this section, the Secretary may give preference to eligible entities that are institutions of higher education that are--

(A) educating regular education personnel to meet the needs of children with disabilities in integrated settings;

(B) educating special education personnel to work in collaboration with regular educators in integrated settings; and

(C) successfully recruiting and preparing individuals with disabilities and individuals from groups that are underrepresented in the profession for which the institution of higher education is preparing individuals.

(g) Scholarships

The Secretary may include funds for scholarships, with necessary stipends and allowances, in awards under subsections (b), (c), and (d).

(h) Service obligation

(1) In general

Each application for assistance under subsections (b), (c), and (d) shall include an assurance that the eligible entity will ensure that individuals who receive a scholarship under the proposed project agree to subsequently provide special education and related services to children with disabilities, or in the case of leadership personnel to subsequently work in the appropriate field, for a period of 2 years for every year for which the scholarship was received or repay all or part of the amount of the scholarship, in accordance with regulations issued by the Secretary.

(2) Special rule

Notwithstanding paragraph (1), the Secretary may reduce or waive the service obligation requirement under paragraph (1) if the Secretary determines that the service obligation is acting as a deterrent to the recruitment of students into special education or a related field.

(3) Secretary's responsibility

The Secretary--

(A) shall ensure that individuals described in paragraph (1) comply with the requirements of that paragraph; and

(B) may use not more than 0.5 percent of the funds appropriated under subsection (i) for each fiscal year, to carry out subparagraph (A), in addition to any other funds that are available for that purpose.

(i) Authorization of appropriations

There are authorized to be appropriated to carry out this section such sums as may be necessary for each of the fiscal years 2005 through 2010.

SEC. 663. TECHNICAL ASSISTANCE, DEMONSTRATION PROJECTS, DISSEMINATION OF INFORMATION, AND IMPLEMENTATION OF SCIENTIFICALLY BASED RESEARCH.

(a) In general

The Secretary shall make competitive grants to, or enter into contracts or cooperative agreements with, eligible entities to provide technical assistance, support model demonstration projects, disseminate useful information, and implement activities that are supported by scientifically based research.

(b) Required activities

Funds received under this section shall be used to support activities to improve services provided under this chapter, including the practices of professionals and others involved in providing such services to children with disabilities, that promote academic achievement and improve results for children with disabilities through--

(1) implementing effective strategies for addressing inappropriate behavior of students with disabilities in schools, including strategies to prevent children with emotional and behavioral problems from developing emotional disturbances that require the provision of special education and related services;

(2) improving the alignment, compatibility, and development of valid and reliable assessments and alternate assessments for assessing student academic achievement, as described under section 6311(b)(2) of this title;

(3) providing training for both regular education teachers and special education teachers to address the needs of students with different learning styles;

(4) disseminating information about innovative, effective, and efficient curricula designs, instructional approaches, and strategies, and identifying positive academic and social learning opportunities, that--

(A) provide effective transitions between educational settings or from school to post school settings; and

(B) improve educational and transitional results at all levels of the educational system in which the activities are carried out and, in particular, that improve the progress of children with disabilities, as measured by assessments within the general education curriculum involved; and

(5) applying scientifically based findings to facilitate systemic changes, related to the provision of services to children with disabilities, in policy, procedure, practice, and the training and use of personnel.

(c) Authorized activities

Activities that may be carried out under this section include activities to improve services provided under this chapter, including the practices of professionals and others involved in providing such services to children with disabilities, that promote academic achievement and improve results for children with disabilities through--

(1) applying and testing research findings in typical settings where children with disabilities receive services to determine the usefulness, effectiveness, and general applicability of such research findings in such areas as improving instructional methods, curricula, and tools, such as textbooks and media;

(2) supporting and promoting the coordination of early intervention and educational services for children with disabilities with services provided by health,

rehabilitation, and social service agencies;

(3) promoting improved alignment and compatibility of general and special education reforms concerned with curricular and instructional reform, and evaluation of such reforms;

(4) enabling professionals, parents of children with disabilities, and other persons to learn about, and implement, the findings of scientifically based research, and successful practices developed in model demonstration projects, relating to the provision of services to children with disabilities;

(5) conducting outreach, and disseminating information, relating to successful approaches to overcoming systemic barriers to the effective and efficient delivery of early intervention, educational, and transitional services to personnel who provide services to children with disabilities;

(6) assisting States and local educational agencies with the process of planning systemic changes that will promote improved early intervention, educational, and transitional results for children with disabilities;

(7) promoting change through a multistate or regional framework that benefits States, local educational agencies, and other participants in partnerships that are in the process of achieving systemic-change outcomes;

(8) focusing on the needs and issues that are specific to a population of children with disabilities, such as providing single-State and multi-State technical assistance and in-service training--

(A) to schools and agencies serving deaf-blind children and their families;

(B) to programs and agencies serving other groups of children with low incidence disabilities and their families;

(C) addressing the postsecondary education needs of individuals who are deaf or hard-of-hearing; and

(D) to schools and personnel providing special education and related services for children with autism spectrum disorders;

(9) demonstrating models of personnel preparation to ensure appropriate placements and services for all students and to reduce disproportionality in eligibility, placement, and disciplinary actions for minority and limited English proficient children; and

(10) disseminating information on how to reduce inappropriate racial and ethnic disproportionalities identified under section 1418 of this title.

(d) Balance among activities and age ranges

In carrying out this section, the Secretary shall ensure that there is an appropriate balance across all age ranges of children with disabilities.

(e) Linking States to information sources

In carrying out this section, the Secretary shall support projects that link States to technical assistance resources, including special education and general education resources, and shall make research and related products available through libraries, electronic networks, parent training projects, and other information sources, including through the activities of the National Center for Education Evaluation and Regional Assistance established under part D of the Education Sciences Reform Act of 2002.

(f) Applications

(1) In general

An eligible entity that wishes to receive a grant, or enter into a contract or cooperative agreement, under this section shall submit an application to the Secretary at such time, in such manner, and containing such information as the Secretary may require.

(2) Standards

To the maximum extent feasible, each eligible entity shall demonstrate that the project described in the eligible entity's application is supported by scientifically valid research that has been carried out in accordance with the standards for the conduct and evaluation of all relevant research and development established by the National Center for Education Research.

(3) Priority

As appropriate, the Secretary shall give priority to applications that propose to serve teachers and school personnel directly in the school environment.

SEC. 664. STUDIES AND EVALUATIONS.

(a) STUDIES AND EVALUATIONS-

(1) DELEGATION- The Secretary shall delegate to the Director of the Institute of Education Sciences responsibility to carry out this section, other than subsections (d) and (f).

(2) ASSESSMENT- The Secretary shall, directly or through grants, contracts, or cooperative agreements awarded to eligible entities on a competitive basis, assess the progress in the implementation of this title, including the effectiveness of State and local efforts to provide—

(A) a free appropriate public education to children with disabilities; and

(B) early intervention services to infants and toddlers with disabilities, and infants and toddlers who would be at risk of having substantial developmental delays if early intervention services were not provided to the infants and toddlers.

(b) ASSESSMENT OF NATIONAL ACTIVITIES-

(1) IN GENERAL- The Secretary shall carry out a national assessment of activities carried out with Federal funds under this title in order—

(A) to determine the effectiveness of this title in achieving the purposes of this title;

(B) to provide timely information to the President, Congress, the States, local educational agencies, and the public on how to implement this title more effectively; and

(C) to provide the President and Congress with information that will be useful in developing legislation to achieve the purposes of this title more effectively.

(2) SCOPE OF ASSESSMENT- The national assessment shall assess activities supported under this title, including—

(A) the implementation of programs assisted under this title and the impact of such programs on addressing the developmental needs of, and improving the academic achievement of, children with disabilities to enable the children to reach challenging developmental goals and challenging State academic content standards based on State academic assessments;

(B) the types of programs and services that have demonstrated the greatest likelihood of helping students reach the challenging State academic content standards and developmental goals;

(C) the implementation of the professional development activities assisted under this title and the impact on instruction, student academic achievement, and teacher qualifications to enhance the ability of special education teachers and regular education teachers to improve results for children with disabilities; and

(D) the effectiveness of schools, local educational agencies, States, other recipients of assistance under this title, and the Secretary in achieving the purposes of this title by—

(i) improving the academic achievement of children with disabilities and their performance on regular statewide assessments as compared to nondisabled children, and the performance of children with disabilities on alternate assessments;

(ii) improving the participation of children with disabilities in the general education curriculum;

(iii) improving the transitions of children with disabilities at natural transition points;

(iv) placing and serving children with disabilities, including minority children, in the least restrictive environment appropriate;

(v) preventing children with disabilities, especially children with emotional disturbances and specific learning disabilities, from dropping out of school;

(vi) addressing the reading and literacy needs of children with disabilities;

(vii) reducing the inappropriate overidentification of children, especially minority and limited English proficient children, as having a disability;

(viii) improving the participation of parents of children with disabilities in the education of their children; and

(ix) resolving disagreements between education personnel and parents through alternate dispute resolution activities, including mediation.

(3) INTERIM AND FINAL REPORTS- The Secretary shall submit to the President and Congress—

(A) an interim report that summarizes the preliminary findings of the assessment not later than 3 years after the date of enactment of the Individuals with Disabilities Education Improvement Act of 2004; and

(B) a final report of the findings of the assessment not later than 5 years after the date of enactment of such Act.

(c) STUDY ON ENSURING ACCOUNTABILITY FOR STUDENTS WHO ARE HELD TO ALTERNATIVE ACHIEVEMENT STANDARDS- The Secretary shall carry out a national study or studies to examine—

(1) the criteria that States use to determine—

(A) eligibility for alternate assessments; and

(B) the number and type of children who take those assessments and are held accountable to alternative achievement standards;

(2) the validity and reliability of alternate assessment instruments and procedures;

(3) the alignment of alternate assessments and alternative achievement standards to State academic content standards in reading, mathematics, and science; and

(4) the use and effectiveness of alternate assessments in appropriately measuring student progress and outcomes specific to individualized instructional need.

(d) ANNUAL REPORT- The Secretary shall provide an annual report to Congress that—

(1) summarizes the research conducted under part E of the Education Sciences Reform Act of 2002;

(2) analyzes and summarizes the data reported by the States and the Secretary of the

Interior under section 618;

(3) summarizes the studies and evaluations conducted under this section and the timeline for their completion;

(4) describes the extent and progress of the assessment of national activities; and

(5) describes the findings and determinations resulting from reviews of State implementation of this title.

(e) AUTHORIZED ACTIVITIES- In carrying out this section, the Secretary may support objective studies, evaluations, and assessments, including studies that—

(1) analyze measurable impact, outcomes, and results achieved by State educational agencies and local educational agencies through their activities to reform policies, procedures, and practices designed to improve educational and transitional services and results for children with disabilities;

(2) analyze State and local needs for professional development, parent training, and other appropriate activities that can reduce the need for disciplinary actions involving children with disabilities;

(3) assess educational and transitional services and results for children with disabilities from minority backgrounds, including—

(A) data on—

(i) the number of minority children who are referred for special education evaluation;

(ii) the number of minority children who are receiving special education and related services and their educational or other service placement;

(iii) the number of minority children who graduated from secondary programs with a regular diploma in the standard number of years; and

(iv) the number of minority children who drop out of the educational system; and

(B) the performance of children with disabilities from minority backgrounds on State assessments and other performance indicators established for all students;

(4) measure educational and transitional services and results for children with disabilities served under this title, including longitudinal studies that—

(A) examine educational and transitional services and results for children with disabilities who are 3 through 17 years of age and are receiving special education and related services under this title, using a national, representative sample of distinct age cohorts and disability categories; and

(B) examine educational results, transition services, postsecondary placement, and employment status for individuals with disabilities, 18 through 21 years of age, who are receiving or have received special education and related services under this title; and

(5) identify and report on the placement of children with disabilities by disability category.

(f) STUDY- The Secretary shall study, and report to Congress regarding, the extent to which States adopt policies described in section 635(c)(1) and on the effects of those policies.

SEC. 665. INTERIM ALTERNATIVE EDUCATIONAL SETTINGS, BEHAVIORAL SUPPORTS, AND SYSTEMIC SCHOOL INTERVENTIONS.

(a) PROGRAM AUTHORIZED- The Secretary may award grants, and enter into contracts and cooperative agreements, to support safe learning environments that support academic achievement for all students by—

(1) improving the quality of interim alternative educational settings; and

(2) providing increased behavioral supports and research-based, systemic interventions in schools.

(b) AUTHORIZED ACTIVITIES- In carrying out this section, the Secretary may support activities to—

(1) establish, expand, or increase the scope of behavioral supports and systemic interventions by providing for effective, research-based practices, including—

(A) training for school staff on early identification, prereferral, and referral procedures;

(B) training for administrators, teachers, related services personnel, behavioral specialists, and other school staff in positive behavioral interventions and supports, behavioral intervention planning, and classroom and student management techniques;

(C) joint training for administrators, parents, teachers, related services personnel, behavioral specialists, and other school staff on effective strategies for positive behavioral interventions and behavior management strategies that focus on the prevention of behavior problems;

(D) developing or implementing specific curricula, programs, or interventions aimed at addressing behavioral problems;

(E) stronger linkages between school-based services and community-based resources, such as community mental health and primary care providers; or

(F) using behavioral specialists, related services personnel, and other staff necessary to implement behavioral supports; or

(2) improve interim alternative educational settings by—

(A) improving the training of administrators, teachers, related services personnel, behavioral specialists, and other school staff (including ongoing mentoring of new teachers) in behavioral supports and interventions;

(B) attracting and retaining a high quality, diverse staff;

(C) providing for referral to counseling services;

(D) utilizing research-based interventions, curriculum, and practices;

(E) allowing students to use instructional technology that provides individualized instruction;

(F) ensuring that the services are fully consistent with the goals of the individual student's IEP;

(G) promoting effective case management and collaboration among parents, teachers, physicians, related services personnel, behavioral specialists, principals, administrators, and other school staff;

(H) promoting interagency coordination and coordinated service delivery among schools, juvenile courts, child welfare agencies, community mental health providers, primary care providers, public recreation agencies, and community-based organizations; or

(I) providing for behavioral specialists to help students transitioning from interim alternative educational settings reintegrate into their regular classrooms.

(c) DEFINITION OF ELIGIBLE ENTITY- In this section, the term eligible entity' means—

(1) a local educational agency; or

(2) a consortium consisting of a local educational agency and 1 or more of the following entities:

(A) Another local educational agency.

(B) A community-based organization with a demonstrated record of effectiveness in helping children with disabilities who have behavioral challenges succeed.

(C) An institution of higher education.

(D) A community mental health provider.

(E) An educational service agency.

(d) APPLICATIONS- Any eligible entity that wishes to receive a grant, or enter into a contract or cooperative agreement, under this section shall—

(1) submit an application to the Secretary at such time, in such manner, and containing such information as the Secretary may require; and

(2) involve parents of participating students in the design and implementation of the activities funded under this section.

(e) REPORT AND EVALUATION- Each eligible entity receiving a grant under this section shall prepare and submit annually to the Secretary a report on the outcomes of the activities assisted under the grant.

SEC. 667. AUTHORIZATION OF APPROPRIATIONS.

(a) IN GENERAL- There are authorized to be appropriated to carry out this subpart (other than section 662) such sums as may be necessary for each of the fiscal years 2005 through 2010.

(b) RESERVATION- From amounts appropriated under subsection (a) for fiscal year 2005, the Secretary shall reserve $1,000,000 to carry out the study authorized in section 664(c). From amounts appropriated under subsection (a) for a succeeding fiscal year, the Secretary may reserve an additional amount to carry out such study if the Secretary determines the additional amount is necessary.

Subpart 3—Supports To Improve Results for Children With Disabilities

SEC. 670. PURPOSES.

The purposes of this subpart are to ensure that—

(1) children with disabilities and their parents receive training and information designed to assist the children in meeting developmental and functional goals, and challenging academic achievement goals, and in preparing to lead productive independent adult lives;

(2) children with disabilities and their parents receive training and information on their rights, responsibilities, and protections under this title, in order to develop the skills necessary to cooperatively and effectively participate in planning and decision making relating to early intervention, educational, and transitional services;

(3) parents, teachers, administrators, early intervention personnel, related services personnel, and transition personnel receive coordinated and accessible technical assistance and information to assist such personnel in improving early intervention, educational, and transitional services and results for children with disabilities and their families; and

(4) appropriate technology and media are researched, developed, and demonstrated, to improve and implement early intervention, educational, and transitional services and results for children with disabilities and their families.

SEC. 671. PARENT TRAINING AND INFORMATION CENTERS.

(a) PROGRAM AUTHORIZED-

(1) IN GENERAL- The Secretary may award grants to, and enter into contracts and cooperative agreements with, parent organizations to support parent training and information centers to carry out activities under this section.

(2) DEFINITION OF PARENT ORGANIZATION- In this section, the term parent organization' means a private nonprofit organization (other than an institution of higher education) that—

(A) has a board of directors—

(i) the majority of whom are parents of children with disabilities ages birth through 26;

(ii) that includes—

(I) individuals working in the fields of special education, related services, and early intervention; and

(II) individuals with disabilities; and

(iii) the parent and professional members of which are broadly representative of the population to be served, including low-income parents and parents of limited English proficient children; and

(B) has as its mission serving families of children with disabilities who—

(i) are ages birth through 26; and

(ii) have the full range of disabilities described in section 602(3).

(b) REQUIRED ACTIVITIES- Each parent training and information center that receives assistance under this section shall—

(1) provide training and information that meets the needs of parents of children with disabilities living in the area served by the center, particularly underserved parents and parents of children who may be inappropriately identified, to enable their children with disabilities to—

(A) meet developmental and functional goals, and challenging academic achievement goals that have been established for all children; and

(B) be prepared to lead productive independent adult lives, to the maximum extent possible;

(2) serve the parents of infants, toddlers, and children with the full range of disabilities described in section 602(3);

(3) ensure that the training and information provided meets the needs of low-income parents and parents of limited English proficient children;

(4) assist parents to—

(A) better understand the nature of their children's disabilities and their educational, developmental, and transitional needs;

(B) communicate effectively and work collaboratively with personnel responsible for providing special education, early intervention services, transition services, and related services;

(C) participate in decisionmaking processes and the development of individualized education programs under part B and individualized family service plans under part C;

(D) obtain appropriate information about the range, type, and quality of—

(i) options, programs, services, technologies, practices and interventions based on scientifically based research, to the extent practicable; and

(ii) resources available to assist children with disabilities and their families in school and at home;

(E) understand the provisions of this title for the education of, and the provision of early intervention services to, children with disabilities;

(F) participate in activities at the school level that benefit their children; and

(G) participate in school reform activities;

(5) in States where the State elects to contract with the parent training and information center, contract with State educational agencies to provide, consistent with subparagraphs (B) and (D) of section 615(e)(2), individuals who meet with parents to explain the mediation process to the parents;

(6) assist parents in resolving disputes in the most expeditious and effective way possible, including encouraging the use, and explaining the benefits, of alternative methods of dispute resolution, such as the mediation process described in section 615(e);

(7) assist parents and students with disabilities to understand their rights and responsibilities under this title, including those under section 615(m) upon the student's reaching the age of majority (as appropriate under State law);

(8) assist parents to understand the availability of, and how to effectively use, procedural safeguards under this title, including the resolution session described in section 615(e);

(9) assist parents in understanding, preparing for, and participating in, the process described in section 615(f)(1)(B);

(10) establish cooperative partnerships with community parent resource centers funded under section 672;

(11) network with appropriate clearinghouses, including organizations conducting national dissemination activities under section 663 and the Institute of Education Sciences, and with other national, State, and local organizations and agencies, such as protection and advocacy agencies, that serve parents and families of children with the full range of disabilities described in section 602(3); and

(12) annually report to the Secretary on—

(A) the number and demographics of parents to whom the center provided information and training in the most recently concluded fiscal year;

(B) the effectiveness of strategies used to reach and serve parents, including underserved parents of children with disabilities; and

(C) the number of parents served who have resolved disputes through alternative methods of dispute resolution.

(c) OPTIONAL ACTIVITIES- A parent training and information center that receives assistance under this section may provide information to teachers and other professionals to assist the teachers and professionals in improving results for children with disabilities.

(d) APPLICATION REQUIREMENTS- Each application for assistance under this section shall identify with specificity the special efforts that the parent organization will undertake—

(1) to ensure that the needs for training and information of underserved parents of children with disabilities in the area to be served are effectively met; and

(2) to work with community based organizations, including community based organizations that work with low-income parents and parents of limited English proficient children.

(e) DISTRIBUTION OF FUNDS-

(1) IN GENERAL- The Secretary shall—

(A) make not less than 1 award to a parent organization in each State for a parent training and information center that is designated as the statewide parent training and information center; or

(B) in the case of a large State, make awards to multiple parent training and information centers, but only if the centers demonstrate that coordinated services and supports will occur among the multiple centers.

(2) SELECTION REQUIREMENT- The Secretary shall select among applications submitted by parent organizations in a State in a manner that ensures the most effective assistance to parents, including parents in urban and rural areas, in the State.

(f) QUARTERLY REVIEW-

(1) MEETINGS- The board of directors of each parent organization that receives an award under this section shall meet not less than once in each calendar quarter to review the activities for which the award was made.

(2) CONTINUATION AWARD- When a parent organization requests a continuation award under this section, the board of directors shall submit to the Secretary a written review of the parent training and information program conducted by the parent organization during the preceding fiscal year.

SEC. 672. COMMUNITY PARENT RESOURCE CENTERS.

(a) PROGRAM AUTHORIZED-

(1) IN GENERAL- The Secretary may award grants to, and enter into contracts and cooperative agreements with, local parent organizations to support community parent resource centers that will help ensure that underserved parents of children with disabilities, including low income parents, parents of limited English proficient children, and parents with disabilities, have the training and information the parents need to enable the parents to participate effectively in helping their children with disabilities—

(A) to meet developmental and functional goals, and challenging academic achievement goals that have been established for all children; and

(B) to be prepared to lead productive independent adult lives, to the maximum extent possible.

(2) DEFINITION OF LOCAL PARENT ORGANIZATION- In this section, the term local parent organization' means a parent organization, as defined in section 671(a)(2), that—

(A) has a board of directors the majority of whom are parents of children with disabilities ages birth through 26 from the community to be served; and

(B) has as its mission serving parents of children with disabilities who—

(i) are ages birth through 26; and

(ii) have the full range of disabilities described in section 602(3).

(b) REQUIRED ACTIVITIES- Each

community parent resource center assisted under this section shall—

(1) provide training and information that meets the training and information needs of parents of children with disabilities proposed to be served by the grant, contract, or cooperative agreement;

(2) carry out the activities required of parent training and information centers under paragraphs (2) through (9) of section 671(b);

(3) establish cooperative partnerships with the parent training and information centers funded under section 671; and

(4) be designed to meet the specific needs of families who experience significant isolation from available sources of information and support.

SEC. 673. TECHNICAL ASSISTANCE FOR PARENT TRAINING AND INFORMATION CENTERS.

(a) PROGRAM AUTHORIZED-

(1) IN GENERAL- The Secretary may, directly or through awards to eligible entities, provide technical assistance for developing, assisting, and coordinating parent training and information programs carried out by parent training and information centers receiving assistance under section 671 and community parent resource centers receiving assistance under section 672.

(2) DEFINITION OF ELIGIBLE ENTITY- In this section, the term eligible entity' has the meaning given the term in section 661(b).

(b) AUTHORIZED ACTIVITIES- The Secretary may provide technical assistance to a parent training and information center or a community parent resource center under this section in areas such as—

(1) effective coordination of parent training efforts;

(2) dissemination of scientifically based research and information;

(3) promotion of the use of technology, including assistive technology devices and assistive technology services;

(4) reaching underserved populations, including parents of low-income and limited English proficient children with disabilities;

(5) including children with disabilities in general education programs;

(6) facilitation of transitions from—

(A) early intervention services to preschool;

(B) preschool to elementary school;

(C) elementary school to secondary school; and

(D) secondary school to postsecondary

environments; and

(7) promotion of alternative methods of dispute resolution, including mediation.

(c) COLLABORATION WITH THE RESOURCE CENTERS- Each eligible entity receiving an award under subsection (a) shall develop collaborative agreements with the geographically appropriate regional resource center and, as appropriate, the regional educational laboratory supported under section 174 of the Education Sciences Reform Act of 2002, to further parent and professional collaboration.

SEC. 674. TECHNOLOGY DEVELOPMENT, DEMONSTRATION, AND UTILIZATION; MEDIA SERVICES; AND INSTRUCTIONAL MATERIALS.

(a) PROGRAM AUTHORIZED-

(1) IN GENERAL- The Secretary, on a competitive basis, shall award grants to, and enter into contracts and cooperative agreements with, eligible entities to support activities described in subsections (b) and (c).

(2) DEFINITION OF ELIGIBLE ENTITY- In this section, the term eligible entity' has the meaning given the term in section 661(b).

(b) TECHNOLOGY DEVELOPMENT, DEMONSTRATION, AND USE-

(1) IN GENERAL- In carrying out this section, the Secretary shall support activities to promote the development, demonstration, and use of technology.

(2) AUTHORIZED ACTIVITIES- The following activities may be carried out under this subsection:

(A) Conducting research on and promoting the demonstration and use of innovative, emerging, and universally designed technologies for children with disabilities, by improving the transfer of technology from research and development to practice.

(B) Supporting research, development, and dissemination of technology with universal design features, so that the technology is accessible to the broadest range of individuals with disabilities without further modification or adaptation.

(C) Demonstrating the use of systems to provide parents and teachers with information and training concerning early diagnosis of, intervention for, and effective teaching strategies for, young children with reading disabilities.

(D) Supporting the use of Internet-based communications for students with cognitive disabilities in order to maximize their academic and functional skills.

(c) EDUCATIONAL MEDIA SERVICES-

(1) IN GENERAL- In carrying out this section, the Secretary shall support—

(A) educational media activities that are designed to be of educational value in the classroom setting to children with disabilities;

(B) providing video description, open captioning, or closed captioning, that is appropriate for use in the classroom setting, of—

(i) television programs;

(ii) videos;

(iii) other materials, including programs and materials associated with new and emerging technologies, such as CDs, DVDs, video streaming, and other forms of multimedia; or

(iv) news (but only until September 30, 2006);

(C) distributing materials described in subparagraphs (A) and (B) through such mechanisms as a loan service; and

(D) providing free educational materials, including textbooks, in accessible media for visually impaired and print disabled students in elementary schools and secondary schools, postsecondary schools, and graduate schools.

(2) LIMITATION- The video description, open captioning, or closed captioning described in paragraph (1)(B) shall be provided only when the description or captioning has not been previously provided by the producer or distributor, or has not been fully funded by other sources.

(d) APPLICATIONS-

(1) IN GENERAL- Any eligible entity that wishes to receive a grant, or enter into a contract or cooperative agreement, under subsection (b) or (c) shall submit an application to the Secretary at such time, in such manner, and containing such information as the Secretary may require.

(2) SPECIAL RULE- For the purpose of an application for an award to carry out activities described in subsection (c)(1)(D), such eligible entity shall—

(A) be a national, nonprofit entity with a proven track record of meeting the needs of students with print disabilities through services described in subsection (c)(1)(D);

(B) have the capacity to produce, maintain, and distribute in a timely fashion, up-to-date textbooks in digital audio formats to qualified students; and

(C) have a demonstrated ability to significantly leverage Federal funds through other public and private contributions, as well as through the expansive use of volunteers.

(e) NATIONAL INSTRUCTIONAL MATERIALS ACCESS CENTER-

(1) IN GENERAL- The Secretary shall establish and support, through the American Printing House for the Blind, a center to be known as the National Instructional Materials Access Center' not later than 1 year after the date of enactment of the Individuals with Disabilities Education Improvement Act of 2004.

(2) DUTIES- The duties of the National Instructional Materials Access Center are the following:

(A) To receive and maintain a catalog of print instructional materials prepared in the National Instructional Materials Accessibility Standard, as established by the Secretary, made available to such center by the textbook publishing industry, State educational agencies, and local educational agencies.

(B) To provide access to print instructional materials, including textbooks, in accessible media, free of charge, to blind or other persons with print disabilities in elementary schools and secondary schools, in accordance with such terms and procedures as the National Instructional Materials Access Center may prescribe.

(C) To develop, adopt and publish procedures to protect against copyright infringement, with respect to the print instructional materials provided under sections 612(a)(23) and 613(a)(6).

(3) DEFINITIONS- In this subsection:

(A) BLIND OR OTHER PERSONS WITH PRINT DISABILITIES- The term blind or other persons with print disabilities' means children served under this Act and who may qualify in accordance with the Act entitled An Act to provide books for the adult blind', approved March 3, 1931 (2 U.S.C. 135a; 46 Stat. 1487) to receive books and other publications produced in specialized formats.

(B) NATIONAL INSTRUCTIONAL MATERIALS ACCESSIBILITY STANDARD- The term National Instructional Materials Accessibility Standard' means the standard established by the Secretary to be used in the preparation of electronic files suitable and used solely for efficient conversion into specialized formats.

(C) PRINT INSTRUCTIONAL MATERIALS- The term print instructional materials' means printed textbooks and related printed core materials that are written and published primarily for use in elementary school and secondary school instruction and are required by a State educational agency or local educational agency for use by students in the classroom.

(D) SPECIALIZED FORMATS- The term specialized formats' has the meaning given the term in section 121(d)(3) of title 17, United States Code.

(4) APPLICABILITY- This subsection shall apply to print instructional materials published after the date on which the final rule establishing the National Instructional Materials Accessibility Standard was published in the Federal Register.

(5) LIABILITY OF THE SECRETARY- Nothing in this subsection shall be construed to establish a private right of action against the Secretary for failure to provide instructional materials directly, or for failure by the National Instructional Materials Access Center to perform the duties of such center, or to otherwise authorize a private right of action related to the performance by such center, including through the application of the rights of children and parents established under this Act.

(6) INAPPLICABILITY- Subsections (a) through (d) shall not apply to this subsection.

SEC. 675. AUTHORIZATION OF APPROPRIATIONS.

There are authorized to be appropriated to carry out this subpart such sums as may be necessary for each of the fiscal years 2005 through 2010.

Subpart 4—General Provisions

SEC. 681. Comprehensive plan for subparts 2 and 3.

(a) Comprehensive plan

(1) In general

After receiving input from interested individuals with relevant expertise, the Secretary shall develop and implement a comprehensive plan for activities carried out under parts B and C in order to enhance the provision of early intervention services, educational services, related services, and transitional services to children with disabilities under subchapters II and III. To the extent practicable, the plan shall be coordinated with the plan developed pursuant to section 9567b(c)1 of this title and shall include mechanisms to address early intervention, educational, related service and transitional needs identified by State educational agencies in applications submitted for State personnel development grants under part A and for grants under parts B and C.

(2) Public comment

The Secretary shall provide a public comment period of not less than 45 days on the plan.

(3) Distribution of funds

In implementing the plan, the Secretary shall, to the extent appropriate, ensure that funds awarded under parts B and C are used to carry out activities that benefit, directly or indirectly, children with the full range of disabilities and of all ages.

(4) Reports to Congress

The Secretary shall annually report to Congress on the Secretary's activities under parts B and C, including an initial report not later than 12 months after December 3, 2004.

(b) Assistance authorized

The Secretary is authorized to award grants to, or enter into contracts or cooperative agreements with, eligible entities to enable the eligible entities to carry out the purposes of such parts in accordance with the comprehensive plan described in subsection (a).

(c) Special populations

(1) Application requirement

In making an award of a grant, contract, or cooperative agreement under part B or C, the Secretary shall, as appropriate, require an eligible entity to demonstrate how the eligible entity will address the needs of children with disabilities from minority backgrounds.

(2) Required outreach and technical assistance

Notwithstanding any other provision of this chapter, the Secretary shall reserve not less than 2 percent of the total amount of funds appropriated to carry out parts B and C for either or both of the following activities:

(A) Providing outreach and technical assistance to historically Black colleges and universities, and to institutions of higher education with minority enrollments of not less than 25 percent, to promote the participation of such colleges, universities, and institutions in activities under this part.

(B) Enabling historically Black colleges and universities, and the institutions described in subparagraph (A), to assist other colleges, universities, institutions, and agencies in improving educational and transitional results for children with disabilities, if the historically Black colleges and universities and the institutions of higher education described in subparagraph (A) meet the criteria established by the Secretary under this part.

(d) Priorities

The Secretary, in making an award of

a grant, contract, or cooperative agreement under part B or C, may, without regard to the rulemaking procedures under section 553 of Title 5, limit competitions to, or otherwise give priority to--

(1) projects that address 1 or more--

(A) age ranges;

(B) disabilities;

(C) school grades;

(D) types of educational placements or early intervention environments;

(E) types of services;

(F) content areas, such as reading; or

(G) effective strategies for helping children with disabilities learn appropriate behavior in the school and other community based educational settings;

(2) projects that address the needs of children based on the severity or incidence of their disability;

(3) projects that address the needs of--

(A) low achieving students;

(B) underserved populations;

(C) children from low income families;

(D) limited English proficient children;

(E) unserved and underserved areas;

(F) rural or urban areas;

(G) children whose behavior interferes with their learning and socialization;

(H) children with reading difficulties;

(I) children in public charter schools;

(J) children who are gifted and talented; or

(K) children with disabilities served by local educational agencies that receive payments under title VII of the Elementary and Secondary Education Act of 1965;

(4) projects to reduce inappropriate identification of children as children with disabilities, particularly among minority children;

(5) projects that are carried out in particular areas of the country, to ensure broad geographic coverage;

(6) projects that promote the development and use of technologies with universal design, assistive technology devices, and assistive technology services to maximize children with disabilities' access to and participation in the general education curriculum; and

(7) any activity that is authorized in part B or C.

(e) Eligibility for financial assistance

No State or local educational agency, or other public institution or agency, may receive a grant or enter into a contract or cooperative agreement under part B or C that relates exclusively to programs, projects, and activities pertaining to children aged 3 through 5, inclusive, unless the State is eligible to receive a grant under section 1419(b) of this title.

SEC. 682. Administrative provisions.

(a) Applicant and recipient responsibilities

(1) Development and assessment of projects

The Secretary shall require that an applicant for, and a recipient of, a grant, contract, or cooperative agreement for a project under part B or C--

(A) involve individuals with disabilities or parents of individuals with disabilities ages birth through 26 in planning, implementing, and evaluating the project; and

(B) where appropriate, determine whether the project has any potential for replication and adoption by other entities.

(2) Additional responsibilities

The Secretary may require a recipient of a grant, contract, or cooperative agreement under part B or C to--

(A) share in the cost of the project;

(B) prepare any findings and products from the project in formats that are useful for specific audiences, including parents, administrators, teachers, early intervention personnel, related services personnel, and individuals with disabilities;

(C) disseminate such findings and products; and

(D) collaborate with other such recipients in carrying out subparagraphs (B) and (C).

(b) Application management

(1) Standing panel

(A) In general

The Secretary shall establish and use a standing panel of experts who are qualified, by virtue of their training, expertise, or experience, to evaluate each application under part B or C that requests more than $75,000 per year in Federal financial assistance.

(B) Membership

The standing panel shall include, at a minimum--

(i) individuals who are representatives of institutions of higher education that plan, develop, and carry out high quality programs of personnel preparation;

(ii) individuals who design and carry out scientifically based research targeted to the improvement of special education programs and services;

(iii) individuals who have recognized experience and knowledge necessary to integrate and apply scientifically based research findings to improve educational and transitional results for children with disabilities;

(iv) individuals who administer programs at the State or local level in which children with disabilities participate;

(v) individuals who prepare parents of children with disabilities to participate in making decisions about the education of their children;

(vi) individuals who establish policies that affect the delivery of services to children with disabilities;

(vii) individuals who are parents of children with disabilities ages birth through 26 who are benefiting, or have benefited, from coordinated research, personnel preparation, and technical assistance; and

(viii) individuals with disabilities.

(C) Term

No individual shall serve on the standing panel for more than 3 consecutive years.

(2) Peer-review panels for particular competitions

(A) Composition

The Secretary shall ensure that each subpanel selected from the standing panel that reviews an application under part B or C includes--

(i) individuals with knowledge and expertise on the issues addressed by the activities described in the application; and

(ii) to the extent practicable, parents of children with disabilities ages birth through 26, individuals with disabilities, and persons from diverse backgrounds.

(B) Federal employment limitation

A majority of the individuals on each subpanel that reviews an application under part B or C shall be individuals who are not employees of the Federal Government.

(3) Use of discretionary funds for administrative purposes

(A) Expenses and fees of non-Federal panel members

The Secretary may use funds available under part B or C to pay the expenses and fees of the panel members who are not officers or employees of the Federal Government.

(B) Administrative support

The Secretary may use not more than 1 percent of the funds appropriated to carry out part B or C to pay non-Federal entities for administrative support related to management of applications submitted under part B or C, respectively.

(c) Program evaluation

The Secretary may use funds made available to carry out part B or C to evaluate activities carried out under part B or C, respectively.

(d) Minimum funding required

(1) In general

Subject to paragraph (2), the Secretary shall ensure that, for each fiscal year, not less than the following amounts are provided under parts B and C to address the following needs:

(A) $12,832,000 to address the educational, related services, transitional, and early intervention needs of children with deaf-blindness.

(B) $4,000,000 to address the postsecondary, vocational, technical, continuing, and adult education needs of individuals with deafness.

(C) $4,000,000 to address the educational, related services, and transitional needs of children with an emotional disturbance and those who are at risk of developing an emotional disturbance.

(2) Ratable reduction

If the sum of the amount appropriated to carry out parts B and C and part E of the Education Sciences Reform Act of 2002 for any fiscal year is less than $130,000,000, the amounts listed in paragraph (1) shall be ratably reduced for the fiscal year:

****

See   www.gpo.gov/fdsys/pkg/FR-2006-08-14/pdf/06-6656.pdf to view the Federal Regulations Implementing the IDEA.

APPENDIX B

Table of Special Education Cases
Decided by the U.S. Supreme Court

Title and Citation (in chronological order)

Southeastern Community College v. Davis, 442 U.S. 397, 99 S.Ct. 2361, 60 L.Ed.2d 980 (1979).

Univ. of Texas v. Camenisch, 451 U.S. 390, 101 S.Ct. 1830, 68 L.Ed.2d 175 (1981).

Pennhurst State School and Hospital v. Halderman, 451 U.S. 1, 101 S.Ct. 1531, 67 L.Ed.2d 694 (1981) (*Pennhurst I*).

Board of Educ. v. Rowley, 458 U.S. 176, 102 S.Ct. 3034, 73 L.Ed.2d 690 (1982).

Pennhurst State School and Hospital v. Halderman, 465 U.S. 89, 104 S.Ct. 900, 79 L.Ed.2d 67 (1984) (*Pennhurst II*).

Irving Independent School Dist. v. Tatro, 468 U.S. 883, 104 S.Ct. 3371, 82 L.Ed.2d 664 (1984).

Smith v. Robinson, 468 U.S. 992, 104 S.Ct. 3457, 82 L.Ed.2d 746 (1984).

Honig v. Students of California School for the Blind, 471 U.S. 148, 105 S.Ct. 1820, 85 L.Ed.2d 114 (1985).

Burlington School Committee v. Dep't of Educ. of Massachusetts, 471 U.S. 359, 105 S.Ct. 1996, 85 L.Ed.2d 385 (1985).

City of Cleburne, Texas v. Cleburne Living Center, 473 U.S. 432, 105 S.Ct. 3249, 87 L.Ed.2d 313 (1985).

Witters v. Washington Dep't of Services for the Blind, 474 U.S. 481, 106 S.Ct. 748, 88 L.Ed.2d 846 (1986).

School Board of Nassau County v. Arline, 480 U.S. 273, 107 S.Ct. 1123, 94 L.Ed.2d 307 (1987).

Honig v. Doe, 484 U.S. 305, 108 S.Ct. 592, 98 L.Ed.2d 686 (1988).

Traynor v. Turnage, 485 U.S. 535, 108 S.Ct. 1372, 99 L.Ed.2d 618 (1988).

Dellmuth v. Muth, 491 U.S. 223, 109 S.Ct. 2397, 105 L.Ed.2d 181 (1989).

Zobrest v. Catalina Foothills School Dist., 509 U.S. 1, 113 S.Ct. 2462, 125 L.Ed.2d 1 (1993).

Florence County School Dist. Four v. Carter, 510 U.S. 7, 114 S.Ct. 361, 126 L.Ed.2d 284 (1993).

Board of Educ. of Kiryas Joel Village School Dist. v. Grumet, 512 U.S. 687, 114 S.Ct. 2481, 129 L.Ed.2d 546 (1994).

Cedar Rapids Community School Dist. v. Garret F., 526 U.S. 66, 119 S.Ct. 992, 143 L.Ed.2d 154 (1999).

Owasso Independent School Dist. No. I-011 v. Falvo, 534 U.S. 426, 122 S.Ct. 934, 151 L.Ed.2d 896 (2002).

Locke v. Davey, 540 U.S. 712, 124 S.Ct. 1307, 158 L.Ed.2d 1 (2004).

Schaffer v. Weast, 546 U.S. 49, 126 S.Ct. 528, 163 L.Ed.2d 387 (2005).

Arlington Cent. School Dist. Board of Educ. v. Murphy, 548 U.S. 291, 126 S.Ct. 2455, 165 L.Ed.2d 526 (2006).

Winkelman v. Parma City School Dist., 550 U.S. 516, 127 S.Ct. 1994, 167 L.Ed.2d 904 (2007).

Fitzgerald v. Barnstable School Committee, 555 U.S. 246, 129 S.Ct. 788, 172 L.Ed.2d 582 (2009).

Ysursa v. Pocatello Educ. Ass'n, 555 U.S. 353, 129 S.Ct. 1093, 172 L.Ed.2d 770 (2009).

Forest Grove School Dist. v. T.A., 557 U.S. 230, 129 S.Ct. 2484, 174 L.Ed.2d 168 (2009).

Fry v. Napoleon Community Schools, 137 S.Ct. 743, 197 L.Ed.2d 46 (2017).

Endrew F. v. Douglas County School Dist. RE-1, 137 S.Ct. 988, 197 L.Ed.2d 335 (2017).

Trinity Lutheran Church of Columbia v. Comer,, 137 S.Ct. 2012, 198 L.Ed.2d 551 (U.S. 2017).

THE JUDICIAL SYSTEM

In order to allow you to determine the relative importance of a judicial decision, the cases included in *Students with Disabilities and Special Education Law* identify the particular court from which a decision has been issued. For example, a case decided by a state supreme court generally will be of greater significance than a state circuit court case. Hence, a basic knowledge of the structure of our judicial system is important to an understanding of school law.

Almost all the reports in this volume are taken from appellate court decisions. Although most education law decisions occur at trial court and administrative levels, appellate court decisions have the effect of binding lower courts and administrators so that appellate court decisions have the effect of law within their court systems.

State and federal court systems generally function independently of each other. Each court system applies its own law according to statutes and the determinations of its highest court. However, judges at all levels often consider opinions from other court systems to settle issues which are new or arise under unique fact situations. Similarly, lawyers look at the opinions of many courts to locate authority that supports their clients' cases.

Once a lawsuit is filed in a particular court system, that system retains the matter until its conclusion. Unsuccessful parties at the administrative or trial court level generally have the right to appeal unfavorable determinations of law to appellate courts within the system. When federal law issues or constitutional grounds are present, lawsuits may be appropriately filed in the federal court system. In those cases, the lawsuit is filed initially in the federal district court for that area.

On rare occasions, the U.S. Supreme Court considers appeals from the highest courts of the states if a distinct federal question exists and at least four justices agree on the question's importance. The federal courts occasionally send cases to state courts for application of state law. These situations are infrequent and, in general, the state and federal court systems should be considered separate from each other.

The most common system, used by nearly all states and also the federal judiciary, is as follows: a legal action is commenced in district court (sometimes called trial court, county court, common pleas court or superior court) where a decision is initially reached. The case may then be appealed to the court of appeals (or appellate court), and, in turn, this decision may be appealed to the supreme court.

Several states, however, do not have a court of appeals; lower court decisions are appealed directly to the state's supreme court. Additionally, some states have labeled their courts in a nonstandard fashion.

In Maryland, the highest state court is called the Court of Appeals. In the state of New York, the trial court is called the Supreme Court. Decisions of this court may be appealed to the Supreme Court, Appellate Division. The highest court in New York is the Court of Appeals. Pennsylvania has perhaps the most complex court system. The lowest state court is the Court of Common Pleas. Depending on the circumstances of the case, appeals may be taken to either the Commonwealth Court or the Superior Court. In certain instances the Commonwealth Court functions as a trial court as well as an appellate court. The Superior Court, however, is strictly an intermediate appellate court. The highest court in Pennsylvania is the Supreme Court.

While supreme court decisions are generally regarded as the last word in legal matters, it is important to remember that trial and appeals court decisions also create important legal precedents. For the hierarchy of typical state and federal court systems, please see the diagram below.

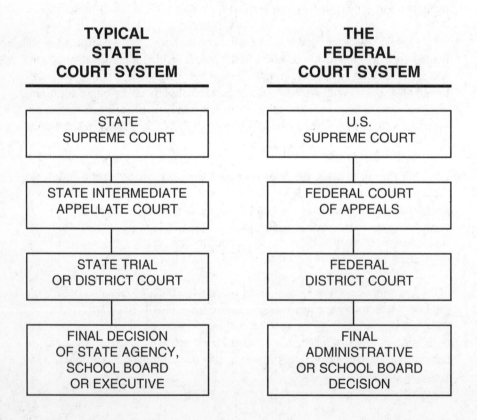

TYPICAL STATE COURT SYSTEM	THE FEDERAL COURT SYSTEM
STATE SUPREME COURT	U.S. SUPREME COURT
STATE INTERMEDIATE APPELLATE COURT	FEDERAL COURT OF APPEALS
STATE TRIAL OR DISTRICT COURT	FEDERAL DISTRICT COURT
FINAL DECISION OF STATE AGENCY, SCHOOL BOARD OR EXECUTIVE	FINAL ADMINISTRATIVE OR SCHOOL BOARD DECISION

Federal courts of appeals hear appeals from the district courts that are located in their circuits. Below is a list of states matched to the federal circuits in which they are located.

First Circuit	— Puerto Rico, Maine, New Hampshire, Massachusetts, Rhode Island
Second Circuit	— New York, Vermont, Connecticut
Third Circuit	— Pennsylvania, New Jersey, Delaware, Virgin Islands
Fourth Circuit	— West Virginia, Maryland, Virginia, North Carolina, South Carolina
Fifth Circuit	— Texas, Louisiana, Mississippi
Sixth Circuit	— Ohio, Kentucky, Tennessee, Michigan
Seventh Circuit	— Wisconsin, Indiana, Illinois
Eighth Circuit	— North Dakota, South Dakota, Nebraska, Arkansas, Missouri, Iowa, Minnesota
Ninth Circuit	— Alaska, Washington, Oregon, California, Hawaii, Arizona, Nevada, Idaho, Montana, Northern Mariana Islands, Guam
Tenth Circuit	— Wyoming, Utah, Colorado, Kansas, Oklahoma, New Mexico
Eleventh Circuit	— Alabama, Georgia, Florida
District of Columbia Circuit	— Hears cases from the U.S. District Court for the District of Columbia.
Federal Circuit	— Sitting in Washington, D.C., the U.S. Court of Appeals, Federal Circuit hears patent and trade appeals and certain appeals on claims brought against the federal government and its agencies.

HOW TO READ A CASE CITATION

Generally, court decisions can be located in case reporters at law school or governmental law libraries. Some cases can also be located on the Internet through legal websites or official court websites.

Each case summary contains the citation, or legal reference, to the full text of the case. The diagram below illustrates how to read a case citation.

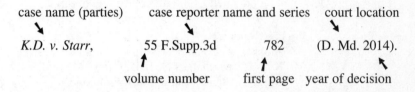

Some cases may have two or three reporter names such as U.S. Supreme Court cases and cases reported in regional case reporters as well as state case reporters. For example, a U.S. Supreme Court case usually contains three case reporter citations.

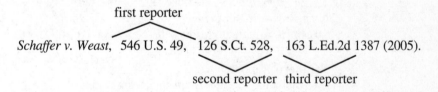

The citations are still read in the same manner as if only one citation has been listed.

Occasionally, a case may contain a citation which does not reference a case reporter. For example, a citation may contain a reference such as:

case name   year of decision   first page

J.Y. v. Dothan City Board of Educ., 2014   WL   1320187,
No. 1:12cv347-SRW   (M.D. Ala. 3/27/14).

court file number   court location   date of decision   Westlaw®[1]

---

[1] Westlaw® is a computerized database of court cases available for a fee.

The court file number indicates the specific number assigned to a case by the particular court system deciding the case. In our example, the Sixth Circuit Court has assigned the case of *Amy S. v. Danbury Local School District* the case number of "No. 04-1279JTM," which will serve as the reference number for the case and any matter relating to the case. Locating a case on the Internet generally requires either the case name and date of the decision, and/or the court file number.

Below, we have listed the full names of the regional reporters. As mentioned previously, many states have individual state reporters. The names of those reporters may be obtained from a reference law librarian.

P.	**Pacific Reporter**
	Alaska, Arizona, California, Colorado, Hawaii, Idaho, Kansas, Montana, Nevada, New Mexico, Oklahoma, Oregon, Utah, Washington, Wyoming
A.	**Atlantic Reporter**
	Connecticut, Delaware, District of Columbia, Maine, Maryland, New Hampshire, New Jersey, Pennsylvania, Rhode Island, Vermont
N.E.	**Northeastern Reporter**
	Illinois, Indiana, Massachusetts, New York, Ohio
N.W.	**Northwestern Reporter**
	Iowa, Michigan, Minnesota, Nebraska, North Dakota, South Dakota, Wisconsin
So.	**Southern Reporter**
	Alabama, Florida, Louisiana, Mississippi
S.E.	**Southeastern Reporter**
	Georgia, North Carolina, South Carolina, Virginia, West Virginia
S.W.	**Southwestern Reporter**
	Arkansas, Kentucky, Missouri, Tennessee, Texas
F.	**Federal Reporter**
	The thirteen federal judicial circuits courts of appeals decisions. See *The Judicial System*, p. 517, for specific state circuits.
F.Supp.	**Federal Supplement**
	The thirteen federal judicial circuits district court decisions.
Fed.Appx.	**Federal Appendix**
	Contains unpublished opinions of the U.S. Circuit Courts of Appeal. See *The Judicial System*, p. 517, for specific state circuits.
U.S.	**United States Reports**
S.Ct.	**Supreme Court Reporter** > U.S. Supreme Court Decisions
L.Ed.	**Lawyers' Edition**

GLOSSARY

Age Discrimination in Employment Act (ADEA) – The ADEA, 29 U.S.C. § 621 *et seq.*, is part of the Fair Labor Standards Act. It prohibits discrimination against persons who are at least 40 years old, and applies to employers that have 20 or more employees and that affect interstate commerce.

Americans with Disabilities Act (ADA) – Key provisions of the ADA, 42 U.S.C. § 12101 *et seq.*, went into effect on July 26, 1992. Among other things, it prohibits discrimination against a qualified individual with a disability because of that person's disability with respect to job application procedures, the hiring, advancement or discharge of employees, employee compensation, job training, and other terms, conditions and privileges of employment.

Bona Fide – Latin term meaning "good faith." Generally used to note a party's lack of bad intent or fraudulent purpose.

Class Action Suit – Federal Rule of Civil Procedure 23 allows members of a class to sue as representatives on behalf of the whole class provided that the class is so large that joinder of all parties is impractical, there are questions of law or fact common to the class, the claims or defenses of the representatives are typical of the claims or defenses of the class, and the representative parties will adequately protect the interests of the class. In addition, there must be some danger of inconsistent verdicts or adjudications if the class action were prosecuted as separate actions. Most states also allow class actions under the same or similar circumstances.

Collateral Estoppel – Also known as issue preclusion. The idea that once an issue has been litigated, it may not be re-tried. Similar to the doctrine of *Res Judicata* (see below).

Due Process Clause – The clauses of the Fifth and Fourteenth Amendments to the Constitution that guarantee the citizens of the United States "due process of law" (see below). The Fifth Amendment's Due Process Clause applies to the federal government, and the Fourteenth Amendment's Due Process Clause applies to the states.

Due Process of Law – The idea of "fair play" in the government's application of law to its citizens, guaranteed by the Fifth and Fourteenth Amendments. Substantive due process is just plain *fairness*, and procedural due process is accorded when the government utilizes adequate procedural safeguards for the protection of an individual's liberty or property interests.

Education for All Handicapped Children Act (EAHCA) – See Individuals with Disabilities Education Act (IDEA).

Education of the Handicapped Act (EHA) – See Individuals with Disabilities Education Act (IDEA).

Enjoin – See Injunction.

Equal Pay Act – Federal legislation which is part of the Fair Labor Standards Act. It applies to discrimination in wages that is based on gender. For race discrimination, employees paid unequally must utilize Title VII or 42 U.S.C. § 1981. Unlike many labor statutes, there is no minimum number of employees necessary to invoke the act's protection.

Equal Protection Clause – The clause of the Fourteenth Amendment that prohibits a state from denying any person within its jurisdiction equal protection of its laws. Also, the Due Process Clause of the Fifth Amendment that pertains to the federal government. This has been interpreted by the Supreme Court to grant equal protection even though there is no explicit grant in the Constitution.

Establishment Clause – The clause of the First Amendment that prohibits Congress from making "any law respecting an establishment of religion." This clause has been interpreted as creating a "wall of separation" between church and state. The test now used to determine whether government action violates the Establishment Clause, referred to as the *Lemon* test, asks whether the action has a secular purpose, whether its primary effect promotes or inhibits religion, and whether it requires excessive entanglement between church and state.

Fair Labor Standards Act (FLSA) – Federal legislation that mandates the payment of minimum wages and overtime compensation to covered employees. The overtime provisions require employers to pay at least time-and-one-half to employees who work more than 40 hours per week.

Federal Tort Claims Act – Federal legislation that determines the circumstances under which the United States waives its sovereign immunity (see below) and agrees to be sued in court for money damages. The government retains its immunity in cases of intentional torts committed by its employees or agents, and where the tort is the result of a "discretionary function" of a federal employee or agency. Many states have similar acts.

42 U.S.C. §§ 1981, 1983 – Section 1983 of the federal Civil Rights Act prohibits any person acting under color of state law from depriving any other person of rights protected by the Constitution or by federal laws. A vast majority of lawsuits claiming constitutional violations are brought under § 1983. Section 1981 provides that all persons enjoy the same right to make and enforce contracts as "white citizens." Section 1981 applies to employment contracts. Further, unlike § 1983, § 1981 applies even to private actors. It is not limited to those acting under color of state law. These sections do not apply to the federal government, though the government may be sued directly under the Constitution for any violations.

Free Appropriate Public Education (FAPE) – The IDEA requires local educational agencies to provide students with disabilities with a free appropriate public education. Under the federal FAPE standard, a student receives a FAPE through an individually developed education program that allows the student to receive educational benefit. States can enact higher standards under the IDEA, but at a minimum must comply with the federal standard governing the provision of a FAPE.

Free Exercise Clause – The clause of the First Amendment that prohibits Congress from interfering with citizens' rights to the free exercise of their religion. Through the Fourteenth Amendment, it has also been made applicable to the states and their sub-entities. The Supreme Court has held that laws of general applicability that have an incidental effect on persons' free exercise rights are not violative of the Free Exercise Clause.

Handicapped Children's Protection Act (HCPA) – (See also Individuals with Disabilities Education Act (IDEA).) The HCPA, enacted as an amendment to the EHA, provides for the payment of attorneys' fees to a prevailing parent or guardian in a lawsuit brought under the EHA (IDEA).

Hearing Officer – Also known as an administrative law judge. The hearing officer decides disputes that arise *at the administrative level*, and has the power to administer oaths, take testimony, rule on evidentiary questions, and make determinations of fact.

Immunity (Sovereign Immunity) – Federal, state and local governments are free from liability for torts committed except in cases in which they have consented to be sued (by statute or by court decisions).

Incorporation Doctrine – By its own terms, the Bill of Rights applies only to the federal government. The Incorporation Doctrine states that the Fourteenth Amendment makes the Bill of Rights applicable to the states.

Individuals with Disabilities Education Act (IDEA) – Also known as the Education of the Handicapped Act (EHA), the Education for All Handicapped Children Act (EAHCA), and the Handicapped Children's Protection Act (HCPA). Originally enacted as the EHA, the IDEA is the federal legislation that provides for the free appropriate public education of all children with disabilities.

Individualized Education Program (IEP) – The IEP is designed to give children with disabilities a free appropriate education. It is updated annually, with the participation of the child's parents or guardian.

Injunction – An equitable remedy (see Remedies) wherein a court orders a party to do or refrain from doing some particular action.

Issue Preclusion – Also known as collateral estoppel, the legal rule that prohibits a court from reconsideration of a particular issue in litigation arising from the same set of facts, involving the same parties and requesting similar relief to a matter previously heard by the court.

Jurisdiction – The power of a court to determine cases and controversies. The Supreme Court's jurisdiction extends to cases arising under the Constitution and under federal law. Federal courts have the power to hear cases where there is diversity of citizenship or where a federal question is involved.

Least Restrictive Environment/Mainstreaming – Part of what is required for a free appropriate education is that each child with a disability be educated in the "least restrictive environment." To the extent that disabled children are educated with non-disabled children in regular education classes, those children are being mainstreamed.

Negligence per se – Negligence on its face. Usually, the violation of an ordinance or statute will be treated as negligence per se because no careful person would have been guilty of it.

Per Curiam – Latin phrase meaning "by the court." Used in court reports to note an opinion written by the court rather than by a single judge or justice.

Placement – A special education student's placement must be appropriate (as well as responsive to the particular child's needs). Under the IDEA's "stay-put" provision, school officials may not remove a special education child from his or her "then current placement" over the parents' objections until the completion of administrative or judicial review proceedings.

Preemption Doctrine – Doctrine which states that when federal and state law attempt to regulate the same subject matter, federal law prevents the state law from operating. Based on the Supremacy Clause of Article VI, Clause 2, of the Constitution.

Pro Se – A party appearing in court, without the benefit of an attorney, is said to be appearing pro se.

Rehabilitation Act – Section 504 of the Rehabilitation Act prohibits employers who receive federal financial assistance from discriminating against otherwise qualified individuals with handicaps solely because of their handicaps. An otherwise qualified individual is one who can perform the "essential functions" of the job with "reasonable accommodation."

Related Services – As part of the free appropriate education due to children with disabilities, school districts may have to provide related services such as transportation, physical and occupational therapy, and medical services that are for diagnostic or evaluative purposes relating to education.

Remand – The act of an appellate court in returning a case to the court from which it came for further action.

Remedies – There are two general categories of remedies, or relief: legal remedies, which consist of money damages, and equitable remedies, which consist of a court mandate that a specific action be prohibited or required. For example, a claim for compensatory and punitive damages seeks a legal remedy; a claim for an injunction seeks an equitable remedy. Equitable remedies are generally unavailable unless legal remedies are inadequate to address the harm.

Res Judicata – The judicial notion that a claim or action may not be tried twice or re-litigated, or that all causes of action arising out of the same set of operative facts should be tried at one time. Also known as claim preclusion.

Section 1981 & Section 1983 – (see 42 U.S.C. §§ 1981, 1983).

Sovereign Immunity – The idea that the government cannot be sued without its consent. It stems from the English notion that "the King can do no wrong." This immunity from suit has been abrogated in most states and by the federal government through legislative acts known as "tort claims acts."

Standing – The judicial doctrine which states that in order to maintain a lawsuit a party must have some real interest at stake in the outcome of the trial.

Statute of Limitations – A statute of limitation provides the time period in which a specific cause of action may be brought.

Summary Judgment – Federal Rule of Civil Procedure 56 provides for the summary adjudication of a case before trial if either party can show that there is no genuine issue as to any material fact and that, given the facts agreed upon, the party is entitled to judgment as a matter of law. In general, summary judgment is used to dispose of claims which do not support a legally recognized claim.

Supremacy Clause – Clause in Article VI of the Constitution, which states that federal legislation is the supreme law of the land. This clause is used to support the Preemption Doctrine (see above).

Title VII, Civil Rights Act of 1964 (Title VII) – Title VII prohibits discrimination in employment based upon race, color, sex, national origin, or religion. It applies to any employer having fifteen or more employees. Under Title VII, where an employer intentionally discriminates, employees may obtain money damages unless the claim is for race discrimination. For those claims, monetary relief is available under 42 U.S.C. § 1981.

Tort – A tort is a civil wrong, other than breach of contract. Torts include negligence, assault, battery, trespass, defamation, infliction of emotional distress and wrongful death.

U.S. Equal Employment Opportunity Commission (EEOC) – The EEOC is the government entity that is empowered to enforce Title VII (see above) and other federal laws against discrimination through investigation and/or lawsuits. Private individuals alleging discrimination must pursue administrative remedies within the EEOC before they are allowed to file suit under Title VII.

Vacate – The act of annulling the judgment of a court either by an appellate court or by the court itself. The Supreme Court will generally vacate a lower court's judgment without deciding the case itself, and remand the case to the lower court for further consideration in light of some recent controlling decision.

Writ of Certiorari – The device used by the Supreme Court to transfer cases from the appellate court's docket to its own. Since the Supreme Court's appellate jurisdiction is largely discretionary, it need only issue such a writ when it desires to rule in the case.

INDEX